FLEA MARKET TRADER

Sixteenth Edition

NOW IN FULL COLOR!

THOUSANDS OF ITEMS
WITH
CURRENT VALUES

COLLECTOR BOOKS

A Division of Schroeder Publishing Co., Inc.

Editors:
Donna Newnum and Loretta Suiters
Contributing Editor:
Sharon Huxford
Editorial Assistants:
Jessica Woodrow, Kim Vincent
Cover Design:
Beth Summers
Layout:
Heather Warren

Collector Books
P.O. Box 3009
Paducah, KY 42002-3009

The current values in this book should be used only as a guide. They are not intended to set prices, which vary from one section of the country to another. Auction prices as well as dealer prices vary greatly and are affected by condition and demand. Neither the editors nor the publisher assumes responsibility for any losses which might be incurred as a result of consulting this guide.

Searching For a Publisher?

We are always looking for people knowledgeable within their fields. If you feel there is a real need for a book on your collectible subject and have a large comprehensive collection, contact Collector Books.

Proudly printed and bound in the
United States of America

Introduction

The *Flea Market Trader*, being specifically designed for the flea market shopper, includes several categories receiving new interest from collectors. With focus on categories not usually found in general price guides and omitting those not commonly found at flea markets, we hope to introduce you to collectibles that are currently coming on. We know the best and often the only source of this information is the market place itself. As all of us who constantly pursue the circuits know, flea markets are among the most exciting places in the world to shop. This excitement may turn to doubt (or sometimes dismay) unless you are well informed on current values. Overpriced items may be purchased, or those 'really great buys' may remain on the table. As in most lifetime pursuits, preparation has its own rewards. It is our intention to provide you with the basic tools of education and awareness toward wise purchasing.

Please bear in mind that the prices in this guide are meant to indicate only general values. Many factors determine actual selling prices; values vary from one region to another. Dealers pay various wholesale prices for their wares, and your bargaining skill is important too.

We have organized our listings into general categories for easy use. If you have trouble locating an item, refer to the index. Unless noted otherwise, the values we have suggested reflect prices of items in mint condition. NM stands for minimal damage or wear. VG indicates that the items will bring 40% to 60% of its mint price. EX should be somewhere between the two. Glassware is assumed clear unless a color is noted. Only generally accepted abbreviations have been used.

Abbreviations

dia — diameter	NRFB — never removed from box
ea — each	pc — piece
EX — excellent	pr — pair
gal — gallon	pt — pint
L — long	qt — quart
lb — pound	rnd — round
lg — large	sm — small
med — medium	sq — square
M — mint	VG — very good
MIB — mint in box	(+) — has been reproduced

Action Figures

The first line of action figures Hasbro developed in 1964 was GI Joe. It met with such huge success that Mego, Kenner, Mattel, and a host of other manufacturers soon began producing their own lines. GI Joe, Marx's Best of the West series, and several of Mego's figures were 12", others were 8" or 9" tall, and the most popular size in the last few years has been 3¾". Many lines came with accessory items such as vehicles, clothing, guns, etc. Original packaging (most now come on cards) is critical when it comes to evaluating your action figures, especially the more recent issues. Values given for MIB or MOC can be reduced by as much as 60% when appraising a 'loose' figure in even the best condition.

For more information refer to *Schroeder's Collectible Toys, Antique to Modern,* published by Collector Books. See also GI Joe; Star Wars.

Bionic Woman, figure, Jaime Sommers, Kenner, MIB, from $125.00 to $150.00.

A-Team, accessory, Combat Headquarters (w/4 figures), Galoob, MIB **50.00**
A-Team, accessory, Patrol Boat (w/Hannibal figure), Galoob, MIB **30.00**

A-Team, 3¾" figure set, Bad Guys, 4-pc, MOC........................ **55.00**
A-Team, 3¾" figure set, Soldiers of Fortune, 4-pc, Galoob, MOC.............................. **45.00**
A-Team, 6½" figure, Amy Allen, Galoob, MOC................... **30.00**
A-Team, 6½" figure, BA Baracus, Galoob, MOC.................... **35.00**
A-Team, 6½" figure, Cobra, Python, Rattler, Viper, Galoob, MOC, ea...................................... **14.00**
A-Team, 6½" figure, Face, Hannibal or Murdock, Galoob, MOC, ea......................... **22.00**
Action Jackson, accessory, Campmobile, Mego, MIB. **75.00**
Action Jackson, accessory, Scramble Cycle, Mego, MIB............. **45.00**
Action Jackson, figure, any except Black figure, 8", MIB...... **28.00**
Action Jackson, figure, Black, 8", MIB.................................. **55.00**
Action Jackson, outfit, any, Mego, MIP, ea.............................. **12.00**
Alien, figure, Kenner, 18", M. **175.00**
Alien, figure, Kenner, 18", MIP. **450.00**
Aliens, accessory, Evac Fighter or Hovertread, Kenner, MIP, ea. **18.00**
Aliens, figure, Flying Queen Alien, MOC................................. **16.00**
Aliens, figure, King Alien or Predator, MOC, ea **22.00**
Aliens, figure, Queen Alien, MOC.............................. **20.00**
Aliens, figure set, Alien vs Predator, Kenner, MOC **32.00**
Avengers, any figure from any series, Toy Biz, MIP, ea **8.00**
Avengers, any figure gift set, Toy Biz, MIP, ea...................... **22.00**
Banana Splits, any figure, Sutton, 1970s, MIP, ea............... **125.00**

Batman (Animated), accessory, Batcave, Kenner, MIP... **115.00**

Batman (Animated), accessory, Batmobile, Kenner, MIP. **55.00**

Batman (Animated), accessory, Robin's Dragster, Kenner, MOC.............**300.00**

Batman (Animated), figure, Anti-Freeze, Bane or Bruce Wayne, MOC, ea.............**12.00**

Batman (Animated), figure, Battle Helmet Batman or Poison Ivy, MOC, ea.............**35.00**

Batman & Robin, 5" figure, Batgirl, MIP.............**6.00**

Batman & Robin, 5" figure, Batman (Neon Armor), MIP.........**10.00**

Batman & Robin, 5" figure, Bruce Wayne (Battle Gear), MIP.............**10.00**

Batman & Robin, 5" figure, Mr Freeze (Ultimate Armor w/ring), MIP..................**15.00**

Batman & Robin, 12" figure, Batgirl, MIB..................**30.00**

Batman & Robin, 12" figure, Batman, Kenner, MIB **20.00**

Batman & Robin, 12" figure, Ultimate Batman or Ultimate Robin, MIB, ea.............**18.00**

Batman Crime Squad, accessory, Attack Jet, Kenner, MOC. **14.00**

Batman Crime Squad, figure, Air Assault Batman, MOC ...**14.00**

Batman Crime Squad, figure, Disaster Patrol Batman, Kenner, MOC..................**26.00**

Batman Forever, accessory, Batboat or Batwing, Kenner, MIB, ea.............**25.00**

Batman Forever, accessory, Batcave or Batmobile, Kenner, MIB, ea.............**38.00**

Batman Forever, figure, Attack Wing Batman, Kenner, MOC.............**22.00**

Batman Forever, figure, Blast Cap Batman, Kenner, MOC...**14.00**

Batman Forever, figure, Catwoman, Penguin or Robin, Kenner, MOC, ea.............**22.00**

Battlestar Galactica, accessory, Colonial Scarab, Mattel, 1970s, MIB.............**65.00**

Battlestar Galactica, 3¾" figure, any from 1978, Mattel, MOC, ea..**32.00**

Battlestar Galactica, 3¾" figure, any from 1979, Mattel, MOC, ea.............**95.00**

Battlestar Galactica, 12" figure, any, Mattel, 1979, MIB...**75.00**

Best of the West, accessory, Circle X Ranch, Marx, MIB, from $150 to.............**175.00**

Best of the West, figure, Geronimo w/Storm Cloud (horse), Marx, MIB.............**175.00**

Best of the West, figure, Jamie West, Marx, MIB, from $75 to.............**110.00**

Best of the West, figure, Jane West, Marx, MIB, from $100 to..**125.00**

Big Jim, accessory, Boat & Buggy Set, Mattel, MIB, from $45 to.............**55.00**

Big Jim, accessory, Sky Commander, Mattel, M, from $40 to ...**50.00**

Big Jim, figure, Big Jack (Gold Medal), from $70 to **80.00**

Big Jim, figure, Big Jim, MIB, from $65 to.............**85.00**

Big Jim's PACK, accessory, Beast, Mattel, MIB, from $85 to.**110.00**

Big Jim's PACK, figure, Big Jim (Double Trouble), Mattel, from $150 to.............**175.00**

Bionic Woman, accessory, House Playset, Kenner, MIP, from $25 to **50.00**

Bionic Woman, accessory, Sports Car, Kenner, MIB, from $90 to **110.00**

Black Hole, 3¾" figure, Capt Holland or Kate McCrae, Mego, MOC, ea **22.00**

Black Hole, 3¾" figure, Humanoid, Mego, MOC **650.00**

Black Hole, 3¾" figure, Maximillion, Mego, MOC, from $70 to .. **80.00**

Black Hole, 12" figure, Dr Durant or Dr Reinhardt, Mego, MIB, ea **75.00**

Bonanza, accessory, 4-in-1 Wagon, American Character, MIB, from $75 to **110.00**

Bonanza, any figure, American Character, MIB, ea from $125 to **175.00**

Bonanza, any figure w/horse, American Character, MIB, ea **200.00**

Bonanza, any horse, American Character, MIB, ea **30.00**

Buck Rogers, accessory, Star Fighter Command Center, Mego, MIB **100.00**

Buck Rogers, 3¾" figure, Buck Rogers, MOC, from $55 to **65.00**

Buck Rogers, 12" figure, any except Tiger Man, MIB, ea from $65 to **75.00**

Buck Rogers, 12" figure, Tiger Man, Mego, MIB, from $120 to **130.00**

Captain Action, accessory, Survival Kit, Ideal, MIB, from $225 to................**250.00**

Captain Action, figure, Captain Action, Ideal, MIB (Lone Ranger box) **500.00**

Captain Action, outfit, Captain Action, Ideal, MIB (photo box)............... **850.00**

Charlie's Angel's (Movie), any figure, Jakks Pacific, MIB, ea...... **40.00**

Charlie's Angels (TV Series), any figure, Hasbro, MOC....... **80.00**

CHiPs, 3¾" accessory, motorcycle, Mego, MIP **28.00**

CHiPs, 3¾" figure, Jon, Mego, MOC, from $18 to **22.00**

CHiPs, 3¾" figure, Ponch, Mego, MOC, from $15 to **18.00**

CHiPs, 8" accessory, motorcycle, Mego, MIP **72.00**

CHiPs, 8" figure, Jon, Mego, MOC **52.00**

CHiPs, 8" figure, Ponch, Mego, MOC................................ **42.00**

Commando (Schwarzenegger), 3¾" figure, any except Matrix, MOC, ea........................... **12.00**

Commando (Schwarzenegger), 3¾" figure, Matrix, MOC, from $35 to **45.00**

Commando (Schwarzenegger), 6" figure, Matrix, MIP, from $35 to **45.00**

Dukes of Hazzard, 3¾" accessory, Cadillac or Cop Car, MIP, ea .**80.00**

Dukes of Hazzard, 3¾" figure, Uncle Jesse, MOC, from $14 to. **18.00**

Dukes of Hazzard, 8" figure, Bo or Luke, Mego, MOC, from $28 to **32.00**

Dukes of Hazzard, 8" figure, Luke, MOC, from $18 to **22.00**

Happy Days, accessory, Fonzie's Garage, Mego, MIB, from $140 to **160.00**

Happy Days, accessory, Fonzie's Jalopy or Motorcycle, Mego, MIB, ea **80.00**

Happy Days, any figure, Mego, MOC, ea from $75 to **85.00**

Indiana Jones & the Temple of Doom, figure, Indiana, LJN, MOC, $145 to **165.00**

Indiana Jones in the Raiders of the Lost Ark, accessory, Map Room, MIB **100.00**

Indiana Jones in the Raiders of the Lost Ark, figure, Indiana, MOC.............................. **225.00**

Knight Rider, Knight 2000 Voice Car w/Michael figure, MIB...... **55.00**

Legend of the Lone Ranger, accessory, Western Town, Gabriel, MIB................................. **80.00**

Legend of the Lone Ranger, figure, Lone Ranger, Gabriel, MOC..............................**26.00**

Lord of the Rings, any figure, Toy Vault, 1998-99, MOC, ea from $12 to **18.00**

Lost in Space, figure, Judy (Cryo Chamber), Trendmasters, MOC................................. **10.00**

M*A*S*H, 3¾" accessory, Ambulance/Hawkeye figure, Tri-Star, MIP................... **30.00**

M*A*S*H, 3¾" figure, any except Hot Lips or Klinger, Tri-Star, MOC, ea........................... **18.00**

M*A*S*H, 3¾" figure, Hot Lips, Tri-Star, MOC, from $20 to **25.00**

M*A*S*H, 3¾" figure, Klinger (in dress), Tri-Star, MOC, from $25 to.............................. **35.00**

M*A*S*H, 8" figure, BJ, Hawkeye, Hot Lips, Tri-Star, MOC, ea from $55 to...................... **65.00**

Major Matt Mason, accessory, Space Station, Mattel, MIB, from $250 to.................. **300.00**

Major Matt Mason, figure, Doug Davis (w/helmet), Mattel, MOC.............................. **260.00**

Man From UNCLE, accessory, Jumpsuit Set, Gilbert, MIP, from $40 to...................... **50.00**

Man From UNCLE, figure, Illya or Napleon, MIB, ea from $325 to.................................. **375.00**

Marvel Super Heroes, accessory, Training Center, Toy Biz, MIB **30.00**

Marvel Super Heroes, figure, Capt America, Toy Biz, MOC, from $18 to.............................. **22.00**

Marvel Super Heroes (Secret Wars), accessory, Doom Copter, Mattel, MIP.................... **35.00**

Marvel Super Heroes (Secret Wars), figure, Captain America, MOC **26.00**

Masters of the Universe, accessory, Battle Cat, Mattel, MIP........................... **50.00**

Masters of the Universe, figure, He-Man (original), Mattel, MOC **125.00**

Masters of the Universe, figure, He-Man (Thunder Punch), Mattel, MOC................................. **65.00**

Masters of the Universe, figure, Ram Man, Mattel, MOC, from $55 to.............................. **65.00**

Micronauts, accessory, Microrail City, Mego, MIB, from $40 to **45.00**

Micronauts, figure, Baron Karza, Mego, MIB, from $30 to **35.00**

Micronauts, figure, Centaurus, Mego, MOC, from $150 to.......... **175.00**

Micronauts, figure, Membros, Mego, MOC, from $75 to.......... **100.00**

Planet of the Apes, accessory, Fortress Treehouse (w/5 figures), MIB 200.00

Planet of the Apes, figure, Alan Verdon, Mego, 1975, 8", MIP, $125.00.

Planet of the Apes, 7" figures, any, Hasbro, 1999, MIP, ea from $5 to 8.00

Planet of the Apes, 8" figure, any astronaut, Mego, 1970s, MIB 225.00

Planet of the Apes, 8" figure, any astronaut, Mego, 1970s, MOC, ea....................................110.00

Planet of the Apes, 8" figure, Cornelius, Mego, 1970s, MIB 185.00

Planet of the Apes, 8" figure, Cornelius, Mego, 1970s, MOC 110.00

Planet of the Apes, 12" figure, any, Hasbro, 1999, MIP, from $18 to 22.00

Pocket Super Heroes, figure, Spider-Man, Mego, MOC (red card)...............................55.00

Pocket Super Heroes, figure, Spider-Man, Mego, MOC (white card)..................110.00

Power Rangers in Space, accessory, any, Bandai, 1998, MIP, ea. 8.00

Power Rangers in Space, 5" figure, any, MIP, ea.....................8.00

Power Rangers Turbo, 4" figure, any, Bandai, MIP, ea.......10.00

Power Rangers Turbo, 5" figure, any, Bandai, 1997, MIP, ea........8.00

Rambo, accessory, Skywolf Assault Jet, Coleco, MIB, from $18 to...................22.00

Rambo, figure, Rambo or Rambo w/Fire Power, Coleco, MOC, ea...................................10.00

Six Million Dollar Man, accessory, Mission Control Center, Kenner, MIB....................65.00

Six Million Dollar Man, figure, Steve Austin, Kenner, MIB.....115.00

Starsky & Hutch, any figure, Mego, MOC, ea from $40 to 50.00

Starsky & Hutch, car, Mego, from $150 to...........................175.00

Super Heroes, 5" figure, Penguin (Bend 'n Flex), Mego, MOC..........135.00

Super Heroes, 8" figure, Batman (Fist-Fighting), Mego, MIB 425.00

Super Heroes, 8" figure, Green Goblin, Mego, MIB, from $225 to 250.00

Super Heroes, 8" figure, Mego, MOC, from $75 to 100.00

Super Heroes, 8" figure, Robin (painted mask), Mego, MOC, from $75 to 100.00

Super Powers, accessory, Supermobile, Kenner, MIB, from $25 to 35.00

Super Powers, 3¾" figure, Aquaman, Kenner, MOC, from $45 to 50.00

Super Powers, 3¾" figure, Clark Kent, Kenner (mail-in), MIP 75.00

Super Powers, 3¾" figure, Green Lantern, Kenner, MOC, from $45 to 50.00

Super Powers, 3¾" figure, Shazam, Kenner, from $50 to **60.00**

Super Powers, 8" figure, Aquaman, Mego, MIB (window box) or MOC, ea **155.00**

Wonder Woman (TV Series), figure, Steve Trevor, Mego, MIB, from $90 to **115.00**

Wonder Woman (TV Series), figure, Wonder Woman w/DP outfit, MIB **200.00**

WWF, figure, Akeem, MOC, from $35 to **40.00**

WWF, figure, Capt Lou Albano (Manager), LJN, 1985, MOC **15.00**

WWF, figure, Honky Tonk Man, Hasbro, MOC, from $18 to **22.00**

WWF, figure, Hulk Hogan, Hasbro, 1990, MOC **22.00**

WWF, figure, Iron Sheik, LJN, 1985, MOC **25.00**

WWF, figure, Junkyard Dog, LJN, 1985, MOC **25.00**

WWF, figure, Kane, Jakks, 7", NM **20.00**

WWF, figure, Mr Wonderful, LJN, 1985, MOC **20.00**

WWF, figure set, Nasty Boys, MOC (2-pack), from $70 to **75.00**

X-Men/X-Force, figure, Deadpool (1995), or Domino, Toy Biz, MOC, ea **12.00**

X-Men/X-Force, figure, Silver Samuari, Toy Biz, MOC, from $15 to **18.00**

X-Men/X-Force, figure, X-Treme, Toy Biz, MOC, from $16 to **18.00**

Zorro (Cartoon Series), figure, Tempest or Picaro, Gabriel, MOC, ea **22.00**

Zorro (Cartoon Series), figure, Zorro or Amigo, Gabriel, MOC, ea **18.00**

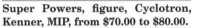

Super Powers, figure, Cyclotron, Kenner, MIP, from $70.00 to $80.00.

Advertising Collectibles

As far back as the turn of the century, manufacturers used characters that identified with their products. They were always personable, endearing, amusing, and usually succeeded in achieving just the effect the producer had in mind, which was to make their product line more visual, more familiar, and therefore one the customer would more often than not choose over the competition. Magazine ads, display signs, product cartons, and TV provided just the right exposure for these ad characters. Elsie the Cow became so well known that at one point during a random survey, more people recognized her photo than one of the president!

There are scores of advertising characters, and many have been promoted on a grand scale. Today's collectors search for the dolls, banks, cookie jars, mugs, plates, and scores of other items modeled after or bearing the likenesses of their favorites, several of which are featured in our listings.

Condition plays a vital role in evaluating vintage advertising pieces. Try to be very objective when you assess wear and damage.

For more information we recommend *Antique and Collectible Advertising Memorabilia* by B.J. Summers.

See also Ashtrays; Automobilia; Breweriana; Bubble Bath Containers; Character and Promotional Drinking Glasses; Coca-Cola; Gas Station Collectibles; Novelty Radios; Pin-Back Buttons; Soda Pop. See Clubs and Newsletters for information concerning *The Prize Insider* newsletter for Cracker Jack collectors; Peanut Pals, a club for collectors of Planters Peanuts; and the Soup Collector Club (Campbell's Soups).

A&W Root Beer, bear, beanbag plush, Alpha Kids, 1997, 6", M **8.00**

A&W Root Beer, bear, plush, Canasia Toys, 8", M **6.00**

A&W Root Beer, bear, plush, 1980s, 12", M **10.00**

A&W Root Beer, beverage container, bear-shape w/pull-out straw, 9", M **3.00**

AC Spark Plugs, figure, AC Man in green hat, 6", EXIB **150.00**

AC Spark Plugs, figure, Sparky the horse, inflatable, 1960s, 24", EX **100.00**

Aflac, figure, duck, plush, talking, 6", NM **8.00**

Aflac, nodder, duck on base, 5½", NM **15.00**

Alka-Seltzer, figure, Speedy, vinyl, 1960s, 5½", EX **275.00**

Alpo, Dan the Dog windup figure, 1970s, 3", EX+ **12.00**

Arithromax, hand puppet, zebra in white coat, Sasco **5.00**

Aunt Jemima, Breakfast Bear, plush, 13", M **175.00**

Aunt Jemima, doll, cloth, red & white checked dress, 1950s, 13", EX **55.00**

Aunt Jemima, paper plate, 9", NM, $35.00.

Aunt Jemima, place mat, Story of../6 views on white, scalloped, 1950s **35.00**

Baskin Robins, Pinky the Spoon figure, bendable vinyl, 1990s, 5", NM+ **6.00**

Big Boy, bank, plastic figure in red & white overalls, 1970s, 9", NM **20.00**

Big Boy, doll, cloth, T-shirt/overalls, 15", MIP (Yes, I'm Your Pal) **25.00**

Big Boy, figure on surfboard w/wave, PVC, 1990, 3", EX **5.00**

Blue Bonnet Margarine, doll, Sue, cloth w/yarn hair, 1980s, NM **5.00**

Blue Bonnet Margarine, shakers, Blue Bonnet Sue, 1989, range size, MIB **35.00**

Borden, bank, Beauregard figure, red plastic, Irwin, 1950s, 5", EX **65.00**

Borden, charm, Elsie's head in circle, gold-tone plastic, 1950s, EX 15.00

Borden, Elsie, creamer and sugar bowl, molded plastic, M, 3½", $65.00.
(Photo courtesy Lee Garmon)

Borden, figure, Elsie, plush w/vinyl head, moo sound, 1950s, 12", VG+ 50.00

Borden, figure, Elsie, PVC, 3½", M, from $10 to 20.00

Borden, figure, Elsie, vinyl in aqua dress, felt shoes & bib, 22", EX+ 100.00

Borden, nightlight, Elsie, rubber composition head figure, 9", NM 175.00

Borden, place mat, Elsie Says.. retro border around 5 scenes, 11x17" 18.00

Borden, postcard, Elsie & Beauregard in Person, unused, EX 18.00

Borden, push-button puppet, Elsie, wood, EX 125.00

Borden, shakers, Beulah/ Beauregard figures, ceramic, 1950s, 3½", M, pr 75.00

Bosco Chocolate, Bosco the Clown doll, vinyl, EX+ 50.00

Bradford House Resturants, squeeze toy, Bucky Bradford, 1970s, 9", NM 35.00

Bud Lite, Spuds McKenzie dog, plush, Applause, 7", NM ... 6.00

Burger Chef, hand puppet, cloth w/vinyl head, 1970s, EX . 10.00

Burger Chef, pillow figure, stuffed printed cloth, 1970s, EX 12.00

Burger King, doll, Burger King, stuffed printed cloth, 1970s, 16", M 10.00

Buster Brown Shoes, doll, Buster Brown, stuffed cloth, 1974, 14", NM 40.00

Butterfinger Candy Bar, Butterfinger Bear, plush, 1987, 15", M 25.00

Camel Cigarettes, shakers, Max, Ray figures, plastic, 1993, 4", EX, pr 35.00

Campbell's Soup, book, Alphabet Soup, image of Campbell Kid, 2002, NM 4.00

Campbell's Soup, book, The Campbell Kids at Home, Rand McNalley — Elf Book, 1934, EX, from $20.00 to $30.00.
(Photo courtesy Dan Young)

Campbell's Soup, dolls, Alphabet Soup, beanbag w/yarn hair, 7", EX, ea 6.00

Campbell's Soup, dolls, farm kids (boy & girl), cloth, 2000, 7", MIP 12.00

Campbell's Soup, dolls, Paul Revere & Betsy Ross, 1976, 10", M, ea 50.00

Campbell's Soup, mug, white ceramic w/Campbell Kid face, 1998, M 8.00

Campbell's Soup, wristwatch, Campbell girl, 1981 Anniversary, NM+ 135.00

Cap'n Crunch, doll, plush, 1990, 18", M 20.00

Carnation, Mighty Dog, plush w/ cape & shash, Dakin, 1986, 10", EX 5.00

Cheer, doll, Cheer Girl, plastic w/cloth outfit, P&G, 1960, 10", NM 20.00

Cheetos, figure, Chester Cheeta, bendable PVC, 4½", M 4.00

Cheetos, figure, Chester Cheeta, plush, 18", NM (w/original tag) 40.00

Chicken of the Sea, carry-all bag, green vinyl w/mermaid logo, 18", EX 5.00

Chiquita Bananas, doll, Chiquita Girl, stuffed print cloth, 16", M 30.00

Chuck-E-Cheese, bank, vinyl figure, 7", EX 10.00

Chuck-E-Cheese, doll, plush, Show Biz Pizza Time, 1996, 10", M 10.00

Chuck-E-Cheese, hand puppet, plush, 1992, 9", EX 12.00

Clark Bar, figure, boy in striped shirt, vinyl, 1960s, 9", NM 175.00

Count Chocula, mask, plastic, 1970s, NM 35.00

Cracker Jack, doll, Jack, vinyl & cloth, Vogue Dolls, 1980, NM 22.00

Cracker Jack, dolls, Jack, Bingo, 100th anniversary, 1996, 16", NM, pr 22.00

Crayola, Bear, plush, 7½", EX .. 15.00

Crayola, doll, Ballerina, plush, Gund, 14", M 10.00

Curel Lotion, Curel Baby, plastic w/jointed arms & legs, 1980, 6", EX 20.00

Curad, bank, Taped Crusader figure, plastic, 8", M 10.00

Dairy Queen, figure, Kid, stuffed cloth, 1974, EX 20.00

Dairy Queen, figure, Marsh Mallo the moose, plush, 1980s, 7", EX 12.00

Dairy Queen, figure, Sweet Nell, plush, 1974, 12", EX 20.00

Del Monte, figure, Shoo Shoo the scarecrow, plush, 1983, 14", EX 8.00

Del Monte, ornament, plush pineapple, Christmas Yumkins, 1991, 4", EX 3.00

Dominos Pizza, figure, Noid, plush, 1988, 19", MIP 20.00

Dominos Pizza, figure, Noid as sorcerer, PVC, 1980s, 2½", MIP. 6.00

Dutch Boy Paint, hand puppet, cloth w/vinyl head, 1960, MIP (sealed) 50.00

Eagle Snacks, figure, Eagle, plush, 21", NM 8.00

Energizer Batteries, Christmas stocking, plush bunny figure, 26", M 10.00

Energizer Batteries, figure, Bunny, beanbag plush, 7", EX 6.00

Eveready Batteries, bank, vinyl black cat, 1981, 5½x8" L, EX 28.00

Flavorite, figure, Riley, beanbag plush, white fuzzy beard, 8", M 5.00

Fruit Stripe Gum, figure, gum pack on motorcycle, vinyl, 1967, 7", EX+ 175.00

Fruit Stripe Gum, figure, Yipes, plush, 15", EX **50.00**

Funny Face, mug, watermelon face w/red hair & gasses, 1974, 3", EX **25.00**

General Electric, shakers, milk glass refrigerators, 1940s, 3", pr..................................... **60.00**

Green Giant, bank, Little Sprout, ceramic, unmarked, M, 8¼", $35.00. (Photo courtesy Jim and Beverly Mangus)

Green Giant, bank, Little Sprout, composition, musical, 8½", EX... **50.00**

Green Giant, book, Sprout's Valley Adventure, Susan Shimshak, 1992, EX **3.00**

Green Giant, doll, Sprout, green plush w/round head, 1992, 11", EX **12.00**

Green Giant, figure, Little Sprout, talker, MIP **55.00**

Hamburger Helper, Helping Hand figure, plush, 14", M **10.00**

Hardee's, any California Raisins from 1st or 2nd promo, ea from $1 to **3.00**

Hardee's, doll, Gilbert Giddyup, stuffed print cloth, 1971, EX............ **25.00**

Harley-Davidson, figure, bulldog, plush w/leather cap & shoes, 10", M **8.00**

Harley-Davidson, figure, Harley Hog, 9", M........................ **25.00**

Hawaiian Punch, doll, Punchy, beanbag type, 1997, 10", MIP... **15.00**

Heinz Ketchup, shakers, red plastic ketchup bottles, 4¼", M pr **20.00**

Hilton Hotels, figure, pink flamingo, plush w/plastic legs, 12", EX..................................... **6.00**

Hush Puppies, dog, beanbag plush, Applause, 2000, M **5.00**

Idaho Potato, potato figure, Growth in Idaho on pink shirt, 16", M **6.00**

Keebler, figure, Doc (chef), beanbag plush, 12", M..................... **8.00**

Kellogg's, figure, Dig 'Em, plush frog, dated 1998, 7½", NM **12.00**

Kellogg's Fruit Loops, figure, Toucan Sam, plush, 1994-96, 8", NM............................. **12.00**

Kentucky Fried Chicken, hand puppet, the Colonel, plastic, 1960s, EX **20.00**

Kentucky Fried Chicken, shaker, white plastic bust, 1972, 4", EX **45.00**

Kentucky Fried Chicken, Wacky Wobbler, PVC Colonel figure, MIB **25.00**

Kodak, bear, Max Film, plush, 1998, 13", M **8.00**

Kodak, figure, Kolorkins 'Flash' Critter, white beanbag plush, 6", M **5.00**

Kool Aid, pitcher figure lifting weights/tennis player, PVC, 2", M, ea **2.50**

Kool Aid, sports bottle, pitcher man as magician graphics, 7½", M............................. **4.00**

Kraft, key chain, Cheesasaurus Rex, orange PVC figure, 2¾", M **3.00**

Land 'O Lakes, cow figure standing upright, soft vinyl, 5", M .. **4.00**

Life Savers, figure, Green Life Saver, bendable PVC, 2½", M **3.00**

Life Savers, figure, Green Life Saver, plush, Art's Toy, 11", M **8.00**

Little Debbie, doll, vinyl w/cloth dress & straw hat, 1980s, 11", NM **85.00**

M&M, book, Counting Board, 1997, M **3.00**

M&M, Burger King promotional figures, any, M, ea **2.00**

M&M, dispenser, green figure w/red & white striped hat, 3½", M **3.00**

M&M, dispenser, red peanut on brown base w/white arm raised, 9", M **10.00**

M&M, dispenser, red plain candy piece kicking present, hard-to-find color, M, $50.00.

M&M, key chain, Action Sports, Basic Fun, 2000, MOC **3.00**

M&M, party paper plates, 8-pack, 1988, 7", MIP (sealed) **3.00**

M&M, plush figure, black & white sneakers, Ace Novelty, 2000, 10", M **8.00**

M&M, plush figure, black vinyl cape & mask, Nanco, 2001, 12", M **10.00**

M&M, trinket box, ceramic heart w/red candy figure on lid, 6", M **8.00**

Mack Trucks, tie clip, diecast enamel image of bulldog mascot, 2x½" **15.00**

Maypo Oat Cereal, bank, Marky Maypo figure, plastic, 1960s, EX **100.00**

McDonald's, bank, Grimace, composition, 1985, NM **15.00**

McDonald's, bank, Ronald McDonald bust, plastic, Taiwan, 1993, EX **40.00**

McDonald's, doll, Grimace, plush, plastic eyes, 8", M **10.00**

McDonald's, doll, Ronald McDonald, stuffed print cloth, 1970s, 17", EX **20.00**

McDonald's, hand puppet, Ronald McDonald, cloth w/vinyl head, 1993, MIB **45.00**

Mr Clean, figure, standing w/arms crossed, vinyl, P&G, 1960s, 8", EX **75.00**

Nabisco, doll, Mr Salty, stuffed cloth, 1983, NM, minimum value **25.00**

Nestle, figure, Milky in straw hat & neckerchief, Trudy Co, 9", M **6.00**

Nestle, figure, P Nutty plush w/ curly-Q top, Trudy, 1984, 8½", EX **6.00**

Nestle, figure, Semi-Sweet Morsel, plush w/heart on bib, 8", NM **6.00**

Nestle, wristwatch, Little Hans, Piet, NM **175.00**

Nestle Quik, Bunny, plush w/black 'N,' Ram Int Group, 18", M **10.00**

Neutrogena, bear, white plush w/pink T-shirt, Logo Bear, 1985, 8", EX **5.00**

Oreo Cookies, cookie figure w/white topknot, arms, legs, PVC, 2½", M **3.00**

Oscar Mayer, Weinermobile beanie, plush, 6½" L, EX **6.00**

PG&E, Magilla Gorilla Kite Fun Book, w/Reddy Kilowatt, 1963, NM **32.00**

Pillsbury, cookie jar, Doughboy, ceramic, 12" **30.00**

Pillsbury, figure, Doughboy, beanbag plush, 9", NM **6.00**

Pillsbury, figure, Doughboy w/plate of biscuits, ceramic, 6¾", M ... **10.00**

Pillsbury, figure, Poppie Fresh, white vinyl w/blue, ca 1971, 5½", M **15.00**

Pillsbury, planter, Doughboy by open bag, ceramic, M **15.00**

Pillsbury, utensil holder, Doughboy, ceramic, Benjamin Medwin Inc., ca 1992, 8", M, from $18.00 to $22.00.

Pizza Hut, bank, Pizza Hut Pete, plastic, 1969, 8", EX+ **25.00**

Planters, ballpoint pin, Bic, white w/blue Mr Peanut graphic, 1980s, EX **10.00**

Planters, doll, Mr Peanut, cloth, Chase Bag Co, 1970, 18", NM **25.00**

Planters, golf set, divet mixer, ball marker, wooden tee, 1970s, EX **12.00**

Planters, iron-on transfer, Mr Peanut figure, Planters, 1970s, 9", M **12.00**

Planters, jar, Mr Peanut embossed on glass lid & bottom, 1982, 9", M **15.00**

Planters, lighter, Bic, Mr Peanut image, 1970s, 3", EX **15.00**

Planters, retractable razor cutter, Mr Peanut image, 1970s-80s, 4", EX **8.00**

Planters, shakers, Mr Peanut figures, pink plastic, rare, 3", EX, pr **28.00**

Planters, whistle, plastic Mr Peanut figure, 1970s, NM **6.00**

Planters, yo-yo, Mr Peanut image, Humphery, 1976, NM **12.00**

Post Sugar Crisp, ornament, Sugar Bear figure as Santa, 3", NM **5.00**

Post Sugar Crisp, Sugar Bear, plush in shorts & aqua T-Shirt, 5", EX **4.00**

Quisp Cereal, bank, Quisp figure, ceramic, 1960s, NM **100.00**

Raid, Bug figure, plush, 1980, EX+ **25.00**

Red Robin, hand puppet, plush, 12", EX **5.00**

Reddy Whip, hand puppet, boy w/crew cut, vinyl & cloth, 1960s, EX **75.00**

Sambos, tiger, beanbag plush, Dakin, 1977, NM............. **10.00**

Scrubbing Bubbles, caddy, white plastic w/3 bubble figures, oblong, NM **6.00**

Smokey Bear, see US Dept of Ag

Snickers, doll, fits into bag resembling candy bar, 1990s, 12", EX **12.00**

Snuggle Fabric Softener, bear, beanbag plush, 1999, 8", EX...... **8.00**

Snuggle Fabric Softener, bear, plush, Russ Berrie, 1985, 15", EX.**12.00**

Spillers Flour, scale measure spoons, Fred figure, multi-pc, 1972, EX **125.00**

Spillers Flour, spice shaker, plastic Flour Fred figure, 9", VG. **40.00**

Star-Kist Tuna, bank, Charlie on tuna can, ceramic, 1988, 9½", NM **20.00**

Star-Kist Tuna, lamp base, Charlie figure, plaster, 1970s, 13", EX+ **65.00**

Star-Kist Tuna, Talkin' Patter Pillow, stuffed, Mattel, 1970s, 15", NM **25.00**

Star–Kist Tuna, Wacky Wobbler, Charlie the Tuna, PVC, M, $15.00.

State Farm Insurance, Good Neighbor Bear, plush, 10", NM **6.00**

Sun Maid Raisins, Play Book, 2 dogs on front, Little Simon, 1999, EX **3.00**

Sunbeam Bread, doll, Little Miss Sunbeam, stuffed cloth, 17", NM **35.00**

Taco Bell, bongo drum w/chihuahua dog detail, 5", NM **4.00**

Taco Bell, coin purse, Yo Quiero Taco Bell!, dog, vinyl, belt clip, 4".. **4.00**

Taco Bell, dog figure, Yo Quiero, plush w/beret, Applause, 6½", MIP **6.00**

Target Stores, dog, The In Thing, white plush w/red detail, 7", EX **5.00**

Target Stores, dog, The In Thing, white plush w/red detail, 14", M **10.00**

Teddy Grahams, doll, plush bear w/purple velvet jacket & shoes, 10", M **15.00**

Toys R Us, Geoffrey, plush in Statue of Liberty outfit, 2001, 10", NM **6.00**

Toys R Us, Geoffrey, PVC figure, jointed, any 3¾" figure, M, ea **2.00**

Tyson Foods, chicken, plush, soldier outfit & Tyson dogtag, 9½", M **10.00**

Tyson Foods, chicken, white bean-bag plush w/brown & red details, 6", M **5.00**

Tyson Foods, figure, Chicken Quick, stuffed cloth, 13", VG...... **15.00**

US Dept of Ag, bank, Smokey Bear, red plastic, 1950s, 5", EX. **50.00**

US Dept of Ag, bank, Woodsy Owl, ceramic, 1970s, 8½", EX. **50.00**

US Dept of Ag, book, ...Story of the Forest, softcover, 1968, EX.**22.00**

US Dept of Ag, book, Smokey Bear's Story of the Forest, 1968, VG **15.00**

US Dept of Ag, ruler, Smokey Bear w/6" ruler on reverse, 1962, 8", EX **18.00**

US Postal Service, pull toy, 3-wheeled mail car w/Mr Zip driver, VG+ **85.00**

Vlasic Pickles, figure, stork, white fur, 1989, 22", NM........... **40.00**

Washington Mutual Insurance, star-shaped slinky toy, white plastic, M **3.00**

Wells Fargo, horse, white & black beanbag plush, Toys R Us, 12", M **8.00**

Advertising Tins

Attractive packaging has always been a powerful marketing tool; today those colorful tin containers that once held products ranging from cookies and peanut butter to coffee and tea are popular collectibles. See also Gas Station Collectibles; Tobacco Collectibles.

Big Buster Yellow Pop Corn, parade drummer on blue canister, 10-oz, EX 100.00

Big Sister Peanut Butter, pail, night blue w/graphics, 1-lb, EX. 475.00

Butter-Nut Coffee, key-wind, red & white, 1-lb, EX 30.00

Cashmere Bouquet Talc, sample, 1940s, unopened, 2", NM..125.00

Chase & Sanborn Coffee, dated Aug 8th on paper label, 1930s, 1-lb, NM 100.00

Chicken Bones (Candy), pry lid, 1930s-40s, 1-lb, VG+ 75.00

Cook's Breakfast Cocoa, sq, slip lid, paper label, 6", EX 35.00

Curad Battle Ribbon Plastic Bandages, 1950s, 4", EX. 25.00

Derby's Peter Pan Peanut Butter, sample tin, screw lid, 2-oz, NM 75.00

Desitin Medicinal & Nursery Powder, sample, sq, 2½", VG 25.00

Hershey's Cocoa, shows baby in cocoa bean, dated 1984, sq, 4½", NM 15.00

Hershey's Kisses, A Kiss for You, round canister, 1980, 6", NM. 8.00

Hill's Cascara Quinine Cold Tablets 29c, pocket tin, red, 2x1½", EX 12.00

Jolly Time Giant Yellow Pop Corn, red canister, 1946, 5", EX 65.00

Keebler Holiday Cookies, elf graphics, 1998, 2x6x8", NM 5.00

Life Savers, round canister w/slip lid & handle, 10", EX 75.00

Lipton Tea, Planter Ceylon, sq canister w/slip lid, 4", EX+ 6.00

Luzianne Coffee & Chicory, sample tin, screw lid, white, 1930s, EX+ 110.00

Mammy's Favorite Brand Coffee, CD Kenny Co, canister, bail, 11", VG+ 150.00

Master-Phona Needles (Montgomery Ward), red hinged lid, 2½", NM 65.00

Mennen Quinsana Powder, sq, shaker top, 5", EX........... 25.00

Milky Way, 'Snack Bars' round canister, late 1990s, 6", M...... 5.00

Monarch Coffee, key-wind, light blue, 1-lb, NM+ 100.00

Monarch Popcorn, pail, lithographed label, 14-ounce, EX+, $300.00. (Photo courtesy Wm. Morford Auctions)

Moonlight Mallos, slip lid, blue, 1930s, 5x10" dia, EX....... 75.00

Nature's Remedy All Vegetable Laxative, red, white, blue, 1x3x½", EX 15.00

Nestle Toll House Cookies, sq canister, lady w/cookie plate, 6", EX 5.00

Nustad's Pointer Brand Coffee, name above pointer dog, multicolor, key-wind lid, EX, $60.00.

Old Dutch Coffee, key-wind, brown, 1-lb, EX+ 40.00

Oreo Cookies, holiday, any from the 1990s, 2x6x8", NM 4.00

Pickanny Brand Peanut Butter, pail, yellow, 1-lb, EX 250.00

Sanders Satin Candies, pail, graphics on yellow, 2½-lb, EX 130.00

Silvertone Needles (Sears), silver w/blue detail, 2½", NM ... 35.00

Tru-Lax Chocolate Minted Laxative, sq w/rounded corners, 1¾", EX 25.00

Valley Queen Cloves, sq w/round slip lid, graphics, 1910, 1-oz, EX+ 75.00

White House Coffee, key-wind, white on blue, 1-lb, VG ... 75.00

ZeaSorb Medicated Powder, sample, round, shaker top, 2½", EX 10.00

Aluminum

From the late 1930s until early in the 1950s, kitchenwares and household items were often crafted of aluminum, usually with relief-molded fruit or flowers on a hammered background. Today many find that these diversified items make an attractive collection. Especially desirable are those examples marked with the manufacturer's backstamp or the designer's signature.

You've probably also seen the anodized (colored) aluminum pitchers, tumblers, sherbet holders, etc., that were popular in the late '50s, early '60s. Interest in these items has exploded, as prices on eBay sales attest. Be sure to check condition, though, as scratching and wear reduce values drastically. The more uncommon forms are especially collectible.

For more information refer to *Collectible Aluminum, An Identification and Value Guide* (Collector Books), by Everett Grist. Unless noted otherwise, our values are for examples in mint to near-mint condition.

Ashtray, Arthur Armour, water lilies & lotus pads, 6" sq 30.00

Ashtray, Everlast, bamboo, single holder, 5" dia 150.00

Ashtray, unmarked, flying duck scene, 6" dia 10.00

Basket, Cromwell, allover fruit/ flowers, twisted/knotted handle, 10" 10.00

Basket, Everlast, floral & leaf band, fluted rim, smooth handle, 9" 10.00

Basket, Everlast, tomato band at edge, serrated lip, knot handle, 11" 10.00

Basket, Forman, mums, scalloped bowl w/sq handle twisted in center, 8" 10.00

Beverage server, Kromex, plain bottle w/ring design, ball stopper, 11" **25.00**

Bookends, Bruce Cox, leaping fish w/sprays, 7x5x3" **185.00**

Bowl, Buenilum, daisy ring in center, 8-petal serrated rim, 6½".... **5.00**

Bowl, Cellini Craft, hammered, footed, berries along scallops, 11½" **85.00**

Bowl, DePonceau, bittersweet pattern, notched rim, 11" **20.00**

Bowl, McClelland, hammered effect w/uneven scalloped edge, 1½x6" **5.00**

Bowl, R Kent, tulips on hammered ground, serrated rim, handled, 10" **25.00**

Bowl, W August Forge, dogwood, wide flared/fluted rim, 7" **35.00**

Bowl, Warrented, mixed blossoms & leaves, scalloped & fluted rim, 11" **5.00**

Buffet server/bun warmer, II Farberware, S-shaped feet w/tulip design **20.00**

Butter dish, Everlast, bamboo pattern & finial on lid, 7x4x4" **10.00**

Butter dish, R Kent, Crisscross glass lid, tulip finial, aluminum tray **20.00**

Butter dish, unmarked, scroll design w/folded-leaf finial, 7" L **8.00**

Cake stand, Wilson, tall pedestal, band of shields, serrated rim, 12" **15.00**

Candlestick, Kensington, anodized, polished, crystal ball, ea. **45.00**

Candlesticks, Everlast, hammered, scalloped base, fluted bobeche, 3", pr **20.00**

Candlesticks, II Farberware, S-shaped floral w/beaded cups & bases, pr **45.00**

Candy dish, Buenilum, pointed leaf w/smooth rim, twisted handle, 9" **5.00**

Candy dish, Buenilum, 2 hammered leaves w/common looped handle, 6x5" **10.00**

Candy dish, II Farberware, round, hammered, beaded rim, S handle, 8" **5.00**

Candy dish, Neocraft, double dish w/butterfly pattern, anodized gold **15.00**

Canister set, Century, 4-pc w/coppertone lids, black knobs.......... **12.00**

Casserole, Everlast, bamboo, handled, w/lid, 7" dia **10.00**

Casserole, Everlast, floral band on lid, rolled handles, 11" dia. **6.00**

Casserole, R Kent, hammered, handled, lid w/tulip finial, 8" dia **10.00**

Chocolate pot, mum design, ear handle, beaded base, petal finial, 10" . **85.00**

Cigarette box, W August Forge, bittersweet design, hinged lid, 3x5" **75.00**

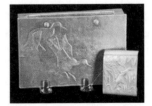

Cigarette case, Wendall August Forge, flying geese, 5¼x3½", $100.00; Matcholder, Wendall August Forge, flying geese, $25.00.

Coaster, unmarked, grapes w/leaves, 5" dia **3.00**

Coaster set, Everlast, 5-petal floral, serrated rim, boxed set of 8. **25.00**

Compote, Continental, rose pattern, serrated rim, tall stem foot, 5x5".......................... **20.00**

Compote, unmarked, hammered, deep w/flared rim, 5x6"... **10.00**

Creamer & sugar bowl w/tray, Buenilum, polished, looped handles **15.00**

Crumb brush & tray, unmarked, tulip & ribbon design on hammered ground.................. **25.00**

Crumber, Everlast, tray w/hanging brush, rose........................ **35.00**

Dresser dish, Farberware, beaded glass, aluminum lid, black finial, sq **10.00**

Gravy boat & underplate, Continental, mums, hammered, serrated, handled **25.00**

Ice bucket, Buenilum, open, hammered inside, serrated, decorative handle........................ **10.00**

Ice bucket, Continental, mums, mushroom & leaf finial... **40.00**

Ice bucket, Everlast, open, hammered, flared/fluted rim, handled **15.00**

Ice bucket, Heller Hostess Ware, Big Apple Ice Vault, 7", M...... **65.00**

Lazy Susan, Cromwell, 2-tier tidbit, fruit & flowers, scalloped............................. **10.00**

Lazy Susan, unmarked, acorns, serrated, 2 applied floral decorations.............................. **15.00**

Measuring scoops, set of 3, ½-cup, ⅓-cup & ¼-cup, anodized............................... **20.00**

Mint dish, unmarked, mums on 1 side of serrated 3-petal form w/finial............................. **20.00**

Napkin holder, W August Forge, dogwood on book shape w/concave sides......................... **30.00**

Pitcher, Continental, wild rose, hammered, serrated, ear handle, 8".............................. **35.00**

Pitcher, Continental Silver Co., mums, $50.00; Tumbler, $15.00.

Pitcher, Gailstyn, hammered, ice lip, ear handle, rolled rim, 8"..................................... **5.00**

Plate, Arthur Armour, dogwood branch & butterfly, fluted, 10"......... **45.00**

Popcorn popper, W August Forge, ducks on lid, black handle, 9"................................... **75.00**

Salad fork & spoon set, unmarked, hammered, rived handles, 12"................................. **45.00**

Salad set, Bascal, lg bowl & 8 footed individuals, anodized **65.00**

Silent butlers, any maker & design, most from $10 to............. **20.00**

Syrup pitcher, Stratford-on-Avon, hammered tankard w/black handle, 6" **15.00**

Tidbit, Designed Aluminum, dogwood, fluted rim, loop handle, 6" dia................................ **5.00**

Tidbit, Everlast, 2-tier, grapevine bands, open circle finial, 11". **5.00**

Tray, bar; Everlast, anchor, rope, sea gulls, applied bar handles, 9x15"................................ **30.00**

Tray, bar; Everlast, pine cone pattern, wide flat rim, 8x20". **10.00**

Tray, bar; unmarked, 2 ducks & cattails, full-length tab ends, 9x16"................................**30.00**

Tray, bread; Continental, wild roses, serrated, tab ends, oval, 6x13"................................**15.00**

Tray, Bruce Fox, lobster form w/ enlarged pinchers, 11x15". **35.00**

Tray, cheese & cracker; Continental, acorns, leaves on bowl, 15" dia............ **15.00**

Tray, sandwich; Admiration, dogwood, tightly fluted rim, 10" dia......................................**5.00**

Tray, sandwich; unmarked, irises on hammered oval w/fluted rim, 10x12"......................**15.00**

Tray, sandwich; W August Forge, bittersweet, notched rim, 8x11"................................**35.00**

Tray, serving; Everlast, apple blossoms, hammered, fluted rim, 10x16"................................**5.00**

Tray, serving; Kensington, polished, hunt scenes on handles, 14x23"..............................**15.00**

Tray, serving; Keystoneware, fold-up w/handle, fruit, hammered, 7x11" **25.00**

Tray, snack; SA Wagner, quail over pond on scalloped oval, 7x9".**60.00**

Tumblers, Zephry Ware, various anodized colors, 5", set of 8..........**50.00**

Anchor Hocking

From the 1930s until the 1970s Anchor Hocking (Lancaster, Ohio) produced a wide and varied assortment of glassware including kitchen items such as reamers, mixing bowls, measuring cups, etc., in many lovely colors. Many patterns of dinnerware were made as well. Their Fire-King line was formulated to produce heat-proof glassware so durable that it was guaranteed for two years against breakage caused by heat. Colors included Jade-ite, Azur-ite, Turquoise and Sapphire Blue, Ivory, milk white (often decorated with fired-on patterns), Royal Ruby, and Forest Green. Collectors are beginning to reassemble sets, and for the most part, prices are relatively low, except for some of the rarer items. For more information, we recommend *Anchor Hocking's Fire-King & More, Third Edition,* by Gene and Cathy Florence (Collector Books).

Alice, cup, Vitrick, blue rim... **10.00**

Alice, plate, Vitrock, 9½"........**15.00**

Alice, saucer, Vitrock, red rim. **7.00**

Anniversary Rose, bowl, dessert; 4½" **15.00**

Anniversary Rose, cup, 8-oz **7.50**

Anniversary Rose, platter, 9x12" .**25.00**

Anniversay Rose, snack tray... **8.00**

Blue Mosaic, bowl, vegetable, 8¼" **20.00**

Blue Mosaic, plate, 7½"............ **8.00**

Blue Mosaic, sugar bowl, open **7.00**

Bubble, bowl, cereal; crystal, 5¼".**10.00**

Bubble, candlesticks, Forest Green, pr....................................**37.50**

Bubble, platter, Sapphire Blue, oval, 12" **16.00**

Bubble, stem, crystal, 4-oz **4.50**

Bubble, tumbler, 12-oz, 4½"... **12.50**

Charm, bowl, dessert; Ruby, 4¾".**8.00**

Charm, creamer, Jade-ite or Ivory, ea.....................................**25.00**

Charm, plate, Forest Green, 9¼" . **28.00**

Charm, sugar bowl, Azur-ite or white, open, ea **12.00**

Early American Prescut, ashtray, 5" **10.00**

Early American Prescut, bowl, #787, 8¾" **9.00**

Early American Prescut, bowl, console; #797, crystal, 9" **12.00**

Early American Prescut, bowl, dessert; #765, 5⅜" **2.50**

Early American Prescut, bowl, oval, #776, 9" L **6.00**

Early American Prescut, bowl, round, #767, 7¼" **5.00**

Early American Prescut, bowl, scalloped rim, #775, crystal, 5¼" **7.00**

Early American Prescut, cake plate, footed, #706, crystal, 13½"..**30.00**

Early American Prescut, candy dish, w/lid, #774, crystal, 5¼" **10.00**

Early American Prescut, cruet, #711, crystal, 7¾" **6.00**

Early American Prescut, lazy Susan, 9-pc, #700/713..... **50.00**

Early American Prescut, oil lamp **295.00**

Early American Prescut, pitcher, sq, 40-oz............................ **45.00**

Early American Prescut, plate, crystal, 11"....................... **12.00**

Early American Prescut, plate, snack; #780, 10" **10.00**

Early American Prescut, plate, 11" **12.00**

Early American Prescut, punch set, 15-pc **35.00**

Early American Prescut, relish, 5-part, crystal, 13½"........... **25.00**

Early American Prescut, relish, 5-part, 13½" **30.00**

Early American Prescut, shakers, plastic tops, #725, crystal, pr **5.00**

Early American Prescut, syrup pitcher, #707, 12-oz........ **20.00**

Early American Prescut, tumbler, juice; #730, 5-oz, 4" **3.00**

Early American Prescut, vase, #742, 10"........................... **12.50**

Early American Prescut, vase, bud; footed, 5"........................ **595.00**

Fleurette, bowl, dessert; 4½" ... **3.00**

Fleurette, creamer **5.00**

Fleurette, plate, 7½" **10.00**

Fleurette, platter, 9x12" **14.00**

Forest Green, ashtray, hexagonal, 5¾" **8.00**

Forest Green, bud vase, 9" **10.00**

Forest Green, compote, 6½"... **50.00**

Forest Green, tumbler, fancy, 9-oz **6.00**

Forest Green, water bottle, screw-on lid, $145.00. (Photo courtesy Gene and Cathy Florence)

Game Bird, ashtray, white w/decal, 5¼" **15.00**

Game Bird, bowl, soup or cereal; white w/decal, 5" **8.00**

Game Bird, mug, white w/decal, 8-oz...................................... **8.00**

Game Bird, plate, white w/decal, 9⅛" **6.50**

Game Bird, tumbler, 11-oz **11.00**

Gray Laurel, bowl, dessert; 5". **7.00**

Gray Laurel, creamer, footed .. **5.00**

Gray Laurel, plate, 11" **16.00**

Gray Laurel, saucer, 5¾" 3.00
Harvest, bowl, soup plate; 6½".. 8.00
Harvest, plate, 10" 6.00
Harvest, sugar bowl, w/lid..... 12.00
Hobnail, cookie jar, w/lid, Milk
  White 25.00
Hobnail, pitcher, Milk White. 12.50
Homestead, bowl, vegetable; white
  w/decal, 8¼"..................... 20.00
Homestead, plate, white w/decal,
  10" 8.00
Honeysuckle, cup, white w/decal,
  8-oz.................................. 4.00
Honeysuckle, plate, white w/decal,
  9⅛" 6.00
Honeysuckle, platter, white w/decal,
  9x12" 16.00
Honeysuckle, relish, 3-part, white
  w/decal, 9¾"................... 125.00
Honeysuckle, tumbler, white w/decal,
  5-oz................................. 20.00
Ivory Glass (Fish Scale), bowl, deep
  cereal; 5½" 12.00
Ivory Glass (Fish Scale), cup, w/blue,
  8-oz................................. 28.00
Ivory Glass (Fish Scale), cup, w/red,
  8-oz................................. 10.00
Ivory Glass (Fish Scale), plate,
  9¼"................................. 13.00
Jane Ray (Jade-ite), bowl, oatmeal,
  6" 16.00
Jane Ray (Jade-ite), bowl, vegeta-
  ble, 8¼" 22.00
Jane Ray (Jade-ite), creamer .. 10.00
Jane Ray (Jade-ite), plate, 9⅛"... 10.00
Jane Ray (Jade-ite), platter,
  9x12"............................... 18.00
Lace Edge, cake plate, plain Milk
  White, 13"........................ 15.00
Lace Edge, compote, plain Milk
  White, 3½x7" 6.00
Meadow Green, cake dish, sq, white
  w/decal, 8" 6.00

Meadow Green, casserole, white
  w/decal, crystal lid, 2-qt ... 9.00
Meadow Green, plate, white w/decal,
  10"................................... 4.00
Peach Blossom, bowl, vegetable;
  8¼" 50.00
Peach Blossom, plate, 9"........ 25.00
Peach Lustre, cup, 8-oz............ 3.50
Peach Lustre (Laurel), bowl, soup
  plate; 7½".......................... 10.00
Peach Lustre (Laurel), creamer or
  sugar bowl, footed, ea 4.00
Peach Lustre (Laurel), plate,
  7½".................................. 9.00
Prescut (Oatmeal), bowl, berry;
  crystal, 4¼"........................ 2.00
Prescut (Oatmeal), tumbler, crys-
  tal, 9-oz 2.00
Prescut (Pineapple), milk pitcher,
  white, 12-oz 10.00
Prescut (Pineapple), shakers, pr. 10.00
Primrose, baking pan, white w/decal,
  w/lid, 5x9" 18.00
Primrose, casserole, white w/decal,
  w/knob lid, 2-qt 16.00
Primrose, creamer or sugar bowl,
  white w/decal, ea.............. 5.00
Primrose, plate, white w/decal,
  7½".................................. 5.00

**Primrose, tumblers: 11-ounce,
$25.00; 9½-ounce (4"), rare, $95.00;
and 5-ounce, $30.00.** (Photo courtesy
Gene and Cathy Florence)

Rainbow, bowl, fruit; primary color,
  6"................................... 22.00

Rainbow, creamer, footed, pastel colors.................................**15.00**

Rainbow, platter, primary colors, 11".......................................**65.00**

Restaurant Ware, cup, straight, #G215, Jade-ite, 6-oz........**9.00**

Restaurant Ware, mug, #G212, crystal or white, 7-oz........**7.50**

Restaurant Ware, mug, #G212, Jade-ite, 7-oz...................**15.00**

Restaurant Ware, plate, #G315, Jade-ite, 5½".....................**14.00**

Restaurant Ware, plate, 3-part, tab or no tab, #G292, Jade-ite, 9½"...................................**28.00**

Royal Ruby, ice bucket...........**35.00**

Royal Ruby, pitcher, tilted or swirled, 3-qt.....................**50.00**

Royal Ruby, plate, dinner; 9".**11.00**

Royal Ruby, sugar bowl, flat, w/lid.............................**22.00**

Royal Ruby, sugar bowl, footed, w/lid.................................**17.50**

Royal Ruby, tumbler, 9-oz........**6.50**

Royal Ruby, vase, 9", $17.50.
(Photo courtesy Gene and Cathy Florence)

Sandwich, bowl, scalloped, Ruby, 6½".....................................**27.50**

Sandwich, bowl, smooth, pink, 5¼".................................... **7.00**

Sandwich, cookie jar, w/lid, crystal....................................**40.00**

Sandwich, custard cup.............**3.50**

Sandwich, plate, crystal, 9"...**20.00**

Sandwich, plate, Desert Gold, 9".**10.00**

Sandwich, saucer, Forest Green.**20.00**

Sapphire Blue, baker, round, 1½-qt......................................**16.00**

Sapphire Blue, measuring cup, 1 spout, 8-oz.......................**32.00**

Sapphire Blue, pie plate, 8½" or 9½", ea.............................**10.00**

Shell, bowl, cereal; Golden, 6⅜".**10.00**

Shell, bowl, dessert; Jade-ite, 4¾"................................**14.00**

Shell, creamer or sugar bowl, footed, Peach Lustre, ea.......**10.00**

Shell, cup, Golden, 8-oz...........**3.25**

Shell, cup, Jade-ite, 8-oz........**10.00**

Shell, cup, Peach Lustre, 8-oz.**5.00**

Shell, plate, Jade-ite, 7¼"......**20.00**

Soreno, ashtray, Aquamarine, 8".**10.00**

Soreno, plate, Avocado or Milk White, 10"...........................**3.00**

Swirl, bowl, cereal; Azur-ite, 6"..**18.00**

Swirl, bowl, cereal; Ivory, 6"...**20.00**

Swirl, bowl, soup plate; Golden Anniversary, 7½".............**10.00**

Swirl, cup, Azur-ite, 8-oz.........**6.00**

Swirl, cup, Azur-ite or pink, 8-oz, ea...**6.00**

Swirl, cup, Jade-ite, 8-oz.......**30.00**

Swirl, plate, Anchorwhite, Azur-ite, Ivory or Sunrise, 7", ea.....**8.00**

Swirl, plate, Anchorwhite, Ivory, pink or Sunrise, 9⅛", ea .**10.00**

Swirl, platter, Anchorwhite, Azur-ite or Ivory, 9x12", ea......**20.00**

Swirl, platter, Jade-ite, 9x12"..**425.00**

Thousand Line, bowl, deep vegetable; crystal, 8"............**12.00**

Thousand Line, candy dish, w/lid, crystal..............................**17.00**

Thousand Line, tray, sandwich; crystal, 12½.....................**12.00**

Turquoise Blue, bowl, vegetable; 8".....................................**25.00**

Turquoise Blue, egg plate, 9¾". **22.00**
Turquoise Blue, mug, 8-oz..... **15.00**
Turquoise Blue, relish, 3-part, 11⅛".................................. **13.00**
Vienna Lace, bowl, cereal/soup; 6½" **8.00**
Vienna Lace, cup, no design.... **4.00**
Vienna Lace, plate, 10"............ **7.00**
Wheat, bowl, vegetable; white w/decal, 8¼".................... **12.00**
Wheat, casserole, w/knob lid, white w/decal, 2-qt **15.00**
Wheat, custard, white w/decal, 6-oz **3.00**
Wheat, loaf pan, white w/decal, 5x9"................................. **12.00**
Wheat, platter, white w/decal, 9x12".............................. **15.00**

Aprons

Vintage aprons evoke nostalgic memories — grandma in her kitchen, gentle heat radiating from the cookstove, a child tugging on her apron strings — and even if collectors can't relate to that scene personally, they still want to cherish and preserve those old aprons. Some are basic and functional, perhaps made of flour sack material, while others are embroidered and trimmed with lace or appliqués. Commercial-made aprons are collectible as well, and those that retain their original tags command the higer prices. Remember, condition is critical, and as a general rule, those that are made by hand are preferred over machine-made or commercial-made aprons. Values are for examples in excellent condition unless otherwise noted.

Bib, cotton, print, adjustable waist, Carmen Lee tag **25.00**
Bib, cotton, print, patch pocket, pleated flounce sides, sash ties, 1950 .... **22.00**
Bib, cotton, print, sweetheart-shaped front, sheer ruffle, 1940s............................... **30.00**
Bib, cotton, solid color w/tatting & embroidery, 1920s........... **50.00**
Bib, cotton, white w/appliqué, rickrack trim, 1940s, from $35 to...... **45.00**
Bib, cotton, white w/bright multi-colored embroidery, trimmed pocket............................... **22.00**
Bib, cotton, white w/embroidered Scottie dogs, 1950s, from $35 to **50.00**

Bib, organdy, with tie back and small triangle pockets, ruffled hem, 1940s, from $28.00 (Photo courtesy La Ree Johnson Bruton)

Bib, silk type, Chinese design of lg fan w/rhinestones............ **55.00**
Bib, wraparound that ties in front, 1940s-50s......................... **22.00**
Pinafore, cotton print w/bias-tape trim, 1930s **25.00**
Waist, cotton canvas w/Disneyland name & printed scene, 1950s, EX **35.00**
Waist, crocheted cotton w/dainty work **15.00**
Waist, gingham w/smocking at waist, 1950s.................... **18.00**

Waist, handkerchiefs pieced together & satin ties, 1940s...... **40.00**

Waist, linen w/allover embroidered dots & Battenburg lace trim............................... **30.00**

Waist, nylon w/lace trim & satin bow at pocket, 1960s, from $10 to **15.00**

Waist, organdy & eyelet, Carmen Lee tag............................ **24.00**

Waist, organdy w/chintz-like trim & rickrack........................ **25.00**

Waist, organdy w/diagonal handkerchiefs along hem........ **18.00**

Waist, plastic w/rooster & barnyard scene, ruffled bottom **40.00**

Waist, polished cotton w/multicolored voile roses & rickrack trim **22.00**

Waist, cotton with organdy ruffle trimmed in rickrack, 1950s, from $10.00 to $15.00. (Photo courtesy La Ree Johnson Bruton)

Ashtrays

Even though smoking may be frowned upon these days, ashtrays themselves are beginning to be noticed favorably by collectors, who perhaps view them as an 'endangered species'! Some of the more desirable examples are those with embossed or intaglio designs,

applied decorations, added figures of animals or people, Art Deco styling, an interesting advertising message, and an easily recognizable manufacturer's mark.

Novelty, chrome sailboat and blue glass tray, F.D. Co., 5" diameter, $45.00. (Photo courtesy Mary Frank Gaston)

Advertising, Big Boy, red logo in round glass dish, 3 rests, 4", EX **28.00**

Advertising, Breyers Ice Cream, ceramic, white w/logo, 5½" dia.................................. **20.00**

Advertising, Bush Bavarian, painted & stamped steel, 2 rests, 6" L... **8.00**

Advertising, Canadian Club Whiskey, ceramic, green lettering, 5½" **21.00**

Advertising, Chrysler Belvidere Assembly, metal, center logo, 5"...................................... **28.00**

Advertising, Corning Glass Works, man in center, 1960s-70s, 7x5", EX **22.00**

Advertising, Disneyland, ceramic, Magic Kingdom/Tinkerbell, 5".................................... **25.00**

Advertising, GE 75th Anniversary, 1878-1953, ceramic, 5½" . **22.00**

Advertising, Hamm's Beer, clear glass w/decals, 6" dia...... **10.00**

Advertising, Honda, ceramic helmet form, 4".................... **25.00**

Advertising, Kodak 50th Anniversary, smoky glass kidney shape, 6", EX............ **15.00**

Advertising, Rubbermaid, 25th Anniversary, 1934-59, dustpan shape, 5" **20.00**

Advertising, Stork Club, ceramic w/ name on rise, 4 rests, 5½"...**45.00**

Decorative, bone china w/dragon pattern, Wedgwood, 4½" . **15.00**

Decorative, ceramic Hummel-like boy, Music Maker, Napco-Japan, 5½" **25.00**

Decorative, glass w/5 flowers in paperweight base, St Clair, 4" **70.00**

Decorative, metal arrowhead shape w/copper plating, 5½" **15.00**

Fraternal, Masonic, ceramic w/gold trim, 1960s, 5" **8.00**

Novelty, card suit shapes, ceramic, set of 4 from 4" to 5" **18.00**

Novelty, clown face w/big mouth, rest pivots, Treasure Craft, 1960, 5" **45.00**

Novelty, Columbia Space Flight (7), Engle-Truly, 5¼" sq **8.00**

Novelty, Dutch shoe, Delft from Holland, 2 rests, 5¼" L ... **20.00**

Novelty, frog w/butterfly on nose, brass ash dump, 4½" **22.00**

Novelty, white elephant with multi-colored design, black ears and tail atop rectangular tray, 4½", from $20.00 to $35.00. (Photo courtesy Carol Bess White)

Tire Ashtrays

Tire ashtrays were introduced ca 1910 as advertising items. The very early all-glass or glass-and-metal types were replaced in the early 1920s by the more familiar rubber-tired varieties. Hundreds of different examples have been produced over the years. They are still distributed (by the larger tire companies only), but no longer display the detail or color of the pre-World War II tire ashtrays. Although the common ones bring modest prices, rare examples sometimes sell for several hundred dollars. For more information we recommend *Tire Ashtray Collector's Guide* by Jeff McVey; he is listed in the Directory under Idaho.

Allstate SR Balloon, amber glass disk wheel 5-lug insert, 5½" **32.00**

Cooper Cobra Radial GT 75th Anniversary, clear imprinted insert............................... **25.00**

Falls Evergreen Tube That Sentenced Air..., Weller Pottery insert . **175.00**

Firestone, red & black plastic insert, 3 extended rests, 6" **10.00**

Firestone Transport 100 (F in shield) Tubeless, embossed clear insert **25.00**

General, Streamline Jumbo, green insert w/Goes Along..., 5". **65.00**

Gillette Super Traction, embossed bear on clear glass insert, 7"........ **65.00**

Good Year, 1991 Farm Progress Show tractor tire, Dalton City IL, 7"............................... **45.00**

Goodyear, Hi-Miler Cross Rib, nylon, clear insert w/blue logo, 6¼" **20.00**

Hood Arrow, Heavy Duty 6 Ply, 500-20, 6½" **65.00**
Hood Balloon Tires, red, white, blue on clear glass insert, 4½". **45.00**
Kelly Springfield, Voyager, Aramid..., clear insert w/green decal, 6" **20.00**
Ohio Rubber Co Long Beach Calif 5.25x1.00, purple glass insert, 5" **30.00**

Pennsylvania Gold Standard Balloon Tires, 33x6.00 six-ply cord, $60.00. (Photo courtesy Jeff McVey)

Pennsylvania Tires, pink glass insert, 5¼" **50.00**
Pennsylvania Vacuum Cup, 33x5, reproduction in modern colors, 6" ea **20.00**
Riverside WR-20 Hi-TRAC, Montgomery Ward decal on clear insert, 6½" **35.00**
Royal US Heavy Duty Six, US Tires embossed on amber glass insert, 7" **75.00**

Automobilia

Many are fascinated with vintage automobiles, but to own one of those 'classy chassis' is a luxury not all can afford! So instead they enjoy collecting related memorabilia such as advertising, owners' manuals, horns, emblems, and hood ornaments. The decade of the 1930s produced the items that are most in demand today, but the '50s models have their own band of devoted fans as well as do the muscle cars of the '60s.

Ashtray, Ford, shield logo in red & white on clear glass, sq, NM **20.00**
Ashtray, Grand Auto Stores, glass, sq, 2½x2½", NM **12.00**
Bank, Chevrolet the Symbol of Savings..., tin globe, Chein, 5", VG+ **50.00**
Bank, Ford, shaggy dog figure w/Ford collar, Florence Ceramics, 8", M **45.00**
Book, American Automobile, John B Rae, 1st edition, 1965, EX..**12.00**
Book, Chevrolet, 75 Years of..., Dammann/Crestline Publishing, 1987, G **30.00**
Book, Ford Mechanic's Handbook, 1949, 36 pages, EX **40.00**
Book, Ford V-8 instruction booklet, 1932, 62 pages, VG **120.00**
Book, GMC 2½-ton 6x6 Parts List, 1942, 202 pages, G **30.00**
Booklet, Buick Stereo User's Guide, 1973, 16 pages, 4x8", EX.. **8.00**
Booklet, Cadillac, Gentle Art of Motoring, 1948, 12 pages, EX **12.00**
Booklet, Lincoln V-8 Engine, 1950, 12 pages, EX................... **10.00**
Booklet, Mercury Station Wagon, 1972, 8 pages, 9x12", EX... **12.00**
Brochure, Chevrolet Corvette, 1960, unfolds to 25½x10", NM ... **30.00**
Brochure, Plymouth, 1956, unfolds to 35x9", G **28.00**
Calendar, Chevrolet Motor Cars, 1920, paper, framed, 33½", EX................................. **80.00**

Calendar, Federal Trucks, 1942, complete, 34x16", EX...... 50.00

Calendar, Nash, 1951, complete, EX 10.00

Catalog, Pep Boys Auto & Radio Supplies..., Summer/Fall, 1940, EX 65.00

Chart, Cadillac Eldorado Tune-Up, 1956, EX 25.00

Clock, Cadillac, sq desk-type light-up w/emblem, 1960, 9x10", NM 200.00

Clock, Cadillac, yellow plastic with glass lens, $165.00. (Photo courtesy B.J. Summers and Wayne Priddy)

Clock, Nash, octagonal w/metal frame, painted tin face, 18x18", G 75.00

Coaster/ashtray, Graham, aluminum, 4" dia, EX............... 30.00

Cup & saucer, Ford logo, Shenango China, 1950s-60s, EX ... 120.00

Display, wood w/1960 Buick on glass front, hinged lid, lights up, EX.............................. 50.00

Display rack, Ford Color Patch, 3 stepped shelves w/marquee, 19", G 100.00

Emblem, body; Thunderbird, 10x2¼", EX 80.00

Emblem, hood; Frazer, 1940s, multicolored, 1940s, 5½x3⅜", VG 90.00

Emblem, radiator; Ford, 1931, oval, VG 60.00

Gearshift knob, simulated onyx w/brass St Christopher medallion, EX............................ 25.00

Hood ornament, chrome nude figure w/windblown hair, 5", VG. 50.00

Horn, Spartan SOS Deluxe, 6-volt, 16" L, EX 60.00

Key chain, '66 Olds Super Salesman, EX 15.00

Magazine, Ford Times, 1955, EX+ 8.00

Magazine, Motor Magazine's Annual, Oct 1939, cover by Radchaugh, VG 30.00

Manual, owner's; Chevrolet, 1955, G 40.00

Manual, owner's; Chevy Nova, 1960, VG 12.00

Manual, owner's; Corvette, 1969, NM 40.00

Manual, owner's; Ford Mustang, 1967, VG 20.00

Manual, owner's; Ford Pinto, 1973, EX 12.00

Manual, owner's; Oldsmobile Toronado, 1969, EX......... 20.00

Manual, shop; Chevrolet, 1938, 272 pages, VG 40.00

Manual, shop; Chevrolet, 1958, 800 pages, VG 40.00

Paperweight, GM Golden Milestones, 1908-1958, token in Lucite cube, EX 45.00

Pocket mirror, Mack-Leading Gasoline Truck..., 2½" dia, EX+ 350.00

Postcard, Buick factory photo, black & white, 1950, EX............. 6.00

Poster, Fordor Sedan, cardboard, 1940s, vehicle, framed, 25x37", EX+ 75.00

Promotional vehicle, Chevy pickup, 1972, NM 150.00

Promotional vehicle, Ford Thunderbird, 1965, VG.. **115.00**
Promotional vehicle, Ford Thunderbird convertible, 1959, EX **150.00**
Ruler, Chevrolet, celluloid, 1930s, 6", M **28.00**
Sign, Buick Quick Service, white, black on red, white, blue bands, 16x26", EX **250.00**
Sign, Cadillac Authorized Service, porcelain, white, black, 48x48", EX **650.00**
Sign, Plymouth, neon, flag shape w/block lettering, 22x25", NM **325.00**
Thermometer, Lincoln Cab Co-Call a Lincoln, wood, arched top, 15", VG **80.00**
Tire gauge, US Gauge Co, measures up to 50 psi, w/leather pouch, VG **32.00**
Token, 1954 General Motors Motorama, VG **18.00**
Tray, Ford & V-8 logo embossed on stainless steel, 12x18", EX .**75.00**
Wrench, open-end; Fiat, 6½", G. **8.00**

Autumn Leaf

Autumn Leaf dinnerware was a product of the Hall China Company, who produced this extensive line from 1933 until 1978 for exclusive distribution by the Jewel Tea Company. The Libbey Glass Company made co-ordinating pitchers, tumblers, and stemware. Metal, cloth, plastic, and paper items were also available. Today, though very rare pieces are expensive and a challenge to acquire, new collectors may easily reassemble an attractive, usable set at a reason-

able price. Hall has produced special club pieces (for the NALCC) as well as some limited editions for an Ohio company, but these are well marked and easily identified as such. Refer to *The Collector's Encyclopedia of Hall China* by Margaret and Kenn Whitmyer (Collector Books) for more information. See Clubs and Newsletters for information concerning the *Autumn Leaf* newsletter.

Baker, individual, Fort Pitt, oval, 12-oz **225.00**
Baker/souffle, 4½" **80.00**
Bowl, cream soup **35.00**
Bowl, salad; 9" **20.00**
Bowl, soup; Melmac **20.00**
Bread box, metal, from $400 to. **800.00**
Butter dish, ruffled lid, regular, 1-lb **500.00**
Butter dish, ruffled lid, regular, ¼-lb, from $175 to **250.00**
Cake plate, w/metal stand... **180.00**
Candy dish, metal base, from $500 to **600.00**
Canister set, copper lids, 4-pc set, from $600 to **1,200.00**
Casserole, Dunbar, Heatflow clear glass, oval, w/lid, 1½-qt... **60.00**
Casserole, Heatflow, clear, round, w/lid, Dunbar, 1½-qt **60.00**
Coaster, metal, 3⅛" **8.00**
Coffeepot, electric percolator, all china, 4-pc **400.00**
Coffeepot, Rayed, 9-cup **45.00**

Covered dish, 1940 – 1976, from $50.00 to $70.00. Gravy boat with underplate, $55.00.

Creamer & sugar bowl, Nautilus..**125.00**

Creamer & sugar bowl, Rayed, 1930s style........................**80.00**

Cup, coffee; Jewell's Best.......**25.00**

Cup, St Denis..........................**37.50**

Dutch oven, metal & porcelain, w/lid, 5-qt........................**160.00**

Flatware, stainless steel, ea pc from $25 to..............................**30.00**

Hot pad, metal back, round, 7¼", from $15 to.......................**25.00**

Marmalade, w/underplate & lid, from $100 to..................**125.00**

Mug, conic, $65.00.

Mustard, 3-pc, from $100 to..**120.00**

Plate, salad; Melmac, 7"........**20.00**

Plate, 6", from $5 to.................**8.00**

Plate, 8", scarce.......................**18.00**

Platter, oval, 11½", from $20 to..**28.00**

Platter, oval, 13½"...................**28.00**

Salt & pepper shakers, Casper, ruffled, regular, pr..........**30.00**

Shelf liner, 108" roll...............**50.00**

Sifter, metal...........................**400.00**

Towel, tea; cotton, 16x33"......**60.00**

Tray, metal, oval...................**100.00**

Tumbler, Brockway, 13-oz......**45.00**

Tumbler, iced-tea; Libbey, frosted, 5½"....................................**20.00**

Tumbler, Libbey, flat or footed, gold frost etching, 15-oz, ea....**65.00**

Vase, bud; regular decal, 6".**350.00**

Avon

Originally founded in 1886 under the title California Perfume Company, the firm became officially known as Avon Products Inc. in 1939. Avon offers something for almost everyone such as cross-collectibles including jewelry, Fostoria, Wedgwood, commerative plates, Ceramarte steins, and hundreds of other quality items. Among the most popular items are the Mrs. P.F.E. Albee figurines. Mrs. Albee was the first Avon lady, ringing doorbells and selling their products in the very early years of the company's history. The figurines are issued each year and awarded only to Avon's most successful representatives. Each are elegantly attired in magnificent period fashions. The workmanship is remarkable. Also sought are product samples, magazine ads, jewelry, and catalogs. Their Cape Cod glassware has been sold in vast quantities since the '70s and is becoming a common sight at flea markets and antique malls. For more information we recommend *Hastin's Avon Collector's Price Guide* by Bud Hastin. See also Cape Cod. For information concerning the National Association of Avon Collectors and the newsletter *Avon Times*, see Clubs and Newsletters. Values are for mint-condition examples unless noted otherwise. Mint-in-box items bring much higher prices than those without their original boxes.

After shave, Wild Country, 1923 Star Station Wagon, designed by William C. Durant, 7", MIB, $35.00.
(Photo courtesy Monsen & Baer)

Albee figurine, #02, 1979, standing w/satchel over arm, MIB. **50.00**

Albee figurine, #05, 1982, seated in chair, MIB........................ **40.00**

Albee figurine, #09, 1986, standing next to chair, MIB........... **50.00**

Albee figurine, #19, 1996, standing w/hand to hat, MIB......... **35.00**

Bath brush, Imp the Chimp, plastic, 1980, 10", MIB............ **4.00**

Bell, Christmas 1986, white porcelain w/gold trim, 5", MIB. **15.00**

Bell, Giving Thanks, porcelain pumpkin & pilgrim, 1990, 4½", MIB.................................. **15.00**

Bell, Treasured Moments, Fostoria, 1984, 5", MIB **11.00**

Bubble Bath, Christmas Sparkler, colors, 1968-69, 4-oz, MIB, ea **13.00**

Bubble Bath, Schroeder figure, plastic, 1970-72, 6-oz, MIB (piano box)........................ **9.00**

Bubble Bath, Tub Sub, yellow plastic, 1978-79, 6-oz, 10" L, MIB **3.00**

Candle, Mr Snowlight (snowman), 1981, 5½", MIB.................. **5.00**

Candle, Sparkling Turtle Candlette, glass, 1976-79, 4½" L, MIB. **9.00**

Candleholder, Fireplace Friends, 1988, 3½", MIB , ea......... **10.00**

Candleholder, Fostoria goblet votive, blue, 1975-77, MIB, ea **14.00**

Candleholders, Holiday Hostess, glass w/holly decal, 1981, 3", MIB, pr **12.00**

Decanter, Bird of Paradise, glass w/gold head, 1970-72, 8", MIB **12.00**

Decanter, Compote, milk glass fruit stack w/gold cap, 5-oz, MIB .**8.00**

Decanter, Cornucopia, milk glass w/gold cap, 1971-76, 5½", MIB **9.00**

Decanter, Eiffel Tower, glass w/gold cap, 1970, 3-oz, MIB **10.00**

Decanter, French Telephone, milk glass w/gold cap, 1971, 6-oz, MIB................................. **30.00**

Decanter, Hurricane Lamp, milk glass w/glass shade, 1973-74, 6-oz, MIB **13.00**

Decanter, It All Adds Up Calculator, black glass, 1979-80, 4-oz, MIB.................................. **8.00**

Decanter, Little Bo Peep, painted milk glass & plastic, 1976-78, MIB.................................. **8.00**

Decanter, Packard Roadster, amber glass, 1970-72, 6-oz, 6½" L, MIB.................................. **13.00**

Decanter, Partridge, milk glass w/plastic cap, 1973-75, 5-oz, MIB **6.00**

Decanter, Snoopy Surprise, milk glass w/yellow or black caps, MIB................................. **12.00**

Decanter, Wise Choice Owl, amber glass, silver top, 1969-70, 4-oz, MIB.................................. **10.00**

Doll, Howdy Partner, 5th in Childhood Dreams series, 1993, 10", MIB **40.00**

Doll, Southern Belle, porcelain, 1988, 8¼", MIB **30.00**

Egg, Four Seasons, 4 different, porcelain w/wood base, 1984, MIB, ea **10.00**

Egg, Majestic, crystal w/pewter base, 1993, 4½", MIB **30.00**

Heart box, Forget Me Not, porcelain, 1989, MIB **8.00**

Ornament, Hummingbird, 1986, crystal w/etched design, 3½", MIB **12.00**

Ornament, Melvin P Merrymouse, plastic, 2nd series, 1983, 2¾", MIB **8.00**

Perfume, Icicle, glass w/gold cap, 1967-68, 1 dram, MIB **8.00**

Perfume, La Belle Telephone, clear, glass w/gold top, 1974-76, 1-oz, MIB **9.00**

Perfume, Love Bird, 1973-74, ¼-oz, MIB **10.00**

Perfume, Petite Mouse, frosted glass w/gold plastic head, ¼-oz, MIB **18.00**

Perfume, Purse, embossed glass w/gold cap & chain, 1½-oz, MIB **10.00**

Perfume, Rollin' Roller Skate, glass, red ball top, 1980-81, 2-oz, MIB **5.00**

Perfume, Strawberry, red glass w/silver cap, 1974-76, ⅛-oz, MIB **6.00**

Plate, Christmas 1987, Magic That Santa Brings, porcelain, 8", MIB **25.00**

Plate, Easter 1994, porcelain, 5", MIB **10.00**

Plate, Let Freedom Ring-Martin Luther King Jr, porcelain, 1995, 5", MIB **10.00**

Platter, Holiday Hostess, glass w/holly decal, 1981, 11" dia, MIB **15.00**

Soap, Christmas Classics set, 3 ornament shapes, 1993, MIB **3.00**

Soap, Soap Savers, 1973, 9-oz, MIB **10.00**

Soap & soap dish, Fostoria egg dish, clear glass, 4½", 1977, MIB **18.00**

Soap & soap dish, Sittin' Kittens, milk glass dish, 1973-75, MIB **10.00**

Banks

After the Depression, everyone was aware that saving 'for a rainy day' would help during bad times. Children of the '40s, '50s, and '60s were given piggy banks in forms of favorite characters to reinforce the idea of saving. They were made to realize that by saving money they could buy that expensive bicycle or a toy they were particularly longing for.

Today on the flea market circuit, figural banks are popular collectibles, especially those that are character-related — advertising characters and Disney in particular.

Interest has recently developed in glass banks, and you may be surprised at the prices some of the harder-to-find examples are bringing. Charlie Reynolds has written the glass bank 'bible,' called *Collector's Guide to Glass Banks*, which you'll want to read if you think you'd like to collect them. It's published by Collector Books. In our listings, the glass banks we've included will have punched factory slots or molded, raised slots. There are other types as well. Because of limited space, values listed below are mid range. Expect to pay as much as 50% more or less than our suggested prices.

Ceramic

Pig in dancing costume with indented dots, full outline footing with center stopper, unmarked (American Bisque), 4¾", from $35.00 to $45.00.

Black woman w/apron, US, 1940s............................**100.00**
Cat, porcelain, black & white, Japan, 1930s, 5"............ **100.00**
Cat snarling, pottery, US (?), 1930s, 5".....................................**100.00**
Dog w/pups on books, overpainted porcelain, Japan, 1930s, 5".....**125.00**
Dutch boy, pottery, Germany, 1930s.............................**175.00**
Egg man, red or green cap, pottery, US, 1940s, 3¾"..............**100.00**
Elephant in tutu, pottery, US, 1940s................................**80.00**
Elephant trumpeting, US (?), 1930s, 5½"......................................**80.00**
Girl's head, pottery, US (?), 1930s, 4"......................................**100.00**
Horse, stylized, porcelain, Occupied Japan, 1950s, 3¼"...........**80.00**

King on throne, pottery, US (?), 1930s, 5".........................**150.00**
Pig standing upright in overalls & neck bow, USA 1940s......**40.00**
Scottie dog, US Tudor Potteries, Hollywood Ware, 1930s, 4¾"..........................**200.00**

Character

Alvin (Chipmunks), vinyl figure in cap & turtleneck w/lg A, M........**25.00**
Andy Panda, composition figure, Crown Toy, 1940s, 5", EX.**85.00**
Andy Panda, plastic figure, 1970s, 7", NM+..........................**45.00**
Barney, purple vinyl figure, 7½", NM+..................................**8.00**
Betty Boop, painted chalkware figure, 1950s-60s, 14", VG.**125.00**
Big Bird, ceramic figure seated next to toy box, Applause, 7", MIB.................................**18.00**
Bionic Woman, vinyl figure running, Animals Plus, 1976, 10", EX+..................................**25.00**
Bozo the Clown, plastic figure on star base, Star, 1960s-70s, 6", EXIB.................................**30.00**
Bullwinkle, molded vinyl figure, Imco, 1977, 10", EX........**75.00**
Cabbage Patch Kids, girl w/piggy bank in hands, 1980s, 7", NM......**10.00**
Cabbage Patch Kids, vinyl baby in diaper, Appalachian Artworks, 6", NM..............................**10.00**
Cecil (Beany & Cecil), molded plastic head, NM....................**35.00**
Cookie Monster, sitting in pile of cookies, ceramic, 7", MIB.**18.00**
Mister Magoo, yellow vinyl, black & blue trim, Renzi, 1960, 17", M **150.00**

Schroeder (Peanuts), ceramic figure, 7", M **100.00**

Scooby Doo, vinyl figure seated on haunches, 1980s, 6", EX+. **20.00**

She-Ra Princess of Power, vinyl head, HG Toys/Hong Kong, MIB **10.00**

Snoopy Bank, tin globe w/sporting Snoopy graphics, EX+ **30.00**

Tasmanian Devil, vinyl figure, w/ or w/o base, NM **75.00**

Topo Gigio, nodder figure w/pineapple, M **125.00**

Wizard of Oz, any ceramic character figure, 1960s, NM, ea **75.00**

Woodstock, ceramic, yellow, signed Schulz, 1970s, 6", M **40.00**

Woody Woodpecker, hard vinyl figure, Imco, 1977, 10", MIP **100.00**

Yogi Bear, playing harmonica, composition, 6½", EX **75.00**

California Raisin with saxophone, ceramic, unmarked, 6½", from $25.00 to $30.00. (Photo courtesy Jim and Beverly Mangus)

Glass

Baseball, Boston Braves, white w/red letters, black base, 3½".... **110.00**

Be Wise Owl, dark amber, Anchor Hocking, 7", from $150 to .**200.00**

Bear, Honey Money, clear w/plastic straw hat, red bow tie w/gold band **100.00**

Clown, Louisiana Vinegar paper label, 7", from $35 to **50.00**

Liberty Bell, amber glass, Anchor Hocking, 3¾" **225.00**

Lincoln bust, For Your Lincoln Pennies, twist-off lid, 9". **115.00**

Lucky Barrel, carnival glass, raised slot, 4½" **55.00**

Milk Bottle, Whitestone Farms (red pyro), steel lid w/lock, ½-pt..**110.00**

Penny Trust Co., from $125.00 to $150.00.

Teddy Bear, seated wearing bow tie, pink or clear, 6¼", from $75 to **100.00**

World Globe, embossed continents, Pat Applied For, 5¼" **55.00**

Metal Still Banks

Airplane Spirit of St Louis, steel, EX **500.00**

Andy Gump, cast iron, EX.**1,500.00**

Baby in Cradle, nickel-plated cast iron, EX **2,200.00**

Barrel of Fun Bank, white metal, kids embossed on front, 3½", NM.**100.00**

Bear standing w/right foot forward, cast iron, Hubley, 6¼", EX.**225.00**

Billiken Bank, cast iron, EX .**85.00**

Camel, cast iron, embossed moon & stars on blanket, AC Williams, 7", EX............................ **300.00**

Campbell's Soup Kids, gold-painted cast iron, AC Williams, 3x4", EX **175.00**

Cat crouching w/ball, cast iron, AC Williams, 5½", VG **250.00**

Clown in pointed hat standing, gold or silver on cast iron, 6", VG.**150.00**

Columbia Tower, japanned cast iron, Grey Iron, 7", EX.. **275.00**

Elephant w/Howdah, swinging trunk, bronze tone, AC Williams, 5x7", VG.......... **75.00**

Give Me a Penny (Sharecropper), painted cast iron, 5½", EX+.......... **275.00**

Globe, spins on base, red-painted cast iron, Grey Iron, 5", EX **150.00**

Horse, Tally Ho, cast iron, EX..**200.00**

Horse (Circus) w/front feet on tub, cast iron, AC Williams, 5½", EX **150.00**

Horse Shoe, Good Luck, cast iron, EX **300.00**

House, 2-story, cast iron, silver & gold w/red or green roof, 4", EX **125.00**

Indian Scout w/tomahawk, painted cast iron, 6", EX............ **300.00**

Liberty Bell (1905), electroplated copper, John Harper, 3¾", EX **175.00**

Liberty Bell w/George Washington, cast iron, red w/gold trim, 3", VG.................................... **75.00**

Money Bag (100,000), cast iron, silver w/gold trim, 3½", EX+...... **300.00**

Pass 'Round the Hat (Derby Hat), cast iron, brown w/gold trim, EX **300.00**

Security Safe Deposit Safe, japanned cast iron w/gold trim, 6", EX............................. **150.00**

State Bank Building, japanned cast iron, Kenton, 5½", VG... **175.00**

Statue of Liberty, cast iron, silver w/gold accents, 10", VG. **450.00**

Teddy (Roosevelt) Bust, cast iron, gold w/silver glasses, 5", NM... **350.00**

Turkey, japanned cast iron w/red detail on head, AC Williams, 4", EX+........................... **300.00**

Wise Monkeys (See/Hear/Speak No Evil), cast iron, gold, 3x3½", VG................................. **175.00**

Boston Bull Dog seated, Hubley, 4", EX+, $275.00. (Photo courtesy Bertoia Auctions)

Barbie Dolls

Barbie was first introduced in 1959, and soon Mattel found themselves producing not only dolls but tiny garments, fashion accessories, houses, cars, horses, books, and games as well. Today's Barbie collectors want them all. Though the early Barbie dolls are very hard to find, there are many of her successors still around. The trend today is toward Barbie exclusives — Holiday Barbie dolls and Bob Mackie dolls are all very 'hot' items. So are special-event Barbie dolls.

When buying the older dolls, you'll need to do a lot of studying and comparisons to learn to distinguish one Barbie from another, but this is the key to making sound buys and good investments. Remember, though, collectors are sticklers concerning condition; compared to a doll mint in box, they'll often give an additional 20% if that box has never been opened! As a general rule, a mint-in-box doll is worth twice as much as one mint, no box. The same doll, played with and in only good condition is worth half as much (or even less).

If you want a good source for study, refer to one of these fine books: *Barbie Doll Fashion, Volumes I, II,* and *III,* by Sarah Sink Eames; *Collector's Encyclopedia of Barbie Doll Exclusives* by J. Michael Augustyniak; *Collector's Encyclopedia of Barbie Doll Collector's Editions* by J. Michael Augustyniak; *Barbie, The First 30 Years,* by Stefanie Deutsch; *The Barbie Doll Years,* by Patrick C. and Joyce L. Olds; and *Schroeder's Collectible Toys, Antique to Modern* (Collector Books).

Dolls

Barbie, bubble cut, American Airlines Stewardess, VGIB, $275.00.

Allan, 1965, bendable legs, MIB. **300.00**
Barbie, #4, 1960, blond or brunette, MIB, ea from $425 to.... **450.00**
Barbie, #6, blond, brunette or titian, MIB, ea **425.00**
Barbie, American Girl, 1964, platinum hair, original swimsuit, NM **650.00**
Barbie, Angel Lights, 1993, NRFB **100.00**

Barbie, Arctic, 1996, Dolls of the World, NRFB.................. **25.00**
Barbie, Autumn in London, 1999, City Season Collection, NRFB............................ **45.00**
Barbie, Brazilian, 1989, Dolls of the World, NRFB **75.00**
Barbie, Calvin Klein, 1996, Bloomingdale's, NRFB.... **40.00**
Barbie, Dream Glow, black, 1986, MIB................................ **30.00**
Barbie, Enchanted Evening, 1991, JC Penney, NRFB **50.00**
Barbie, Fabulous Fur, 1986, NRFB............................ **65.00**
Barbie, Holiday, 1989, NRFB. **250.00**
Barbie, Holiday, 1992, NRFB. **150.00**
Barbie, Holiday, 1996, NRFB. **50.00**
Barbie, Indiana, 1998, University Barbie, NRFB.................. **15.00**
Barbie, Island Fun, 1988, NRFB. **20.00**
Barbie, Miss America, 1972, Kellogg Co, NRFB **175.00**
Barbie, My First Barbie, 1981, NRFB............................... **25.00**
Barbie, Nutcracker, 1992, Musical Ballet Series, NRFB **150.00**
Barbie, Oreo Fun, 1997, NRFB ...**35.00**
Barbie, Peach Pretty, 1989, K-Mart, MIB **35.00**
Barbie, Perfume Party, 1988, NRFB............................... **30.00**
Barbie, Polly Pockets, 1994, Hill's, NRFB............................... **30.00**
Barbie, Safari, 1983, Disney, MIB **25.00**
Barbie, Standard, 1967, any hair color, MIB, ea **475.00**
Barbie, Stars & Stripes, 1993, Army Desert Storm, Black or white, NRFB **30.00**
Barbie, Sunset Malibu, 1971, NRFB............................... **65.00**

Barbie, Swirl Ponytail, 1964, blond or brunette, NRFB........ **650.00**

Barbie, Ten Speeder, 1973, NRFB **30.00**

Barbie, Twirly Curls, 1983, MIB............................. **45.00**

Barbie, Twist 'n Turn, 1966, blond, MIB................................ **600.00**

Brad, Talking, 1970, NRFB. **225.00**

Casey, Twist 'n Turn, 1968, blond or brunette, NRFB **300.00**

Chris, 1967, any hair color, MIB. **200.00**

Christie, Beauty Secrets, 1980, MIB................................... **60.00**

Christie, Superstar, 1977, MIB .**80.00**

Francie, Malibu, 1971, NRFB. **75.00**

Francie, Twist 'n Turn, 1969, blond or brunette, short hair, MIB **465.00**

Francie, 30th Anniversary, 1996, NRFB............................... **65.00**

Ginger, Growing Up, 1977, MIB. **100.00**

Kelley, Quick Curl, 1972, NRFB. **175.00**

Ken, 1961, flocked hair, straight legs, MIB, ea **125.00**

Ken, 1962, painted blond or brunette hair, MIB **125.00**

Ken, Arabian Nights, 1964, NRFB........................... **425.00**

Ken, Beach Blast, 1989, NRFB.. **15.00**

Ken, California Dream, 1988, NRFB............................... **25.00**

Ken, Dream Date, 1983, NRFB.**30.00**

Ken, Hawaiian, 1979, MIB.... **55.00**

Ken, Jewel Secrets, 1987, NRFB.**30.00**

Ken, Rhett Butler, 1994, Hollywood Legends, NRFB............... **55.00**

Ken, Sport & Shave, 1980, MIB. **40.00**

Ken, Western, 1982, MIB **45.00**

Midge, 1963, brunette, straight legs, MIB **150.00**

Midge, 1965, any hair color, bendable legs, MIB **450.00**

Midge, Cool Times, 1989, NRFB .**30.00**

Midge, Winter Sports, 1995, Toys R Us, MIB **40.00**

Nikki, Animal Lovin', 1989, NRFB **30.00**

PJ, Fashion Photo, 1978, MIB. **95.00**

PJ, Sun Lovin' Malibu, 1979, MIB **50.00**

Ricky, 1965, MIB.................. **150.00**

Scott, 1980, MIB **55.00**

Skipper, 1964, any hair color, straight legs, MIB **130.00**

Skipper, 1965, any hair color, MIB **175.00**

Skipper, Dramatic New Living, 1970, MIB...................... **130.00**

Skipper, Totally Hair, 1991, NRFB **30.00**

Skipper, Western, 1982, NRFB .**40.00**

Skipper Dream Date, 1990, NRFB............................. **25.00**

Skooter, 1966, any hair color, bendable legs, MIB **275.00**

Stacey, Talking, any hair color, MIB................................ **400.00**

Stacey, Twist 'n Turn, 1969, any hair color, NRFB **500.00**

Teresa, California Dream, 1988, MIB................................. **30.00**

Tutti, 1967, any hair color, MIB .**165.00**

Whitney, Style Magic, 1989, NRFB **35.00**

Cases

Barbie, red vinyl, Barbie pictures on 4 different outfits, 1961, EX..**35.00**

Barbie, Stacey, Francie & Skipper, pink hard plastic, NM, from $75 to **100.00**

Barbie & Ken, black vinyl, Party Date/Sat Night Date outfits, 1961, EX **65.00**

Barbie & Stacey, 1967, vinyl, NM, from $65 to **75.00**

Circus Star Barbie, FAO Schwarz, 1995, M **25.00**

Fashion Queen Barbie, 1963, red vinyl, w/mirror & wig stand, EX. **100.00**

Francie & Casey, vinyl, NM, from $65 to **75.00**

Ken, gold vinyl w/black plastic handle, NM **35.00**

Skipper, round, $150.00. (Photo courtesy Stefanie Deutsch)

Tutti Play Case, blue or pink vinyl, EX, ea from $30 to **40.00**

Clothing and Accessories

Barbie, Bermuda Holidays, 1967 – 1968, #1810, $175.00. (Photo courtesy Sarah Sink Eames)

Barbie, All Turned Out, #4822, 1984, NRFP **20.00**

Barbie, Barbie in Hawaii, #1605, 1964, NRFB **300.00**

Barbie, Cinderella, #872, 1964, NRFP **475.00**

Barbie, City Fun, #5717, 1983, NRFP **10.00**

Barbie, Day & Night, #1723, 1965, NRFP **75.00**

Barbie, Disco Dazzle, #1011, 1979, NRFP **15.00**

Barbie, Galaxy A Go-Go, #2742, 1986, NRFP **30.00**

Barbie, Gold Spun, #1957, 1981, NRFP **15.00**

Barbie, Indian Print Separates, #7241, 1975, NRFP **35.00**

Barbie, My First Picnic, #5611, 1983, NRFP **10.00**

Barbie, Picnic in the Park, #16077, 1996, NRFP **30.00**

Barbie, Walking Pretty Pak, 1971, NRFP **130.00**

Barbie, White Delight, #3799, 1982, NRFP **15.00**

Francie, Cheerleading Outfit, #7711, 1973, NRFP **80.00**

Francie, Little Knits, #3275, 1972, NRFP **125.00**

Francie, Pretty Frilly, #3366, 1972, MIB **200.00**

Francie, Striped Types, #1243, 1970, NRFP **75.00**

Ken, Date With Barbie, #5824, 1983, NRFP **10.00**

Ken, Evening Elegance, #1415, 1980, NRFP **15.00**

Ken, Fountain Boy, #1407, 1964, NRFP **150.00**

Ken, Rain or Shine, #4999, 1984, NRFP **10.00**

Ken, Safari, #7706, 1973, NRFP.. **70.00**

Ken, United Airlines Pilot Uniform, #7707, 1973, NRFP **100.00**

Ken & Brad, Way Out West, #1720, 1972, MIP **175.00**

Skipper, Ice Skatin', #3470, 1971-72, MIB **150.00**

Skipper, Little Miss Midi, #3468, 1971, NRFP **70.00**

Skipper, School's Cool, #1976, 1969-70, MIP **200.00**

Tutti, Clowning Around, #3606, 1967, NRFP **195.00**

Houses, Furnishings, and Vehicles

Barbie & the Beat Cafe, 1990, MIB **35.00**

Barbie Beauty Boutique, 1976, MIB **40.00**

Barbie Dream Armoire, 1980, NRFB **35.00**

Barbie Dream Glow Vanity, 1986, MIB **20.00**

Barbie's Apartment, 1975, MIB **140.00**

Barbie's Mercedes, Irwin, EX. **150.00**

Barbie Silver 'Vette, MIB **30.00**

Barbie Teen Dream Bedroom, MIB **50.00**

Beach Bus, 1974, MIB **45.00**

California Dream Barbie Hot Dog Stand, 1988, NRFB **50.00**

Dream Glow Vanity, 1986, MIB **20.00**

Francie House, 1966, complete, M **150.00**

Go-Together Chaise Lounge, MIB **75.00**

Living Pretty, Cooking Center, 1988, MIB **25.00**

Magical Mansion, 1989, MIB. **125.00**

Movietime Prop Shop, 1989, MIB **50.00**

Pink Sparkles Starlight Bed, 1990, MIB **30.00**

Starlight Motorhome, 1994, MIB **45.00**

Workout Center, 1985, MIB .. **30.00**

Gift Sets

Army Barbie & Ken, 1993, Stars 'n Stripes, MIB **60.00**

Ballerina Barbie on Tour, 1976, MIB **175.00**

Barbie & Ken Campin' Out, 1983, MIB **75.00**

Barbie Loves Elvis, 1996, NRFB. **75.00**

Barbie's Olympic Ski Village, MIB **75.00**

Dance Sensation Barbie, 1985, MIB **35.00**

Halloween Party Barbie & Ken, Target, 1998, NRFB **65.00**

Happy Meal Stacy & Whitney, JC Penney Exclusive, 1994, MIB **30.00**

Hollywood Hair Barbie, #10928, 1993, MIB **35.00**

Malibu Barbie Fashion Combo, 1978, NRFB **80.00**

Malibu Ken Surf's Up, Sears Exclusive, 1971, MIB.... **350.00**

Pretty Pairs Nan 'n Fran, 1970, NRFB **25.00**

Stacy & Butterfly Pony, 1993, NRFB **30.00**

Travelin' Sisters, 1995, NRFB. **70.00**

Walking Jamie Strollin' in Style, NRFB **450.00**

Wedding Party Midge, 1990, NRFB **150.00**

Workin' Out Barbie Fashions, BJ's Wholesale Clubs, 1997, NRFB **25.00**

Miscellaneous

Barbie & Ken Sew Magic Add-Ons, 1973-74, complete, MIB.. **55.00**

Barbie Make-Up Case, 1963, NM **25.00**

Barbie Shrinky Dinks, 1979, MIB 30.00

Booklet, World of Barbie Fashion, 1968, M 10.00

Diary, black vinyl w/image of Barbie in long gown & fur stole, EX.100.00

Fashion Designer Set, Mattel, 1969, NM (EX+ box) 50.00

Picture Maker Designer Fashion Set, Mattel, 1969, NMIB.40.00

Pillow, lavender vinyl w/Barbie & Ken graphics, 11½" dia, VG 25.00

Purse, Barbie & the Rockers, vinyl, w/comb & cologne, M 15.00

Tea set, Barbie, 16-pc china set, Chilton Globe, 1989, NRFB 30.00

Wagon, Camp Barbie, 1995, 34", EX 50.00

Wallet, pink vinyl w/bust of Barbie encircled by her name, 1976, G..20.00

Wristwatch, 30th Anniversary, 1989, MIB........................80.00

Bauer

The Bauer Company moved from Kentucky to California in 1909, producing crocks, gardenware, and vases until after the Depression when they introduced their first line of dinnerware. From 1932 until the early 1960s, they successfully marketed several lines of solid-color wares that are today very collectible. Some of their most popular lines are Ring, Plain Ware, and Monterey Modern.

Art Pottery, fan vase, Matt Carlton, 3¾", from $75 to 150.00

Art Pottery, orange red, Matt Carlton, sq, 2½x6".........150.00

Art Pottery, vase, #10 stock, chartreuse, Hi-Fire..............125.00

Art Pottery, vase, Ring cylinder, Hi-Fire, 10", from $125 to..175.00

Brusche Al Fresco, creamer & sugar bowl, speckled or solid....25.00

Brusche Al Fresco, cup, pink speckled 10.00

Brusche Al Fresco, French casserole, Dubonnet, 2-qt......100.00

Brusche Al Fresco, mug, solid colors, handled, 8-oz............10.00

Brusche Al Fresco, salt & pepper shakers, Coffee Brown, jumbo, pr.......................................30.00

Brusche Contempo, pitcher, Indio Brown, 1-pt......................30.00

Brusche Contempo, plate, Spicy Green, 10".........................10.00

Brusche Contempo, teapot, beige.65.00

Cal-Art, bowl, florist's; Brusche Contempo Spicy Green ...40.00

Cal-Art, flowerpot, Pinnacle, olive green, 10"..........................85.00

Cal-Art, jardiniere, #4, speckled colors, 4", from $18 to 25.00

Cal-Art, pot, 3-step, glossy white, 4".....................................40.00

Cal-Art, Spanish pot, speckled green, 4"...........................20.00

Gloss, baker, all colors, scarce, 11½x6½" 45.00

Gloss, casserole, olive green, 1-qt 45.00

Gloss, pitcher, all colors, w/ice lip, 2-qt, from $75 to 90.00

Montery, bowl, batter............90.00

Montery, egg cup 45.00

Montery, ramekin...................30.00

Montery, teapot, old style, 6-cup.85.00

Montery Moderne, buffet server.15.00

Montery Moderne, coffee server, cobalt, open 90.00

Montery Moderne, pitcher, chocolate, 1-pt **30.00**

Plain Ware, bowl, salad; 8¼", from $80 to **120.00**

Plain Ware, butter pat, black, 4½" **125.00**

Plain Ware, pitcher, 5" **195.00**

Ring, two-quart batter bowl, from $85.00 to $125.00; Less common one-quart batter bowl, $400.00.
(Photo courtesy Jack Chipman)

Ring, bowl, low salad; orange-red, 9" **75.00**

Ring, candlestick, orange-red, dark blue or burgundy, 2½", ea ...**65.00**

Ring, creamer & sugar bowl, ivory **95.00**

Ring, cup & saucer, Delph Blue.**45.00**

Ring, plate, Jade Green, 9½". **35.00**

Ring, relish plate, Delph Blue, from $85 to **125.00**

Ring, salt & pepper shakers, Jade Green, squat style, pr **45.00**

Speckled Kitchenware, bowl, low salad; speckled yellow, 8½".**35.00**

Speckled Kitchenware, bowl, mixing; speckled white, #36, sm......**25.00**

Speckled Kitchenware, buffet server, speckled brown **45.00**

Speckled kitchenware, coffeepot, blue, #608, 7", from $50.00 to $65.00.

Speckled Kitchenware, mug, speckled green, 8-oz **15.00**

Beanie Babies

Beanie Babies first came on the scene in 1994, and from 1996 until 2000, they were highly collectible. Since then the 'collecting frenzy' has cooled considerably, and you can find Beanie Babies by the score at most large flea markets. Values given are for some of the more desirable, retired Beanie Babies with all tags in mint to near mint condition.

Ally the alligator, #4032 .... **20.00**

Baldy the eagle, #4074, from $6 to **12.00**

Bessie the cow, #4009 .... **15.00**

Blackie the bear, #4011.......... **10.00**

Bones the dog, #4001 .... **10.00**

Bongo the monkey, #4067, 2nd issue, tan tail, from $10 to **15.00**

Bronty the brontosaurus, #4085, blue, minimum value.... **100.00**

Brownie the bear, #4010, minimum value **200.00**

Bubbles the fish, #4078, minimum value **10.00**

Bumble the bee, #4045, minimum value **50.00**

Caw the crow, minimum value..**50.00**

Chilly the polar bear, #4012, minimum value..................... **200.00**

Chops the lamb, #4019 .... **20.00**

Coral the fish, #4079, tie-dyed. **10.00**

Daisy the cow, #4006 .... **15.00**

Derby the horse, #4008, 2nd issue, coarse mane & tail.......... **10.00**

Digger the crab, #4027, 1st issue, orange **50.00**

Digger the crab, #4027, 2nd issue, red **10.00**

Flash the dolphin, #4021, minimum value **15.00**

Flashy the peacock, #4339 ..... **10.00**

Flip the cat, #4012, white **10.00**

Flutter the butterfly, #4043, tie-dyed, minimum value **50.00**

Garcia the bear, #4051, tie-dyed, minimum value **20.00**

Glory the Bear, #4188, A m e r i c a n Bear with stars, retired, from $8.00 to $10.00.

Goldie the goldfish, #4023 .... **8.00**

Grunt the razorback pig, #4092, minimum value **20.00**

Happy the hippo, 1st issue, gray, minimum value **50.00**

Happy the hippo, 2nd issue, lavender, #4061 .... **8.00**

Holiday Teddy, any from 1997 to 2002, ea **10.00**

Inch the worm, #4004, yarn antenna, from $7 to **10.00**

Inch the worm, #4044, felt antenna **20.00**

Inky the octopus, #4028, 3rd issue, pink, from $6 to **10.00**

Kiwi the toucan, #4070, minimum value **30.00**

Lefty the donkey, #4087, gray . **20.00**

Libearty the bear, #4057, w/ American flag, white, minimum value **50.00**

Liberty the bear, #4531, 3 versions, red, white & blue heads, from $7 to **10.00**

Lizzy the lizard, #4033, 1st issue, tie-dyed, minimum value . **50.00**

Lizzy the lizard, #4033, 2nd issue, blue, from $10 to **20.00**

Lucky the ladybug, 3rd issue, 11 spots, from $10 to **15.00**

Magic the dragon, #4088, from $10 to **20.00**

Manny the manatee, #4081, minimum value **20.00**

Mystic the unicorn, #4007, 2nd issue, coarse mane & brown horn, from $10 to **15.00**

Nectar the hummingbird, #4361, from $10 to **20.00**

Nip the cat, #4003, 3rd issue, gold w/white paws, from $10 to .**25.00**

Patti the platypus, #4025, 2nd issue, purple, from $10 to **20.00**

Peanut the elephant, #4062, light blue, from $7 to **15.00**

Peking the panda bear, #4013, minimum value **100.00**

Pinchers the lobster, #4026 ... **15.00**

Princess the bear, #4300, purple, from $7 to **10.00**

Quackers the duck, #4024, 1st issue, no wings, minimum value **450.00**

Quackers the duck, #4024, 2nd issue, w/wings, from $10 to **20.00**

Radar the bat, #4091, black, minimum value **30.00**

Rex the tyrannosarus, minimum value **100.00**

Righty the elephant, #4085, gray **20.00**

Ringo the raccoon, #4014, from $10 to **15.00**

Rover the dog, #4101, from $10 to **15.00**

Sammy the bear, #4215, tie-dyed. **10.00**

Santa, #4203, from $10 to **12.00**

Seamore the seal, #4029, white, minimum value **20.00**

Slither the snake, #4031, minimum value **200.00**

Snowball, #4201, from $10 to . **12.00**

Snowgirl, #4333, from $10 to . **12.00**

Sparky the dalmatian, #4100, minimum value **15.00**

Speedy the turtle, #4030, from $10 to **15.00**

Splash, #4022, minimum value. **15.00**

Spooky the Ghost, #4090, orange neck ribbon, retired, minimum value, $10.00.

Spot the dog, #4000, 2nd issue, spot on back............................. **30.00**

Steg the stegosaurus, minimum value **100.00**

Sting the stingray, #4077, minimum value........................ **20.00**

Tabasco the bull, #4002, red feet, minimum value **20.00**

Tank the armadillo, #4031, 1st issue, no shell, 7 lines, minimum value........................ **40.00**

Teddy the bear, #4050, brown, new face, from $15 to **30.00**

The End the bear, #4265, black. **10.00**

Trap the mouse, #4042, minimum value **100.00**

Velvet the panther, #4064, minimum value........................ **10.00**

Waddle the penguin **10.00**

Web the spider, #4041, black, minimum value..................... **100.00**

Ziggy the zebra, #4063........... **15.00**

Zip the cat, #4004, 3rd issue, black w/white paws.................. **10.00**

Beer Cans

Beer has been sold in cans since 1935, when the Continental Can Company developed a method of coating the inside of the can with plastic. The first style was the flat top that came with instructions on how to open it. Because most breweries were not equipped to fill a flat can, most went to the 'cone top,' but by the 1950s, even that was obsolete. Can openers were the order of the day until the 1960s, when tabtop cans came along. The heyday of beer can collecting was during the 1970s, but the number of collectors has since receded, leaving a huge supply of beer cans, most of which are worth no more than a few dollars each. Our listings represent a sampling of higher-end cans. The basic rule of thumb is to concentrate your collecting on cans made prior to 1970. Remember, condition is critical. Values are based on cans in conditions as stated.

A-1 Pilsner, flat top, 12-oz, Phoenix AZ, 1957, EX **35.00**

ABC Extra Pale Dry Beer, flat top, 12-oz, Los Angeles, CA, 1958, NM+ **85.00**

Aero Club Pale Select, cone top, 12-oz, Pocatello ID, 1953, EX+... **300.00**

Altes 'Brisk' Lager, cone top, 12-oz, San Diego CA, 1953, EX+. **150.00**

Altes Lager, cone top, 12-oz, Detroit MI, 1948, VG................. **100.00**

Amber Brau Lager, pull tab, 12-oz, Los Angeles CA, 1968, NM. **30.00**

Atlas Lager, cone top, 12-oz, Detroit MI, 1948, EX **95.00**

Ballantine King Size, pull tab, 16-oz, Newark NJ, NM **32.00**

Banner Extra Dry Premium, flat top, 12-oz, Akron OH, NM **70.00**

Bavarian Beer, cone top, 12-oz, Pottsville PA, 1951, EX+. **200.00**

Berghoff, cone top, 12-oz, Fort Wayne IN, 1945, EX+ **12.00**

Beverwyck Irish Brand Cream Ale, cone top, 12-oz, Albany NY, 1939, NM **300.00**

Blackhawk Premium Beer, flat top, 12-oz, Buffalo NY, 1955, NM **175.00**

Blackhawk Topping, cone top, 12-oz, Davenport IA, 1948, NM **300.00**

Blatz Milwaukee Beer, cone top, 12-oz, Milwaukee WI, 1937, EX+ **125.00**

Blatz Old Heidelberg Pilsener, cone top, 12-oz, Milwaukee WI, EX+ **125.00**

Budweiser Big Size, flat top, 16-oz, St Louis MO, 1958, NM.. **50.00**

Bull Dog Malt Liquor, flat top, 8-oz, Altas Brewing, 1957, NM. **35.00**

Bull Dog Malt Liquor Half Quart, pull tab, 16-oz, Los Angeles, NM **25.00**

Busch Bavarian Half Quart, flat top, 16-oz, St Louis MO, 1958, EX+ **30.00**

Carling Black Label, pull tab, 16-oz, Natick MA, 1964, NM...... **35.00**

Carling Pilsener, pull tab, 12-oz, British Columbia Canada, 1968, NM **30.00**

Charrington Toby, pull tab, 12-oz, British Columbia Canada, 1965, NM **40.00**

Colt 45 Malt Liquor, pull tab, 16-oz, Miami FL, 1964, NM+.. **200.00**

Coors, flat top, 7-oz, Golden CO, 1960, NM **25.00**

Cremo Sparkling Beer, crown-tainer, 12-oz, New Britain CT, 1947, NM+ **350.00**

Crowntainer, Ebling Premium Beer, Ebling Brewing, New York, 1940s, G, $50.00; Cone top, National Bohemian Pale Beer, National Brewing, Baltimore, 1940s, VG, $55.00; Cone top, Falstaff Beer, Falstaff Brewing, St. Louis, 1940s, EX, $65.00. (Photo courtesy Frank's Auctions)

El Rancho Lite, pull tab, 12-oz, Los Angeles CA, 1971, NM+ . **30.00**

Falstaff King Size, flat top, 16-oz, Fort Wayne IN, 1957, EX+ **30.00**

Fitzgerald's Pale Ale, crowntainer, 12-oz, silver, Troy NY, 1940, NM+ **175.00**

Gluek's Stite, crowntainer, 12-oz, striped, Minneapolis MN, 1952, EX+ **175.00**

Gluek's Stite Malt Liquor, flat top, 8-oz, Minneapolis MN, 1955, NM **85.00**

Gobel Bantam, flat top, 8-oz, Detroit MI, 1955, EX+ **25.00**

Gobel Light Lager Luxury Beer, flat top, 8-oz, Detroit MI, 1954, VG **35.00**

Heileman's Special Export Malt.., flat top, 8-oz, La Crosse, 1959, NM **45.00**

Iroquois Indian Head Beer, crown-tainer, 12-oz, Buffalo NY, 1952, VG+ **100.00**

Kingsbury Pale Beer, crowntainer, 12-oz, Sheboygan WI, 1946, EX+ **45.00**

Maier Pale Dry 102, flat top, 12-oz, Los Angeles CA, 1953, NM **100.00**

Neuweiler Light Lager Beer, flat top, 8-oz, Allentown PA, 1957, NM **30.00**

Olympia, pull tab, 7-oz, Tumwater WA, 1964, NM+ **22.00**

Pearl Light Lager, pull tab, 8-oz, San Antonio TX, 1976, NM+ **8.00**

Rheingold Extra Dry, pull tab, 7-oz, New York NY, 1968, NM+ .. **15.00**

Ruppert Knickerbocker Little Knick, flat top, 7-oz, NY, 1996, NM **35.00**

Schlitz Half Quart, flat top, 16-oz, Los Angeles CA, 1954, NM **125.00**

Birthday Angels

Here's a collection that's a lot of fun, inexpensive, and takes relatively little space to display. They're not at all hard to find, but there are several series, so completing 12-month sets of them all can provide a bit of a challenge. Generally speaking, angels are priced by the following factors: 1) company — look for Lefton, Napco, Norcrest, and Enesco marks or labels (unmarked or unknown sets are of less value); 2) application of flowers, bows, gold trim, etc. (the more detail, the more valuable); 3) use of rhinestones, which will also increase price; 4) age; and 5) quality of the workman-ship involved, detail, and accuracy of painting.

Arnet, Kewpies in choir robes w/ rhinestones, 4½", ea from $12 to **15.00**

Enesco, angels on bases w/flowers of the month, gold trim, ea from $15 to **18.00**

High Mountain Quality, colored hair, 7", ea from $30 to ... **32.00**

Japan, months or days of the week, 4½", ea from $20 to **25.00**

Kelvin, #C-230, holding flower of the month, 4½", ea from $15 to. **20.00**

Lefton, #130, Kewpie, 4½", ea from $35 to **40.00**

Lefton, #489, holding basket of flow-ers, 4", ea from $25 to **35.00**

Lefton, #556, boy of the month, 5½", ea from $25 to **30.00**

Lefton, #985, flower of the month, 5", ea from $30 to **35.00**

Lefton, #1411, angel of the month, 4", ea from $28 to **32.00**

Lefton, Angel of the Month (November and December shown), #3332, 4", from $25.00 to $30.00 each. (Photo courtesy Loretta DeLozier)

Lefton, #1987J, w/rhinestones, 4½", ea from $30 to **40.00**

Lefton, #2600, birthstone on skirt, 3¼", ea from $25 to **30.00**

Lefton, #5146, birthstone on skirt, 4½", ea from $22 to **28.00**

Lefton, #6883, days of the week & months in sq frame, 3¼x4", ea from $28 to **32.00**

Lefton, #6985, musical, sm, ea from $40 to **45.00**

Mahana Importing, #1194/#1294, month series, white hair, 5", ea from $20 to **22.00**

Napco, #A1360-1372, angel of the month, ea from $20 to **30.00**

Napco, #A4307, angel of the month, sm, ea from $22 to **25.00**

Napco, #C1921-1933, boy angel of the month, ea from $20 to........**25.00**

Napco, #S0429, day of the week (also available as planters), ea from $25 to **30.00**

Napco, #S1291, day of the week 'Belle,' ea from $22 to **25.00**

Napco, #S1361-1372, angel of the month, ea from $20 to **25.00**

Napco, #S1392, angel of the month on oval frame, ea from $25 to **30.00**

Norcrest, #F-023, day of the week, 4½", ea from $18 to **22.00**

Norcrest, #F-167, bell of the month, 2¾", ea from $8 to **12.00**

Norcrest, #F-535, angel of the month, 4½", ea from $20 to............ **25.00**

Relco, 4¼", ea from $15 to **18.00**

Relco, 6", ea from $18 to........ **22.00**

Schmid, boy sitting w/gift, label, 1950s, 3½"......................... **29.00**

TMJ, angel of the month w/flower, ea from $20 to **25.00**

Ucago, white hair, 5¾", ea from $12 to.. **15.00**

Black Americana

This is a wide and varied field of collector interest. Advertising, toys, banks, sheet music, kitchenware items, movie items, and even the fine arts are areas that offer Black Americana buffs many opportunities to add to their collections. Caution! Because some pieces have become so valuable, reproductions abound. Watch for a lot of new ceramic items, less detailed in both the modeling and the painting.

Ashtray, Afrobar advertising on white on clear glass, 1940s, sq, EX **35.00**

Ashtray, Dinah's Shack, ceramic, Dinah's portrait on white, Japan, 5".......................... **75.00**

Ashtray, man's head w/mouth wide open & bug eyes, ceramic, 4", NM **55.00**

Bell, Aunt Jemima in red & white apron lettered New Orleans, 3¼" **15.00**

Bell, girl on knees praying in white gown/bows, porcelain, 1950s, 4"..................................... **35.00**

Book, Beloved Belindy, Johnny Gruelle, Bobbs Merrill, 1960 later edition, 95 pages, VG, $60.00.

Book, I Have a Dream, editors of Time-Life Books, 1968, EX.**50.00**

Book, Kids of Many Colors, 1901, hardback, 156 pages, EX+ **225.00**

Book, Little Black Sambo, Kellogg's Story Book of Games, 1931, EX **60.00**

Book, The Pop-Up Little Black Sambo, Blue Ribbon, 1934, NM **275.00**

Book, Well Done Noddy!, by Enid Blayton, hardback, EX+ . **30.00**

Book, You Funny Little Noddy, by Enid Blayton, hardback, 1950, EX **28.00**

Bookends, clowns w/instruments, ceramic, 1935-45, 5½", NM, pr **85.00**

Bowl, boy in center, flat rim, Brownie Downing China, 1962, 6", EX **45.00**

Brooch, lady's face, black turban w/ rhinestones, green stone eyes, 2" **35.00**

Card, Missed Yo' Birthday, man behind 8-ball, 1950s, 6x5", EX **18.00**

Card, valentine, Mammy graphics, stand-up, Tuck, EX **45.00**

Card game, Tops & Tails, ethnic caricature, 48 cards, EX . **75.00**

Cookie jar, Coon Chicken Inn, caricature face, Copyright '92, USA **135.00**

Cookie jar, Topsy seated looking up in white dress/blue apron, Metlox **600.00**

Cream of Wheat box, sample size, chef w/bowl, 1940s, 3x2x1¼", EX **75.00**

Doll, Mammy, Norah Wellings, velvet w/glass eyes & mohair wig, 13", VG **150.00**

Doll, Pretty Pairs (Nan 'n Fran), flannel nighties, NRFC. **200.00**

Egg cup, golliwog & teddy bear, porcelain w/unglazed bottom, 2½" **95.00**

Fan, Smoking Sambo, die-cut figure w/wooden handle, 1930s, 13½", NM **150.00**

Figurine, angel seated on white cloud & rock, bisque, 1950s, 5"....**32.00**

Figurine, baby girl, heavy pottery, hollow bottom, 1950s, 4½" **35.00**

Figurine, guitar player in plaid jacket, ceramic, Italy, 3¾" **50.00**

Game, Snake Eyes, Selchow & Righter, 1940s, EXIB **75.00**

Label, Small Black Zinfandel/Victor Fruit Growers, baby on red, 4x13" **18.00**

Matchbook, M&M Cafeterias, waiters w/trays on cover, EX. **22.00**

Measuring cup, Aunt Jemima Pancake Mix, 1980s, ¼-cup.**35.00**

Menu, Club Plantation souvenir, naughty lady cover, 1940s, 5x6½" **65.00**

Nodder, chef w/arms extended, ceramic, EX **225.00**

Noisemaker, tin litho, minstrel, US Metal..., 5½x3", EX **29.00**

Novelty, chenille native/tree on barkwood base, Japan, 1950s, 4", EX................................. **15.00**

Paint book, Golly's Magic, 8-page booklet, w/coupon, 1970s, 4½x6" **35.00**

Paper dolls, Oh Susanna, w/unbreakable record/color book, 1950, EX **65.00**

Pin, plastic, Black face winking, white hat, bow tie, 1 earring, 3", EX............................... **25.00**

Place mat, Aunt Jemima Restaurant, Disneyland, 1955, 14x10", M......................... **45.00**

Plate, Mammy's Shanty Restaurant, 7¼", NM **30.00**

Postcard, Busy Line, couple on phones w/Black Cupid on wire, 1920s, EX **25.00**

Print, Catching Trout, Currier & Ives 1952 repro, 8½x13½" image **18.00**

Program, Louis Armstrong & His All Stars, mid-1960s, 22 pages, EX **48.00**

Puzzle, Coon Chicken Inn souvenir, optical illusion, 1940s, EX. **125.00**

Recipe book, Kentucky Fare, Mammy at kettle, 1953, 28 pages, EX......................... **40.00**

Shakers, Aunt Jemima & Uncle Mose, F&F Mold Co, 3½", EX+, pr...................................... **50.00**

Shakers, boys riding ears of corn, Japan, 2¼x3¾", pr......... **100.00**

Shakers, golliwog driving yellow car, pottery, England, 1990s, 3x5" **110.00**

Shakers, Mammy & Chef, ceramic, Japan, 1950s, 2½", pr...... **30.00**

Shakers, natives riding hippos, hand-painted details, Japan, 1950s, pr........................ **175.00**

Shakers, praying hands, ceramic, w/ gold, Japan, 1950s, EX, pr..**65.00**

Shakers, 2 ceramic bongo shakers in wire native holder, Japan, 1950s............................... **60.00**

Squeeze toy, golliwog, rubber, marmalade premium, 1950s, 4", EX+ **100.00**

Tablecloth, printed caricature figures along yellow border, 51" sq, NM **225.00**

Teapot, Mammy figure, ceramic, Japan, 1980s, 7".............. **75.00**

Towel, Mammy w/cake & spoon embroidered on white, 1950s, 24x15", EX...................... **35.00**

Vase, female native's head, pottery, black w/gold trim, 1950s, 6", EX **30.00**

Wall pocket, chef on stove, ceramic, Hollywood, $65.00.

Wall pocket, lady's head w/metal coil necklace, ceramic, Horton, 1950s............................... **35.00**

Black Cats

This line of fancy felines was marketed mainly by the Shafford (importing) Company, although black cat lovers accept similarly modeled, shiny glazed kitties of other importing firms into their collections as well. Because eBay offers an over supply of mid-century collectibles, the value structure for these cats has widened, with prices for common items showing a marked decline. At the same time, items that are truely rare, such as the triangle spice set and the wireware cat face spice set have shot upwards. Values that follow are for examples in mint (or nearly mint) paint, an important consideration in determining a fair market price. Shafford items are often minus their white whiskers and eyebrows, and this type of loss should be reflected in your evaluation. An item in poor paint may be worth even less than half of given estimates. Note: Unless 'Shafford' is included in the descriptions, values are for cats that were imported by other companies.

Pitcher, Shafford, 5" with 14½" circumference, rare, $90.00.

Ashtray, flat face, Shafford, 4¾", from $18 to **25.00**

Ashtray, head shape, Shafford, 3", from $22 to **35.00**

Condiment set, upright, yellow eyes, 2 bottles & shakers in wire frame **95.00**

Cookie jar, head form, Shafford. **100.00**

Creamer, Shafford, from $20 to.**30.00**

Creamer, upraised paw is spout, yellow eyes, gold trim, 6½x6" **40.00**

Creamer & sugar bowl, head lids are shakers, yellow eyes, 5½".. **50.00**

Cruets, upright, she w/'V' eyes, he w/'O' eyes, Shafford, pr from $65 to............................. **85.00**

Decanter, long cat w/red fish on mouth as stopper **75.00**

Decanter, upright cat holds bottle w/cork stopper, Shafford, from $50 to **65.00**

Demitasse pot, tail handle, bow finial, Shafford, 7½", from $175 to **200.00**

Egg cup, cat face bowl, pedestal foot, Shafford, from $50 to **65.00**

Ice bucket, cylinder w/embossed yellow-eyed cat, 2 sizes, ea.... **75.00**

Mug, cat's head above rim, Shafford, standard, 3½", from $50 to **60.00**

Mug, Shafford, hard to find, 4", from $65 to **75.00**

Pincushion, cushion on back, tongue measure **25.00**

Pitcher, squatting cat, pour through mouth, Shafford, rare, 4½".**75.00**

Pitcher, squatting cat, pour through mouth, Shafford, rare, 5".**90.00**

Planter, upright, Shafford, from $35 to **45.00**

Pot holder caddy, 'teapot' cat, 3 hooks, Shafford, minimum value **150.00**

Shaker, long & crouching (shaker at each end), Shafford, 10", from $75 to **100.00**

Shakers, round-bodied 'teapot' cats, Shafford, pr from $60 to. **75.00**

Shakers, upright, Shafford, 3¾" (or slightly smaller), pr from $22 to **28.00**

Shakers, upright range type, Shafford, 5", pr............... **45.00**

Spice set, 6 pcs in wood frame, yellow eyes, Wales, from $80 to.................................. **95.00**

Spice set, 9 pcs in wood frame, yellow eyes, Wales, from $95 to. **110.00**

Sugar bowl, Shafford, from $25 to................................... **35.00**

Teapot, ball-shaped body, head lid, Shafford, 4" to 4½", ea from $20 to.................... **25.00**

Teapot, ball-shaped body, head lid, Shafford, 5" to 6½", ea from $25 to.................... **35.00**

Teapot, ball-shaped body, head lid, Shafford, 7", from $50 to . **60.00**

Tray, flat face, wicker handle, Shafford, scarce, from $75 to **100.00**

Utensil rack, flat-back cat w/3 slots for utensils, cat only, Shafford...................... **100.00**

T e a p o t , embossed cat face with yellow eyes, wire bail handle, $65.00.

Blade Banks

In 1903 the safety razor was invented, making it easier for men to shave at home. But the old, used razor blades were troublesome, because for the next 22 years, nobody knew what to do with them. In 1925 the first patent was filed for a razor blade bank, a container designed to hold old blades until it became full, in which event it was to be thrown away. Most razor blade banks are 3" or 4" tall, similar to a coin bank with a slot in the top but no outlet in the bottom to remove the old blades. These banks were produced from 1925 to 1950. Some were issued by men's toiletry companies and were often filled with shaving soap or cream. Many were made of tin and printed with an advertising message. An assortment of blade banks made from a variety of materials — ceramic, wood, plastic, or metal — could also be purchased at five-and-dime stores.

For information on blade banks as well as many other types of interesting figural items from the same era, we recommend *Collectibles for the Kitchen, Bath & Beyond* (featuring napkin dolls, egg timers, string holders, children's whistle cups, baby feeder dishes, pie birds, and laundry sprinkler bottles) by Ellen Bercovici, Bobbie Zucker Bryson, and Deborah Gillham (available through Antique Trader Books).

Barber, bust only, mustache, hair, white shirt w/black sleeves, 5½" **75.00**
Barber chair, sm, from $100 to.**125.00**
Barber head, different colors on collar, Cleminson, from $25 to.......**35.00**
Barber holding pole, marked Blades on back, Occupied Japan, 4", from $65 to **75.00**
Barber pole, red & white w/ or w/out attachments/various titles, from $20 to **25.00**
Barber pole w/face, red & white, from $30 to **40.00**
Barbershop quartet, 4 singing barber heads, from $95 to..**125.00**
Dandy Dans, plastic w/brush holders, from $25 to **35.00**
Friar Tuck, marked Razor Blade Holder on back, Goebel.**300.00**
Frog, green, For Used Blades, from $60 to **70.00**
Grinding stone, For Dull Ones, from $80 to **100.00**

Half barber pole, wall mount, from $40.00 to $60.00.
(Photo courtesy Debbie Gillham)

Half shaving cup, hangs on wall, Gay Blades, floral design, from $75 to **100.00**

Indian head, porcelain, Japan, 4"..**25.00**

Listerine donkey, from $20 to. **30.00**

Listerine elephant, from $25 to.**35.00**

Listerine frog, from $15 to..... **25.00**

Looie, right-hand or left-hand version, from $85 to **110.00**

Man shaving, mushroom shape, Cleminson, personalized, from $45 to **55.00**

Outhouse, For Gay Old Blades, wood, w/state names, Crosby, from $35 to **45.00**

Outhouse, white w/Used Blades on bottom, from $75 to **90.00**

Razor Bum, from $85 to **100.00**

Safe, green, Blade Safe on front, from $40 to **60.00**

Shaving brush, white w/red Blades on front, red bottom, 5½". **40.00**

Tony the Barber, Ceramic Arts Studio, from $85 to **95.00**

Blair Dinnerware

American dinnerware has been a popular field of collecting for several years, and the uniquely styled lines of Blair are very appealing, though not often seen except in the Midwest (and it's there that prices are the strongest). Blair was located in Ozark, Missouri, manufacturing dinnerware from the mid-1940s until the early 1950s. Gay Plaid, recognized by its squared-off shapes and brush-stroke design (in lime, green, brown, and dark green on white), is the pattern you'll find most often. Several other lines were made as well. You'll be able to rec-ognized all of them easily enough, since most pieces (except for the smaller items) are marked.

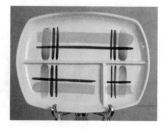

Divided tray, Highland (yellow plaid), from $40.00 to $50.00.
(Photo courtesy Jo Cunningham)

Bowl, cereal; Gay Plaid, from $8 to **10.00**

Bowl, cereal; Spiced Pear, from $15 to **20.00**

Bowl, Gay Plaid, teardrop form, 10".................................... **18.00**

Bowl, serving; Primitive Bird, lg **65.00**

Casserole, individual, w/lid, Leaves, from $20 to **25.00**

Creamer, Gay Plaid, from $20 to.**25.00**

Creamer, Yellow & Gray Plaid, from $10 to **12.00**

Cup & saucer, Brick, from $15 to **20.00**

Cup & saucer, Gay Plaid, from $8 to **10.00**

Cup & saucer, Leaves, from $10 to................................... **12.00**

Pitcher, Spiced Pear, w/ice lip, from $125 to **150.00**

Plate, dessert; Brick, 6½"......... **7.00**

Plate, dessert; Primitive Bird, 6½" **20.00**

Plate, dinner; Gay Plaid, from $8 to **10.00**

Plate, dinner; Leaves, from $10 to................................. **15.00**

Plate, dinner; Primitive Bird, from $40 to **50.00**

Plate, dinner; Spiced Pear, from $20 to **25.00**

Platter, Brick, sq, 10", from $18 to **20.00**

Platter, Gay plaid, sq, 10", from $15 to **18.00**

Relish dish, oblong, Gay Plaid, from $18 to **20.00**

Salt & pepper shakers, Yellow & Gray Plaid, short, pr from $12 to **15.00**

Sugar bowl, Gay Plaid, w/lid, from $20 to **25.00**

Sugar bowl, Yellow & Gray Plaid, w/lid, from $20 to **25.00**

Tumblers, Gay Plaid, from $10.00 to $12.00 each.

Water cooler, Gay Plaid, 5-gal, minimum value **200.00**

Water cooler, Primitive Bird, 5-gal, rare, minimum value **225.00**

Blue Garland

This lovely line of dinnerware was offered as premiums through grocery store chains during the decades of the '60s and '70s. It has delicate garlands of tiny blue flowers on a white background trimmed in platinum. Rims are scalloped and handles are gracefully curved. Though the 'Haviland' backstamp might suggest otherwise, this china has no connection with the famous Haviland company of Limoges. 'Johann Haviland' (as contained in the mark) was actually the founding company that later became Philip Rosenthal & Co., the German manufacturer who produced chinaware for export to the USA from the mid-1930s until as late as the 1980s.

This line may also be found with the Thailand Johann Haviland backstamp, a later issue. Our values are for the line with the Bavarian mark; expect to pay at least 30% less for the Thailand issue.

Bell, 5½x3¼" **40.00**

Bowl, coupe soup; 7½" **12.00**

Bowl, fruit; 5⅛" **5.00**

Bowl, oval, 11¼", from $60 to. **75.00**

Bowl, vegetable; round, 8½" .. **35.00**

Butter dish, ¼-lb, from $35 to.. **45.00**

Butter pat/coaster, 3½" **5.00**

Casserole, metal, stick handle, w/lid, 3-qt, 8¼", from $35 to **50.00**

Casserole, metal, tab handles, w/lid, 3-qt, from $20 to **28.00**

Casserole, metal, w/lid, 4-qt, 9¾", from $40 to **50.00**

Casserole, w/lid, 1½-qt, 5x8", from $50 to **60.00**

Casserole/soup tureen, w/lid . **50.00**

Clock plate, from $25 to **50.00**

Coffeepot/beverage server, 11", $45.00.

Creamer, 9-oz, 4¼" **15.00**

Cup & saucer, flat or footed..... **5.00**
Fondue pot, w/lid, from $50 to. **65.00**
Goblet, glass, 6¾", set of 6..... **40.00**
Gravy boat, w/attached or separate underplate, 10" L, from $20 to **30.00**
Nut dish, footed, w/handles... **30.00**
Plate, dinner; 10" **7.00**
Plate, salad; 7¾"....................... **6.00**
Platter, serving; oval, 13"...... **30.00**
Platter, serving; oval, 14½".... **40.00**
Roaster, metal, oval, 13", from $50 to **75.00**
Salt & pepper shakers, pr **22.00**
Saucepan, metal, w/lid, 1½-qt, 2 styles, ea from $30 to...... **40.00**
Skillet, metal, w/lid, 8½", from $35 to **45.00**
Sugar bowl, w/lid, 5½x7"........ **18.00**
Teapot, 8".............................. **45.00**
Tray, tidbit; 2-tier.................. **35.00**
Tray, tidbit; 3-tier.................. **40.00**

Blue Ridge

Some of the most attractive American dinnerware made in the twentieth century is Blue Ridge, produced by Southern Potteries of Erwin, Tennessee, from the late 1930s until 1956. More than 400 patterns were hand painted on eight basic shapes. Elaborate or appealing lines are represented by the high end of our range; use the lower side to evaluate simple patterns. The Quimper-like peasant-decorated line is one of the most treasured and should be priced at double the amounts recommended for the higher-end patterns.

Ashtray, individual, from $20 to **24.00**

Bonbon, flat shell, china, from $55 to **65.00**
Bowl, hot cereal; from $20 to. **25.00**
Bowl, salad; 10½" or 11½", from $50 to **65.00**
Bowl, vegetable; oval, 9", from $35 to **40.00**
Box, Rose Step, pearlized, from $85 to **100.00**
Box, Seaside, china, from $125 to **150.00**
Cake tray, Maple Leaf, china, from $50 to.............................. **65.00**

Chocolate pot, Williamsburg Bouquet, from $150.00 to $225.00.
(Photo courtesy Betty and Bill Newbound)

Cigarette box, sq, from $85 to. **90.00**
Creamer, Charm House, from $70 to **85.00**
Creamer, Waffle shape, from $15 to **18.00**
Cup & saucer, regular shapes, ea from $20 to **25.00**
Egg cup, double, from $25 to. **35.00**
Gravy boat, from $15 to......... **20.00**
Jug, character; Daniel Boone, from $450 to **500.00**
Leftover, w/lid, med, from $50 to **65.00**
Pitcher, Abby, china, from $175 to **200.00**
Pitcher, Milady, china, from $125 to **185.00**

Pitcher, Sculptured Fruit, china, from $75 to 100.00

Plate, dinner; 10½", from $20 to. 25.00

Plate, salad; flower & fruit, 8½", from $25 to 30.00

Plate, sq, novelty pattern, 6", from $65 to 75.00

Plate, 11½" or 12", ea from $50 to 65.00

Platter, 12½" or 13", ea from $25 to 30.00

Pot, demitasse; china, from $250 to 300.00

Relish dish, loop handle, china, from $65 to 75.00

Salt & pepper shakers, Apple, 1¼", pr from $50 to 55.00

Salt & pepper shakers, range; pr from $40 to 45.00

Sugar bowl, Colonial, eared, from $15 to 20.00

Teapot, ball shape, Premium, from $200 to 250.00

Teapot, Palisades, from $125 to............................. 150.00

Tidbit, 3-tier, from $40 to 50.00

Tray, Fox Grape, leaf form, china, from $40.00 to $50.00. (Photo courtesy Betty and Bill Newbound)

Tumbler, glass, from $15 to ... 20.00

Vase, ruffled top, china, 9½", from $100 to 125.00

Wall sconce, from $70 to 75.00

Blue Willow

Inspired by the lovely blue and white Chinese exports, the Willow pattern has been made by many English, American, and Japanese firms from 1950 until the present. Many variations of the pattern have been noted — mauve, black, green, and multicolor Willow ware can be found in limited amounts. The design has been applied to tinware, linens, glassware, and paper goods, all of which are treasured by today's collectors. Refer to *Gaston's Blue Willow, 3rd Edition*, by Mary Frank Gaston (Collector Books) for more information. See also Royal China. See Clubs and Newsletters for information concerning *The Willow Review* newsletter.

Coffeepot, Burgess and Leigh, England, 1930s, five-cup, from $40.00 to $50.00. (Photo courtesy Mary Frank Gaston)

Ashtray, figural fish, Japan, 1970s, 5", from $20 to................. 35.00

Ashtray, sq, Japan, 7½", from $45 to 55.00

Bank, stacked pigs (3), Japan, 1970s-80s, from $70 to.... 80.00

Bowl, cereal; Johnson Bros, from $20 to 35.00

Bowl, vegetable; oval, Japan, from
$30 to **40.00**
Bowl, vegetable; w/lid, Japan, from
$100 to **125.00**
Butter pat, Made in England, from
$35 to **45.00**
Carafe & warmer, Japan, from $250
to **300.00**
Coffeepot, Johnson Bros, 9", from
$125 to **145.00**
Creamer, Albert Meakin, 1920s,
from $75 to **100.00**
Creamer, individual; Shenango
Hotel Ware, from $30 to . **35.00**
Cruets, oil & vinegar; Japan, pr
from $100 to **125.00**
Cup, chili; Japan (unmarked),
4x4½", from $45 to **50.00**
Cup, chili; w/liner plate, Japan . **75.00**
Cup & saucer, demitasse; Johnson
Bros, from $35 to **45.00**
Cup & saucer, Shenango China,
from $15 to **20.00**
Egg cup, double; Japan, 4", from
$30 to **40.00**
Mug, Japan (unmarked), 3½", from
$10 to **15.00**
Plate, dessert/bread & butter;
Japan **5.00**
Plate, dinner; Johnson Bros, from
$25 to **35.00**
Plate, grill; Made in Occupied
Japan, 10", from $50 to .. **60.00**
Plate, salad; red, Wallace
China **8.00**
Platter, James Kent, 1950s, 14x11",
from $100 to **125.00**
Relish, divided, w/lug handles,
Adderly, 1929-47, 8"...... **130.00**
Salt & pepper shakers, jug form,
Japan, 13", pr from $40 to.. **50.00**
Salt box, wall-mount w/wood lid,
Japan (unmarked), 5"... **110.00**

Spoon rest, double, Japan, from
$40 to **50.00**
Sugar bowl, w/lid, Japan **15.00**
Tea set, Japan, stacking 2-cup pot,
creamer & sugar bowl, from
$150 to **175.00**
Teapot, musical base, Japan
(unmarked), from $130 to. **150.00**
Tumbler, juice; glass, Jeannette,
3½" or 5½", ea.................. **12.00**

Bookends

Bookends have come into their
own as a separate category of collectibles. They are so diversified in styling, it's easy to find some that appeal
to you, no matter what your personal tastes and preferences. Metal
examples seem to be most popular,
especially those with the mark of
their manufacturer, and can still be
had at reasonable prices. Glass and
ceramic bookends by noted makers,
however, may be more costly — for
example, those made by Roseville or
Cambridge, which have a cross-over
collector appeal.

Louis Kuritzky and Charles De
Costa have written an informative
book titled *Collector's Encyclopedia
of Bookends* (Collector Books); Louis
Kuritzky is listed in the Directory
under Florida. See Clubs and
Newsletters for information concerning the Bookends Collectors Club. All
our values are for a pair of bookends
in at least excellent condition.

Alamo, cast iron, Alamo Iron Works
Safety, dated 4/1/30, 4" . **200.00**
Anchor, gray metal, Dodge, 1940s,
6" **45.00**

Blacksmith w/arm raised at anvil, cast iron, Littco, 1920s, 5"..........**175.00**

Bust, Deco style, gray metal, Abbot, 1940s, 7" **150.00**

Cocker spaniel, Frankart, 1930s, 6"..........**150.00**

Discus thrower, Littco, 1920s, 7"..**110.00**

Eagle, patriotic style, chalkware, black & gold paint, 1970s.**20.00**

Elephants, cast iron, marked Verona Pat, ca 1920, 5¼", $140.00.
(Photo courtesy Louis Kuritzky)

Elephants trumpeting, cast iron, Connecticut Foundry, 1930s, 6" **75.00**

End of the Trail, gray metal, Ronson, 1930s, 6"..........**110.00**

Gate, country type, cast iron, Bradley & Hubbard, 1930s, 5".....**125.00**

Golfer, gray metal, Ronson, 1930, 6½" **175.00**

Hall's Bookcase, Bakelite, SW Hall, 1920s, 6" **135.00**

Heraldic eagle, pressed wood, Syrocco, 1930s, 6" **30.00**

Lily pad, gray metal, Dodge, 1940s, 4½" **65.00**

Lincoln seated, marked Solid Bronze, 4" **90.00**

Lion, glass, Cambridge, 1940s, 6"..........**200.00**

Man reading, chalk on stone base, marked HBH.RUHK, 1930s, 4½" **125.00**

Oak leaf, gray metal, PM Craftsman, 1960s, 6½"..........**45.00**

Parrot on book, K&O, 1920s, 6", pr **125.00**

Patriotic eagle, coated chalk, 1970s, 5" **20.00**

Pirate couple, multicolored enamel on gray metal, K&O, 1930s, 11" **175.00**

Polo player on white horse, Littco, 1920s, 5½"..........**85.00**

Primrose, Syroco, Syracuse Ornamental, ca 1930, 6", $75.00.
(Photo courtesy Louis Kuritzky)

Sailboat, cast iron, Littco, late 1920s, 7½"..........**100.00**

Sailor boy & dog, Frankfort, 1930s, 7"..........**185.00**

Scottie dog on fence, bronze, 1920s, 6" **175.00**

Swimmer, gray metal, Dodge, 1940s, 6" **85.00**

Trout leaping, gray metal, unmarked, 6½" **125.00**

Bottles

Bottles have been used as containers for commercial products since the late 1800s. Specimens from as early as 1845 may still be occasionally found today (watch for a rough pontil to indicate this early production date). Some of the most collectible are bitters bottles, used for 'medicine' that was mostly alcohol, a ploy to avoid paying the stiff tax levied on liquor sales. Spirit flasks from the 1800s were blown in the mold and were often designed to convey a historic, political, or symbolic message. Refer to *Bottle Pricing Guide* by Hugh Cleveland (Collector Books) for more information.

Dairy Bottles

The storage and distribution of fluid milk in glass bottles became commonplace around the turn of the century. They were replaced by paper and plastic containers in the mid-1950s. Perhaps 5% of all US dairies are still using some glass, and glass bottles are still widely used in Mexico and some Canadian provinces.

Milk-packaging and distribution plants hauled trailer loads of glass bottles to dumping grounds during the conversion to the throw-away cartons now in general use. Because of this practice, milk bottles and jars are scarce today. Most collectors search for bottles from hometown dairies; some have completed a 50-state collection in the three popular sizes.

Bottles from 1900 to 1920 had the name of the dairy, town, and state embossed in the glass. Nearly all of the bottles produced after this period had the copy painted and then pyro-glazed onto the surface of the bottle. This enabled the dairy-man to use colors and pictures of his dairy farm or cows on the bottles. Collectors have been fortunate that there have been no serious attempts at this point to reproduce a particularly rare bottle!

¼-pt, 3¢ Store, clear embossed, heavy **14.00**

⅓-qt, Marble Farms Dairy, Marble Kid on back, sq, orange pyro **9.00**

½-pt, Asgard Dairy, sq, green pryo cow **8.00**

½-pt, Buy Burn Boost, Anthracite Coal, pyro, 1945 .... **15.00**

½-pt, Cloverleaf, Stockton CA, ribbed cream top, pyro.... **18.00**

½-pt, Cole Farm Dairy, Biddeford Main, sq/squat, black pyro. **9.00**

½-pt, Howell & Demarest Farm Dairies, embossed, wire bail, ca 1900 .... **30.00**

½-pt, Mid Valley Dairy Farm, sq, green pryo **8.00**

½-pt, Smith's Dairy Farm, Erie PA, maroon pyro **10.00**

½-pt, Sunnymede Farm, Missouri Pacific Lines, squat, red pyro **22.00**

½-pt, Sunshine Goat Milk, embossed standing goat.................... **70.00**

½-pt, University of Georgia, pyro, ca 1950............................. **12.00**

1-pt, Deerfoot Farm, pear form w/screw lid, embossed, ca 1900............................. **30.00**

1-pt, Dublin Coop..., You Owe It to Your Country..., squat, red pyro **30.00**

1-pt, Gibb's Dairy Farm, Rochester MA, embossed name **5.00**

1-pt, Gillet & Sons..., America First Last Always, eagle, orange pyro **35.00**

1-pt, Hope Dairy...Mulberry St, embossed **12.00**

1-pt, Lueck Dairy, pyro............ **8.00**

1-qt, Badger Farms Creameries, orange pyro..................... **15.00**

1-qt, Beaulac's Ideal Bakery, green pyro **14.00**

1-qt, Blais Dairy Farm, Lewiston ME, black & orange pyro. **24.00**

1-qt, Cloverleaf Blue Ribbon Farm, Stockton CA, cream top, red pyro **25.00**

1-qt, Eastside Creamery, Saratoga Springs NY, embossed name . **8.00**

One-quart, Ellerman Dairy, red pyro, $15.00.

1-qt, FE White, orange pyro.. **35.00**

One-quart, Ferndale Dairy... Grand Lodge Mich., white pyro on amber, $12.00.

1-qt, Harlow's Jerseydale Farm, Amhurst MA, red pyro ... **45.00**

1-qt, Highland Dairy, squat, green & black pyro **35.00**

1-qt, Indian Hill Farms, Greenville ME, orange pyro **28.00**

1-qt, It's Hoods, sq, orange pyro. **5.00**

1-qt, Maple City Dairy, Monmouth IL, cream top, red pyro... **32.00**

1-qt, Meadow Brook, Clarksville NY, sq, pyro **8.00**

1-qt, Newsom's Pride Dairy, Milk the Champion of Drinks, black pyro **30.00**

1-qt, North Chatham Dairy, North Chatham NY, maroon pyro..**42.00**

1-qt, Quality Dairy The Best..., Gloversvill NY, sq, pyro.. **28.00**

1-qt, Shade's Dairy, Sante Fe NM, pyro, ca 1940 .... **17.50**

1-qt, Wilson Goat Farm, San Bernadino CA, pyro, ca 1950......... **30.00**

½-gal, Cloyed's Dairy Farm, pyro lettering **25.00**

½-gal, Land-O-Sun, Phoenix AZ, pyro, 1950s **20.00**

½-gal, Rojeck's Delicious Sour Cream, wide mouth, pyro.............. **10.00**

1-gal, Wallas Dairy, New Castle PA, pyro **30.00**

Soda Bottles With Applied Color Labels

This is a specialized area of advertising collectibles that holds the interest of bottle collectors as well as those who search for soda pop items; both fields attract a good number of followers, so the market for these bottles is fairly strong right now. See also Coca-Cola; Soda Pop.

A&W Root Beer, clear, 10-oz . **10.00**

Ace High, clear, 12-oz **22.00**

Brookdale, green, 8-oz **10.00**

Buckeye Sparkling Beverages, green, 7-oz **10.00**

Buffalo Rock, clear, 7-oz **15.00**

Bull's Eye Sparkling Beverages, clear, 12-oz...................... **24.00**

Choc-ola, clear, 9-oz **10.00**

Cleo Cola, red and white label on green, Vess Co., 12-ounce, from $125.00 to $140.00.

Clicquot Club, clear, 7-oz **10.00**
Crown Club, clear, 7-oz **15.00**
Cuban Dry Beverages, clear, 9-oz **18.00**
De Swett's, clear, 12-oz **10.00**
Freshway Fresh Fruit...Beverages, amber, 10-oz **15.00**
Frontenac, clear, 1-qt **15.00**
Frosty Root Beer, amber, 10-oz .. **18.00**
Grantman Beverages, clear, 8-oz **10.00**
Grapeteen, clear, 6-oz **50.00**
Jet-up, green, 7-oz **24.00**
La Grape/La Orange Cola, clear, 9-oz **24.00**
Lindy Beverage, clear, 10-oz . **24.00**
Moo Cho, clear, 7-oz **20.00**
Mountain Dew, green, 7-oz **28.00**
Phoenix, clear 1-qt **15.00**
Royal Crown Cola, aqua, 12-oz .. **28.00**
Sky High, clear, 12-oz **30.00**
Smack, clear, 12-oz **40.00**
Sody-Licious Famous Brand, clear, 7-oz **25.00**
Sun Crest, clear, King Size, 1964 .... **5.00**
Sun Spot, clear, 12-oz **10.00**
Twang Root Beer, clear, 7-oz . **10.00**
Veep, green, 12-oz **10.00**
Verner's, clear, 12-oz **10.00**

Vic's Beverages, clear, 10-oz .. **34.00**
Walsh's, green, 7-oz **10.00**
Yacht Club, clear, 7½-oz **15.00**

Miscellaneous

Ayer's Compound Extract Sarsaparilla, clear **10.00**
Benjamin's Wonder Oil, rare . **35.00**
Carl Schultz, aqua, 10-pin soda . **75.00**
Chamberlin's Immediate Relief... Elkhart IN, aqua, dug **90.00**
Dr G Barber's Instantaneous Relief From Pain, aqua **175.00**
Dr Kennedy's Medical Discovery, aqua, smooth base, 9" **13.00**
Dr Thacher's Worm Syrup, aqua, smooth base, 4¼" **10.00**
Dr Ward's Cremola, lotion, clear, 5¼" **8.00**
F Brown's Ess of Jamaica Ginger, aqua, smooth base, 5½" **7.00**
FA Sherwin Pharmacist Ashland OR, amethyst, 4¼" **8.00**
Hirch's Malt Whiskey Reliable Stimulant, amber, cylinder . **40.00**
Johnson's Chill & Fever Tonic, clear, rectangular, 6" **4.00**
Lashes Kidney & Liver Bitters Best Cathartic, honey amber to amber, NM **35.00**
Lyon's Katheron for the Hair, aqua, open pontil, minor stain . **35.00**
R Riddle Philada, squat, green .. **20.00**
Sapo Elixir Dry Cleaner, clear, 6" **3.00**
Schenck's Pulmonic Syrup Philda, aqua **12.00**
Star Anchor Bitters, sq, amber, 9" **225.00**
Union Clasped Hands, E Wormser, flask, blue, blob lip, aqua, 1-qt **140.00**

Warner's Safe Kidney & Liver Cure Rochester NY, amber, left-handed **79.00**

Owl on mortar and pestle, T.O.D.C. Trade Mark embossed on dark cobalt blue, square, W.T. & Co. USA on smooth base, 6¼", $125.00; Poison — Bowman's Drug Store — Poison, cobalt blue, irregular hexagon, smooth base, 6¼", $850.00. (Photo courtesy Glass-Works Auctions)

Boyd's Crystal Art Glass

Since it was established in 1978, this small glasshouse located in Cambridge, Ohio, has bought molds from other companies as they went out of business, and they have designed many of their own as well. They may produce several limited runs of a particular shape in a number of the lovely colors of glass they themselves formulate, none of which are ever reissued. Of course, all of the glass is handmade, and each piece is marked with their 'B-in-diamond' logo. See Clubs and Newsletters for information concerning a Boyd's Crystal Art Glass newsletter.

Airplane, Banana Cream Carnival (1995) or Classic Black (1991), ea...................................... **20.00**

Baby Shoe, Alpine Blue (1998) or Peacock Blue (1999), ea.. **10.00**

Baby Shoe, Boyd's Butterscotch, ca 1979, 2x2¾", $15.00. (Photo courtesy Earlene Wheatley)

Baby Shoe, Lemon Splash, 2002 . **10.00**
Basket Toothpick, Cobalt Blue. **10.00**
Bernie Eagle, Cobalt Blue (1992) or Columbus White Carnival, ea..................................... **12.00**
Bow Slipper, Crystal Carnival (1996) or Marshmallow (1997), ea..................................... **12.00**
Brian Bunny, Alpine Blue (1998) or Bamboo (1986), ea........... **15.00**
Bunny Salt, Cornsilk #5 or English Yew #2, 1983, ea.............. **25.00**
Bunny Salt, Crystal Carnival, 1996 .... **15.00**
Chuckles the Clown, Caramel Slag, Sea Green or Thistlebloom, 1987, ea **15.00**
Chuckles the Clown, Heavenly Blue (reissued color)............... **12.50**
Debbie Duck, Cobalt Blue, 1981 .... **12.00**
Debbie the Duck, Alice Blue (1983) or Furr Green (1981), ea .. **8.00**
Forget-Me-Not Toothpick, Carmine #1, 1978 .... **25.00**
Forget-Me-Not Toothpick, Rubena, 1979 .... **15.00**
Fuzzy Bear, Orange Calico, 1988.......................... **15.00**

Fuzzy Bear, Plum (black amethyst), hand-painted, 1988 .... **18.00**

Heart toothpick, Aqua, 1978 . **10.00**

Hen on Nest Covered Dish, Delphinium Blue #35, 1980.. **35.00**

Hen on Nest Covered Dish, Misty Cale #78, 1986 .... **25.00**

Kitten on Pillow, Butterscotch, 1979 .... **20.00**

Kitten on Pillow, Pippin Green #43, 1982 .... **15.00**

Melissa Doll, Peacock Blue, 1999. **10.00**

Owl, Black Walnut (1979) or Mandarin (1986), ea **20.00**

Owl, Delphinium (1981) or Willow Blue (1980), ea **15.00**

Pooche, Sandpiper, 1981 .... **15.00**

Sammy Squirrel, Cambridge Blue, 1988 .... **15.00**

Skippy Dog, Golden Delight (1982) or Lemonade (1985), ea .. **15.00**

Sonny the Gorilla, Crystal Carnival, 1996 .... **10.00**

Sportscar, Nightwatch Black #15 (2001) or Rosie Pink #4 (1999), ea..................................... **15.00**

Teddy Tugboat, Cornsilk, 1983 .. **12.00**

Virgil the Two-Faced Clown, Nile Green, 1993 .... **25.00**

Willie Mouse, Peach #11 (1991) or Spinnaker Blue (1990), ea.. **10.00**

Breweriana

Beer can collectors and antique advertising buffs alike enjoy looking for beer-related memorabilia such as tap knobs, beer trays, coasters, signs, and such. While the smaller items of a more recent vintage are quite affordable, signs and trays from defunct breweries often bring three-digit prices.

Condition is important in evaluating early advertising items of any type.

Ashtray, Anheuser-Busch, brass w/embossed & painted eagle, EX................................... **60.00**

Ashtray, Coors, white ceramic round dish, Brewed With Pure..., 6", EX **22.00**

Ashtray, Hamm's bear on shield on pop-up pocket type, gold-tone, 1973 .... **20.00**

Ashtray, Pearl Lager, white ceramic w/red detail, 1963, 6x7½", NM+................................. **30.00**

Ashtray, Say Bud's Beer/Peter Bud Brewery, round w/2 rests, 1957, unused **40.00**

Ashtray/coaster, Schmidt's City Club, Tastes Sooooo Good!, 1953, NM+...................... **35.00**

Bar-B-Que Mitt, Budweiser, allover advertising, MIP (sealed) . **6.00**

Blotter, Pabst Blue Ribbon Beer, bottle/frothy glass, 1932, 2x4", EX **25.00**

Blotter, Schmidt's City Club, scene under tree, 1939, 3x6", NM+.............................. **25.00**

Bolo tie, Budweiser logo on gold medallion, red tie, 1966, NM **20.00**

Bottle carrier, Edelweiss, cardboard 6-pack, 1956, NM+.......... **15.00**

Bow tie, Lone Star Beer, cloth, 1963, NM **15.00**

Box, Kamm's in Cans, cardboard, holds 12 12-oz crowntainers, 1951, VG......................... **25.00**

Brochure, Lemps, Gesundheit, diecut foldout w/animation, 1906, NM **125.00**

Checkbook holder, Falstaff, vinyl, 1966, 11½", EX+ 10.00

Clock, Dawson's Beer, image of king, metal frame, glass front, EX 65.00

Clock, Falstaff, logo on glass front, metal frame, 1953, 12x13", NM 75.00

Clock, Mitchell's Premium, glass face, 15" dia, EX 220.00

Cooler, Storz, paper pulp w/wire handle, red logo, 1948, EX+ 20.00

Corncob pipe, Falstaff, 1945, NM+ 10.00

Display, Blatz Man w/mug on tray, 1960s, 16", EX 65.00

Display, Rolling Rock Premium Beer, molded waterfall, 1952, NM 50.00

Drawstring bag, Budweiser, cloth w/allover advertising, 19x17", EX 12.00

Earrings, Falstaff logos, gold-tone, clip-on backs, 1960, MOC, pr 25.00

Earrings, Falstaff logos, gold-tone, screw backs, 1949, 1", EX+, pr 15.00

Figurine, Hamm's bear frying fish on campfire, porcelain, 1979, 6", NM 45.00

Flashlight, Schlitz, bottle shape, 1969, MIB 12.00

Miniature beer bottle, amber glass w/foil label, w/cap, 1953, 4", NM 15.00

Miniature beer bottle, Coors, cream porcelain, long neck, 1937, NM+ 18.00

Miniature beer bottle, Coors, cream porcelain, short neck, 1936, NM+ 25.00

Miniature beer can, Coors, 1969, 1½", NM 8.00

Miniature beer can/bank, Miller High Life, 1957, 3½", NM+ 20.00

Mirror, Weidemann Fine Beer, reverse-painted glass, 1981, 14x20" 5.00

Nail clippers, Heinekin, metal w/ chain, 1975, NM+ 8.00

Paperweight, Schlitz, brewery scene encased in glass, EX 100.00

Pocket mirror, Anthracite Brewing Co, bust image of girl, VG 65.00

Salt & pepper shakers, Ballentine Ale, w/cardboard tote, 1960, NM, pr 12.00

Salt & pepper shakers, bears w/ Hamm's Beer signs, 1959, NM, pr................................... 100.00

Salt & pepper shakers, Schell's Beer..., wooden barrels, 1945, NM, pr 115.00

Shakers, Bud Man form, ceramic, Ceramarte, 3¾", pr........ 250.00

Sign, Budweiser Draught, light-up, team of horses and wagon before frosty mug, 16½" diameter, NM, $85.00. (Photo courtesy B.J. Summers)

Sign, Duquesne, self-framed cardboard, couple/dog, 1957, 17x23", NM...................... 60.00

Sign, Enjoy Goebel Beer, tin/cardboard, bottle, glass, 1941, 14x11", NM.................... 135.00

Sign, Hamms, light-up motion, From the Land..., 1958, rectangular, EX+ **250.00**

Sign, Miller $1,000 Beer, coach light wall sconce, 1969, EX **50.00**

Sign, New York's Famous Knickerbocker Beer, round light-up, 1953, NM+ **350.00**

Sign, Pabst...in Bottles, reverse-painted glass, 1954, 6x12", EX.................................... **75.00**

Sign, Schlitz, lighted metal bottle form, 20", EX.................. **175.00**

Sign, Schlitz Beer, blue light-up globe w/band, 1958, 22" dia, NM................................... **65.00**

Sign, Schlitz Lager, die-cut cardboard, hand opening bottle, 1935, EX+........................ **75.00**

Sign, V Loewer's Gambrinus Brewery, embossed tin barrel shape, 26", G **300.00**

Tap knob, Cook's Goldblume, ball-type w/flat orange top, 1948, NM+.............................. **125.00**

Tap knob, Fort Pitt Beer, blue plastic w/flat white top, 1950, EX+ **75.00**

Tap knob, Hamm's, white porcelain ball on gold-tone base, 1970, EX..................................... **25.00**

Tap knob, Miller, maroon Bakelite ball, flat red top, 1941, EX . **30.00**

Tap knob, Mitchell's Premium, black Bakelite w/metal insert, G....................................... **80.00**

Tattoos, temporary; Hamm's bear in various poses on 1 sheet, 1967, NM........................... **8.00**

Telephone, Busch Beer can w/dial on bottom, 1983, NM **25.00**

Thermometer, Bud Lite/Spuds McKenzie, 12" dia, EX.... **12.00**

Tie clip, Falstaff logo, gold-plated, 1949, VG............................ **8.00**

Tip tray, Budweiser, Custer's Last Stand, oval, 1979, 4½x6", NM+................................. **15.00**

Tip tray, Frank Jones Homestead Ale, round, 1935, NM+ ... **75.00**

Tip tray, Goldschmidt Bros, litho tin, triangle logo, 4", EX. **40.00**

Tip tray, Hamm's Preferred, rectangular, 1953, 4½x6½", NM...............................**25.00**

Tip tray, Red Raven, red raven by bottle and glass, tin litho, Chas. Shonk Litho Co, Chicago, EX, **$100.00.**

Tip tray, Tech Beer/None Better, rectangular, 1913, 7x5", NM............................ **90.00**

Tray, Ambassador Export...Beer, white, round w/deep rim, 1961, 12", NM+ **35.00**

Tray, Beck's Beer, 2 bottles & frothy mug, round w/deep rim, 1975, 13", NM............................ **18.00**

Tray, Bevo, coaching scene, rectangular, 1917, VG+........... **125.00**

Tray, Dawson's, couple at table, round w/deep rim, 1943, 12", NM+.............................. **125.00**

Tray, Fox Head, fox head on blue, round w/deep rim, 1947, 13", NM+.............................. **135.00**

Tray, Kurth's Beer, The Old Favorite, rectangular, 1938, EX+ **250.00**

Tumbler, Iroquois Brewing, Indian logo on clear glass, 3½"... **50.00**

Breyer Horses

Breyer collecting has grown in popularity over the past several years. Though horses dominate the market, cattle and other farm animals, dogs, cats, and wildlife have also been produced, all with exacting details and lifelike coloration. They've been made since the early 1950s in both glossy and matt finishes. (Earlier models were glossy, but from 1968 until the 1990s when both glossy and semigloss colors were revived for special runs, matt colors were preferred.) Breyer also manufactures dolls, tack, and accessories such as barns for their animals. For more information we recommend *Schroeder's Collectible Toys, Antique to Modern* (Collector Books).

Andalusian Mare, Classic Andalusian Family, dapple gray, 1979-93 .... **11.00**

Angus Bull, no markings, 1978-current **25.00**

Appaloosa, Stablemates, chestnut pinto w/details, 1999-2001 .. **9.00**

Appaloosa Performance Horse (Stallion), Traditional, JC Penney, 1984 .... **44.00**

Arabian Mare, Stablemates, dapple gray w/details, 1975-76 .. **22.00**

Arabian Stallion, Classic Arabian Family, brown bay w/details, 1984-85 .... **18.00**

Big Ben, Traditional, chestnut w/details, 1997-current **31.00**

Cantering Foal, Stablemates, flocked appaloosa, BreyerFest, 2001 .... **12.00**

Clydesdale, Paddock Pals, chestnut w/details, 1984-88 .... **9.00**

Clydesdale, Stablemates, Red Stable Set, dun, 2003-current **23.00**

Cow, Holstein, 2001-current .. **24.00**

El Pastor, Traditional, bay w/black points, 1987 .... **124.00**

Fighting Stallion mold as Ponokah-Eematah, 1996, $32.00.

Five Gaiter, Traditional, American Saddlebred, dapple gray, 1987-88 .... **39.00**

Indian Pony, Traditional, alabaster, red hand print on haunch, 1970-71 .... **211.00**

Kelso, Classic, dark bay w/details, 1975-90 .... **17.00**

Lying Down Foal, Traditional, black appaloosa w/bald face, 1969-84 .... **19.00**

Majestic Arabian Stallion, Traditional, leopard appaloosa, 1989-90 .... **25.00**

Man O' War, Classic, red chestnut w/stripe or star, 1975-90. **17.00**

Mesteno, Classic, Pirro, chestnut pinto, Wal-Mart, 2001..... **13.00**

Montana Mountain Goat, alabaster w/shading, black horns, 1989 reissue **37.00**

Morgan, Traditional, black w/bald face, socks & stockings, 1965-87 . **38.00**

Morgan Stallion, Paddock Pals, seal brown w/black points, 1984-88 .... **8.00**

Mustang Stallion, Classic, Mustang Family, buckskin, Sears, 1985 .... **15.00**

Pony of Americas, Traditional, chestnut leopard appaloosa, 1976-80 .... **28.00**

Rearing Stallion, Classic, bay w/bald face, stockings, 1965-80.... **17.00**

Ruffian, Classic, dark bay, 1977-90 .... **13.00**

Scratching Foal, Traditional, alabaster, JC Penney, 1991 . **21.00**

Silky Sullivan, Classic, Ladies of the Bluegrass, dark gray, 1996-99 .... **15.00**

Terrang, Classic, dark brown, 1975-90 .... **17.00**

Trakehner, Traditional, bay w/black points & brand on left thigh, 1979-84 .... **30.00**

Western Horse, Traditional, palomino w/saddle, QVC, 1995.... **26.00**

Bubble Bath Containers

Figural bubble bath containers were popular in the 1960s and have become highly collectible today. The Colgate-Palmolive Company produced the widest variety called Soakies. Purex's Bubble Club characters were also popular. Most Soaky bottles came with detachable heads made of brittle plastic which cracked easily. Purex bottles were made of a softer plastic but lost their paint easier. Condition affects price considerably.

The interest collectors displayed in the old bottles prompted many to notice foreign-made products. Some of the same characters have been licensed by companies in Canada, Italy, the UK, Germany, and Japan, and the bottles they've designed have excellent detail. They're usually a little larger than domestic bottles and though fairly recent are often reminiscent of those made in the US during the 1960s.

For more information, we recommend *Schroeder's Collectible Toys, Antique to Modern*, published by Collector Books.

Deputy Dog, Terrytoons, Soaky, 1966, 9¾", EX, from $20.00 to $25.00.

Anastasia, Kid Care, 1997, NM. **8.00**

Baba Looey, Purex, 1960s, NM .**35.00**

Bamm-Bamm, Purex, NM **35.00**

Batman, Kid Care, 1995, M .. **10.00**

Bozo the Clown, Colgate-Palmolive, 1960s, NM **30.00**

Broom Hilda, 1977, EX.......... **30.00**

Bugs Bunny, light blue & white, Colgate-Palmolive, NM... **25.00**

Bullwinkle, Colgate-Palmolive, NM **45.00**

Casper the Friendly Ghost, Colgate-Palmolive, EX.................. **30.00**

Cinderella, Colgate-Palmolive, 1960s, NM **30.00**

Darth Vader, Omni, 1981, NM. **20.00**

Dick Tracy, Colgate-Palmolive, 1965, NM 50.00

Dopey, Colgate-Palmolive, 1960s, NM 20.00

Elmer Fudd, hunting outfit, Colgate-Palmolive, 1960s, NM................................. 25.00

Elmo, Kid Care, 1997, NM 10.00

Fozzie Bear, Muppet Treasue Island, Calgon, 1996, NM 10.00

Frankenstein, Colgate-Palmolive, 1963, NM, from $100 to.125.00

Garfield, lying in tub, Kid Care, NM 10.00

Gumby, M&L Creative Packaging, 1987, NM.........................30.00

Incredible Hulk, Benjamin Ansehl, M......................................25.00

Jiminy Cricket, Colgate-Palmolive, 1960s, EX+ 30.00

Kermit the Frog, Calgon, Muppet Treasure Island, Calgon, M .8.00

Little Mermaid, Kid Care, 1991, NM....................................10.00

Magilla Gorilla, Purex, 1960s, NM 60.00

Mickey Mouse, Avon, 1969, MIB .30.00

Mighty Mouse, Colgate-Palmolive, EX 25.00

Miss Piggy, Muppet Treasure Island, Calgon, 1996.......10.00

Pebbles Flintstone, Purex, 1960s, EX 35.00

Pinocchio, Colgate-Palmolive, 1960s, NM 20.00

Popeye, Colgate-Palmolive, 1977, NM....................................35.00

Power Rangers, any character, Kid Care, 1994, M, ea..............8.00

Raggedy Ann, Lander, 1960s, NM..............................50.00

Robin, Colgate-Palmolive, 1966, EX, from $75 to.............100.00

Secret Squirrel, Purex, 1966, rare, VG, from $40 to...............60.00

Simba, Kid Care, M 6.00

Smokey Bear, Colgate-Palmolive, 1960s, NM 25.00

Snoopy, Flying Ace, Avon, 1969, MIB.................................20.00

Snoopy, in tub of bubbles, Avon, 1971, MIB.......................20.00

Snow White, movable arms, Colgate-Palmolive, 1960s, from $20.00 to $25.00.

Speedy Gonzales, Colgate-Palmolive, 1960s, EX......25.00

Splash Down Space Capsule, Avon, 1970, MIB........................20.00

Spouty Whale, Roclar (Purex), M..................................20.00

Superman, Avon, 1978, MIB .35.00

Superman, Colgate-Palmolive, 1965, EX..........................50.00

Sylvester the Cat, holding Tweety Bird, DuCair Bioscence, 1988, M......................................20.00

Sylvester the Cat, w/microphone, Colgate-Palmolive, 1960s, EX..............................30.00

Tasmanian Devil in inner tube, Kid Care, 1992, EX.................8.00

Teenage Mutant Ninja Turtles, any character, Kid Care, 1990, M, ea.......................................8.00

Three Little Pigs, any character, Tubby Times, 1960s, M, ea.40.00

Thumper, Colgate-Palmolive, 1960s, EX **25.00**

Top Cat, Colgate-Palmolive, 1963, EX **30.00**

Touche Turtle, Purex, NM **45.00**

Wally Gator, Purex, 1963, rare, NM, from $45 to **60.00**

Wendy the Witch, Colgate-Palmolive, 1960s, NM..... **30.00**

Winnie the Pooh, Johnson & Johnson, 1997, NM **6.00**

Winsome Witch, Purex, 1965, rare, NM **30.00**

Woodsy Owl, Lander, early, 1970s, EX **35.00**

Woody Woodpecker, Colgate-Palmolive, 1977, NM **45.00**

Yoda (Star Wars), Omni, 1981, NM **20.00**

Cake Toppers

The first cake toppers appeared on wedding cakes in the 1880s and were made almost entirely of sugar. The early 1900s saw toppers carved from wood and affixed to ornate plaster pedestal bases and backgrounds. A few single-mold toppers were even made from poured lead. From the 1920s to the 1950s bisque, porcelain, and chalkware figures reigned supreme. The faces and features on many of these were very realistic and lifelike. The beautiful Art Deco era was also in evidence.

Celluloid Kewpie types made a brief appearance from the late 1930s to the 1940s. These were quite fragile because the celluloid they were made of could be easily dented and cracked. The true Rose O'Neill Kewpie look-alike also appeared for awhile during this period. During and after World War II and into the Korean Conflict of the 1950s, groom figures in military dress appeared. Only a limited amount was ever produced; they are quite rare. From the 1950s into the 1970s, plastics were used almost exclusively. Toppers took on a vacant, assembly-line appearance with no specific attention to detail or fashion.

In the 1970s, bisque returned and plastic disappeared. Toppers were again more lifelike. For the most part, they remain that way today. Wedding cakes now often display elegant and elaborate toppers such as those made by Royal Doulton and Lladro.

Toppers should not be confused with the bride and groom doll sets of the same earlier periods. While some smaller dolls could and did serve as toppers, they were usually too unbalanced to stay upright on a cake. The true topper consisted of a small bride and groom anchored to (or a part of) a round flat base which made it extremely stable for resting on a soft, frosted cake surface. Cake toppers never did double-duty as play items.

1900s couple under bower of cloth flowers, plaster base **90.00**

1920s couple arm-in-arm under bower of flowers, lead single mold **50.00**

1920s couple w/bride in drop-waist gown, bisque, 4" **50.00**

1920s couple w/bride in wide collar, chalkware & gum paste, 7" **110.00**

1930s couple, bisque, chalkware base conceals music box, 11".............................**175.00**

1930s couple under crepe-paper fringe, goggle-eyed, bisque, 6"...............................**125.00**

1930s Kewpie couple embracing, porcelain in crepe-paper attire, 3"......................................**50.00**

1930s Kewpie couple, porcelain on cardboard base, wire and crepe-paper archway, $50.00.
(Photo courtesy Jeannie Greenfield)

1940s couple, 3 lg bells as backdrop, floral trim...............**40.00**

1940s couple holding hands before table w/ring, plaster & chalkware.................................**50.00**

1940s military couple arm-in-arm, chalkware, 3¾"................**50.00**

1950s couple under lg heart w/netting, heart-theme base, plastic....**20.00**

California Potteries

In recent years, pottery designed by many of the artists who worked in their own small studios in California during the 1940s through the 1960s has become highly sought after. Values continue to be impressive, though slightly compromised by the influence of the Internet. Among the more popular studios are Kay Finch, Florence Ceramics, Brayton, Howard Pierce, and Sascha Brastoff; but Matthew Adams, Marc Bellair, and deLee are attracting their share of attention as well, and there are others.

It's a fascinating field, one covered very well in Jack Chipman's *Collector's Encyclopedia of California Pottery,* and *California Pottery Scrapbook* both published by Collector Books. Mike Nickel and Cynthia Horvath have written *Kay Finch Ceramics, Her Enchanted World* (Schiffer), a must for collectors interested in Kay Finch ceramics; and to learn more about Florence ceramics, you'll want to read *The Complete Book of Florence Ceramics: A Labor of Love,* written by Margaret Wehrspaun and Sue and Jerry Kline. They are listed in the Directory under Tennessee. See also Bauer; Cookie Jars; Franciscan; Metlox.

Adams, Matthew

Ashtray, walrus, star shape, 10x12"..............................**95.00**

Ashtray, walrus on turquoise, hooded, 5½".............................**75.00**

Bowl, polar bear on green, freeform, 7½" L.....................**40.00**

Charger, caribou on dark blue, 18"..............................**150.00**

Cigarette lighter, cabin on stilts, 5x5"..................................**50.00**

Creamer, seal, #144, 5x5¼" ...**20.00**

Dish, Eskimo child w/igloo beyond, #190A, 2x8" **65.00**

Ginger jar, walrus on turquoise, w/lid, 6½" **90.00**
Tray, polar bear, sq, #122, 12½"..**90.00**
Vase, walrus on ice floe, gold trim, 11½" **110.00**

Bellaire, Marc

Ashtray, Friendly Island, bowl form, 11" dia.................... **25.00**
Ashtray, girl & butterfly, freeform, marked Cortillian B 51-15, 10x15" **45.00**
Bowl, Beachcomber, shallow egg shape, 8x10½"................. **45.00**
Cake plate, Friendly Island, pedestal foot, 4½x9" dia **100.00**
Dish, Balinese Dancers, B50-L, w/lid, 2⅞x12¾x5"................. **60.00**
Jar, Stick People, conical w/wide top, w/lid, 5x5" **135.00**

Brastoff, Sascha

Ashtray, copper w/enameled blue & white flowers, ¾x5½".......**35.00**
Bowl, Americana, 5½" **50.00**
Candleholder, orange resin, grapes & leaves in relief, 9½", ea.**25.00**
Figurine, seal, aquamarine resin, 7x9"................................**135.00**
Mug, Arabian woman on gray w/purple, #070, 5x3"......... **235.00**
Plate, island & palm tree, 8½".**65.00**

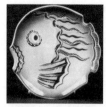

Tray, fish form, pink, blue, and brown, 8", $95.00.

Vase, Aztec Horse, bulbous, #066, 5½x8½" **30.00**

Wine coaster, orange resin w/grape leaves, 2¼x5½".................**25.00**

Brayton Laguna

Bookends, clowns seated, 5¾". **75.00**
Box, oval w/knobed lid, pink & beige w/molded fern-like fronds, 5½" **15.00**
Figurine, Anne, seated, 4".....**85.00**
Figurine, cats, stylized, white, 4½x5½", pr **45.00**
Figurine, cow, seated, brown, 4".**35.00**
Figurine, Inger, 7"................. **50.00**
Figurine, swan, turquoise w/orange beak & feet, 1940............ **25.00**
Figurine/planter, Frances, 8"..**60.00**
Flower holder, blond w/basket, blue-green dress, marked 1942, 8½"......................... **25.00**
Pitcher, African mask shape, black, 8x7"................................. **90.00**
Salt & pepper shakers, cat (floral) & dog (plaid), seated, pr.**40.00**

Salt and pepper shakers, Mammy and Chef, 4½", $45.00 for the pair.

Teapot, white & yellow flowers w/green leaves on black, 6½".............. **45.00**

Cleminson Pottery

Ashtray, You're the Big Wheel, 8"..**15.00**

Butter dish, Distlefink, bird form, 4½x6½"............................ **40.00**

Cheese dish, figural lady, 6½x7½", from $50 to **70.00**

Cleanser shaker, Katrina, 6¼", from $40 to **50.00**

Creamer, figural rooster, 5½", from $40 to **58.00**

Gravy boat, Distlefink, figural bird, 5¾x6" **35.00**

Pitcher, honey; Queen Bee, 5½" .**75.00**

Ring holder, worm in apple ... **60.00**

Salt & pepper shakers, bowling pin shape, 5½", pr.................. **40.00**

String holder, heart shape w/verse ..**45.00**

Tea bag holder, teapot shape, 3x4¼" **15.00**

Wall pocket, Antoine, 7¼" **75.00**

Wall pocket, pink kettle w/heart & verse................................. **40.00**

Wall pocket, red long johns ... **42.50**

Finch, Kay

Canister, Santa, 10½" **110.00**

Cup, Kitten Face, Toby, 3".....**75.00**

Figurine, Choir Boy, kneeling, #211, 5½" **40.00**

Figurine, Goodey Man & Lady, #122, 9½", pr.................. **100.00**

Figurine, Jezebel, contented cat, #179, 6x9"...................... **175.00**

Figurine, Kneeling Madonna, #4900, 6"........................... **85.00**

Figurine, Peep & Jeep (ducks), #178a & #178b, pr **65.00**

Figurine, Polly Penguin, #467, 4¾"............................... **100.00**

Figurine, Sassy, pig looking up, #166, 3¾x4" **50.00**

Figurine, Squirrel Family, #108A, B & C, 3½" adults & 1¾" baby **110.00**

Figurine, Toot (owl), #188, 5¾". **60.00**

Figurine, Tootsie (owl), #189, 3¾" **25.00**

Plate, Santa face, 6½" **50.00**

Tea tile, Yorkshire terrier in relief, 5½" sq............................... **85.00**

Toby mug, Santa Claus, stamped mark, 4¼", $75.00.
(Photo courtesy Jack Chipman)

Toby mug, Santa, w/hat lid, 5½".**125.00**

Florence Ceramics

Note: The amount of applied decoration — lace, flowers, etc. — has a great deal of influence on values. Our ranges reflect this factor.

Ann, pink & white w/gold trim, 6", from $40 to **50.00**

Belle, 8", from $140 to **150.00**

Charles, 8¾", from $300 to ..**325.00**

David, 7½", from $125 to **140.00**

Emily, flower holder, 8", from $40 to **50.00**

Grace, blue, plain, 10", from $200 to **225.00**

Jim, child, 6¼", from $125 to. **140.00**

Kay, fur trim w/gold, 6", from $125 to **140.00**

Lillian, 7¼", from $135 to **150.00**

May, flower holder, from $40 to.**50.00**

Patsy, flower holder, 6", from $40 to **50.00**

Rebecca, 7", from $225 to **250.00**

Sally, white hat, hat in left hand, flower holder, 6", from $65 to **70.00**

Sue Ellen, 8¼", from $160 to. **175.00**

Violet, wall pocket, w/gold, 7", from $150 to **160.00**

Keeler, Brad

Bowl, green leaves form bowl, Lobster line (no lobster), #859, 11¾" **36.00**

Figurine, bluebirds, #718 & #719, ea 5", pr **75.00**

Figurine, cat in basket, 3¾" .. **50.00**

Figurine, fawn, 3½", from $20 to.. **25.00**

Figurine, kitten lying on side in playful pose, brown tones, #773, 7" **40.00**

Figurine, quail, male (head up) & female (head down), 3½", pr **45.00**

Figurine, rabbit, creamy white w/pink accents, foil label, 6½" **50.00**

Platter, green leaves form, Lobster line (no lobster), #892, 13½" **52.00**

Salt & pepper shakers, crab, ruby red, rubber stoppers, pr . **125.00**

Vase, 2 budgie parakeets perched on cornucopia-like form, #854, 5x7" **45.00**

Schoop, Hedi

Ashtray, marbleized green & white, 6-sided, 11" **42.50**

Console/planter, 2 ducks joined at back, white w/gold specks, 7x13" **150.00**

Figurine, deer lying w/head turned over back, gold & white, 12" **55.00**

Figurine, Dutch girl in green holds apron in right hand, 10¾". **50.00**

Flower holder, Black boy angel, right hand to lips, 8" **150.00**

Flower holder, Dutch boy in light blue, hands in pockets, 10" **145.00**

Lamp base/flower holder, lady w/2 baskets, ca 1940, 11½", NM **75.00**

Vase, rooster crowing, stylized, rosy pink, green & white, 14x11" **100.00**

Twin Winton

Ashtray, Bronco Group, cowboy kneeling beside saddle, B-208, 5½" H **75.00**

Ashtray, Ladies of the Mountain, lady, 4¼" sq **20.00**

Bank, Dobbin, TW-410, 8" **40.00**

Bank, poodle, 8" **65.00**

Candy jar, elephant, TW-356, 6x9" **54.00**

Canister, Flour House, TW-101, 1957-58, 7x11" **125.00**

Canister, Pot O' Tea, TW-124, 4x5" **20.00**

Decanter, Irishman, Alberta mark, 12½" **50.00**

Decanter, Robin Hood, 10½" .. **40.00**

Figurine, Asian girl holding books, T-16, 5½" **100.00**

Figurine, cat holding up paw, early, 3" **30.00**

Figurine, elf on snail pulling cart, 5" **100.00**

Figurine, Mickey the Sorcerer, Disney, 8" **150.00**

Figurine, squirrel w/mallet, dated 1940-45, 3x5" **40.00**

Ice bucket, 1969 Hillbilly line modeled after 1947 line, Bottoms Up, TW-32, 14x7½", $250.00.

Miniature, Democrat Donkey, #408 .... **20.00**
Miniature, fawn standing, #401. **11.00**
Miniature, ram, #405 .... **9.00**
Mug, Wood Grain Line, rope & spur handle, 4" **40.00**
Pitcher, Men of the Mountain, H-101, 5½" **75.00**
Planter, rabbit crouching beside sq basketweave planter, 5x8" .**85.00**
Salt & pepper shakers, apples, pr **75.00**
Salt & pepper shakers, cookie pot, pr **30.00**
Salt & pepper shakers, goose, pr.. **45.00**
Stein, Ladies of the Mountain, 8" **70.00**

Weil Ware

Bowl, aqua w/coral interior, incurvate rim, 3x6½" **20.00**
Bowl, Bambu, divided, rectangular.**35.00**
Flower holder, Asian girl sitting beside vase, #4021 .... **75.00**
Flower holder, lady holding 2 conical baskets, blue scarf, 10"..... **55.00**
Flower holder, lady in braids w/left hand holding apron, 11" . **35.00**

Flower holder, lady w/flowers in hand & vase at left side, #4030 .... **60.00**
Toothbrush holder, Dutch boy, holes in pants pockets, M/W mark, 6½" **50.00**
Vase, Ming Tree, sq sides, incurvate rim, 8x4".................. **45.00**
Vase, pink nautilus shell, #720, 6x9½x4"............................ **47.50**

Yona

Box, octagonal w/applied fruit & leaves on lid, paper label.**35.00**
Figurine, clown lying on chest w/feet high in air, 5¼" **15.00**
Figurine, girl w/basket, lg pink hair bow, green skirt, #16, 8½".**50.00**
Figurine, Siamese dancers, 10", pr **35.00**
Napkin holder, chef appears to be looking over top of side, 7x5" **32.00**
Ornament set, 3 choir boys, pierced at hair for hanging, 4¼", EXIB **32.50**
Pill jar, plump lady w/hair as lid, Shafford label, ca 1960 ... **45.00**
Tumbler, Country Club, cold-painted red stripes, 5", NM..... **20.00**

Cameras

Whether buying a camera for personal use, adding to a collection, or for resale, use caution. Complex usable late-model cameras are difficult to check out at sales, and you should be familiar with the camera model or have confidence in the seller's claims before purchasing one for your personal use. If you are just beginning a camera collection, there are a multitude of different types and models and special features to select from in building your collection; you should have on hand some of the available guide books listing various models and types. Camera collecting can be a very enjoyable hobby and can be done within your particular funding ability.

Buying for resale can be a very profitable experience if you are careful in your selection and have made arrangements with buyers who have made their requirements known to you. Generally, buying low-cost, mass-produced cameras is not advisable; you may have a difficult time finding a buyer for such cameras. Of these low-cost types, only those that are mint or new in the original box have any appreciable appeal to collectors. Very old cameras are not necessarily valuable — it all depends on availability. The major criterion is quality; prices offered for mint-condition cameras may be double or triple those of average-wear items. You can expect to find that foreign-made cameras are preferred by most buyers because of the general perception that their lenses and shutters are superior. The German- and Japanese-made cameras dominate the 'classic' camera market. Polaroid cameras and movie cameras have yet to gain a significant collector's market.

The cameras listed here represent only a very small cross section of thousands of cameras available. Values are given for examples with average wear and in good working order; they represent average retail prices with limited guarantees. It is very important to note that purchase prices at flea markets, garage sales, or estate sales would have to be far less for them to be profitable to a resaler who has the significant expense of servicing the camera, testing it, and guaranteeing it to a user or a collector.

Adfa, Optima, 1960s, from $15 to **35.00**
Agfa, Billy, 1930s **15.00**
Agfa, Isolette **20.00**
Alpa, Standard, 1946-52, Swiss, from $700 to **1,500.00**
Ansco, Folding, Nr 1 to Nr 10, ea from $5 to **30.00**
Ansco, Memo, 1927 type **100.00**
Argoflex, Seventy-Five, TLR, 1949-58 .... **7.00**
Argus A2 F, 1940, from $10 to . **20.00**
Asahi Pentax, Original, 1957 . **200.00**
Baldi, by Balda-Werk, 1930s . **30.00**
Bell & Howell Dial 35 .... **40.00**
Bosley B2 .... **20.00**
Burke & James Cub, 1914 .... **20.00**
Canon A-1, from $100 to **130.00**
Canon AE-IP, from $70 to **125.00**
Canon AE-1, from $40 to **80.00**
Canon F-1 .... **225.00**
Canon III **250.00**
Canon L-1, 1956-57 .... **400.00**
Canon P, 1958-61, from $250 to .. **350.00**
Canon Rangefinder IIF, ca 1954, from $200 .... **350.00**
Canon S-II, 1947-49 .... **375.00**
Canon TL, from $40 to **60.00**
Canon VT, 1956-57, from $250 to **300.00**
Canonet QL1, from $25 to **40.00**

Conley, 4x5 Folding Plate, 1905, from $90 to **140.00**

Contessa 35, 1950-55, from $100 to **150.00**

Detrola Model D, Detroit Corp, 1938-40 .... **20.00**

Eastman Folding Brownie Size-20 .... **12.00**

Eastman Kodak Bantam, Art Deco, 1935-38 .... **35.00**

Eastman Kodak Retina II **60.00**

Eastman Kodak Retina IIa ... **80.00**

Eastman Kodak Signet 35..... **35.00**

Eastman Kodak 35, 1940-51 . **25.00**

Eastman View Camera, early 1900s, from $100 to **200.00**

Exakta, Kine with round magnifier, 1936, from $175.00 to $250.00.
(Photo courtesy C.E. Cataldo)

Exakta VX, 1951, from $75 to. **85.00**

Fujica AX-3 .... **80.00**

Fujica AX-5 .... **115.00**

Herbert George, Donald Duck, 1946 .... **35.00**

Konica FS-1 .... **60.00**

Kowa H, 1963-67................... **25.00**

Lecia IID, 1932-38, from $250 to **400.00**

Mamiya-Sekor 500TL, 1966 .. **20.00**

Minolta Autocord, TLR **100.00**

Minolta SR-7 .... **50.00**

Minolta SRT-202, from $50 to.. **90.00**

Minolta X-700, from $90 to . **135.00**

Minolta XD-11, 1977............ **140.00**

Minox B, spy camera **125.00**

Nikon EM, from $45 to.......... **75.00**

Nikon FG **100.00**

Nikon S2 Rangefinder, 1954-58, from $700 to **1,000.00**

Olympus OM-1, from $90 to. **120.00**

Olympus OM-10, from $40 to. **60.00**

Pax M3, 1957......................... **30.00**

Pentax ME, from $50 to **75.00**

Petri FT, FT-1000, FT-EE & similar models, ea........................ **70.00**

Petri 7, 1961......................... **20.00**

Polaroid, most models, ea from $5 to **10.00**

Polaroid SX-70....................... **35.00**

Praktica FX, 1952-57............. **30.00**

Regula, King, fixed lens, various models, ea........................ **25.00**

Regula, King, interchangable lens, various models, ea **75.00**

Ricoh Diacord 1, TLR, built-in meter, 1958..................... **75.00**

Ricoh Singlex, 1965, from $50 to **80.00**

Rolleiflex SL35M, 1978, from $75 to **100.00**

Samoca 35, 1950s.................. **25.00**

Taron 35, 1955....................... **25.00**

Topcon Super D, 1963-75..... **125.00**

Tower 45, w/Nickkor lens, Sears. **200.00**

Tower 50, w/Cassar lens, Sears.**20.00**

Univex-A, Univ Camera Co, 1933 .... **25.00**

Voightlander Bessa, various folding models, 1931-49, ea from. **35.00**

Yashica Electro-35, 1966 .... **25.00**

Yashica FX-70......................... **60.00**

Zeiss Ikon Super Ikonta B, 1937-56 .... **150.00**

Candlewick

Candlewick was one of the all-time bestselling lines of The Imperial

Glass Company of Bellaire, Ohio. It was produced from 1936 until the company closed in 1982. More than 741 items were made over the years; and though many are still easy to find today, some (such as the desk calendar, the chip and dip set, and the dresser set) are a challenge to collect. Candlewick is easily identified by its beaded stems, handles, and rims characteristic of the tufted needlework of our pioneer women for which it was named. For a complete listing of the Candlewick line, we recommend *Elegant Glassware of the Depression Era* by Gene and Cathy Florence (Collector Books).

Ashtray, heart, #400/173, 5½". **12.00**
Ashtray, sq, #400/652, 4½" **35.00**
Bowl, finger; #3400, footed **35.00**
Bowl, finger; #3800 .... **35.00**
Bowl, oval, divided, #400/125A, 11" **350.00**
Bowl, oval, 2 handles, #400/217, 10" **40.00**
Bowl, pickle/celery, #400/57, 7½". **27.50**
Bowl, relish; #400/60, 7" **25.00**
Bowl, round, #400/69B, 8½"... **35.00**
Bowl, round, 2 handles, #400/42B. **12.50**
Bowl, round, 2 handles, #400/62B, 7" **17.50**
Bowl, sauce; deep, #400/243, 5½". **40.00**
Bowl, sq, #400/231, 5" **95.00**
Bowl, 3-footed, #400/183, 6" .. **60.00**
Butter dish, bead top, #400/61, ¼-lb **30.00**
Cake stand, high foot, #400/103D, 11" **75.00**
Candleholder, rolled edge, #400/79R, ea........................ **17.50**
Candleholder, 2-light, #400/100, ea **24.00**

Candleholder #400/40S, 3" x 6", $35.00. (Photo courtesy Gene and Cathy Florence)

Candy box, divided, w/lid, #400/110, 7" **125.00**
Cigarette box, w/lid, #400/134 . **35.00**
Coaster, #400/78, 4" **10.00**
Coaster, w/spoon rest, #400/226. **18.00**
Compote, 2-bead stem, #400/66B, 5½" **22.00**
Compote, 4-bead stem, #400/45, 5½" **30.00**
Cordial, #3400, 1-oz **40.00**
Creamer, plain foot, #400/31 ... **9.00**
Cruet, etched 'Oil,' w/stopper, #400/121 .... **75.00**
Cruet, etched 'Vinegar,' w/stopper, #400/121 .... **75.00**
Cup, after dinner; #400/77 .... **20.00**
Cup, tea; #400/35 .... **8.00**
Goblet, #4000, 11-oz.............. **35.00**
Ice tub, #400/63, 5½x8" dia.. **135.00**
Mayonnaise set, 2-pc, #400/23 . **400.00**
Mustard jar, w/spoon, #400/156. **40.00**
Parfait, #3400, 6-oz **60.00**
Pitcher, plain, #400/416, 20-oz . **40.00**
Pitcher, plain, #400/424, 64-oz. **60.00**
Plate, #1400/10D, 10½" **45.00**
Plate, #400/3D, 7" **9.00**
Plate, #400/5D, 8" **10.00**
Plate, #400/7D, 9" **15.00**
Plate, #400/92D, 14" **50.00**
Plate, handles, #400/145D, 12".. **45.00**
Plate, oval, #400/38, 9" **45.00**
Relish dish, 5-part, 5 handles, #400/56, 10½" **75.00**

Salt & pepper shakers, straight & footed, chrome top, #400/247, pr............................... **20.00**

Salt cellar, #400/61, 2" **11.00**

Sauceboat, #400/169 .... **115.00**

Saucer, after dinner; #400/77AD . **5.00**

Sherbet, tall #400/190, 5-oz... **15.00**

Sugar bowl, flat, bead handle, #400/126 .... **35.00**

Tidbit, 2-tier, cupped, #400/2701.. **60.00**

Tray, 5-part, #400/102, 13" **65.00**

Tumbler, #3800, 9-oz.............. **28.00**

Tumbler, old-fashioned; #400/18, 7-oz................................ **70.00**

Tumbler, wine; footed, #400/19, 3-oz **22.00**

Vase, fan; bead handle, #400/87F, 8"...................................... **35.00**

Vase, rolled rim, bead handle, #400/87R, 7" **45.00**

Wine, #3800, 6-oz **28.00**

Cape Cod by Avon

Though now discontinued, the Avon company sold this dark ruby red glassware through their catalogs since the '70s, and there seems to be a good supply of it around today. In addition to the place settings (there are plates in three sizes, soup and dessert bowls, a cup and saucer, tumblers in two sizes, three different goblets, a mug, and a wine glass), there are many lovely accessory items as well. Among them you'll find a cake plate, a pitcher, a platter, a hurricane-type candle lamp, a butter dish, napkin rings, and a pie plate server. Note: Mint-in-box items are worth about 20% more than the same piece with no box.

Bell, hostess; marked Christmas 1979, 6½" **18.00**

Bell, hostess; unmarked, 1979-80, 6½" **17.50**

Bowl, dessert; 1978-90, 6½"... **10.00**

Bowl, rimmed soup; 1991, 7½". **22.00**

Bowl, vegetable; marked Centennial Edition 1886-1986, 8¾"... **30.00**

Box, heart form, w/lid, 1989-90, 4"................................... **15.00**

Butter dish, 1983-84, ¼-lb, 7" L, from $20 to **22.00**

Cake knife, red plastic handle, Regent Sheffield, 1981-84, 8".................................... **39.50**

Cake plate, pedestal foot, 1991, 10¾" dia **48.00**

Candleholder, hurricane type w/clear chimney, 1985.................... **39.50**

Candlesticks, 1975 – 1980, 8¾", $12.00 each.

Candlestick, 1983-84, 2½", ea.. **8.00**

Candy dish, 1987-90, 3½x6" dia.**19.50**

Creamer, footed, 1981-84, 4" . **10.00**

Cruet, w/stopper, 1975-80, 5-oz .**12.50**

Cup & saucer, 15th Anniversary, marked 1975-90 on cup, 7-oz **20.00**

Cup & saucer, 1990-93, 7-oz.. **15.50**

Goblet, claret; 1992, 5-oz, 5¼", from $10 to **14.00**

Goblet, saucer champagne; 1991, 8-oz, 5¼"........................... **14.00**

Goblet, water; 1976-90, 9-oz.... **9.00**

Goblet, wine; 1976-80, 3-oz **2.00**

Mug, pedestal foot, 1982-84, 5-oz, 5", from $8 to.................. **12.00**

Napkin ring, 1989-90, 1¾".....**10.00**

Ornament, 6-sided, marked Christmas 1990, 3¼".......**12.50**

Pie plate/server, 1992-93, 10¾" dia, from $20 to **25.00**

Pitcher, water; footed, 1984-85, 60-oz, from $40 to.................**45.00**

Plate, bread & butter; 1992-93, 5½" **8.00**

Plate, dessert; 1980-90, 7½" **7.50**

Plate, dinner; 1982-90, 11", from $20 to...............................**25.00**

Platter, oval, 1986, 13"...........**48.00**

Relish, rectangular, 2-part, 1985-86, 9½" **15.00**

Salt & pepper shaker, marked May 1978, ea **7.50**

Salt & pepper shaker, unmarked, 1978-80, ea **6.00**

Sauce bowl, footed, 1988, 8" L. **28.00**

Sugar bowl, footed, 1980-83, 3½", from $7 to **10.00**

Tidbit tray, 2-tiered (7" & 10" dia), 1987, 9¾" H, from $30 to.**40.00**

Tumbler, straight-sided, footed, 1988, 8-oz, 3½" **10.00**

Tumbler, straight-sided, 1990, 12-oz, 5½" **14.00**

Vase, footed, 1985, 8", from $15 to..................................**20.00**

Carnival Chalkware

Chalkware statues of Kewpies, glamour girls, assorted dogs, horses, etc., were given to winners of carnival games from about 1910 until the 1950s. Today's collectors especially value those representing well-known personalities such as Disney characters and comic book heroes. Refer to *The Carnival Chalk Prize* by Tom Morris.

Mickey Mouse, no mark, ca 1930 – 1935, rare, 8½", $175.00.

Abe Lincoln bust, 1940-50, 12"..**55.00**

Air-raid warden standing holding American flag, 1940s **95.00**

Apache Babe, original marks, 1936-45, 15"..............................**90.00**

Bell Hop, marked, 1940s, 13". **85.00**

Call Me Papa, 1935-45, 14"... **15.00**

Cat sitting & looking into fishbowl, 1940-50, 9½" **75.00**

Clown standing w/hand in pockets, 1940s-50s, 9½"................**45.00**

Colonial lady standing w/dog, 1935-45, 11¼"...........................**55.00**

Cowboy holding hat, 1935-45, 8½" **35.00**

Dog (aka Bonzo/Bimbo/Bozo) sitting, some marked Jenkins, 1920s-40s, 9" **65.00**

Donald Duck, 1934-50, 14".... **70.00**

Gorilla (King Kong) w/fists on chest, flat back, 1930s-40s, 6"... **30.00**

Horse & rider jumping barrier, 1935-45, 9"......................**45.00**

Horse w/feather plume on head, 1935-45, 11"....................**40.00**

Horse w/sad face, 1945-50, 5". **20.00**

Indian chief standing w/arms crossed, 1930-45, 19" **45.00**

Kewpie w/both hands on fat tummy, 1935-45, 7½" **20.00**

Lady w/jointed arms in crepe-paper dress & wig, 1920-30, 12".**185.00**

Lighthouse, 1935-40, 12" **45.00**

Lion standing & growling, ca 1940-50, 9x12".............................**45.00**
Popeye standing w/fists together, 1940-50, 13½"..................**100.00**
Remember Pearl Harbor, sailor saluting at base of cannon, 1940s, 11"........................**95.00**

Soldier Boy, JY Jenkins, copyright 1944, 9", $45.00.

Westward Ho Cowboy, 1945-50, 10"......................................**35.00**
Wimpy standing holding mug of beer, marked Jenkins Studio, 1946, 10"...........................**80.00**

Cat-Tail Dinnerware

Cat-Tail was a dinnerware pattern popular during the late 1920s until sometime in the 1940s. So popular, in fact, that ovenware, glassware, tinware, and even a kitchen table was made to coordinate with it. The dinnerware was made primarily by Universal potteries of Cambridge, Ohio, though a catalog from Hall China Co., circa 1927, shows a three-piece coffee service, and there may have been other pieces made by Hall as well. Cattail was sold for years by Sears Roebuck and Company, and some items bear a mark with their name.

The pattern is unmistakable — a cluster of red cattails (usually six but sometimes only one or two) with black stems on creamy white. Shapes certainly vary; Universal used a minimum of three of their standard mold designs — Camwood, Old Holland, Laurella — and there were possibly others. Some pieces are marked 'Wheelock' on the bottom. Wheelock was a department store in Peoria, Illinois.

If you are trying to decorate a '40s vintage kitchen, no other design could afford you more to work with. To see many of the pieces that are available and to learn more about the line, read *The Collector's Encyclopedia of American Dinnerware* by Jo Cunningham (Collector Books).

Note: Assume that suggested prices for tinware items are for examples in excellent condition. For ceramic items, assume that they are at least near mint.

Bowl, footed, 9½"....................**20.00**
Bowl, mixing; 8"......................**23.00**
Bowl, Old Holland shape, Wheelock, 6"..**7.00**
Bowl, salad; lg.........................**25.00**
Bowl, sauce; Camwood Ivory, 5¼"................................**6.00**
Bowl, soup; flat rim, 7¾"........**15.00**
Bowl, soup; tab handles, 8"...**17.50**
Bowl, straight sides, 6¼".......**12.00**
Bowl, vegetable; oval, 9"........**27.50**
Bowl, vegetable; Universal, 8¾".**25.00**
Bread box, tin, 12x13½", VG.**50.00**
Butter dish, ¼-lb....................**55.00**
Butter dish, 1-lb.....................**30.00**
Cake keeper, w/copper-colored lid & knob, EX+....................**65.00**

Cake plate, Mt Vernon........... **25.00**
Canister set, tin, 4-pc **60.00**
Casserole, w/lid, 3¾x7", from $25 to **30.00**
Casserole, w/lid, 4¼x8¼"........ **45.00**
Coffeepot, electric................. **150.00**
Coffeepot, 3-pc........................ **70.00**
Cookie jar, w/lid, 9", from $100 to **125.00**
Creamer, Laurella shape, from $16 to **20.00**
Creamer & sugar bowl, w/lid, Camwood Ivory, 3¾x5¼" . **45.00**
Custard cup **9.00**
Gravy boat, from $18 to......... **25.00**
Gravy boat, w/underplate, from $35 to............................. **40.00**
Ice box jar, round bowl shape w/lid, 4"...................................... **20.00**
Ice box jar, round bowl shape w/lid, 5"...................................... **25.00**
Ice box jar, round bowl shape w/lid, 6"...................................... **28.00**
Jug, ball; cork stopper, from $30 to **35.00**
Jug, canteen; sq, flat-sided, ceramic-topped cork stopper, from $30 to.............................. **35.00**
Match holder, tin.................... **45.00**
Pickle dish/gravy boat liner... **20.00**
Pie plate................................ **30.00**
Pie server, hole in handle for hanging, from $20 to............... **25.00**
Pitcher, clear glass w/Cat-Tail pattern, ribbed neck & base, 9"...................................**65.00**
Plate, dinner; Laurella shape, 10", from $10 to **15.00**
Plate, luncheon; 9", from $7 to. **8.50**
Plate, salad or dessert; round, from $5 to **6.50**
Plate, sq, 7¾"............................ **7.00**
Plate, tab handles, 11"........... **30.00**

Platter, oval, tab handles, Camwood Ivory, 14½" **35.00**
Platter, oval, tab handles, 13½".**30.00**
Platter, oval, 11½", from $15 to..**20.00**
Relish tray, oval, Cat-Tail pattern repeated 4 times at rim, 9x5" **50.00**
Salad set (bowl, fork & spoon), from $50 to **60.00**
Salt & pepper shakers, various styles, ea pr from $25 to. **40.00**
Saucer, Old Holland shape, marked Wheelock, from $4 to **6.00**
Scales, metal **45.00**
Shaker set, 4-pc (salt, pepper, flour, sugar), glass, red metal tops/ tray **75.00**
Sugar bowl, w/lid, from $20 to. **25.00**
Tablecloth **90.00**
Teapot, 4-cup **35.00**
Tumbler, juice; glass, 3¾", from $18 to **25.00**
Tumbler, marked Universal Potteries, scarce, from $65 to **70.00**
Tumbler, water; glass............. **35.00**
Waste can, step-on, tin **45.00**

Plate, dinner; square, 10", $20.00.

Ceramic Arts Studio

Whether you're a collector of American pottery or not, chances are you'll like the distinctive styling of the figurines, salt and pepper shakers, and other novelty items made by the Ceramic Arts Studio of Madison, Wisconsin, from about 1938 until approximately 1952. They're not especially hard to find — a trip to any good flea market will usually produce at least one good buy from among their vast array of products. They're easily spotted, once you've seen a few examples; but if you're not sure, check for the trademark — most are marked.

For more information we recommend *Ceramic Arts Studio, The Legacy of Betty Harrington,* by Donald-Brian Johnson, Timothy J. Holthaus, and James E. Petzold (Schiffer). See the Directory for information concerning the CAS Collector's Association, listed under Clubs and Newsletters.

Ashtray, hippo, 3½x5" **135.00**
Bank, Skunky, 4", from $260 to.. **280.00**
Bowl, Bonita, paisley shape, 3¾" L **75.00**
Candleholders, bedtime boy & girl, 4¾", pr from $150 to **190.00**
Figurine, Al the Hunter, 6¼" . **100.00**
Figurine, Annie (baby elephant) & Benny, 3" & 3¾", pr from $115 to **160.00**
Figurine, Bright Eyes (cat), 3", from $30 to **40.00**
Figurine, child w/towel, 5", from $300 to **350.00**
Figurine, chipmunk, 2" **45.00**
Figurine, Cupid, 5", from $325 to **375.00**
Figurine, fawn, from Indian group, 4¼" **50.00**

Figurine, Fire Man, 11¼", from $185 to **200.00**
Figurine, Frisky the baby lamb, 3", from $25 to **35.00**
Figurine, frog singing, 2" **45.00**
Figurine, Gay 90's couple #2, 6½" & 6¾", pr from $110 to **150.00**
Figurine, girl praying, 3" **50.00**
Figurine, Isaac & Rebekah, 10", pr from $140 to **200.00**
Figurine, King's Flutist & Lutist Jesters, 12", pr from $250 to **350.00**
Figurine, Lover Boy, 4½" **85.00**
Figurine, Our Lady of Fatima, 9", from $260 to **285.00**
Figurine, panda w/hat, 2¾", from $200 to **225.00**
Figurine, Petrov & Petruska, 5" & 5½", pr from $120 to **150.00**
Figurine, Ralph the goat, 4".. **95.00**
Figurine, shepherd & shepherdess, 8" & 8½", pr from $180 to **220.00**
Figurine, Spanish dancers, 7" & 7½", pr **190.00**
Figurine, Spring Sue, 5" **85.00**
Figurine, swan w/neck up, 6". **110.00**
Figurine, Wee Piggy boy & girl, 3¼" & 3½", pr from $50 to **70.00**
Head vase, Barbie, 7", from $125 to **150.00**
Head vase, Becky, 5¼", from $100 to **125.00**

Head vase, Bonnie, from $125.00 to $150.00.

Head vase, Svea, 6" **215.00**

Metal accessory, arched window for religious figure, 6½" **150.00**

Metal accessory, circle bench w/crescent planter, 9" dia, from $200 to **245.00**

Metal accessory, garden shelf for Mary Contrary, 4x12", from $100 to **120.00**

Metal accessory, ladder for Jack, rare, 13", from $125 to.. **150.00**

Metal accessory, sofa for Maurice & Michelle, 7½" L, from $250 to................................. **275.00**

Miniature, pitcher, Adam & Eve 'Autumn', 3", from $40 to. **50.00**

Miniature, pitcher, George Washington & stars, white on blue **65.00**

Miniature, pitcher, pine cone, 3¾" **65.00**

Miniature, vase, flying ducks, round, 2", from $75 to..... **85.00**

Plaque, Dutch boy & girl dancing, pr..................................... **145.00**

Plaque, Manchu & Lotus, 8", pr **190.00**

Plaque, mask, Tragedy, 5", from $80 to **90.00**

Shakers, baby chick in nest, pr .**50.00**

Shakers, covered wagon & ox, 3" L, pr from $100 to **135.00**

Shakers, fish on tail, pr **125.00**

Shakers, horse's head, pr....... **95.00**

Shakers, Paul Bunyan & evergreen, 2½" & 4½", pr from $200 to.**250.00**

Shakers, Santa Claus & Christmas tree, 2¼", pr from $325 to .**375.00**

Shakers, sea horse & coral, 3" & 3½", pr from $100 to **140.00**

Shakers, Suzette the poodle on pillow, pr **250.00**

Shelf sitter, Budgie & Pudgie parakeets, 6", pr from $100 to..**120.00**

Shelf sitter, Chinese boy & girl, 4", pr from $30 to **40.00**

Shelf sitter, Fluffy & Tuffy cats, 7", pr from $120 to **160.00**

Shelf sitter, girl w/cat, 4¼" **75.00**

Shelf sitter, Persian mother cat, green eyes, 4¼"............... **125.00**

Shelf sitter, Smi-Li & Mo-Pi, chubby man & woman, 6", pr from $50 to............................... **80.00**

Character and Promotional Glassware

Once routinely given away by fast-food restaurants and soft-drink companies, these glasses have become very collectible; and though they're being snapped up by avid collectors everywhere, you'll still find there are bargains to be had. The more expensive are those with Disney or Walter Lantz cartoon characters, super-heroes, sports greats, or personalities from Star Trek or the old movies. For more information refer to *The Collector's Guide to Cartoon and Promotional Drinking Glasses* by John Hervey (L-W Book Sales) and *McDonald's Drinkware* by Michael J. Kelly (Collector Books). See Clubs and Newsletters for information on *Collector Glass News*.

Al Capp, 1975, flat bottom, any character, ea from $35 to **50.00**

Al Capp, 1975, footed, any except Joe Btsfplk, ea from $35 to **50.00**

Al Capp, 1975, footed, Joe Btsfplk, from $40 to **60.00**

Battlestar Galactica, 1979, 4 different, ea from $7 to............ **10.00**

Burger King, Collector Series, 1979, 5 different, ea from $3 to.. **5.00**

California Raisins, Applause, 1989, juice, 12-oz, or 16-oz, ea from $4 to **6.00**

California Raisins, Applause, 1989, 32-oz, from $6 to **8.00**

Dick Tracy, Domino's Pizza, from $100 to **125.00**

ET, Pizza Hut, 1982, footed, 4 different, from $2 to **4.00**

Happy Days, Dr Pepper or Dr Pepper/Pizza Hut, 1977, any, ea from $6 to **10.00**

Harvey Cartoon Characters, Pepsi, 1970s, any action pose, ea from $8 to **10.00**

Harvey Cartoon Characters, Pepsi, 1970s, any static pose, ea from $12 to **30.00**

Hopalong Cassidy's Western Series, ea from $25 to **30.00**

Howdy Doody, Welch's/Kagran, 1960s, 6 different, ea from $10 to .**15.00**

James Bond 007, 1985, 4 different, ea from $10 to **15.00**

Leonardo TTV Collector Series, Pepsi, 3 different, 5", ea from $6 to **10.00**

Leonardo TTV Collector Series, Pepsi, 4 different, 6", ea from $10 to **15.00**

Little Mermaid, 1991, 3 different sizes, ea from $6 to **10.00**

Masters of the Universe, Mattel, 1983, 4 different, ea from $5 to **10.00**

Masters of the Universe, Mattel, 1986, 4 different, ea from $3 to **5.00**

MGM Collector Series, Pepsi, 1975, Barney, Droopy, Spike, 6", ea from $5 to **10.00**

MGM Collector Series, Pepsi, 1975, Tom, Jerry or Tuff, 6", ea from $6 to **10.00**

MGM Collector Series, Pepsi, 1975, Tom or Jerry, 5", ea from $6 to **10.00**

Mickey Mouse, Happy Birthday, Pepsi, 1978, 8 different, ea from $5 to **7.00**

Mickey Mouse Club, 4 different w/filmstrips top & bottom, ea from $10 to **20.00**

Mister Magoo, Polomar Jelly, different variations & style, ea from $25 to **35.00**

Pac-Man, Arby's Collector Series, 1980, rocks glass, from $2 to **4.00**

Pac-Man, Bally Midway, MFG/AAFES/Libbey, 1980 or 1982, any, ea from $2 to **6.00**

PAT Ward, Holly Farms, Boris, Natasha, or Rocky, 1975, 6¼", each from $20.00 to $40.00. (Photo courtesy Collector Glass News)

PAT Ward, Pepsi, 1970s, action, Bullwinkle w/balloons, from $5 to **10.00**

PAT Ward, Pepsi, 1970s, static, Boris, Natasha, or Peabody, 5", ea from $10 to **15.00**

PAT Ward, Pepsi, 1970s, static, Boris & Natasha, 6", from $15 to **20.00**

PAT Ward, Pepsi, 1970s, static, Bullwinkle, 5", from $15 to.**20.00**

Peanuts Characters, McDonald's, 1983, Camp Snoopy, plastic, ea from $5 to **8.00**

Peanuts Characters, Smuckers, 1994, 3 different, ea from $2 to **4.00**

Popeye, Popeye's Famous Fried Chicken, 1978, Pals, any, ea from $10 to **15.00**

Rescuers, Pepsi, 1977, any except Madame Medusa or Rufus, ea from $5 to **10.00**

Rescuers, Pepsi, 1977, Madame Medusa or Rufus, ea from $15 to **25.00**

Roy Rogers Restaurant, 1883-1983 logo, from $3 to **5.00**

Sleeping Beauty, American, late 1950s, 6 different, ea from $8 to **15.00**

Sleeping Beauty, Canadian, late 1950s, 12 different, ea from $10 to **15.00**

Smurf's, Hardee's, 1982 (8 different) & 1983 (6 different), ea from $1 to **3.00**

Star Trek, Dr Pepper, 1976, 4 different, ea from $15 to **20.00**

Star Trek, Dr Pepper, 1978, 4 different, ea from $25 to **30.00**

Star Trek: The Motion Picture, Coca-Cola, 1980, 3 different, ea from $10 to **15.00**

Super Heroes, Marvel, 1978, flat bottom, any except Spider-Woman, from $40 .... **75.00**

Super Heroes, Marvel, 1978, flat bottom, Spider-Woman, from $100 to **150.00**

Super Heroes, Marvel/7-11, footed, Spider-Man, from $25 to . **30.00**

Super Heroes, Marvel/7-11, 1977, footed, any except Spider-Man, from $10 to **15.00**

Super Heroes, Pepsi Super (Moon) Series/DC Comics, 1976, ea from $20 to **30.00**

Super Heroes, Pepsi Super (Moon) Series/DC Comics-NPP, 1976, ea from $10 to **20.00**

Super Heroes, Pepsi Super (Moon) Series/NPP, 1976, any, ea from $20 to **30.00**

Super Heroes, Pepsi/DC Comics, 1978, flat bottom, any, ea from $8 to **15.00**

Super Heroes, Pepsi/DC Comics, 1978, round bottom, ea from $15 to........................... **25.00**

Superman, NPP/M Polanar & Son, 1964, 6 different, 4" & 6", ea from $20 to **25.00**

Universal Monsters, Universal Studio, 1980, footed, any, from $125 to **150.00**

Walter Lantz, Pepsi, 1970s, Chilly Willy or Wally Walrus, ea from $25 to **45.00**

Walter Lantz, Pepsi, 1970s, Space Mouse, from $150 to **200.00**

Walter Lantz, Pepsi, 1970s, Woody Woodpecker, from $7 to **15.00**

Warner Bros, Arby's, 1988, footed, Bugs, Daffy, etc, ea from $25 to **30.00**

Warner Bros, Pepsi, 1976, Bugs & Yosemite Sam w/cannon, from $10 to **15.00**

Warner Bros, Pepsi, 1979, round bottom, any, ea from $7 to **10.00**

Warner Bros, Pepsi, 1980, heads on stars, names on bands, any, ea from $6 to **10.00**

Warner Bros, 1996, repeated characters on backgorund, any of 8, ea from $4 to **6.00**

Western Heroes, Annie Oakley, Buffalo Bill or Bill Hickok, ea from $8 to **12.00**

Western Heroes, Lone Ranger, from $10 to **15.00**

Western Heroes, Wyatt Earp, fight scene or OK Corral gunfight, ea from $12 to **22.00**

Wild West Series, Coca-Cola, Buffalo Bill or Calamity Jane, ea from $10 to **15.00**

Wonderful World of Disney, Pepsi, 1980s, any, ea from $15 to..**20.00**

Ziggy, Number Series, 1-8, ea from $4 to **8.00**

Ziggy, 7-Up Collector Series, 1977, Here's to Good Friends, any, from $3 to **5.00**

Character Collectibles

One of the most active areas of collecting today is the field of character collectibles. Flea markets usually yield some of the more common items. Toys, books, lunch boxes, children's dishes, and games of all types are for the most part quite readily found. Disney characters, television personalities, and comic book heroes are among the most sought after.

For more information, refer to *Schroeder's Collectible Toys, Antique to Modern*; *Cartoon Toys & Collectibles* by David Longest; *Star War's Collector's Wish Book* by Geoffery T. Carlton; *G-Men and FBI Toys and Collectibles* by Harry and Jody Whitworth;

and *The World of Raggedy Ann Collectibles* by Kim Avery. All are published by Collector Books. See also Advertising; Banks; Bubble Bath Containers; Character and Promotional Glassware; Children's Books; Cookie Jars; Dakin; Disney; Games; Garfield; Kliban Cat; Lunch Boxes; Novelty Telephones; Puzzles; Radios; Star Trek; Star Wars; Western Heroes.

Charlie Brown, figure, push down head and body pivots, EX, $35.00.

Addams Family, hand puppets, any character, Ideal, 1965, EX, ea **75.00**

Alf, finger puppet, Coleco, 1987, MIB **15.00**

Alf, hand puppet, Cookin' w/Alf, Alien Products, 1988, MIP (sealed) **22.00**

Alvin & the Chipmunks, figure, Theodore, cloth & vinyl, musical, EX+ **85.00**

Alvin & the Chipmunks, harmonica, Plastic Inject Corp, 1959, 4", MOC **85.00**

Alvin & the Chipmunks, jack-in-the-box, Child Guidance, 1983, NM **35.00**

Archies, stencil set, 1983, MOC.**15.00**

Aristocats, Colorforms, 1960s, NMIB **40.00**

Astro Boy, figure, vinyl w/jointed arms & neck, NM............ **50.00**

Banana Splits, Kut-Up Kit, Larami, 1973, MIB (sealed).......... **10.00**

Banana Splits, tambourine, plastic & cardboard, 1970s, MIP. **35.00**

Batman, figure, plush & vinyl, black & red, Play-By-Play, 2001, 13", M **10.00**

Batman, figure, stuffed cloth, blue & black, Justice League, 17", M **10.00**

Batman, figure, vinyl, jointed, cloth outfit, Presents, 1988, 15", M **40.00**

Batman, push-button puppet, Kohner, 1960s, NM **100.00**

Batman Returns, Accessory Pak for 4, Unique, 1991, MIP **5.00**

Beatle Bailey, putty stickers, Ja-Ru, 1983, MIP (sealed) ... **20.00**

Ben Casey, notebook, 3-ring binder, photo cover, Hasbro, 1960s, EX+ **85.00**

Ben Casey, Paint-by-Number Water Color Set, Transogram, 1962, MIB **38.00**

Ben Casey, Sweater Guard, 5 charms on chain w/faux pearls, 1962, NMOC **50.00**

Betty Boop, figure, bendable, NJ Croce, 1988, 8", MOC **15.00**

Blondie, doll, vinyl w/molded hair, cloth dress, Presents, 1985, 18", NM **30.00**

Bozo the Clown, figure, cloth & vinyl, Eegee, 1970s, 12", NM **25.00**

Bozo the Clown, planter, ceramic box w/embossed Bozo at piano, 5", NM **125.00**

Bozo the Clown, wristwatch, image & name in red, vinyl band, 1960s, EX **50.00**

Brady Bunch, banjo, Larami, 1973, 15", MIP **65.00**

Bugs Bunny, ball cap, Space Jam's Hare Jordan, Nike, 1990s, EX **5.00**

Bugs Bunny, figure, Chatter Chum, 1976, string missing, VG. **10.00**

Bugs Bunny, figure, plush, sheriff outfit, Six Flags, 1999, 20", NM **10.00**

Bugs Bunny, mug, gray molded plastic face w/toothy grin, 4", NM **15.00**

Bugs Bunny, pennant, BB Follies, character graphics, 1978, 30", EX **18.00**

Bugs Bunny, plate, Mother's Day 1977, MIB **38.00**

Bullwinkle & Rocky, wallet, brown vinyl w/white stitching, graphics, EX **25.00**

Captain America, Flashmite, Janex, 1970s, MOC **75.00**

Captain America, hand puppet, Ideal, 1960s, NM **50.00**

Captain America, hand puppet, vinyl, Imperial, 1978, MIP **50.00**

Captain Kangaroo, hand puppet, cloth w/vinyl head, Rushton, 1950s, M **75.00**

Car 54 Where Are You?, hand puppet, officer, cloth & vinyl, 1961, EX **175.00**

Care Bears, phonograph, 1983, MIB **125.00**

Casper the Ghost, baseball hat & ball set, inflatable vinyl, MOC **15.00**

Charlie's Angels, magic slate, Whitman, 1977, M, from $25 to **30.00**

Charlie's Angels, sunglasses, Fleetwood, MOC (photo card w/Farrah) **50.00**

CHiPs, Emergency Medical Kit, Empire, 1980, MIB **30.00**

Curious George, magic slate, Fairchild, 1968, 9x12", M. **10.00**

Daffy Duck, figurine, ceramic, Shaw & Co, 1940s, 5½", VG...... **75.00**

Daffy Duck, wall plaque, ceramic figure, black & orange, 15", M.................................. **75.00**

Dennis the Menace, doll, Stuff 'n Lace, Standard Toycraft, MIP **40.00**

Dick Tracy, transfer, Tracy holding up shield, 1940s, unused, NM.................................. **15.00**

Dr Dolittle, figure, bendable vinyl w/cloth outfit & parrot, 6", EX................................... **50.00**

Dr Dolittle, figure, periscope, Bat-Zam #609, NMIP............. **30.00**

Dr Seuss, figure, Cat in Hat, plush, w/umbrella, Coleco, 1983, 26", NM..................................**30.00**

Dr Seuss, wristwatch, Cat in the Hat, 1972, NM **150.00**

Dukes of Hazzard, Acrylic Paint Set, Craft Master #N48001, MIB.................................. **75.00**

Dukes of Hazzard, ID Set, Grand Toy, MOC **10.00**

Elmer Fudd, wall plaque, ceramic face in hunting hat, 11", M................................. **80.00**

Emergency, fire helmet, plastic, Playco, 1975, EX+........... **30.00**

ET, pillow, blue or purple, EX, ea **20.00**

Evel Knievel, bike flags, Schaper, 10x15", MIP..................... **18.00**

Evel Knievel, wristwatch, vinyl band, Bradley, 1976, EX............ **150.00**

Family Affair, doll, Buffy w/Mrs Beasley, talker, Mattel, 1967, 10", M **150.00**

Family Affair, tea set, Buffy, plastic, Chilton Toys, 46 pcs, M **75.00**

Fat Albert, figure, vinyl, 1973, 7", VG **10.00**

Felix the Cat, alarm clock, Felix & mouse, Bright Ideas, 1989, NMIB **65.00**

Felix the Cat, figure, bendable, w/satchel, Applause, 1990, 5", M **15.00**

Felix the Cat, figure, squeeze rubber, lg green eyes, 1962, 6", EX+.. **100.00**

Flintstones, coin purse, Barney, 1975, NM **25.00**

Flintstones, figure, Pebbles & Dino hugging, vinyl, NM......... **80.00**

Flintstones, finger puppet, Fred, Knickerbocker, MOC....... **20.00**

Flintstones, iron-on transfer, Fred, Wilma & Pebbles, Holoubek, 1976, MIP **20.00**

Flintstones, lamp, Fred figure, vinyl, 11", NM **50.00**

Flintstones, nightlight, Fred figure, 1975, NMOC.................... **20.00**

Flintstones, pencil topper, Bamm-Bamm, green, Hong Kong, 1970s, M **15.00**

Flipper, figure, plush, Knickerbocker, 1976, scarce, 19", M **100.00**

Flying Nun, Weaving Loom Set, Hasbro, 1967, 12x12", MIB, from $100.00 to $125.00. (Photo courtesy Greg Davis and Bill Morgan)

Foghorn Leghorn, figure, ceramic, 1970s, NM **30.00**

Green Hornet, display card for flicker rings, 12 different, 8x8", EX+ **275.00**

Grizzly Adams, wastebasket, photo image on metal, 13", EX+. **50.00**

Gumby, figure, Perma Toys and Lewco Toys Ltd., 1984, 12"; Pokey, sitting figure, Perma Toys, JESCO, 9", each from $10.00 to $12.00.

Happy Days, guitar, Fonzie, 1976, MIB (sealed) **75.00**

Heckle & Jeckle, hand puppet, plush & vinyl, Rushton Star, 1950s, EX **75.00**

Howdy Doody, bath mitt, terry w/Howdy graphics, w/hang loop, EX **75.00**

Howdy Doody, Birthday Cake Decorations, Tee Vee Products, 1950s, MOC **175.00**

Howdy Doody, hand puppet, cloth body w/vinyl head, goggle eyes, VG+ **75.00**

HR Pufnstuff, Milton Bradley #4108, 1971, NMIB **75.00**

Huckleberry Hound, figure, fireman Huck, squeeze vinyl, Dell, 9", NM **75.00**

Huckleberry Hound, Flip Show, 1961, EXIB **40.00**

Huckleberry Hound, magic slate, Paper Saver, Whitman #4465, 1960, NM **25.00**

Humpty Dumpty, hanger, stamped-out images on plastic, Clarolyte, 1950s **18.00**

Humpty Dumpty, tea set, litho tin, 7-pc set, 1960s, EX **45.00**

Incredible Hulk, Crazy Foam, 1979, VG+ **25.00**

Incredible Hulk, Halloween candy pail, green plastic head, 1979, EX **45.00**

Incredible Hulk, hand puppet, green vinyl, Imperial, 1978, EX **35.00**

James Bond 007, wall clock, Roger Moore image, 1981, NM+. **50.00**

Jetsons, Pocket Flix, Rosey the Robot, Ideal, 1978, MOC (sealed) **50.00**

Josie & the Pussycats, guitar, Larami, plastic, 1973, MOC **75.00**

Knight Rider, sticker & album set, Goody, MOC **8.00**

Land of the Lost, Direction Finder, Larami, 1975, MOC **30.00**

Land of the Lost, Secret Lookout (Periscope), Laramie, 1975, MOC **35.00**

Laverne & Shirley, iron-on transfers, several different, 1970s, MIP **15.00**

Little Lulu, coin purse, red or white vinyl, Hallmark, 1960s, 5x3", M **35.00**

Little Lulu, face mask, Kleenex premium, 1950s, unused, M.. **30.00**

Little Lulu, magic slate, features Tubby, Whitman #4921, 1972, VG+ **40.00**

Love Boat, Poster Art Kit, Craft Master, 1978, MIP **40.00**

Lucy (Peanuts) at desk, ceramic, NM **20.00**

Magilla Gorilla, figure, cloth body w/ vinyl head, Ideal, 7½", NM..**100.00**

Magnum PI, wallet, black vinyl w/white whipstitching & graphics, NM **42.00**

Man From UNCLE, Secret Print Putty, Colorforms, 1960s, MOC **75.00**

Marvel Super Heroes, Colorforms, 1983, complete, MIB **165.00**

Masters of the Universe, tray, metal w/fold-down legs, 1982, 12x18", M **20.00**

Mighty Mouse, Presto-Paints, Kenner, 1963, complete, EXIB **65.00**

Mork & Mindy, Acrylic Paint-by-Number, Craft Master, 1979, MIB **38.00**

Mork & Mindy, Figurine Painting Set, Crafts by Whiting, 1979, MOC **60.00**

Mr Ed, hand puppet, pull-string talker, Mattel, 1962, MIB **200.00**

Muppets, figure, Kermit the Frog, stuffed, Fisher-Price, 1977-83, NM **12.00**

Muppets, figure, Miss Piggy, bendable, Just Toys, 5", EX **5.00**

Muppets, figure, Muppet Babies, McDonald's issue, 1996, EX, set of 4 .... **10.00**

Muppets, jack-in-the-box, Big Bird, 1980s, EX+ **15.00**

Mushmouse, doll, Ideal, 1960s, 9", EX **75.00**

Oswald the Rabbit, figure, squeeze vinyl, Vinfloat Prod, 1960s, 7", VG **40.00**

Peanuts, alarm clock, character faces as numbers, metal case, MIB **60.00**

Peanuts, figure, Charlie Brown, plastic, Hungerford, 1958, 9", EX **175.00**

Peanuts, figure, Charlie Brown, stuffed print cloth, 1963, EX............................... **40.00**

Peanuts, figure, Sally, squeeze vinyl, Con Agra, 1990s, 6", NM **8.00**

Peanuts, figure, Snoopy, Dress Me, Knickerbocker, 1983, EX+..**25.00**

Peanuts, finger puppets, Ideal/ Determined, MIB, set of 6..**35.00**

Peanuts, friction toy, Lucy & Her Doctor Booth, Aviva, 1974, 7", MIB **85.00**

Peanuts, game, Monopoly, Peanuts version, MIB **35.00**

Peanuts, guitar, Snoopy, plastic w/crank handle, Aviva, 1980, EX **25.00**

Peanuts, kaleidoscope, Snoopy Disco, Determined, 1979, EX **20.00**

Peanuts, ornament, Peppermint Patty w/guitar, Determined, 1977, 3", NM **65.00**

Peanuts, plate, Valentines 1980, Woodstock & Snoopy blowing bubbles, MIB **35.00**

Peanuts, pull toy, Snoopy Copter, Romper Room, 1980, NM+.**12.00**

Peanuts, Push 'n Fly Snoopy, Romper Room/Hasbro, 1980s, EX **15.00**

Peanuts, push-button puppet, Lucy, Ideal, 1970s, EX.............. **25.00**

Peanuts, push-button puppet, Snoopy as Joe Cool, Ideal, 1970s, 4", NM.................. **85.00**

Peanuts, tea set, litho tin, Chein, 1970s, complete, EXIB....**75.00**

Peanuts, top, litho tin, Chein, 1969, MIB **75.00**

Penguin (Batman), doll, plush w/vinyl head, Play-by-Play, 1998, 10", M **8.00**

Peter Pan, figure, molded rubber, Sun Rubber, 1950s, 10", EX............................... **75.00**

Peter Potamus, figure, plush & vinyl, bendable arms, Ideal, 7", EX............................ **75.00**

Petunia Pig, figurine, ceramic, Shaw, 1940, M............... **125.00**

Pink Panther, Cartoonarama, 1970, complete, EXIB **60.00**

Pink Panther, figure, Chatter Chum, 1976, 6", EX+ **45.00**

Pixie & Dixie, figurine, pr in old shoe w/names, Ideas, 1961, 4", NM **150.00**

Pixie & Dixie, squeeze toy, pr on cheese wedge, Mexico, 1960s, 5", EX............................ **100.00**

Popeye, figure, Olive Oyle, Jesco, 1988, 7", MOC (Bendable/ Posable) **25.00**

Popeye, figure, Popeye, cloth & vinyl, Uneeda, 1979, 8", MIB...... **50.00**

Popeye, figure, Popeye, Jesco, 1988, 6½", MOC (Bendable/ Posable) **25.00**

Popeye, mug, plastic head, thermo liner, 1990s, EX............... **20.00**

Popeye, wristwatch, green case, Bradley #308, 1964, EXIB. **200.00**

Porky Pig, print, Porky & Petunia, Dell premium, 1940s-50s, 8x10", EX+...................... **35.00**

Porky Pig, wall plaque, ceramic face, 10", M...................... **80.00**

Quick Draw McGraw, 2-D figure on base, World's Greatest Friend, 6", NM............................. **35.00**

Ricochet Rabbit, push puppet, Kohner, EX..................... **40.00**

Rocky the Squirrel, figure, plush w/vinyl face, dated 1966, 10", VG................................. **150.00**

Rookies, Emergency First Aid Kit, Fleetwood, 1975, MOC ... **32.00**

Santa Claus, push puppet, holding bell, Kohner, 1960s, EX.. **75.00**

Secret Squirrel, Tricky Trapeze, Kohner, NM..................... **85.00**

Sesame Street, figure, Guy Smiley, plush beanbag type, Tyco, 1997, M............................ **10.00**

Sesame Street, figure, Honker, beanbag type, Tyco, 1997, EX **6.00**

Sesame Street, figures, PVC, Applause, 1993, M, set of 8,................... **20.00**

Sesame Street, Lacing Puppets, Big Bird & Ernie, Fisher-Price, 1984, MIB....................... **10.00**

Sesame Street, puppet, Big Bird, plush, Child Guidance, 1980, NM **18.00**

Simpsons, Bendable Figures, Jesco, 1990, M(ea sealed)IB **50.00**

Simpsons, doll, any, Burger King promo, 1990, Marge is 12", NM+, ea........................... **10.00**

Simpsons, doll, Bart in nightshirt w/toothbrush, Dan-Dee, 1990, 24", M **20.00**

Simpsons, Fun Dough Maker, MIB **30.00**

Simpsons, key chain, Bart figure, PVC, 3½", 1990, EX **5.00**

Simpsons, Paint-by-Number, Rose Art, unused, MIB............ **10.00**

Simpsons, Wash It Dude Bath Soap, Bart, Cosrich, 1990, 5", NRFB **12.00**

Six Million Dollar Man, waste can, metal w/lithoed images, 1976, EX **25.00**

Smurfs, bank, Peyo, molded plastic character, 1980s, NM...... **35.00**

Smurfs, figure, grandpa Smurf on skateboard, PVC, Applause, 3", NM **12.00**

Smurfs, push puppet, red sq base, TM, 1970s, 4", EX **40.00**

Smurfs, record player, Vanity Fair, 1982, EXIB **75.00**

Speedy Gonzales, ceramic full-figure wall plaque, 12", M .. **80.00**

Spider-Man, Code Breaker, Gordy, 1980, MOC **35.00**

Spider-Man, sunglasses, Nasta, 1986, MOC **10.00**

Starsky & Hutch, Poster Put-Ons, Bi-Rite, 1976, unused, MIP, ea **10.00**

Superman, push puppet, Kohner, 1960s, EX **120.00**

Superman, wallet, brown w/embossed colored images, Croydon, 1950s, EX+ **75.00**

Superman, water pistol, plastic, Multiple Toys, 1960s, unused, MIP **175.00**

Sylvester the Cat, pencil topper, blue head, dated 1975, 1", EX **10.00**

Tasmanian Devil, figure, as vampire, plush, 1998, 4½", EX...............................**12.00**

Tom & Jerry, figures, bendable, MOC, ea........................... **10.00**

Tweety Bird, flasher ring, silver plastic, gumball prize, EX **15.00**

Underdog, harmonica, yellow & green plastic w/figural ends, 1975, 8", NM **50.00**

Underdog, pillow, inflatable vinyl, EX **15.00**

Waltons, farmhouse play set, Amsco, 1975, MIB........................ **75.00**

Welcome Back Kotter, magic slate, Whitman, 1977, M................**20.00**

Whistle, Woodstock, Hallmark, 1976, MIP........................ **45.00**

Wizard of Oz, figure, Cowardly Lion or Scarecrow, Mego, 1974, MIB, ea............................ **75.00**

Wizard of Oz, figure, Dorothy, bendable, Multiple Toy, 1960s, 6", EX **50.00**

Wizard of Oz, ornament, Glenda the good witch, Bradford Novelty, MIP **12.00**

Wolfman, figure, Playco Products, 1991, 10", MIB **12.00**

Wonder Woman, figure, inflatable vinyl, ca 1979, 24", MIP . **30.00**

Wonder Woman, iron-on transfers, several different, 1970s, MIP, ea. **15.00**

Woody (Toy Story), pocket watch, Fossil, 1996, MIB **125.00**

Woody Woodpecker, harmonica, plastic figure, early, 6", EX...... **30.00**

Yogi Bear, figure, standing on base w/name, ceramic, 1960s, 5½", M **100.00**

Yogi Bear, Tricky Trapeze, Kohner, EX+ **75.00**

Yogi Bear & Boo Boo, handkerchief, 1960s, 8" sq, EX.............. **10.00**

Yosemite Sam, coffee cup, stuffing basketball into hoop, dated 1994, M........................... **12.00**

Ziggy, figure, plush w/vinyl face, Tom Wilson, 1988, EX..... **18.00**

Cherished Teddies

First appearing on dealers' shelves in the spring of 1992, Cherished Teddies found instant collector appeal. They were designed by artist Priscilla Hillman and produced in the Orient for the Enesco company. Besides the figurines, the line includes waterballs, frames, plaques, and bells.

#203432, Charity, I Found a Friend in Ewe, 1993, retired in 1996, MIB, $70.00.

#102914, O Canada!, musical....**95.00**
#104662, A Girl With Style.... **25.00**
#104664, Are We There Yet?... **25.00**
#107021, My Garden Is a Little Piece 'o Heaven **25.00**
#107036, Sprinkle a Little Love Wherever You Go **15.00**
#107071, I Am the Queen...... **22.00**
#109242, Georgia **45.00**
#109636, Hooray for the USA!...**25.00**
#109637, Smile, You Have a Friend! **20.00**
#110009, Love Spans All Nations........................ **15.00**
#110010, Our Little Angel, boy or girl, ea............................. **10.00**
#219177, Santa Express **30.00**
#629618, Jingle Bells............. **65.00**

#651362, A Christmas Carol (Cratchits house nightlight) **28.00**
#904309, Nativity Camel pull toy **20.00**
#950793, Rocking Reindeer ornament................................. **45.00**
#4001552, Alana Abbey Express..**30.00**
#4001916, Heath **25.00**
#4002844, Let Your Love Shine.**22.00**
#6610095, Cow **35.00**

Children's Books

Books were popular gifts for children in the latter 1800s; many were beautifully illustrated, some by notable artists such as Frances Brundage and Maxfield Parrish. From this century tales of Tarzan by Burroughs are very collectible, as are those familiar childhood series books — for example, The Bobbsey Twins and Nancy Drew.

Big Little Books

Probably everyone who is now 60 and over owned a few Big Little Books as a child. Today these thick hand-sized adventures bring prices from $10.00 to $75.00 and upwards. The first was published in 1933 by Whitman Publishing Company. Dick Tracy was the featured character. Kids of the early '50s preferred the format of the comic book, and the Big Little Books were gradually phased out. Stories about super heroes and Disney characters bring the highest prices, especially those with an early copyright.

Beasts of Tarzan, #1410, 1937, EX+.................................. **50.00**

Blondie & Dagwood in Some Fun, #703-10, 1949, EX+......... **35.00**

Blondie in Cookie & Daisy's Pups, #1491, 1943, EX+............ **45.00**

Buck Jones in Ride 'Em Cowboy, #116, 1937, EX+.............. **75.00**

Buck Jones in the Roaring West, #1174, 1935, EX+............ **55.00**

Buck Rogers & the Planetoid Plot, #1197, EX+...................... **85.00**

Bullet Benton, #1169, 1939, NM+.............................. **35.00**

Captain Midnight & the Secret Squadron, #1488, 1941, NM............................ **65.00**

Cinderella, #711-10, 1950, VG. **20.00**

Corley of the Wilderness Trails, #1607, 1937, EX+............ **35.00**

Donald Duck & the Green Serpent, #1432, 1947, VG+............ **45.00**

Donald Duck Up in the Air, #1486, 1945, VG+........................ **35.00**

Dumbo — Only His Ears Grew, #1400, 1941, scarce, VG . **75.00**

Flame Boy & the Indians' Secret, #1464, 1938, EX.............. **40.00**

Frank Merriwell at Yale, #1121, 1935, VG+....................... **35.00**

Gene Autry & the Gun-Smoke Reckoning, #1434, 1943, EX+.............................. **50.00**

Gulliver's Travels, #1172, 1939, VG.................................... **45.00**

Jackie Cooper in Peck's Bad Boy, #1314, 1934, VG+............ **45.00**

John Carter of Mars, #1402, 1940, NM................................. **150.00**

Kayo & Moon Mullins & the One Man Gang, #1415, 1939, EX+.....**40.00**

Little Lord Fauntleroy, #1598, 1936, VG+....................... **35.00**

Mother Goose (576 Pages of), #725, 1934, G **50.00**

Popeye & the Quest for the Rainbird, #1459, 1943, EX+............ **45.00**

Scrappy, #112, 1934, very scarce, VG+................................. **60.00**

Smilin' Jack & the Stratosphere Ascent, #1152, 1927, VG+. **25.00**

Spike Kelly of the Commandos, #1467, 1943, EX+............ **45.00**

Tarzan & the Jewels of Opar, #1495, 1941, VG...................... **25.00**

Tarzan and the Lost Empire, #1442, 1948, EX, $25.00.

Tarzan Lord of the Jungle, #1407, VG.................................... **35.00**

Terry Lee Flight Officer USA, #1492, 1944, EX+............ **40.00**

Texas Kid, #1429, 1937, VG.... **20.00**

Tim McCoy in the Westerner, #1193, 1938, EX.......................... **35.00**

Tom Mix Plays a Lone Hand, #1173, 1935, VG+........................ **35.00**

Wings of the USA, #1407, 1940, EX.................................... **35.00**

Little Golden Books

Little Golden Books (a registered trademark of Western Publishing Company Inc.), introduced in October of 1942, were an overnight success. First published with a blue paper spine, the later spines were of gold foil. Parents and grandparents born in the '40s, '50s, and '60s are now trying to find the titles they had as children. From 1942 to the early 1970s, the books were numbered from 1 to 600, while books published later had no numerical order. Depending on where you find the book, prices can vary from 25¢ to $30.00 plus. The most expensive are those with dust jackets from the early '40s or books with paper dolls and activities. The three primary series of books are the Regular (1 – 600), Disney (1 – 140), and Activity (1 – 52).

Television's influence became apparent in the '50s with stories like the Lone Ranger, Howdy Doody, Hopalong Cassidy, Gene Autry, and Rootie Kazootie. The '60s brought us Yogi Bear, Huckleberry Hound, Magilla Gorilla, and Quick Draw McGraw, to name but a few. Condition is very important when purchasing a book. You normally don't want to purchase a book with large tears, crayon or ink marks, or missing pages.

As with any collectible book, a first edition is always going to bring the higher price. To determine what edition you have on the 25¢ and 29¢ cover price books, look on the title page or the last page of the book. If it is not on the title page, there will be a code of 1/(a letter of the alphabet) on the bottom right corner of the last page. A is for first edition, Z would refer to the twenty-sixth printing.

There isn't an easy way of determining the condition of a book. What is 'good' to one might be 'fair' to another. A played-with book in average condition is gen-

erally worth only half as much as one in mint, like-new condition. To find out more about Little Golden Books, we recommend *Collecting Little Golden Books* (published by Books Americana) by Steve Santi.

Baby Looks, #404, A edition, 1960, EX+ 10.00

Buffalo Bill Jr, #254, A edition, 1956, VG 18.00

Busy Timmy, #50, F edition, 1948, EX 16.00

Chicken Little, #413, A edition, 1960, EX 8.00

Cleo, #287, A edition, 1957, scarce, VG 38.00

Country Rhymes, #361, A edition, 1960, EX 10.00

Doctor Dan the Bandage Man, #111, A edition, 1950, G+ .. 8.00

Emerald City of Oz, #151, A edition, 1952, EX 40.00

Hansel & Gretel, #17, A edition, 1943, EX 25.00

Heroes of the Bible, #236, A edition, 1955, EX 20.00

House that Jack Built, #218, A edition, 1954, EX 12.00

Howdy Doody in Funland, #172, A edition, 1953, EX+ 35.00

I'm an Indian Today, #425, A edition, 1961, NM, EX+ 20.00

Kitten's Surprise, #107, A edition, 1951, EX+ 15.00

Lippy the Lion & Hardy Har Har, #508, A edition, 1963, NM .. 35.00

Littlest Racoon, #459, A edition, 1961, NM 18.00

Lively Little Rabbit, #15, L edition, 1943, VG 18.00

My Little Golden Dictionary, #90, A edition, 1949, NM 16.00

Night Before Christmas, #20, L edition, 1949, NM **12.00**

Three Little Kittens, #1, O edition, 1942, VG **15.00**

Top Cat, #453, A edition, 1962, EX **35.00**

We Help Daddy, #468, A edition, 1962, NM **20.00**

Whitman

The Whitman Company produced several series of children's books, many of which centered around radio, TV, and comic strips. Among them were Tell-A-Tales, Tiny-Tot-Tales, Top-Top-Tales, and Big Little Books (which are in their own subcategory).

Buffy and the New Girl, **Tell-A-Tale, 1969, EX, from $10.00 to $15.00.**

Andy Panda's Rescue, Tiny-Tot-Tale #2942, 1949, EX **20.00**

Beverly Hillbillies in Saga at Wildcat Creek, 1963, hardcover, NM. **12.00**

Big Golden Animal ABC, #10457, last printing, 1954, NM .. **18.00**

Bongo, Story Hour #803, 1948, VG+ **25.00**

Crusader Rabbit in Bubble Trouble, Top-Top-Tales #2468, 1960, EX **45.00**

Dopey He Don't Talk None, #955, 1938, NM+ **150.00**

F Troop in The Great Indian Uprising, #1544, 1967, hardback, VG+ **12.00**

Flintstones at the Circus, Tell-A-Tale #2552, 1963, NM **25.00**

Funny Company & Shy Shrinkin' Violette, Top-Top-Tales #2471, 1964, EX+ **35.00**

Gene Autry & the Golden Ladder Gang, 1950, EX **18.00**

Jetsons in The Birthday Surprise, Top-Top-Tales #2484, 1963, NM.. **25.00**

Jungle Book, Giant Classic #11299, 1964, EX **35.00**

King Leonardo & the Royal Contest, Top-Top-Tales #2472, 1962, EX+ **32.00**

Little Lulu & the Birthday Mystery, Tell-A-Tale #3502, 1974, EX+ **30.00**

Little Lulu Lucky Landlady, Tip-Top-Tales #2473, 1960, VG+ **35.00**

Little Lulu Uses Her Head, Tell-A-Tale #2567, 1955, NM **45.00**

Loopy de Loop Odd Jobber, Tell-A-Tale #2611, 1964, EX+ **25.00**

Mother Pluto, #1058, 1939, NM. **50.00**

Munsters & the Great Camera Caper, #1510, 1965, EX .. **15.00**

Mushmouse & Punkin Puss Country Cousins, Tell-A-Tale #2552, 1964, EX+ **25.00**

One Hundred & One Dalmatians, Tell-A-Tale #2622-15, 1960s, EX **10.00**

Peter Potamus Meets the Black Knight, Tell-A-Tale #2506, 1965, NM **32.00**

Pixie & Dixie & Make-Believe Mouse, Top-Top-Tales #2464, 1961, EX **32.00**

Popeye Calls on Olive Oyl, #884, 1937, scarce, VG+ **175.00**

Porky Pig in All Picture Comics, #1408, 1942, VG **35.00**

Ricochet Rabbit Showdown at Gopher Gulch Bakery, Tell-A-Tale #2622, NM **25.00**

Snagglepuss The Way To Be King, Top-Top-Tales #2488, EX+ .. **28.00**

Top Cat, Top-Top-Tales #2468, 1963, NM **40.00**

Touche Turtle & the Fire Dog, Top-Top-Tales #2485, 1963, NM **40.00**

Woody Woodpecker's Pogo Stick Adventures, Tell-A-Tale #2562, 1954, EX **20.00**

Woody Woodpecker Shoots the Works, Tell-A-Tale #2562, 1955, EX+ **22.00**

Wonder Books

Though the first were a little larger, the Wonder Books printed since 1948 have all measured 6½" x 8". They've been distributed by Random House, Grosset Dunlap, and Wonder Books Inc. They're becoming very collectible, especially those based on favorite TV and cartoon characters. Steve Santi's book *Collecting Little Golden Books* includes a section on Wonder Books as well.

Billy & His Steam Roller, #557, 1951, EX+ **15.00**

Black Beauty, #595, 1952, VG+. **8.00**

Choo Choo Train, #718, 1958, EX **12.00**

Deputy Dawg & the Space Man, #773, 1961, M **35.00**

Deputy Dawg's Big Catch, #770, 1961, EX **20.00**

Felix on Television, A Flip-It Book, #716, 1956, by Irwin Shapiro, NM **30.00**

Heckle & Jeckle, #694, 1957, NM+ **35.00**

Hector Heathcoate & the Knights, #840, EX **28.00**

Hector Heathcoate the Minute-&-A-Half Man, #758, 1960, EX.. **30.00**

House That Popeye Built, #750, 1960, EX **25.00**

How the Clown Got His Smile, #566, 1951, EX **10.00**

Magilla Gorilla & the Super Kite, #707, 1976, EX+ **12.00**

Mighty Mouse Dinky Learns To Fly, #677, 1953, M **35.00**

Pecos Bill, #767, 1961, EX **10.00**

Peter Pan, #597, 1952, EX+ .. **12.00**

Peter Rabbit & Reddy Fox, #611, 1954, NM **25.00**

Rolling Wheels, #762, 1950, EX+ **20.00**

Who Goes There?, #779, 1961, EX+ **25.00**

Miscellaneous

Adventures of Andy Panda, Dell Fast Action, NM **75.00**

Batman — Three Villians of Doom, Signet, 1966, 160 pages, EX+ **20.00**

Bullwinkle Book, Golden Press #5954, 1976, head shape, EX **25.00**

Butter Battle Book, Dr Seuss, Random House, 1984, M . **10.00**

Dale Evans Prayer Book for Children, Big Golden Book, 1956, VG+ **10.00**

Disney on Parade, Mary Poppins cover, 1973, 12x8½", EX.. **28.00**

Disney Storybook Collection, Disney Press, 1998, 1st edition, EX............................. **18.00**

Donald Duck Takes It on the Chin, Dell Fast-Action, 1941, EX................................. **75.00**

***Donkey Work*, Doreen Tovey, drawings by Maurice Wilson, Doubleday first edition, blue hardcover, 138 pages, $15.00 ($30.00 with dust jacket).** (Photo courtesy Diane McClure Jones and Rosemary Jones)

Emerald City of Oz, Rand McNally Jr Edition #301, 1939, EX..... **45.00**

Felix the Cat, Treasure Book, #872, 1953, EX+........................ **35.00**

Helen Keller The Story of My Life, Helen Keller, 1969, softcover, VG.................................... **10.00**

Here's to You Charlie Brown, Charles Schulz, 1970, hardback, EX+ **8.00**

Hop on Pop, Dr Seuss, Random House Beginner Books, 1990s, M.. **6.00**

It's a Dog's Life Charlie Brown, Holt Rinehart Winston, 1967, NM..**6.00**

Lassie Come Home, Eric Knight, 1st edition of reissue, 1978, EX+ **18.00**

Little Lulu & the Magic Paints, Golden Press #10498, 1974, EX **40.00**

Little Tiger, Mabel Watts, Rand McNally Jr Elf #8097, 1962, EX+ **10.00**

My First Golden Dictionary, Golden Press #10417, A edition, 1963, NM **12.00**

My Many Colored Days, Dr Seuss, A Knof, 1996, NM+ **12.00**

Puss 'n Boots Pop Ups With Moving Figures, Artia Prague, 1973, EX **20.00**

Sgt Preston & Yukon King, MH Comfort, Rand McNally, 1955, NM+ **10.00**

Shirly Temple's Favorite Poems, Saalfield #1720, 1936, EX+. **30.00**

Speak Up Charlie Brown Talking Storybook, Mattel #4812, 1971, NM+.............................. **125.00**

Strawberry Shortcake & the Fake Cake Surprise, Little Pop-Up, 1982, NM **10.00**

Winnie the Pooh A Tight Squeeze, Big Golden Book, 1974, EX+ **12.00**

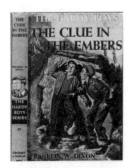

The Hardy Boys, *The Clue in the Embers,* Franklin W. Dixon, Grossett & Dunlap, with dust jacket, 1955, $20.00. (Photo courtesy Diane McClure Jones and Rosemary Jones)

Christmas Collectibles

No other holiday season is celebrated to such an extravagant extent as Christmas, and vintage decorations provide a warmth and charm that none from today can match. Ornaments from before 1870 were imported from Dresden, Germany. They were usually made of cardboard and sparkled with tinsel trim. Later, blown glass ornaments were made there in literally thousands of shapes such as fruits and vegetables, clowns, Santas, angels, and animals. Kugles, heavy glass balls (though you'll sometimes find fruit and vegetable forms as well) were made from about 1820 to late in the century in sizes up to 14". Early Santa figures are treasured, especially those in robes other than red. Figural bulbs from the '20s and '30s are popular, those that are character related in particular. Refer to *Pictorial Guide to Christmas Ornaments & Collectibles* by George Johnson and *Collector's Encyclopedia of Electric Christmas Lighting* by Cindy Chipps and Greg Olson, both published by Collector Books.

Bubble lights, Paramount, oil, ca 1947 – 1948, from $40.00 to $50.00; Paramount, methelene chloride, 1948 – 1950, from $8.00 to $12.00; Noma Tulip, ca 1948 – 1960, from $7.00 to $10.00. (Photo courtesy George Johnson)

Bulb, boy playing drum, milk glass, Japan, 1950s, 2½" **80.00**

Bulb, faceted, clear glass, Japan, 1950s, 1½-2" **18.00**

Bulb, Jiminy Cricket, milk glass, Diamond Brite, Japan, 1970s, 2½" **16.00**

Bulb, lantern, clear glass, 4-panel, Mazda, 1940s, 2¼" **65.00**

Bulb, Mother Goose riding a goose, milk glass, 1950s, 5" **55.00**

Bulb, Santa w/toy bag on back, Goodlite Electric, 1950s.. **10.00**

Bulb, soccer player, milk glass, Japan, 1950s, 2½" **80.00**

Bulb, star, gold-tone w/5 green-light points, Japan, 1935, 3" **25.00**

Bulb set, Walt Disney Character Lites, Raylite #899, 1958, NMIB. **100.00**

Candelabra, 2-socket candles w/angel light in center, Thomas, 1950s **25.00**

Candelabra, 3-socket candles on base, US Electric, 1950s. **15.00**

Candy container, boot, red plastic, 1950s, 2¾" **10.00**

Candy container, drum, paper, 2x3" dia **100.00**

Candy container, Santa in sleigh, plastic, 1950s, 4x4", EX.. **35.00**

Decoration, pine tree, cardboard standup, Germany, 12" ... **40.00**

Decoration, Santa head wall display, papier-mâché, eye inserts, 17" **125.00**

Decoration, tree w/bubble lights, round pedestal holder, 1950s, 20" **100.00**

Flashlight, Santa head, plastic, Hong Kong, 1960s, EX (in cone box) **20.00**

Garland, plastic faceted beads, 1960s-70s **10.00**

Garland, round colored glass beads **12.00**

Lantern, Santa head on round base, 5", MIB **65.00**

Lantern, snowman head on round base, plastic, Japan, 1950s, MIB **50.00**

Light set, Bubble Lites, 8 miniature, World Wide #2502, 1960, NMIB **50.00**

Light set, Glow Bells, set of 6, American Plastics, 1950s, EXIB **25.00**

Light set, Misty Glow, set of 15 outdoor, Renown #7015, 1960s, EXIB **35.00**

Light set, Sno-Ball, set of 7, Noma #3437, 1959, EXIB **25.00**

Motion lamp, Santa & sleigh in plastic cylinder, pedestal foot, 1965, 9" **225.00**

Nightlight, Santa figure, plastic, Japan, 1960s **5.00**

Novelty light, Blinking Christmas Bell, battery-op, Dan-Dee, 1960 .... **20.00**

Novelty light, candy cane w/red bow, Royal Electric #860, 1954, 24" **40.00**

Novelty light, choir girl w/candle light, Japan, 1960s, 9½" . **15.00**

Novelty light, Christmas tree, wall hanging, Vinylite, 1950s, 22" **50.00**

Novelty light, crèche, wall hanging, Vinylite, 1958, 16" L **15.00**

Novelty light, Rudolph head w/red light-up nose, #JC-341, 1960, 11" **20.00**

Novelty light, Santa face, plastic, wall mount, Noma #551, 1948, 15".**15.00**

Novelty light, Santa figure w/red light-up nose, rubber, 1960s **20.00**

Novelty light, Santa in chair, plastic, USA, 1960s, 7½".........**20.00**

Ornament, clay, mushroom & gnome, 3", from $50 to....**65.00**

Ornament, Dresden, circus elephant, silvered/multicolored, 9½" **130.00**

Ornament, foil, cone shape w/scalloped edge, colored, 1950s, 5½" **5.00**

Ornament, foil, star, 6-point, goldtone, 1950s, 3"................... **4.00**

Ornament, glass, ball w/swan indent, 1950s, 2¾" dia **25.00**

Ornament, glass, basket of daisies, 1980s, 2¾"........................**35.00**

Ornament, glass, dog's head, double-faced, 1½"...................**80.00**

Ornament, glass, frog, silver w/ red eyes & mouth, 1990s, 3½" **95.00**

Ornament, glass, pine cone form w/embossed bird & pine tree, 1950s, 3" **20.00**

Ornament, glass, rabbit eating carrot, Germany, 1980s, 3"..**70.00**

Ornament, Kugel, ribbed ball, silvered, 1¾".......................**125.00**

Ornament, metal, pine cone, 6".**25.00**

Ornament, scrap, Santa head, 2¼" **3.00**

Ornament, scrap, star w/Santa face & string, 3¾" **100.00**

Tree topper, angel w/star wand, Noma #701, 1950s...........**20.00**

Tree topper, Sparkling Tree Top Star, Noma #431, 1959...**15.00**

Tree topper, star, foil, holds center bulb, National Tensil, 1940s, 9" **2.00**

Wreath light, cellophane w/ Santa & poinsettia, Goodlite, 1955 ....**30.00**

Wreath light, chenille w/candle in center, M Propp Co #210, 1928 .... **45.00**

Cigarette Lighters

Pocket lighters were invented sometime after 1908 and were at their peak from about 1925 to the 1930s. Dunhill, Zippo, Colibri, Ronson, Dupont, and Evans are some of the major manufacturers. An early Dunhill Unique model, if found in its original box, would be valued at hundreds of dollars. Quality metal and metal-plated lighters were made from the 1950s to about 1960. Around that time disposable lighters never needing a flint were introduced, causing a decline in sales of figurals, novelties, and high-quality lighters.

What makes a lighter collectible? — novelty of design, type of mechanism (flint and fuel, flint and gas, battery, etc.), and manufacturer (and whether or not the company is still in business). For further information we recommend *The Big Book of Cigarette Lighters* by James Flanagan.

Advertising, Coors, table, painted metal, 1970s, 3½", from $10 to **20.00**

Advertising, GE Supply Co, brass & enamel, Park Industries, 1950s **15.00**

Advertising, Jim Beam, plastic butane, Korea, 1980s, from $5 to **10.00**

Advertising, Lucky Strike, painted chromium, 1950s, 4½x3". **25.00**

Advertising, Mack Trucks, brass lift-arm butane, Korea, 1960s, 2½" **15.00**

Advertising, Phillips 66, slim chromium & enamel, Park, 1960s, 2", from $15 .... **25.00**

Advertising, Winston, red & white enamel, Penguin, 1960s, 2", from $15 to **25.00**

Japan, chromium pistol with mother-of-pearl grips, early 1950s, 1½x2", from $25.00 to $40.00. (Photo courtesy James Flanagan)

Pocket, Clark, gold-plated, left arm, w/gift box, 1930s, 2", from $50 to **70.00**

Pocket, Colibri, gold-plated, 1950s, 1½", from $30 to **50.00**

Pocket, Continental, chromium & enamel, 1950s, from $20 to. **30.00**

Pocket, Crown, gold-plated, musical, 1940s, 2½x2", from $60 to **85.00**

Pocket, Elgin American, brass w/ostrich band, 1950s, 1½", from $40 to **60.00**

Pocket, Elgin American, chromium & brass, 1940s, 2", from $25 to **40.00**

Pocket, Evans, chromium w/floral design, 1940s, 2½x1", from $35 to **50.00**

Pocket, Evans, silver-plated w/swirl design, 1930s, 2", from $20 to. **40.00**

Pocket, Gulton, rechargable electric, 1950s, MIB, from $50 to 75.00

Pocket, Match King, chromium striker type, 1940s, 2½x1", from $15 to 25.00

Pocket, Perfecto, chromium, 1930s, 2½", from $40 to 55.00

Pocket, Pigeon, brass w/ivory colored bands, 1960s, 1½", from $15 to 25.00

Pocket, Ronson, blue enamel w/ivory cherubs, 1950s, 2", from $25 to................... 40.00

Pocket, Ronson Comet, chromium & red plastic, 1950s, 2¼", from $10 to 15.00

Pocket, Ronson Princess, chromium w/green leather, 1950s, w/box, 2" 50.00

Pocket, Ronson Varaflame, chromium butane, 1960s, w/box, from from $30 to 50.00

Pocket, Savinelli, chromium butane pipe, 1970s, 2¾x1⅛", from $25 to 40.00

Pocket, Wisner, brass & rhinestone, 1950s, 1½x1¾", from $25 to 40.00

Pocket, Zippo, chromium w/ etched lady, 1990s, 2", from $20 to 30.00

Table, boat motor, chromium & enamel, Swank, 1960s, 5x2½", from $75 to 125.00

Table, cowboy boot, silver-plated, Occupied Japan, 1950s, from $50 to............................. 70.00

Table, elephant figure, painted, 1940s, Strikalite, 3x3½", from $25 to 40.00

Table, horse on base, Japan, 1950s, 5½", from $15 to 25.00

Table, horse rearing, chromium, butane, Japan, 1980s, 7x4½", from $25 to 35.00

Table, machine gun on tripod, chromium & metal, 1980s, 12", from $50 to 70.00

Table, nautical, bronze & copper, Ronson, ca 1939, 5x3", from $225 to 300.00

Table, owl, silver-plate, glass eyes, Occupied Japan, 1940s, from $80 to 100.00

Table, penguin figure, gold & silver-plated, 1960s, 2", from $40 to 70.00

Table, Scottie dog figure, painted metal, 2½x3", from $25 to. 40.00

Table, ship's wheel, chromium, Dunhill, 1930s, 5x3", from $175 to 250.00

Table, tankard, chromium, 1980s, 4x3", from $20 to............. 30.00

Table, television, Swank, 1960s, 2¾x4", from $25 to 40.00

Table, floral and gold trim, brass, late 1940s, 4⅞x2¼", from $25.00 to $40.00. (Photo courtesy James Flanagan)

Clothes Sprinkler Bottles

From the time we first had irons, clothes were sprinkled with water before ironing for the best results. During the 1930s and until the 1950s when the steam iron became a home staple, some of us merely took sprinkler tops and stuck them into old glass bottles to accomplish this task, while the more imaginative bought and enjoyed bottles made in figural shapes. The most popular, of course, were the Chinese men marked 'Sprinkle Plenty.' Some bottles were made by American Bisque, Cleminson of California, and other famous figural pottery makers. Many were made in Japan for the export market.

Cat, ceramic, handmade, variety of designs & colors, from $75 to **125.00**

Cat, ceramic, marble eyes, Cardinal USA, 8" **250.00**

Cat with marble eyes, American Bisque, $400.00. (Photo courtesy Ellen Bercovici)

Chinese man, ceramic, removable head, from $250 to **400.00**

Chinese man, ceramic, Sprinkle Plenty, holding iron, 8½", from $125 to **175.00**

Chinese man, ceramic, towel over arm, from $300 to **350.00**

Chinese man, ceramic, white & aqua, California Cleminsons **85.00**

Chinese man, hand-made, various types made, from $50.00 to $150.00. (Photo courtesy Ellen Bercovici)

Clothespin, ceramic, w/facial features, Cardinal **400.00**

Clothespin, plastic, red, yellow & green, from $20 to **40.00**

Dearie Is Weary, ceramic, Enesco, from $350 to **500.00**

Dutch boy, ceramic, green & white **275.00**

Dutch girl, ceramic, white w/green & pink trim, wetter-downer, from $175 to **250.00**

Elephant, ceramic, pink & gray . **165.00**

Iron, ceramic, blue flowers, from $100 to **150.00**

Iron, ceramic, farm couple, from $200 to **275.00**

Iron, ceramic, green ivy, from $95 to **125.00**

Iron, ceramic, lady ironing **95.00**

Iron, ceramic, white w/black rooster decoration, metal lid, 6½" **100.00**

Iron, ceramic, lady cleaning . **125.00**

Iron, ceramic, souvenir, Florida, pink flamingo **300.00**

Iron, ceramic, souvenir, San Marcos TX, Aquarena Springs, from $200 to **300.00**

Iron, ceramic, souvenir, San Marcos TX, Wonder Cave **300.00**

Iron, plastic, green, from $35 to............................... **75.00**

Lady w/embossed apron, cobalt glass w/metal sprinkler cap, 7" **60.00**

Mammy, ceramic **450.00**

Mary Maid, plastic, all colors, Reliance, from $20 to **35.00**

Mary Poppins, ceramic, Cleminsons, from $300 to **450.00**

Myrtle, ceramic, Pfaltzgraff, from $350 to **300.00**

Peasant woman, ceramic, w/laundry poem on label, from $200 to **300.00**

Poodle, ceramic, gray, pink & white, from $200 to **300.00**

Rooster, ceramic, green, tan & red on white, Sierra Vista... **125.00**

Coca-Cola

Introduced in 1886, Coca-Cola advertising has literally saturated our lives with a never-ending variety of items. Some of the earlier calendars and trays have been known to bring prices well into the four figures. Because of these heady prices and extreme collector demand for good Coke items, reproductions are everywhere, so beware! In addition to reproductions, 'fantasy' items have also been made, the difference being that a 'fantasy' never existed as an original. Don't be deceived. Belt buckles are 'fantasies.' So are glass doorknobs with an etched trademark, bottle-shaped knives, pocketknives, and there are others.

When the company celebrated its 100th anniversary in 1986, many 'centennial' items were issued. They all carry the '100th Anniversary' logo. Many of them are collectible in their own right, and some are already high priced.

If you'd really like to study this subject, we recommend these books: *Goldstein's Coca-Cola Collectibles* by Sheldon Goldstein; *Collectors's Guide to Coca-Cola Items, Vols. I* and *II,* by Al Wilson; *Petretti's Coca-Cola Collectibles Price Guide* by Allan Petretti; and *B.J. Summers' Guide to Coca-Cola.*

Ashtray, glass w/gold lettering, 3 raised rests, EX............... **20.00**

Blotter, party scene, 1950s, EX .**25.00**

Bottle, amber, 75th Anniversary, 1974, G **55.00**

Bottle carrier, metal & wire w/wire handles, red/white, 1950s-60s, G..................................... **45.00**

Bottle, glass, first version of the straight-sided throw-away bottle, embossed diamond, 1960s, 10-ounce, NM, $25.00. (Photo courtesy Sam and Vivian Merryman)

Bottle opener, flat metal bottle shape, 1950s, EX............. **35.00**

Calendar, 1952, Coke Adds Zest, complete, EX **150.00**

Calendar, 1956, There's Nothing Like a Coke, complete, EX....... **125.00**

Calendar, 1973, cloth w/Lillian Nordica standing by table, M.................................. **10.00**

Calendar, 1980, sports scenes, complete, M............................20.00

Christmas card, Season's Greetings, silver ornament on red, 1976, M......................................10.00

Clock, light-up, fishtail w/white background, 1960s, EX.200.00

Clock, light-up, white lettering on red button on front, 1950s, NM.................................600.00

Clock, regular, wood, 1980s reproduction, 23", M..............225.00

Cookie jar, Hollywood Polar Bear, 2nd in series, 1996, M....35.00

Cooler, airline; red, chrome handle, side opener, 1950s, 12x17x6", EX...................................350.00

Decal, foil, Enjoy Coca-Cola, 1960s, 6x13", M...........................10.00

Door push, metal, Coke Adds Life, wave logo, 1970s-80s, NM..75.00

Fan, paper w/wooden handle, spotlight on bottle in center, 1950s, EX.....................................75.00

Fan, wicker, Compliments of Waycross, 1950s, EX+...100.00

Frisbee, plastic w/wave logo, EX................................15.00

Game, checkers, wooden, logo on tops, 1940s-50s, complete, NM...50.00

Lighter, can-shaped w/wave logo, M......................................35.00

Menu board, cardboard standup, Refreshing Your Best, 1960s, EX..................................175.00

Menu board, tin, arched top w/embossed fishtail logo, NM 450.00

Menu board, w/clock, light-up, 1960s, EX 150.00

Plate, bottle & glass on white, logos on rim, Knowles, 1930s, 7", EX+.................................225.00

Playing cards, white & red w/bottle, 1963, complete, EXIB.....50.00

Radio, can form w/wave logo, 1960s, EX+...................................50.00

Sign, cardboard, Enjoy..., for bottle rack, red & white, 1970s, EX..................................25.00

Sign, cardboard, Pick Up the Fixins, Enjoy Coke, 1957, 20x14", NM 55.00

Sign, cardboard, Refresh, majorette, 1952, 20x26", VG..475.00

Sign, cardboard, Refreshing New Feeling, 1960s, 32x67", EX.135.00

Sign, cardboard standup, Santa, Norman Rockwell art, 1960s, 20", EX+...........................30.00

Sign, cardboard, 'You taste its quality,' lady drinking from bottle under flowering tree branch, 20x36", EX, $485.00.

Sign, die-cut cardboard 6-pack, 1954, EX 750.00

Sign, plastic, Here's the Real Thing, Coke, wave logo, 1970s, 51x7", M......................................30.00

Sign, tin, Sign of..., fishtail, bottle, green rolled rim, 1960s, 32x56"............................275.00

Sign, tin button, Drink...in Bottles, white on red, 1954, 12", EX 250.00

Sign, tin flange, Drink..., bottle on yellow dot, 1940s, 20x24", EX.550.00

Syrup jug, clear glass w/applied label, 1950, 1-gal, VG 25.00

Thermometer, cardboard, gauge on left, chart on right, 1960s, VG..................................**65.00**

Thermometer, dial-type, Things Go Better..., Pam, 1960s, 12" dia, NM..................................**250.00**

Thermometer, die-cut metal bottle, 1956, 17x5", EX+...........**150.00**

Thermometer, plastic & metal, Drink..., green on white, 1960s, NM..................................**375.00**

Toy top, plastic, Coke Adds..., 1960s, VG...................................**15.00**

Tray, 1958, pull cart w/picnic basket, 13x11", EX................**10.00**

Tray, 1961, Pansy Garden, 13x10", NM...................................**30.00**

Tray, 1972, Duster Girl, 15x11", EX.....................................**15.00**

Tray, 1977, shows various sporting events, 15x11", NM+.......**50.00**

Tray, Running Girl, 1937, 13¼x10½", NM, $425.00.

Coin Glass

Coin Glass was originally produced in crystal, ruby, blue, emerald green, olive green, and amber. Lancaster Colony bought the Fostoria Company in the mid-1980s and reproduced this line in crystal, green, blue, amber, and red. Except for the red and crystal, the colors are off enough to be pretty obvious, but the red is so close it's impossible to determine old from new. Here are some (probably not all) of the items made after that time: bowl, 8" diameter; bowl, 9" oval; candlesticks, 4½"; candy jar with lid, 6¼"; cigarette box with lid, 5¾" x 4½"; creamer and sugar bowl; footed comport; decanter, 10¼"; jelly; nappy with handle, 5¼"; footed salver, 6½"; footed urn with lid, 12¾"; and wedding bowl, 8¼". Know your dealer!

Emerald green is most desired by collectors. You may also find some crystal pieces with gold-decorated coins. These will be valued at about double the price of plain crystal if the gold is not worn. (When the gold is worn or faded, value is minimal.) Numbers included in our descriptions were company-assigned stock numbers that collectors use as a means to distinguish variations in stems and shapes. For further information we recommend *Collectible Glassware from the 40s, 50s & 60s*, by Gene and Cathy Florence (Collector Books).

Ashtray, #1372/114, amber, crystal or ruby, round, 7½".........**20.00**

Ashtray, #1372/123, amber, crystal or olive, 5".........................**15.00**

Ashtray, #1372/123, emerald green, 5".......................................**30.00**

Bowl, #1372/189, amber or crystal, oval, 9"..............................**30.00**

Bowl, #1372/199, blue, footed, 8½"..............................**90.00**

105

Bowl, #1372/212, emerald green, footed, w/lid, 8½" **225.00**

Bowl, ruby with frosted coins, oval, 9", $50.00.

Candleholders, #1372/316, amber or olive, 4½", pr **30.00**

Candleholders, #1372/316, emerald green or ruby, 4½", pr **50.00**

Candleholders, #1372/326, amber, crystal or olive, 8", pr **50.00**

Candy box, #1372/354, blue or ruby................................. **60.00**

Candy box, #1372/354, emerald green, 4"........................... **100.00**

Cigarette box, #1372/374, crystal, 5½x4½"............................ **40.00**

Condiment set, #1372/737, amber, 4-pc w/2 shakers, cruet & tray............................. **225.00**

Condiment set, #1372/737, crystal, 4-pc w/2 shakers, cruet & tray............................. **135.00**

Decanter, #1372/400, crystal, w/stopper, 1-pt, 10½"....... **95.00**

Goblet, #1372/2, ruby, 10½-oz.**95.00**

Jelly dish, #1372/448, blue or ruby **25.00**

Lamp, coach; #1372/321, amber, electric, 13½" **145.00**

Lamp, patio; #1372/46, amber, electric, 16½"........................ **175.00**

Lamp chimney, coach or patio; #1372/461, amber............ **50.00**

Nappy, #1372/495, crystal, 4½"..**22.00**

Pitcher, #1372/453, amber or crystal, 32-oz, 6¼".................. **48.00**

Plate, #1372/550, crystal or olive, 8"..................................... **20.00**

Plate, #1372/550, ruby, 8"...... **40.00**

Punch bowl, #1372/600, crystal, 14"................................. **150.00**

Punch bowl base, #1372/602, crystal.................................. **150.00**

Punch cup, #1372/615, crystal. **30.00**

Salt & pepper shakers, #1372/652, amber or olive, chrome tops, 3", pr...................................... **30.00**

Sugar bowl, #1372/673, amber or olive, w/lid **35.00**

Sugar bowl, #1372/675, blue or ruby, w/lid........................ **45.00**

Tumbler, #1372/64, crystal, 12-oz, 5"...................................... **28.00**

Tumbler, #1372/81, crystal, 9-oz, 3½" **22.00**

Vase, #1372/818, crystal, footed, 10"..................................... **45.00**

Vase, bud; #1372/799, blue, 8". **40.00**

Vase, bud; #1372/799, emerald green, 8"........................... **60.00**

Wine stem, #1372/26, crystal, 5-oz, 4"...................................... **33.00**

Coloring Books

Throughout the 1950s and even into the 1970s, coloring and activity books were produced by the thousands. Whitman, Saalfield, and Watkins-Strathmore were some of the largest publishers. The most popular were those that pictured well-known TV, movie, and comic book characters, and these are the ones that are bringing top dollar today. Condition is also an important worth-assessing factor.

Compared to a coloring book that was never used, one that's only partially colored is worth from 50% to 70% less.

Diahann Caroll as Julia, blue or red cover, Saalfield #9252, 1968, NM, from $20.00 to $25.00. (Photo courtesy Greg Davis and Bill Morgan)

Adventures of Batman, Whitman, 1966, some use, EX+....... 25.00

Alice in Wonderland, Playmore, 1975, unused, EX............ 15.00

Around the World w/The Jetsons, Charlton #509, 1972, unused, NM.................................. 45.00

Augie Doggie, Whitman #1186, 1960, some use, EX......... 35.00

Batman Paint-By-Number Book, Whitman, 1966, some use, EX+.................................. 25.00

Bewitched Fun & Activity Book, Treasure Books #8908, 1965, unused, M....................... 30.00

Big Jim, Whitman, 1975, some use, EX+.................................. 20.00

Blondie Paint Book, 1940, some use, VG 45.00

Buffalo Bill Jr, Whitman #1316, 1956, some use, NM........ 18.00

Bugs Bunny Book To Color, 1951, some use, VG.................. 20.00

Calling Dr Kildare for Fun & Games, Lowe #3092, 1960s, unused, EX...................... 50.00

Captain Gallant, Lowe #2505, 1956, unused, NM..................... 85.00

Captain Kangaroo, 1960, some use, EX+................................. 30.00

Chilly Willy Paint Book, Whitman #2946, 1960, some use, EX+. 35.00

Crusader Rabbit A Story Coloring Book, Treasure Books #298, 1957, EX 65.00

Donna Reed Coloring Book, Saalfield, 1964, unused, M................. 30.00

Dukes of Hazzard New Adventure Coloring & Activity Book, 1981, unused, M....................... 35.00

Fantasic Four, Whitman, 1977, some use, EX.................... 20.00

Flintstones Great Big Punchout Book, Whitman, 1961, some use, EX 30.00

Flipper, Watkins-Strathmore #1851, 1965, some use, VG 20.00

Frankenstein Jr, Whitman #1115, 1967, unused, EX............ 75.00

Gene Autry, Whitman #1124, 1950, unused, VG..................... 18.00

Goofy Dots, 1952, some use, EX+ 20.00

Hey There It's Yogi Bear Sticker Fun, Whitman #2190, 1964, unused, NM..................... 65.00

Howdy Doody, Whitman #1188, 1956, some use, VG......... 15.00

Howdy Doody Fun Book, Whitman #2187, 1950s, some use, VG 20.00

Incredible Hulk, Whitman, 1977, unused, M......................... 25.00

Knight Rider Activity Book, Modern Publishing, 1983, unused, EX+ 8.00

Lassie, Whitman #1151-2, 1982, unused, EX **15.00**

Lassie Coloring Book, Whitman #1151, 1982, unused, EX. **15.00**

Little Lulu, Whitman #1663, 1974, unused, M **45.00**

Love Bug, Disney/Hunt's Catsup promo, 1969, some use, EX. **22.00**

Magilla Gorilla 128-Page Coloring Book, Whitman #1113, 1964, unused, M **50.00**

Mickey Mouse Club/Old McDonald's Had a Farm, 1955, some use, EX **22.00**

Mumbly Super Sleuth, Rand McNally #06440, 1977, some use, NM **50.00**

Munsters Sticker Fun Book, Whitman, 1965, some use, EX................................... **75.00**

Peanuts Featuring Linus, Artcraft #4650, 1972, some use, EX. **10.00**

Popeye, Bonnie Books #2964, 1958, unused, EX+ **60.00**

Popeye, Lowe #2834, 1962, unused, EX+ **50.00**

Popeye Paint With Water Book, Whitman, 1981, unused, NM+ **10.00**

Popeye Secret Pictures, Lowe #3097, 1964, unused, VG. **45.00**

Ramar of the Jungle, Saalfield #1029, 1955, unused, NM+ **65.00**

Range Rider, Lowe #2528, 1956, unused, M **30.00**

Ripcord Pictures To Color, Saalfield #9629, 1963, unused, NM. **38.00**

Scooby Doo Funtime Paint With Water, Whitman, 1984, unused, M **22.00**

Six Million Dollar Man Dot-to-Dot, #C2412, 1977, unused, NM+ **35.00**

Superman Sticker Book, Whitman/DC Comics, 1977, unused, M **22.00**

Three Stooges, Whitman #1135, 1964, some use, EX......... **35.00**

Wally Walrus, Saalfield #4547, 1962, unused, NM+......... **55.00**

Walt Disney Presents The Jungle Book, Mowgli and Baloo, A Golden Book by Western Publishing Co., #1138, copyright 1967, NM, $20.00. (Photo courtesy Diane Zillner)

Waltons Sticker Book, Whitman, 1975, unused, NM+......... **50.00**

Wonderbug, Whitman, 1978, unused, M........................ **35.00**

Woody Woodpecker's Fun-O-Rama Punch-Out Book, 1972, unused, NM+ **30.00**

Comic Books

Factors that make a comic book valuable are condition, content, and rarity, not necessarily age. In fact, comics printed between 1950 and the late 1970s are most in demand by collectors who prefer those they had as children to the earlier comics. Issues where the hero is first introduced are treasured. While some may go for hundreds, even thousands of dollars, many are worth very little; so if you plan to collect, you'll need a good comic book price guide such as *Overstreet's* to assess your holdings. Condition is extremely important. Compared to a book in excellent condition, a mint issue might be worth six to eight times as much, while one in only good condition should be priced at less than half the price of the excellent example. For more information see *Schroeder's Collectible Toys, Antique to Modern* (Collector Books).

Amazing Spider-Man, Marvel #43, 1966, VG 35.00

Amazing Spider Man, #129, EX, from $350.00 to $400.00.

Aquaman, Dell #1, 1962, EX. 200.00
Around the World in 80 Days, Dell Golden Picture Classic, 1957, EX+ 20.00
Batman, DC Comics #183, 1966, VG 20.00
Batman, DC Comics #188, 1966, VG 15.00
Batman, DC Comics #193, 1967, EX+ 16.00
Beany & Cecil, Dell #2, 1962, rare, EX 35.00

Bewitched, Dell #2, 1965, NM. 50.00
Bionic Woman, Charlton #1, 1977, NM 15.00
Black Rider, Marvel #8, EX+. 20.00
Bonanza, Dell #20, 1962, EX. 50.00
Buffalo Bill Jr, Dell #742, 1956, VG+ 18.00
Captain Marvel, Marvel #1, 1968, NM 150.00
Cisco Kid, Dell #14, 1953, VG+ .25.00
Colt .45, Dell #9, 1961, VG.... 18.00
Elmer Fudd, Dell #689, NM.. 25.00
Gene Autry, Fawcett #6, G+. 100.00
Get Smart, Dell #1, 1966, NM. 65.00
Gunslinger, Dell #1220, 1961, photo cover, EX+ 75.00
Hogan's Heroes, Dell #4, 1966, NM 25.00
Hopalong Cassidy, Fawcett #24, VG 32.00
I Love Lucy, Dell #5, 1955, EX+. 85.00
Jetsons, Gold Key #35, EX 15.00
Kid Montana, Charlton #10, EX+ 15.00
Lassie, Dell #27, NM 25.00
Lone Ranger, Dell #37, EX+.. 45.00
Marvel Tales, Dell #121, 1954, VG 50.00
Maverick, Dell #980, EX........ 65.00
Munsters, Gold Key #4, 1965, EX 20.00
Old Yeller, Dell #869, 1957, EX .30.00
Partridge Family, Charlton #19, 1973, EX 15.00
Rawhide, Dell #1160, 1960, VG+ .30.00
Red Ryder, Dell #39, VG........ 25.00
Robin Hood, Dell #1, 1963, EX+. 15.00
Scooby Doo, Marvel #1, 1977, NM+ 25.00
Super Duck, MLJ #36, 1951, VG 16.00
Superman, DC Comics #191, 1966, VG 15.00

Superman, DC Comics #199, 1967, Superman/Flash, VG+ **45.00**

Tales To Astonish, Atlas #22, 1961, VG **35.00**

Tarzan's Jungle Annual, Dell #2, 1953, EX **40.00**

Tex Ritter Western, Fawcett #2, 1954, EX **60.00**

Tom & Jerry, Dell #115, EX... **20.00**

Tweety & Sylvester, Dell #11, NM **25.00**

Underworld Crime, Fawcett #3, 1952, EX+ **60.00**

Voyage to the Bottom of the Sea, Gold Key #6, 1966, EX ... **15.00**

Walt Disney Presents the Swamp Fox, Dell, Leslie Neilson cover, EX+ **35.00**

Walt Disney's Picnic Party, Dell Giant #8, 1957, VG+ **50.00**

Welcome Back Kotter, DC Comics #1, 1976, EX+ **15.00**

Western Tales, Dell #32, 1956, EX+ **80.00**

Wild Wild West, Gold Key #2, 1966, G+ **12.00**

Wonder Woman, NPP #100, 1958, EX **45.00**

Woody Woodpecker, Whitman #188, EX **8.00**

Wyatt Earp, Dell #860, NM... **75.00**

X-Men, Marvel #13, 1965, VG. **45.00**

Zane Grey's Stories of the West, Dell #511, 1954, EX **25.00**

Compacts

Prior to World War I, the use of cosmetics was frowned upon. It was not until after the war when women became liberated and entered the work force that makeup became acceptable. A compact became a necessity as a portable container for cosmetics and usually contained a puff and mirror. They were made in many different styles, shapes, and motifs and from every type of natural and man-made material. The fine jewelry houses made compacts in all of the precious metals — some studded with precious stones. The most sought-after compacts today are those made of plastic, Art Deco styles, figural styles, and any that incorporate gadgets. Compacts that are combined with other accessories are also very desirable.

See Clubs and Newsletters for information concerning the *Powder Puff.*

Basket shape, black enamel w/gold-tone trim, no handle, Henriette, 2" **100.00**

Book shape, tooled leather w/floral & urn decor, Mondaine, from $80 to **125.00**

Envelope shape, cobra covering, Wadsworth, from $120 to .**150.00**

Fan shape, gondola enameled on cracked eggshell, Melissa, 4½" **125.00**

Flared sides, stylized orange floral on gold-tone, Elgin American on puff, 3¼" wide, $25.00.

Hand mirror, plastic, lipstick in handle, Coty, from $50 to **75.00**

Hand mirror, silver-plated, lipstick in handle, Hoechst, from $125 to **175.00**

Harlequin shape, light blue w/cutout eyes, Elizabeth Arden, 1940s **150.00**

Heart shape, gold-tone, Cherie w/jeweled crown, 1950s, from $50 to **80.00**

Heart shape, gold-tone, embossed key on red enamel, 3", from $125 to **200.00**

Heart shape, gold-tone, engraved lid, American Maid, from $40 to **60.00**

Heart shape, gold-tone, stylized, Halston/Elsa Peretti, 2" . **175.00**

Horseshoe shape, leather w/zipper closure, lipstick sleeve, from $80 to **100.00**

Oblong, 1 end rounded, blue tooled leather, Mondaine, from $40 to **80.00**

Octagonal, sailing ship painted on foil, Gwenda, from $40 to **80.00**

Oval, cream enamel w/gold-tone monogram, Rex Fifth Ave, 3x2", from $45 to **60.00**

Oval, gold-tone (antiqued) encrusted w/faux jewels, Evans . **60.00**

Oval, gold-tone w/black enamel harlequin mask, Dorothy Gray, 1940s **90.00**

Round, enameled w/gold dots & center diamond motif, Coty, 3", from $45 to **60.00**

Round, gold-tone, pierced w/faux jewels, Elizabeth Arden, 4", from $150 to **175.00**

Round, gold-tone flapjack w/embossed hat, Dorothy Gray, 4", from $150 to... **175.00**

Round, gold-tone ribs w/Coty crest, French Flair label, 2½", from $15 to **25.00**

Round, gold-tone w/'On Your Toes' painted design, Estee Lauder, 2" **55.00**

Round, silver-tone on glossy gold-tone, center logo, Lucor, 3", from $25 to **30.00**

Round, silver-tone w/gold-tone scene, Disneyland souvenir, from $60 to **100.00**

Round, wood flapjack w/horse ornament on plastic inset, Zell, 4", from $75 .... **100.00**

Square, beaded flowers on beaded sunburst design, France, from $75 to **100.00**

Square, clear Lucite with molded and gold-painted sunburst, Roger and Gallet, from $125.00 to $225.00.
(Photo courtesy Alvin Gerson)

Square, gilt w/floral decor at 4 corners on black enamel, Volupte **100.00**

Square, gilt w/raised tulip design, w/lipstick, Richard Hudnut, from $40 to **60.00**

Square, gold-tone (brushed) w/ applied rhinestones, Eisenberg, from $125 to **200.00**

Square, gold-tone (hammered) w/rhinestone bell, Elgin American, 3" **75.00**

Square, gold-tone (satin) w/courting scene under dome, Daniel, from $80 to **125.00**

Square, gold-tone w/chased niello sterling rococo & mother-of-pearl **100.00**

Square, gold-tone w/Deco flower basket motif, Rhojan, 3½", from $125 to **150.00**

Square, gold-tone w/embossed lattice band, Volupte, 2½", from $25 to........................... **50.00**

Square, gold-tone w/tooled leather, Italy, sm, from $30 to...... **50.00**

Square, Lucite w/applied gold medallion, Roger & Gallet, from $125 to **225.00**

Square, marbleized metal w/portrait transfer, 2¾", from $40 to **60.00**

Square, silver w/allover embossed Adam & Eve motif, Volupte, from $60 to **80.00**

Square, wood w/stylized lid, Evening in Paris, from $40 to................................... **60.00**

Suitcase shape, blue enamel, Alwyn, from $80 to **120.00**

Vanity, egg shape, yellow w/monogram, Richelieu, from $40 to **60.00**

Vanity, oblong, gold-tone, engraved, w/tassel & chain, Melba, from $40 to **60.00**

Vanity, oblong, gold-tone, w/sliding mirror, Yardley, from $60 to........**80.00**

Vanity, octagonal, polished nickel, Coty, from $60 to............. **80.00**

Cookbooks

Cookbook collecting can be traced back to the turn of the century. Good food and recipes on how to prepare it are timeless. Cookbooks fall into many subclassifications with emphasis on various aspects of cooking. Some specialize in regional or ethnic food; during the World Wars, conservation and cost-cutting measures were popular themes. Because this field is so varied, you may want to decide what field is most interesting and specialize. Hardcover or softcover, Betty Crocker or Julia Childs, Pillsbury or Gold Medal — the choice is yours!

Cookbooks featuring specific food items are plentiful. Some are die-cut to represent the product — for instance, a pickle or a slice of bread. Some feature a famous personality, perhaps from a radio show sponsored by the food company. Appliance companies often published their own cookbooks, and these appeal to advertising buffs and cookbook collectors alike, especially if they illustrate pre-1970s kitchen appliances.

Perhaps no single event in the 1950s attracted more favorable attention for the Pillsbury Flour Company than the one first staged in 1949. Early in the year, company officials took the proposal to its advertising agency. Together they came up with a plan that would become an American institution, the Pillsbury Bake-Off contest.

For more information, we recommend *Collector's Guide to Cookbooks* by Frank Daniels, published by Collector Books. When no condition is noted, our values are for examples in near-mint condition.

Peanuts Cook Book, 1968, $8.00.
(Photo courtesy Colonel Bob Allen)

America's Cook Book, NY Herald Tribune, 1945, hardback, 1,032 pgs 30.00

Art of Cooking & Serving, Sarah Field Splint, 1932, hardback, 252 pgs 15.00

Baking Made Easy, Margaret B Baker, 1922, paperback, 55 pgs 15.00

Betty Crocker's Cake Mix Magic, 1950, 28 pgs 12.00

Blondie's Cook Book, Chic Young, 1946, hardback/jacket, 142 pgs 45.00

Catering for Special Occasions, Fannie Farmer, 1911, hardback, 249 pgs 60.00

Cooking Out-of-Doors, Girl Scouts, 1960, spiral paperback, 212 pgs 12.00

Creative Cooking Course, Charlotte Turgeon, 1975, hardback/jacket 10.00

Deep South Cookbook, Southern Living, 1972, hardback, 192 pgs 6.00

Down on the Farm Cook Book, H Worth, 1943, hardback/jacket, 322 pgs............................ 25.00

Electric Refrigerator Recipes, A Bradley, 1927, hardback, 136 pgs 15.00

Elsie's Cook Book, Harry Botsford, 1952, hardback/jacket, 374 pgs 50.00

Farmer Journal's Complete Pie Cookbook, Nell Nichols, 1965, hardback 20.00

Fit for a King, Merle Armitage, 1939, hardback, 256 pgs. 30.00

General Foods Cookbook, 1937, 5th printing, hardback, 370 pgs 10.00

Good Houskeeping Cook Book, 1933, hardback, 254 pgs. 20.00

Hershey's Recipes, 1940, paperback, 32 pgs 12.00

How America Eats, Clementine Paddleford, 1960, hardback, 179 pgs............................ 50.00

How To Cook Your Catch, Rube Allyn, 1963, 80 pgs 3.00

Jolly Times Cook Book, MN Osborn, 1934, hardback, 64 pgs 15.00

Joys of Jell-O Brand Gelatin, 1981, spiral hardback, 128 pgs .. 3.00

Kitchen Tested Recipes, Sunbeam Mixmaster, 1933, paperback, 40 pgs.............................. 12.00

Ladies' Home Journal Cookbook, Carol Truax, 1963, hardback, 728 pgs.............................. 6.00

Low-Carbohydrate Diet Menus & Recipes, Culinary Arts Institute, 1966................. 12.00

Mary Dunbar's Favorite Recipes, Jewel Tea, 1936, paperback, 80 pgs.................................... 6.00

McCall's Cook Book, Random House, 1963, hardback, 786 pgs.................................... 10.00

New American Cook Book, Lily Wallace, 1941, hardback, 931 pgs.................................... 15.00

Newman's Own Cookbook, Simon & Schuster, 1998, hardback, 222 pgs................................ **8.00**

Old Favorite Honey Recipes, American Honey Institute, 1945, paperback **5.00**

Omelette Originals, Irena Kirshman, 1970, paperback, 47 pgs................................. **3.00**

Peter Pan Peanut Butter Cook Book, 1963, paperback, 26 pgs **8.00**

Pillsbury's Best New Butter Cookie Cookbook, Vol II, 1958, 48 pgs **5.00**

Praise for the Cook, Crisco, 1959, spiral paperback, 120 pgs.. **6.00**

Quantity Cookery, L Richards & N Treat, 1925, hardback, 200 pgs.. **8.00**

Queen of Hearts Cook Book, Peter Pauper Press, 1955, hardback, 64 pgs.................................. **5.00**

Royal Cook Book, Royal Baking Powder, 1929, paperback, 49 pgs...................................... **6.00**

Rumford Complete Cook Book, LH Wallace, 1936, hardback, 209 pgs..................................... **10.00**

Someone's in the Kitchen With Dinah, D Shore, 1972, hardback, 1979 pgs................. **10.00**

Southern Cooking, Mrs SR Dull, 1928, hardback/jacket, 384 pgs.................................... **45.00**

Tempting Kosher Dishes, Manischewitz Co, 1930, hardback, 156 pgs................. **125.00**

Tested Recipes, Guardian Service, 1950, paperback, 72 pgs. **30.00**

Treasury of Outdoor Cooking, James Bears, hardback/jacket, 282 pgs............................. **15.00**

Walt Disney's Mickey Mouse Cookbook, 1975, hardback, 93 pgs.................................... **15.00**

Walton Family Cook Book, Sylvia Resnick, 1975, paperback, 148 pgs.................................... **50.00**

Watergate Cookbook, NY Alplaus, 1973, paperback, 92 pgs. **12.00**

Watkins Cook Book, 1928, spiral hardback, 288 pgs........... **20.00**

Young Wife's Own Cook Book, 1890, hardback, 124 pgs........... **40.00**

Your Frigidaire Recipes, 1955, paperback, 48 pgs **8.00**

20 Minute Cookbook, Michael Reise, 1953, hardback/jacket, 252 pgs............................ **12.00**

500-Plus Ideas for Freezing & Canning, E Henley, 1964, paperback **5.00**

The White House Cookbook, Janet Holliday Ervin, Follett Publishing Co., 1964, first printing, hardback, $20.00.

Cookie Cutters and Shapers

Cookie cutters have come into their own in recent years as worthy kitchen collectibles. Prices on many have risen astronomically, but a practiced eye can still sort out a good bargain. Advertising cutters and product premiums, especially in plastic, can still be found without too much effort. Aluminum cutters with painted wooden handles are usually worth several dollars each if in good condition. Red and green are the usual handle colors, but other colors are more highly prized by many. Hallmark plastic cookie cutters, especially those with painted backs, are always worth considering, if in good condition.

Be wary of modern tin cutters being sold for antique. Many present-day tinsmiths chemically antique their cutters, especially those done in a primitive style. These are often sold by others as 'very old.' Look closely, because most tinsmiths today sign and date these cutters.

Female symbol, dark green plastic outline, $4.00. (Photo courtesy Rosemary Henry)

Card suit shapes, aluminum w/handles, 2½", set of 4 .... **6.00**
Cat, flat back, tin, 1930s, 3½x4", EX **12.00**
Chick, tin, flat back, unusual handle, 3x4" **28.00**
Christmas stocking, plastic, Rudolph series, Domar, 1940s-50s, MOC **45.00**
Crescent moon, Nutbrown Products, 3" **10.00**
Crow, tin, flat back, w/handle, 5¾x2½" **95.00**
Dinosaur, tin, flat back, recent, 4x2½" **13.00**
Disney characters, Tupperware, set of 4, MIP **40.00**

Dog, tin, flat back, no handle, 2¾x4" **25.00**
Donald Duck, head only, yellow plastic, Hallmark, 1970s, 4½", MIP. **18.00**
Duck, red plastic, HRM, MIP.. **8.00**
Flower, tin, flat back w/center hole, 4½" dia **28.00**

Friar Tuck, orange plastic, Robin Hood Flour ad, 4", $6.50.

Gingerbread man, tin, flat back, no handle, 10x5½" **40.00**
Guitar, tin, flat back, 4¾x1¾" . **40.00**
Hand, tin, flat back, w/handle, 2½x3½" **15.00**
Hobby horse, tin, flat back, 4½x3¼" **15.00**
Horse, tin, Davis Baking Powder, 3¾x3" **35.00**
Horse leaping, tin, flat back, no handle, 3x4½" **30.00**
Humpty Dumpty, red plastic, 3¼", EX **10.00**
Looney Tunes cartoon charaters, Wilton, 1996, 2" ea, set of 4, MIP **80.00**
MGM cartoon characters, Tom & Jerry, etc, plastic, 1956, set of 6, EX **15.00**
Mr Peanut, full figure, plastic, Planters, 1990, 4½", M.... **40.00**
Owl, tin, flat back, 4½x2½"....**22.50**
Rabbit, tin, flat back, Formay, 6", EX **14.00**
Raccoon, orange plastic, Our Kids Club, 3¼" **20.00**

Reddy Kilowatt, red plastic, 3" dia,
MIB.................................. **25.00**

Rooster, tin, flat back, no handle,
2½x2¾"............................ **22.50**

Santa, aluminum w/wooden handle **13.00**

Santa & Rudolph, red plastic, HRM,
pr.. **18.00**

Scooby Doo, head only, yellow
plastic, Hallmark, 1970s,
4x3", M **15.00**

Snoopy as Santa holding ornament
in his mouth, red plastic, 1958,
3".. **60.00**

Snoopy on jack-o'-lantern, red plastic, 6½", from $60 to........ **80.00**

Texas state shape, tin, 4½" **13.00**

Thomas the Tank Engine, blue
plastic, NM...................... **15.00**

Twelve Days of Christmas set, red
plastic, handled, Chilton, 1978,
MIB................................... **16.00**

Unicorn, aluminum, flat back, 4x6
12", EX............................. **23.00**

West Virginia state shape, tin, 3",
M.. **25.00**

Windmill, copper, 4".............. **10.00**

Winnie the Pooh, orange plastic,
Hallmark, 1979............... **15.00**

Witch riding broom, copper-colored
aluminum, 5¼x5" **15.00**

Cookie Jars

McCoy, Metlox, Twin Winton,
Robinson Ransbottom, Brush, and
American Bisque were among the
largest producers of cookie jars
in the country. Many firms made
them to a lesser extent. Figural
jars are the most common (and the
most valuable), made in an endless
variety of subjects. Early jars from
the 1920s and 1930s were often
decorated in 'cold paint' over the
glaze. This type of color is easily
removed — take care that you use
very gentle cleaning methods. A
damp cloth and a light touch is the
safest approach.

For further information we recommend *Collector's Encyclopedia of
Metlox Potteries* by Carl Gibbs, *The
Ultimate Collector's Encyclopedia
of Cookie Jars* by Joyce and Fred
Roerig, and *An Illustrated Value
Guide to Cookie Jars* by Ermagene
Westfall (all published by Collector
Books). Values are for jars in mint
condition unless otherwise noted.
Beware of modern reproductions!

A Little Company, Edmund,
1992 .... **125.00**

A Little Company, Indian Couple,
1991 .... **150.00**

Abingdon, Bo Peep, #694..... **235.00**

Abingdon, Choo Choo, #651, $145.00.
(Photo courtesy Ermagene Westfall)

Abingdon, Clock, #653, 1949. **90.00**

Abingdon, Hobby Horse, #602 .**175.00**

Abingdon, Jack-in-the-Box,
#611 .... **245.00**

Abingdon, Miss Muffet, #622. **225.00**

Abingdon, Mother Goose, #695. **275.00**

Abingdon, Pineapple, #664.... **65.00**

Abingdon, Three Bears........ **100.00**

Abingdon, Windmill, #678 ... **200.00**

American Bisque, Bear, #CJ-701 .... **50.00**

American Bisque, Churn, USA .**25.00**

American Bisque, Fire Chief. **125.00**

American Bisque, Kitten & Beehive, USA, 1958 .... **45.00**

American Bisque, Puppy, #CJ-754 .... **60.00**

Applause, Sylvester Head w/Tweety..**95.00**

Brush, Dog & Basket **225.00**

Brush, Donkey Cart, #W33, ears down, gray **350.00**

Brush, Gas Lamp, #K1 .... **75.00**

Brush, Happy Bunny, #W25, white **200.00**

Brush, Night Owl **125.00**

Brush, Owl, stylized **325.00**

Brush, Panda, #W21 (+) **225.00**

Brush, Peter Peter Pumpkin Eater, #W24 .... **275.00**

Brush, Raggedy Ann, #W16..**450.00**

Brush, Treasure Chest, #W28..**150.00**

California Originals, Fire Truck, #841 .... **225.00**

California Originals, Sheriff, brown stain, marked USA **45.00**

Clay Art, Chihuahua, in sombrero & serape, 12" **50.00**

Clay Art, Humpty Dumpty, 1991 .... **125.00**

Clay Art, Queen of Cats, 13" . **45.00**

DeForest of California, Hen in Bonnet **150.00**

DeForest of California, Poodle, 1960, from $45 to **55.00**

Dept 56, Gone Fishin' Bear ... **60.00**

Dept 56, Vegetable House, 1990.**55.00**

Doranne of California, Dragon, USA............................... **175.00**

Doranne of California, Hippo.. **100.00**

Doranne of California, Snowman, #J52 .... **175.00**

Enesco, Cookie Monster, 1993, from $55 to **85.00**

Enesco, Owl, Whoo's Eating Owl Cookies?, #E-9227 .... **30.00**

Harry James, Yogi Bear, from $300 to **325.00**

Hirsch, Chef, Lots'a Goodies . **100.00**

Hirsch, Hen, Peck O' Cookies. **100.00**

Hirsch, Rabbit, #58, from $30.00 to $35.00. (Photo courtesy Joyce Roerig)

Lefton, Chef/Fat Boy, #552, 8½".. **175.00**

Lefton, French Girl, #1174, 9½".. **250.00**

Maddux of California, Humpty Dumpty, #2113, 11" **40.00**

Maddux of California, Queen, from $100 to **125.00**

McCoy, Apples on Basketweave.**70.00**

McCoy, Barnum's Animals... **150.00**

McCoy, Baseball Boy **150.00**

McCoy, Bugs Bunny **125.00**

McCoy, Caboose **125.00**

McCoy, Chilly Willy **65.00**

McCoy, Coca-Cola Can **150.00**

McCoy, Coffee Grinder **45.00**

McCoy, Cookie Bank, 1961 .. **125.00**

McCoy, Cookie Cabin **80.00**

McCoy, Cookie Mug **45.00**

McCoy, Cookie Safe **65.00**

McCoy, Covered Wagon **95.00**

McCoy, Dog on Basketweave. **75.00**

McCoy, Fortune Cookies **50.00**

McCoy, Frog on Stump **75.00**

McCoy, Grandfather Clock **75.00**

McCoy, Ice Cream Cone **45.00**

McCoy, Keebler Tree House... **70.00**
McCoy, Koala Bear................. **85.00**
McCoy, Little Clown............... **75.00**
McCoy, Monk........................... **50.00**
McCoy, Mouse on Clock **40.00**
McCoy, Mushroom on Stump. **55.00**
McCoy, Orange **55.00**
McCoy, Picnic Basket............. **75.00**
McCoy, Pine Cones on Basket . **70.00**
McCoy, Pirate's Chest **95.00**
McCoy, Raggedy Ann **110.00**
McCoy, Strawberry, 1955-57.. **65.00**
McCoy, Strawberry, 1971-75.. **45.00**
McCoy, Tomato **60.00**
McCoy, Tudor Cookie House.. **95.00**
McCoy, WC Fields **150.00**
McCoy, Woodsy Owl **200.00**
Metlox, Apple, from $75 to **85.00**
Metlox, Basket, natural, basket lid, from $35 to **45.00**
Metlox, Basket, white w/red apple lid, from $40 to................ **50.00**
Metlox, Clown, white w/black accents, from $200 to.... **225.00**
Metlox, Frog Prince, from $175 to.................................**200.00**
Metlox, Grapefruit, 2-qt, from $150 to **175.00**
Metlox, Koala Bear, from $100 to **125.00**
Metlox, Lucy Goose, from $125 to **150.00**
Metlox, Miller's Sack, from $50 to................................... **75.00**
Metlox, Rabbit on Cabbage, from $125 to **150.00**
Metlox, Sun, from $150 to ... **175.00**
Metlox, Teddy Bear, bisque, from $40 to **45.00**
Regal, Cat, from $340 to...... **385.00**
Regal, Fisherman, from $650 to.**720.00**
Regal, Humpty Dumpty, red. **250.00**
Regal, Tulip, from $200 to ... **225.00**

Robinson Ransbottom, Cookie, white w/blue.................... **40.00**
Robinson Ransbottom, Jack (sailor), EX........................... **200.00**
Shawnee, Fruit Basket, #84, 8", from $185 to **225.00**
Shawnee, Jack, yellow pants, USA, from $80 to **100.00**
Shawnee, Winnie the Pig, green collar, USA, from $425 to ... **475.00**
Sierra Vista, ABC Bear........ **125.00**
Sierra Vista, Dog on Drum.... **50.00**
Sierra Vista, Train **75.00**
Sigma, Beaver Fireman....... **250.00**
Sigma, Chicago Cubs Bear.... **50.00**

Star Jars, Cowardly Lion, from $250.00 to $300.00. (Photo courtesy Joyce Roerig)

Treasure Craft, Bart Simpson, USA, 1995 only, from $100 to **125.00**
Treasure Craft, Cookieville ... **45.00**
Treasure Craft, Genie (Aladdin). **75.00**
Treasure Craft, Jukebox, original style, 1970s, from $45 to. **50.00**
Treasure Craft, Noah's Ark, Winton, 1970s, from $25 to **30.00**
Treasure Craft, Smokey the Bear, from $225 to **250.00**
Treasure Craft, Soccer Ball, from $50 to **60.00**
Treasure Craft, 101 Dalmatians pup, MIB **85.00**

Twin Winton, Bambi **175.00**
Twin Winton, Chipmunk **75.00**
Twin Winton, Cookie Guard . **350.00**
Twin Winton, Cookie Time, clock w/mouse finial **45.00**
Twin Winton, Fire Engine **75.00**
Twin Winton, Raccoon **50.00**
Twin Winton, Ranger Bear, no badge **50.00**
Twin Winton, Ranger Bear, w/badge **90.00**
Twin Winton, Snail **150.00**
Twin Winton, Squirrel **55.00**
Twin Winton, Wheelbarrow . **350.00**
Warner Bros, Batmobile, DC Comics, 1997, MIB **80.00**
Warner Bros, Bugs Bunny as Santa, Certified International ... **80.00**
Warner Bros, Scooby Doo Snacks, MIB **70.00**
Warner Bros, Sylvester the Cat on Cookie Can, 1994 .... **65.00**
Warner Bros, Tasmanian Devil on motorcycle, 1998, MIB.... **80.00**
Warner Bros, Tweety Bird Head, from $40 to **50.00**

Coppercraft Guild

Sold during the 1960s and 1970s through the home party plan, these decorative items are once again finding favor with the buying public. The Coppercraft Guild of Taunton, Massachusetts, made a wonderful variety of wall plaques, bowls, pitchers, trays, etc. Not all were made of copper, some were of molded plastic. Glass, cloth, mirror, and brass accents added to the texture. When uncompromised by chemical damage or abuse, the finish they used on their copper items has proven remarkably enduring. Collectors are beginning to take notice, but prices are still remarkably low. If you enjoy the look, now is the time to begin your collection.

Bowl, footed, plain, 4x9" **12.00**
Bread tray, 12x7" **20.00**
Candlabrum, 4-arm, 5-light, MIB **40.00**
Candleholders, flared bottoms, 4x3¾", pr from $15 to **20.00**
Carafe, glass w/copper collar & stand, 13" **20.00**
Creamer & sugar bowl w/tray, brass handles, 6x9½" tray **25.00**
Demitasse pot, 7½" **15.00**
Fondue pot, w/warmer & metal stand, from $25 to **30.00**
Gravy boat, w/stand **28.00**
Hurricane lamp (candleholder), glass globe, 9½" **15.00**
Ice bucket, w/lid, 2 ring handles, 5½x8" **9.00**
Lazy Susan, w/6 glass serving pcs, 13" dia.............................. **15.00**
Leaf dish, 9x6"........................ **22.00**
Mirror w/eagle finial, molded w/copper-tone finish, 21x14½" **35.00**
Mugs, brass handles, set of 4. **15.00**
Napkin holder, 4½x7", from $15 to................................... **20.00**
Planter, pot w/3 chains on footed hanger.............................. **18.00**
Plaque, Last Supper embossed on copper w/wood frame, 10x21"........................... **20.00**
Plaque, log cabin scene on embossed copper plate, 14" dia **15.00**
Plaque, sailing ship, Syroco, 16x13" **12.00**

Plaque, sailing ship, Syroco, 29x22" **25.00**

Plate, hunting scene, 6½", $10.00.

Punch set, 12" bowl & 6 3" cups on 18" tray **45.00**
Stein, 5" **15.00**
Teapot, 4x5" **20.00**
Tidbit tray, 2-tiered **15.00**

Corning Ware and Visions Cookware

In late 1957, Corning Glass Works introduced a new line of cookware called Corning Ware. This new line of very durable cookware consisted of a skillet, three saucepans, and lids. A metal cradle and detachable handle were included for easy handling of the dishes. Blue Cornflower was the first design, and to the collectors' delight, many new designs have since been added.

Visions Cookware first appeared in the United States in 1981. It was imported from France, and 'France' is marked on the top part of the handle. Eventually, it was made in the U.S. in Martinsburg, West Virginia. In 1989 a non-stick surface was added to Visions, because food had a tendency to stick during cooking. In 1992 the Cranberry color was added. In 1993 there was the addition of the Healthy Basics line, then in 1994, the Healthy Basics Versa-Pots were added. This new version of Visions was not very popular and is now extremely rare.

For more in-depth information and listings, see *The Complete Guide to Corning Ware & Visions Cookware* by Kyle Coroneos (Collector Books).

Corning Ware

Black Trefoil, party buffet, glass lid, 1961-65, from $8 to .. **10.00**
Black Trefoil, percolator, 1963-65, 6-cup, from $20 to **25.00**
Blue Cornflower, Dutch oven, glass lid, 1972-78, 5-qt, from $20 to **25.00**
Blue Cornflower, loaf pan, 1967-?, 2-qt, from $12 to **15.00**
Blue Cornflower, percolator, either style, 1960-76, 6-cup, from $20 to **25.00**
Blue Cornflower, petite pan, glass lid, 1963-70, 1½-cup, from $5 to **10.00**
Blue Cornflower, petite pan, plastic lid, 1963-70, 1½-cup, from $2 to **4.00**
Blue Cornflower, platter, 1972-78, 13", from $8 to **10.00**
Blue Cornflower, saucepan, glass lid, 1959-71, 2½", from $12 to **15.00**
Blue Cornflower, skillet, fin or glass knob lid, 1959-71, 7", from $8 to **10.00**
Forever Yours, casserole, amber glass lid, 1990-93, 1½-qt, from $8 to.............................. **10.00**

Fresh Cut, roaster, glass lid, 1997, 4-qt, from $12 to **15.00**

Fresh Cut, saucepan, glass lid, 1997, 2-qt, from $8 to **10.00**

Friendship, casserole, glass lid, 1996-97, 1½-qt, from $8 to **10.00**

Friendship, saucepan, glass lid, 1996-97, 5-qt, from $30 to **35.00**

Indian Summer, casserole, oval, glass lid, 1976-77, 1½-qt, from $5 to . **7.00**

Nature's Bounty, loaf pan, plastic lid, 1971, 2-qt, from $10 to **12.00**

Pastel Bouquet, petite pan, plastic lid, 1985-?, 2¾", from $3 to . **5.00**

Peony, saucepan, glass lid, 1989, 2½-qt, from $20 to **25.00**

Peony, skillet, glass lid, 1989, 10", from $12 to **15.00**

Renaissance, tray w/serving cradle, 1979, 16", from $20 to **25.00**

Spice O' Life, baking dish, glass lid, 1974-?, 1½-qt, from $6 to .. **8.00**

Spice O' Life, skillet, glass lid, 1972-?, from $10 to **12.00**

Wildflower, skillet, glass lid, 1977-?, 6½", from $5 to **7.00**

Spice O' Life, covered saucepan, 1972 – 1987, five-quart, from $35.00 to $40.00. (Photo courtesy Kyle Coroneos)

Visions

Amber, casserole, round, ribbed, w/lid, 1989-?, 1-qt, from $10 to **12.00**

Amber, double boiler, Sculptured, 3-pc w/lid, 1989-?, 1½-qt, from $25 to **30.00**

Amber, double boiler, 3-pc w/lid, 1983-?, 1½-qt, from $15 to **20.00**

Amber, Dutch oven, non-stick, tab handles, w/lid, 1992-?, 5-qt, from $25 to **30.00**

Amber, Dutch oven, Scupltured, tab handles, lid, 1989-?, 5-qt, from $35 to **40.00**

Amber, Dutch oven, tab handles, w/lid, 1983-?, 3½-qt, from $35 to **40.00**

Amber, Dutch oven, tab handles, w/lid, 1983-?, 5-qt, from $35 to **40.00**

Amber, Dutch oven/stewpot, tab handles, w/lid, 1992-?, 5-qt, from $40 to **50.00**

Amber, Heat 'n Eat dish, w/handle & flat glass lid, 1987, 15-oz, from $6 to **8.00**

Amber, Heat 'n Eat dish, w/handle & plastic lid, 1988-?, 15-oz, from $4 to **6.00**

Amber, roaster, oval, ribbed, w/lid, 1989-?, 4-qt, from $25 to **30.00**

Amber, saucepan, Sculptured, w/lid, 1989-?, 2½-qt, from $15 to **20.00**

Amber, saucepan, Sculptured, w/lid, 1989-?, 1½-qt, from $15 to **20.00**

Amber, saucepan, side spout, w/lid, 1980-?, 1-qt, from $15 to. **20.00**

Amber, saucepan, w/lid, 1983-?, 1½-qt, from $15 to **20.00**

Amber, saucepan, w/lid, 1983-?, 1-pt, from $10 to **12.00**

Amber, saucepan, w/lid, 1983-?, 2½-qt, from $15 to **20.00**

Amber, skillet, non-stick, open, 1989-?, 10", from $8 to.... **10.00**

Amber, skillet, non-stick, w/or w/out lid, 1989-?, 7", from $2 to **4.00**

Amber, skillet, open, 1985-89, 7", from $2 to **4.00**

Cranberry, casserole, round, ribbed, w/lid, 1992-?, 1-qt, from $12 to **15.00**

Cranberry, Heat 'n Serve dish, plain, handle, plastic lid, 15-oz **5.00**

Cranberry, skillet, non-stick, open, 1992-?, 10", from $6 to...... **8.00**

Cranberry, skillet, non-stick, open, 1992-?, 7", from $2 to........ **4.00**

Covered lipped non-stick saucepan, 1992 – ?, 1 L (one-quart), from $12.00 to $15.00. (Photo courtesy Kyle Coroneos)

Cracker Jack

The name Cracker Jack was first used in 1896. The trademark as well as the slogan 'The more you eat, the more you want' were registered at that time. Prizes first appeared in Cracker Jack boxes in 1912. Prior to then, prizes or gifts could be ordered through catalogs. In 1910, coupons that could be redeemed for many gifts were inserted in the boxes.

The Cracker Jack boy and his dog Bingo came on the scene in 1916 and have remained one of the world's most well-known trademarks. Prizes themselves came in a variety of materials, from paper and tin to pot metal and plastic. The beauty of Cracker Jack prizes is that they depict what was happening in the world at the time they were made.

To learn more about the subject, you'll want to read *Cracker Jack Toys, The Complete Unofficial Guide for Collectors*, and *Cracker Jack Advertising Collectibles*, both by Larry White, who is listed in the Directory under Massachusetts.

First row: metal Man-in-the Moon plate, $95.00; metal patriotic whistle, $85.00; plastic astronaut, $10.00; Second row: Cracker Jack Air Corp stud, 95.00; Third row: plastic and paper rising moon palm puzzle, $85.00; metal Mary Lu Quick Delivery truck, $78.00; plastic invisible magic picture, $9.00. (Photo courtesy Mary and Larry White)

A-Maze Puzzle, plastic & paper, various designs & colors, ea **3.50**

Bank, metal book shape **275.00**

Baseball player, plastic, any of 11, ea.. **9.00**

Book, Animated Jungle Book, paper............................... **90.00**

Book, Hello, 1980, paper, any of 20, ea.. **7.50**

Booklet, Words of Wisdom, paper.**145.00**

Bookmarks, metal, figural, any of 4, ea **9.50**

Breakfast Set, agateware in matchbox.................................... **25.00**

Candleholder, single, metal, gold color, ea.............................. **3.75**

Charm, man eating watermelon, white metal **2.75**

Chicken figure, chenille........... **7.50**

Compass, paper & metal, 1½" dia **98.00**

Eyeglasses, Cracker Jack Wherever You Look, paper w/celluloid insert............................. **72.50**

Flip-Action Movie, various subjects, paper............................... **11.50**

Fortune Teller, Cracker Jack, paper............................... **95.00**

Game, Cracker Jack Magnik Question Box, paper **33.50**

Globe, metal **60.00**

Hat, Me for Cracker Jack, paper **295.00**

Locomotive, Cracker Jack Line #512, metal, 1920s, 2", EX........ **125.00**

Pencil sharpener, clock face, white metal............................... **39.00**

Picture Panorama, any of 14, ea..**15.50**

Pinball game, w/graphics, Gordy, 1995, 5x10", MIP............... **6.00**

Puzzle, image of early toys, 500 pcs, complete, unused, MIB... **10.00**

Spinner, Cracker Jack Golf, paper & wood........................... **125.00**

Spinner, Keep 'Em Flying, metal.**55.00**

Squeeze Faces, paper, any of 9, ea **15.00**

Stickers, glow-in-the-dark, paper, any of 56, ea...................... **1.75**

Tele-Viz, paper, any of 10 ...... **65.00**

Train, Kerchoo, plastic, various colors, ea **5.25**

Trick Mustache, paper punch-out card **13.50**

Trophy, World Famous Musician, etc, plastic, ea.................... **5.50**

Visor, Cracker Jack, paper ..**325.00**

Whistle, dirigible, litho tin **42.50**

Zodiac coin, plastic, various colors, any of 12, ea **5.50**

Crackle Glass

Most of the crackle glass you see on the market today was made from about 1930 until the 1970s. At the height of its popularity, almost 500 glasshouses produced it; today it is still being made by Blenko, and a few pieces are coming in from Taiwan and China. It's hard to date, since many pieces were made for years. Some colors, such as red, amberina, cobalt, and cranberry, were more expensive to produce; so today these are scarce and therefore more expensive. Smoke gray was made for only a short time, and you can expect to pay a premium for that color as well. For more information we recommend *Crackle Glass From Around the World* by Stan and Arlene Weitman (Collector Books).

Basket, amber w/crystal handle, ruffled, Kanawha, 6", from $85 to **115.00**

Bowl, sea green, applied decor at rim, Blenko, 2½x4½", from $60 to **80.00**

Candy dish, ruby, flared & curved rim, Bishoff, 4½x5", from $85 to **115.00**

Cruet, blue, clear teardrop handle & stopper, Rainbow, 6½", from $75 to **100.00**

Decanter, crystal w/blue stopper, pinched, Blenko, 11", from $125 to **150.00**

Decanter, green, blue handle & stopper, Rainbow, 14½", from $200 to **300.00**

Decanter, topaz, waisted w/ball stopper, Pilgrim, 8", from $125 to **150.00**

Fruit, pear, rose crystal, Blenko, 5", from $125 to **150.00**

Goblet, amber, long stem, Blenko, 11½", from $125 to **150.00**

Lamp shade, hurricane; amberina, Kanawha, 7", from $100 to. **125.00**

Pitcher, amberina, flared w/drop-over handle, Kanawha, 3", from $45 to **50.00**

Pitcher, amberina w/amber drop-over handle, Rainbow, from $85 to **95.00**

Pitcher, amethyst (desirable color), clear drop-over handle, Pilgrim, 3¼", from $35.00 to $40.00. (Photo courtesy Stan and Arlene Weitman)

Pitcher, blue, pinched, drop-over handle, Greenwich, 6", from $65 to **70.00**

Pitcher, emerald green, waisted, drop-over handle, Pilgrim, 4", from $50 to **55.00**

Pitcher, gold, mold-blown w/pulled-back handle, Kanawha, 5", from $50 to **60.00**

Pitcher, lemon lime, teardrop w/drop-over handle, Pilgrim, 4", from $45 to **50.00**

Pitcher, orange w/clear drop-over handle, Blenko, 13", from $135 to **160.00**

Pitcher, ruby, drop-over handle, Pilgrim, 3¼", from $50 to. **55.00**

Rose bowl, topaz, folded rim, Blenko, 5", from $110 to.............. **135.00**

Swan dish, orange & clear, heart-shaped body, Kanawha, 7", from $100 to **125.00**

Syrup pitcher, amethyst, pulled-back handle, Kanawha, 6", from $85 to **110.00**

Tumbler, topaz, unknown maker, 6¾", from $50 to **60.00**

Vase, amberina, applied serpentine neck, Hamon, from $110 to **120.00**

Vase, cranberry, trumpet neck w/ruffled rim, Rainbow, 5", from $70 to **80.00**

Vase, crystal w/applied blue rosettes, Blenko, from $110 to................................. **150.00**

Vase, crystal/applied olive green leaves, flared, Blenko, 10", from $150 to **175.00**

Vase, gold, pinched, Blenko, 17½", from $160 to **180.00**

Vase, olive, applied serpentine along stick neck, Pilgrim, 7", from $75 to **85.00**

Vase, orange, ruffled rim, Rainbow, 5", from $50 to................ **65.00**

Vase, smoke gray, slim waisted, Blenko, 16", from $175 to..**200.00**

Czechoslovakian Glass

Czechoslovakia was established as a country in 1918. It was an area rich in the natural resources needed to produce both pottery and glassware. Wonderful cut and pressed scent bottles were made in a variety of colors with unbelievably well-detailed intaglio stoppers. Vases in vivid hues were decorated with contrasting applications or enamel work. See Clubs and Newsletters for information concerning the *Czechoslovakian Collectors Guild International.*

Bowl, cased autumn-colored mottling, sm foot, 4½" **60.00**

Box, crystal w/geometric cuttings, acid-etched signature, 2½x3" **120.00**

Candlestick, pale pink w/applied serpentine trim, 8½" **65.00**

Candlestick, red w/black & white enameled design, 10½" ... **85.00**

Candy basket, light green w/med green stripes, green handle, 8"....**200.00**

Candy jar, multicolored geometrics, w/lid, 3¾" **175.00**

Cocktail shaker, green w/enameled rooster, chrome lid, 8¾" .**125.00**

Compote, white opaque w/maroon lid, ruffled rim, 6" **150.00**

Decanter, 'bubbly' green w/hand-painted hunt scene, 9½"..**175.00**

Decanter, orange cased w/silver bird decor, 12" **135.00**

Decanter, topaz stain w/hand-painted carriage scene, 10"....**140.00**

Dresser jar, reverse-painted cottage scene on yellow, 1920s-30s, 3x2" **35.00**

Figurine, man holding brown ball, black tie and pants, 6¾", from $150.00 to $200.00.

Perfume bottle, blue, geometric cuttings, 3" **145.00**

Perfume bottle, clear, geometric cuttings, red stopper, 5" **195.00**

Perfume bottle, clear w/silver filigree & tiny purple glass jewels, 1½" **100.00**

Pin/card tray, frosted scene of 3 Grecian women on clear, 1930s, 3¾" **95.00**

Pitcher, orange cased, w/cobalt tricorner rim & handle, 5"..**85.00**

Powder box, green pressed pattern, octagonal, 1940s, 3½x4"..**65.00**

Rose bowl, pink mercury glass, 1930s, 4¾"........................ **50.00**

Salt & pepper shakers, crystal w/porcelain duck-head tops, 2", pr....................................... **45.00**

Tumbler, exotic birds & flowers enameled on orange, 5¼".**85.00**

Vase, black w/orange spirals, cylindrical, 6½"........................ **75.00**

Vase, cranberry w/controlled bubbles, 1920s-30s, 5"........**275.00**

Vase, exotic bird on black glass w/silver & gold trim, 13½" **225.00**

Vase, floral design w/white trim on green flared stick form, 8½" **160.00**

Vase, floral in green & gold enamel on green, 1940s-50s, 12" **60.00**

Vase, green spatter, 10" **165.00**

Vase, multicolored mottling, 8½"..**65.00**

Vase, red & black spider-web pattern, 1930s, 11½"........... **250.00**

Vase, red-orange w/black rim, 1930s, 7" **85.00**

Vase, red-orange w/black overlay at foot, 9½" **150.00**

Vase, swirls embossed on pink, 3 cobalt handles, 8".......... **200.00**

Vase, opaque green w/black trim, 6-footed, 6½" **110.00**

Wine, red cased w/black stem & foot, silver trim, 7½" **65.00**

Perfume, cut crystal, footed oblong with cut facets and stars, cut snowflake stopper, 6⅞", **$250.00.** (Photo courtesy Monsen and Baer)

Dakin

From about 1968 through the late 1970s, the R. Dakin Company produced a line of hollow vinyl advertising and comic characters licensed by companies such as Warner Brothers, Hanna-Barbera, and the Disney corporation. Some figures had molded-on clothing; others had felt clothes and accessory items. Inspiration for characters came from TV cartoon shows, comic strips, or special advertising promotions. Dakins were offered in different types of packaging. Those in colorful 'Cartoon Theatre' boxes command higher prices than those that came in clear plastic bags. Plush figures were also produced, but the examples we've listed below are the most collectible. Assume all to be complete with clothes, accessories, and original tags unless otherwise noted. For further information and more listings we recommend *Schroeder's Collectible Toys, Antique to Modern* (Collector Books).

Bamm Bamm, vinyl, cloth outfit, w/club, 1970s, MIP.......... **50.00**

Barney Rubble, vinyl, cloth outfit, 1970s, MIP **50.00**

Benji (dog), plush, plastic collar, metal tag, NM+.............. **30.00**

Big Boy, vinyl, cloth outfit, tag marked No 2040/Dream Dolls, MIP **50.00**

Bozo the Clown, vinyl, Larry Harmon, 1974, NM **50.00**

Bugs Bunny, vinyl, standing on Happy Birthday base, 1970s, VG **18.00**

Bullwinkle, plush, red sweater w/green B, 1978, M **45.00**

Bullwinkle, vinyl, jointed, 1970s, VG **22.00**

Daffy Duck, vinyl, 1976, EXIB (TV Cartoon Theater box)...... **35.00**

Dino the Dinosaur, vinyl, 1970, MIP **75.00**

Drooper Dog, plush, 1970s, G. **45.00**

Elmer Fudd, vinyl, hunting outfit, M **125.00**

Elmer Fudd, vinyl, in tuxedo & hat, EX+ **20.00**

Foghorn Leghorn, vinyl, 1970, NM+.............................. **100.00**

Foofur the Dog, blue plush, VG .**32.00**

Fred Flintstone, vinyl, cloth outfit, 1970, MIP **50.00**

Freddy Fast, vinyl, MIP (sealed)..**60.00**

Goofy, vinyl, cloth outfit, #2247 on orange hang tag, EX+ **30.00**

Honolulu Harry, Dream Pets, #353, plush, 1970, EX **18.00**

Mariner Monkey, plush, Dream Pets, VG **35.00**

Merlin the Lion, plush, EX....**50.00**

Merlin the Mouse, vinyl, Goofy Gram, I'll Drink to That!, MIP **50.00**

Monkey, Dream Pet, plush, red & tan, early, NM **25.00**

Olive Oyl, vinyl, cloth outfit, NM+IP **30.00**

Pepe Lepew, vinyl, Goofy Gram, You're a Real Stinker!, NM **75.00**

Pink Panther, vinyl, jointed arms & legs, w/pink hang tag, 1971, EX **25.00**

Porky Pig, vinyl, 1976, EXIB (TV Cartoon Theater box)......**35.00**

Scottie Dog, Dream Pets, #118, plush, 1950s, VG.............**25.00**

Second Banana, vinyl, MIP...**40.00**

Smokey Bear, vinyl, MIP.......**25.00**

Snagglepuss, 1971, EX, $100.00.

Speedy Gonzalez, vinyl, cloth outfit & hat, 1968, EX **30.00**

Tweety Bird, plush, no hair tuft, NM **30.00**

Tweety Bird, plush, w/hair tuft, EX+ **40.00**

Wile E Coyote, vinyl & plastic, jointed limbs, 1969, MIP.........**25.00**

Yosemite Sam, vinyl, 1976, MIP (sealed Funny Farm Bag). **40.00**

Zip Chimp, plush, cloth outfit, 1984 Lee Ecuyer Fun Farm tag, EX **30.00**

Decanters

The James Beam Distilling Company produced its first ceramic whiskey decanter in 1953 and remained the only major producer of these decanters throughout the decade. By the late 1960s, other companies such as Ezra Brooks, Lionstone, and Cyrus Noble were also becoming involved in their production. Today these fancy liquor containers are attracting many collectors.

Beam, Army Jeep, green, 1986..**50.00**

Beam, Baseball, Chicago Cubs, 1985 ....**120.00**

Beam, Bell Ringer Plaid Apron, 1970 ....**10.00**

Beam, Bird, Owl, gray, 1979 .**19.00**

Beam, Bird, Robin, 1969..........**9.00**

Beam, Catfish, 1981...............**40.00**

Beam, Charlie McCarthy, 1976.**35.00**

Beam, Chevy Corvette (1955), copper-bronze, 1989............**125.00**

Beam, Colorado, 1959............**22.00**

Beam, Dodge, '70 Hot Rod, yellow, 1992 ....**55.00**

Beam, Ducks Unlimited, #02 Wood Duck, 1975......................**38.00**

Beam, Dump Truck, sand & gravel, 1992 ....**50.00**

Beam, Ford Model A Phaeton, green, 1982...................... **75.00**

Beam, General Train Series, Wood Tender #3, 1988............. **145.00**

Beam, Gulf Cart, blue, 1986 . **45.00**

Beam, Harold's Club Nevada, silver, 1964 .... **100.00**

Beam, JB Turner Train Series, Caboose, yellow #285, 1985. **90.00**

Beam, Labrador Retriever, 1987 .... **30.00**

Beam, Marine Bulldog, Devil Dog, 1979 .... **45.00**

Beam, Seal, Harp, 1986......... **20.00**

Beam, Walleye Pike, 1977 ..... **28.00**

Brooks, '56 Ford T-Bird, yellow, 1976 .... **59.00**

Brooks, American Legion, Chicago, 1972 .... **48.00**

Brooks, Clown w/Accordion, 1971 .... **32.00**

Brooks, Golf, Greensboro Open, 1972 .... **28.00**

Brooks, Kansas Jayhawk, 1969.**25.00**

Brooks, Weirton Steel, 1975 .. **18.00**

Budweiser, Bud Man, mini.... **79.00**

Budweiser, Clydesdale, 1978. **89.00**

Collectors Art, Charlois Bull, 1974 .... **25.00**

Collectors Art, Corvette Stingray, blue, 1971 .... **59.00**

Cyrus Noble, Carousel Lion, 1979 .... **55.00**

Cyrus Noble, Moose & Calf #1, 1976 .... **95.00**

Cyrus Noble, Violinist, 1976.. **39.00**

Dant, Mt Rushmore, 1969....... **9.00**

Dant, Washington at Delaware, 1969 .... **8.00**

Dugs Nevada Miniatures, Cherry Patch, 1988..................... **65.00**

Dugs Nevada Miniatures, Sagebrush Ranch, 1984.. **22.00**

Famous First, Dewitt Clinton Engine, 1969 .... **32.00**

Famous First, Honda Motorcycle, 1975 .... **62.00**

Famous First, Yacht America, 1970 .... **69.00**

Garnier, Cardinal, 1969......... **15.00**

Garnier, Cocker Spaniel, 1970. **19.00**

Garnier, London Police, 1970. **18.00**

Grenadier, American Thoroughbred, 1978 .... **59.00**

Grenadier, Scots Fusileer Officer, 1971 .... **25.00**

Grenadier, Ulysses S Grant, 1975.**29.00**

Grenadier, 11th Indiana Zouave, 1975, mini........................ **14.00**

Hoffman, AJ Foyte, #2, 1972. **125.00**

Hoffman, Bartender, Mr Lucky Series #3, 1975................ **36.00**

Hoffman, Carpenter, Mr Lucky Series #4, 1979................ **32.00**

Hoffman, Cowboy, CM Russell Series #2, 1978................ **40.00**

Hoffman, Fox & the Grapes, 1978 .... **22.00**

Hoffman, Missouri Tigers, Helmets, 1981 .... **29.00**

Hoffman, Shepherd, 1980...... **45.00**

Hoffman, Wood Ducks, 1980 . **24.00**

Jack Daniels, Barrel House 1, 1994 .... **25.00**

Jack Daniels, Riverboat Captain, 1987 .... **25.00**

Kontinental, Innkeeper, 1978. **26.00**

Lionstone, Alaskan Malamute, 1977, mini........................ **25.00**

Lionstone, Bartender, 1969 ... **30.00**

Lionstone, Betsy Ross, 1975.. **26.00**

Lionstone, Burmese Girl, 1973.. **25.00**

Lionstone, Fireman #1, red hat, 1972 .... **98.00**

Lionstone, Gazelles, 1977, mini.**20.00**

Lionstone, Molly Brown, 1973. **22.00**

Lionstone, Railroad Engineer, 1969 .... **29.00**

Lionstone, Stutz Bearcat, 1978, mini **29.00**

McCormick, Air Race Propeller, 1971 .... **21.00**

McCormick, Brahama Bull, 1973 . **33.00**

McCormick, Charles Lindbergh, 1977 .... **42.00**

McCormick, Cowboy Hall of Fame, 1983 .... **89.00**

McCormick, Hank Williams Jr, 1980 .... **95.00**

McCormick, Patrick Henry, 1975 .... **25.00**

McCormick, Paul Bunyan, 1979 .... **32.00**

McCormick, Texas Tech Raiders, 1972 .... **42.00**

Michters, Halloween Witch, 1979 .... **55.00**

Mike Wayne, John Wayne Bust, 1980 .... **55.00**

Old Commonwealth, Coal Miner #1, 1975 .... **89.00**

Old Commonwealth, Fireman #3, On Call, yellow hat, 1983 .... **72.00**

Old Commonwealth, Leprechaun #1, Elusive, 1980 .... **39.00**

Old Mr Boston, Bingo in Illinois, 1974 .... **12.00**

Old Mr Boston, Deadwood South Dakota, 1975 .... **15.00**

Old Mr Boston, Steelhead Trout, 1976 .... **15.00**

Ski Country, Barn Owl, 1979 . **86.00**

Ski Country, Bobcat, 1981 ..... **75.00**

Ski Country, Bull Rider, 1980 . **87.00**

Ski Country, Circus Lion, 1975 . **49.00**

Ski Country, Cowboy Joe, University of Wyoming, 1980 .... **200.00**

Ski Country, Fighting Pheasants, 1977 .... **115.00**

Ski Country, Jaguar, 1983 ... **180.00**

Ski Country, Meadowlark, 1980. **63.00**

Ski Country, Pronghorn Antelope, 1979 .... **70.00**

Ski Country, Rainbow Dancer, 1984 .... **98.00**

Ski Country, Scrooge, 1979.... **67.00**

Ski Country, Whooping Crane, 1984 .... **65.00**

Wild Turkey, Series #1, #8 Turkey Strutting, 1983, mini **30.00**

Wild Turkey, Series #2, Turkey Lore #1, 1979, $32.00.

Wild Turkey, Series #3, #1 Turkey in Flight, 1983 .... **110.00**

Wild Turkey, Series #3, #5 Turkey & Raccoon, 1984 .... **95.00**

Wild Turkey, Series #3, #9 Turkey & Cubs, 1985 .... **95.00**

Degenhart

Elizabeth Degenhart and her husband John produced glassware in their studio at Cambridge, Ohio, from 1947 until John died in 1964. Elizabeth restructured the company and hired Zack Boyd who had previously worked for the Cambridge Glass Company, to help her formulate almost 150 unique and original colors which they used to press small-scale bird and animal figures, boxes, wines, covered dishes, and toothpick holders. Degenhart glass is marked with a 'D in heart' trademark. After her death and at her request, this mark was removed from the molds, some of which were bequeathed to the Degenhart museum. The remaining molds were acquired by Boyd, who added his own logo to them and continued to press glassware very similar to Mrs. Degenhart's.

Bird Salt, Lavender Green Slag.**35.00**
Bird Toothpick Holder, Custard Slag **25.00**
Buzz Saw Wine, Light Blue... **20.00**
Elephant Toothpick Holder, Amber **25.00**
Elizabeth Degenhart Portrait Plate, Clear, 5½" **30.00**
Forget-Me-Not Toothpick Holder, Amber **30.00**

Forget-Me-Not Toothpick, Misty Green, $22.50.

Forget-Me-Not Toothpick Holder, Pearl Gray **25.00**
Gypsy Pot, Amethyst **15.00**
Gypsy Pot, Cobalt **15.00**
Hand, Amethyst **25.00**
Heart Jewel Box, Nile Green. **25.00**
Heart Toothpick Holder, Amberina **15.00**
Hen Covered Dish, Charcoal. **28.00**
High-Button Shoe, Green **25.00**
Hobo Baby Shoe, Caramel Custard Slag **20.00**

Hobo Baby Shoe, Vaseline **12.00**
Liberty Bell, Lemonade **15.00**
Owl, Chad's Blue **50.00**
Owl, Dark Sahara Sand **50.00**
Owl, Misty Blue **55.00**
Owl, Spiced Brown **50.00**
Paperweight, 5 flowers each w/bubble centers, John Degenhart, 2½" **175.00**
Pooch, Brown Gray Slag **20.00**
Pooch, Dark Amber **25.00**
Priscilla, Amethyst Heather Bloom **100.00**
Priscilla, Cobalt **100.00**
Priscilla, Milk Blue **150.00**
Skate Boot (Roller Skate), Vaseline **30.00**
Sweetheart Toothpick Holder, April Green **25.00**

Texas Boot, Amethyst, 2⅝", $15.00.

Tomahawk, Custard **40.00**

Department 56 Inc.

In 1976 this company introduced their original line of six handcrafted ceramic buildings. The Original Snow Village quickly won the hearts of young and old alike, and the light that sparkled from their windows added charm and warmth to Christmas celebrations everywhere. Accessories followed, and the line was expanded. Over the years, new villages have been developed — the Dickens Series, New England, Alpine, Christmas in the City, and Bethlehem. Offerings in the '90s included the North Pole, Disney Parks, and Seasons Bay. Their popular Snowbabies assortment was introduced in 1986, and today they're collectible as well.

Church, Dickens' Village, 1985, unused, MIB **75.00**
Flower Shop (Flowers), 1983, M. **85.00**
Ford Uptown Motors, Snow Village, #54941, complete 3-pc set, MIB **100.00**
Ghostly Carousel, Snow Village, #55317, MIB **125.00**
Golden Gate Bridge, #59241, MIB **75.00**
Halloween Hauntsburg House, Snow Village, MIB **60.00**
Harley-Davidson Motorcycle Shop, complete, MIB **100.00**
Haunted Mansion, #54035, MIB **300.00**
Haversham House, Snow Village, #5008-3, 1986, M............. **35.00**
Lily's Easter & Gifts, EX **35.00**
M&M Candy House, 2005, MIB **20.00**
McDonald's, Snow Village, #54925/ #54926, both EXIB.......... **85.00**
Mickey's Dining Car, Snow Village, 1986, EX **190.00**
Mountain Creek Waterfall, M. **45.00**
Pillsbury Doughboy Bake Shop, Snow Village, #55342, MIB **50.00**
Plantation House, Snow Village, #50474, 1985-87, MIB **65.00**
Play Doh Sculpting Studio, North Pole Series, #56746, 2002, MIB................................ **40.00**

Ramsford Palace Set, Dickens' Village, #08624, 1996, MIB **125.00**
Santa's Workshop, North Pole Series, MIB **75.00**
Shelly's Diner, Snow Village, MIB **50.00**
Starbucks Coffee Shop, Snow Village, #544859, EXIB . **190.00**
Statue of Liberty (Liberty Enlighting the World), #57708, MIB **55.00**
Village Pets Sales & Service, Snow Village, #55365, MIB **45.00**
Yummy Gummy Gumdrop Factory, North Pole Series, #56771, MIB **50.00**

Depression Glass

Depression glass, named for the era when it sold through dime stores or was given away as premiums, can be found in such varied colors as amber, green, pink, blue, red, yellow, white, and crystal. Mass produced by many different companies in hundreds of patterns, Depression glass is one of the most sought-after collectibles in the United States today. For more information refer to *Pocket Guide to Depression Glass & More; Collector's Encyclopedia of Depression Glass;* and *Treasures of Very Rare Depression Glass;* all are by Gene and Cathy Florence (Collector Books). See also Anchor Hocking/Fire-King. See Clubs and Newsletters for information concerning the National Depression Glass Association.

Adam, ashtray, pink, 4½"....... **30.00**
Adam, bowl, green, 7¾" **30.00**

Adam, coaster, green, 3¾"...... **20.00**

Adam, platter, green, 11¾" **33.00**

American Pioneer, bowl, green, w/lid, 9¼" **150.00**

American Pioneer, creamer, crystal or pink, 2¾" **25.00**

American Pioneer, sugar bowl, green, 3½"........................ **22.00**

American Sweetheart, bowl, cereal; Monax, 6"......................... **20.00**

American Sweetheart, cup, pink **18.00**

American Sweetheart, plate, luncheon; Monax, 9"......... **12.00**

American Sweetheart, platter, pink, oval, 13" **55.00**

American Sweetheart, tumbler, pink, 9-oz, 4¼" **125.00**

Aunt Polly, bowl, berry; green or iridescent, 4¾".................... **8.00**

Aunt Polly, plate, luncheon; blue, 8" **20.00**

Aurora, bowl, cereal; cobalt or pink, 5½" **18.50**

Aurora, plate, cobalt or pink, 6½" **12.50**

Avocado, all pieces in green: cup, $35.00; saucer, $24.00; luncheon plate, 8¼", $22.00; sherbet plate, $18.00; sugar bowl, $40.00; and tumbler, rare, $325.00. (Photo courtesy Gene and Cathy Florence)

Beaded Block, bowl, deep, crystal, green or pink, 6" **25.00**

Beaded Block, pitcher, jug; amber, crystal, green or pink, 1-pt, 5".. **110.00**

Block Optic, candy jar, yellow, w/lid, 2¼" **75.00**

Block Optic, goblet, wine; green, 4½" **40.00**

Block Optic, salt & pepper shakers, green, footed, pr **45.00**

Bowknot, bowl, berry; green, 4½". **25.00**

Bowknot, plate, salad; green, 7". **15.00**

Cameo, bowl, cereal; yellow, 5½". **35.00**

Cameo, bowl, rimmed soup; green, 9"....................................... **75.00**

Cameo, cookie jar, green........ **65.00**

Cameo, domino tray, green, 7" w/3" indentation **225.00**

Cameo, plate, luncheon; yellow, 8"....................................... **11.00**

Cameo, tumbler, green, 15-oz, 5¼" **80.00**

Cherry Blossom, cake plate, green, 3-legged, 10¼" **40.00**

Cherry Blossom, plate, dinner; green, 9"........................... **28.00**

Cherry Blossom, platter, pink, oval, 11" **60.00**

Chinx Classic, bowl, soup; decal decorated, 7¾" **25.00**

Chinx Classic, creamer, castle decal................................. **20.00**

Colonial, bowl, berry; pink, 4½". **18.00**

Colonial, plate, luncheon; green, 8½" **11.00**

Colonial, stem, water; crystal, 8½-oz, 5¾"............................. **25.00**

Diamond Quilted, bowl, blue or black, crimped edge, 7"... **22.00**

Diamond Quilted, candy jar, green or pink, footed, w/lid....... **65.00**

Diana, plate, bread & butter; pink, 6"....................................... **5.00**

Diana, salt & pepper shakers, crystal, pr **30.00**

Dogwood, bowl, cereal; pink, 5½"............................ 25.00

Dogwood, plate, dinner; pink, 9¼"...............................38.00

Dogwood, sugar bowl, green, thin, 2½"................................. 45.00

Doric, bowl, cereal; pink, 5½".80.00

Doric, pitcher, green, 36-ounce, $55.00.

Doric, plate, dinner; pink, 9".20.00

Doric, platter, green, oval, 12".30.00

Doric, tumbler, pink, footed, 12-oz, 5"..................................90.00

English Hobnail, bowl, green or pink, flared rim, 10"........40.00

English Hobnail, ice tub, ice blue or turquoise, 4".....................90.00

Florentine No 1, bowl, cereal; green, 6"....................................25.00

Florentine No 1, pitcher, yellow, 36-oz, 6½"..............................45.00

Florentine No 1, plate, salad; yellow, 8½"............................12.00

Florentine No 1, platter, yellow, oval, 11½".........................25.00

Florentine No 1, tumbler, iced-tea; green, footed, 12-oz, 5¼".28.00

Florentine No 2, butter dish, yellow..................................165.00

Florentine No 2, creamer, yellow............................. 12.00

Florentine No 2, cup, green..... 9.00

Florentine No 2, pitcher, green, 48-oz, 7½"..............................75.00

Florentine No 2, sugar bowl, green 10.00

Fruits, sherbet, green............ 12.00

Fruits, tumbler, pink, 4"........22.00

Hex Optic, platter, green or pink, round, 11"........................15.00

Hex Optic, tumbler, green or pink, footed, 5¾".......................10.00

Holiday, tumbler, pink, footed, 4"................................. 50.00

Indiana Custard, bowl, berry; ivory, 5½" 13.00

Indiana Custard, creamer, ivory.16.00

Indiana Custard, plate, dinner; ivory, 9¾" 32.00

Indiana Custard, sherbet, ivory.105.00

Iris, bowl, salad; iridescent, 9½".13.00

Iris, candlesticks, crystal, pr.40.00

Iris, cup, crystal 15.00

Iris, goblet, iridescent, 4-oz, 5½"..495.00

Iris, saucer, iridescent............. 8.00

Iris, tumbler, crystal, flat, 4"..135.00

Iris, tumbler, crystal, footed, 6"..20.00

Jubilee, cup, yellow............... 13.00

Jubilee, plate, sandwich; yellow, 13½" 50.00

Laced Edge, bowl, blue or green, 5" 36.00

Laced Edge, candlestick, double; blue or green 175.00

Laced Edge, creamer, blue or green 40.00

Laced Edge, sugar bowl, blue or green 40.00

Lake Como, bowl, vegetable, 9¾".45.00

Lake Como, platter, 11" 75.00

Laurel, bowl, cereal; ivory, 6".12.00

Laurel, cup, jade 15.00

Laurel, plate, sherbet; ivory, 6"..10.00

Laurel, sherbet, ivory 12.00

Lincoln Inn, ashtray, blue 18.00

Lincoln Inn, compote, red...... **30.00**
Lincoln Inn, goblet, water; red. **30.00**
Lincoln Inn, plate, red, 6"........ **9.00**
Lorain, bowl, cereal; yellow, 6". **70.00**
Lorain, plate, dinner; green, 10¼" **60.00**
Lorain, saucer, yellow.............. **6.00**
Madrid, ashtray, green, sq, 6". **450.00**

Madrid, butter dish, amber, $70.00.

Madrid, cookie jar, amber...... **45.00**
Madrid, hot dish coaster, green .**95.00**
Madrid, plate, grill; green, 10½".**20.00**
Madrid, platter, amber, oval, 11½" **16.00**
Madrid, saucer, green **5.00**
Madrid, sugar bowl, amber **8.00**
Manhattan, bowl, salad; crystal, 9" **30.00**
Manhattan, pitcher, crystal, 24-oz.......................... **40.00**
Manhattan, plate, dinner; pink, 10¼" **250.00**
Manhattan, relish tray w/inserts, pink, 14" **85.00**

Mayfair, candy dish, blue, $310.00.

Mayfair (Federal), bowl, sauce; green, 5".......................... **12.00**
Mayfair (Federal), tumbler, amber, 9-oz, 4½"........................... **30.00**
Mayfair (Federal), tumbler, crystal, 9-oz, 4½"........................... **15.00**
Mayfair (Open Rose), bowl, vegetable; pink, 7" **30.00**
Mayfair (Open Rose), creamer, pink, footed...................... **32.00**
Mayfair (Open Rose), plate, dinner; pink, 9½"........................... **60.00**
Mayfair (Open Rose), tumbler, juice; pink, 5-oz, 3½" **50.00**
Miss America, bowl, berry; pink, 6¼" **30.00**
Miss America, cake plate, pink, footed, 12"........................ **65.00**
Miss America, coaster, crystal, 5¾".................................... **16.00**
Miss America, cup, green **15.00**
Moderntone, bowl, cream soup; cobalt, ruffled, 5"............. **70.00**
Moderntone, cobalt **12.00**
Moderntone, plate, luncheon; amethyst, 7¾"........................... **9.00**
Moderntone, saucer, cobalt...... **4.00**
Moderntone, whiskey, cobalt, 1½-oz **45.00**
Moondrops, candy dish, colors other than blue or red, ruffled, 8". **20.00**
Moondrops, compote, blue or red, 4" **27.00**
Moondrops, goblet, wine; blue or red, 4-oz, 4"...................... **25.00**
Moondrops, plate, dinner; colors other than blue or red, 9½"..........**20.00**
Moondrops, plate, luncheon; blue or red, 8½" **15.00**
Moondrops, sugar bowl, colors other than blue or red, 4"......... **11.00**
Mt Pleasant, bowl, fruit; amethyst, sq, footed, 4".................... **20.00**

Mt Pleasant, cup, black **12.00**

Mt Pleasant, plate, cobalt, w/handles, 8" **18.00**

Mt Pleasant, sugar bowl, black..**20.00**

New Century, cup, pink **20.00**

New Century, plate, breakfast; crystal, 7"......................... **10.00**

New Century, plate, grill; green, 10" **20.00**

New Century, platter, green, oval, 11" **25.00**

New Century, tumbler, green, footed, 5-oz, 4" **22.00**

Newport, bowl, berry; cobalt, 4¼" **22.00**

Newport, cup, cobalt **14.00**

Newport, saucer, cobalt **5.00**

No 610 Pyramid, bowl, berry; pink, 4¾" **20.00**

No 610 Pyramid, bowl, yellow, oval, 9½" **65.00**

No 610 Pyramid, pitcher, pink.**395.00**

No 610 Pyramid, sugar bowl, yellow................................... **40.00**

No 612 Horseshoe, cup, green.. **12.00**

No 612 Horseshoe, plate, grill; green, 10⅜".....................**125.00**

No 612 Horseshoe, tumbler, yellow, footed, 9-oz **32.00**

No 616 Vernon, cup, yellow ... **18.00**

No 616 Vernon, plate, luncheon; green, 8".......................... **10.00**

No 616 Vernon, plate, sandwich; yellow, 11"...................... **27.00**

No 618 Pineapple & Floral, bowl, salad; amber, 7"............... **25.00**

No 618 Pineapple & Floral, compote, red, diamond shape . **8.00**

No 618 Pineapple & Floral, platter, amber, closed handles, 11" .**18.00**

No 622 Pretzel, creamer, crystal .**5.00**

No 622 Pretzel, tumbler, juice; crystal, 5-oz **45.00**

Normandie, creamer, iridescent, footed **10.00**

Normandie, plate, grill; pink, 11" **25.00**

Normandie, salt & pepper shakers, amber, pr **55.00**

Old Cafe, bowl, berry; pink, 3¾".**14.00**

Old Cafe, cup, red **8.00**

Old Cafe, plate, dinner; pink, 10"................................. **65.00**

Old Cafe, tumbler, juice; red, 3".**20.00**

Old English, creamer, all colors.**20.00**

Old English (Threading), tumblers, any color, footed, 5½", $40.00; 4½", $28.00. (Photo courtesy Gene and Cathy Florence)

Old English, vase, fan; all colors, 7" **65.00**

Ovide, bowl, berry; decorated white, 4½" **7.00**

Ovide, creamer, green.............. **5.00**

Ovide, saucer, green................. **2.00**

Oyster & Pearl, bowl, fruit; red, deep, 10½"........................ **60.00**

Oyster & Pearl, relish dish, crystal or pink, oblong, divided, 10½" **18.00**

Parrot, bowl, berry; green, 5" **30.00**

Parrot, cup, green **42.00**

Parrot, saucer, green.............. **15.00**

Parrot, sugar bowl, amber..... **50.00**

Patrician, bowl, cereal; green, 6" **32.00**

Patrician, pitcher, amber, 75-oz, 8" **125.00**

Patrician, tumbler, amber, 14-oz, 5½" **48.00**

Patrick, bowl, console; yellow, 11" **145.00**

Patrick, creamer, pink **65.00**

Patrick, cup, yellow **35.00**

Patrick, plate, luncheon; yellow, 8" **25.00**

Patrick, tray, pink, w/handles, 11" **75.00**

Petalware, bowl, cream soup; pink, 4½" **18.00**

Petalware, plate, dinner; pink, 9". **13.00**

Petalware, sugar bowl, Monax, footed **8.00**

Primo, bowl, green, 4½" **25.00**

Primo, creamer, yellow **12.00**

Primo, plate, dinner; yellow, 10". **30.00**

Primo, plate, grill; green, 10". **18.00**

Princess, bowl, berry; green, 4½" **30.00**

Princess, cake stand, pink, 10"..**35.00**

Princess, plate, salad; green, 8".**20.00**

Princess, sugar bowl, green... **10.00**

Princess, vase, pink, 8" **65.00**

Queen Mary, bowl, cereal; pink, 6" **25.00**

Queen Mary, compote, pink, 5¾".**25.00**

Queen Mary, cup, crystal **5.00**

Queen Mary, tumbler, water; crystal, 9-oz, 4" **7.00**

Raindrops, bowl, cereal; green, 6" **14.00**

Raindrops, plate, luncheon; green, 8" **6.00**

Raindrops, plate, sherbet; green, 6" **3.00**

Raindrops, sugar bowl, green. **10.00**

Ribbon, bowl, cereal; green, 5". **45.00**

Ribbon, plate, luncheon; black, 8" **14.00**

Ribbon, salt & pepper shakers, black, pr **45.00**

Ring, bowl, soup; crystal, 7".. **11.00**

Ring, ice bucket, crystal w/decoration **35.00**

Ring, pitcher, green, 60-oz, 8". **25.00**

Ring, tumbler, iced-tea; crystal, footed, 6½" **10.00**

Ring, vase, green, 8" **38.00**

Rock Crystal, bowl, salad; red, scalloped edge, 8" **75.00**

Rock Crystal, compote, red, 7".**95.00**

Rock Crystal, plate, dinner; scalloped edge, crystal, 10½".**50.00**

Rock Crystal, relish dish, crystal, 6-part, 14" **50.00**

Rock Crystal, tumbler, juice; crystal, 5-oz **22.00**

Rose Cameo, bowl, cereal; green, 5" **24.00**

Rose Cameo, plate, salad; green, 7" **15.00**

Rosemary, bowl, cream soup; green, 5" **30.00**

Rosemary, plate, dinner; green..**15.00**

Rosemary, platter, amber, oval, 12" **15.00**

Roulette, bowl, fruit; pink, 9". **25.00**

Roulette, plate, sandwich; green, 12" **18.00**

Roulette, tumbler, juice; pink, 5-oz, 3¼" **28.00**

Round Robin, bowl, berry; iridescent, 4" **9.00**

Round Robin, plate, luncheon; iridescent, 8" **4.00**

Round Robin, sugar bowl, green. **12.00**

Roxana, plate, yellow, 6" **9.00**

Roxana, tumbler, yellow, 9-oz, 4" .**22.00**

Royal Lace, bowl, cream soup; blue, 4¾" **49.00**

Royal Lace, creamer, pink, footed **22.00**

Royal Lace, platter, blue, oval, 13". **65.00**
Royal Ruby, bowl, berry; red, 4¼" **5.50**
Royal Ruby, bowl, vegetable; oval, red, 8" **32.00**
Royal Ruby, plate, salad; red, 7"..**5.00**
Royal Ruby, tumbler, iced-tea; red, 2 styles, 5-oz, ea **7.50**
S Pattern, bowl, cereal; amber, 5½" **9.00**
S Pattern, plate, grill; crystal . **6.50**
Sandwich (Hocking), pitcher, juice; crystal, 7" **75.00**
Sandwich (Hocking), plate, dinner; green, 9" **130.00**
Sharon, bowl, berry; pink, 5" . **14.00**
Sharon, bowl, cereal; amber, 6" .**24.00**
Sharon, cup, amber **8.00**
Sharon, platter, pink, oval, 12½". **32.00**
Sharon, tumbler, pink, footed, 15-oz, 6½" **55.00**
Ships, cocktail shaker, blue/white **40.00**
Ships, tumbler, iced-tea; blue/white, 12-oz **25.00**
Sierra, bowl, cereal; green, 5½" .**18.00**
Sierra, cup, pink **15.00**
Spiral, bowl, mixing; green, 7". **15.00**
Spiral, ice tub, green **32.00**
Spiral, vase, green, footed, 5¾"..**55.00**
Starlight, bowl, berry; crystal, 4".**6.00**
Starlight, plate, dinner; crystal, 9" **8.00**
Strawberry, compote, green, 5¾"..**30.00**
Strawberry, olive dish, pink, w/ handles, 5" **20.00**
Strawberry, pickle dish, green. **20.00**
Sunburst, relish dish, crystal, 2-part **12.00**
Sunburst, sugar bowl, crystal . **10.00**
Sunflower, creamer, green **25.00**
Sunflower, plate, dinner; pink, 9" **24.00**

Swirl, bowl, cereal; pink, 5¼" . **14.00**
Swirl, plate, salad; pink, 8" ... **10.00**
Swirl, vase, ultramarine, footed, 8½" **28.00**
Tea Room, creamer, pink, 4"..**28.00**
Tea Room, cup, green **60.00**
Tea Room, ice bucket, pink.... **55.00**
Tea Room, sugar bowl, green, 4". **25.00**
Tea Room, tumbler, green, footed, 12-oz **75.00**
Thistle, plate, luncheon; green, 8" **20.00**
Thistle, saucer, pink **12.00**
Tulip, creamer, amethyst **24.00**
Tulip, plate, blue, 6" **11.00**
Tulip, plate, green, 10" **34.00**
Twisted Optic, bowl, cereal; green, 5" **9.00**
Twisted Optic, cup, pink **5.00**
Twisted Optic, pitcher, green, 64-oz **45.00**
Twisted Optic, saucer, green ... **2.00**
US Swirl, bowl, berry; green, 4½" **6.00**
US Swirl, bowl, pink, oval, 8". **45.00**
US Swirl, tumbler, green, 12-oz, 4½" **14.00**
Victory, bonbon, pink, 7" **12.00**
Victory, plate, dinner; blue, 9". **50.00**
Victory, sugar bowl, pink **15.00**
Vitrock, cup, white **5.00**
Vitrock, plate, dinner; white, 10" **10.00**
Vitrock, plate, soup; white, 9". **33.00**
Waterford, ashtray, crystal **7.50**
Waterford, coaster, crystal, 4" . **4.00**
Waterford, goblet, crystal, 5¼". **16.00**
Waterford, sugar bowl, pink.. **12.50**
Windsor, butter dish, crystal. **30.00**
Windsor, cup, crystal **2.50**
Windsor, plate, chop; crystal, 13½" **16.00**
Windsor, plate, dinner; pink, 9". **27.00**

Windsor, tumbler, pink, 12-oz, 5" **35.00**

Desert Storm

On August 2, 1990, Saddam Hussien invaded Kuwait, taking control of that small nation in less than four hours and capturing nearly a fourth of the world's oil supplies. Saudia Arabia seemed to be his next goal. After a plea for protection by the Saudis, President Bush set a January 15, 1991, deadline for the removal of Iraqi soldiers from Kuwait. January 16 saw the bombing of Bagdad and other military targets, followed by SCUD missile attacks. The brief but bloody war ended in March 1991 with Iraqi soldiers leaving Kuwait and US combat forces returning home.

Many Desert Storm related items were created as remembrances of this brief time in history. Topps published a series of Desert Storn trading cards, and Mattel got in on the action with Barbie and Ken in Desert Storm uniforms. Many other items were issued as well. Actual battle-related items are extremely scarce but highly coveted by collectors.

Bayonet, M7, w/scabbard, EX. **35.00**
Belt buckle, cast metal eagle, shield & banner, enameled, Operation..., M **15.00**
Book, Remembering the Gulf War, Keith F Girard, NM........ **20.00**
Boots, combat; Belleville 390 DES Hot Weather, tan leather, NM................................. **5.00**

Evasion Chart EVC NG-38A, EX............................... **25.00**
Gas mask, MCU-2P 864-55, w/canvas carrying case, EX **35.00**
Helmet, Iraqi soldier's; tan w/green netting, VG...................... **35.00**
Jacket, navy flight; nylon, several patches on back, EX **100.00**
Knife, EK Commando, EK Commando Knife Co, Virginia, 12¾" overall, EX............ **200.00**
Knife, Remington, limited edition, case covered w/camo material & logo.............................. **95.00**
Patch, Desert Storm Nevada, for the 152nd TRG/RF-4C Phantom II, tan, M **22.00**
Patch, F-4G Phantom II Wild Weasel 3552, tan, 3½" dia, M **22.00**
Playset, Desert Storm Liberation, Marx, 1991 limited edition, NMIB.............................. **45.00**
Sleeping bag, Iraqi; roll-up type, EX **50.00**
Spare tire cover, tan camo cloth, VG.................................... **20.00**
Trading cards, Desert Storm Pro Set, sealed case w/36 packs, M **15.00**
Video game, Conflict, X-Box, all original, M...................... **10.00**
Wristwatch, Marathon US Military, 1991, black nylon strap, EX.**55.00**
Wristwatch, Seiko, aviator dial, black nylon band, VG+ ... **50.00**

Disney Collectibles

As soon as the newest Disney film is released, toy makers scurry to create merchandise featuring the film's characters. From gum wrappers to the very high-end items, collectors vie to own them. Of course, examples from the 1930s and 1940s are often hard to find and bring the higher prices, but even later Disney-related merchandise is often collectible as well, as each newly created personality attracts their own cult following.

Alarm clock, Mickey's ears atop round case, Bradley, 1960s, EXIB 85.00

Ashtray, white ceramic w/Donald Duck head in center, 1960s, 7" sq, EX 75.00

Bank, Pinocchio head form, vinyl, Play Pal, 1970s, 10", NM+ .25.00

Bell, white ceramic w/various characters, blue trim, Schmid #231, 6" 25.00

Book, Disney on Parade ('73), Mary Poppins Cover, 1973, M.. 30.00

Candy dispensers, Toy Story characters, sold at McDonald's, 1999, NM 5.00

Creamer, Mad Hatter, figural, Fitz & Floyd, 1992, 5" 30.00

Figure, Belle (Beauty & Beast), bendable PVC, Just Toys, 4½", NM 5.00

Figure, Donald Duck, ceramic, as pirate, WD Prod/Japan, 1970s, 3½" 28.00

Figure, Donald Duck, rubber, standing w/arms & legs out, 1970s, 5", EX 15.00

Figure, Genie (Aladdin), ceramic, copyright Disney Japan, 7", M... 28.00

Figure, Mickey, Chatter Chum, 1976, 6", EX..................... 40.00

Figure, Mickey, hard plastic, on tricycle, Gabriel, 1977, EX... 40.00

Figure, Mickey, stuffed cloth & vinyl, Applause #8528, 1981, 10½", EX+ 15.00

Figure, Minnie Mouse, plush, Teach-Me Doll, Mattel, 1992, 14", EX+ 10.00

Figure, Petunia, wood bead type, late 1930s, 4½", VG 75.00

Figure, Pinocchio, ceramic, WD Prod, 1970s, 5¼", EX 35.00

Figure, Roger Rabbit, bendable, dated 1987, 14½", NM 18.00

Figure, Roger Rabbit, ceramic, copyright Disney Japan, 4¾", M.. 28.00

Figure, Roger Rabbit, plush, Applause, 1987, 12", EX+. 15.00

Figure, Simba (Lion King), plush, Mattel, 1993, EX............. 12.00

Figure, Tigger, plush, McDonald's issue, 12", EX 15.00

Figure, Woody (Toy Story), pull-string talker, cloth with vinyl head and hands, Thinkway, MIB, $45.00. (Photo courtesy Mark Mazzetti)

Growth Chart, Ready Set Grow!, Mickey, Donald & Pluto, 1970s, 60", EX.............................. 18.00

Hand puppet, Beast or Belle, rubber, Pizza Hut issue, 1992, 7", EX, ea 6.00

Hand puppet, Esmerelda, Hugo, Phoebus or Quasimodo, Burger King, 1996, ea 5.00

Hand puppet, Minnie Mouse, plush, purple dress, WD Productions, 10", M **10.00**

Handkerchief, nautical image of Donald in boat, 1950s, 8" sq, EX **25.00**

Napkin ring, figural 'Santa' Mickey next to ring, 1970s, 3", NM. **18.00**

Ornament, Ariel (Little Mermaid), figural, 3¾", EX **18.00**

Ornament, The Disney Family, Christmas 1975, Schmid, EXIB **18.00**

Party decorations, Sword in the Stone, Dennison, 1963, 3-pc, MIP **18.00**

Pin, Goofy as fife player, enameled, Kodak premium, 1989, 1½", EX **20.00**

Pin, Little Mermaid, cloisonne, Disney/Arthus Bertrand, 1½", EX **10.00**

Pincushion, Tinkerbell atop velvet cushion w/gold base, 1960s-70s, 3" dia **30.00**

Posters To Color, Toy Story, Golden Books, 1996, MIP **5.00**

Push puppet, Donald Duck's Nephew, Wara, 1960s, 3", VG+ **45.00**

Push puppet, Mickey inside lg top hat, Kohner, 1960s, NM . **50.00**

Push puppet, Pinocchio inside tree stump, Kohner, 1960s, EX.. **45.00**

Spoon, Donald Duck ceramic handle, marked Disney, Stainless, Japan, 6" **15.00**

Squeeze toy, Donald Duck, Sun Rubber, 1950s, 8", EX **75.00**

Squeeze toy, elephant (Jungle Book), vinyl, white & yellow, '60s, 6", EX **25.00**

Straws, Donald Duck, 100 Sunshine Straws, American Seal-Kap Corp, EXIB **15.00**

Tea set, Mary Poppins, litho tin, Chein, 1960s, complete, NM+ **100.00**

Ventriloquist doll, Mickey Mouse, Horsman, 1973, NM **75.00**

Wall clock, lg battery-op wristwatch w/Mickey, Bradley, 26" L, NM **85.00**

Dollhouse Furnishings

Collecting antique dollhouses and building new ones is a popular hobby with many today, and all who collect houses delight in furnishing them right down to the vase on the table and the scarf on the piano! Flea markets are a good source of dollhouse furnishings, especially those from the 1940s through the 1960s made by Strombecker, Tootsietoy, Renwal, or the Petite Princess line by Ideal. For an expanded listing, see *Schroeder's Collectible Toys, Antique to Modern.*

Ideal Petite Princess, Fantasy Furniture, grandfather clock, no folding screen (came with one), MIB, $35.00.

Acme/Thomas, baby carriage, any color combination, ea **6.00**

Acme/Thomas, doll, baby w/diaper, 2".. **4.00**

Allied Pyro, floor radio, yellow. **8.00**

Best, doll, baby standing or sitting, hard plastic, ea **2.00**

Fisher-Price, doll, Mother, #276, 1983-85, MOC **3.00**

Fisher-Price, dresser w/mirror, white................................ **5.00**

Fisher-Price, kitchen chair, white & yellow............................ **2.00**

Fisher-Price, stove w/hood, yellow **5.00**

Ideal, bathtub, ivory w/black .. **10.00**

Ideal, buffet, red..................... **15.00**

Ideal, china closet, red........... **20.00**

Ideal, dishwasher, w/lettering. **20.00**

Ideal, highchair, collapsible, blue or pink, ea............................ **25.00**

Ideal, piano w/bench, caramel swirl................................. **35.00**

Ideal Petite Princess, bed, blue or pink, #4416-4, w/original box, ea.. **30.00**

Ideal Petite Princess, grand piano & bench, Royal #4425-5.. **25.00**

Ideal Petite Princess, grandfather clock, #4423-0.................. **10.00**

Ideal Petite Princess, grandfather clock, #4423-0, w/screen & box **20.00**

Ideal Young Decorator, kitchen table or chair, white, ea.. **10.00**

Ideal Young Decorator, sectional sofa, rose, ea section **12.00**

Jaydon, kitchen sink, ivory w/ black **15.00**

Jaydon, living room chair, ivory w/brown base..................... **8.00**

Marx Little Hostess, double dresser, ivory............................ **8.00**

Marx Little Hostess, occasional chair, yellow **12.00**

Mattel Littles, drop-leaf table w/4 plates & cups................... **15.00**

Mattel Littles, sofa................... **5.00**

Plasco, bathroom set, complete in original box..................... **50.00**

Plasco, kitchen table, pink **5.00**

Reliable, dining room chair, rust.............................. **5.00**

Reliable, dining room table, rust.............................. **20.00**

Renwal, bathroom sink, dark turquoise & black.................. **8.00**

Renwal, buffet, non-opening drawer, brown............................ **6.00**

Renwal, folding table & chairs set, gold & red...................... **120.00**

Renwal, Jolly Twins living room set, complete, MIB, from $100 to **125.00**

Renwal, mantel clock, ivory or red, ea............................... **10.00**

Renwal, radio, brown or red table model, ea **15.00**

Renwal, server, opening door, brown................................. **8.00**

Renwal, toilet, turquoise w/black handle............................... **8.00**

Sounds Like Home, breakfront, brown................................. **6.00**

Sounds Like Home, kitchen table **5.00**

Strombecker, floor lamp, unfinished, ¾" scale **10.00**

Strombecker, sofa, green flocked, 1940s, ¾" scale **18.00**

Strombecker, sofa, green flocked, 1950s, 1" scale................. **25.00**

Tomy-Smaller Homes, canopy bed **15.00**

Tomy-Smaller Homes, end table........................... **8.00**

Tomy-Smaller Homes, refrigerator, w/drawers...................... **12.00**

Tootsietoy, living room set, 2 chairs, side table, stool & floor lamp **65.00**

Tootsietoy, nightstand, pink .. **10.00**

Tootsietoy, table, rectangular, brown **22.00**

Tootsietoy, vanity, black **18.00**

Dollhouses

Flea markets are a great place to find those old toys of your childhood, including dollhouses. Many are mansions in miniature, finished out with great care and detail. Our listings represent a sampling of dollhouses from the 1930s through the 1980s made by many different manufacturers.

Brumberger, 2-story colonial w/5 rooms, wood composition, 1970, 20x24" **60.00**

Fisher-Price, 2-story, Loving Family, plastic, w/accessories, 1997, EX **75.00**

Fisher-Price, 3 story w/5 rooms, battery-op, #280, 1981-84, M . **30.00**

Fisher-Price, 3-story w/5 rooms, spiral staircase, #250, 1978-80, M **40.00**

Jayline, 2 story w/5 rooms, litho tin, 1949, 14½x18½", VG **50.00**

Marx, split-level w/patio above garage, red w/gray roof, VG **65.00**

Marx, 2-story brick, flat-roofed side room, bay window, 13x8x25" L, EX **50.00**

Marx, 2-story colonial w/breezeway, clapboard over brick, 1960s, NM **75.00**

Marx, 2-story w/2 side single rooms, litho tin, 15x43" L, EX.... **40.00**

Meritoy, Cape Cod, litho tin w/plastic window inserts, 1949, 21x14", M **150.00**

Rich, bungalow, litho cardboard, 1930s, 32x21", VG......... **200.00**

T Cohn, litho tin, blue shutters/red roof, furnished, 1951, 16x24", VG **200.00**

Wolverine, colonial mansion, no garage, ½" scale, EX........ **50.00**

Wolverine, country cottage, #800, 1986, ½" scale, EX........... **50.00**

Marx, two-story house, tin litho, with 40+ pieces of plastic furniture, EX, $95.00. (Photo courtesy Apple Pie Collectibles)

Dolls and Accessories

Doll collecting is no doubt one of the most active fields today. Antique as well as modern dolls are treasured, and limited edition or artists' dolls often bring prices in excess of several hundred dollars. Investment potential is considered excellent in all areas. Dolls have been made from many materials — early to middle nineteenth-century dolls were carved of wood, poured in wax, and molded in bisque or china. Primitive cloth dolls were sewn at home for the enjoyment of little girls when fancier dolls were unavailable. In this century from 1925 to about 1945, composition was used. Made of a mixture of sawdust, clay, fiber, and a binding agent, it was tough and durable. Modern dolls are usually made of vinyl or molded plastic.

Learn to check your intended purchases for damage which could jeopardize your investment. In the listings, values are for dolls in excellent to near mint condition unless another condition is noted in the line or in the subcategory narrative. They are priced 'mint in box' only when so indicated. Played-with, soiled dolls are worth from 50% to 75% less, depending on wear. Many are worthless.

For more information we recommend *Small Dolls of the 40s & 50s* by Carol Stover and two volumes of *Collector's Encyclopedia of American Composition Dolls* by Ursula R. Mertz, all published by Collector Books. See also Action Figures; Advertising Collectibles; Character Collectibles; Holly Hobbie and Friends. See Clubs and Newsletters for information on *Doll Castle News* Magazine.

American Character

In business by 1918, this company made both composition and plastic dolls, all of excellent quality. Many collectors count them among the most desirable American dolls ever made. The company closed in 1968, and all of their molds were sold to other companies. The hard plastic dolls of the 1950s are much in demand today. See also Betsy McCall. For more information we recommend *American Character Dolls* by Judith Izen (Collector Books).

Eloise, cloth w/painted features, yarn hair, 15", G **30.00**
Little Miss Echo, 1964, 28", MIB **225.00**
Magic Make-Up, vinyl, grow hair, 1965-66, 9", EX **75.00**
Miss America, 1963, EX.........**60.00**
Sweet Sue, rooted hair, all original, 30", EX..........................**200.00**
Tiny Tears, molded hair, bottle mouth, 1950s, 12", EX ..**235.00**
Tiny Tears, rooted hair, bottle mouth, 1950s, 11", EXIB.............**290.00**
Toni, rooted hair, ballerina outfit, ca 1958, 14", MIB..........**300.00**
Toodles, rooted hair, pink checked sundress, white shoes, 1959, 22", NM..........................**140.00**

Annalee

Annalee Davis Thorndike made her first commercially sold dolls in the late 1950s. They're characterized by their painted felt faces and the meticulous workmanship involved in their manufacture. Most are made entirely of felt, though Santas and rabbits may have flannel bodies. All are constructed around a wire framework that allows them to be positioned in imaginative poses. Depending on rarity, appeal, and condition, some of the older dolls have increased in value more than 10 times their original price. Dolls from the 1950s carried a long white red-embroidered tag with no date. The same tag was in use from 1959 until 1964, but there was a copyright date in the upper right-hand corner. In 1970 a transition period began. The company changed its tag to a white satiny tag with a date preceded by a copyright symbol in the upper right-hand corner. In 1975 they made another change to a long white cotton strip with a copyright date. In 1982 the white tag was folded over, making it shorter. Many people mistake the copyright date as the date the doll was made — not so! It wasn't until 1986 that they finally began to date the tags with the year of manufacture, making it much easier for collectors to identify their dolls. Besides the red-lettered white Annalee tags, numerous others were used in the 1990s, but all reflect the year the doll was actually made. For more information refer to *Teddy Bears, Annalee's, and Steiff Animals* by Margaret Fox Mandel, and *Garage Sale and Flea Market Annual*. Both are published by Collector Books. Values are given for dolls in clean, near-mint condition.

Artist rabbit painting Easter egg w/paint brush, 1987, 11", M **45.00**
Chick, yellow w/orange beak & feet, wisps of fur, 1972/1982, 5", EX.............................. **35.00**
Christmas child w/bear & train on rug, Annalee Doll Society, 1989, 5x6", M **28.00**
Clown, Annalee Doll Society logo, 1990, complete w/pin, 9", NM **28.00**

Clown winking, 1971, approximately 21", NM **50.00**
Cowboy clown w/styrofoam-ball belly, 1980, 8", EX........... **38.00**
Frog w/pink ribbon & white eyelet 'skirt,' 1969, 8", M **45.00**
Mrs Claus w/skis, 1963, 6¼", EX.**35.00**
Victory Skier, 'Eagle' medal, dated 1/11/91 R20230, #9913, 9", M............................. **38.00**

Windsurfer mouse (Annalee birthdate on sail), 1982, 7", $150.00. (Photo courtesy Jane Holt)

Betsy McCall

Tiny 8" Betsy McCall was manufactured by the American Character Doll Company from 1957 until 1963. She was made from fine quality hard plastic with a bisque-like finish and had hand-painted features. Betsy came with four hair colors — tosca, blond, red, and brown. She has blue sleep eyes, molded lashes, a winsome smile, and a fully jointed body with bendable knees. On her back is an identification circle which reads "©McCall Corp." The basic doll could be purchased for $2.25 and wore a sheer chemise, white taffeta panties, nylon socks, and Maryjane-style shoes.

There were two different materials used for tiny Betsy's hair.

The first was soft mohair sewn onto mesh. Later the rubber skullcap was rooted with saran which was more suitable for washing and combing.

Betsy McCall had an extensive wardrobe with nearly 100 outfits, each of which could be purchased separately. They were made from wonderful fabrics such as velvet, felt, taffeta, and even real mink fur. Each ensemble came with the appropriate footware and was priced under $3.00. Since none of Betsy's clothing is tagged, it is often difficult to identify other than by its square snap closures (although these were used by other companies as well).

Betsy McCall is a highly collectible doll today but is still fairly easy to find at doll shows. The prices remain reasonable for this beautiful clotheshorse and her many accessories, some of which we've included below. For further information we recommend *Betsy McCall, A Collector's Guide* by Marci Van Ausdall. See Clubs and Newsletters for information concerning the Betsy McCall's Fan Club.

American Character, hard plastic, glued on saran hair, in first white nylon chemise, 1957, 8", MIB, $275.00. (Photo courtesy Judith Izen)

American Character, plastic, rooted hair, in chemise, 1958, 8", MIB **275.00**

American Character, vinyl, jointed limbs, swivel waist, 1961, 29", EX **300.00**

American Character, vinyl, swivel waist or 1-pc, 1958, 14", EX, ea.................................... **500.00**

American Character, vinyl w/Patti Playpal-style body, 1959, 36", EX **325.00**

Horsman, plastic teen body w/vinyl head, 1974, 29", MIB **275.00**

Horsman, plastic w/vinyl head, extra hair & accessories, 1974, 12½", EX **50.00**

Ideal, 14", hard plastic, original gray & white checked dress, EX **200.00**

Uneeda, vinyl, wore 'hip' outfits, 1964, 11½", EX, minimum value. **100.00**

Celebrity Dolls

Dolls that represent movie or TV personalities, fictional characters, or famous sports figures are very popular collectibles and can usually be found for well under $100.00. Mego, Horsman, Ideal, and Mattel are among the largest producers. Condition is vital. To price a doll in mint condition but without the box, deduct about 65% from the value of one mint-in-the-box. Dolls in only good or poorer condition drop at a very rapid pace. For more information see *Schroeder's Collectible Toys, Antique to Modern*, and *Collector's Guide to Celebrity Dolls* by David Spurgeon; both are published by Collector Books.

145

Alan Jackson (Country Music Stars), Exclusive Premiere, 1998, 9", MIB **30.00**

Brooke Shields, pink & gray casual outfit, LJN, 1982, 11½", MIB.......**55.00**

Debbie Boone, Mattel, 1978, 11½", MIB **100.00**

Dennis Rodman, Street Players, 1990s, 12", MIB............... **30.00**

Dolly Parton, plastic and vinyl with painted features, Eegee/Goldberger, 1987 only, 17", M, $75.00.

Dorothy Hamill, Ideal, 1977, 11½", MIB **100.00**

Ginger Rogers, World Doll, 1976, limited edition, MIB **100.00**

Humphrey Bogart (Casablanca), Effanbee, 1989, 16", MIB..**150.00**

James Cagney, Effanbee, 1987, 16", MIB **125.00**

John Travolta (On Stage...), Chemtoy, 1977, 12", MIB **100.00**

Kristi Yamaguchi, Playmates, 1998, 11½", MIB **25.00**

Leann Rimes (Country Music Stars), Exclusive Premiere, 1998, 9", MIB **30.00**

Lucille Ball, Effanbee, 1985, 15", MIB **175.00**

Mae West, Hamilton Gifts, 1991, 17", M **50.00**

Mandy Moore, Play Along, 2000, 11½", MIB **20.00**

Marylin Monroe, DSI, 1993, 11½", MIB **50.00**

Muhammad Ali, Hasbro, 1997, 12", MIB **45.00**

Muhammad Ali, Mego, 1976, 9", MOC............................... **150.00**

Robert Crippen (Astronaut), Kenner, 1997, 12", MIB .. **45.00**

Selena, Arm Enterprises, 1996, 11½", MIB **85.00**

Eegee

The Goldberger company made these dolls, Eegee (E.G.) being the initials of the company's founder. Dolls marked 'Made in China' were made in 1986.

Andy, molded & painted hair, 1963, 12" **35.00**

Annette, vinyl, rooted hair, teen fashion, 1963, 11½", EX.. **50.00**

Babette, 1962, 11½", M **75.00**

Baby Luv, 1973, 15", VG........**25.00**

Baby Susan, 1958, 8½", EX+ . **25.00**

Ballerina, hard plastic w/vinyl head, 1964, 31", EX **100.00**

Little Debutantes, swivel waist & high-heeled feet, 1958, 18", EX.... **50.00**

Miss Sunbeam, plastic & vinyl, 1968, 17", M **25.00**

Posey Playmate, foam & vinyl, 1969, 18", M **20.00**

Shelly, grow hair, 1964, 12"... **18.00**

Susan Stroller, walker, ca 1955, 26", EX............................... **8.00**

Tandy Talks, pull-string talker, 1961, 20", EX................... **55.00**

Effanbee

This company has been in business since 1910, continually producing high quality dolls, some of all composition, some composition and cloth, and a few in plastic and vinyl. In excellent condition, some of the older dolls often bring $300.00 and up.

Alyssa, walker, 1960-61, 23" . **90.00**
Andy, 1963, 12", EX **35.00**
Baby Lisa Grows Up, 1983, M in trunk w/wardrobe **150.00**
Honey, 1949-55, 14", M **500.00**
Miss Chips, 1966-81, 17", EX . **35.00**
Miss Chips (Black), 15", EX .. **45.00**

Patsyette Red Riding Hood, all composition, molded and painted hair, five-piece body, original clothes, 9", EXIB, $550.00. (Photo courtesy McMasters Doll Auctions)

Polka Dotty, 1954, 21", M **165.00**
Pun'kin, 1966-83, 11", M **30.00**
Suzie Sunshine, 1961-79, 18", M **50.00**

Fisher-Price

Since the mid-1970s, this well-known American toy company has been making a variety of dolls. Many have vinyl heads, rooted hair, and cloth bodies. Most are marked and dated.

Doll, Audrey, #203, 1974-76, EX **25.00**
Doll, Billie, #242, 1978-80, EX. **10.00**
Doll, Elizabeth (Black), #205, 1974-76, EX **25.00**
Doll, Mary, #200, 1974-77, EX. **25.00**
Doll, Muffy, #241, 1979-80, EX.. **10.00**
Doll, My Friend Mandy, #216, 1984 only, EX **35.00**
Doll, My Friend Mikey, #205, 1982-84, EX **30.00**
Doll, Natalie, #202, 1974-76, EX **25.00**
Outfit, Let's Go Camping, #222, 1978-79, EX **10.00**
Outfit, Valentine Party Dress, #238, 1984-85, EX **10.00**

Horsman

During the 1930s, this company produced composition dolls of the highest quality. Today many of their dolls are vinyl. Hard plastic dolls marked '170' are also Horsmans.

Answer Doll, 1966, 10", EX ... **15.00**
Baby Tweaks, 1960s, 20", EX.. **30.00**
Betty, 1951, 14", EX **60.00**
Cindy Kay, 1950s+, 15", M **80.00**
Gold Medal Doll, 1953, 26".... **45.00**
Jackie, 1961, 25", M **125.00**
Lady Lee, Storybook Series #442, 1988, 8" **65.00**
Peggy Pen Pal, 1970s, 18", EX. **25.00**
Pippi Longstocking, 1972, 18", M **25.00**

Poor Pitiful Pearl, 1964, 11", VG..**35.00**
Tuffie, 1966, 16", EX+ **20.00**
Tynie Baby, 1950s, 15", EXIB..**110.00**

Ideal

For more than 80 years, this company produced quality dolls that were easily affordable by the average American family. Their Shirley Temple and Toni dolls were highly successful. They're also the company who made Miss Revlon, Betsy Wetsy, and Tiny Tears. For more information see *Collector's Guide to Ideal Dolls* by Judith Izen. See also Dolls, Shirley Temple and Tammy.

Baby Giggles, 1967, 15", MIB. **100.00**
Johnny Playpal, 1959, 24", NM **425.00**
Kissy, 1960s, 22", MIB, from $100 to **125.00**
Miss Ideal (The Photographer's Model), w/Playway Kit, 25", MIB **275.00**
Newborn Thumbelina, 1967, pull string & she wiggles & squirms, 10", M **50.00**
Patti Playful, 1970, 16", EX, from $45 to **65.00**
Patti Prays, 1957, NM **55.00**
Pretty Curls, 1981-82, all original, EX **25.00**
Thumbelina, 18", NMIB, from $150 to **200.00**
Tiny Thumbelina, 1962-68, 14", MIB............................... **185.00**
Toddler Thumbelina, 1960s, complete w/walker, NMIB, from $75 to **100.00**
Upsy Dazy, 1972, 15", EX...... **40.00**

Kenner

This company's dolls range from the 12" jointed teenage glamour dolls to the tiny 3" Mini-Kins with the snap-on changeable clothing and synthetic 'hair' ponytails. (Value for the latter: doll only, $8.00; doll with one outfit, $15.00; complete set, $70.00.)

Baby Bundles, white, 16", M. **20.00**
Baby Yawnie, 1975, 15", M.... **20.00**
Crumpet, 1970, 18", M........... **28.00**
Darcy Cover Girl, 1978, 12½", M **30.00**
Dusty, 12", M......................... **18.00**
Gabbigale, black, 1972, 18", M..**45.00**
Garden Gal, 1972, 6½", M **10.00**
Jenny Jones & Baby, 1972, 9" & 2½", M............................. **20.00**
Rose Petal, scented, 1984, 7", M **20.00**
Steve Scout, 1974, 9", M........ **20.00**
Sweet Cookie, 1972, 18", M...**28.00**

Liddle Kiddles

Produced by Mattel between 1966 and 1971, Liddle Kiddle dolls and accessories were designed to suggest the typical 'little kid' in the typical neighborhood. These dolls can be found in sizes ranging from ¾" to 4", all with poseable bodies and rooted hair that can be restyled. Later, two more series were designed that represented storybook and nursery rhyme characters. The animal kingdom was represented by the Animiddles and Zoolery Jewelry Kiddles. There was even a set of extraterrestrials. And lastly, in 1979 Sweet Treets dolls were marketed.

Items mint on card or mint in box are worth about 50% more than one in mint condition but with none of the original packaging. Based on mint value, deduct 50% for dolls that are dressed but lack accessories. For further information we recommend *Dolls of the 1960s and 1970s, Volumes I* and *II,* by Cindy Sabulis, and *Schroeder's Collectible Toys, Antique to Modern*; both are published by Collector Books.

mint to near-mint condition. For further information, we recommend *Collector's Encyclopedia of Madame Alexander Dolls, 1948 – 1965, Madame Alexander Store Exclusives & Limited Editions,* and *Madame Alexander Collector's Doll Price Guide*; all are by Linda Crowsey and published by Collector Books.

**Pierrot, hard plastic with sleep eyes, walker, original clothes, Alexanderkins #561, 1956, 8",
MIB, $375.00.** (Photo courtesy McMasters Doll Auctions)

Accessory, Liddle Kiddles Klub, #3301, M............................**20.00**
Accessory, Snap-Happy Bedroom, #5172, complete, M.........**15.00**
Doll, Greta Griddle, #3508, complete **85.00**
Doll, Laffy lemon, #3732, MIP.**85.00**
Doll, Lolli-Mint, #3658, MIP . **75.00**
Doll, Santa Kiddle, #3595, MIP.**40.00**
Doll, Shirley Skediddle, #3766, MIP **75.00**
Doll, Sleeping Biddle, #3527, MOC **300.00**
Doll, Windy Fliddle, #3514, complete, M............................**85.00**

Madame Alexander

Founded in 1923, Beatrice Alexander began her company by producing an Alice in Wonderland doll which was all cloth with an oil-painted face. By the 1950s there were over 600 employees making dolls of various materials. The company is still producing lovely dolls today. In the listings that follow, values are for dolls in

Alice in Wonderland, hard plastic, blue w/lace trim, organdy pinafore, 1995, 8" **65.00**
Baseball boy, red & white baseball outfit, 1997, #16313, 8"...**50.00**
Charlene, cloth & vinyl, 1991-92 only, 18" **100.00**
Cissy Bride, porcelain portrait, #52011, 1994 only, 21" ..**350.00**
Dionne Quints, hard plastic, 75th Anniversary set w/carousel, #12230, 1998, 8", complete ..**450.00**
Geranium, vinyl toddler, red organdy dress & bonnet, 1953 only, 9" **100.00**
Indian girl, hard plastic, bent knees, Wendy Ann, #721, 1966 only, 8" **400.00**

Little Women, plastic & vinyl, Nancy Drew, 1969-82, 12", ea **65.00**

Muffin, cloth, 1966 only, 19". **100.00**

Rebecca, plastic & vinyl, Classic Series, 2-tiered pink skirt, Mary Ann, #1485, 1968-69, 14".................................. **150.00**

Smiley, cloth & vinyl, Happy, 1971 only, 20" **250.00**

Tommy, hard plastic, Lissy, 1962 only, 12" **800.00**

Mattel

Though most famous, of course, for Barbie and her friends, the Mattel company also made celebrity dolls, Liddle Kiddles, Chatty Cathy, talking dolls, lots of action figures (the Major Matt Mason line and She-Ra, Princess of Power, for example), and in more recent years, Baby Tenderlove and P.J. Sparkles. See also Barbie; Dolls, Liddle Kiddles. They are listed in the Directory under California.

Baby First Step, 1964, M **95.00**

Baby Fun, 1968, 7", complete, EX, from $30 to **35.00**

Baby Tender Love, 1971, 16", complete, VG.......................... **35.00**

Baby Tippee Toes, 1967, 16", MIB **100.00**

Chatty Cathy, black, 1960s, 15", EX **185.00**

Chatty Cathy, holes in chest, early 1960s, 20", EX, from $250 to **300.00**

Chatty Cathy, 1970 reissue, MIB, from $75 to **100.00**

Dancerella, 1976, 15", MIB ... **75.00**

Magic Baby Tender Love, 1978, 14", MIB.................................. **45.00**

Tearful Tender Love, 1971, 16", VG+................................. **50.00**

Tiny Chatty Baby, EX, from $35 to **50.00**

Nancy Ann Storybook

Nancy Ann Abbott was a multifaceted, multitalented Californian who seemed to excel at whatever was her passion at the moment. Eventually she settled on designing costumes for dolls. This burgeoned into a full-fledged and very successful doll company which she founded in 1937. Early on, her 5" dolls were imported from Japan, but very soon she was making her own dolls, the first of which had jointed legs, while those made in the early '40s had legs molded as part of the body (frozen). But it was their costumes that made the dolls so popular. Many series were designed around various themes — storybook characters; the flower series; Around the World Dolls of every ethnic persuasion; the American girls; sports and family series; and dolls representing seasons, days of the week, and the months of the year. Ms. Abbott died in 1964, and within a year the company closed. To learn more about this extensive line, we recommend *Encyclopedia of Bisque Nancy Ann Storybook Dolls* by Elaine M. Pardee and Jackie Robertson (Collector Books).

Audrey Ann, toddler, 6", VG. **250.00**

Beauty (Beauty & the Beast), lavender dress, #156, M **45.00**

Debut, Commencement Series, all original, 5", NMIB, minimum value **75.00**

Little Betty Blue Wore Her Holiday Show, #190, M **135.00**

Mistress Mary Quite Contrary, #119 .... **50.00**

Muffie, 1953-56, 8", M **185.00**

Over the Hills, #114, M **135.00**

See Saw Marjorie Daw, #177, M.. **55.00**

Silks & Satin, fabric w/painted stripes, #168, M **500.09**

Talking Snow White, MIB... **150.00**

Raggedy Ann and Andy

Designed by Johnny Gruelle in 1915, Raggedy Ann was named by combining two James Whitcomb Riley poem titles, *The Raggedy Man* and *Orphan Annie*. The early cloth dolls he made were dated and had painted-on features. Though these dolls are practically nonexistent, they're easily identified by the mark, 'Patented Sept. 7, 1915.' P.F. Volland made these dolls from 1920 to 1934; theirs were very similar in appearance to the originals. The Mollye Doll Outfitters were the first to print the now-familiar red heart on her chest, and they added a black outline around her nose. These dolls carry the handwritten inscription 'Raggedy Ann and Andy Doll/Manufactured by Mollye Doll Outfitters.' Georgene Averill made them ca 1938 to 1950, sewing their label into the seam of the dolls. Knickerbocker dolls (1963 to 1982) also carry a company label. The Applause Toy Company made these dolls for two years in the early 1980s, and they were finally taken over by Hasbro, the current producer, in 1983.

Besides the dolls, scores of other Raggedy Ann and Andy items have been marketed, including books, radios, games, clocks, bedspreads, and clothing. For more information see *The World of Raggedy Ann Collectibles* by Kim Avery.

Volland, ca 1920s, Ann, 16", $1,350.00; Andy, 17", $750.00. (Photo courtesy McMasters Harris Doll Auctions)

Doll, Applause, Sleepytime, 17", EX, ea from $30 to **35.00**

Doll, Applause, 8", EX, ea from $8 to **12.00**

Doll, Applause, 20", EX, ea from $45 to **55.00**

Doll, Applause, 36", EX, ea from $75 to **80.00**

Doll, Georgene, flowered dress, 1946-63, 19", EX, from $100 to **145.00**

Doll, Georgene, 1946-63, 15", EX, ea from $180 to **210.00**

Doll, Knickerbocker, Korea, 15", EX, ea from $30 to **40.00**

Doll, Knickerbocker, Taiwan, 6", ea from $12 to **15.00**

Doll, Knickerbocker, Taiwan, 15", EX, ea from $50 to **65.00**

Doll, Knickerbocker, Taiwan, 19", EX, ea from $40 to **45.00**

Doll, Knickerbocker, talker, 1974, 12", EX **100.00**

Doll, Knickerbocker, Teach & Dress, 1970s, 20", M, ea from $45 to **50.00**

Doll, Playskool, Christmas Edition, 1990, 12", MIB **40.00**

Doll, Playskool, Heart-to-Heart, battery-operated, 1992, 17" .. **40.00**

Hand puppet, Andy, yarn hair, Knickerbocker, 1960s, EX. **50.00**

Remco

The plastic and vinyl dolls made by Remco during the 1960s and 1970s are gaining popularity with collectors today. Many have mechanical features that were activated either by a button on their back or batteries. The Littlechap Family of dolls (1964), Dr. John, his wife Lisa, and their two children, Judy and Libby, came with clothing and fashion accessories of the highest quality. Children found the family less interesting than the more glamorous fashion dolls on the market at that time, and as a result, production was limited. These dolls in excellent condition are valued at about $15.00 to $20.00 each, while their outfits range from about $30.00 (loose and complete) to a minimum of $50.00 (MIB).

Baby Crawl Along, 1967, 20", MIB **25.00**

Baby Grow a Tooth, 1968, 15", MIB **25.00**

Growing Sally, 6", MIB **45.00**

Jumpsy, 1970, 14", MIB........ **20.00**

Mimi, battery-operated singer, white or Black, 1973, 19", MIB, from $50 to **60.00**

Pip, 1967, 6", EX **20.00**

Tipp Tumbles, 1968, 16", MIB. **55.00**

Shirley Temple

The public's fascination with Shirley was more than enough reason for toy companies to literally deluge the market with merchandise of all types decorated with her likeness. Dolls were a big part of that market, and the earlier composition dolls in excellent condition are often priced at a minimum of $600.00 on today's market. Many were made by the Ideal Company, who in the 1950s also issued a line of dolls made of vinyl. For more information, we recommend *The Complete Guide to Shirley Temple Dolls and Collectibles* by Tonya Bervaldi-Camaratta.

Bisque, Armand Marseille, jointed, white dress w/red dots, 22", VGIB **135.00**

Composition, wig, chubby face w/6 teeth, pinafore, 13", VGIB. **400.00**

Composition, wig, sleep eyes, white dress w/blue dots, 17", EX **750.00**

Composition, wig, sleep eyes, white dress w/red dots, 27", VGIB **900.00**

Plastic, Ideal, white dress w/red dots, 1973, 17", MIB **40.00**

Vinyl, rooted hair, black & white velvet dress, w/purse, 19", EX **375.00**

Vinyl, rooted hair, sleep eyes, blue dress w/flocking, 15", NM.**200.00**

Vinyl, rooted hair, sleep eyes, pink taffeta dress, 36", EX....**900.00**

Vinyl, rooted hair, sleep eyes, Scottish outfit, 1957, 22", NM.............................. **250.00**

Vinyl, rooted hair, sleep eyes, w/print pinafore & purse, 12", NM.................................**350.00**

Vinyl, Wards Yesterday's Darling, 1972, 15", MIB **125.00**

Strawberry Shortcake

Strawberry Shortcake and friends came onto the market around 1980 and quickly captured the hearts of little girls everywhere. A line of accessories and related merchandise were soon added. Strawberry Shortcake vanished from the scene in the mid-1980s but has currently reappeared. The originals have become highly collectible.

Big Berry Trolly, 1982, EX **40.00**

Doll, Almond Tea, 6", MIB..... **30.00**

Doll, Angel Cake & Souffle, 6", NRFB.............................. **40.00**

Doll, Apple Dumpling, cloth w/yarn hair, 12", EX+.................. **25.00**

Doll, Apricot, 15", NM............**35.00**

Doll, Baby Needs a Name, 15", NM **35.00**

Doll, Berry Baby Orange Blossom, 6", MIB **35.00**

Doll, Butter Cookie, 6", MIB .**25.00**

Doll, Cafe Olé, 6", MIB **45.00**

Doll, Cherry Cuddler, 6", NRFB.**45.00**

Doll, Huckleberry Pie, flat hands, 6", MIB **45.00**

Doll, Lemon Meringue, cloth w/yarn hair, 15", EX **24.00**

Doll, Lemon Meringue, 6", MIB.**45.00**

Doll, Lime Chiffon, 6", MIB... **45.00**

Doll, Mint Tulip, 6", MIB....... **50.00**

Doll, Orange Blossom & Marmalade, 6", MIB **45.00**

Doll, Peach Blush & Melonie Belle, 6", MIB **115.00**

Doll, Purple Pieman w/Berry Bird, poseable, MIB................. **35.00**

Strawberry Shortcake doll of 1980, came with cat named Custard, 5½", EX, $25.00 (NRFB, $125.00).

Doll, Strawberry Shortcake & Custard, 6", NRFB........ **150.00**

Doll, Strawberry Shortcake & Strawberrykin, 6", NRFB **295.00**

Dollhouse, no accessories, M.**200.00**

Figurine, Strawberry Shortcake, ceramic, 5", EX.................. **8.00**

Ice skates, EX.......................... **35.00**

Miniature figure, Almond Tea w/Marza Panda, PVC, 1", MOC.......... **15.00**

Miniature figure, Cherry Cuddler w/Gooseberry, PVC, 1", MOC **18.00**

Miniature figure, Lemon Chiffon w/balloons, PVC, 1", MOC.............. **15.00**

Miniature figure, Lemon Meringue w/Frappo, PVC, 1", MOC .**15.00**

Miniature figure, Merry Berry Worm, MIB **35.00**

Miniature figure, Mint Tulip w/March Mallard, PVC, 1", MOC **15.00**

Miniature figure, Raspberry Tart w/bowl of cherries, PVC, 1", MOC................................. **15.00**

Miniature figure, Sour Grapes w/Dregs, PVC, 1", MOC.. **18.00**

Pillow doll, Huckleberry Pie, 9", EX **10.00**

Roller skates, EX **35.00**

Sleeping bag, EX.................... **25.00**

Storybook Play Case, M......... **35.00**

Stroller, Coleco, 1981, M........ **85.00**

Telephone, Strawberry Shortcake figure, battery-operated, EX . **85.00**

Tammy

In 1962 the Ideal Novelty & Toy Company introduced their teenage Tammy doll. Slightly pudgy and not quite as sophisticated as some of the teen fashion dolls on the market at the time, Tammy's innocent charm captivated consumers. Her extensive wardrobe and numerous accessories added to her popularity with children. Tammy had everything including a car, a house, and a catamaran. In addition, a large number of companies obtained licenses to issue products using the 'Tammy' name. Everything from paper dolls to nurse's kits were made with Tammy's image on them. Tammy's success was not confined to the United States. She was also successful in Canada and in several European countries. Doll values listed here are for mint-in-

box examples. (Loose dolls are generally about half mint-in-box value as they are relatively common.) Other values are for mint-condition items without their original packaging. (Such items with their original packaging or in less-than-mint condition would then vary up or down accordingly.)

Accessory, Hot Dog Stand, #5002, complete, M **25.00**

Accessory Pak, Misty Hair Color Kit, #9828-5, MIB **75.00**

Accessory Pak, poodle on a leash, #9186-80, NRFB.............. **25.00**

Case, Dodi, green background, EX................................... **30.00**

Case, Misty, pink & white, EX. **25.00**

Case, Tammy Model Miss, hatbox style, blue or black, EX... **30.00**

Doll, Dodi, MIB **75.00**

Doll, Misty, MIB................... **100.00**

Doll, Patti, MIB.................... **200.00**

Doll, Pos'n Pepper, MIB......... **75.00**

Doll, Tammy, MIB.................. **85.00**

Doll, Tammy (Grown-Up), MIB .**85.00**

Doll, Tammy's Dad, MIB **65.00**

Doll, Tammy's Mom, MIB...... **75.00**

Doll, Ted, MIB **50.00**

Outfit, Dad & Ted, sweater, shorts & socks, #9476-3, MIP.... **25.00**

Outfit, Tammy, Private Secretary, #9939-0, MIP................. **100.00**

Outfit, Tammy's Mom, Lazy Days, #9418-5, MIP................... **50.00**

Vogue

This is the company that made the Ginny doll famous. She was first made in composition during the late 1940s, and if you could find her in mint condition, she'd bring about $450.00 on today's market. (Played with and in relatively sad condition, she's still worth about $90.00.) Ginnys from the 1950s were made of rigid vinyl. The last Ginny came out in 1969. Tonka bought the rights in 1973, but the dolls they produced sold poorly. After a series of other owners, Dakin purchased the rights in 1986 and began producing a vinyl doll that resembled the 1950-style Ginny very closely. For more information, we recommend *Collector's Encyclopedia of Vogue Dolls* by Judith Izen and Carol Stover (Collector Books).

Baby Dear, original, 1960s, 16",
   EX **165.00**
Cheryl (Tiny Miss), 8", EX... **400.00**
Crib Crowd, baby w/curved legs,
   poodle-cut wig, 1950, 8". **175.00**
Ginette, open mouth w/painted
   eyes, 1955-69, 8" **50.00**

Ginny, Far-Away Lands series, missing original hat, Made in Hong Kong, copyright 1972, 8", from $20.00 to $25.00.

Ginny (Gym Kids), walker, ca 1956-
   57, 8" **150.00**
Ginny (Nurse), walker, 1956, 8",
   EX **325.00**

Ginny (Sasson), slimmer body,
   1981-82, 8", EX **35.00**
Jan, rigid body w/swivel waist,
   1958-60, 10½", EX......... **150.00**
Kay (Kindergarten Series), 1952,
   8", EX............................. **450.00**
Miss Ginny, soft vinyl head that
   tilts, 1962-64, 15", EX+ .. **50.00**

Doorstops

Doorstops, once called door porters, were popular from the Civil War period until after 1930. They were used to prop the doors open during the hot summer months so that the cooler air could circulate. Though some were made of brass, wood, and chalk, cast iron was by far the most preferred material, usually molded in amusing figurals — dogs, flower baskets, frogs, etc. Hubley was one of the largest producers. Beware of reproductions! All of the examples in the listing that follows are made of cast iron and are priced relative to the condition code in the description. See Clubs and Newsletters for information concerning the Doorstop Collectors of America.

Aunt Jemima, hands on hips, Littco
   Products, 13½", EX+ **550.00**
Bellhop, flat-sided, CJO, 9",
   EX+ **400.00**
Bird dog (Setter) pointing on grassy
   base, National Foundry, 6x12",
   EX **475.00**
Bobby Blake holding teddy bear,
   Grace Dayton design, Hubley,
   9", EX............................. **250.00**

Cape Cod cottage w/white picket fence, Eastern Specialty Co, 6x9", NM........................**475.00**

Cat w/hunched back and tail up, 10½x7½", NM.................**375.00**

Cats (white girl/black boy) arm-in-arm, marked 73, 7", EX+..**525.00**

Dog w/spots, striding, flat-sided, stylized, Taylor Cook, 8", EX+............................. **400.00**

Drum major, 13½", EX+.......**325.00**

Elephant w/tusks getting coconut from palm tree, flat, 14x10", EX **325.00**

Equestrian girl jumping hurdle, flat-sided, 7x7", EX+.....**500.00**

Fireplace w/lady at spinning wheel, flat-sided, 6x8", EX **200.00**

Flower basket w/ribbon bow 'handle,' multicolored, Hubley, 11", EX+...............................**250.00**

Fruit bowl, multicolored, Hubley, 7x6½", NM **165.00**

Geese (3), side-view, white w/orange beaks, 8x8", EX+...........**400.00**

Girl on round rug holding bonnet at side, Waverly Studio, 8", EX.................................**525.00**

Gnome w/pipe in mouth reclining, no base, 10" L, EX+ **375.00**

Iris (3) bouquet on base, Hubley, marked 469, 10½x7", EX+.**400.00**

Koala bear on log, stylized, No 5 copy, Taylor Cook, 1930, 8" L, EX+ **850.00**

Lady standing holding skis in crook of arm, 12½", EX+ **1,300.00**

Lady w/fan, poofed skirt w/layers of scallops, hair plume, 9½", NM **350.00**

Organ grinder w/monkey at feet, double-sided side view, 10", NM+............................**1,000.00**

Pansies in footed bowl, multicolored, Hubley, 7x6½", EX+.........**165.00**

Pheasant w/head turned back, realistic, Fred Everett, 8½x7½", NM **450.00**

Rabbit in tails & top hat, flat-sided side view, Albany, 10", EX+ **700.00**

Rooster crowing, flat-sided side view w/leafy base, 10x6", EX+.**550.00**

Scottie dog seated w/embossed red collar, Hubley, 11x15", NM **975.00**

Sea Serpent, S-shaped wedge style, Spencer design, 10½", EX.**100.00**

Stork w/beak resting on chest, no base, realistic, Hubley, 12", EX...**400.00**

Swallows (2) on stump w/red berries, flat-sided, Hubley, 8½", EX+.**8.50**

Terrier standing on base, Spencer, 5¼x6", EX **100.00**

Windmill, National Foundry #10 Cape Cod, 6¾x7", EX....**200.00**

Woman w/hand-held basket on head, colorful apron, 12", NM.**1,100.00**

Lantern, realistic paint, metal handle, 13x5", M, $175.00; The Constitution in ocean waves, A.M. Greenblatt Studios, 1924, 11¾x8½", VG/EX, $165.00.

Dragon Ware

Dragon ware is fairly accessible and still being made today. The new Dragon ware is distinguishable by the lack of detail in the dragon, which will appear flat.

Colors are primary, referring to background color, not the color of the dragon. New pieces are shinier than old. New colors include green, lavender, yellow, pink, blue, pearlized, and orange as well as the classic blue/black. Many cups have lithophanes in the bottom. Nude lithophanes are found but are scarce. New pieces may have lithophanes; but again, these tend to be without detail and flat.

Items listed below are unmarked unless noted otherwise. Ranges are given for pieces that are currently being produced. Be sure to examine unmarked items well; in particular, look for good detail. Newer pieces lack the quality of workmanship evident in earlier items and should not command the prices of the older ware. Use the low end to evaluate any item you feel may be new.

Aladdin lamp, 3-legged, orange, 6", from $20 to **35.00**
Ashtray, ball form, gray w/gold, Occupied Japan, 2½x4", from $40 to **55.00**
Biscuit jar, footed, orange, 6", from $35 to **50.00**
Chocolate pot, gray, MIJ, 7", from $25 to **50.00**
Cigarette box w/2 ashtrays, gray, marked Hand Painted, from $50 to **75.00**
Condiment set, tray w/8 pcs (including lids), gray, from $75 to **150.00**
Cup & saucer, child size, green, D China, from $10 to **20.00**

Cup & saucer, 6-sided, gray, from $10 to **20.00**

Demitasse cup and saucer, gray with lithophane, 2¼", 4", from $45.00 to $60.00.

Dish, gray, divided, TT HH Jade in Japan, 8x6", from, $75 to **125.00**
Dresser box, footed, MIJ, 4½x5¼", from $50 to **60.00**
Ginger jar, orange, 6", from $25 to **75.00**
Hatpin holder, gray, Nippon, 5", from $50 to **175.00**
Incense burner, black w/gold handles & finial, 3x3¼", from $15 to **45.00**
Juice set, elephant decanter & 4 cups, black & white **250.00**
Lamp, blue lustre, Napco, miniature, from $15 to **20.00**
Nappy, blue, from $20 to **60.00**
Pitcher, dark blue, miniature, 2¼", from $10 to **20.00**
Planter, hanging, gray, marked Hand Painted Japan, 6", from $75 to **125.00**
Salt & pepper shakers, gray, 6", pr from $15 to **25.00**
Teapot, gray, from $50 to **75.00**
Trinket box, pink lustre, 1½x5", from $20 to **40.00**
Vase, bulbous, black, 3¼" **45.00**
Vase, w/handle, yellow, 3", from $10 to **25.00**

Wall pocket, orange, Made in Japan, 9", from $50 to **75.00**

Egg Timers

The origin of the figural egg timer appears to be Germany, circa 1920s or 1930s, with Japan following their lead in the 1940s. Some American companies may have begun producing figural timers at about the same time, but evidence is scarce in terms of pottery marks or company logos.

Figural timers can be found in a wide range of storybook characters (Oliver Twist), animals (pigs, ducks, rabbits), career and vocational uniformed people (chef, London Bobby, housemaid), or people in native costume.

All types of timers were a fairly uniform height of 3" to 4". If a figural timer no longer has its sand tube, it can be recognized by the hole which usually goes through the back of the figure or the stub of a hand. Most timers were made of ceramic (china or bisque), but a few are of cast iron and carved wood. They can be detailed or quite plain. Listings below are for timers with their sand tubes completely intact.

Boy with yellow hat, red scarf, and blue pants beside timer, black Japan mark, 5", from $30.00 to $45.00. (Photo courtesy Carol Bess White)

Bellhop on phone, Japan, 3".. **50.00**
Black cat & grandfather clock w/timer beside, painted composition, 4" **45.00**
Chef (Black), seated w/timer in right hand, German mark, 3½" .. **75.00**
Chicken on nest, green plastic, England, 2½" **25.00**
Chimney sweep w/ladder in 1 hand, timer in other, porcelain, 3". **75.00**
Dutch boy in yellow hat w/timer in left hand, Japan, 2½" **45.00**
Elf standing beside mushroom on base, plastic, Casdon/England, 3x5" **35.00**
Little Red Riding Hood w/wolf at feet, porcelain, Germany, 1930s, 3" **60.00**
Maid w/towel over left arm, timer in right hand, Japan, 1940s-50s, 4" **70.00**
Monks (2) on base w/timer in between, Goebel, full bee mark, 3¾" **175.00**
Mrs Santa w/timer in toy bag. **75.00**
Pixie w/arm extended holding timer, Enesco, 5¾x3" **60.00**
Sailboat, plastic, Made in Great Britian, 1950s-60s, 4½"... **38.00**
Santa Claus & present, Sonsco, Japan, 5½" **75.00**
Sea gull, lustre, Germany ... **100.00**
Shoe (wooden) holds 3-minute timer w/pink sand, Lewis 101/11, 6" **32.00**
Sultan holding glass timer w/pink sand, porcelain, Germany, 1920s-30s **90.00**

Elegant Glass

To quote Gene and Cathy Florence, Elegant glassware 'refers

mostly to hand-worked, acid-etched glassware that was sold by better departmant and jewelry stores during the Depression era through the 1950s, differentiating it from dime store and give-away glass that has become known as Depression glass. Cambridge, Duncan & Miller, Fostoria, Heisey, Imperial, Morgantown, New Martinsville, Paden City, Tiffin, U.S. Glass, and Westmoreland were major producers. For further information we recommend *Elegant Glassware of the Depression Era,* by Gene and Cathy Florence (Collector Books).

Cambridge

Mt. Vernon, candlestick, amber, footed, 4 x 4½", from $15.00 to $22.00.
(Photo courtesy Gene and Cathy Florence)

Apple Blossom, bowl, baker; green or pink, 10".....................**110.00**
Apple Blossom, bowl, cereal; crystal, 6" **35.00**
Apple Blossom, plate, bread & butter; amber or yellow, 6" ..**10.00**
Apple Blossom, plate, dinner; green or pink, 9½" **115.00**
Candlelight, bonbon, crystal, w/handles, footed, #3900/130, 7"...................................**40.00**

Candlelight, cup, crystal, #3900/17.........................**33.00**
Candlelight, plate, salad; crystal, #3900/22, 8".....................**22.00**
Candlelight, vase, crystal, footed, #279, 13".........................**175.00**
Caprice, coaster, pink, #13, 3½" **35.00**
Caprice, pitcher, crystal, ball shape, #179, 32-oz **135.00**
Caprice, tumbler, blue, footed, #9, 12-oz................................**50.00**
Chantilly, candlestick, crystal, 5"..................................**28.00**
Chantilly, cocktail stem, crystal, #3600, 2½-oz.....................**26.00**
Chantilly, vase, crystal, footed, 13".............................. **150.00**
Cleo, bowl, fruit; amber, green, pink or yellow, 5½"...................**25.00**
Cleo, ice pail, amber, green, pink or yellow..............................**125.00**
Cleo, platter, blue, 12" **195.00**
Daffodil, saucer, crystal, #1170.**5.00**
Daffodil, tumbler, crystal, footed, #1937, 5-oz......................**22.00**
Decagon, bowl, berry; blue, 10".**50.00**
Decagon, compote, pastel colors, 5¾".................................**20.00**
Decagon, cup, blue **11.00**
Decagon, plate, salad; pastel colors, 8½" **15.00**
Diane, bowl, berry; crystal, 5".**32.00**
Diane, plate, crystal, 8½".......**20.00**
Diane, tumbler, crystal, 13-oz.**35.00**
Elaine, candlestick, crystal, 5"............................**35.00**
Elaine, plate, dinner; crystal, 10½".............................. **85.00**
Elaine, tumbler, crystal, #1402, 12-oz..**40.00**
Gloria, bowl, crystal, oval, 4-footed, 12"....................................**85.00**

Gloria, compote, green, pink or yellow, 4" **33.00**

Gloria, plate, dinner; green, pink or yellow, 9½" **110.00**

Gloria, sugar bowl, crystal, footed **20.00**

Imperial Hunt Scene, ice tub, crystal **65.00**

Imperial Hunt Scene, plate, colors, 8" **22.50**

Mt Vernon, candlestick, amber or crystal, #35, 8" **27.50**

Mt Vernon, celery dish, amber or crystal, #98, 11" **17.50**

Mt Vernon, creamer, amber or crystal, footed, 8" **10.00**

Number 520, bowl, cream soup; green or Peach Blo **25.00**

Number 520, cheese plate, all colors, #468 .... **35.00**

Portia, bowl, cranberry; crystal, 3½" **45.00**

Portia, goblet, crystal, #3124, 10-oz **28.00**

Portia, plate, salad; crystal, 8" . **15.00**

Rosalie, bowl, amber or crystal, 11" **40.00**

Rosalie, celery dish, blue, green or pink, 11" **40.00**

Rosalie, platter, amber or crystal, 15" **100.00**

Rosalie, sugar bowl, green or black, footed **20.00**

Rose Point, candlestick, crystal, #3121, 7", ea **110.00**

Rose Point, creamer, crystal, #3500/14 .... **30.00**

Rose Point, relish dish, crystal, 5-part, #3400/67, 12" **90.00**

Tally Ho, ashtray, amber or crystal, 4" **12.50**

Tally Ho, saucer, Carmen or Royal **5.00**

Valencia, ashtray, crystal, round, #3500/124, 3¼" **12.00**

Valencia, bowl, crystal, #1402/88, 11" **50.00**

Valencia, saucer, crystal, #3500/1. **3.00**

Wildflower, candlestick, #3400/646, 5", ea **45.00**

Wildflower, plate, crystal, #3400/176, 7½" **10.00**

Duncan and Miller

Canterbury, basket, crystal, 9x10x7" **55.00**

Canterbury, cake plate, crystal, 14" **25.00**

Canterbury, celery dish, crystal, w/handles, 9x4x1¼" **22.50**

Canterbury, cup, crystal **8.00**

Caribbean, bowl, salad; blue, 9". **75.00**

Caribbean, cruet, crystal **45.00**

Caribbean, plate, salad; crystal, 7½" **10.00**

First Love, bowl, crystal, #115, 3½"..**25.00**

First Love, creamer, crystal, #111, 10-oz, 3" **18.00**

First Love, plate, crystal, 14".. **50.00**

First Love, vase, crystal, footed, #507, 12" **155.00**

Nautical, ashtray, blue, 3" **30.00**

Nautical, plate, crystal, 8" **10.00**

Nautical, sugar bowl, blue..... **45.00**

Plaza, cocktail stem, amber or crystal **12.50**

Plaza, cup, green or pink....... **12.00**

Plaza, parfait, amber or crystal. **15.00**

Sandwich, bowl, nut; crystal, 3½" **10.00**

Sandwich, coaster, crystal, 5".. **12.00**

Sandwich, plate, crystal, 7" **9.00**

Sandwich, tray, crystal, oval, 8". **18.00**

Spiral Flutes, candleholder, amber, green or pink, 3½", ea **25.00**

Spiral Flutes, nappy, amber, pink or green, 7".................. **15.00**

Spiral Flutes, pie plate, amber, green or pink, 6" **3.00**

Spiral Flutes, platter, amber, green or pink, 13"..................... **60.00**

Tear Drop, ashtray, crystal, 5". **8.00**

Tear Drop, bowl, salad; crystal, 12"................................. **40.00**

Tear Drop, ice bucket, crystal, 5½"................................ **85.00**

Tear Drop, sugar bowl, crystal, 6-oz.................................. **6.00**

Terrace, cup, cobalt or red **40.00**

Terrace, plate, amber or crystal, 11"....................................... **30.00**

Terrace, plate, cobalt or red... **25.00**

Fostoria

For more information we recommend *The Fostoria Value Guide* by Milbra Long and Emily Seate, published by Collector Books.

Alexis, nappy, crystal, 5" **15.00**

Alexis, nut bowl, crystal **15.00**

Alexis, spooner, crystal **30.00**

Alexis, toothpick holder, crystal. **15.00**

American, bonbon, crystal, 3-footed, 8"................................. **17.50**

American, bowl, crystal, footed, 8"....................................... **90.00**

American, coaster, crystal, 3¾". **9.00**

Baroque, candlestick, blue, 4". **52.50**

Baroque, pickle dish, crystal, 8". **15.00**

Baroque, saucer, blue............... **7.00**

Baroque, tray, crystal, oval, 12½". **40.00**

Brocade/#73 Palm Leaf, compote, green or rose, #2400, 6". **125.00**

Brocade/#73 Palm Leaf, vase, green or rose, footed, #2421, 10½"... **285.00**

Colony, bowl, crystal, oval, 10½". **60.00**

Colony, ice bucket, crystal **85.00**

Colony, platter, crystal, 12" ... **52.50**

Fairfax, celery dish, green or topaz, 11½"................................ **18.00**

Fairfax, compote, amber, 7"... **15.00**

Fairfax, cup, blue, orchid or rose, footed **14.00**

Fairfax, ice bowl, blue, orchid or rose **25.00**

Fairfax, plate, grill; amber, 10¼"..**18.00**

Fuchsia, bonbon, #2470 .... **33.00**

Fuchsia, bowl, wisteria, #2470, 12" **175.00**

Fuchsia, plate, dinner; crystal, #2440, 9"........................... **67.50**

Fuchsia, tumbler, wisteria, footed, #6004, 12-oz..................... **60.00**

Hermitage, bowl, soup; wisteria, #2449½, 7" **45.00**

Hermitage, relish dish, azure, #2449, 8"........................... **17.50**

June, bowl, blue or rose, 10". **150.00**

June, creamer, crystal, footed . **15.00**

June, tumbler, topaz, footed, 5-oz, 4½" **30.00**

Kashmir, ashtray, green or yellow **25.00**

Kashmir, plate, dinner; blue, 10". **70.00**

Lafayette, bowl, fruit; green, rose or topaz, 5" **22.50**

Lafayette, platter, amber or crystal, 15" **50.00**

Lafayette, saucer, burgundy.... **8.00**

Navarre, candlestick, crystal, #2496, 4", ea.................... **95.00**

Navarre, creamer, footed, crystal, #2440, 4¼" **20.00**

Navarre, saucer, crystal, #2440. **5.00**

New Garland, plate, rose, 9". **35.00**

New Garland, platter, amber or topaz, 15"......................... **50.00**

New Garland, vase, rose, 8" .. **85.00**

Pioneer, cup, blue, flat **15.00**

Pioneer, egg cup, amber, crystal or green **20.00**

Pioneer, plate, ebony, 9" **14.00**

Pioneer, relish dish, azure or orchid, round, 3-part **17.50**

Rogene, cocktail stem, crystal, #5082, 3-oz **18.00**

Rogene, jelly dish, crystal, #825 . **22.50**

Rogene, nappy, crystal, footed, #5078, 7" **30.00**

Royal, ashtray, amber or green, #2350, 3½" **22.50**

Royal, bowl, baker, amber or green, oval, #2350, 9" **45.00**

Royal, chop plate, amber or green, #2350, 13" **35.00**

Royal, tumbler, amber or green, footed, #5000, 12-oz **27.50**

Seville, bowl, cereal; green, #2350, 6½" **25.00**

Seville, candlestick, amber, #2324, 2", ea **18.00**

Seville, egg cup, green, #2350 .. **35.00**

Seville, grapefruit, green, #945½", $30.00. (Photo courtesy Gene and Cathy Florence)

Sun Ray, coaster, crystal, 4" **8.00**

Sun Ray, cup, crystal **12.00**

Sun Ray, jelly dish, crystal **16.00**

Sun Ray, vase, crystal, 7" **50.00**

Trojan, bowl, baker, topaz, #2375, 9" **75.00**

Trojan, candlestick, rose, #2394, 2", ea **25.00**

Trojan, sauceboat, topaz, #2375 .. **105.00**

Versailles, ashtray, green or pink, #2350 .... **30.00**

Versailles, candlestick, yellow, #2394, 2", ea **30.00**

Versailles, ice bucket, blue, #2375 .... **125.00**

Vesper, ashtray, green, #2350, 4" . **24.00**

Vesper, bowl, fruit; amber, #2350, 5½" **18.00**

Vesper, creamer, green, footed, #2350½" **16.00**

Heisey

For more information we recommend *Heisey Glass, 1896 – 1957,* by Neila and Tom Bredehoft, published by Collector Books.

Charter Oak, compote, Flamingo, footed, #3362, 7" **65.00**

Charter Oak (Acorn & Leaves), plate, salad; Hawthorne, #1246, 6" .. **20.00**

Chintz, bowl, cream soup; crystal **18.00**

Chintz, cup, Sahara **25.00**

Chintz, oil bottle, crystal, 4-oz . **60.00**

Chintz, platter, Sahara, oval, 14" . **85.00**

Empress, ashtray, Flamingo . **175.00**

Empress, bonbon, Sahara, 6" .. **25.00**

Greek Key, coaster, crystal **20.00**

Greek Key, finger bowl, crystal .. **40.00**

Ipswich, creamer, green **125.00**

Ipswich, sugar bowl, Sahara . **90.00**

Lariat, cup, crystal **20.00**

Lariat, nappy, crystal, 7" **20.00**

Lariat, plate, salad; crystal, 7" . **14.00**

Minuet, bowl, oval, crystal, #1514, 12" **65.00**

Minuet, plate, salad; crystal, 7" . **18.00**

Minuet, tumbler, fruit juice; crystal, #5010, 5-oz **34.00**

New Era, creamer, crystal..... **37.50**
New Era, sugar bowl, crystal . **37.50**
Octagon, creamer, Flamingo, #500 .... **30.00**
Octagon, plate, Moongleam, 14". **35.00**
Octagon, plate, sandwich; Sahara, #1229, 10" **25.00**
Old Colony, celery tray, Sahara, 10" **30.00**
Old Colony, nappy, Sahara, 4½". **14.00**
Old Colony, plate, Sahara, round 12" **75.00**
Old Sandwich, compote, Flamingo, 6" **95.00**
Old Sandwich, finger bowl, crystal **12.00**
Old Sandwich, plate, Sahara, sq, 7" **25.00**
Old Sandwich, saucer, Moongleam **25.00**
Pleat & Panel, creamer, hotel; Flamingo.......................... **25.00**
Pleat & Panel, plate, crystal, 6". **4.00**
Pleat & Panel, vase, Moongleam, 8" **100.00**
Provincial, mustard, crystal. **140.00**
Provincial, plate, luncheon; Limelight Green, 8" **50.00**
Provincial, vase, sweet pea; crystal, 6" **45.00**
Queen Ann, jug, crystal, footed, 3-pt **100.00**
Queen Ann, platter, crystal, 14".**30.00**
Queen Ann, vase, crystal, flared, 8" **55.00**
Ridgeleigh, ashtray, crystal, round **14.00**
Ridgeleigh, celery tray, crystal, 12" **40.00**
Ridgeleigh, cheese dish, crystal, w/handles, 6" **22.00**
Saturn, ashtray, Limelight Green or Zircon **150.00**

Saturn, finger bowl, crystal... **15.00**
Saturn, plate, luncheon; crystal, 8" **10.00**
Stanhope, bowl, salad; crystal, 11" **90.00**
Stanhope, plate, crystal, 7" ... **20.00**
Twist, claret, crystal, 4-oz...... **15.00**
Twist, ice tub, Sahara.......... **125.00**
Victorian, plate, sandwich; crystal, 13" **90.00**
Victorian, vase, crystal, footed, 6" **100.00**
Waverly, cup, crystal.............. **14.00**
Waverly, saucer, crystal **4.00**
Yeoman, celery tray, Flamingo, 9" **14.00**
Yeoman, plate, Marigold, 6".. **15.00**
Yeoman, tumbler, Sahara, 12-oz **25.00**

Imperial

Beaded Block, creamer & sugar bowl, pink........................ **50.00**
Beaded Block, plate, ice blue, 7¾" **80.00**
Cape Cod, bowl, crystal, tab handles, 6½"........................... **40.00**
Cape Cod, bowl, vegetable; crystal, oval, 11" **65.00**
Cape Cod, cake plate, crystal, 4-toed, 10"........................ **100.00**
Cape Cod, candy dish, crystal, w/lid, 1-lb........................ **85.00**
Cape Cod, cologne bottle, w/stopper **75.00**
Cape Cod, cruet, amber, w/stopper **30.00**
Cape Cod, mint dish, crystal, w/handles, 3".................. **20.00**
Cape Cod, pepper mill, crystal. **30.00**
Cape Cod, puff box, crystal, w/lid **80.00**

Cape Cod, relish dish, crystal, 5-part, 11" **55.00**

Cape Cod, tumbler, crystal, 10-oz.. **10.00**

Crocheted Crystal, basket, 7½".. **30.00**

Crocheted Crystal, celery dish, oval, 10" **25.00**

Crocheted Crystal, console bowl, 12" **35.00**

Crocheted Crystal, hurricane lamp, 11" **75.00**

Crocheted Crystal, mayonnaise plate, 7½" **7.50**

Crocheted Crystal, sherbet, 6-oz, 5" **30.00**

Hobstar, butter dish, marigold carnival, 8" **50.00**

Mt Vernon, bonbon, crystal, footed, #10, 7" **12.50**

Mt Vernon, claret, crystal, 4½". **13.50**

Mt Vernon, compote, belled, 6½". **22.50**

Mt Vernon, plate, salad; crystal, 8½" **7.00**

Zippered Heart, bowl, amethyst carnival, 5" **55.00**

Crucifix candlestick, amethyst, $150.00 each. (Photo courtesy Gene and Cathy Florence)

Morgantown

Golf Ball, bell, colors other than cobalt, green or red **60.00**

Golf Ball, creamer, green or red **175.00**

Golf ball, stem, aquamarine, 3⅞", $30.00. (Photo courtesy Gene and Cathy Florence)

Golf Ball, stem, cocktail; green or red, 3½-oz, 4½" **26.00**

Janice, basket, blue or red, 11". **215.00**

Janice, plate, crystal, 15" **40.00**

Meadow Wreath, bowl, crystal, crimped, #4220/26, 10" ... **40.00**

Meadow Wreath, plate, crystal, #42/26, 14" **45.00**

Queen Louise, plate, salad; crystal w/pink **150.00**

Queen Louise, water goblet, crystal w/pink, 9-oz **400.00**

Sunrise Medallion, cup, crystal.. **40.00**

Sunrise Medallion, sherbet, blue............................. **20.00**

Sunrise Medallion, tumbler, green or pink, footed, 4-oz, 3½" . **35.00**

Sunrise Medallion, tumbler, green or pink, footed, 9-oz, 4¾" . **40.00**

Tinkerbell, vase, azure, ruffled rim, footed, Uranus #26, 10". **350.00**

Tinkerbell, wine goblet, azure or green, 2½-oz................... **135.00**

New Martinsville

Addie, candlestick, black, cobalt, jade or red, 3½" **30.00**

Janice, basket, crystal, 11".... **75.00**

Janice, creamer, blue or red, 6-oz................................. **20.00**

Janice, ice pail, crystal, w/handles, 10".....................................85.00

Janice, platter, blue or red, oval, 13".....................................90.00

Janice, syrup, crystal.............75.00

Meadow Wreath, bowl, crystal, flat, crimped, #4212, 12".........45.00

Moondrops, decanter, blue or red, 8½".....................................70.00

Moondrops, mug, blue or red, 12-oz, 5⅛".....................................40.00

Prelude, bowl, crystal, shallow, 13".45.00

Prelude, plate, crystal, 3-footed, 10".30.00

Prelude, plate, crystal, 8"............10.00

Prelude, saucer, crystal.................5.00

Paden City

Black Forest, cake plate, amber, 2" pedestal foot.....................75.00

Black Forest, candy dish, amber, w/lid, several styles, ea.135.00

Black Forest, egg cup, green.150.00

Black Forest, finger bowl, green, 4½".....................................40.00

Black Forest, tumbler, old-fashioned; green or pink, 8-oz, 4"......65.00

Black Forest, water goblet, crystal, 9-oz, 6".............................22.50

Black Forest, wine goblet, crystal, 2-oz, 4¼"...........................17.50

Gazebo, cake stand, crystal...65.00

Gazebo, candlestick, crystal, 5¼", ea......................................45.00

Gazebo, plate, crystal, 10¾"..45.00

Gazebo, relish dish, blue, 3-part, 9¾".....................................60.00

Tiffin

Cadena, bowl, cream soup; crystal...................................25.00

Cadena, finger bowl, crystal..25.00

Cadena, plate, crystal, 9¼"....45.00

Cadena, plate, pink or yellow, 6".................................12.00

Cherokee Rose, plate, crystal, 8"..15.00

Cherokee Rose, table bell, crystal................................75.00

Classic, bud vase, crystal, 6½".27.50

Classic, cup, crystal..............60.00

Classic, plate, pink, 8"..........20.00

Flanders, ashtray, crystal, 2¼x3¾"..........................55.00

Flanders, compote, yellow, 6".95.00

Flanders, fan vase, pink......250.00

Flanders, relish dish, pink, 3-part..............................90.00

Fontaine, candlestick, amber, green or pink, low, #9758, ea....35.00

Fontaine, cup, Twilight, #8869.125.00

Fontaine, plate, amber, green or pink, #8818, 10"..............65.00

Fuchsia, saucer, crystal, #5831..15.00

Julia, cream pitcher, amber trim............................30.00

Julia, plate, dessert; amber trim............................12.00

Julia, sugar bowl, amber.......35.00

June Night, bowl, crystal, crimped, 12"....................................65.00

June Night, parfait stem, crystal, 4½-oz...............................38.00

June Night, relish dish, crystal, 3-part, 6½".........................35.00

Jungle Assortment, basket, any color, #151, 6".................85.00

Jungle Assortment, candy jar, any color, footed, #15179.......55.00

Jungle Assortment, wall vase, any color, #320.......................75.00

Elvis Presley

The king of rock 'n roll, the greatest entertainer of all time (and not many would disagree with that), Elvis remains just as popular today as he was in the height of his career. Over the past few years, values for Elvis collectibles have skyrocketed. The early items marked 'Elvis Presley Enterprises' bearing a 1956 or 1957 date are the most valuable. Paper goods such as magazines, menus from Las Vegas hotels, ticket stubs, etc., make up a large part of any Elvis collection and are much less expensive. His 45s were sold in abundance, so unless you find an original Sun label, a colored vinyl or a promotional cut, or EPs in wonderful condition, don't pay much! The picture sleeves are usually worth much more than the record itself! Albums are very collectible, and even though you see some stiff prices on them at antique malls, there's not many you can't buy for well under $25.00 at any Elvis convention. Remember, the early mark is 'Elvis Presley Enterprises'; the 'Boxcar' mark was used from 1974 to 1977, and the 'Boxcar/Factors' mark from then until 1981. In 1982, the trademark reverted back to Graceland. For more information, we recommend *Elvis Presley Memorabilia* by Sean O'Neal (Schiffer).

Bracelet, wide gold mesh band w/5 oval portraits, 1960s **40.00**
Christmas ornament, gold figure w/guitar, Hallmark, 1979, MIB **22.00**
Clock, Love Me Tender, Unique Time Co, 1977 .... **80.00**
Clutch purse, vinyl, EPE, 1956, 4½x3½", M **365.00**

Dog tags, Elvis standing on record w/guitar, EPE, 1956, MOC.**70.00**

Doll, **Eugene Doll Co., Elvis Presley Enterprises, 1984, 12",
MIB, $55.00.**

Doll, Teen Idol, Hasbro, 1993, NRFB............................... **45.00**
Fan club publication, Elvis for Everyone, 1967, M **18.00**
Game, The Elvis Presley Game, 1956, MIB................... **1,350.00**
Handkerchief, blue border, EPE, 1956, M **450.00**
Mobile, cardboard, in white jumpsuit, RCA, 24x18", M **40.00**
Photo, promotional, black & white, 1956, 8x10", M **50.00**
Plate, Graceland: Memphis Tennessee, Bradford Exchange #13782A, MIB **30.00**
Postcard, Blue Hawaii scene, unused, M......................... **40.00**
Postcard, West Germany, in color, M, from $10 to................. **12.00**
Punching bag balloon, King Galahad, EX.................... **65.00**
Radio, figural, dressed in white, AM, 1970s, M **40.00**
Record, That's All Right/Blue Moon..., Sun #209, original, G **500.00**
Scarf, silky, concert giveaway, M..**40.00**

Ticket, Madison Square Garden, June 1972, EX............... **320.00**

Trading card, Go Go Elvis, #1 of 66, Bubbles Inc, 1956, EX **30.00**

McCormick Decanters

1978, Elvis '77, Love Me Tender, 750 ml............................ **125.00**

1979, Elvis '77 Mini, Love Me Tender, 50 ml.................... **55.00**

1984, Elvis & Rising Sun, Green Green Grass of Home, 750 ml................................ **495.00**

1984, Elvis Designer I Gold, Are You Lonesome Tonight, 750 ml **150.00**

1984, Elvis Designer II Gold, It's Now or Never, 750 ml... **195.00**

1984, Elvis 50th Anniversary, I Want You, I Need You..., 750 ml **495.00**

1985, Elvis Designer I White, Are You Lonesome Tonight, 50 ml............................ **125.00**

1985 Elvis Designer III Gold, Crying in the Chapel, 750 ml **250.00**

1986, Elvis & Gates of Graceland, Welcome to My World, 750 ml................................ **150.00**

1986, Elvis Designer I Gold Mini, Are You Lonesome Tonight, 50 ml **150.00**

1986, Elvis 50th Anniversary Mini, I Want You, I Need You..., 50 ml **250.00**

Enesco

Enesco is an importing company based in Elk Grove, Illinois. They're distributors of ceramic novelties made for them in Japan. There are several lines styled around a particular character or group, and with the emphasis collectors currently place on figurals, they're finding these especially fascinating. During the 1960s, they sold a line of novelties originally called 'Mother-in-the Kitchen.' Today's collectors refer to them as 'Kitchen Prayer Ladies.' Ranging from large items such as canisters and cookie jars to toothpick holders and small picture frames, the line was fairly extensive. Some of the pieces are very hard to find, and those with blue dresses are much scarcer than those in pink. Where we've given ranges, pink is represented by the lower end, blue by the high side. If you find a white piece with blue trim, add another 10% to 20% to the high end.

Another Enesco line that has become very collectible is called 'Kitchen Independence.' It features George Washington with the Declaration of Independence scroll held at his side, and Betsy Ross wearing a blue dress and holding a large flag. See also Cookie Jars.

**Bank, Elmo in Train, Jim Henson Productions, copyright 1993, 5¾",
$45.00.**

Bell, Golden Girl, hood shaped like a rose **15.00**

Bookends, black panther on black w/gold highlights, 5½".....**90.00**

Bookends, boy & girl holding cat by tail, cold paint, 1950s, EX+.**25.00**

Creamer, Kitchen Prayer Lady, 4", from $45 to **60.00**

Creamer & sugar bowl, Chip 'n Dale, 1979, 3" & 4" **85.00**

Creamer & sugar bowl, Snappy the Snail, 4½", pr................... **65.00**

Cup & saucer, water lily on pearl lustre, silver sticker........ **17.50**

Decanter, Sad Hound, hound dog w/hot-water bottle, 1960s-70s, 9½" **25.00**

Egg timer, Kitchen Prayer Lady, from $100 to **140.00**

Figurine, beagle pup, realistic detail, 3¾x5".....................**30.00**

Figurine, Cookie the Cookie Maker, North Pole Village, 2¼", MIB **45.00**

Figurine, Eggbert, chick coming out of egg w/boxing gloves, 1989, MIB................................. **20.00**

Figurine, Eggbert, Eggstinguisher, fireman, 1989, MIB......... **20.00**

Figurine, Eggbert, Running Quack, football player, 1989, MIB..**20.00**

Figurine, Growing Up, young girl in blue dress holding hat, 6½".**12.00**

Figurine, Ivan the Orator, Borzoi dog (Bar Hound) on bar stool, 6" **65.00**

Figurine, Middle-Age Pro, comic golfing man, 5½".............. **25.00**

Figurine, Pity Kitty, orange & black cat w/lg green eyes, 7" **80.00**

Jack-in-the-box, Cowardly Lion (Wizard of Oz), 1988, 8x8", MIB.................................. **90.00**

Mug, Time To Say We Love You, Memories of Yesterday, 1988............................**10.00**

Music box, bunny & bear by picnic basket, plays Brahm's Lullaby, 1984 .... **25.00**

Music box, Eiffel Tower, plays I Love Paris, 17¼", MIB..**110.00**

Music box, Majestic Ferris Wheel, 16x10x11" **210.00**

Music box, Santa's Workshop, 14"..............................**170.00**

Napkin holder, Kitchen Prayer lady, from $20 to **25.00**

Nightlight, Jesus Loves Me on blue cross shape **15.00**

Ornament, Coca-Cola's Trunk Full of Treasures, MIB **35.00**

Ornament, Minnie Mouse holding teapot & teacup, 3", MIB..**5.00**

Pincushion, rocking chair w/cushion in seat & kitty...........**10.00**

Planter, 3 cocker spaniels standing side by side, 4x6x5½" **15.00**

Salt & pepper shakers, Dear God Kids, pr from $35 to........**40.00**

Salt & pepper shakers, Kitchen Prayer Lady, pr from $15 to.............................. **20.00**

Salt & pepper shakers, pixie on mushroom, green, yellow & brown, 4", pr....................**35.00**

Salt & pepper shakers, swans on base, silver-plated, 3-pc set.**18.00**

Soap dish, Kitchen Prayer Lady, from $25 to **35.00**

Spoon holder, Kitchen Prayer Lady, upright, from $40 to........**50.00**

Spoon holder, old lady figure, No Use Crying Over Spilt Milk, 1950s..............................**25.00**

Spoon rest, Kitchen Prayer Lady, from $30 to **40.00**

Sugar bowl, Kitchen Prayer Lady, w/spoon **70.00**

Tea bag holders, Snappy the Snail, pr **20.00**

Teapot, hands & arms form spout & handle, brick wall base, 7½" **130.00**

Teapot, Snappy the Snail, 7x8" **55.00**

Toothpick holder, donkey w/2 baskets on back, 3½x5" **20.00**

Toothpick holder, Kitchen Prayer Lady, 4½" **20.00**

Spoon holder, Kitchen Independence, Betsy Ross figural, 6", from $30.00 to $35.00.

Ertl Banks

The Ertl company was founded in the mid-'40s by Fred Ertl, Sr., and until the early 1980s, they produced mainly farm tractors. In 1981 they made their first bank, the 1913 Model T Parcel Post Mail Service #9647; since then they've produced thousands of models with the logos of countless companies. The size of each run is dictated by the client and can vary from a few hundred up to several thousand. Some clients will later add a serial number to the vehicle; this is not done by Ertl. Other numbers that appear on the base of each bank are a four-number dating code (the first three indicate the day of the year up to 365, and the fourth number is the last digit of the year, '5' for 1995, for instance). The stock number is shown only on the box, never on the bank, so be sure to keep them in their original boxes. For more information, see *Schroeder's Collectible Toys, Antique to Modern* (Collector Books).

Texaco Delivery Truck, Mack Bulldog Tanker, #9238, 1985, M, $250.00.

Ace Hardware, 1925 Kentworth, #F397 .... **20.00**

Alka Seltzer, 1918 Ford, #9155 .. **95.00**

Aunt Jemima Pancakes, 1923 Ford Delivery Truck, MIB **40.00**

Batman, Joker Van **12.00**

Bell Telephone, 1932 Ford, #9803 .... **35.00**

Borden's Dairy, 1950 Divco Delivery Truck **60.00**

Breyer's Ice Cream, 1905 Ford, #9028 .... **65.00**

Budweiser, Clydesdale 8-Horse Hitch & Wagon, 4x19" **65.00**

Canada Dry, 1913 Ford, #2133. **125.00**

Coca-Cola, 1923 Ford Delivery Truck **40.00**

Coca-Cola, 1925 Kenworth, #B398 .... **25.00**

DuPont, 1923 Chevy, #1353 .. **75.00**

Dutch Girl Ice Cream, 1931 Hawkeye, #9049 .... **30.00**

Granny Goose Chips, 1913 Ford, #9979 .... **50.00**

Grapette, 1932 Ford, #9885... **65.00**

Gulf Oil, 1925 Kenworth Wrecker **75.00**

IGA, 1917 Ford Pickup, #F951.. **20.00**

John Deere Servicegard, 1918 Ford Model T, #104 .... **50.00**

Kodak, 1905 Ford, gold spokes, #9985 .... **225.00**

Lennox, 1905 Ford, #9323 ..... **35.00**

Nestle's Crunch, 1931 Hawkeye, #1316 .... **32.00**

North American Van Lines, 1917 Ford Delivery Van **40.00**

Old Milwaukee Beer, 1918 Ford, #9173 .... **35.00**

Pennzoil, 1918 Ford, #7676 ... **30.00**

Quaker Oats, 1931 Hawkeye, #F569 .... **45.00**

Quaker State Oil, 1913 Ford, #9195 .... **95.00**

RCA, 1926 Mack Truck, #9275.. **45.00**

Reese's Pieces, 1950s Chevy, #9809 .... **28.00**

Sears, 1913 Ford, #2129 .... **45.00**

Sinclair Oil, 1946 White Tilt-Cab Tanker, #8 .... **50.00**

Smokey Bear, 1913 Ford, #9124 .. **85.00**

Texaco, Wings of Texaco 1929 Lockheed Air Express, Series #1 .... **175.00**

Thomas English Muffins, 1932 Ford, #9129 .... **50.00**

True Value, 1926 Mack Delivery Van, MIB **80.00**

US Mail, 1918 Ford, #9843 ... **45.00**

Watkins, 1957 Chevy, MIB **50.00**

Watkins Inc, 1913 Ford, #F435 .**45.00**

Winn Dixie, 1918 Ford, #9166. **25.00**

Wix Filters, 1932 Ford, #9810..**125.00**

Fenton

The Fenton glass company, organized in 1906 in Martin's Ferry, Ohio, is noted for their fine art glass. Over 130 patterns of carnival glass were made in their earlier years, but even their newer glass is considered collectible. Only since 1970 have some of the pieces carried a molded-in logo; before then paper labels were used. For more information we recommend *Fenton Art Glass, 1907 – 1939*; *Fenton Art Glass Patterns, 1939 – 1980; Fenton Art Glass Colors and Hand-Decorated Patterns;* and *Fenton Art Glass Hobnail Pattern*; all are by Margaret and Kenn Whitmyer. Two of Fenton's later lines, Hobnail and Silver Crest, are shown in Gene and Cathy Florence's book called *Collectible Glassware from the 40s, 50s, and 60s*. All are published by Collector Books. See also Glass Animals; Glass, Porcelain, and Pottery Shoes. For information on Fenton Art Glass Collectors of America, see Clubs and Newsletters.

Aqua Crest, basket, #192, 1942-43, 7", from $95 to **125.00**

Black Crest, plate, early 1970s, 6", from $14 to **16.00**

Coin Dot, candleholder, cranberry, #1524, 1947-54, ea from $125 to **150.00**

Coin Dot, vase, honeysuckle, #203, 1948-49, 4½", from $60 to **65.00**

Daisy & Button, boot, custard, #1990-CU, 1972-77, from $12 to **15.00**

Daisy & Button, vase, fan; turquoise, footed, #1959-TU, 1955-56, 8".........................**60.00**

Diamond Optic, creamer, rose, #1502, 1927, from $20 to.**25.00**

Diamond Optic, tumbler, orange juice; aquamarine, #1502, 5"...............................**35.00**

Emerald Crest, basket, #7237, 7"............................. **110.00**

Emerald Crest, bowl, salad; heart shape, 10½".....................**95.00**

Georgian, decanter, amber, from $45 to...............................**50.00**

Hobnail, ashtray, milk glass, round, #3973, 5"...........................**10.00**

Hobnail, basket, blue opal, crimped handle, footed, #389, 9"..**75.00**

Hobnail, basket, milk glass, #3834, 4½".................................**17.50**

Hobnail, basket, milk glass, deep, #3637, 7x7"......................**65.00**

Hobnail, candleholder, ruby, dome base, #3974, 3½", ea........**15.00**

Hobnail, fairy light, orange, #3608, 2-pc, 4½"...........................**28.00**

Hobnail, jardiniere, light green, tapered, scalloped, #3994, 4½"................................. **20.00**

Hobnail, nut dish, milk glass, oval, #3633, 7x3½"....................**14.00**

Hobnail, trinket box (old mustard jar mold), blue topaz, #3969...**20.00**

Hobnail, vanity bottle, milk glass, w/stopper, #3865, 5½".....**50.00**

Hobnail, vase, blue opal, ruffled rim, tapers to smooth base, #389, 8"...........................**55.00**

Honeycomb & Clover, tumbler, amethyst opal, from $40 to.....**45.00**

Jade Green, goblet, #139, 1931, from $10 to.....................**12.00**

Leaf, plate, bl opal, 8", from $35 to **40.00**

Lilac, bowl, crimped rim, footed, #857, 1933, 10", from $80 to **85.00**

Ming, bowl, green satin, crimped rim, #-toed, #249, 1935-36, 10½"................................**45.00**

Peach Crest, vase, #5459-PC, 1959-62, 9", from $75 to...........**85.00**

Pulled Feather, candlestick, #3019, ea from $600 to.............**650.00**

Sheffield #1800, vase, ruby, sq, 1936-38, 10", from $22 to..........**24.00**

Silver Crest, bowl, square, flared foot, #77301, from $110.00 to $130.00. (Photo courtesy Margaret and Kenn Whitmyer)

Silver Crest, cup & saucer, #7209-SC, 1956-65, from $25 to..**32.00**

Silver Crest, vase, #7262-SC, 1956-67, 12", from $100 to.....**145.00**

Spiral Optic, bowl, orchid, flared, 1927-30, 10", from $30 to.........................**35.00**

Spiral Optic, vase, cameo opal, #3157-CO, 1978-80, 6½", from $30 to...............................**35.00**

Stretch, candlestick, Celeste Blue, #649, 10", ea from $110 to.**120.00**

Thumbprint, vase, Colonial Blue, #4454-CB, 1964-74, 8", from $20 to...............................**25.00**

Fiesta

Since it was discontinued by Homer Laughlin in 1973, Fiesta has become one of the most popular collectibles on the market. Values have continued to climb until some of the more hard-to-find items now sell for several hundred dollars each. In 1986 HLC reintroduced a line of new Fiesta. To date these colors have been used: cobalt (darker than the original), rose (a strong pink), black, white, apricot (very pale), yellow (a light creamy tone), turquoise, sea mist (a light mint green), lilac, persimmon, periwinkle (country blue), sapphire blue (very close to the original cobalt), chartreuse (brighter), gray, juniper (teal), cinnabar (maroon), sunflower (yellow), plum (dark bluish-purple), shamrock (similar to the coveted medium green), tangerine, scarlet, and peacock. There is a strong secondary market for limited edition and discontinued pieces and colors of the post-86 Fiesta as well. When old molds were used, the mark will be the same, if it is a molded-in mark such as on pitchers, sugar bowls, etc. The ink stamp differs from the old — now all the letters are upper case.

'Original colors' in the listings indicates values for three of the original six colors — light green, turquoise, and yellow. The listing that follows is incomplete due to space restrictions; refer to *The Collector's Encyclopedia of Fiesta, Tenth Edition*, by Sharon and Bob Huxford (Collector Books) for more information. See also Clubs and Newsletters for information on *Fiesta Collector's Quarterly*.

Ashtray, original colors, from $35 to **60.00**

Bowl, cream soup; '50s colors, from $60 to **75.00**

Bowl, cream soup; original colors, from $30 to **60.00**

Bowl, fruit; 4¾", '50s colors, from $30 to **35.00**

Bowl, fruit; 4¾", med green, minimum value..................... **550.00**

Bowl, fruit; 4¾", original colors, from $20 to **30.00**

Bowl, mixing; #2, original colors, from $100 to **150.00**

Bowl, mixing; #6, original colors, from $230 to **300.00**

Bowl, nappy; 9½", original colors, from $55 to **70.00**

Candleholders, bulb; orignal colors, pr from $80 to **130.00**

Candleholders, tripod, yellow or light green, from $450.00 to $600.00 for the pair.

Casserole, original colors, from $150 to **200.00**

Coffeepot, original colors, from $180 to **265.00**

Creamer, regular; '50s colors, from $35 to **45.00**

Cup, demitasse; original colors, from $70 to **100.00**

Egg cup, '50s colors, from $140 to . **160.00**

Mug, Tom & Jerry; original colors, from $50 to 80.00
Pitcher, disk water; '50s colors, from $200 to 275.00
Pitcher, jug; 2-pt, original colors, from $70 to 105.00
Plate, calendar; 9-10", ea from $45 to 55.00
Plate, chop; 13", '50s colors, from $90 to 95.00
Plate, chop; 13", original colors, from $40 to 55.00
Plate, chop; 15", '50s colors, from $135 to 150.00
Plate, chop; 15", original colors, from $70 to 100.00
Plate, compartment; 10½", '50s colors, from $60 to 70.00
Plate, compartment; 10½", original colors, from $35 to 45.00
Plate, compartment; 12", original colors, from $40 to 60.00
Plate, deep; '50s colors, from $50 to 55.00
Plate, deep; med green, from $130 to 145.00
Plate, deep; original colors, from $35 to 60.00
Plate, 6", '50s colors, from $7 to............................... 10.00
Plate, 6", original colors, from $4 to 7.00
Plate, 7", '50s colors, from $10 to..12.00
Plate, 7", original colors, from $7 to 10.00
Plate, 9", '50s colors, from $20 to..25.00
Plate, 9", med green, from $60 to. 75.00
Plate, 9", original colors, from $10 to 20.00
Plate, 10", '50s colors, from $45 to................................... 50.00
Plate, 10", original colors, from $30 to 45.00

Platter, '50s colors, from $50 to .60.00
Platter, med green, from $175 to 225.00
Platter, original colors, from $40 to 55.00
Relish tray, complete, minimum value 300.00
Salt & pepper shakers, '50s colors, pr from $40 to 45.00
Salt & pepper shakers, original colors, pr from $22 to...... 30.00
Sauceboat, original colors, from $40 to 70.00
Sugar bowl, w/lid, med green, 3¼x3½", from $225 to.... 250.00
Sugar bowl, w/lid, original colors, 3¼x3½", from $50 to........ 75.00
Teacup, '50s colors, from $35 to.40.00
Teacup, original colors, from $15 to 40.00
Teapot, med; original colors, from $15 to 250.00
Tray, utility; original colors, from $40 to 50.00
Tumbler, juice; original colors, from $40 to 50.00
Vase, 8", original colors, from $600 to 800.00

Bowl, mixing; 6" 60.00
Cake plate............................... 35.00
Casserole, individual; from $150 to 160.00
Casserole, 8½" 85.00
Covered jar, med, from $275 to. 300.00
Covered jug, lg, from $275 to. 300.00
Pie plate, 9" or 10" (other than Spruce Green) 40.00
Platter, from $60 to................ 75.00
Salt & pepper shakers, pr from $120 to 150.00

Post '86 Line

Bowl, vegetable; apricot, 39-oz. **20.00**
Candlestick, round (bulb); sapphire, ea............................ **45.00**
Carafe, sapphire, from $40 to. **50.00**

Coffee server, lilac, from $150.00 to $160.00.

Creamer & sugar bowl, lilac, w/lid, no handles, from $110 to...... **125.00**
Pitcher, mini disk; apricot, from $45 to **55.00**
Place setting, apricot, 5-pc, from $55 to **70.00**
Plate, chop; 11¾", lilac **65.00**
Plate, dinner; chartreuse, from $9 to **12.00**
Teapot, apricot, 7½", from $50 to.. **60.00**
Tumbler, apricot..................... **15.00**
Tumbler, sapphire **20.00**
Vase, 10", sapphire, from $150 to **165.00**

Fishbowl Ornaments

Mermaids, divers, and all sorts of castles have been devised to add interest to fishbowls and aquariums, and today they're starting to attract the interest of collectors. Many were made in Japan and imported decades ago to be sold in 5-&-10¢ stores along with the millions of other figural novelties that flooded the market after the war. The condition of the glaze is very important; for more information we recommend *Collector's Encyclopedia of Made in Japan Ceramics* by Carole Bess White (Collector Books). Unless noted otherwise, the examples in the listing that follows were produced in Japan.

Bathing beauty on turtle, red, tan & green on white, 2½" **25.00**
Castle towers w/3 arches, tan lustre w/red, green & white, 5¼". **22.00**
Castle w/arch, multicolored, 2½" or 3½", ea.............................. **20.00**

Castle, multicolor, unmarked (Japan), 4½", from $20.00 to $32.00.
(Photo courtesy Carole Bess White)

Colonade w/palm tree, multicolored, 3¾x4" **20.00**
Diver spearing fish, bubble hole in top, Japan, 5½"................ **45.00**
Doorway, stone entry w/open aqua wood-look door, 2" **15.00**
Fish riding waves, 2 white fish on cobalt waves, 3½x3" **22.00**
Houses & cave, bubble hole in top, Japan, 3½"....................... **15.00**
Houses w/water wheel & bridge, multicolored, 4½x4½" **26.00**

Lighthouse, tan, black, brown & green, 6½x4" 26.00

Mermaid on sea horse, white, green & orange glossy glazes, 3¼" 25.00

No Fishing sign on tree trunk, brown, black & white, 2½x4" 12.00

Nude on starfish, bisque, 4½", from $40 to 50.00

Octopus, pink & brown, Japan, 4" 35.00

Pagoda, triple roof, blue, green & maroon, 5½x3¼" 20.00

Ruins among rocks, aqua, green & brown, Japan, 4x4" 15.00

Torii gate, multicolored glossy glazes, 3¾" 22.00

Fisher-Price

Since about 1930 the Fisher-Price Company has produced distinctive wooden toys covered with brightly colored lithographed paper. Plastic parts were first added in 1949. The most valuable Fisher-Price toys are those modeled after well-known Disney characters and having the Disney logo. A little edge wear and some paint dulling are normal to these well-loved toys and to be expected; our prices are for toys in very good played-with condition. Mint-in-box examples are extremely scarce and worth from 40% to 60% more. For further information we recommend *A Pictorial Guide to the More Popular Toys, Fisher-Price Toys, 1931 – 1990,* by Gary Combs and Brad Cassity; *Fisher-Price, A Historical Rarity Value Guide,* by John J. Murray and Bruce R. Fox (Books Americana); and *Schroeder's Collectible Toys, Antique to Modern* (Collector Books). See also Dolls, Fisher-Price. See Clubs and Newsletters for information on the Fisher-Price Collectors Club.

#8 Bouncy Racer, 1960-62 ..... 30.00

#28 Bunny Egg Cart, 1950 .... 50.00

#111 Play Family Merry-Go-Round, 1972-77 .... 30.00

#120 Cacklin' Hen, 1958-66, white 35.00

#121, Happy Hoppers, 1969 – 1976, $10.00. (Photo courtesy Brad Cassity)

#125 Uncle Timmy Turtle, 1956-58, red shell 75.00

#132 Molly Moo Cow, 1972-78 . 10.00

#135 Play Family Circus, 1974-76, complete 60.00

#136 Play Family Lacing Shoe, 1965-69, complete 60.00

#137 Pony Chime, 1965-67 .... 40.00

#140 Katy Kackler, 1954-56 & Easter 1957 .... 75.00

#145 Humpty Dumpty Truck, 1963-64 & Easter 1965 .... 30.00

#151 Goldilocks & the Three Bears Playhouse, 1967-71 .... 60.00

#151 Happy Hippo, 1962-63 .. 85.00

#164 Mother Goose, 1964-66 . 30.00

#168 Magic Chug-Chug, 1964-69 .... 35.00

#170 Change-A-Tune Carousel, 1981-83 .... 20.00

#177 Oscar the Grouch, 1977-84 . 10.00

#183 Play Family Fun Jet, 1970, 1st version **10.00**

#190 Gabby Duck, 1939-40 & Easter 1941 .... **350.00**

#192 School Bus, 1965-69, new version of #990 .... **125.00**

#301 Shovel Digger, 1975-77 . **15.00**

#304 Chick Basket Cart, 1960-64 .**35.00**

#307 Adventure People Wilderness Patrol, 1975-79 .... **30.00**

#326 Adventure People Alpha Star, 1983-84 .... **20.00**

#337 Husky Rescue Rig, 1982-83. **20.00**

#400 Donald Duck Drum Major, 1946-48 .... **250.00**

#401 Push Bunny Cart, 1942 . **200.00**

#402 Duck Cart, 1943 .... **250.00**

#448 Mini Copter, 1971-84 ...... **5.00**

#454 Donald Duck Drummer, 1949-50 .... **250.00**

#460 Movie Viewer, 1973-85, crank handle **1.00**

#476 Cookie Pig, 1966-70 ...... **40.00**

#477 Dr Doodle, 1940-41 ..... **225.00**

#499 Kitty Bell, 1950-51 ...... **100.00**

#552 Basic Hard Board Puzzle, Nature, 1974-75 .... **15.00**

#621 Suzie Seal, 1965-66, ball on nose **30.00**

#629 Fisher-Price Tractor, 1962-68.**30.00**

#637 Milk Carrier, 1966-65 ... **15.00**

#653 Alli Gator, 1960-61 & Easter 1962 .... **75.00**

#663 Play Family, 1966-70, tan dog, MIP **170.00**

#677 Picnic Basket, 1975-79 . **20.00**

#686 Car & Camper, 1968-70.. **65.00**

#712 Fred Flintstone Xylophone, 1962, Sears only **250.00**

#715 Ducky Flip Flap, 1964-65..**50.00**

#724 Ding-Dong Ducky, 1949-50 .**200.00**

#725 Play Family Bath/Utility Room Set, 1972 .... **10.00**

#734 Teddy Zilo, 1964-66 .... **40.00**

#758 Push-Along Clown, 1980-81 .... **5.00**

#766 Music Box Pocket Radio, 1977-78 .... **10.00**

#780 Snoopy Sniffer, 1955-57 & Easter 1958 .... **50.00**

#789 Lift & Load Builders, 1978-82 .... **15.00**

#853 Scooter, 1978-81, plush hand puppet............................. **10.00**

#855 Miss Piggy Hand Puppet, 1979-80, mouth moves.... **10.00**

#860 Kermit the Frog Hand Puppet, 1979-83 .... **10.00**

#928 Play Family Fire Station, 1980-82, complete **50.00**

#931 Play Family Children's Hospital, 1976-78 .... **115.00**

#934 Play Family Western Town, 1982-84 .... **60.00**

#937 Play Family Sesame Street Clubhouse, 1977-79 .... **70.00**

#960 Woodsey's Log House, 1979-81, complete **20.00**

#972 Fisher-Price Cash Register, 1960-72 .... **20.00**

#985 Play Family House Boat, 1972-76, complete **35.00**

#996 Play Family Airport, 1972-76.................................... **45.00**

#997 Musical Tick-Tock Clock, 1962-63 .... **30.00**

#997 Play Family Village, 1973-77 .... **50.00**

#999 Huffy Puffy Train, 1958-62 .**50.00**

#1006 Floor Train, 1934-38 . **600.00**

#1064 Mother Goose, 1964-66. **30.00**

#2361 Little People Fire Truck..**10.00**

#2500 Little People Main Street, 1986-90 .... **30.00**

#2550 Little People School, 1988-89 .... **20.00**

#2717, Pick-Up and Peek Puzzle, 1985 – 1988, MIB, $15.00. (Photo courtesy Brad Cassity)

#4520 Highway Dump Truck, 1985-86 .... **15.00**
#4550 Chevy S-10 4x4, 1985 . **20.00**
#4581 Power Dump Truck, 1985-86 .... **20.00**
#7001 Zummi Gummi Bear, 1986, any in this line from #7001 to #7006, ea **10.00**

Fishing Collectibles

Very much in evidence at flea markets these days, old fishing gear has become very collectible. Early twentieth century plugs were almost entirely carved from wood, sprayed with several layers of enamel, and finished off with glass eyes. Molded plastics were of a later origin. Some of the more collectible manufacturers are James Heddon, Shakespeare, Rhodes, and Pflueger. Rods, reels, old advertising calendars, and company catalogs are also worth your attention. For more information we recommend *19th Century Fishing Lures* by Arlan Carter; *Fishing Lure Collectibles,* by Dudley Murphy and Rick Edmisten; *Fishing Lure Collectibles,* by Dudley and Deanie Murphy; *Collector's Encyclopedia of*

Creek Chub Lures and Collectibles by Harold E. Smith, MD; *Modern Fishing Lure Collectibles, Volumes 1 – 4,* by Russell E. Lewis; *Spring-Loaded Fish Hooks, Traps & Lures* by William Blauser and Timothy Mierzwa; and *Captain John's Fishing Tackle Price Guide* by John Kolbeck. All are published by Collector Books.

Values are for lures in good average condition. Mint-in-box examples are worth about twice as much.

Lures

Creek Chub, Plunking Dinger #6200, two treble hooks, 1939 – 1953, 4", from $40.00 to $60.00. (Photo courtesy Dudley Murphy and Deanie Murphy)

Arbogast, Jitterbug, green scale w/black plastic lip, EX+.. **35.00**
Arbogast, Sunfish Tin Liz, glass eyes, 1½", EX **200.00**
Bagley Bait Co, Chatter Shad, black & chartreuse, 3", MOC.... **20.00**
Butch Harris, Fas-Bak, staple hardware molded into casting, 2¼", M **15.00**
Clark, Water Scout, tack eyes, black & white ribs, EX+ **30.00**
Creek Chub, Crawdad #300, albino w/red blush on chin, EX . **75.00**
Creek Chub, Giant Jointed Pike #802, glass eyes, white w/red head, MIB **90.00**

Creek Chub, Husky Surfster #7300, silver flash, 6", EX+ **100.00**

Creek Chub, Wigglefish #2400, 1957 & 1974-77, from $40 to **50.00**

Creek Club, Big Bomber, Golden Shiner, 3¾", EX **300.00**

Fin-Wing, round decal type, 3", M, minimum value **50.00**

Heddon, Crazy Crawler, movable wings, 2½", EX **40.00**

Heddon, Dowagiac Minnow #100, fat-body style, 1917, 2½", EX ...**85.00**

Heddon, Giant River Runt #7510, 1939-41, 3¼", from $60 to. **90.00**

Heddon, Lung Frog #3500, VG .**85.00**

Heddon, Torpedo, rainbow finish w/glass eyes, 3½", EX+ ... **50.00**

Hofschneider, Red Eye No 2P-C, 1950s, 2¼", MIB **20.00**

Jamison, Musky Wig-Wag (Gep Bait), 2-part head & body, 6", EX.. **125.00**

Jamison, Twin Spinner Bucktail, 1932, EX **20.00**

JK Rush, Deluxe Tango, metal head plate, 4¼", EX+ **100.00**

Keeling, Crab, black & yellow, EX **55.00**

Les Davis, Herring Dodger #0, MOC, from $8 to **10.00**

Millsite, Wig Wag, 1946, 3", EX.**15.00**

Moonlight/Paw Paw, Moonlight Crawfish, rubber legs, tack eyes, NM **125.00**

Ozark Woodchopper, rainbow colored, ½-oz size, from $12 to **18.00**

Pflueger, Gay Blade, green to yellow, 2 treble hooks, 1960s, 2" **5.00**

Pflueger, Mustang, perch scale, painted eyes, carver gills, VG+ **20.00**

Pflueger, Razum Minnow, rubber w/perch finish, attached keel, 2", VG **30.00**

Shakespeare, Floating Minnow, yellow & green w/6 tiger stripes, EX **100.00**

Shakespeare, Pad-Ler, red & white, musky size, 3¾", VG **80.00**

Shurebite, Shedevil, black & yellow, 1940s, from $15 to ... **20.00**

South Bend, Be Bop #902 YP, yellow perch, MIB **25.00**

South Bend, Minnow #999, glass eyes, tail cap, weighted nose, 1929, EX **55.00**

South Bend, Perch-Oreno, nickel finish, deep front hook cup, EX **55.00**

South Bend, Super Snooper #1960, plastic, 2 treble hooks, 1950s, 3" **18.00**

Turner, Spoon #F1551, red & white, M in 2-pc box, from $20 to .**30.00**

Winchester, Spinner #9783, feathered treble, EX **100.00**

Reels

Abu-Ambassadeur #5000, common model, from $50 to **70.00**

Alcedo #2, spinning, stamped PO 27, EX **75.00**

Benjamin Thumezy Patents Pending, bait casting with mechanical thumb brake, VG, $525.00.

Brookline #16, EX **8.00**

Classic Pflueger Supreme, Patent Pending, MIP **100.00**

Garcia Mitchell #314, EX **20.00**
Hardy, Silex, 1950s, 4", EX . **165.00**
Meek, BF & Son #3, EX **100.00**
Roddy Roddymatic #560, star drag, free spool, NM **25.00**
Shakespeare Model #2065 Spin Wonder, MIB, minimum value **50.00**
Shakespeare Precision, jeweled, EX **15.00**
Utica Reel, early auto fly wheel, values vary by models, from $20 to **60.00**
Winchester #4291, single handle, counterweight, 80-yd, NM. **145.00**

Miscellaneous

Bobber, Kingfish, multicolored, w/instructions, EX+OC... **15.00**
Catalog, South Bend, 1939, multi-colored charts, EX+ **75.00**
Catalog, Weber, 1938, EX+.. **100.00**
Decoy, Carl Christenson, brown trout, glass eyes, 11", EX+ **75.00**
Decoy, Trout, Dennis Wolf, glass eyes, 12", EX+ **200.00**
Fly line cleaner, Orvis, in EX tin container, from $5 to....... **10.00**
Magazines, Field & Stream, 1930s-40s, EX, ea...................... **10.00**
Minnow trap, CF Orvis Manchester VT, all original, EX **85.00**
Plaque, Heddon, wood, black crappie, VG............................. **40.00**
Rod, Gene Edwards, spinning, w/original bag & tube, 78", EX+ **150.00**
Rod, Heddon #105, 2-pc bait casting, 5½", VG..................... **75.00**
Rod, Kitkast Pocket Rod, extendable, MIB........................ **35.00**
Rod, South Bend #59, fly, bamboo, EX **85.00**

Split-shot container, Selby BB, celluloid, round, EX............. **70.00**
Tackle box, aluminum, embossed Gut Cast Box, 4½" dia **42.00**

Flashlights

The flashlight was invented in 1898 and has been produced by the Eveready Company for the past 96 years. Eveready dominated the flashlight market for most of this period, but more than 125 other U.S. flashlight companies have come and gone, providing competition along the way. Add to that number 35 known foreign flashlight manufacturers, and you end up with over 1,000 different models of flashlights to collect. They come in a wide variety of styles, shapes, and sizes. The flashlight field includes tubular, lanterns, figural, novelty, litho, etc. At present, over 45 different categories of flashlights have been identified as collectible. For further information we recommend that you consult Flashlight Collectors of America; see Clubs and Newsletters for contact information.

Bond Vest Pocket, marbleized green, EX......................... **22.00**
Challenger, copper, Made in USA, VG.................................... **25.00**
Daco Lite, WWII, marked Tropical Use, hand energized, 1944, EX **50.00**
Deluxe Lightlaster, chrome bullet shape, 7", EX.................. **30.00**
Eveready Hand Lantern, black, 1908, NM...................... **75.00**

Eveready Liberty Daylo Lantern #3651, blued or nickel finish, NM **20.00**

Eveready Lily Candle, wood base, 1900, EX **110.00**

Eveready Little Captain, MIP. **30.00**

Eveready Masterlite, sq body, red, 7", EX **20.00**

Eveready Midget #1904, w/red glass switch, NM **35.00**

Eveready Strapper, brown leather w/chrome ends, VG+ **25.00**

Franco gun flashlight, black steel, 1913, VG, from $75.00 to $90.00. (Photo courtesy Bill Utley)

Franco Vest Pocket, 2AA-cell, EX **25.00**

GE Automotive Lamp, w/17" L 'snake' neck, EX **25.00**

Genesy Electric Lantern Co Kansas MO, metal w/wood handle, EX **30.00**

Niagara Searchlight Co, chrome-plated brass, dated 4/28/1914, VG+ **25.00**

Philips Red Head, 1925, EX.. **80.00**

Ray-O-Vac, Patented December 3, 1929, working, G+ **25.00**

Ray-O-Vac Miner, 2B-cell, NM. **22.00**

Ray-O-Vac Rotomatic, chrome w/fish-eye glass lens, VG. **30.00**

Ray-O-Vac Sportsman #301, MIB **40.00**

Saja, hand-generated, Bakelite, 4", EX **45.00**

Siemans Handdynamo, squeeze action, VGIB **50.00**

Sterling Candle, 2C-cell, EX. **150.00**

Winchester, chrome-plated brass, dated 1920, 5¾", EX **85.00**

Zoom-Lite Lithograph Flashlight, NM **32.00**

Flower Frogs

Nearly every pottery company and glasshouse in America produced their share of figural flower frogs, and many were imported from Japan as well. They were probably most popular from about 1910 through the 1940s, coinciding not only with the heyday of American glass and ceramics, but with the gracious, much less hectic style of living the times allowed. Way before a silk flower or styrofoam block was ever dreamed of, there were fresh cut flowers on many a dining room sideboard or table, arranged in shallow console bowls with matching frogs such as we've described in the following listings. For further information see *Collector's Encyclopedia of Made in Japan Ceramics, Identification and Values*, by Carole Bess White (Collector Books). See also specific pottery and glass companies.

Acorns (2), Ming Blue, Van Briggle, 1960s+, 3x6x5" **60.00**

Bluebird on peach lustre base, red Japan mark, 2½x1¾" **40.00**

Butterfly on flower, multicolored, ceramic, 7 holes, 2x3" **25.00**

Carnival glass, gold, 8 holes, 1½x2½"............................12.00

Cockatoo, majolica-like, 8 holes, Japan, 7x3"......................22.00

Depression glass, clear, 3 sm glass feet, angled holes, sm.....15.00

Depression glass, green, 16 angled holes, 4½" dia.................20.00

Dome, cast iron, woven-look, 1½x3½" dia.........................8.00

Ducks (2), turquoise, California Faience mark, 5½x5"......85.00

Fawn leaping, multicolored, 12 holes, Rosemeade............28.00

Frog on dome-like base, multicolored, ceramic, Japan, 3½x3½"....35.00

Kingfisher bird beside flower, multicolored, ceramic, 7 holes, 4x3"..................................45.00

Nude standing on base, white, porcelain, Japan, 1930s-50s, 9x5½"............................250.00

Nude with floral decoration, Germany, 7½", $95.00.

Owl on stump, tan & blue lustre, 6 holes, Japan....................55.00

Parrot on stump, multicolored lustre, 5 holes, Japan, 3x2".50.00

Rosebud, mulitcolored lustre, Japan, 2½", from $12 to..22.00

Sailboat, creamy white, ceramic, 6 holes................................65.00

Sunflower in center of stump, multicolored, ceramic, 8 holes, 3"......15.00

Swan, mother-of-pearl lustre, 1930s-50s, 7½x9x6".........25.00

Water lily, silver-plated metal, 3-pc set, Leonard, 3x7"...........22.00

'40s, '50s, and '60s Glassware

Remember the lovely dishes mother used back when you were a child? Many collectors do. With scarcity of the older Depression glassware items that used to be found in every garage sale or flea market, glass collectors have refocused their interests and altered buying habits to include equally interesting glassware from more recent years, often choosing patterns that bring back warm childhood memories.

Note that the listing for King's Crown/Thumbprint pattern is under Indiana although it was originally made by the U.S. Glass Co. The pattern was later made by Tiffin through the early 1960s, and then by Indiana. Our listing is for the later Tiffin and Indiana pieces.

For more information, see *Collectible Glassware from the '40s, '50s, '60s,* and *Hazel-Atlas Glass Identification and Value Guide,* both by Gene and Cathy Florence (Collector Books). See also Anchor Hocking; Indiana Carnival Glass.

Cambridge

Cascade, bonbon, crystal.......13.00

Cascade, bowl, crystal, 4½"......7.50

Cascade, candlestick, crystal, 5" **17.50**

Cascade, candlestick, green or yellow, 5" **35.00**

Cascade, creamer, green or yellow **20.00**

Cascade, plate, crystal, 4-footed, 11½" **30.00**

Cascade, salt & pepper shakers, crystal, pr **20.00**

Cascade, tumbler, crystal, flat or footed, 5-oz, ea **10.00**

Square, creamer, crystal **10.00**

Square, relish dish, crystal, 2-part, 6½" dia **17.50**

Square, stem, crystal, 12-oz .. **12.00**

Square, tumbler, low sherbet, crystal **10.00**

Colony

Harvest, butter dish, w/lid, milk glass, ¼-lb **15.00**

Harvest, cake stand, milk glass, 12" **18.00**

Harvest, candleholder (sherbet design), milk glass, footed. **10.00**

Harvest, console bowl, milk glass, footed, 10" **18.00**

Harvest, creamer, footed, milk glass **5.00**

Harvest, cup, milk glass **4.50**

Harvest, goblet, milk glass **6.00**

Harvest, pitcher, milk glass, 40-oz **20.00**

Harvest, pitcher, milk glass, 65-oz **25.00**

Harvest, plate, milk glass, 6"... **1.00**

Harvest, plate, milk glass, 8"... **3.00**

Harvest, plate, milk glass, 10". **6.00**

Harvest, platter, milk glass, 14½"..**14.00**

Harvest, punch bowl, milk glass, 8-qt.................................... **20.00**

Harvest, punch/snack cup, milk glass, footed **2.50**

Harvest, salt & pepper shakers, milk glass, footed, pr **12.50**

Harvest, saucer, milk glass .... **.50**

Harvest, sherbet, milk glass, footed **5.00**

Harvest, snack tray, milk glass, oval **4.50**

Harvest, sugar bowl, milk glass, footed, no handles **5.00**

Harvest, tray for creamer & sugar bowl, milk glass, w/handles..**4.00**

Harvest, tumbler, milk glass, 5-oz ..**4.00**

Harvest, tumbler, milk glass, 10-oz ..**5.00**

Harvest, tumbler, milk glass, 14-oz ..**8.00**

Duncan and Miller

Festive, bowl, honey or aqua, 6"..**6.00**

Festive, candy dish, w/lid, honey .**45.00**

Festive, creamer, aqua **25.00**

Festive, cruet, honey, 8" **35.00**

Festive, salt & pepper shakers, aqua, pr **25.00**

Festive, vase, honey, 10" **42.00**

Federal Glass Co.

Clover Blossom, bowl, milk glass w/pink & gray decor, 5" **3.50**

Clover Blossom, creamer, milk glass w/pink & gray decor **5.00**

Clover Blossom, plate, coupe; milk glass w/pink & gray decor, 10" **8.00**

Clover Blossom, sugar bowl, milk glass w/pink & gray decor, w/lid **10.00**

Golden Glory, bowl, white w/22k gold trim, rimmed, 8" **12.00**

Golden Glory, bowl, white w/22k gold trim, 5" **4.50**

Golden Glory, plate, white w/22k
gold trim, 10" **7.00**
Golden Glory, platter, white w/22k
gold trim, oval, 12".......... **13.00**
Golden Glory, tumbler, white w/22k
gold trim, 10-oz, 5".......... **10.00**
Heritage, bowl, crystal, 5" **8.00**
Heritage, cup, crystal.............. **6.00**
Heritage, plate, crystal, 9" **12.00**
Heritage, saucer, crystal.......... **2.00**

Fostoria

Argus, bowl, crystal, olive or smoke,
5" **14.00**
Argus, plate, cobalt or ruby, 8". **25.00**
Argus, plate, crystal, olive or smoke,
8" **15.00**
Argus, sherbet, crystal, olive or
smoke, 8-oz, 5" **10.00**
Argus, tumbler, cobalt or ruby, foot-
ed, 13-oz, 6¾".................... **25.00**
Bouquet, bowl, crystal, 5"...... **15.00**
Bouquet, cake plate, crystal, tab
handles **27.50**
Bouquet, plate, crystal, 9½"... **30.00**
Bouquet, tray, muffin; crystal, tab
handles, 9½" **35.00**
Buttercup, candlestick, crystal,
#2324, 4", ea.................... **20.00**
Buttercup, coaster, crystal..... **20.00**
Buttercup, plate, crystal, #2337,
9½".................................. **42.50**
Buttercup, relish dish, crystal,
3-part, #2364, 7x10"........ **35.00**
Buttercup, tray, crystal, center
handle, #2364, 11"........... **35.00**
Camellia, ashtray, crystal, 6". **25.00**
Camellia, bowl, crystal, flared, 8". **35.00**
Camellia, butter dish, crystal,
¼-lb................................. **25.00**
Camellia, plate, salad; crystal,
7½" **10.00**

Camellia, salt & pepper shakers,
crystal, 3⅛", pr **55.00**
Camellia, sugar bowl, crystal, foot-
ed, 4" **14.00**
Century, basket, crystal w/wicker
handle, 6½x10"............... **60.00**
Century, bowl, crystal, footed, rolled
edge, 11" **38.00**
Century, bowl, crystal, 6" **22.00**
Century, cake plate, crystal, han-
dled, 10".......................... **22.00**
Century, pitcher, crystal, 16-oz,
6⅛" **50.00**
Century, platter, crystal, 12". **40.00**
Century, relish dish, crystal, 3-part,
11"................................... **22.00**
Century, wine, crystal, 3½-oz,
4½" **25.00**
Chintz, bowl, crystal, oval, #2496,
9½" **125.00**
Chintz, candy dish, crystal, 3-part,
w/lid, #2496 .... **135.00**

**Chintz, etching #338, candlestick,
crystal, triple, #2496, 6", $60.00 each.**

Chintz, ice bucket, crystal,
#2496......................... **110.00**
Chintz, pickle dish, crystal, #2496,
8".................................... **32.00**
Chintz, plate, cracker; crystal,
#2496, 11" **40.00**
Corsage, bonbon, crystal, 3-footed,
#2496, 7½" **25.00**
Corsage, candelabrum, crystal, 2-
light w/prisms, #2527 ... **120.00**

Corsage, candlestick, duo; crystal, #2496 .... **45.00**

Corsage, compote, crystal, #2496, 5½" **30.00**

Corsage, cup, crystal, #2440 .. **18.00**

Corsage, finger bowl, crystal, #869 .... **30.00**

Corsage, plate, crystal, #2496, 11" **30.00**

Corsage, relish dish, crystal, 3-part, #2496 .... **28.00**

Corsage, saucer, crystal, #2440. **5.00**

Corsage, tumbler, crystal, footed, #6014, 9-oz, 5½" **20.00**

Corsage, vase, crystal, footed, #2470, 10" **150.00**

Corsage, water goblet, crystal, #6014, 9-oz, 7½" **26.00**

Cut Rose, bowl, salad; crystal, 11" **42.50**

Cut Rose, celery dish, crystal, 9" .. **26.00**

Cut Rose, mayonnaise, crystal. **35.00**

Cut Rose, mayonnaise plate, crystal **12.00**

Cut Rose, pitcher, crystal, flat, 32-oz **110.00**

Cut Rose, sherbet, crystal, 6-oz, 4" **9.00**

Cut Rose, sugar bowl, crystal. **20.00**

Cut Rose, tumbler, crystal, footed, 12-oz, 6" **20.00**

Heather, bowl, cereal; crystal, #2470, 6" **28.00**

Heather, bowl, serving; crystal, w/handles, #2470, 9½" **42.50**

Heather, cake plate, crystal, w/handles, #2470, 10" **30.00**

Heather, cocktail, crystal, #6037, 4-oz, 5" **16.00**

Heather, creamer, crystal, #2470, 4¼" **15.00**

Heather, relish dish, crystal, 2-part, #2470, 7½" **20.00**

Heather, sugar bowl, crystal, footed, #2470, 4" **15.00**

Heirloom, basket, all colors, 12". **55.00**

Heirloom, bowl, star shape, all colors, 8½" **40.00**

Heirloom, plate, all colors, 8". **30.00**

Heirloom, vase, all colors, 6". **25.00**

Holly, bowl, salad; crystal, #2364, 9" **30.00**

Holly, compote, crystal, #6030, 5" **25.00**

Holly, creamer, crystal, #2350½, 3¼" **12.00**

Holly, cup, crystal, #2350½ **10.00**

Holly, plate, crystal, #2337, 9½". **35.00**

Holly, sugar bowl, crystal, #21350½", 3⅛" **12.00**

Holly, vase, crystal, #2619½, 6".. **65.00**

Horizon, bowl, cereal; all colors, 5" **12.00**

Horizon, cup, all colors, 8½-oz. **10.00**

Horizon, platter, all colors, 12". **22.00**

Jamestown, bowl, salad; amber or brown, #2719/211, 10"..... **21.00**

Jamestown, pitcher, amethyst, crystal or green, #2719/456, 48-oz.. **40.00**

Jamestown, plate, blue, pink or ruby, #2719/550, 8" **20.00**

Jamestown, relish dish, amber or brown, 2-part, #2719/620, 9" **16.00**

Jamestown, sugar bowl, amethyst, crystal or green, footed, #2719/679 .... **17.50**

Jamestown, tumbler, blue, pink or ruby, #2719/64, 12-oz, 5". **22.00**

Lido, compote, crystal, 5¾" **34.00**

Lido, finger bowl, crystal, #766 . **25.00**

Lido, pickle dish, crystal, 8" .. **17.50**

Lido, plate, crystal, 8½" **12.50**

Lido, plate, crystal, 10¼" **50.00**

Lido, relish dish, crystal, 3-part, 10" **30.00**

Lido, tidbit, crystal, 3-part, flat, 8"...................................20.00

Mayflower, bowl, #2560, handled, crystal, 5"...........................22.50

Mayflower, cake plate, #2560, handled, crystal.....................35.00

Mayflower, candlestick, #2560, crystal, 4½"........................25.00

Mayflower, compote, crystal, 5½".30.00

Mayflower, salt & pepper shakers, crystal, pr.........................75.00

Meadow Rose, bonbon, crystal, 3-footed, 7½".....................27.50

Meadow Rose, candlestick, crystal, 5½", ea..............................32.00

Meadow Rose, plate, crystal, 9½".45.00

Meadow Rose, tray, crystal, center handle, 11".........................35.00

Meadow Rose, vase, crystal, footed, 10"..................................165.00

Navarre, bowl, crystal, footed, w/handles, #2496, 5".......20.00

Navarre, cake plate, crystal, #2440, 10½"..................................65.00

Navarre, candlestick, crystal, #2496, 5½".........................42.00

Navarre, cocktail, crystal, #6106, 3½-oz, 6"...........................22.00

Navarre, plate, crystal, #2440, 7½"..................................14.00

Navarre, plate, crystal, #2440, 9½"..................................47.50

Navarre, salt & pepper shakers, crystal, #2364, 3¼", pr....80.00

Navarre, tumbler, crystal, footed, #6106, 10-oz, 5½"............24.00

Hazel-Atlas

Beehive, bowl, berry; tab handles, crystal, 8½"......................12.00

Beehive, creamer, crystal or white, 9½-oz.................................5.00

Beehive, cup, crystal...............6.00

Beehive, sugar bowl, milk glass, with lid, 11 ounce, $10.00. (Photo courtesy of Gene and Cathy Florence)

Beehive, tumbler, pink, flat, 9-oz.22.50

Capri, ashtray, blue, round, 3¼"..6.00

Capri, bowl, Colony Swirl, blue, 5½".....................................8.00

Capri, candy jar, blue, footed, w/lid................................32.00

Capri, cup, Tulip, blue, round.7.00

Capri, plate, dinner; blue, octagonal, 9¾"..............................9.00

Capri, plate, salad; Hobnail, blue, 7¼".....................................6.00

Capri, tumbler, Colony Swirl, blue, 12-oz, 5"............................10.00

Colonial Couple, bowl, milk glass w/black decor & red trim, 5".......................15.00

Colonial Couple, egg cup, milk gass w/black decor & red trim...............................22.00

Gothic, cup, crystal..................6.00

Gothic, plate, crystal, 8"...........7.50

Gothic, saucer, crystal..............2.00

Gothic, sherbet, crystal, 8-oz, 3½"..3.00

Gothic, tumbler, crystal, footed, 10-oz...................................6.00

Gothic, tumbler, crystal, footed, 7-oz, 5¼"............................20.00

Moderntone Platonite, bowl, cream soup; pastel colors, 4¾".....6.50

Moderntone Platonite, creamer & suger bowl, white w/stripes, ea...................................... **10.00**

Moderntone Platonite, cup, any color, from $7 to **8.00**

Moderntone Platonite, plate, white w/red or blue Willow decor, 9"......................... **30.00**

Moderntone Platonite, saucer, any color, from $4 to **5.00**

Moroccan Amethyst, ashtray, sq, 3½" **8.00**

Moroccan Amethyst, bowl, oval, 7¾" **12.00**

Moroccan Amethyst, candy dish, short, w/lid **35.00**

Moroccan Amethyst, plate, sandwich; w/metal handle, 12"........... **17.50**

Newport, bowl, cream soup; fired-on colors, 4¾".................... **10.00**

Newport, bowl, cream soup; white, 4¾" **5.50**

Newport, plate, fired-on colors, 8½"...................................... **5.00**

Newport, plate, white, 8½" **3.00**

Newport, salt & pepper shakers, white, pr **18.00**

Heisey

Cabochon, bonbon, crystal, sloped sides, sq handle, #1951, 6¼" **24.00**

Cabochon, creamer, crystal, #1951 .... **13.00**

Cabochon, creamer, Dawn, #1951............................ **40.00**

Cabochon, pickle tray, crystal, 8½" **20.00**

Cabochon, plate, sandwich; crystal, #1951, 14"......................... **18.00**

Cabochon, stem, wine; crystal, #6091, 3-oz......................... **8.00**

Cabochon, tumbler, crystal, footed, #6091, 12-oz..................... **10.00**

Lodestar, ashtray, Dawn........ **85.00**

Lodestar, bowl, Dawn, 8"....... **95.00**

Lodestar, bowl, Dawn, crimped, 11", $100.00. (Photo courtesy Gene and Cathy Florence)

Lodestar, creamer & sugar bowl, Dawn, no handles, ea **50.00**

New Era, cordial, crystal, 1-oz . **40.00**

New Era, cup, crystal **10.00**

New Era, goblet, crystal, 10-oz..**16.00**

New Era, plate, crystal, 10x8" . **45.00**

New Era, tumbler, crystal, footed, 14-oz................................. **20.00**

Imperial

Atterbury Scroll, basket, crystal. **22.00**

Atterbury Scroll, compote, crystal.................................**18.00**

Atterbury Scroll, plate, luncheon; crystal **10.00**

Atterbury Scroll, plate, luncheon; jade **18.00**

Atterbury Scroll, sugar bowl, crystal, footed......................... **25.00**

Chroma, cake stand, all colors . **65.00**

Chroma, goblet, all colors, 12-oz. **25.00**

Chroma, plate, all colors, 8".. **15.00**

Chroma, tumbler, all colors, 8-oz............................. **22.50**

Crocheted Crystal, basket, 6". **30.00**

Crocheted Crystal, candleholder, single, 6" wide, ea **20.00**

Crocheted Crystal, creamer, footed 20.00

Crocheted Crystal, plate, 14" .. 25.00

Crocheted Crystal, punch bowl, 14" 65.00

Crocheted Crystal, sugar bowl, footed 20.00

Indiana Glass Co.

Banana Fruit, cake plate, crystal w/flashed colors, footed, 13" 35.00

Banana Fruit, candleholder, double; crystal w/flashed colors, 5½" 25.00

Banana Fruit, plate, crystal w/flashed colors, 7½" 15.00

Christmas Candy, bowl, crystal, 7½" 7.00

Christmas Candy, bowl, teal, 7½" 55.00

Christmas Candy, mayonnaise, crystal, w/ladle & liner ... 20.00

Christmas Candy, plate, sandwich; crystal, 9½" 14.00

Christmas Candy, plate, sandwich; teal, 11", $65.00. (Photo courtesy Gene and Cathy Florence)

Constellation, basket, centerpiece; crystal, 11" 30.00

Constellation, bowl, console; colors, flat rim, footed, 11½" 20.00

Constellation, cake stand, crystal, round 50.00

Constellation, compote, celery; crystal, oval, low centerpiece .. 25.00

Constellation, pitcher, colors, ½-gal, 7½" 60.00

Constellation, pitcher, crystal, ½-gal, 7½" 40.00

Constellation, platter, crystal, oval 22.50

Daisy, bowl, green, 4½" 6.00

Daisy, bowl, vegetable; crystal or green, oval, 10" 10.00

Daisy, plate, amber or red, 7½" . 7.00

Daisy, plate, grill; crystal, 10½" . 5.50

Daisy, sherbet, crystal or green, footed 5.00

Daisy, tumbler, amber or red, footed, 12-oz 35.00

Daisy, tumbler, green, footed, 12-oz 18.00

Diamond Point, bowl, crystal w/ruby, scalloped rim, 6" .. 6.00

Diamond Point, candy dish, crystal w/red, w/lid, 4¾" 10.00

Diamond Point, compote, crystal w/ruby, flat rim, 7¼" H ... 12.50

Diamond Point, pitcher, crystal w/ruby 20.00

Diamond Point, sugar bowl, crystal w/ruby, footed 4.00

King's Crown/Thumbprint, bowl, ruby flashed, 5¾" 20.00

King's Crown/Thumbprint, cake plate, ruby flashed, footed, 12½" dia 80.00

King's Crown/Thumbprint, compote, ruby flashed, footed, 6¼" .. 25.00

King's Crown/Thumbprint, creamer & sugar bowl, ruby flashed, ea 20.00

King's Crown/Thumbprint, plate, ruby flashed, 7½" 12.00

187

King's Crown/Thumbprint, plate, ruby flashed, 10" **42.00**

King's Crown/Thumbprint, relish dish, ruby flashed, 5-part, 14" **135.00**

King's Crown/Thumbprint, tumbler, ruby flashed, 11-oz.. **12.00**

Lily Pons, bonbon, colors other than green, footed, 6½" **6.00**

Lily Pons, bonbon, green, footed, 6½" **15.00**

Lily Pons, creamer & sugar bowl, green **25.00**

Lily Pons, plate, colors other than green, 8" **6.00**

Lily Pons, plate, green, 8" **14.00**

Jeannette

Anniversary, cake plate, crystal, round, w/metal lid **17.50**

Anniversary, creamer, pink, footed **12.50**

Anniversary, plate, crystal or iridescent, 10" **6.00**

Anniversary, plate, iridescent, 12½" **8.00**

Anniversary, relish dish, crystal w/metal base, 4-part **20.00**

Camellia, candleholder, crystal, ea **12.50**

Camellia, nappy, 1 handle, crystal **9.00**

Camellia, plate, sandwich; crystal, 12" **12.00**

Camellia, tidbit, 2-tier; crystal. **20.00**

Dewdrop, bowl, crystal, 10½". **20.00**

Dewdrop, butter dish, crystal . **25.00**

Dewdrop, creamer, crystal **8.00**

Dewdrop, plate, crystal, 11½". **17.50**

Dewdrop, tumbler, crystal, 9-oz.**22.00**

Floragold, bowl, iridescent, sq, 4½" **5.00**

Floragold, candy dish, iridescent, 1 handle **12.00**

Floragold, cup, iridescent **6.00**

Floragold, plate, dinner; iridescent, 8½", $40.00. (Photo courtesy Gene and Cathy Florence)

Floragold, platter, iridescent, 11¼" **25.00**

Floragold, tumbler, iridescent, footed, 10-oz or 11-oz, ea **18.00**

Harp, ashtray/coaster, crystal . **5.00**

Harp, cake stand, ice blue, 9". **45.00**

Harp, plate, crystal, 7" **12.00**

Harp, vase, crystal, 7½" **25.00**

Holiday, bowl, pink, 8½" **35.00**

Holiday, butter dish, pink **50.00**

Holiday, creamer & sugar bowl, pink, ea **10.00**

Holiday, pitcher, iridescent, 16-oz, 4¾" **25.00**

Holiday, plate, pink, 9" **18.00**

Holiday, tumbler, crystal, footed, 5¼-oz, 4¼" **8.00**

Iris & Herringbone, butter dish, w/lid, iridescent.............. **45.00**

Iris & Herringbone, tumbler, footed, crystal or iridescent, 6" ... **17.00**

National, bowl, crystal, 4½" **4.00**

National, pitcher, crystal, 64-oz.**27.50**

National, relish dish, crystal, 6-part, 13" **18.00**

National, salt & pepper shakers, crystal, pr **9.00**

Morgantown

Crinkle, bowl, all colors, 4" or 5",
ea.. 8.00
Crinkle, pitcher, all colors, 34-oz. 75.00
Crinkle, plate, all colors, 9¼". 20.00
Crinkle, tumbler, all colors, 10-
oz................................. 18.00

Paden City

Emerald Glo, bowl, salad; 10". 33.00
Emerald Glo, casserole, w/metal
cover on tray 45.00
Emerald Glo, creamer............ 20.00
Emerald Glo, cruet................ 25.00
Emerald Glo, relish dish, divided,
w/metal handle, 9" 35.00
Emerald Glo, salt & pepper shak-
ers, pr............................. 25.00
Emerald Glo, tray, handled, 8½". 35.00

US Glass

**King's Crown/Thumbprint, butter
dish, rare, from $200.00 to $225.00.**

Manhattan, bowl, crystal, 4½". 4.00
Manhattan, bowl, crystal, 6". 10.00
Manhattan, celery dish, crystal,
9½" 15.00
Manhattan, compote, crystal,
10½" 15.00
Manhattan, creamer & sugar bowl,
crystal, ea 6.00

Manhattan, cup, crystal 4.00
Manhattan, goblet, crystal, 4-oz .. 8.00
Manhattan, goblet, crystal, 6-oz .. 5.00
Manhattan, goblet, crystal, 10-oz. 10.00
Manhattan, goblet, crystal, 12-oz .. 12.00
Manhattan, plate, crystal, 6" ... 5.00
Manhattan, plate, crystal, 11".. 12.00
Manhattan, tumbler, crystal, flat,
8-oz................................. 16.00

Viking

Prelude, bowl, crystal, shallow,
13"................................... 45.00
Prelude, butter dish, crystal, oval,
8½" 35.00
Prelude, cake stand, crystal, footed,
5½x11" dia 55.00
Prelude, creamer & sugar bowl,
crystal, ea 12.50
Prelude, plate, crystal, flat or
turned-up edge, 14" 45.00
Prelude, plate, crystal, tab handles,
13".................................. 40.00
Prelude, relish dish, crystal, 3-part,
2 handles, 10".................. 32.00
Prelude, salt & pepper shakers,
crystal, 3½", pr 40.00
Prelude, vase, crystal, 8" 40.00

Franciscan

When most people think of
the Franciscan name, their Apple
or Desert Rose patterns come to
mind immediately, and without
a doubt these are the most collectible of the hundreds of lines
produced by Gladding McBean.
Located in Los Angeles, they produced quality dinnerware under
the trade name Franciscan from
the mid-1930s until 1984, when

they were bought out by a company from England. Many marks were used; most included the Franciscan name. An 'F' in a square with 'Made in USA' below it dates from 1938, and a double-line script F was used later. Some of this dinnerware is still being produced in England, so be sure to look for the USA mark. For an expanded listing, see *Schroeder's Antiques Price Guide* (Collector Books).

Apple, bowl, cereal; 6".............**16.50**
Apple, bowl, salad; 10"...........**27.50**
Apple, butter dish **50.00**
Apple, plate, side salad..........**38.00**

Apple, platter, 14", $50.00.

Apple, sherbet **22.00**
Apple, teacup & saucer..........**12.00**
Coronado, bowl, cereal; from $10 to **15.00**
Coronado, bowl, serving; oval, 10½", from $20 to **33.00**
Coronado, cigarette box, w/lid, from $40 to...............................**75.00**
Coronado, cup & saucer, jumbo .**32.00**
Coronado, pitcher, 1½-qt, from $25 to **45.00**
Coronado, plate, chop; 14" dia, from $20 to...............................**30.00**
Coronado, plate, 9½", from $10 to **15.00**

Coronado, relish dish, oval, from $12 to **25.00**
Desert Rose, ashtray, sq **15.00**
Desert Rose, bowl, fruit.........**10.00**
Desert Rose, butter dish........**45.00**
Desert Rose, caserole, 1½-qt.. **75.00**
Desert Rose, compote, lg........**55.00**
Desert Rose, cup & saucer, tall..**35.00**
Desert Rose, egg cup..............**35.00**
Desert Rose, jam jar **125.00**
Desert Rose, napkin ring.......**50.00**
Desert Rose, pitcher, milk **65.00**
Desert Rose, plate, grill; from $75 to **95.00**
Desert Rose, sherbet..............**20.00**
Desert Rose, sugar bowl, regular...............................**25.00**
Desert Rose, tumbler, juice; 6-oz **45.00**
Ivy, bowl, fruit **12.00**
Ivy, coffeepot.........................**150.00**
Ivy, creamer, regular..............**22.00**
Ivy, jam jar **150.00**
Ivy, plate, 9½" **22.00**
Ivy, teapot **150.00**
Ivy, tumbler, 10-oz..................**32.50**
Starburst, ashtray, individual.**20.00**
Starburst, bowl, divided, 8", from $25 to **35.00**
Starburst, bowl, soup/cereal; from $15 to **25.00**
Starburst, butter dish, from $50 to **65.00**
Starburst, coffeepot, from $175 to..................................**225.00**
Starburst, creamer, from $22 to................................**25.00**
Starburst, jam dish, from $40 to **50.00**
Starburst, plate, 8", from $10 to **15.00**
Starburst, relish tray, 3-part, 9", from $75 to **95.00**

Starburst, salt & pepper shakers, bullet shape, 3½", pr from $50 to **65.00**

Frankoma

Since 1933 the Frankoma Pottery Company has been producing dinnerware, novelty items, vases, etc. In 1965 they became the first American company to produce a line of collector plates. The body of the ware prior to 1954 was a honey tan that collectors refer to as 'Ada clay.' A brick red clay (called 'Sapulpa') was used from then on, and this and the colors of the glazes help determine the period of production. For more information refer to *Frankoma and Other Oklahoma Potteries* by Phyllis and Tom Bess (Schiffer), and *Frankoma Pottery, Value Guide and More*, by Susan N. Cox. See Clubs and Newsletters for information on the Frankoma Family Collectors Association.

Ashtray, leaf shape, Prairie Green, #226, 6x12" **30.00**
Ashtray, Oklahoma shape, UCT John B Baumen...1968-69, Prairie Green **10.00**
Bean pot, Mayan Aztec, Prairie Green, ... **32.00**
Candleholders, 2-light; Prairie Green, 1950s, 3¾x5", pr.. **60.00**
Candy dish, Desert Gold, 3-section leaf shape, #83, 2x12x8". **25.00**
Christmas card, 1957-60, from $65 to **70.00**
Christmas card, 1973-82, from $25 to **30.00**

Creamer, Wagon Wheel, Prairie Green, 1948, 2½x3x1" **30.00**

Gravy boat and tray, Plainsman, Prairie Green, from $35.00 to $40.00.

Honey pitcher, dark glossy green, #835, 1960s, 8" **27.50**
Honey pot, Desert Gold, #803, 4¾x3¾" **52.50**
Leaf dish, Prairie Green, 1940s, 12x6" **75.00**
Mug, Aztec, white................... **12.00**
Mug, Elephant, 1969, from $40 to. **60.00**
Pitcher, cream; Wagon Wheel, Prairie Green, Ada clay .. **30.00**
Pitcher, Osage Brown, w/ice lip, 1940-42, 7x8¼" **85.00**
Planter, Autumn Yellow, 8-sided, Sapula clay, 5x5¼" **20.00**
Planter/bowl, horn of plenty, Prairie Green, #222, ca 1960, 5x12" **17.50**
Plate, Madonna, Grace Lee Frank, 1977, 8¼" **30.00**
Plate, Oh Come Let Us Adore Him, white, 1981 .... **10.00**
Salt & pepper shakers, Mayan Aztec, Flame Red, 4½", pr **28.00**
Teapot, South Western design, Flame Red **75.00**
Trivet, rooster embossed on blue, 6½" dia **40.00**
Vase, bud; Old Gold, snail form, #331, 1940s, 6½".............. **50.00**

Vase, collector; V-15, 13", from $75 to **85.00**

Wall pocket, cowboy boot, light blue **45.00**

Wall vase, Phoebe, Prairie Green, Ada Clay, #730 .... **150.00**

Fruit Jars

Some of the earliest glass jars used for food preservation were blown, and corks were used for seals. During the nineteenth century, hundreds of manufacturers designed over 4,000 styles of fruit jars. Lids were held in place either by a wax seal, wire bail, or the later screw-on band. Jars were usually made in aqua or clear, though other colors were also used. Amber jars are popular with collectors, milk glass jars are rare, and cobalt and black glass jars often bring $3,000.00 and up, if they can be found! Condition, age, scarcity, and unusual features are also to be considered when evaluating old fruit jars.

Acme Seal (script), clear, regular mouth, qt **50.00**

Amazon Swift Seal (in circle), blue, pt **22.00**

Atlas, E-Z Seal, green, qt **15.00**

Atlas Mason Improved, sky blue, qt **25.00**

Atlas Whole Fruit, clear, qt **2.00**

Ball Improved, blue, pt **12.00**

Ball Improved (dropped A), aqua, qt **4.00**

Ball Perfect Mason, black, 9 ribs, ½-gal **15.00**

Ball Refrigerator & Freezer Jar, clear, pt **3.00**

Ball Special, blue, shoulder seal, qt **50.00**

Ball Sure Seal, black, ½-gal... **12.00**

Bamberger's Mason Jar (in circle), blue, pt **30.00**

Bernardin (script) Underlined Mason, clear, pt **10.00**

Clark's Peerless, aqua, qt **5.00**

Clark's Peerless, aqua, ½-gal. **18.00**

Converse Jar, clear, qt **5.00**

Crown Cordial & Extract & Co New York, clear, ½-gal **12.00**

Crown Mason, clear, qt **2.00**

Double Seal, clear, qt **15.00**

Excelsior, aqua, ½-gal (unlisted size) **65.00**

Foster Sealfast, clear, pt **3.00**

Globe, brillant amber with strong strike, #65 on base, quart, $100.00.

Hazel-Atlas Lightning Seal, aqua, qt **25.00**

Hero, aqua, 2-pc lid, ½-gal..... **80.00**

Ideal, aqua, midget **75.00**

Jewel Jar, clear, made in Canada, qt **5.00**

Kerr 'Self-Sealing' Trade Mark Patented Mason, clear, ½-gal **5.00**

Lamb Mason, clear, zinc lid, qt. **3.00**

Lockport Mason Improved, clear, ½-gal................................. **20.00**

Mason (star) H Jar, clear, pt ... **1.00**

Mason's 14 (underlined) Patent Nov
30th 1858, aqua, ½-gal..... **18.00**
Mountain Mason, clear, round, qt.**22.00**
Presto Supreme Mason, clear, qt. **1.00**
Princess, clear, qt.................... **18.00**
Putnam (base), amber, qt...... **45.00**
Safe Seal (in circle), blue, pt ... **5.00**
Silicon (in circle), aqua, pt..... **18.00**
TM Lightning, aqua, ½-gal.... **15.00**
Trade Mark Banner WM Warrented,
blue, qt.............................. **7.00**
True's Imperial Brand DW True
Portland ME, clear, pt.... **10.00**
Victory (in shield) on lid, clear, twin
side clamps, pt **4.00**
Wears Jar (in circle), clear, qt . **9.00**

Games

The ideal collectible game is
one that combines playability (i.e.,
good strategy, interaction, surprise,
etc.) with interesting graphics and
unique components. Especially
desirable are the very old games
from the nineteenth and early twentieth centuries as well as those relating to early or popular TV shows and
movies. As always, value depends on
rarity and condition of the box and
playing pieces. For a greatly expanded list and more information, see
*Schroeder's Collectible Toys, Antique
to Modern* (Collector Books).

77 Sunset Strip, Lowell, 1960,
EXIB **30.00**
$10,000 Pyramid, Milton Bradley,
1972, NMIB...................... **25.00**
$64,000 Question, Lowell, 1955,
EXIB **25.00**
A-Team, Parker Bros, 1984,
EXIB **25.00**

Addams Family (Cartoon Series), Milton
Bradley, 1974, NMIB..............**35.00**
Advance to Boardwalk, Parker
Bros, 1985, NMIB **15.00**
Alien, Kenner, 1979, EXIB.... **25.00**
All in the Family, Milton Bradley,
1972, NMIB..................... **25.00**
Amazing Spider-Man, Milton
Bradley, 1966, EXIB **50.00**
Annie the Movie Game, Parker
Bros, 1981, NMIB **10.00**
Archies, Whitman, 1969, NMIB. **30.00**
Atom Ant Saves the Day, Trans-
ogram, 1966, NMIB **50.00**
Bamboozle, Milton Bradley, 1962,
NMIB.............................. **30.00**
Baretta, Milton Bradley, 1976,
NMIB.............................. **30.00**
Barney Miller, Parker Bros, 1977,
NMIB.............................. **20.00**
Batman, Milton Bradley, 1966,
NMIB.............................. **50.00**
Battle of the Planets, Milton
Bradley, 1970s, NMIB **30.00**
Beat the Clock, Milton Bradley,
1960s, NMIB **15.00**
Ben Casey, Transogram, 1961,
MIB................................ **20.00**
Beverly Hillbillies Card Game,
Milton Bradley #4332, 1963,
NMIB.............................. **65.00**
Bewitched Card Game, Milton
Bradley, 1965, EX **30.00**
Black Beauty, Transogram, 1957,
NMIB.............................. **25.00**
Bugaloos, Milton Bradley, 1971,
EXIB **30.00**
Bullwinkle's Super Market Game,
Whitman, 1970s, EXIB... **25.00**
Candyland, Milton Bradley, 1955,
NMIB.............................. **20.00**
Captain America, Milton Bradley,
1977, NMIB..................... **20.00**

193

Careers, Parker Bros, 1965, NMIB.**20.00**

Cat & Mouse Game, Parker Bros, 1964, EXIB **10.00**

CHiPs Game, Milton Bradley, 1977, NMIB **10.00**

Clue, Parker Bros, 1972, NMIB.**10.00**

Combat Card Game, Milton Bradley #4539, 1964, EXIB **20.00**

Crazy Clock, Ideal, 1964, NMIB. **50.00**

Dark Shadows, Whitman, 1968, NMIB **50.00**

Davy Crockett Rescue Race, Gabriel, 1950s, EXIB **25.00**

Dr Kildare, Ideal, 1962, NMIB..**40.00**

Emergency!, Milton Bradley, 1973, NMIB **40.00**

Family Ties, Apple Street, 1986, EXIB **15.00**

Flintstones, Milton Bradley, 1971, NMIB **20.00**

Flipper Flips, Mattel #5417, 1965, NMIB **75.00**

Fugitive, Ideal, 1964, NMIB .**75.00**

Garrison's Gorilla's Target Game, Hasbro #5118, 1967, EX+IB **35.00**

George of the Jungle, Parker Bros, 1968, NMIB **110.00**

Gilligan's Island, Game Gems/T Cohn, 1965, EXIB **375.00**

Gomer Pyle, Transogram, 1964, EXIB **35.00**

Gunsmoke, Lowell, 1958, NMIB .**75.00**

Happy Days, Parker Bros, 1976, MIB **28.00**

Hopalong Cassidy, Marx, 1950s, EXIB **115.00**

I Spy, Ideal, 1965, NMIB **85.00**

Ipcress File, Milton Bradley, 1966, MIB **40.00**

Jetson's Fun Pad, Milton Bradley, 1963, NMIB **80.00**

King Kong, Milton Bradley, 1966, NMIB **35.00**

Knight Rider, Parker Bros, 1983, EXIB **18.00**

Land of the Lost, Milton Bradley, 1975, NMIB **30.00**

Little Orphan Annie, Parker Bros, 1981, NMIB **18.00**

Lone Ranger, Milton Bradley, 1966, NMIB **35.00**

Looney Tunes, Milton Bradley, 1968, NMIB **60.00**

Man From UNCLE Card Game, Milton Bradley #4532, 1965, EXIB **50.00**

Man From UNCLE Target Game, Marx, 1965, NM **250.00**

Masquerade Party, Bettye-B, 1955, MIB **110.00**

Miami Vice, Pepper Lane, 1984, EXIB **25.00**

Mickey Mouse Pop-Up Game, Whitman, 1970s, MIB **25.00**

Mission Impossible, Ideal, 1967, EXIB **120.00**

Mister Ed, Parker Bros, 1962, EXIB **55.00**

Mork & Mindy, Milton Bradley, 1978, NMIB **20.00**

Mr Green Jeans Animal Rummy Card Game, Fairchild, 1950s, VGIB **20.00**

Munsters Card Game, Milton Bradley, EXIB **50.00**

Murder She Wrote, Warren, 1985, VGIB **10.00**

My Favorite Martian, Transogram, 1963, VGIB **90.00**

Newlywed Game, Hasbro, 1st Edition, 1967, NMIB **25.00**

Nurses, Ideal, 1963, NMIB....**65.00**

Outer Limits, Milton Bradley, 1964, EXIB **240.00**

Pac-Man, Milton Bradley, 1980s, NMIB **20.00**

Partridge Family, Milton Bradley, 1974, NMIB..................... **45.00**

Patty Duke Show, Milton Bradley, 1963, NMIB..................... **40.00**

Petticoat Junction Game, Standard Toykraft, 1963, NMIB..... **85.00**

Pink Panther, Warren, 1977, NMIB.............................. **25.00**

Planet of the Apes, Milton Bradley, 1974, EXIB...................... **50.00**

Popeye Ring Toss, Transogram, EXIB.............................. **165.00**

PT Boat 109, Ideal, 1963, VGIB. **45.00**

Rat Patrol, Transogram, 1966, NMIB.............................. **90.00**

Road Runner, Milton Bradley, 1968, NMIB.............................. **35.00**

Rocky & His Friends, Milton Bradley, 1960, EXIB....... **75.00**

Sea Hunt, Lowell, 1961, EXIB. **75.00**

Simpsons Don't Have a Cow, Milton Bradley #4025, 1990, NMIB............................ **20.00**

Snoopy Car Game, Ideal, 1965, NMIB.............................. **25.00**

Space: 1999, Milton Bradley, 1975, NMIB.............................. **25.00**

Starsky & Hutch Detective, Milton Bradley, 1977, NMIB...... **25.00**

Stymie Card Game (Bewitched), Milton Bradley #4534, 1964, EXIB.............................. **75.00**

Supercar to the Rescue, Milton Bradley #4216, 1962, EXIB........................ **75.00**

Tom & Jerry, Milton Bradley, 1977, EXIB.............................. **30.00**

Top Cat, Cadaco-Ellis, 1961, NMIB.............................. **70.00**

Uncle Wiggily, Parker Bros, 1979, NMIB.............................. **25.00**

Virginian, Transogram, 1962, EXIB.............................. **100.00**

Voyage to the Bottom of the Sea Card Game, Milton Bradley, 1964, NMIB..................... **50.00**

Wally Gator Game, Transogram, 1963, NMIB.................. **100.00**

Wanted Dead or Alive, Lowell, 1959, EXIB................... **110.00**

Welcome Back Kotter Card Game, Milton Bradley #4635, 1976, NMIB.............................. **40.00**

White Shadow Bas-Ket A Year Round Sports Game, Cadaco, NMIB............................ **125.00**

Who Framed Roger Rabbit?, Milton Bradley, 1987, NMIB...... **50.00**

Wonder Woman, Hasbro, 1967, NMIB.............................. **60.00**

Woody Woodpecker Game, Milton Bradley, 1959, MIB......... **50.00**

Wyatt Earp, Transogram, 1958, EXIB.............................. **70.00**

You Don't Say, Milton Bradley 1963, EXIB.............................. **20.00**

Zorro, Parker Bros, 1966, EXIB. **55.00**

The Brady Bunch Game, Whitman, 1973, MIB, from $150.00 to $200.00.
(Photo courtesy Greg Davis and Bill Morgan)

Garfield

America's favorite grumpy cat, Garfield has his own band of devotees who are able to find a good variety of merchandise modeled after his likeness. Garfield was created in 1976 by Jim Davis. He underwent many changes by the time he debuted in newspapers in 1978. By 1980 his first book was released, followed quickly in 1981 by a line of collectibles by Dakin and Enesco. The stuffed plush animals and ceramic figures were a huge success. There have been thousands of items made since, with many that are hard to find being produced in Germany, the Netherlands, England, and other European countries. Banks, displays, PVCs, and figurines are the most desirable items of import from these countries.

Alarm clock, Sunbeam #883-140, 1978, NMIB...................... **28.00**
Aquarium, plastic figure w/clear plastic tummy bowl, Hawkeye, EX **35.00**
Bank, upright figure w/arms folded, ceramic, Enesco, 6", EX.. **28.00**

Bookends, Garfield© 1978, 1981 United Features Inc. Licensee Enesco, from $50.00 to $60.00. (Photo courtesy Joyce and Fred Roerig)

Candy tin, round, name & image bursting through..., Cheinco, 3½", NM........................... **10.00**
Comb & brush set, orange plastic figural brush, AVON, MIP .**12.00**
Figure, plush, purple nightshirt, cap, slippers, Play-By-Play, 11", NM........................... **10.00**
Figure, plush, Red Hot Lover, Expressions/Paws Inc, 2003, 8", M **6.00**
Figure, plush, w/rabbit in a hat, Dakin, 1981, 9", EX........ **10.00**
Gumball machine, But It Will Cost You, Superior Toy, NM.... **30.00**
Nightlight, plastic, black-outlined image on cloud, Prestigeline, MOC................................ **10.00**
Ornament, Garfield as angel, ceramic, Enesco, 1980s, NM **20.00**
Party horns, paper & plastic, package of 5, Carrousel Party Favors, MIP..................... **10.00**
Playing cards, complete in blue box w/Garfield showing his hand, MIB................................... **5.00**
Wall plaque, framed, You Are What You Eat, wood, Enesco, 5x4", NM................................... **10.00**

Gas Station Collectibles

From the invention of the automobile came the need for gas service stations, which sought to attract customers through a wide variety of advertising methods. Gas and oil companies issued thermometers, signs, calendars, clocks, banks, and scores of other items emblazoned with their logos and catchy slogans. Though a rather specialized area, gas station collectibles encompass a wide variety of items that appeal to automobilia and advertising collectors as well. For further information we recommend *Value Guide to Gas Station Memorabilia* by B.J. Summers and Wayne Priddy (Collector Books).

Badge, Socony Vacuum, place for photo, Pegasus logo below, 2" dia, VG............................175.00

Bank, Phillips 66 embossed on clear glass block, 5x5x3", NM.135.00

Bank, Texaco gas pump, 1920 replica, 1996, MIB................35.00

Banner, New Sinclair Gasoline, Anti-Rust, Super..., 1940s, 56" L, VG 75.00

Blotter, Gargoyle Lubricants, leather w/stitched border, rocker type, EX..............60.00

Calendar, 1937, Richfield dealer, 12 illustrations, 8x7", unused, EX..................................125.00

Calendar, 1939, True Blue, Marathon logo, Brown & Bigelow, 24", EX..............65.00

Calendar, 1956, Dog Gone, Sinclair, Elvgren artwork, complete, 11", EX..............................25.00

Chalkboard, Sinclair H-C Products, green board w/chalk ledge, 24", EX..................................125.00

Clock, Cities Services, green neon, 15" dia, NM+..................75.00

Clock, Conoco, red neon, chrome frame, 15" dia, EX...........50.00

Clock, Sunoco Race Fuels, lights-up, 14" dia, EX..............100.00

Compass, Union 76, suction-cup mount, EX 15.00

Credit card, International Credit Card/Phillips..., 1950s, EX .15.00

Cuff links/tie-bar set, gold cloisonné w/ Shell logo on red, 1960s, M...35.00

Display, Spark Plug Protectors, Perfect Parts, 1960s, w/product, NM...........................30.00

Gas can, Sunoco Sun Oil Co, Mercury Made, 1955, 2½-gal, EX 50.00

Gas globe, American, red, white & blue, 12½", EX...............450.00

Gas globe, Marathon Mile Marker, red, white & blue, Capco frame, EX 250.00

Gas globe, Pure, Capco frame, 1960s, EX 375.00

Gas globe, Sinclair Dino Supreme, white Capco frame, EX.275.00

Gas globe, Texaco Sky Chief, white Capco frame, 1950s, EX.350.00

Gas globe, White Flash, gill body, EX 600.00

Grease can, Mobilgrease #8, cone top, metal, 1940s, 7-oz, NM 20.00

Key chain, Put a Tiger in Your Tank, embossed tiger head, 1½", EX 10.00

Kite, Texaco, lollipop sign w/star logo on white paper, 1950s, M................................. 125.00

Lighter, chrome Zippo pocket type w/yellow & red Shell logo, 1973, EX 40.00

Map, Shell, Golden State International Exposition, 1939, 9x12", VG........................12.00

Map holder, Gulf Oil, w/15 vintage maps, 1950s, 18x9x5", EX.135.00

Map holder, Tourguide/Sinclair logo on red-painted metal, EX.55.00

Mechanical pencil, Gulf, oil can end, blue, white & orange, EX..35.00

Mechanical pencil, Royal Triton Union 76, 1950s, EX.......50.00

Mug, Texaco advertising on milk glass, 1970s, EX..............12.00

Oil bottle, metal cone top, embossed color label, 1-qt................65.00

Oil can, Aero Mobiloil, red gargoyle logo, ca 1934, 1-qt, VG....50.00

Oil can, Agalion Motor Oil, red w/lion head image, 1-gal, VG 350.00

Oil can, Deep-Rock Prize Motor Oil, unused, 1-qt, EX **45.00**

Oil can, Mobiloil, horse logo, red, white & blue, 1-qt, 1940s, EX **45.00**

Oil can, Pennzoil, owl logo on yellow, 5-qt, EX **50.00**

Oil can, Pep Boys Pure As Gold Motor Oil, yellow, 2-gal, EX+...... **100.00**

Oil can, Pioneer Oil, tin, covered wagon scene, 1-gal, EX+.**50.00**

Oil can, Shell Oil, red & yellow, bail handle, 5-gal, EX+ **100.00**

Patch, Sinclair Gasoline H-C, 1960s, 3" dia, EX.............. **15.00**

Patch, Texaco, felt, red star logo on white, 8" dia, NM.......... **100.00**

Pennant, Firestone, orange felt w/blue lettering, 8x28", EX+............**50.00**

Pocket mirror, Metro Gas Mobiloil, red gargoyle logo, EX...... **18.00**

Postcard, Standard, serviceman checking wipers for lady, 1950s, NM+ **12.00**

Premium, mechanical pencil, Skelly Oil, 1940s-50s, VG+ **20.00**

Premium, Sinclair Dinosaurs, set of 4 different, vinyl, MIP **25.00**

Premium, Texaco Fire Chief fireman's hat, molded cellophane, unused, M......................... **45.00**

Radio, early Shell gas pump, red, 10", NM+ **75.00**

Sign, Dunlop Tires, metal, black, red & white, 60x14", EX+..... **100.00**

Sign, Gargoyle Mobiloil, painted tin, red gargoyle, 11" dia, M.... **50.00**

Sign, Phillips 66, porcelain shield, white, black & orange, 46", EX **425.00**

Sign, Put a Tiger In Your Tank & Esso tiger, heavy vinyl, 78x42", EX **85.00**

Thermometer, Champion Spark Plug, die-cut metal, 24", NM **60.00**

Thermometer, Gulf, tin, orange, white & blue, 27x6", EX. **100.00**

Thermometer, Mobilgas in blue, red Pegasus on white, 1990s, 12" dia, NM **30.00**

Toy truck, Gulf Oil 1957 International tow truck, First Gear, 8"............................ **55.00**

Toy fire chief's hat, Texaco Fire Chief, red plastic with center logo, 8", $60.00. (Photo courtesy B.J. Summers and Wayne Priddy)

Gay Fad Glassware

The Gay Fad company started out on a very small scale in the late 1930s, but before long, business was booming! Their first products were hand-decorated kitchenware, but it's their frosted tumblers, trays, pitchers, and decanters that are being sought today. In addition to souvenir items and lines with a holiday theme, they made glassware to coordinate with Royal China's popular dinnerware, Currier and Ives. They're also known for their 'bentware' — quirky cocktail glasses with stems that were actually bent. Look for an interlocking 'G' and 'F' or the name 'Gay Fad,' the latter mark indicating pieces from the late 1950s to the early 1960s. Gay Fad is mentioned in *Hazel-Atlas Glass Identification and Value Guide* by Gene and Cathy Florence (Collector Books). See also Anchor Hocking.

Ashtray, Trout Flies, clear **8.00**
Batter bowl, Fruits, milk white, signed w/F (Federal Glass), handled **55.00**
Bent tray, Phoenix Bird, clear, signed Gay Fad, 13¾" dia **20.00**
Bent tray, Stylized Cats, clear, signed, Gay Fad, 11½" dia **30.00**
Bowl, batter; Fruits, Federal .. **35.00**
Bowl, chili; Fruits, 2¼x5" **12.00**
Canister set, Red Rose, red lids, white interior, 3-pc **60.00**
Cocktail set, metal-frame poodle body w/mixer & glasses, signed ..**60.00**
Cocktail shaker, The Last Hurdle, 32-oz **35.00**
Cruet set, Oil & Vinegar, Cherry, clear **14.00**
Goblet, Bow Pete, Hoffman Beer, 16-oz **15.00**
Ice tub, Gay '90s, frosted **21.00**
Luncheon set, Fantasia Hawaiian flower, 1-place setting, sq. **16.00**
Mix-A-Salad set, Ivy, shaker, garlic press, spoon, recipe book, MIB **75.00**
Mug set, toasts from a different country on ea, frosted, 12-pc... **120.00**
Pilsner set, Gay '90s, character portrait on ea, frosted, 8-pc . **80.00**
Pitcher, Currier & Ives, blue & white, frosted, 86-oz **90.00**
Pitcher, Musical Notes, frosted, 86-oz **55.00**
Plate, Fruits, lace edge, Hazel-Atlas, 8½" **17.50**
Range set, Fighting Cocks, frosted w/red metal caps, 8-oz, 4-pc **120.00**

Salad set, Outlined Fruits, frosted, bowl, 2 cruets & shakers, 5-pc **60.00**
Salt & pepper shakers, Morning Glory, frosted w/red plastic caps, pr **16.00**
Stem, bent cocktail; Souvenir of My Bender, frosted, 3-oz **10.00**
Tom & Jerry set, Christmas bells, milk white, marked GF, bowl & 6 cups **70.00**
Tumbler, Christmas Greetings From Gay Fad, frosted, 4-oz **17.00**
Tumbler, Hors D'oeuvres, clear, 14-oz **10.00**
Tumbler, Pegasus, gold & pink on black, 12-oz **11.00**
Tumbler, Zombie, flamingo, frosted, marked GF, 14-oz **20.00**
Tumbler set, Christmas angels, frosted, 12-oz, 8-pc **72.00**
Tumbler set, French Poodle, clear, 17-oz, 8-pc, original box .. **95.00**
Tumbler set, Ohio Presidents, frosted, 12-oz, 8-pc **55.00**
Vanity set, butterflies in meadow, pink inside, 5-pc **60.00**
Vase, Red Poppy, clear, footed, 10" **24.00**
Waffle set, Little Black Sambo, frosted, 48-oz batter & 11½-oz syrup jug **250.00**
Waffle set, Red Poppy, frosted, 48-oz batter & 11½-oz syrup jug ..**25.00**
Wine set, grapes, decanter & 4 wines, clear, 5-pc **40.00**

Geisha Girl China

More than 65 different patterns of tea services were exported from Japan around the turn of the century, each depicting geishas going about the everyday activities of Japanese life. Mt. Fuji is often featured in the background. Geisha Girl Porcelain is a generic term collectors use to identify them all. Many of our lines contain reference to the color of the rim bands, which many collectors use to tentatively date the ware.

Basket vase, Bamboo Trellis, gold trim, 8½"............................ **75.00**

Biscuit jar, Flower Gathering B, red w/gold, 6½" **45.00**

Bonbon dish, Battledore, olive green, mum shaped **22.00**

Bowl, carp, red w/gold, 6"...... **18.00**

Bowl, chrysanthemum, Parasol C, red w/gold buds, curled handle, 6" **18.00**

Bowl, Samurai Dance, red border w/gold, 3x10" **38.00**

Butter pat, Geisha Dance, 2 geisha w/flowers, gold trim **5.00**

Cake plate, Parasol C, pale cobalt blue, 11¼" **30.00**

Candy dish, Picnic A, gold w/bamboo handle, 5½x6½"......... **25.00**

Celery dish, Foreign Garden, blue border **45.00**

Cocoa pot, Samurai Dance, red border w/gold lacing, fluted, 10" **50.00**

Cup & saucer, Mother & Son A, diaper border, child size . **12.50**

Egg cup, Parasol C, red, modern.**7.00**

Ewer, Garden Bench H, red w/gold lacing **35.00**

Nappy, Leaving Teahouse, multicolored border.................. **22.00**

Plate, Child's Play, cobalt w/gold buds, 6½" **15.00**

Plate, River's Edge, red & gold border, 7¼" **12.00**

Powder jar, Flower Gathering E, red border w/gold lacing, 3½"..**24.00**

Relish dish, Paper Carp, red, fluted edge, cut-out handles...... **12.00**

Salt & pepper shakers, Parasol E, blue border, pr................. **15.00**

Sauce dish, Meeting B, dark apple green, red & gold border..**12.00**

Snack set, Garden Bench D ..**35.00**

Teacup & saucer, Cloud B, red-orange w/yellow............... **14.00**

Teacup & saucer, Writing B, blue w/gold............................... **15.00**

Teapot, Cloud B, red-orange w/yellow, melon ribs **30.00**

Teapot, Grape Arbor, red w/gold.**26.00**

Toothpick holder, Circle Dance, red border, cylindrical **15.00**

Trivet, Prayer Ribbon, red..... **15.00**

Vase, Garden Bench F, green & red border w/gold highlights, Kutani, 5" **32.00**

Refreshment set, Garden Bench D, red border, $35.00. (Photo courtesy Elyce Litts)

GI Joe

Introduced by Hasbro in 1964, 12" GI Joe dolls were offered in four basic packages: Action Soldier, Action Sailor, Action Marine, and Action Pilot. A Black figure was included in the line, and there were representatives of many nations as well. Talking dolls followed a few years later, and scores of accessory items such as vehicles, guns, uniforms, etc., were made to go with them all. Even though the line was discontinued in 1976, it was evident the market was still there, and kids were clamoring for more. So in 1982, Hasbro brought out the 'little' 3¾" GI Joe's, each with his own descriptive name. Sales were unprecedented. The small figures are easy to find, but most of them are 'loose' and played with. Collectors prefer old store stock still in the original packaging; such examples are worth from two to four times more than those without the package, sometimes even more. For more information we recommend *Schroeder's Collectible Toys, Antique to Modern*, published by Collector Books.

12" Figures and Accessories

Accessory, Super Joe Adventure Team, Paths of Danger outfit with binoculars, 1977, MIP, $55.00.

Accessory, Action Pilot Crash Crew Set, #7820, NM 225.00

Accessory, Adventure Soldier Helicopter, #5395, NM.. 275.00

Accessory, Adventure Team Combat Jeep Set w/Trailer, #7000, EX 75.00

Accessory, Adventure Team Rescue Laser, #7311, MOC 75.00

Accessory, Adventure Team Volcano Jumper, #7349, MIP 50.00

Accessory, Army Flag, EX 25.00

Accessory, Astronaut Boots, plastic, VG+, pr 25.00

Accessory, Demolition Armored Suit, EX 15.00

Accessory, Desert Patrol Goggles, amber, EX 75.00

Accessory, Desert Patrol Jeep, #8030, NM 375.00

Accessory, Flame Thrower, green EX 35.00

Accessory, Green Beret Set, #7533, NM 250.00

Accessory, Jackhammer, EX+ . 275.00

Accessory, Landing Signal Officer Coveralls, VG 35.00

Accessory, Marine Pup Tent, EX 25.00

Accessory, Medic Stethoscope, EX 19.00

Accessory, Mobile Support Vehicle, EX+IB 325.00

Accessory, Scuba Gear, orange suit, tanks & fins, NM 150.00

Figure, Action Marine, #7700, EX 115.00

Figure, Action Marine, Demolition Set, #7730, EX................. 60.00

Figure, Action Pilot, Talking, #7890, NM 250.00

Figure, Action Sailor, #7600, NM 250.00

Figure, Action Sailor, Black, #7900, EX 450.00

Figure, Action Sailor, Deep Freeze, #7623, EX **225.00**

Figure, Action Soldier, Command Post Poncho, #7519, 1964, NM...**40.00**

Figure, Action Soldier, Green Beret, #7536, EX **250.00**

Figure, Action Soldier, Snow Troops Set, #7529, NM **50.00**

Figure, Adventure Team, Air Adventurer, #7403, EX. **130.00**

Figure, Adventure Team, Bullet Man, #8026, NM **95.00**

Figure, Adventure Team, Demolition, #7370, EX.... **25.00**

Figure, Adventure Team, Man of Action, Life-Like Hair, #7500, EX **60.00**

Figure, Adventure Team, Volcano Jumper, #7344, MIP **275.00**

Figure, British Commando, #8140, EX **325.00**

3¾" Figures and Accessories

Figure, Cross Country, 1986, NM, $8.00.

Accessory, Ammo Dump Unit, #6129-1, 1985, MIP......... **30.00**

Accessory, Arctic Blast, 1988, EX **12.00**

Accessory, Battlefield Robot Radar Rat, 1989, MIP................ **25.00**

Accessory, CAT Crimson Attack Tank, 1985, Sears, MIP. **110.00**

Accessory, Cobra Night Raven S3P, 1986, MIP **85.00**

Accessory, Crusader Space Shuttle, 1989, MIP **125.00**

Accessory, Ghostrider X-16, Battle Corps, 1993, MOC........... **38.00**

Accessory, Motorized Battle Wagon, 1991, MIP **30.00**

Accessory, Thundercap, 1989, MIB **115.00**

Figure, Aero-Viper, 1989, NM.. **11.00**

Figure, Barbecue, 1985, MOC. **50.00**

Figure, BAT, 1990, MOC **30.00**

Figure, Beach Head, 1986, MOC.**35.00**

Figure, Blocker, 1988, NM **22.00**

Figure, Clutch, 1993, MOC ... **15.00**

Figure, Destro, 1983, MOC ... **65.00**

Figure, Dial-Tone, 1986, MOC. **45.00**

Figure, Hardball, 1988, NM.. **12.00**

Figure, Ken Masters, 1993, MOC **10.00**

Figure, Law & Order, 1987, NM..**20.00**

Figure, Mainframe, 1986, NM. **18.00**

Figure, Ninja Force Bushido, 1993, MOC................................. **10.00**

Figure, Outback, 1987, MOC . **24.00**

Figure, Ranger-Viper, 1990, MOC. **19.00**

Figure, Recoil, 1989, EX.......... **7.00**

Figure, Road Pig, 1988, EX..... **8.00**

Figure, Roadblock, 1984, MOC .**60.00**

Figure, Scoop, 1989, MOC..... **20.00**

Figure, Sneek Peek, 1987, MOC..**25.00**

Figure, Techno-Viper, 1987, MOC............................**23.00**

Figure, Torpedo, 1983, NM.... **30.00**

Figure, Zandar, 1986, NM **18.00**

Glass Animals and Birds

Nearly every glasshouse of note has at some point over the years produced these beautiful models, some of which double for vases, bookends, and flower frogs. Many were made during the '30s through the '50s and '60s, and these are the most collectible. But you'll also be seeing brand new examples, and you need to study to know the difference. A good reference to help you sort them all out is *Glass Animals, Animal & Figural Related Items*, by Dick and Pat Spencer (Collector Books). See also Fenton.

Basset hound, satin, Viking #7965, 1980s, 5x6", from $15 to.**25.00**

Bear (Mama), solid ruby, Viking, Mirror Images, 4x6", from $100 to **150.00**

Butterfly ashtray, frosted, Imperial #5006, 1949-57, from $45 to ..**55.00**

Cat, green, Viking, #1322, 1960s, 8", from $40.00 to $60.00.

Cat, olive green, Fostoria, 1970s, from $30 to **40.00**

Cat (Sassie Susie), black satin, Tiffin, ca 1928-41, from $175 to **200.00**

Chick, amber, New Martinsville #667, 1", from $55 to.......**60.00**

Colt reclining, Fostoria #2589, 2¼x2¾", from $20 to........**35.00**

Dolphin candlestick, amber, Imperial, 1970s-80s, 9", from $40 to **50.00**

Dolphin w/tail up, blue, Fostoria, 1970s, 4½x3¾", from $20 to. **25.00**

Duck ashtray, ice blue, Duncan Miller, Pall Mall line, 4" L, from $225 to **250.00**

Duck w/head up, orange, Viking #1317, 1960s, 13½", from $75 to **85.00**

Eagle, New Martinsville #509, 1930s, from $65 to **75.00**

Giraffe, Heisey, ca 1942-52, 10¾", from $275 to **300.00**

Moth, crystal satin, Cambridge, 1930s, 2¼", from $25 to .. **35.00**

Owl, Fostoria, 1980s-90s, 2½", from $10 to **12.00**

Pelican, Fostoria, ca 1935-44, 4", from $75 to **85.00**

Polar bear, topaz, Fostoria #2431, 1930s, 4½", from $125 to. **150.00**

Polar bear on ice, Paden City #611, 4½", from $60 to **70.00**

Pony kicking, caramel slag, Heisey mold, 4", from $150 to .. **175.00**

Porpoise, New Martinsville #904, 1970s, 6x9", from $25 to. **35.00**

Rabbit head, Heisey, 1940s, 2½x2½", from $300 to **325.00**

Rabbit paperweight, milk glass, Heisey, 1970s, 2¾x3¾", from $35 to............................ **45.00**

Rooster vase, Heisey, 6½" **100.00**

Scottie dog, black satin, Heisey, ca 1979, 6½", from $75 to..**100.00**

Sea gull, flower holder, Cambridge, 8", from $65 to.................. **75.00**

Seal, persimmon, Viking, 9¾" L, from $25 to **35.00**

Sparrow w/head down, yellow satin, LE Smith, 3½", from $20 to. **25.00**

Squirrel, satin, Viking, 1980s, 5x4¾", from $15 to **20.00**

Stork, blue, Fostoria, 1960s, 2x2¾", from $20 to **25.00**

Swan ashtray, ebony body, indents in tail, New Martinsville, from $40 to **45.00**

Sylvan swan, wings spread, opalescent, Duncan Miller, from $325 to **350.00**

Sylvan swan candleholder, Duncan Miller, 5½", ea from $75 to .**85.00**

Glass and Ceramic Shoes

While many miniature shoes were made simply as whimsies, you'll also find thimble holders, perfumes, inkwells, salts, candy containers, and bottles made to resemble shoes of many types. See also Degenhart.

Glass

Baby shoe, frosted, hollow sole, ca 1930, 3⅛x2⅛", $50.00. (Photo courtesy Earlene Wheatley)

Boot, Daisy & Button, canary yellow, Fenton **40.00**

Boot, Daisy & Button, crystal, Duncan & Sons, 4¾" **95.00**

Boot, Daisy & Button on top w/alligator foot, amber, 2½" **25.00**

Boot, embossed w/cow & star, blue w/leather strap, handled . **45.00**

Boot, Hobnail, milk glass, #3002, MI, ca 1971 .... **25.00**

Boot, Santa style, cobalt blue, 1930s, 2½" **20.00**

Boot, textured w/6 embossed side buttons, green, 1970s, 4¾" **15.00**

Bootie, Daisy & Button, French opalescent, Fenton **50.00**

Bottle boot, lady's high-top w/embossed detail, crystal, 1900, 4¼" **50.00**

Bottle shoe, 3 buttons on side, milk glass, ca 1900, 6" **85.00**

Cat slipper, Hobnail, Colonial Blue, Fenton, 1960s, 3x5⅛" **45.00**

Covered shoe, Hobnail, milk glass, w/dome lid, Fenton, 1970s, 6½" **65.00**

Dutch style, blue, 8¼" **125.00**

High heel, round heel plate, amethyst, 1880s, 3¾" **110.00**

High heel, smooth crystal w/gold-trimmed bow, 1980s, 5" .. **25.00**

High-button shoe, 6 buttons, textured, green, ca 1970, 4¾". **15.00**

Skate shoe, Daisy & Square, amber, LE Smith, 1970s, 4¼" **15.00**

Slipper, Daisy & Button, mesh sole, blue, Duncan, lg **55.00**

Slipper, Daisy & Button, pointed toe, jade, Guernsey, ca 1985, 3" **15.00**

Slipper, embossed allover, floral toe decor, dk green, Kanawha, 6" **35.00**

Slipper, embossed bow, any color except yellow, Mosser #109, 4½" **20.00**

Slipper, embossed bow, yellow, Mosser #109, 4½" **25.00**

Slipper, pointed upturned toe, floral on blue w/crystal ruffle, 5" **35.00**

Slipper, Rose Slipper, upturned toe, frosted, Mosser #117, 5¾". **20.00**

Slipper, rounded upturned toe, plain edge, opalescent, Degenhart, 4" **40.00**

Ceramic

Bennington, glossy black w/real brown shoelace, 1920s, 6". **75.00**

Boot, bisque, white over gold w/applied grape cluster, Germany **40.00**

Boot, floral & grape decor on toe, yellow lustre, gold trim, 3¾" **85.00**

Boot, floral & leaf decor on pink lustre, ca 1900, 4½" **55.00**

Boot, gray-blue lustre w/gold applied detail, 6½" **65.00**

Boot, porcelain, white, applied porcelain lace & flowers, gold trim, 3" **45.00**

Boot, tan, Franklin Pottery Co, 2½" **40.00**

Boot, white with flowers, bows, and butterflies, gilded scallops, Germany, 4½x3¾", $35.00. (Photo courtesy Earlene Wheatley)

Bootie, white embossed 'quilted' look w/holes around top, 3" **25.00**

Brogan shoe, porcelain, white w/gold shamrocks & trim, Royal Lara, 4" **45.00**

Cabinet shoe, low cut, white w/embossed gold floral trim, Germany, 6" **75.00**

Dutch shoe, plain green, Metlox, Made in California USA, 1930s, 6" **60.00**

High heel, embossed scroll & floral decor, turquoise, 1950s, 7"..**45.00**

High-button shoe, embossed detail, all white, Red Wing USA 651, 6" **135.00**

Man's shoe, bright yellow, Haegar — Made in the USA........ **45.00**

Slipper, bisque, textured w/applied rose, white w/gold flecks, 4" **45.00**

Slipper, cobalt w/white applied flower, embossed leaves, 5"..... **65.00**

Slipper, Daisy & Button, white w/floral toe decal, lacy edge, 2". **35.00**

Slipper, low back, 4 buttons on both sides, turquoise, 7".......... **45.00**

Slipper, pointed toe, green w/embellished floral toe, 4" **35.00**

Slipper, pointed toe, strap, white w/applied toe decor & gold trim **100.00**

Slipper, upturned toe, applied bow, orange, gold trim, Saxony, 8"................... **450.00**

Slipper, white w/pink airbrushed flowers, embossed gold trim, 6½" **65.00**

Golden Foliage

If you can remember when this glassware came packed in boxes of laundry soap, you're telling your age. Along with 'white' margarine, Golden Foliage was a product of the 1950s. It was made by the Libbey Glass Company, and the line was rather limited; as far as we know, we've listed the entire assortment here. The glassware features a satin band with various leaves and gold trim. (It also came in silver).

Bowl, serving; cone shape...... **15.00**
Creamer & sugar bowl........... **15.00**
Goblet, cocktail; 4-oz................ **6.00**
Goblet, cordial; 1-oz **8.50**
Goblet, pilsner; 11-oz **9.00**
Goblet, sherbet; 6½-oz............. **5.00**
Goblet, water; 9-oz **7.50**
Ice tub, in metal 3-footed frame . **19.50**
Pitcher, w/metal frame, 5¼" .. **16.50**
Salad dressing set, 3 4" bowls & metal caddy..................... **19.50**
Tumbler, beverage; 12½-oz **8.50**

Tumbler, cooler, 14-ounce, $9.50.

Tumbler, jigger; 2-oz **6.50**
Tumbler, juice; 6-oz.................. **5.00**
Tumbler, old-fashioned; 9-oz.... **6.00**
Tumbler, water; 10-oz **8.50**
Tumbler set, 12½-oz, set of 8 in metal frame..................... **60.00**

Granite Ware

Granite Ware is actually a base metal with a coating of enamel. It was first made in the 1870s, but graniteware of all sorts was made well into the 1950s. In fact, some of what you'll find today is brand new. But new pieces are much lighter in weight than the old ones. Look for seamed construction, metal handles, and graniteware lids on such things as tea- and coffeepots. All These are indicators of age. Colors are another, and swirled pieces — cobalt blue and white, green and white, brown and white, and red and white — are generally older, harder to find, and therefore more expensive. For a comprehensive look at this popular collectible, we recommend the *Collector's Encyclopedia of Granite Ware* by Helen Greguire (Collector Books).

Baking pan, blue & white lg swirl, molded handles, eyelet, 2x9x8", EX+ **100.00**
Bean pot, blue & black w/white interior, w/handles & lid, 8x6", NM **125.00**
Bowl, cobalt & white lg mottling, pedestal foot, 8", EX+ ... **150.00**
Bowl, yellow w/white interior, black trim, 3x6" dia, NM.......... **25.00**
Bread pan, aqua & white mottling w/cobalt, Granite Steel Ware, 11", VG............................ **300.00**
Bucket, green veins w/white 'lumpy' effect, green trim, 10", EX.**325.00**
Canister, white w/dark blue trim & lettering, 7½x5", M **85.00**
Chamber pot, blue & white mottling, w/lid, Lisk, 6½x9½", VG **250.00**
Coal hod, black & gray, seamed, 15x10½x18", EX **250.00**

Coffeepot, cream w/green trim, seamed, welded handle, 8", NM **100.00**

Coffeepot, red w/black handles & trim, bulbous, 9", NM ... **100.00**

Colander, white, w/handles, 2½x7½", EX **60.00**

Corn pot, yellow w/brown lid & trim, ceramic on steel, 1988, M **20.00**

Cream can, brown & white fine mottling, seamed, w/handle, 8", NM **140.00**

Cuspidor, blue w/black trim, 4x7½", EX **85.00**

Custard cup, cream w/green trim, 2x3½", NM **55.00**

Egg pan, red, 7 eyes, 10" dia, M **110.00**

Fry pan, red & white lg swirl w/black handle & trim, 1970s, 6½" **185.00**

Funnel, blue & white mottling, gray interior w/blue flecks, 3" dia, EX **165.00**

Kettle, gray large mottle, flared sides, seamless, 7x15¾", G+, $145.00.
(Photo courtesy Helen Greguire)

Mold, ring; yellow w/white interior, 2x8" dia, EX **65.00**

Mug, red & white lg swirl w/white interior, red trim, ca 1970, 3", M .. **30.00**

Pie plate, green & white lg swirl, white interior, cobalt trim, 9", EX **115.00**

Plate, blue & white mottling, black trim, 1x7" dia **75.00**

Pudding pan, white w/cobalt trim, Tru-B1 Quality...label, 7". **35.00**

Roaster, cream w/green trim, 4x9" (w/handles), NM+ **150.00**

Saucepan, blue & white mottling, lipped, 6" dia, G+ **75.00**

Spoon, solid white w/red trim on handle, 13", EX+ **50.00**

Tea steeper, blue & white lg swirl, 6", G **350.00**

Tea strainer, gray med mottling, 1x4" dia, NM+ **100.00**

Teakettle, white w/black trim & knob, bail handle w/wood grip, 8", NM+ **100.00**

Teapot, red & white lg swirl, white interior, seamed, 1950s, 8", NM+ **100.00**

Wash basin, white w/gold bands, black trim, brass eyelet, 12" dia, EX+ **60.00**

Griswold

Cast-iron cooking ware was used extensively in the nineteenth century, and even today lots of folks think no other type of cookware can measure up. But wheather they buy it to use or are strictly collectors, Griswold is the name they hold in highest regard. During the latter part of the nineteenth century the Griswold company began to manufacture the finest cast-iron kitchenware items available at that time. Soon after they became established, they introduced a line of lightweight, cast-aluminum ware that revolutionized the industry. The company enjoyed many prosperous years until its closing in the late 1950s. You'll recognize most items by the marks, which generally will include the Griswold name; for instance, 'Seldon Griswold' and 'Griswold Mfg. Co.' But don't overlook the 'Erie' mark, which the company used as well. See Clubs and Newsletters for information on the Griswold and Cast Iron Cookware Association.

Ashtray, #00, PIN 570, round w/matchbook holder, from $10 to **15.00**

Cake mold, lamb, PIN 866, from $75 to **100.00**

Dutch oven, #6, Tite-Top, block trademark, from $250 to **300.00**

Dutch oven, #8, early Tite-Top, block trademark, from $40 to **60.00**

Dutch oven, #8, early Tite-Top, block trademark, full writing on lid **50.00**

Dutch oven, #10, Tite-Top baster, slant EPU trademark, from $125 to **150.00**

Gem pan, #1, PIN 940, slant EPU trademark, from $200 to . **250.00**

Gem pan, #3, PIN 942, slant trademark, from $250 to **300.00**

Gem pan, #19, fully marked, 6-cup golf ball, from $250 to **300.00**

Gem pan, #100, heart & star, 5 cups, from $600 to **800.00**

Gem pan, #273, cornstick, from $15 to **20.00**

Gem pan, #2700, cornstick, from $275 to **325.00**

Griddle, #8, slant EPU trademark, X-bar support, handle, from $20 to **40.00**

Griddle, #12 Gas & Vapor, marked Erie Gas Griddle, from $275 to **325.00**

Griddle, #14, block trademark, bailed, from $50 to **75.00**

Muffin pan, #3, marked #3 & PIN 943 only, 11-cup, from $150 to.................................... **175.00**

Roaster, #3, block trademarks, lid marked Oval Roaster, from $475 to **525.00**

Roaster, #5, block trademarks, full writing on lid, from $200 to **350.00**

Skillet, #2, slant EPU trademark, heat ring, from $375 to. **425.00**

Skillet, #3, block trademark, no heat ring, from $10 to..... **20.00**

Skillet, #3, PIN 3103 (+), Square Fry Skillet, from $75 to . **115.00**

Skillet, #4, block trademark, heat ring, from $375 to **425.00**

Skillet, #4, block trademark, no heat ring, from $40 to..... **60.00**

Skillet, #5, sm trademark, grooved handle, from $10 to......... **15.00**

Skillet, #6, block trademark, heat ring, from $50 to **75.00**

Skillet, #7, block trademark, heat ring, from $45 to **55.00**

Skillet, #8, block trademark, no heat ring, extra deep, from $50 to **75.00**

Skillet, #9, Victor, fully marked, from $35 to **45.00**

Skillet, #10, block trademark, heat ring, from $50 to **55.00**

Skillet, #10, block trademark, no heat ring, from $40 to..... **60.00**

Skillet, #11, slant EPU trademark, from $250 to **300.00**

Skillet, #14, block trademark, from $125 to **175.00**

Skillet, #55, Made in Sidney OH, sq, from $25 to **35.00**

Skillet lid, #7, block trademark, high dome, smooth, from $40 to **60.00**

**Teakettle, aluminum, two-pint, 7½",
$220.00.**

Teakettle, #8, spider trademark top, from $400 to **500.00**

Trivet, #9, PIN 207, Dutch oven, from $25 to **35.00**

Waffle iron, #2, Savory, sq ... **425.00**

Waffle iron, #7, finger ring, low-handle base, from $100 to **125.00**

Guardian Ware

The Guardian Service company was in business from 1935 until 1955. They produced a very successful line of hammered aluminum that's just as popular today as it ever was. Sold through the home party plan, special hostess gifts were offered as incentives. Until 1940 metal lids were used, bud during the ware when the government restricted the supply of available aluminum, glass lids were introduced.

Be sure to judge condition when evaluating Guardian Service.

Wear, baked-on grease, scratches, and obvious signs of use devaluate its worth. Our prices range from pieces in average to exceptional condition. To be graded exceptional, the interior of the pan must have no pitting and the surface must be bright and clean. An item with a metal lid is worth 25% more than the same piece with a glass lid.

Ashtray, glass, knight & white stars logo, hostess gift, from $10 to **15.00**

Beverage urn (coffeepot), glass lid, screen & dripper, 15", from $50 to **60.00**

Chicken frier, glass lid, 12", from $60 to **80.00**

Coaster set, glass, knight logo, 6 in upright metal carrier **35.00**

Condiment set, 3 glass-lids, 3-legged wire frame w/wood knob, from $175 to **225.00**

Dome cooker, Tom Thumb, glass lid, w/handles, 3½x5" dia, from $25 to **35.00**

Dome cooker, 1-qt, glass lid, w/handles, 6¾" dia, from $30 to . **45.00**

Dome cooker, 2-qt, glass lid, w/ handles, 4½x10½" dia, from $35 to **50.00**

Dome cooker, 4-qt, glass lid, w/handles, 6½x10½" dia, from $35 to **55.00**

**Gravy boat and undertray, from
$30.00 to $45.00.**

Griddle/tray, w/handles, 12½" dia cooking area, 17" wide, from $20 to.............................**30.00**

Ice bucket & liner, w/glass lid, from $45 to..............................**65.00**

Kettle oven, glass lid, bail handle, w/rack, 8x12" dia, from $100 to.....................................**125.00**

Lid, glass, 7" dia, from $15 to . **18.00**

Lid, glass, 10" dia...................**30.00**

Omelet pan, double black handle, from $50 to......................**65.00**

Potato ricer, w/wood pestle, complete, 11"........................**125.00**

Pressure cooker, minimum value......................... **100.00**

Roaster, glass lid, no rack, 16½" L, from $100 to..................**125.00**

Roaster, metal lid, w/rack, 16½" L, from $175 to..................**225.00**

Roaster, metal lid, 4x12½" L, from $60 to..............................**80.00**

Salt & pepper shakers, metal chef figures, hostess gift, 3½", pr.....**45.00**

Steak servers, oval w/tree design in well, set of 4.....................**60.00**

Tray, hammered center, w/handles, 13" dia, from $20 to........**30.00**

Tureen casserole, glass lid, from $65 to...............................**90.00**

Gurley Candles

Santas, choir boys, turkeys, and eagles are among the figural candles made by this company from the 1940s until as late as the 1960s, possibly even longer. They range in size from 2½" to nearly 9", and they're marked 'Gurley' on the bottom. Because they were so appealing, people were reluctant to burn them and instead stored them away and used them again and again. You can still find them today, especially at flea markets and garage sales. Tavern candles (they're marked as well) were made by a company owned by Gurley; they're also collectible.

Birthday, boy, marked Tavern, 3"..**5.00**

Christmas, choir boy, maroon, 7", pr.......................................**24.00**

Christmas, church, white, w/choirboy inside, 6"...................**14.50**

Christmas, evergreen tree, 3¼". **6.00**

Christmas, Nativity, 5-pc, MIP..**35.00**

Christmas, reindeer, marked Tavern, 3½".........................**2.50**

Church with three green trees against starry night background, MOC, $24.50.

Easter, chick, pink or yellow, 3". **6.00**

Easter, egg, pink, w/bunny inside, 3".......................................**10.00**

Easter, lily, white w/blue lip & green candle, 3"................**4.50**

Easter, rabbit w/carrot winking, 3¼".......................................**6.00**

Halloween, black cat w/orange candle beside it, 4"................**22.50**

Halloween, ghost, orange, 5", from $8 to..............................**10.00**

Halloween, jack-o'-lanterns (5) w/white candles, 1950s, unused, MIP.**50.00**

Halloween, owl, orange, cut-out w/black candle behind it.....................**25.00**

Halloween, pumpkin w/black cat, 2½" **9.00**
Halloween, witch holding pumpkin, 8" **25.00**
Halloween, witch in cauldron, 6" **28.00**
Thanksgiving, Pilgrim boy & girl, 5¼" & 5½", pr **15.00**
Thanksgiving, sailing ship, gold, 7½" **12.50**
Thanksgiving, turkey, 2½" **2.50**
Thanksgiving, turkey, 6¼" **12.00**
Wedding, bride & groom, 4½", ea **12.50**

Hagen-Renaker

This California company has been producing quality ceramics since the mid-1940s — mostly detailed, lifelike figurines of animals, though they've made other decorative items as well. Their Designers Workshop line was primarily horses, larger than most of their other figures. Their portrayal of Disney charcters is superb. Other lines collectors seek are their Millesan Drews Pixies, Rock Wall Plaques and Trays (decorated with primitive animals similar to cave drawings), Black Bisque animals, and Little Horribles (qrotesque miniature figures). In the late 1980s, they introduced Stoneware and Specialty lines, larger than the miniatures but smaller than the Designers Workshop line. They continue to make the Specialties yet today.

Black Bisque animal, bull, blue-green enamel, 1959, 4¼". **85.00**

Black Bisque animal, dachshund, black & white, 1959, 9½", rare **250.00**
Designers Workshop figurine, Alex (rooster), glossy red, 1955-72, 7" **125.00**
Designers Workshop figurine, Chester (terrier puppy), 1955, 2¼" **75.00**
Designers Workshop figurine, Ching Wu (Siamese cat), 1954-69, 6½" **75.00**
Designers Workshop figurine, cottontail rabbit, 1954, 2½". **35.00**
Designers Workshop figurine, Jane (squirrel), 1960-72, 5¼" .. **65.00**
Designers Workshop figurine, Timothy (mouse) w/hat, 1958-86, 2½" **45.00**
Designers Workshop figurine, Willy (duckling) seated, 1954-79, 1⅞" **50.00**
Disney miniature, Alice (Alice in Wonderland), 1957, 1¾". **175.00**
Disney miniature, Flower (skunk from Bambi), 1956-57, 1¼" **65.00**
Disney miniature, Gus (mouse from Cinderella), 1956-57, 1¼" **250.00**
Disney miniature, Scamp (Lady & the Tramp), 1955-59, 1".. **40.00**
Little Horribles, Anxious, #443, 1959, 1¾" **260.00**
Little Horribles, Peeping Tom, 1959, 1½" **140.00**
Little Horribles, Vulture, 1958-59, 2" **60.00**
Miniature, Afghan dog, 1992-93, 2⅜" **25.00**
Miniature, bantam rooster, A-94, 1970-79 ...... **15.00**
Miniature, cockatoo on ring, A-897, 1987-88, 1⅞" **40.00**

Miniature, ewe walking, A-13, 1949, rare, 2⅛" 200.00

Miniature, ferret walking, A-3319, current, 1½" 5.00

Miniature, manatee, A-3186, 1995-97, ¾" 15.00

Miniature, rocking horse, A-990, 1981, 2"............................ 20.00

Miniature, wart hog, A-3167, 1995-96, 1¼" 20.00

Specialty figurine, egret, #2095, 1991, 3¾" 50.00

Specialty figurine, gorilla, #3015, 1991-93, 2½" 40.00

Specialty figurine, kudu, #2098, 1991-92, 4¼" 150.00

Wall plaque, butterfly (rock plaque), 1959-60, 8½x14" 80.00

Wall plaque, Siamese cats (rock plaque), 1959-60, 16½x12". 300.00

Zany Zoo, baboon, brown, Aurasperse finish, 1960 only, 3½" 250.00

Hall

Most famous for their extensive lines of teapots and colorful dinnerwares, the Hall China Company still operates in East Liverpool, Ohio, where they were established in 1903. Refer to *Collector's Encyclopedia of Hall China* by Margaret and Kenn Whitmyer (Collector Books) for more information. See Clubs and Newsletters for information on the Hall China Collector's Club. For listings of Hall's most popular dinnerware line, see Autumn Leaf.

Arizona, bowl, coupe soup; Tomorrow's Classic, 9" 10.00

Arizona, platter, 17"............... 38.00

Blue Blossom, bean pot, New England, #4 .... 225.00

Blue Blossom, creamer, New York.. 45.00

Blue Bouquet, bowl, flared, 7¾".45.00

Blue Bouquet, plate, 7¼" 10.00

Blue Garden, ball jug, #1 .... 145.00

Blue Garden, creamer, morning set................................... 55.00

Blue Willow, ashtray.............. 35.00

Bouquet, candlestick, Tomorrow's Classic, 8", ea 50.00

Bouquet, vase, Tomorrow's Classic, 8"....................................... 95.00

Buckingham, casserole, Tomorrow's Classic, 1¼-qt 40.00

Buckingham, plate, Tomorrow's Classic, 6" 6.00

Cactus, bowl, batter; Five Band . 125.00

Cactus, custard, Radiance 24.00

Cameo Rose, bowl, cream soup; E-style, 5"............................ 90.00

Cameo Rose, plate, 10" 25.00

Caprice, egg cup, Tomorrow's Classic............................ 47.00

Caprice, vase, Tomorrow's Classic............................ 75.00

Carrot & Golden Carrot, bowl, Five Band, 6" 25.00

Christmas Tree & Holly, cup . 22.00

Christmas Tree & Holly, platter, 15½" 65.00

Clover & Golden Clover, ball jug, #3 .... 220.00

Clover & Golden Clover, bowl, Thick Rim, 8½"................ 35.00

Crocus, cake plate 42.00

Crocus, pie baker 95.00

Daisy, coffeepot, Cathedral.... 55.00

Dawn, jug, Tomorrow's Classic, 3-qt...................................... 42.00

Eggshell, baker, Dot, fish shape, 13½" 65.00

Eggshell, custard, Plaid or Swag .**22.00**

Fantasy, drip jar, Thick Rim, w/lid..**95.00**

Fantasy, platter, Tomorrow's Classic, 12¼"....................**27.00**

Fern, bowl, fruit; Century, 5¾".. **6.50**

Fern, gravy boat, Century.....**30.00**

Flare-Ware, bowl, salad; Gold Lace, 5".......................................**10.00**

Flare-Ware, casserole, Autumn Leaf, 3-pt..........................**22.00**

Floral Lattice, salt & pepper shakers, canister style, pr **250.00**

Frost Flowers, bowl, onion soup; Tomorrow's Classic, w/lid .**37.00**

Gaillardia, bowl, Radiance, 9" .**30.00**

Gaillardia, teapot, Boston ...**195.00**

Game Bird, casserole, MJ......**85.00**

Game Bird, plate, 9¼"............**45.00**

Garden of Eden, relish, 4-part, Century............................**35.00**

Golden Glo, casserole, basket-weave...............................**50.00**

Golden Oak, bowl, salad........**12.00**

Golden Oak, gravy boat.........**18.00**

Heather Rose, cake plate.......**18.00**

Heather Rose, pie baker........**25.00**

Homewood, coffeepot, Terrace.**75.00**

Homewood, sugar bowl, Art Deco .**30.00**

Meadow Flower, salt and pepper shakers, handles, from $40.00 to $55.00 each. (Photo courtesy Margaret and Kenn Whitmyer)

Medallion, bowl, ruffled, Chinese Red, 9¼"..........................**145.00**

Mums, bowl, Radiance, 6" **22.00**

Mums, canister, Medallion **50.00**

Mums, jug, Simplicity..........**220.00**

No 488, casserole, Sundial **55.00**

No 488, custard, Radiance.....**25.00**

No 488, plate, 9".....................**20.00**

Orange Poppy, cake plate......**45.00**

Orange Poppy, plate, C-style, 9".**30.00**

Orange Poppy, spoon............**120.00**

Pastel Morning Glory, ball jug, #3 & #4 ....**210.00**

Pastel Morning Glory, plate, D-style, 10".....................................**85.00**

Peach Blossom, bowl, coupe soup; Tomorrow's Classic, 9".... **11.00**

Pine Cone, vase, Tomorrow's Classic............................**75.00**

Prairie Grass, creamer **10.00**

Prairie Grass, plate, 7¼"..........**7.50**

Prairie Grass, sugar bowl, w/lid.**18.00**

Primrose, pie baker, E-style ..**25.00**

Primrose, plate, 10" **12.00**

Primrose, platter, oval, E-style, 13¼" **25.00**

Red Poppy, cake plate............**55.00**

Red Poppy, French Baker, fluted...............................**26.00**

Red Poppy, sugar bowl, w/lid.**25.00**

Ribbed, casserole, Russet, 8".**28.00**

Rose White, bean pot, tab handles **95.00**

Sears Arlington, bowl, fruit; 5¼" .. **4.50**

Sears Arlington, platter, oval, E-style, 15½".....................................**25.00**

Sears Fairfax, plate, 8"............**5.50**

Sears Monticello, plate, E-style, 9¼" **9.00**

Sears Monticello, sugar bowl, E-style, w/lid **18.00**

Sears Mount Vernon, bowl, oval, 9¼" **22.00**

Sears Mount Vernon, plate, 10". **8.50**

Sears Richmond/Brown-Eyed Susan, bowl, oval, 9¼".................**22.00**

Sears Richmond/Brown-Eyed Susan, sugar bowl, w/lid **15.00**
Serenade, creamer, Art Deco . **22.00**
Serenade, plate, 9" **11.00**
Shaggy Tulip, pretzel jar **185.00**
Silhouette, bowl, vegetable, round, D-style, 9¼" **32.00**
Silhouette, platter, oval, D-style, 13¼" **30.00**
Silhouette, salt & pepper shakers, w/handles, pr **45.00**
Silhouette, saucer **2.50**
Springtime, bowl, salad; 9" **14.00**
Springtime, plate, 9" **9.50**
Sunglow, plate, Century, 8" **9.50**
Tulip, bowl, oval **37.00**
Tulip, custard, Thick Rim **20.00**
Tulip, plate, 10" **65.00**
Wild Poppy, creamer, Hollywood .. **40.00**
Wildfire, bowl, D-style, 6" **13.00**
Wildfire, gravy boat, D-style . **25.00**
Wildfire, plate, 10" **65.00**
Yellow Rose, bowl, salad; 9" .. **27.00**
Yellow Rose, French baker, fluted **27.00**

Teapots

Nautilus, Cadet Blue, 7x9", from $200.00 to $250.00.

Airflow, cobalt, from $75 to . **100.00**
Aladdin, orchid, from $350 to. **450.00**
Albany, ivory w/standard gold, from $45 to **55.00**
Automobile, turquoise (solid color), from $500 to **550.00**

Baltimore, Marine Blue w/standard gold, from $90 to **110.00**
Boston, cobalt, gold label, from $75 to **85.00**
Boston, turquoise w/standard gold, from $45 to **55.00**
French, Chinese Red (solid color), 8-cup, from $140 to **165.00**
Globe, rose w/standard gold, 6-cup, from $75 to **85.00**
Los Angeles, Dresden w/standard gold, 4- or 8-cup, ea from $50 to **55.00**
Melody, emerald green (solid color), 6-cup, from $200 to **225.00**
Moderne, maroon w/standard gold, 6-cup, from $60 to **75.00**
New York, pink w/standard gold, 6- or 8-cup, ea from $40 to .. **50.00**
Newport, stock green (solid color), from $30 to **35.00**
Parade, warm yellow (solid color), 6-cup, from $60 to **70.00**
Philadelphia, black w/standard gold, 1- or 4-cup, ea from $27 to **32.00**
Regan (Ronald), white, from $100 to **125.00**

Hallmark

Since 1973 the Hallmark Company has made Christmas ornaments, some of which are today worth many times their original price. Our suggested values reflect the worth of those in mint condition and in their original boxes.

Antlers Aweigh/I Love H20, QX5901, figural **18.00**
Babe Ruth 94, QX5323, 1994, 1st in series **18.00**

Baby's First Christmas, QX3126-S, 1982 .... **18.00**

Beary Gifted, Masterpiece 93, QX5762, 1993, figural..... **10.00**

Blessed Family, QLX7564, 2000, lighted porcelain ball...... **18.00**

Bright & Sunny Tepee, QX5247, 1995, Crayola **15.00**

Bugs Bunny, QX5019, 1995, Looney Tunes series, figural **12.00**

Chris Mouse Wreath, QLX7296, 1990, figural, 6th in series............**18.00**

Christmas Brings Us Together, Christmas Plate 2001, QX8285, ceramic **21.00**

Christmas Is Love, XHD1062-N, 1973 .... **30.00**

Christmas Kitty, QX5445, 1989, figural **20.00**

Classic American Car, QX4284, 1992, 1966 Mustang convertible..**30.00**

Classic American Car, QX5422, 1994, 1957 Chevy Bel Air **24.00**

Clauses on Vacation, QX6399, 1999, figural, square dancing... **12.00**

Close Knit Friends 1996, QX5874, figural **15.00**

Cuddly Lamb, QX5199, 1991, figural **10.00**

Dress Reheasal, QX3007, 1983, Norman Rockwell.......... **100.00**

Felicity, QAC6404, 2002, American Girls Collection **18.00**

For Dad 1989, QX4412, figural polar bear **18.00**

From Our Home to Yours, QX2287, glass ball........................... **8.00**

Frosty Friends, QX4822, 1985 . **90.00**

Golf's a Ball 1992, QX5984, golf-ball snowman **18.00**

Gone Fishing, QX4794, 1988, figural **12.00**

Granddaughter, QX2119, 1979..**28.00**

Happy Holidays Barbie, QXC5162, 1997 .... **42.00**

Harry Potter, QXE4381, 2000, Harry flying on broom **30.00**

Heart of Christmas, QX4357, 1991, hinged heart opens to 3-way scene **18.00**

Heathcliff, QX4386, 1986, figural..**16.00**

Holiday Glow, QLX7177, 1991, lighted 3-D scene in ball. **18.00**

Jack-in-the-Box, QX8457, 2003 .**30.00**

Mele Kalikimaka, QX4827, 1987, Windows of the World..... **20.00**

Merry Christmas, QX2079, 1979, glass ball......................... **40.00**

Moonlit Nap, QLX7134, 1988, figural **40.00**

Murray Fire Truck (1955), QBG6909, 1998, figural.. **28.00**

My Third Christmas 1989, QX4695, figural bear...................... **18.00**

Paddington Bear, QX4356/QX4376, 1986, figural **20.00**

Raggedy Ann, QX1591-N, 1975, figural **85.00**

Reindeer Champs, QX4331, 1993.**12.00**

Santa's Countdown to Christmas, QLX7529, 2003................ **18.00**

Snow Buddies, QX4236, figural.**18.00**

Squirrel, QX4466, 1990, Fabulous Decade **25.00**

Swing with Friends, Classical Pooh Collection, Keepsake Ornament, 2000, from $15.00 to $18.00.

Winnie the Pooh, QX5715, 1993,
Pooh on skis **12.00**

Halloween

Halloween items are fast
becoming the most popular holiday-
related collectibles on the market
today. Although originally linked
to pagan rituals and superstitions,
Halloween has long since evolved
into a fun-filled event; and the
masks, noisemakers, and jack-o'-
lanterns of earlier years are great
fun to look for.

Pamela E. Apkarian-Russell
(the Halloween Queen) has written several books on the subject: *Collectible Halloween;*
Salem Witchcraft and Souvenirs;
More Halloween Collectibles;
Halloween: Decorations and
Games; Anthropomorphic Beings
of Halloween; and *The Tastes*
and Smells of Halloween. She
is listed in the Directory under
New Hampshire. See Clubs and
Newsletters for information concerning *The Trick or Treat Trader.*

Die-cut, witch walking, Germany, 15", from $95.00 to $135.00.

Book, Children's Party Book, 1940s,
softcover, 23 pages, EX ... **35.00**

Cake decorations, 3 orange plastic figures w/black trim, 1½",
NM **25.00**
Candy box, cardboard w/image of
owl on branch, EX **45.00**
Candy container, bell-shaped goblin's
head, glass, 1920s, VG **600.00**
Candy container, black cat emerg-
ing from pumpkin, composi-
tion, 6", VG **375.00**
Candy container, devil's head w/
veggie body, composition, 6",
EX **250.00**
Candy container, pumpkin man
seated on tree stump, composi-
tion, 4", VG **345.00**
Candy container, tree trunk,
pressed cardbaord, NM .. **150.00**
Change purse, orange vinyl jack-
o'-lantern form, zipper, chain,
NM+ **50.00**
Costume, Baretta, NMIB **75.00**
Costume, Electra Woman, Ben
Cooper, 1976, MIB **60.00**
Costume, Gumby, green vinyl,
1989, NMIB **25.00**
Costume, Hong Kong Phooey, Ben
Cooper, 1974, NMIB **25.00**
Costume, Jeannie, TV Comic/Ben
Cooper, 1974, EXIB **65.00**
Costume, King Kong, Ben Cooper,
1976, MIB **95.00**
Costume, KISS, Gene Simmons,
Collegeville, 1978, MIB .. **100.00**
Costume, Lemon Meringue
(Strawberry Shortcake), 1981,
EX+IB **25.00**
Costume, Mr Spock, Ben Cooper,
MIB **50.00**
Costume, Space 1999: Commander
Koenig, 1975, MIB **35.00**
Decoration, bat w/movable wings,
paper **6.00**

Decoration, cat face, die-cut cardboard, Germany, 1930s, 8", EX..................................50.00

Decoration, scarecrow w/pumpkin head, die-cut w/crepe limbs, Beistle..............................40.00

Game, Halloween Party, Saalfield #702, unused, NM.........125.00

Hat, orange felt conical form w/painted black cat & jack-o'-lantern, EX......................................15.00

Horn, cardboard litho w/wooden mouthpiece, EX..............50.00

Jack-o'-lantern, composition, with fang insert, Germany, 3½", $250.00.

Lantern, glass jack-o'-lantern globe on black base, battery-op, 5", EX 50.00

Lantern, jack-o'-lantern, litho tin w/metal handle, US Metal, 5", EX 50.00

Lantern, skull, paper pulp, insert eyes & mouth, Germany, 5", VG+...............................850.00

Lantern, witch & owl on 4 panels, cardboard/tissue paper, EX.65.00

Mask, Alfred E Newman, 1964, M.....................................75.00

Nodder, pumpkin man, painted composition, 8½", G.......150.00

Nut cup, jack-o'-lantern, papier-mâché, NM 20.00

Party favor, girl in pumpkin patch, celluloid/crepe, 1930s, 5", EX.........................150.00

Plate, plastic w/Halloween theme, McDonald's, 1995, M 25.00

Roly poly, black cat seated upright w/paws crossed, celluloid, 4", G+ 375.00

Sparkler, witch face, litho tin, Hale-Ness Corp, 1950s, 6½", NMOC.............................50.00

Squeeze toy, Crying Pumpkin, Made in Boston, USA, EX..........45.00

Tambourine, litho tin & textured paper top & festive trim, 1940s, 6", VG+ 50.00

Windup figure, pumpkin girl, composition w/cloth dress, 6½", VG....................................225.00

Yo-yo, skull & crossbones, tin litho, 1960s, MIP 10.00

Handkerchiefs

Lovely to behold, handkerchiefs remain as feminine keepsakes of a time past. Largely replaced by disposable tissues of more modern times, handkerchiefs found today are often those that had special meaning, keepsakes of special occasions, or souvenirs. Many collectible handkerchiefs were never meant for everyday use, but intended to be a feminine addition to the lady's total ensemble. Made in a wide variety of styles and tucked away in grandmother's dresser, handkerchiefs are now being brought out and displayed for their dainty loveliness and fine craftsmanship. For further information we recommend *Ladies' Vintage Accessories,* by LaRee Johnson Bruton, and *Handkerchiefs, A Collector's Guide, Volumes I* and *II,* by Helene Guarnaccia and Barbara Guggenheim (Collector Books).

Arthur Murray...in a Hurry, couples along border form scallop, from $40 to **45.00**

Ballerinas in multicolor tutus form border on navy, from $25 to........**30.00**

Be Cautious...The Enemy Has Ears..., brown & white, 1940s, from $40 to **45.00**

Best Wishes & violets on white cotton, scalloped edge, from $6 to **8.00**

Bon Voyage!, plane & travel itineraries on white, paper label, from $30 to **35.00**

Boston historic sites, black line drawings on pink & white, from $8 to **12.00**

Butterfly specimens w/in 9 squares, yellow border, F Austin, from $20 to **25.00**

Curtain open revealing exotic fish in lg tank, from $12 to.... **15.00**

Feathers of various types & colors float on cream, Monique, from $10 to **15.00**

Florida map, flamingos, sailboats & swordfish, paper label, from $20 to **25.00**

Good Luck, dog looking at 1960 calendar on blue, from $20 to **25.00**

Grand Central Terminal, center scene, name in border, Keefe, from $80 to **90.00**

Happy Birthday, flowers & birthday cakes, blue on white, from $8 to **12.00**

Horses (2) w/heads visible from stall, brown tones, from $10 to **15.00**

Jockey silks on white in center of red & blue stripes, from $10 to.**15.00**

Kangaroos, multicolor on white, Heil, from $10 to **15.00**

Kittens and ball of yarn, printed, cotton, from $10.00 to $15.00. (Photo courtesy Helen Guarnaccia and Barbara Guggenheim)

Kittens, multicolored on yellow, orange & white border, T Keefe............................... **30.00**

Mickey Mouse as Davy Crockett, multicolored, Disney, from $15 to **20.00**

Noah's Ark in center, animals in diamonds along border, from $25 to.............................. **35.00**

Pinwheels on blue, Faith Austin, from $40 to **45.00**

Polka dots, 3 colors on white, white dotted blue border, from $10 to **15.00**

Primrose bouquet w/pink bow on purple, scalloped edge, from $10 to.............................. **15.00**

Restaurants of London, 16 listed, chefs on bl border, Kreier, from $20 to.............................. **25.00**

Rock & Roll, thin dancers in 1950s attire form letters, from $40 to **50.00**

Rose (red) in full bloom, blue leaves form edge, from $10 to.... **15.00**

Sports cars, 15 classic cars on white, Kreier, from $20 to **25.00**

Swallows (stylized) in flight, orange, beige, yellow & white, from $20 to **30.00**

Three Little Kittens..., mitten border, Carl Tait, from $15 to **20.00**

Tricolor of France, red, white & blue, from $15 to **20.00**

Wire-haired terrier at attention on teal green, paper label, from $30 to............................. **35.00**

Woman w/French poodle on red, 1950s, from $15 to **20.00**

Zinnias (3), red, white & blue on black, from $8 to **10.00**

Harker

One of the oldest potteries in the East Liverpool, Ohio, area, the Harker company produced many lines of dinnerware from the late 1920s until it closed around 1970.

Amy, cake lifter **18.00**

Amy, salt and pepper shakers, sky-scraper form, $35.00 for the pair.

Amy, teapot............................. **38.00**
Bridal Rose, fork **28.00**
Cactus, pie baker **25.00**
Calico Ribbon, cake plate, flat. **15.00**
Cameo Rose, tidbit tray, metal center handle **20.00**

Colonial Lady, platter, gold trim, from $12 to **15.00**

Coronet, platter...................... **20.00**
Crayon Apples, batter jug...... **25.00**
Dainty Flower, swirl cup **10.00**
Deco Dahlia, pie baker, 10" ... **25.00**
Deco Dahlia, pie server.......... **22.00**

Dresden, gravy boat, from $65 to **75.00**

Duchess, creamer..................... **8.00**
English Ivy, bowl, mixing...... **40.00**
Godey Print, bowl, fruit........... **3.00**

Heritance, bowl, divided vegetable..................................... **5.00**

Ivy Vine, spoon...................... **28.00**

Ivy Wreath, plate, 10", from $13 to **16.00**

Lovelace, cake lifter **13.00**
Mallow, bowl, 5½".................. **10.00**
Mallow, plate, 6"...................... **5.00**
Modern Tulip, bowl, 7½" **9.00**

Modern Tulip, creamer, 4", from $12 to **15.00**

Oriental Poppy, platter, Melrose, 15"..................................... **20.00**

Petit Point, platter, 12x9"...... **18.00**

Rosebud, shakers, Skyscraper, pr.................................... **22.00**

Ruffled Tulip, tray, tab handles, 12"..................................... **25.00**

Silhouette, bowl, serving; 3x8½".**18.00**

Springtime, platter **20.00**
Vintage, platter **11.00**

Wild Rose, plate, soup; 9¼", from $9 to **12.00**

Wood Song, plate, 7" **8.00**

Hartland

Hartland Plastics Inc. of Hartland, Wisconsin, produced a line of Western and Historic Horseman and Standing Gunfighter figures during the 1950s, which are now very collectible. Using a material called virgin acetate, they molded such well-known characters as Annie Oakley, Bret Maverick, Matt Dillon, and many others, which they painted with highest attention to detail. In addition to these, they made a line of sports greats as well as one featuring religious figures.

Horseman, Lone Ranger, NM, $150.00.

Gunfighter, Bat Masterson, NMIB........................... 500.00
Gunfighter, Bret Maverick, NM.350.00
Gunfighter, Chris Colt, NM.150.00
Gunfighter, Clay Holister....200.00
Gunfighter, Dan Troop, NM..600.00
Gunfighter, Jim Hardy........150.00
Gunfighter, Johnny McKay, NM.......................... 800.00
Gunfighter, Paladin, NM.....400.00
Gunfighter, Vint Bonner, NMIB.850.00
Gunfighter, Wyatt Earp, NM.150.00
Horseman, Alpine Ike, NM..150.00
Horseman, Annie Oakley, NM.275.00
Horseman, Bill Longley, NM.600.00
Horseman, Chief Thunderbird, NM................................150.00
Horseman, Cochise, NM......150.00
Horseman, Davy Crockett, NM..500.00
Horseman, General Custer, NM..........................150.00

Horseman, Hoby Gillman, NM.250.00
Horseman, Jim Hardy, EX+.200.00
Horseman, Paladin, NMIB..350.00
Horseman, Rebel, NM.........250.00
Horseman, Rifleman, NMIB.350.00
Horseman, Seth Adams, NM.275.00
Horseman, Tonto, NM.........150.00
Horseman, Wyatt Earp, NMIB.250.00

Hawaiian Shirts

Vintage shirts made in Hawaii are just one of many retro fads finding favor on today's market. Those with the tag of a top designer can bring hefty prices — the more colorful, the better. Shirts of this type were made in the states as well. Look for grapics that shout 'Hawaii'! Fabrics are typically cotton, rayon, or polyester.

Barfoot Paradise, tiki design in browns & oranges, cotton, 1950s-60s.........................95.00
Betty Lace, rows of blue & red palms on turquoise, coconut buttons...........................68.00
East Wind/Sun Surf, pineapple & trees w/'zebra' trunks on green rayon...............................62.00
Kahala, Fisherman's Paradise name & scene front & back, rayon...............................55.00
Kahanamoku, floral print over blue & white checked design, 1960s 55.00
Kahanamoku, geometrics in gray, black & red on yellow rayon, 1950s..............................225.00
Kalakaua, elongated diamonds & paisley in browns & greens, 1940s................................90.00

Lauhala, palm trees w/blue, green, yellow fronds & clouds on red, 1950s **85.00**

Malihini, red & tan shells, starfish & fishnet on white rayon, 1940s **155.00**

Pataloha, repeated horizontal rows of blue-finned fish, 1 pocket, 1995 .... **65.00**

Penney's, blue volcanos & birds on gray & white surf, tags, 1950s **135.00**

Spooner, rows of exotic flowers in blues & red on green rayon, 1960s **85.00**

Stan Hicks, red, green & blue design on tan cotton, coin buttons, 1950s **70.00**

Sun Surf, fish & coral on light & dark blue rayon **60.00**

Sun Surf, hula girl & pineapple print on red rayon, coconut buttons **65.00**

Surfriders, print in shades of red, black, tan & white, bronze buttons **55.00**

Silk print by Frank MacIntosh, Hookano label, from $600.00 to $800.00. (Collection of John Dowling/copyright John Dowling 1997/model: John Dowling)

Head Vases

Many of them Japanese imports, head vases were made primarily for the florist trade. They were styled as children, teenagers, clowns, and famous people. There are heads of religious figures, Blacks, Orientals, and even some animals. One of the most common types are ladies wearing pearl earrings and necklaces. Refer to *Collecting Head Vases* by David Barron and *Head Vases* by Kathlene Cole (Collector Books) for more information. See Clubs and Newsletters for information concerning the *Head Hunter's Newsletter.*

Girl with umbrella, blue and white, bows in brown hair, Japan, 5" plus umbrella, $100.00.

Baby, blond girl in pink bonnet w/blue phone, #2185, 5". **45.00**

Baby, upright on pillow, #92-USA, 6" **75.00**

Baby in bonnet, head cocked, glancing look, Art Mark, 6" ... **135.00**

Boy, head bowed praying, blond, #E1575, 5¾" **85.00**

Girl, eyes closed, hair up, flower at top of forehead, Japan, 6" **135.00**

Girl, glancing, hands pointing up on chest, ponytail, 6" **105.00**

Lady, black-gloved hand w/fan to face, blond curls, #E1062, 6" **95.00**

Lady, eyes closed, gloved hand to cheek, feathered hat, #2359, 7½" **325.00**

Lady, eyes closed, gloved hand to cheek, flip hairdo, #C6428, 6" **215.00**

Lady, eyes closed, hand to cheek, rose in hair, #E-193/M/A, 6" **270.00**

Lady, eyes closed, picture hat, pearls, #434, 4½" **200.00**

Lady, eyes closed, streaked updo, #C6987, 10½" **950.00**

Lady, eyes closed, updo, brimmed hat, ruffles, pearls, 7" ... **290.00**

Lady, eyes open, gloved hand to chin, streaked updo, #K1633, 7" **320.00**

Lady, Lady Aileen, blond curls w/tiara & necklace, #E1756, 5½" **95.00**

Teen girl, eyes open, hair swept to side, bow headband, #C8493, 6" **235.00**

Umbrella girl, eyes closed, gold trim, #527271, 5" (8" w/umbrella) **215.00**

Young lady, eyes closed, flip, scalloped neckline, pearls, Enesco, 6" **215.00**

Young lady, eyes closed, floral crown, pearl necklace, #C5676, 6½" **215.00**

Young lady, eyes closed, hand to cheek, short hairdo, pearls, Ardco, 6" **215.00**

Young lady, eyes closed, heart-shaped hat, flower earrings, #3515, 8" **310.00**

Young lady, eyes closed, pageboy, 3 flowers at neckline, #C6431, 6" **230.00**

Young lady, eyes closed, short-to-long hair, pearls, #C5939, 6" ... **215.00**

Young lady, eyes closed, streaked curly updo, pearls, #3855, 4½" **170.00**

Young lady, eyes open, lg bow on side, cowl collar, #K1695, 7" **310.00**

Young lady, eyes open, short do, 2 flowers at neckline, Ardco, 6" ... **190.00**

Young lady, eyes open, short hair w/swept bangs, pearls, Ardco, 6" **180.00**

Young lady, eyes open, short swirled do w/side bow, #C8497, 7".**270.00**

Young lady, eyes open, streaked short hair, shoulder bow, #C7294, 8" **320.00**

Holly Hobbie and Friends

Around 1970 a young homemaker and mother, Holly Hobbie, approached the American Greeting Company with some charming country-styled drawings of children. Since that time, hundreds items have been made. Most items are marked HH, H. Hobbie, or Holly Hobbie.

Cup, porcelain, footed, 'A memory is the afterglow...,' WWA, 1974, NM+ **20.00**

Doll, Country Fun Holly Hobbie, 1989, 16", NRFB **20.00**

Doll, Day 'n Night Holly Hobbie, 14", MIB **15.00**

Doll, Dream Along Holly Hobbie, Carrie or Amy, 12", MIB, ea **15.00**

Doll, Grandma Holly, 14", MIB .**20.00**

Doll, Grandma Holly, 24", MIB..**25.00**

Doll, Holly Hobbie, Bicentennial, 12", MIB **25.00**

Doll, Holly Hobbie, Heather, Amy or Carrie, 6", MIB, ea **8.00**

Doll, Holly Hobbie, Heather, Amy or Carrie, 9", MIB, ea **10.00**

Doll, Holly Hobbie, Heather, Amy or Carrie, 16", MIB, ea ...**20.00**

Doll, Holly Hobbie, Heather, Amy or Carrie, 27", MIB, ea ...**25.00**

Doll, Holly Hobbie, Heather, Amy or Carrie, 33", MIB, ea ...**35.00**

Doll, Holly Hobbie Talker, 4 sayings, 16", MIB **25.00**

Doll, Little Girl Holly, 1980, 15", MIB **20.00**

Doll, Robby, 9", MIB...............**15.00**

Doll, Robby, 16", MIB.............**20.00**

Dollhouse, M..........................**200.00**

Ewer, porcelain, 'Start each day in a happy way,' WWA, 1974, 6", NM **23.00**

Trinket box, egg shape, porcelain, 'Fill your world...,' WWA, 1977, M **18.00**

Trinket box, heart shape, porcelain, 'Happiness...,' WWA, 1973, 2x3", NM...........................**16.00**

Vase, porcelain, 'Happiness is having someone...,' WWA, 1973, M **25.00**

Doll, Amy, vinyl, incomplete outfit, otherwise NM, 6", $5.00.
(Photo courtesy Cindy Sabulis)

Holt Howard

This company was an importer of Japanese-made novelty items. From the late 1950s, collectors searched for their pixie kitchenware items such as condiments, etc., all with flat, disk-like pixie heads for stoppers. In the '60s the company designed and distributed a line of roosters — egg cups, napkin holders, salt and pepper shakers, etc. Items with a Christmas theme were distributed in the '70s, and you'll also find a line of white cats collectors call Kozy Kitten. These are only a sampling of the wonderful novelties by this company. Most are not only marked but dated as well.

Bluebird, candle ring, 1958, 1¾". **35.00**

Bride & Groom, shakers, figural, pr..**30.00**

Christmas, ashtray, starry-eyed Santa **34.00**

Christmas, bell, Santa winking, 1958, 4", from $12 to.......**15.00**

Christmas, butter pats, holly leaves & berries, 2¾", set of 4....**32.00**

Christmas, candleholder, Santa in early touring car, 3½", ea.**25.00**

Christmas, candleholder, votive; Santa, dated 1968, 3", ea.**20.00**

Christmas, candleholders, Santa w/bags, w/label, 1958, pr.**32.00**

Christmas, candleholders, Santa, MIB, from $25.00 to $35.00 for the pair.

Christmas, candy container, w/pop-up Santa, 4¼" **50.00**

Christmas, chip & cheese dish, starry-eyed Santa, gold trim, 1960, 12" **20.00**

Christmas, figurine, angel, 'spaghetti' trim at hem, gold trim, 4¼" **25.00**

Christmas, mug, Christmas tree w/Santa handle **10.00**

Christmas, pitcher, Santa winking, embossed features, 1959, 7½" **28.00**

Christmas, planter, candy cane .**20.00**

Christmas, planter, Santa Express, Santa riding train, 6x7½" . **45.00**

Christmas, punch bowl, Santa's head, 6x9" dia.................. **50.00**

Christmas, salt & pepper shakers, Christmas tree w/Santa, pr.................................. **25.00**

Christmas, salt & pepper shakers, Santa w/gifts, 2¼" & 2¾", pr.................................. **15.00**

Christmas, salt & pepper shakers, Santa winking, w/label, pr.**40.00**

Christmas, tray, Christmas tree, 1959, 10" **18.00**

Coin Kitty, bank, nodder, from $175 to **200.00**

Dandy Lion, bank, nodder, 6", from $100 to **150.00**

Jeeves (Butler), dip dish, head as handle, 1960.................... **85.00**

Jeeves (Butler), jars, Onions, Cherries, Olives, ea from $175 to **185.00**

Jeeves (Butler), martini shaker, 9" **200.00**

Jeeves (Butler), tray, 4¾" wide.**150.00**

Kozy Kitten, ashtray, green & white pillow w/brass match holder, 1958 .... **85.00**

Kozy Kitten, butter dish, 2 kittens peek from under lid, 7", from $100 to........................... **125.00**

Kozy Kitten, cheese crock, Stinky Cheese on side, cats kissing on lid **60.00**

Kozy Kitten, cleanser shaker, full figure, 1958, rare, 6½", from $150 to **175.00**

Kozy Kitten, cookie jar, head form, from $40 to **50.00**

Kozy Kitten, cottage cheese dish, 2 cats kissing on lid, from $45 to **60.00**

Kozy Kitten, grocery clip, Kitty Catch, 1958, from $125 to **165.00**

Kozy Kitten, Instant Coffee jar, attached spoon, from $300 to **400.00**

Kozy Kitten, match holder, Match Dandy, 1959, 6" **140.00**

Kozy Kitten, mug, cat on side, w/squeaker, 8-oz.............. **50.00**

Kozy Kitten, pitcher, white w/kitten, 1960, 7½"................ **140.00**

Kozy Kitten, salt & pepper shakers, heads only, male in hat, pr....................................... **45.00**

Kozy Kitten, salt & pepper shakers, noisemaker, 1958, pr from $35 to **45.00**

Kozy Kitten, spice set, stacking, from $150 to **175.00**

Kozy Kitten, string holder, cat head, holds scissors in collar, 1958 .... **50.00**

Kozy Kitten, tape measure/pin box, cat on cushion **50.00**

Kozy Kitten, wall pocket, cat w/hole in head, 1959, 7½", from $30 to **40.00**

Kozy Kitten, wall pocket, cat w/hook tail, 7x3" **60.00**

Pixie Ware, bottle hanger, Scotch, head only, 2½x8½" **300.00**

Pixie Ware, Cherries, head finial, from $145.00 to $185.00.

Pixie Ware, Cocktail Olives jar, green winking head as finial, from $135 to **165.00**

Pixie Ware, Hors d'ouvres, Pixie w/tall green hat in center, 7½x6" **125.00**

Pixie Ware, Jam & Jelly jar Pixie, licking lips as finial **80.00**

Pixie Ware, Ketchup jar, smiling tomato head as finial, 1958, from $75 to **90.00**

Pixie Ware, Mustard jar, scowling head as finial, from $80 to . **110.00**

Pixie Ware, Relish jar, green head as finial **250.00**

Pixie Ware, salt & pepper shakers, Salty & Peppy, wooden handles, pr.................... **160.00**

Pixie Ware, towel hook, orange-haired Pixie **165.00**

Ponytail Princess, candleholder, figure-8 base/flower-head candle cup **45.00**

Ponytail Princess, lipstick holder, from $50 to **65.00**

Ponytail Princess, shakers, 3½x4", pr...................................... **40.00**

Ponytail Princess, tray, girl between 2 joined flower cups, from $50 to **65.00**

Rooster, bowl, 6"....................... **9.00**

Rooster, butter dish, stick style, 1961, from $35 to **45.00**

Rooster, candleholders, figural, 1960, 5x4", pr from $25 to **40.00**

Rooster, coffeepot, electric, 1960. **60.00**

Rooster, cup & saucer **15.00**

Rooster, cutting board, 15x8½". **100.00**

Rooster, napkin holder, 6" **40.00**

Rooster, platter, oval, from $28 to **35.00**

Rooster, recipe box, wood w/painted-on rooster.................... **75.00**

Rooster, vase, figural, 6", from $35 to **45.00**

Homer Laughlin

The Homer Laughlin China Company has produced millions of pieces of dinnerware, toiletry items, art china, children's dishes, and hotel ware since its inception in 1874. On most pieces the backstamp includes company name, date, and plant where the piece was produced, and nearly always the shape name is included. We have listed samples from many of the decaled lines; some of the more desirable patterns will go considerably higher. Refer to *Collector's Encyclopedia of Homer Laughlin China* by Joanne Jasper; *Homer Laughlin China Company, A Giant Among Dishes,* by Jo Cunningham; and *The Collector's Encyclopedia of Fiesta* by Sharon and Bob Huxford. See Clubs and Newsletters for information concerning *The Laughlin*

Eagle, a newsletter for collectors of Homer Laughlin dinnerware. See also Fiesta.

Angelus Shape

Bowl, fruit; 5", from $4 to........ **6.00**
Bowl, nappy, 8", from $15 to . **20.00**
Casserole, w/lid, 9¼", from $40 to. **45.00**
Creamer, from $15 to............. **20.00**
Jug, lg, from $45 to................. **55.00**
Plate, 10¼", from $10 to **12.00**
Saucer, from $8 to.................. **10.00**
Sugar bowl, w/lid, from $20 to . **25.00**
Teacup, from $10 to................ **15.00**
Teapot, 3-pt, from $65 to **75.00**

Century

Bowl, deep, 1-pt, from $23 to. **32.00**
Butter dish, from $125 to **150.00**
Casserole, w/lid, from $65 to. **85.00**
Cup, from $10 to **15.00**
Plate, rim soup; from $10 to.. **13.00**
Plate, 8", from $11 to **14.00**
Plate, 10", from $18 to........... **21.00**
Platter, 10", from $22 to **26.00**
Teacup, from $6 to.................... **8.00**

Eggshell Georgian

Bowl, fruit; 5", from $4 to........ **8.00**
Bowl, nappy/salad; from $15 to. **20.00**
Creamer, from $12 to............. **15.00**
Cup & saucer, from $14 to..... **21.00**
Pickle dish, from $6 to............. **8.00**
Plate, 7", from $6 to **10.00**
Sugar bowl, from $25 to **30.00**

Eggshell Nautilus

Bowl, baker, 9", from $14 to.. **16.00**
Bowl, cream soup; from $10 to. **15.00**

Bowl, 15", from $16 to **26.00**
Creamer, from $15 to............. **25.00**
Egg cup, double (Swing); from $12 to **16.00**
Plate, 8", from $9 to **12.00**
Sugar bowl, w/lid, from $20 to. **30.00**

Empress

Bone dish, from $6 to............... **8.00**
Bowl, baker, 8", from $10 to .. **12.00**
Bowl, 10", from $12 to **16.00**
Celery tray, 11", from $20 to . **28.00**
Gravy boat, from $20 to......... **28.00**
Oyster tureen, 8", from $45 to. **50.00**
Plate, 10", from $9 to **12.00**
Sauce tureen, from $45 to **55.00**
Sugar bowl, w/lid, from $18 to. **25.00**
Teapot, from $75 to **95.00**

Marigold

Bowl, flat soup; from $12 to .. **18.00**
Bowl, oatmeal; from $6 to **8.00**
Butter dish (Jade), from $40 to. **50.00**
Egg cup, double, from $14 to. **16.00**
Platter, from $20 to................ **30.00**
Teacup & saucer, from $14 to. **16.00**

Nautilus

Bouquet pattern, teacup and saucer, from $10.00 to $13.00; plate, 6", from $5.00 to $7.00; creamer, from $8.00 to $12.00.

Baker, 10", from $22 to.......... **28.00**
Bowl, soup; 7", from $6 to........ **8.00**

Butter dish (Jade), from $50 to............................. **65.00**

Casserole, w/lid, from $20 to.**24.00**

Cup & saucer, demitasse; from $18 to..................................... **20.00**

Plate, 10", from $7 to............. **10.00**

Platter, 12", from $15 to........ **18.00**

Sauceboat, from $12 to **14.00**

Sugar bowl, w/lid, from $10 to. **12.00**

Tea saucer, from to................... **4.00**

Teacup, from $4 to................... **6.00**

Republic Shape (available in Jean, Calais, Priscilla, and Wayside)

Bone dish, from $15 to........... **18.00**

Bowl, baker, 7", from $10 to.. **15.00**

Bowl, fruit; 5", from $5 to........ **8.00**

Butter dish, from $30 to........ **35.00**

Plate, 7", from $5 to................. **7.00**

Plate, 10", from $8 to............. **10.00**

Platter, 10", from $12 to........ **18.00**

Sauceboat, from $15 to **18.00**

Sugar bowl, w/lid, from $10 to. **15.00**

Teapot, from $40 to **45.00**

Rhythm

Bowl, coupe soup; 8", from $8 to **10.00**

Bowl, vegetable; round, 8½", from $12 to............................... **15.00**

Casserole, w/lid, from $35 to.**40.00**

Plate, 7", from $6 to................. **8.00**

Plate, 10", from $10 to........... **12.00**

Platter, oval, 13½", from $15 to .**18.00**

Sauceboat, from $12 to **14.00**

Saucer, from $3 to.................... **5.00**

Sugar bowl, w/lid, from $14 to. **16.00**

Teacup, from $6 to................... **8.00**

Teapot, from $40 to **45.00**

Water jug, 2-qt, from $40 to.. **45.00**

Swing

Bowl, baker, from $25 to........**32.00**

Bowl, fruit; from $9 to **12.00**

Bowl, oatmeal; from $6 to **10.00**

Bowl, soup; from $15 to......... **18.00**

Casserole, w/lid, from $35 to.**45.00**

Egg cup, double, from $12 to.**18.00**

Sugar bowl, w/lid, from $14 to.**18.00**

Virginia Rose

Values are for Moss Rose (JJ59) and Fluffy Rose (VR128); for other patterns deduct 65%.

Bowl, coupe soup; from $20 to.**25.00**

Bowl, lug soup; from $20 to...**25.00**

Casserole, w/lid, from $85 to.**135.00**

Jug, 5", from $65 to............... **80.00**

Nappy, 8", from $24 to **35.00**

Plate, rare, 8", from $15 to....**18.00**

Plate, 7", from $8 to.............. **11.00**

Salt & pepper shakers, Kitchen Kraft, scarce, pr from $160 to.... **185.00**

Salt & pepper shakers, regular, scarce, pr from $125 to.**150.00**

Wells

Bowl, bouillon; from $10 to ...**12.00**

Cake plate, from $18 to **24.00**

Casserole, from $35 to...........**45.00**

Chop plate, from $18 to **24.00**

Plate, 7", from $9 to.............. **12.00**

Platter, 15", from $18 to........**22.00**

Teacup & saucer, from $9 to..**14.00**

Teapot, from $50 to **60.00**

Hot Wheels

An instant success in 1968, Hot Wheels are known for their

fastest model cars on the market. Keeping up with new trends in the big car industry, Hot Wheels also included futuristic vehicles, muscle cars, trucks, hot rods, racers, and some military vehicles. A lot of these can be found for very little, but if you want to buy the older models (collectors call them 'redlines' because of their red sidewall tires), it's going to cost you a little more, though many can still be found under $25.00. By 1971, earlier on some models, black-wall tires had become the standard.

Though recent re-releases have dampened the collector market somewhat, cars mint in the original packages are holding their values and still moving well. Near-mint examples (no package) are worth about 50% to 60% less than those mint and still in their original package, excellent condition about 65% to 75% less. For further information we recommend *Hot Wheels, The Ultimate Redline Guide, Volumes 1 and 2,* by Jack Clark and Robert P. Wicker (Collector Books).

'31 Doozie, 1986, white walls, maroon w/red-brown fenders, MIP **12.00**

'56 Flasher Pickup, 1990s, black walls, turquoise, MIP **5.00**

'57 Chevy, 1984, yellow w/flame accents, MIP **20.00**

American Hauler, 1976, redline, dark blue w/red & blue tampo, M. **40.00**

American Tipper, 1976, redline, red, M **55.00**

Blown Camaro, 1980s, black walls, turquoise, MOC.............. **10.00**

Boss Hoss, 1971, redline, chocolate brown, rare, MOC **550.00**

Boss Hoss, 1971, redline, metallic aqua, #2 tampo, M **150.00**

Breakaway Bucket, 1974, redline, blue, M **100.00**

Bywayman, 1979, black walls, light blue, NM+ **15.00**

Camaro Z-28, 1984, black walls, metal-flaked red, MIP..... **10.00**

Captain America, 1970, black walls, red, white & blue, NM.... **20.00**

Captain America Hot Bird, 1975, NM, $25.00.

Carabo, 1970, redline, yellow, NM+ **48.00**

Chapparal 2G, 1969, redline, yellow, NM+ **35.00**

Chief's Special, 1976, redline, red w/red bar, NM **45.00**

Classic '31 Ford Woody, 1969, redline, orange, M **45.00**

Classic '32 Ford Vicky, 1968, redline, rose w/white interior, NM+ **48.00**

Classic Cobra, 1990s, black walls, red, MOC **8.00**

Classic Cord, 1971, redline, blue, NM+ **250.00**

Classic Nomad, 1970, redline, magenta, NM+ **135.00**

Custom AMX, 1969, redline, blue, NM+ **85.00**

Custom AMX, 1969, redline, yellow, NM+ **90.00**

Custom Continental Mark III, 1969, redline, gold, NM+ **65.00**

Custom Eldorado, 1968, redline, olive w/white interior, NM+ **100.00**

Custom Firebird, 1968, redline, red w/brown interior, M **100.00**

Custom T-Bird, 1968, redline, gold, NM **600.00**

Custom Volkswagen, 1968, orange, NM+ **75.00**

Double Vision, 1973, redline, light green, NM+ **180.00**

Dumpin' A, 1983, black walls, gray w/chrome motor, M **50.00**

Dumpin' A, 1983, black walls, gray w/gray motor, M **15.00**

Dune Daddy, 1973, redline, light green, NM+ **90.00**

Ferarri 312P, 1973, redline, pink, NM+ **400.00**

Ferrari 312P, 1970, redline, red, M **45.00**

Fire Eater, 1977, redline, red, M..**20.00**

Ford J-Car, 1968, redline, white, NM+ **65.00**

Gun Slinger, 1975, redline, light olive, M **55.00**

Hairy Hauler, 1971, redline, magenta, NM+ **55.00**

Heavy Chevy, 1970, redline, purple & white, NM **135.00**

Heavyweight Scooper, 1971, redline, blue, NM+ **135.00**

Hiway Robber, 1973, redline, red, NM+ **135.00**

Hot Heap, 1968, redline, orange, NM+ **45.00**

Indy Eagle, 1969, redline, aqua w/black interior, NM+..... **30.00**

Inside Story, 1980, black walls, yellow, MIP.......................... **10.00**

Lamborghini Diablo, red, MIP. **12.00**

Mantis, 1970, redline, metallic yellow w/cream interior, NM+ **35.00**

Mercedes 540K, black, MIP... **10.00**

Mod Quad, 1970, redline, magenta, scarce, M......................... **120.00**

Mongoose Funny Car, 1970, redline, red, NM+ **75.00**

Mutt Mobile, 1971, redline, magenta, NM+ **200.00**

Mutt Mobile, 1971, redline, metallic aqua, complete, NM.. **50.00**

Nitty Gritty Kitty, 1970, redline, metallic brown, NM **120.00**

Omni 024, 1981, black walls, gray, MIP..................................... **8.00**

Paramedic, 1975, redline, yellow w/red tampo, MIP........... **65.00**

Pit Crew Car, 1971, redline, white w/gray interior, NM+.... **115.00**

Purple Passion, 1990, white walls, purple w/2-tone green tampo, NM **11.00**

Python, 1968, redline, yellow w/white interior, NM+ **55.00**

Road King Truck, 1974, redline, yellow w/original trailer, rear, EX+ . **475.00**

Rocket Bye Buster, 1971, redline, aqua, NM+........................ **68.00**

Sand Crab, 1970, redline, yellow, NM+ **30.00**

Shadow Jet, yellow w/maroon accents, MIP.................... **10.00**

Short Order, 1971, redline, gold w/black interior, M.......... **80.00**

Side Kick, 1972, redline, magenta, NM+ **150.00**

Silhouette, 1968, redline, light green, M........................ **165.00**

Snake 2, 1971, redline, white, NM **65.00**

Spider-Man, 1979, black walls, black, M **15.00**

Sting Rod, 1988, black walls, olive, MIP **12.00**

SWAT Van Scene, 1979, black walls, dark blue, VG **20.00**

Thor Van, 1979, black walls, yellow, M **12.00**

Thunderbird Stocker, 1984, black walls, white, MIP **35.00**

TNT Bird, 1970, redline, metallic blue w/#3 tampo, NM **65.00**

Tow Truck, 1970, redline, metallic green w/black interior, NM **45.00**

Turbo Mustang, 1982, black walls, red, MIP **10.00**

Turismo, 1983, black walls, yellow, MIP **10.00**

Waste Wagon, 1971, redline, metallic aqua, NM **80.00**

Hull

Established in Zanesville, Ohio, in 1905, Hull manufactured stoneware, florist ware, art pottery, and tile until about 1935, when they began to produce lines of pastel matt-glazed artware which are today very collectible. The pottery was destroyed by flood and fire in 1950. The factory was rebuilt and equipped with the most modern machinery which they soon discovered was not geared to duplicate the matt glazes. As a result, new lines — Parchment and Pine and Ebb Tide, for example — were introduced in a glossy finish. During the '40s and into the '50s their kitchenware and novelty lines were very successful. Refer to *Robert's Ultimate Encyclopedia of Hull Pottery* and *The Companion Guide,* both by Brenda Roberts (Walsworth Publishing), for more information. Brenda also has authored *The Collector's Encyclopedia of Hull Pottery* and *The Collector's Ultimate Encyclopedia of Hull Pottery,* both of which are published by Collector Books.

Bow-Knot, creamer, #B-021, 4", from $200 to **225.00**

Bow-Knot, vase, #B-2, 5", from $175 to **225.00**

Calla Lilly, cornucopia, #570/33, 8", from $130 to **160.00**

Calla Lilly, vase, #540/33, 6", from $140 to **165.00**

Cinderella Kitchenware, pitcher, Blossom, #29, 16-oz, from $45 to **70.00**

Dogwood, candleholder, #512, 3¾", ea from $135 to **155.00**

Dogwood, cornucopia, #533, 3¾", from $110 to **135.00**

Ebb Tide, shell basket, E-11, 16½", from $210.00 to $265.00.

Iris, basket, #408, 7", from $285 to **365.00**

Iris, vase, #403, w/handles, 5", from $40 to **60.00**

Magnolia, basket, #10, matt, 10½", from $375 to **425.00**

Magnolia, creamer, #H-21, glossy, 3¾", from $50 to **70.00**

Magnolia, teapot, #23, matt, 6½", from $240 to **275.00**

Novelty, basket girl planter, #954, glossy, 8", from $35 to..... **45.00**

Novelty, kitten planter, #61, 1940s, 7½", from $40 to.............. **55.00**

Novelty, parrot planter, #60, 9½x6", from $45 to...................... **65.00**

Open Rose, hanging basket, #132, 7", from $260 to............. **325.00**

Orchid, candleholder, #315, 4", ea from $135 to **160.00**

Orchid, vase, #304, w/handles, 6", from $150 to **180.00**

Poppy, vase, #606, upturned handles, 10½", from $450 to.**550.00**

Rosella, creamer, #R-3, ivory, 5½", from $45 to **65.00**

Serenade, candy dish, #S-3, 8¼", from $155 to **200.00**

Serenade, ewer, #S-13, 13¼", from $360 to **460.00**

Sueno Tulip, ewer, #109-33, ornate handle, 13", from $465 to..**540.00**

Sunglow, bowl, #50, 8", from $35 to **45.00**

Sunglow, pitcher, #52, 24-oz, from $45 to **65.00**

Sunglow, vase, #89, rim-to-hip handles, 5½", from $35 to **50.00**

Tokay, vase, #8, w/handles, 10", from $105 to **135.00**

Tuscany, basket, green and cream, 8¼", from $75.00 to $100.00.

Utility, flowerpot, green, 4" ... **50.00**

Water Lily, creamer, #L-19, 5", from $80 to **110.00**

Water Lily, jardiniere, #L-23, 5½", from $130 to **170.00**

Wildflower, console bowl, #W-21, 12", from $225 to........... **265.00**

Wildflower, console bowl, #70, 12", from $400 to **500.00**

Woodland, candleholder, #W-30, branch handle, 3½", ea from $140 to **170.00**

Woodland, vase, #W-8, 7½", from $140 to **175.00**

Dinnerware

Avocado, bowl, vegetable; divided, 11x7", from $8 to............. **12.00**

Avocado, jug, 2-pt, from $18 to. **25.00**

Avocado, salt & pepper shakers, w/cork, 3¾", pr................. **12.00**

Avocado, saucer, 6".................. **4.00**

Centennial, casserole, 4½x11"..**110.00**

Centennial, salt & pepper shakers, unmarked, 3", ea............. **30.00**

Centennial Brown, mug, unmarked, 4", from $40 to................. **50.00**

Country Belle, gravy boat, w/tray..**28.00**

Country Belle, sq baker......... **18.00**

Country Squire, water jug, 5-pt/80-oz................................. **32.00**

Crestone, carafe, 2-cup, 6½", from $50 to **65.00**

Crestone, coffeepot, w/lid, 60-oz.**55.00**

Crestone, gravy boat, 10-oz ... **20.00**

Crestone, mug, 9-oz, from $4 to. **6.00**

Crestone, plate, 10¼", from $10 to.................................... **12.00**

Gingerbread Man, coaster, gray, 5x5" **30.00**

Gingerbread Man, server, gray or sand, 10x10".................... **50.00**

Heartland, bowl, soup/salad; 12-oz, from $7 to **9.00**

Heartland, pitcher, 66-oz **57.00**

Heartland, quiche dish, from $18 to **28.00**

Mirror Almond, bean pot, 2-qt, from $30 to **40.00**

Mirror Almond, cruet, vinegar; 5¾", from $22 to **30.00**

Mirror Almond, plate, 9½", from $8 to **10.00**

Mirror Almond, plate, 10¼", from $9 to **12.00**

Mirror Almond, ramekin, 2½-oz, from $7 to **8.00**

Mirror Almond, sauceboat, 5½", from $20 to **30.00**

Mirror Brown, bowl, mixing; 8", from $10 to **12.00**

Mirror Brown, butter dish, ¼-lb, from $20 to **25.00**

Mirror Brown, carafe, 2-cup, from $18 to **22.00**

Mirror Brown, casserole, w/lid, oval, 2-pt, from $14 to **18.00**

Mirror Brown, cookie jar, w/lid, 94-oz, from $18 to **25.00**

Mirror Brown, gravy boat & saucer, from $17 to **22.00**

Mirror Brown, pie plate, 9¼", from $18 to **25.00**

Mirror Brown, plate, 8½", from $7 to **9.00**

Mirror Brown, plate, 10¼", from $8 to **10.00**

Mirror Brown, sugar bowl, w/lid, 12-oz, from $3 to **5.00**

Mirror Brown, tidbit, 2-tiered, from $22 to **28.00**

Provencial, bowl, mixing; 8¼", from $19 to **23.00**

Provencial, coffeepot, w/lid, 8-cup **50.00**

Provencial, plate, 10¼" **15.00**

Rainbow, coffee cup, 6-oz, from $4 to **6.00**

Rainbow, plate, 8½", from $6 to . **8.00**

Rainbow, tidbit, 2-tiered, from $25 to **32.00**

Ridge, plate, 10¼" **8.00**

Ridge, sugar bowl, w/lid, 8-oz.. **10.00**

Ring, bean pot, w/lid **35.00**

Ring, coffeepot, stemmed **9.00**

Ring, salt & pepper shakers, w/handles, pr **28.00**

Tangerine, bowl, soup/salad; 6½", from $5 to **9.00**

Tangerine, jug, 2-pt, from $24 to **30.00**

Tangerine, plate, 6½" **5.00**

Mirror Brown, Gingerbread man cookie jar, 1984, 12", from $150.00 to $250.00.

Indiana Carnival Glass

Though this glass looks old, it really isn't. It's very reminiscent of old Northwood carnival glass with its grape clusters and detailed leaves and vines, but this line was actually introduced in 1972! Made by the Indiana Glass Company, Harvest (the pattern name assigned by the company) was produced in blue, lime green, and marigold.

Although they made a few other carnival patterns in addition to this one, none are as collectible or as easy to recognize. (You'll find an identical line in milk glass, and though it was produced by Indiana, it was never marketed in their catalogs. Instead it was sold through the parent company, Colony.)

This glassware is a little difficult to evaluate as there seems to be a wide range of 'asking' prices simply because some dealers are unsure of its age and therefore its value. If you like it, now is the time to buy it! Harvest values given below are based on items in blue. Adjust them downward a price point or two for lime green and even a little more so for marigold. For further information we recommend *Garage Sale & Flea Market Annual* (Collector Books).

Iridescent Amethyst (Heritage)

Basket, footed, 9x5x7" **40.00**
Butter dish, 5x7½" dia, from $40 to **50.00**
Candleholders, Harvest, compote style, embossed grapes, 4", pr, from $22 to **28.00**
Candleholders, 5½", pr from $30 to.................................... **35.00**
Center bowl, 4¾x8½", from $30 to **40.00**
Goblet, 8-oz, from $12 to **18.00**
Pitcher, 8¼", from $40 to **60.00**
Punch set, 10" bowl, 8 cups, no pedestal, from $90 to **135.00**
Punch set, 10" bowl, 8 cups, w/pedestal, ladle, 11-pc, from $150 to **200.00**

Swung vase, slender & footed w/irregular rim, 11x3", from $30 to **40.00**

Iridescent Blue

Basket, Canterbury, waffle pattern, flared sides, 11x8x12", from $50 to **65.00**
Basket, Monticello, allover faceted embossed diamonds, 7x6" sq, from $25 to **35.00**
Bowl, Harvest, embossed grapes, paneled sides, scalloped rim, 2x6" **60.00**
Butter dish, Harvest, embossed grapes, ¼-lb, 8" L, from $25 to.................................. **35.00**
Candleholders, Harvest, compote style, embossed grapes, 4" pr, from $20 to **30.00**
Candy dish, Harvest, embossed grapes, lacy rim, w/lid, 6½", from $35 to **45.00**
Candy dish, Princess, pointed faceted finial, 6x6" dia, from $10 to **15.00**
Candy dish, rectangle, lacy rim, embossed ribs, foot, lid, 7", from $30 to **40.00**
Canister/Candy jar, Harvest, embossed grapes, 7", from $30 to **45.00**
Canister/Snack jar, Harvest, embossed grapes, 8", from $120 to... **150.00**
Canister/Snack jar, Harvest, embossed grapes, 9", from $125 to **175.00**
Center bowl, Harvest, embossed grapes, paneled, 4-footed, 12", from $20 to **30.00**
Compote, Harvest, embossed grapes, scalloped rim, w/lid, 10", from $20 to.............. **30.00**

Creamer & sugar bowl on tray, Harvest, embossed grapes, 3-pc **30.00**

Goblet, Harvest, embossed grapes, 9-oz, from $10 to **15.00**

Hen on nest, from $18 to **25.00**

Pitcher, Harvest, embossed grapes, common, 10½", from $25 to **35.00**

Plate, Bicentennial; American Eagle, from $15 to **18.00**

Tumbler, Harvest, embossed grapes, 14-oz, from $9 to **12.00**

Iridescent Gold

Basket, Canterbury, waffle pattern, 10x11x9", from $35 to **55.00**

Center bowl, Harvest, oval, pan-eled w/embossed grapes, 12", from $12 to **15.00**

Egg plate, 11", from $18 to **25.00**

Pitcher, Harvest, embossed grapes, 10½", from $30 to **35.00**

Plate, hostess; shallow, crimped & flared, embossed diamonds, 10", from $12 to **18.00**

Relish tray, Vintage, 6 sections, 9x13", from $15 to **18.00**

Salad set, Vintage, apple shape, 3-pc w/spoon & fork, 13", from $15 to **20.00**

Iridescent Lime

Candy box, Harvest, embossed grapes, 6½", from $20.00 to $30.00.

Candleholders, Harvest, compote style, 4x4½", pr from $25 to **35.00**

Console bowl, Harvest, embossed grapes, stemmed foot, 7½x10" **45.00**

Creamer & sugar bowl on tray, Harvest, embossed grapes, 3-pc, from $25 to **30.00**

Hen on nest, from $15 to **22.00**

Pitcher, Harvest, embossed grapes, 10½", from $35 to **45.00**

Snack set, Harvest, embossed grapes, 4 plates & 4 cups, from $50 to **70.00**

Tumbler, Harvest, embossed grapes, 6" **12.50**

Iridescent Sunset (Amberina)

Wedding bowl, Harvest, embossed grapes, 8x8½", from $22.00 to $25.00.

Basket, footed, 9x5x7", from $30 to **45.00**

Bowl, crimped, 3¾x10", from $32 to **40.00**

Butter dish, 5x7½ dia, from $32 to.................................... **38.00**

Dessert set, 2-pc, 8½" bowl & 12" plate, from $40 to............ **45.00**

Goblet, 8-oz, from $10 to **15.00**

Pitcher, 8", from $45 to **50.00**

Plate, 12", from $30 to **35.00**

Rose bowl, 4½x6½", from $25 to. **30.00**

Tumbler, 3½", from $15 to **18.00**

Japan Ceramics

Though Japanese ceramics marked Nippon, Noritake, and Occupied Japan have long been collected, some of the newest fun-type collectibles on today's market are the figural ashtrays, pincushions, wall pockets, toothbrush holders, etc., that are marked 'Made in Japan' or simply 'Japan.' In her book called *Collector's Encyclopedia of Made in Japan Ceramics*, Carole Bess White explains the pitfalls you will encounter when you try to determine production dates. Collectors refer to anything produced before WWII as 'old' and anything made after 1952 as 'new.' You'll find all you need to know to be a wise shopper in her books. See also Black Cats; Blue Willow; Egg Timers; Enesco; Fishbowl Ornaments; Flower Frogs; Geisha Girl; Head Vases; Holt Howard; Lefton; Moss Rose; Nippon; Noritake; Occupied Japan; Rooster and Roses; Sewing Items; Toothbrush Holders; Wall Pockets.

Ashtray, card suit, stacking set of 4, multicolored lustre, 3", from $25 to **45.00**

Ashtray, dog & dish form, multicolored lustre, 2½", from $20 to **30.00**

Ashtray, dog w/water barrel, white & multicolored, 4", from $150 to **200.00**

Ashtray, frog in water, multicolored, 5", from $18 to **28.00**

Ashtray, house, stylized, multicolored lustre, 3¼", from $15 to.......**22.00**

Bank, money-bag form w/dollar symbol, gray lustre w/red trim, 4½" **22.00**

Basket, ovoid w/gazelle-like handle, scalloped rim, lustre, 8", from $20 to **35.00**

Basket, wishing well w/bird, branch handle, washed glazes, 5", from $15 to **25.00**

Baskets, miniature; various styles & glazes, 2" to 2½", ea from $5 to **8.00**

Bell, colonial lady figure, multicolored, 3½", from $12 to..... **20.00**

Biscuit jar, card suit motif, animal finial, reed handle, 5½" ... **65.00**

Biscuit jar, fruit on cream crackle, 7", from $48 to................. **68.00**

Biscuit jar, sq w/apple motif on green gloss, reed handle, 8", from $30 to **55.00**

Bookends, boat anchors in orange on white round fluted bases, 5" **40.00**

Bookends, colonial couple, blue rhinestone eyes, 6¼", from $25 to **40.00**

Bookends, dog head, green airbrushing, 5", pr from $28 to...... **48.00**

Bookends, siesta figures, glossy & lustre, 4", pr from $28 to.............................. **48.00**

Bowl, applied flowers & butterflies, angled w/scalloped rim, 6½" **45.00**

Bowl, floral, multicolored lustre, 3-footed, 4 scallops, 7½", from $20 to **35.00**

Bowl, house scene, multicolored on teal lustre, lug handles, from $25 to **55.00**

Bowl, multicolored geometric lustre, 8-sided w/reeded handles, 8" **35.00**

Bowl, 12 multicolored panels, lustre, 9½" dia, from $35 to. **55.00**

Cache pot, bird perched next to nest, glossy colors, 4" H, from $10 to **18.00**

Cache pot, girl w/umbrella (white), blue beaded pot, glossy, 6", from $20 to **35.00**

Cache pot, gnome by palm trees pot, glossy, 4½", from $12 to ... **20.00**

Cache pot, pixie seated on upright leaves, glossy, 5¼", from $20 to **35.00**

Cake plate, floral, multicolored lustre, 9½", from $35 to **55.00**

Candlesticks, flowers & berries on blue trumpet form, 7½", pr **145.00**

Candy dish, Deco floral w/lustre on urn shape, 7½", from $60 to **80.00**

Candy dish, elephant heads (3) form bowl, w/lid, 9", from $75 to **125.00**

Cigarette set, cherry blossoms w/lustre, holder, ashtray & tray, from $50 to **75.00**

Cigarette set, Scottie dog figural box w/4 ashtrays, from $50 to **60.00**

Coal scuttle, white w/floral motif, black trim, glossy, 5", from $15 to **20.00**

Compote, floral motif, glossy, w/handles, 6¾", from $35 to **55.00**

Condiment set, fish (3) on fish tray, airbrushed blue & white, from $35 to **55.00**

Condiment set, girl w/flowers in center of tray, 3¾", from $125 to **150.00**

Creamer & sugar bowl, dog figures w/yellow eyes, 6¾", from $100 to **150.00**

Figurine, boy fishing (barefoot), multicolored, 4¾", from $35 to **50.00**

Figurine, football player in early helmet, bisque, 5", from $18 to .. **28.00**

Figurine, lady skier, matt colors, 7¾" **60.00**

Figurine, pheasant, majolica style, glossy, 6", from $35 to **55.00**

Figurine set, musician trio, multicolored, 2¾", from $10 to . **18.00**

Flower bowl, swans form bowl, blue & tan lustre, 8½", from $85 to **135.00**

Flower frog, bird perched on stump, multicolored lustre, 7", from $50 to **75.00**

Flowerpot, Dutch girl scene on tapered sq pot w/saucer, 3½" **25.00**

Incense burner, Geisha seated w/arm resting on pot, lustre, 4", from $40 to **55.00**

Lamp, sailboat on glossy white, 6¾" to top of ceramic post, from $25 to **35.00**

Leaf dish, 2 overlapping 2-tone green leaves w/gold handle, 7¾".. **8.00**

Lemon server, Mexican motif, multicolored, 5½", from $25 to .. **35.00**

Liquor flask, girl & dog, multicolored bisque, 4", from $75 to **135.00**

Marmalade pot, fruit motif, w/handles, 4¾", from $25 to **35.00**

Pincushion, black cat next to white basket, 2", from $18 to.... **28.00**

Pincushion, sailor boy, painted bisque, 3¼", from $23 to . **33.00**

Pincushion, stagecoach, yellow w/black & brown trim, 4" L, from $18 to **28.00**

Pitcher, floral motif, multicolored w/orange handle, 7¾", from $45 to **75.00**

Sandwich server, floral w/lustre, center handle, 10", from $45 to **75.00**

Shakers, sq range style, Moriyama, 5", pr from $25 to **45.00**

Spice set, 5 ceramic containers on wooden lazy Susan, 4" dia, from $20 to **35.00**

Spice set, 6 ceramic books on wooden wall shelf, various motifs, from $25 to **35.00**

Teapot, floral motif, blue & tan lustre, 6½", from $35 to **50.00**

Teapot, river scene, multicolored lustre, dome lid, 7", from $35 to **50.00**

Tray, Deco floral w/lustre, coval, tab handles, 11", from $25 to . **45.00**

Vase, Deco geometrics w/lustre on fan shape, from $75 to.. **125.00**

Creamer and sugar bowl, dogs with multicolored lustre, black mark, 6½", from $85.00 to $100.00. (Photo courtesy Carole Bess White)

Jewelry

Anyone interested in buying jewelry will soon find out that antique gems are the best values. Not only are prices from one-third to one-half less than on comparable new jewelry, but the older pieces display a degree of craftsmanship and and styling seldom seen in modern-day jewelry. Costume jewelry from all periods is popular, especially Art Nouveau and Art Deco examples. Signed pieces are particularly good, such as those by Miriam Haskell, Eisenberg, Trifari, Hollycraft, and Weiss, among others.

There are some excellent reference books available if you'd like more information. Marcia 'Sparkles' Brown has written *Unsigned Beauties of Costume Jewelry; Signed Beauties of Costume Jewelry, Volumes I* and *II*; and *Coro Jewelry*. Lillian Baker has written *Plastic Jewelry of the Twentieth Century; 50 Years of Collectible Fashion Jewelry;* and *100 Years of Collectible Jewelry.* Books by other authors include *Costume Jewelry* and *Collectible Silver Jewelry* by Fred Rezazadeh; *Collectible Costume Jewelry* by Cherri Simonds; *Christmas Pins, Past & Present,* by Jill Gallina; *Costume Jewelry 101* by Julia C. Carroll; *Inside the Jewelry Box* by Ann Mitchell Pitman; *Vintage Jewelry for Investment & Casual Wear* by Karen Edeen; and *Brilliant Rhinestones* and *20th Century Costume Jewelry,* both by Ronna Lee Aikins. All of these books are published by Collector Books. See Clubs and Newsletters for information on the *Vintage Fashion & Costume Jewelry* newsletter and club.

Bracelet, Ciner, black Bakelite & gilded brass links, 1950s, from $135 to **150.00**

Bracelet, Coro, flexible w/lg topaz-colored jewel & pearls, from $50 to **70.00**

Bracelet, Emmons, silver-tone lacy chain w/opaque black stones **30.00**

Bracelet, Kramer, single strand of clear rhinestones, from $35 to **50.00**

Bracelet, Miriam Haskell, 3 strands of white glass beads w/rhinestones **135.00**

Bracelet, Napier, gold-plated flexible mesh w/faux jade stone at clasp **55.00**

Bracelet, Sarah Coventry, wheat shocks design, gold-tone, 1950s **10.00**

Bracelet & earrings, Marvella, faceted iridescent glass beads, from $50 to **70.00**

Brooch, Alice Caviness, green & blue pronged stones, 2¼". **85.00**

Brooch, Art, dragonfly, gold-tone w/enamel flowers, from $50 to **75.00**

Brooch, Baldwin, silver leaf w/autumn-like enameling, from $30 to **40.00**

Brooch, BSK, bird on perch, gold-tone w/faux ruby accents, 1950s, sm **35.00**

Brooch, bug, silver w/multicolored rhinestones, lg, from $75 to **100.00**

Brooch, Castlecliff, crown, sterling w/red & white rhinestones, 2" **170.00**

Brooch, Coro, peacock, gold-plated w/enameling & rhinestones, 1950s **65.00**

Brooch, Danecraft, floral design, silver, from $35 to **45.00**

Brooch, Emmons, bobcat's face, gold-tone w/green eyes, 1950s **75.00**

Brooch, Gerry's, rooster, gold-tone w/enameled details, from $12 to **35.00**

Brooch, Gorham, dragonfly, silver, 2½" **175.00**

Brooch, Hattie Carnegie, giraffe running, gold-tone w/rhinestones **75.00**

Brooch, JJ, owl w/jewel middle, from $30 to **45.00**

Brooch, Krementz, flower form w/cultured pearls, from $65 to **95.00**

Brooch, Lea Stein Paris, vintage car w/long hood, celluloid **85.00**

Brooch, Sarah Coventry, snowflake, clear rhinestones, from $25 to **35.00**

Brooch, Trifari, butterfly, colored stones, sm, from $45 to... **55.00**

Brooch, Trifari, poodle w/mother-of-pearl body **25.00**

Brooch, unsigned, basket of topaz with hand-set rhinestone petals encircling citrine chatons, $95.00. (Photo courtesy Marcia Brown)

Brooch, Weiss, apple form, black metal w/red rhinestones. **75.00**

Brooch & earrings, Sherman, floral shape w/topaz rhinestones, from $65 to **95.00**

Brooch & earrings, Trifari, gold-plated w/white rhinestones **95.00**

Brooch & earrings, Weiss, daisies, enameled, from $50 to **75.00**

Brooch & earrings, Weiss, red stones form strawberries, from $80 to **110.00**

Earrings, Albion, leaves, gold-washed metal w/faux pearls, from $10 to **15.00**

Earrings, Chanel, clustered aurora borealis stones, 1950s **20.00**

Earrings, Coro, cluster of plastic flowers w/rhinestones, from $40 to **75.00**

Earrings, Coro, leaf shape, rhinestones, screw backs, from $20 to **30.00**

Earrings, George Jensen, sterling doves **130.00**

Earrings, Kramer, grape cluster, clear rhinestones, sm, from $25 to **30.00**

Earrings, Kramer, pearl & rhinestone beads, clips **10.00**

Earrings, Laguna, cut crystal drops, from $25 to **30.00**

Earrings, Marvella, leaf shape gold-tone w/faux pearls, from $15 to **20.00**

Earrings, Regency, blue iridescent rhinestones, from $90 to **125.00**

Earrings, Weiss, flower w/white glass petals & black center **40.00**

Earrings, Weiss, green baguette stones, from $35 to **50.00**

Necklace, Avon, gold-tone w/faux pearl insets, from $15 to.. **20.00**

Necklace, BSK, gold-tone floral design w/pink rhinestones **45.00**

Necklace, Coro, gold-tone chains w/gold-tone spatter-look beads **12.00**

Necklace, Emmons, cross, rhodium w/faux turquoise & cultured pearls **55.00**

Necklace, Hobé, cross w/antiqued gold filigree & garnets, from $175 to **225.00**

Necklace, Hollywood Stars, carved wooden beads **40.00**

Necklace, Miriam Haskell, 6 stands of amber beads **175.00**

Necklace, Monet, choker w/Art Moderne rhodium links, 1950s **45.00**

Necklace, Pam, floral design w/iridescent stones & enameling, from $40 to **60.00**

Necklace & earrings, Trifari, gold-tone w/plastic inserts & enameling **75.00**

Pendant, Vendome, rhinestones form flower, from $80 to. **140.00**

Ring, Avon, inset faux stone, from $10 to **25.00**

Ring, Emmons, aurora borealis rhinestones set in gold-tone, 1970 .... **30.00**

Ring, Emmons, simulated pearls & turquoise, from $30 to **45.00**

Ring, Emmons, turquoise & faux pearls, from $30 to.......... **45.00**

Ring, Hattie Carnegie, ram's head, Lucite w/rhinestones & faux coral **175.00**

Ring, Miriam Haskell, seed pearl cluster, adjustable......... **145.00**

Ring, Sarah Coventry, silver w/hematite stone, from $25 to................................. **35.00**

Johnson Brothers

Dinnerware marked Johnson Brothers, Staffordshire, is bought and sold with considerable fervor on today's market, and for good reason. They made many lovely patterns, some scenic and some florals. Most are decorated with multicolor transfer designs, though you'll see blue or red transferware as well. Some, such as Friendly Village (one of their most popular lines), are still being produced, but the lines are much less extensive now, so the secondary market is being tapped to replace broken items that are no longer available anywhere else.

Some lines are more valuable than others. Unless a pattern is included in the following two categories, use the base values below as a guide. (Some of the most popular base-value lines are Bird of Paradise, Mount Vernon, Castle on the Lake, Old Bradury, Day in June, Nordic, Devon Sprays, Old Mill, Empire Grape, Pastorale, Haddon Hall, Pomona, Harvest Time, Road Home, Indian Tree, Vintage [older version], Melody, and Windsor Fruit.) One-Star patterns are basically 10% to 20% higher and include Autumn's Delight, Coaching Scenes, Devonshire, Fish, Friendly Village, Gamebirds, Garden Bouquet, Hearts and Flowers, Heritage Hall, Indies, Millstream, Olde English Countryside, Rose Bouquet, Sheraton, Tulip Time, and Winchester. Two-Star lines include Barnyard King, Century of Progress, Chintz, Victorian, Dorchester, English Chippendale, Harvest Fruit, His Majesty, Historical America, Merry Christmas, Old Britain Castles, Persian Tulip, Rose Chintz,

Strawberry Fair, Tally Ho, Twelve Days of Christmas, and Wild Turkeys. These patterns are from 25% to 35% higher than our base values. For more information refer to *Johnson Brothers Dinnerware* by Mary J. Finegan.

Trio, Friendly Village (One-Star pattern), $25.00.

Bowl, berry/fruit	**8.00**
Bowl, cereal/soup (sq, round or lug)	**10.00**
Bowl, rimmed soup	**14.00**
Bowl, vegetable; round	**25.00**
Bowl, vegetable; w/lid	**50.00**
Butter dish	**40.00**
Cake/chop plate	**50.00**
Coffee mug, minimum value	**20.00**
Coffeepot, minimum value	**90.00**
Creamer	**30.00**
Cup & saucer, jumbo	**30.00**
Cup & saucer, tea	**15.00**
Egg cup	**15.00**
Pitcher/jug, minimum value	**45.00**
Plate, buffet; 10½-11"	**26.00**
Plate, dinner	**14.00**
Plate, luncheon	**12.00**
Platter, 12"-14", minimum value	**45.00**
Salt & pepper shakers, pr, minimum value	**40.00**
Sauceboat	**40.00**
Sauceboat base/relish tray	**20.00**
Sugar bowl, open	**30.00**

Sugar bowl, w/lid 40.00
Teacup & saucer, minimum value. 15.00
Teapot 90.00
Tureen.................................. 200.00

Kentucky Derby Glasses

Kentucky Derby glasses are the official souvenir glasses that are filled with mint juleps and sold on Derby Day. The first glass (1938), picturing a black horse within a black and white rose garland and the Churchill Downs stadium in the background, is said to have either been given away as a souvenir or used for drinks among the elite at the Downs. This glass, the 1939, and two glasses said to have been used in 1940 are worth thousands and are nearly impossible to find at any price.

1975, $16.00.

1940, aluminum 1,000.00
1940, French Lick, aluminum .1,000.00
1941-44, plastic Beetlware, ea from
    $2,500 to 4,000.00
1945, jigger, I have Seen Them All,
    green horse head........ 1,000.00
1945, regular, green horse head facing right, horseshoe ... 1,600.00
1945, tall, green horse head facing right, horsehoe 450.00

1946-47, frosted w/frosted bottom,
    L in circle....................... 100.00
1948, clear bottom, green horse head in horseshoe, horse on reverse 225.00
1948, frosted bottom, green horse head in horseshoe, horse on reverse 250.00
1949, He Has Seen Them All, Matt Winn, green on frosted . 225.00
1950, green horses running on track, Churchill Downs behind 450.00
1951, Where Turf Champions Are Crowned, green winner's circle............................... 650.00
1952, black horse facing left, rose garland 200.00
1952, Kentucky Derby Gold Cup, Gold Derby Trophy 225.00
1954, green twin spires 225.00
1955, The Fastest Runners, green & yellow horses,............ 175.00
1956, 1 star, 2 tails, brown horses, twin spires..................... 275.00
1956, 1 star, 3 tails, brown horses, twin spires..................... 400.00
1956, 2 stars, 2 tails, brown horses, twin spires..................... 200.00
1956, 2 stars, 3 tails, brown horses, twin spires..................... 250.00
1957, gold & black, horse & jockey facing right.................... 125.00
1958, Gold Bar, solid gold insignia w/horse, jockey & 1 spire 175.00
1958, Iron Liege, same as 1957 w/'Iron Liege' added...... 225.00
1959-60, black & gold, ea 100.00
1961, black horses on track, jockey in red, gold winners...... 110.00
1962, Churchill Downs, red, gold & black 70.00

1963, brown horse, jocky #7, gold lettering **70.00**

1964, brown horse head, gold lettering **55.00**

1965, brown horses & twin spires, red lettering **85.00**

1966-68, black, black & blue respectively, ea............................ **60.00**

1969, green jockey in horseshoe, red lettering **65.00**

1970, green shield, gold lettering **70.00**

1971, green twin spires, horses at bottom, red lettering **55.00**

1972, 2 black horses, orange & green print........................ **55.00**

1973, white, black twin spires, red & green lettering............. **60.00**

1974, Federal, brown & gold, regular or mistake................ **200.00**

1974, mistake (Canonero in 1971 listing on back), Libbey .. **18.00**

1974, regular (Canonero II in 1971 listing on back)................ **16.00**

1976, plastic tumbler or regular glass, ea **16.00**

1978-79, ea **16.00**

1980.. **22.00**

1981-82, ea **15.00**

1983-85, ea **12.00**

1986, $14.00.

1986 ('85 copy)........................ **20.00**

1987-89, ea **12.00**

1990-92, ea **10.00**

1993-95, ea **9.00**

1996-98, ea **8.00**

1999-2000, ea **6.00**

2001-2002, ea **5.00**

2003... **4.00**

2003, mistake........................... **6.00**

2004... **3.50**

2005... **3.00**

Kitchen Collectibles

From the early patented apple peelers, cherry pitters, and food hoppers to the gadgets of the '20s through the '40s, many collectors find special appeal in kitchen tools. Refer to *Kitchen Antiques, 1790 – 1940,* by Kathryn McNerney and *Kitchen Glassware of the Depression Years* by Gene and Cathy Florence for more information. Both are published by Collector Books. See also Aluminum; Clothes Sprinkler Bottles; Cookie Cutters; Egg Timers; Enesco; Graniteware; Griswold.

Angel food cake pan, Glasbake, crystal **15.00**

Baker, Glasbake, oval, crystal, 6½x4¼" **10.00**

Batter jug, McKee................ **150.00**

Blender, Handy Hot Blendette, Silex, sq pink base, EX... **40.00**

Blender, Vitamix Mark 20, 2-speed, stainless steel, plastic handles, NM **70.00**

Bread box, Kromax, aluminum w/aqua trim, 1940s-50s, EX.............. **70.00**

Bread slicer, Breadman, wooden, collapsible, EX................. **55.00**

Butter dish, Hocking, Block Optic, green, from $50 to........... **65.00**

Can opener, Sunbeam, pink w/ chrome trim, countertop, 1950s, EX......20.00

Canister, Hazel-Atlas, transparent green, from $60 to......65.00

Canister, McKee, dots on white, screw-on lid, lg, from $75 to......85.00

Casserole, McKee, Glasbake, fired-on color, w/lid, 1-qt......16.00

Casserole, McKee, Glasbake, white, w/lid, 2-qt, w/metal holder, from $45 to......55.00

Chopper, Lorraine Metal Mfg, green glass w/metal top, 12", EX......30.00

Coffeepot, McKee, clear w/silver rings, from $25 to......30.00

Colander, pink enamel on metal, footed, 1½-qt, NM......55.00

Cookie jar, LE Smith, peacock blue, from $75 to......100.00

Cookie press, Deluxe Cookie King, Nordic, copper-colored metal, MIB......40.00

Cookie press, Hamilton Beach Super Shooter, cordless, 8 disks, MIB......25.00

Drippings bowl, Hazel-Atlas, ships on white, 8-oz, from $55 to.75.00

Egg beater, Androck, crank handle, 12", EX......45.00

Egg beater, Turbine, ca 1930, 9½", $25.00.

Egg cooker, Sunbeam Model E, holds 6 eggs, 1940s, EX..65.00

French-fry cutter, Bloomfield Mfg Co Chicago IL, cast iron, EX.45.00

Grater, Lorraine Metal Mfg, crank handle, 8½x5", EX......20.00

Hot plate, Westinghouse, double burner, 1950s, 6x23x10½", NM......25.00

Ice bucket, Cambridge, Mt Vernon, from $95 to......110.00

Ice-cream freezer, White Mountain, electric, wooden bucket, 5-qt, EX......125.00

Juicer, Chicago Electric Mfg Co, milk glass reamer, 1930-35, EX......75.00

Juicer, Landers Frary & Clark, aluminum, 4-footed, EX......20.00

Juicer/press, National Juice-King Juicer, 1935-40, EX......25.00

Knife holder, Nuway, green & white plastic, mounts on wall, 1930s, EX......28.00

Measuring cup, Anchor Hocking, Sapphire Blue Ovenware, 1 spout, 8-oz......26.00

Measuring cup, Jeannette, pink, fluted sides, smooth rim, 1-cup, from $70 to......75.00

Measuring cup, McKee, Delphite Blue, 2-cup, from $110 to.125.00

Mixer, hand-held; GE, aqua, 1960s, EX......20.00

Mixer, Sunbeam 7B Mixmaster, Jade-ite bowls, EX......125.00

Mixing bowl, Hazel-Atlas, ships on white, 9", from $40 to.....45.00

Mixing bowl, Pyrex, American Heritage, brown on white, 4-qt......12.00

Mixing bowl set, Jeannette, pink, 3-pc, from $200 to......225.00

Napkin holder, Serv-All, green clam-broth, from $200 to......225.00

Nut chopper, Anchor Hocking, glass w/crank handle, 1930s-40s, EX......25.00

Nutmeg grater, grating blade in green wooden box frame, 8½" L, EX................................ 25.00

Organizer/rack, Lincoln, for paper towels, foil & waxed paper, 1970s, EX 15.00

Pastry blender, curved wires attached to wooden handle, 1940s, EX 10.00

Percolator, Proctor-Silex, gold starbursts on glass sides, EX . 35.00

Popcorn popper, Sears, yellow enameling, glass lid, EX. 55.00

Potato masher, wooden handle, 1940s................................ 15.00

Ramekin, Fry, pearl or lime, ea from $15 to 18.00

Range set, anodized aluminum, lime green, grease jar and shakers, from $35.00 to $45.00 for the set.

Reamer, Jeannette, fluted sides w/smooth rim, crystal, from $85 to 100.00

Refrigerator dish, Hazel-Atlas, ships on white, 4x5", from $35 to . 40.00

Refrigerator dish, McKee, dots on custard, 5x8", from $50 to. 55.00

Ricer/masher, cast-iron hinged press w/removable basket, 4x10", EX.......................... 16.00

Roaster, Fry, Pearl Ovenware, domed lid, 7½x14x10", from $200 to.............................. 225.00

Rolling pin, Rowoco USA, wooden, 24x3" dia, EX 25.00

Scale, Hanson, green enamel, original labels, 10", NM 100.00

Sifter, Androck Hand-I-Sift, mother & child in kitchen scene, 1950s, EX 40.00

Skillet/fry pan, Sunbeam FP-MO45903, 1950s-60s, 10½" sq, EX 38.00

Slicer/grater/chopper, Saladmaster, stainless steel, 5 cones, EX.60.00

Stack set, Hazel-Atlas, Skating Dutch, 3-pc, from $75 to. 80.00

Stack set, Jeannette, Hex Optic, pink, w/lid, 3-pc, from $75 to 85.00

Sugar shaker, Hazel-Atlas, Skating Dutch, from $35 to.......... 38.00

Syrup pitcher, Paden City, green w/metal top, from $55 to . 60.00

Teakettle, Glasbake, glass handle, from $30 to 35.00

Toaster, Sunbeam Model T-20C, chrome, 2-slice, 1950s, EX..45.00

Utility dish, Anchor Hocking, sapphire blue, 12½x8", from $100 to 125.00

Waffle iron/grill, Sunbeam Model CG-1, chrome & black, 1950s, EX 55.00

Water bottle, Hazel-Atlas, Crisscross, crystal, 32-oz, from $35 to 40.00

Kliban

B. Kliban, artist and satirist, was extremely fond of cats and usually had more than one as companion to him in his California home. This led to his first book (published in 1975), simply titled *Cat*. The popularity of the Kliban cat led to sales of various types of merchandising featuring his likeness. Among the items you may encounter are calendars, mugs, note pads, Christmas cards, stuffed toys, and many other items, the majority of which are of recent production.

Apron, cat chef flipping mice & cheese in skillet on white cotton, MIP............................25.00
Bank, cat in print shirt w/'Aloha' at bottom, 7", M....................20.00
Bank, walking figure wearing red sneakers, Sigma, 1970s, M...47.00
Book, Catchristmas, by B Kliban, NM.....................................12.00
Candleholder, figural cat climbing tree trunk, 8", NM, ea....28.00
Candy jar/canister, 2 cats in single pr of white pants, Sigma, 8¼"................................90.00
Clock, die-cut cat on roller skates above round clock face, 15x14", EX....................................70.00

Cookie jar, 10", from $90.00 to $115.00.

Creamer, full figure w/tail handle, Sigma, 3¾", M, from $40 to.50.00
Drinking glasses, cat as reindeer on clear glass, 14-oz, M, set of 6.....................................22.00

Jar, cat playing guitar (lid) atop red stool (bottom), EX+.........65.00
Jar, figural black & white cat in black top hat, 1970s-80s, 8", EX..................................150.00
Mug, Bah, Humbug! in red on white w/black Kliban, 1970s-80s, 3½", M........................7.50
Mug, plump black & white cat figure w/red bow tie, EX.....15.00
Ornament, cat hugging ball, painted glass, Hawaii, 3x4", NM...15.00
Ornament, cat in Santa's hat w/presents in white car, ceramic, NM......50.00
Picture frame, Love a Cat, cat at side, Sigma, from $75 to.90.00
Pillow, stuffed cat figure, 22"..22.00
Plate, cat in shoes repeated around border on white ceramic, 9", EX....................................18.00
Plush cat figure, red bow tie, 1989, 13" L w/chubby 25" waist, NM.................................20.00
Sleeping bag, cat in red sneakers, 78", M.............................20.00
Stationery, 12 sheets ea of 4 designs w/25 envelopes, MIB.......15.00
Sugar bowl, cat, mostly black w/white, red bow, w/lid, NM..............35.00
Teapot, cat in red Santa's hat & red bow on tail, 8", NM.........85.00
Tumbler, plastic, 4½", NM.....28.00

Kreiss

These novelties were imported from Japan during the 1950s. There are several lines. One is a totally off-the-wall group of caricatures called Psycho Ceramics. There's a Beatnik series, Bums, and Cave People (all of which are strange little creatures), as well as some that are very well done and tasteful. Others you find will be inset with colored 'jewels.' Many are marked either with an ink stamp or an in-mold trademark (some are dated). Unless noted otherwise, our values are for examples in mint condition.

Ashtray/dish, Big Mouth, head w/open toothy mouth, rhinestone eye **60.00**

Ashtray/dish, reddish figure w/white fingertips, rhinestone eyes, 5" **25.00**

Ashtray/dish, Suicide Guy, Psycho Ceramics, green, 1960s, 5", EX **50.00**

Bank, pig winking, pink, You Save... Pig's Eye on belly, 6" **25.00**

Bank, Santa, grumpy, 7" **25.00**

Bell, choir girl w/'spaghetti' decor on dress, 4½" **15.00**

Candleholder, boy & girl angels w/Noel banner, 3x6", ea .. **25.00**

Cup & saucer, Bridge set, king & queen on white **18.00**

Egg cups, Santa & Mrs Claus, 2¼", pr **20.00**

Figurine, Beatnik, 'Man, My Philosophy Is Easy, To Heck With Everything,' 5¾", from $50.00 to $60.00. (Photo courtesy Jim and Beverly Mangus)

Figurine, Blue & Forlorn, sad blue figure w/lg white eyes, 5½".**10.00**

Figurine, Christmas elf on spread knees w/'spaghetti' trim, 3".**11.00**

Figurine, elf w/present behind back, 6" **20.00**

Figurine, fellow in red & white smoking jacket & red tam, lg ears, 7" **60.00**

Figurine, Four Eyes, white eyes w/blue rhinestones, w/hair, 5" **100.00**

Figurine, frowning pink figure w/hands to head, blue hair, 5" **90.00**

Figurine, Little Champ, gold trim, 5", NM **12.00**

Figurine, Moon Being, brownish tan creature w/hair, blue eyes, 4½" **100.00**

Figurine, Santa, Psycho-Ceramic, 5", NM **15.00**

Figurine, Some Days I Go All to Pieces, yellow w/blond hair............**100.00**

Figurine, Suicide Guy, gun to head, green, 5½" **60.00**

Figurine, water bottle on head, green, red bottle w/antenna, 4½" **100.00**

Figurine, 2-headed purple figure w/brown hair, 5" **135.00**

Mug, Santa w/rhinestone eyes, 2½" **10.00**

Napkin doll, green & yellow airbrushed dress, brimmed hat, 10", VG **25.00**

Salt & pepper shakers, reindeer seated, 4", pr **20.00**

Salt & pepper shakers, skunks in Santa hats, 1960s, 3½", pr..**10.00**

Lava Lamps

These were totally cool in the '60s — no self-respecting love child was without one. Like so many good ideas, this one's been revived and is popular again today. In fact, more are being sold this time around than were sold 40 years ago. We've listed only vintage examples.

Bullet style w/flared aluminum base, pink liquid, 1960s, 16", M **25.00**

Celestial lamp, sun/moon face on base, blue liquid, #5524, MIB **75.00**

Ceramic Series II, purple tie-dyed look ceramic base, #5924, MIB **70.00**

Dinosaur lamp, #LP-10D, 17½", EX **30.00**

Hourglass style, gold finish, light holes in base, blue liquid, 1960s **65.00**

Hourglass style, pink & white swirl top & base, EX **30.00**

Lantern type, copper finish, blue water, 1960s **225.00**

Rocket ship, blue liquid, Haggerty Enterprises, #5424, MIB. **100.00**

Lefton China

Since 1940 the Lefton China Co. has been importing and producing ceramic giftware which may be found in shops throughout the world. Because of the quality of the workmanship and the beauty of these items, they are eagerly sought by collectors of today. Lefton pieces are usually marked with a fired-on trademark or a paper label. See Clubs and Newsletters for information concerning the National Society of Lefton Collectors.

Ashtray, White Holly, leaf shape, #6056 .... **15.00**

Bone dish, Rose Chintz, #637, 8", from $12 to **18.00**

Bookends, dogs, #7484, 4¾", from $40 to **45.00**

Candleholder, Green Holly, #717, ea **15.00**

Candleholder, White Holly, #6052, 5" **30.00**

Candy dish, Green Holly, from $45.00 to $55.00.

Candy dish, Misty Rose, #5538, from $275 to **325.00**

Cheese dish, Americana, #958, from $55 to **65.00**

Coffeepot, To a Wild Rose, #3564, from $95 to **125.00**

Compote, Misty Rose, #5696, 5", from $22 to **28.00**

Compote, Rose Chintz, #650, from $45 to **55.00**

Creamer & sugar bowl, Cuddles, #1449, w/lid, from $35 to. **45.00**

Creamer & sugar bowl, Lilac Chintz, #694, from $38 to **42.00**

Cup & saucer, Green Holly, #2047, from $20 to **25.00**

Cup & saucer, Poinsetta, #4392, from $25 to **35.00**

Egg cup, Lilac Chintz, #698, from $12 to **18.00**

Egg cup, Pink Clover, #2493, 3½", from $10 to **15.00**

Figurine, Colonial couple on base, #3047, 9", from $150 to.**175.00**

Figurine, Dutch girl, #5096, 6", from $18 to **22.00**

Figurine, Jeanne, ruffled skirt, umbrella, #5741, 7½", from $125 to **150.00**

Figurine, Madeline, fancy blue dress, #5745, 7½", from $125 to.**175.00**

Figurine, policeman w/open book, #538, 8¼", from $45 to **55.00**

Figurine, Santa & Mrs Claus dancing, #023139, 3½", pr from $20 to.**30.00**

Figurine, Sunday angel, #255, 4", from $25 to **35.00**

Figurine, Valentine girl, #7173, 4", from $12 to **15.00**

Hors d'oevres, Green Holly, musical, #1365, 8½", from $60.00 to $75.00.
(Photo courtesy Loretta DeLozier)

Jam jar, Bossie the Cow, #6509, from $25 to **30.00**

Jam jar, White Christmas, #605, from $30 to **35.00**

Mug, Fruits of Italy, #1209, from $5 to **10.00**

Mug, Miss Priss, #1503, 4", from $65 to **75.00**

Music box, Christmas angel on bell, #637, 7", from $50 to.......**60.00**

Nappy, violets w/gold, #2334, from $30 to **35.00**

Nightlight, clown, #01890, 7", from $42 to **48.00**

Pitcher, Bluebird, #287, 4½", from $75 to **95.00**

Pitcher, Green Heritage, #796, from $100 to **150.00**

Pitcher, Misty Rose, #5692, 7", from $95 to **135.00**

Pitcher & bowl, White Holly, #6076, 5¼", from $35 to **45.00**

Planter, cardinal, matt, #570, from $18 to **28.00**

Planter, clown's head, #4498, 4", from $45 to **55.00**

Planter, egg w/chick on top, #7880, 4½", from $10 to **15.00**

Plaques, mermaids, #4574, 6", pr from $50 to **75.00**

Plaques, Mr & Mrs Toodles, #2032, 7", pr from $22 to............**28.00**

Plate, Rose Chintz, #658, 7", from $22 to **28.00**

Relish dish, White Holly, #6057, 12", from $25 to...............**30.00**

Salt & pepper shakers, Christmas candles, #1556, 4", pr from $18 to **22.00**

Salt & pepper shakers, Fruits of Italy, #1207, pr from $12 to.........**15.00**

Salt & pepper shakers, Mammy & Chef, #2046, 3¼", pr from $35 to **35.00**

Salt & pepper shakers, To a Wild Rose, #2584, pr from $20 to...........**25.00**

Sleigh, White Christmas, #1408, from $35 to **45.00**

Spice jar, Sweet Violets, #2876, 5", from $45 to **55.00**

Teabag holder, Violet Chintz, #1793, from $25 to **35.00**

Teapot, Cuddles, bow finial, #1448, from $85 to **95.00**

Teapot, Thumbelina, butterfly finial, #1695, from $145 to.**195.00**

Tidbit, Green Holly, 2-tiered, #1364, from $30 to **30.00**

Vase, Green Heritage, #4072, 8½", from $55 to **65.00**

Wall pocket, girl w/basket, #50264, 7", from $130 to **150.00**

Wall pockets, Mr & Mrs Bluebird, #283, pr from $275 to ... **350.00**

Liberty Blue

'Take home a piece of American history!,' stated an ad from the 1970s for this dinnerware made in Staffordshire, England. Blue and white depictions of George Washington at Valley Forge, Paul Revere, Independence Hall — fourteen historic scenes in all — were offered on different pieces. The ad goes on to describe this 'unique... truly unusual museum-quality... future family heirloom.'

For every five dollars spent on groceries you could purchase a basic piece (dinner plate, bread and butter plate, cup, saucer, or dessert dish) for 59¢ on alternate weeks of the promotion. During the promotion, completer pieces could also be purchased. The soup tureen was the most expensive item, originally selling for $24.99. Nineteen completer pieces in all were offered along with a five-year open stock guarantee. For more information we recommend Jo Cunningham's book, *The Best of Collectible Dinnerware*.

Bowl, cereal; 6½" **10.00**

Bowl, flat soup; 8¾", from $18 to **20.00**

Bowl, fruit; 5" **2.50**

Bowl, vegetable; oval, from $30 to **35.00**

Butter dish, ¼-lb **45.00**

Casserole, w/lid, from $115 to. **135.00**

Coaster **7.50**

Creamer, from $18 to **22.00**

Creamer & sugar bowl, w/lid, original box **80.00**

Cup & saucer **3.50**

Gravy boat **45.00**

Gravy boat liner **25.00**

Mug **10.00**

Pitcher, 7½", from $85 to **95.00**

Plate, dessert; 6" **2.00**

Plate, dinner; 10", from $5 to.. **7.00**

Plate, luncheon; scarce, 8¾" .. **20.00**

Plate, scarce, 7" **9.00**

Platter, 12", from $35 to **45.00**

Platter, 14", from $65.00 to $85.00.

Salt & pepper shakers, pr **35.00**

Soup ladle, plain white, no decal, from $30 to **35.00**

Soup tureen, w/lid **225.00**

Sugar bowl, no lid **10.00**

Sugar bowl, w/lid **28.00**

Teapot, w/lid, from $85 to **95.00**

License Plates

Early porcelain license plates are treasured by collectors and often sell for more than $500.00 per pair when found in excellent condition. The best examples are first-year plates from each state, but some of the more modern plates with special graphics are collectible too. Prices given below are for plates in good or better condition.

Alaska, 1953 .... **75.00**
Arizona, 1933, copper **100.00**
Arkansas, 1986-89, ea **3.50**
California, 1940 .... **30.00**
Connecticut, 1926 .... **14.50**
Delaware, 1982 .... **5.50**
Florida, 1938 .... **30.00**
Georgia, 1990, peach **3.50**
Hawaii, 1981 .... **6.00**
Idaho, 1941 .... **40.00**
Illinois, 1940 .... **9.50**
Iowa, 1911, fair **100.00**
Kansas, 1943, tab **8.00**
Kentucky, 1961 .... **10.50**
Maine, 1941 .... **25.00**
Massachussetts, 1918-19, ea . **25.00**
Michigan, 1940 .... **15.00**
Minnesota, 1943, tab **5.00**
Mississippi, 1974 .... **6.00**
Montana, 1963 .... **7.50**
Nebraska, 1930 .... **15.00**
Nevada, 1933 .... **30.00**
New Hampshire, 1926, pr ... **125.00**
New Jersey, 1923 .... **15.50**
New Mexico, 1983 .... **5.00**

New York, 1961, tab **3.00**
North Carolina, 1981, First in Freedom **10.00**
North Dakota, 1988, Teddy **9.50**
Ohio, 1959 .... **8.00**
Oklahoma, 1977 .... **5.00**
Oregon, 1948 .... **18.00**
Pennsylvania, 1938 .... **11.50**
Rhode Island, 1959 .... **10.00**
South Carolina, 1968 .... **6.00**
South Dakota, 1926 .... **15.00**
Tennessee, 1961 .... **10.50**
Texas, 1958, pr **18.00**
Utah, 1973 .... **3.00**
Vermont, 1995 .... **10.50**
Virginia, 1969 .... **5.00**
Washington DC, 1965 .... **10.00**
West Virginia, 1996 .... **7.50**
Wisconsin, 1941 .... **20.00**
Wyoming, 1958 .... **8.00**

Little Red Riding Hood

This line of novelties and kitchenware has always commanded good prices on the collectibles market. In fact, it became valuable enough to make it attractive to counterfeiters, and now you'll see reproductions everywhere. They're easy to spot, though, watch for one-color eyes. Though there are other differences, you should be able to identify the imposters armed with this information alone.

Little Red Riding Hood was produced from 1943 to 1957. The Regal China Company was by far the major manufacturer of this line, though a rather insignificant number of items were made by the Hull Pottery of Crooksville, Ohio, who sent their whiteware to the Royal China

New York, World's Fair, 1939, $40.00 each.

and Novelty Company (a division of Regal China) of Chicago, Illinois, to be decorated. For further information we recommend *The Ultimate Collector's Encyclopedia of Cookie Jars* by Joyce and Fred Roerig; and *The Collector's Encyclopedia of Hull Pottery* and *The Collector's Ultimate Encyclopedia of Hull Pottery*, both by Brenda Roberts. All of these books are published by Collector Books.

Bank, standing, 7", from $900 to **1,350.00**
Butter dish, 5½", from $350 to . **400.00**
Canister, Cereal, 10" **1,375.00**
Canister, Flour or Sugar, 10", ea from $600 to **700.00**
Canister, Tea, 10" **700.00**
Cookie jar, fan-shaped flower basket, 13", from $450 to ... **650.00**
Cookie jar, round basket, no apron, 13", from $600 to **900.00**
Cookie jar, round basket, 13", from $400 to **500.00**
Cracker jar, unmarked, from $600 to **750.00**
Creamer, side pour, from $150 to. **225.00**
Creamer, top pour, no handle, from $400 to **425.00**
Dresser jar, 8¾", from $450 to .. **475.00**
Jar, Red Riding Hood lid, 9", from $450 to **575.00**
Jar, wolf lid, red base, from $925 to **1,000.00**
Jar, wolf lid, yellow base, 6", from $750 to **850.00**
Matchbox, wall-mount, 5¼", from $400 to **650.00**
Mustard jar, w/spoon, 5¼", from $375 to **460.00**
Pitcher, 7", from $450 to **675.00**

Pitcher, 8", from $550 to **850.00**
Planter, wall-mount, 9", from $400 to **500.00**
Salt & pepper shakers, 3¼", pr from $95 to **140.00**
Salt & pepper shakers, 5½", pr from $185 to **225.00**
Spice jar, sq base, from $650 to. **750.00**
Sugar bowl, crawling, no lid, from $300 to **450.00**
Sugar bowl, standing, no lid, from $175 to **225.00**
Sugar bowl lid, minimum value. **175.00**
Teapot, 8", from $400 to **450.00**

Lu Ray Pastels

Introduced in 1938 by Taylor, Smith, and Taylor of East Liverpool, Ohio, Lu-Ray Pastels is today a very sought-after line of collectible American dinnerware. It was first made in these solid colors: Windsor Blue, Surf Green, Persian Cream, and Sharon Pink. Chatham Gray was introduced in 1948 and is today priced higher than the other colors.

Platter, 13", $24.00.

Bowl, coupe soup; flat **18.00**
Bowl, cream soup **70.00**
Bowl, fruit; Chatham Gray, 5" . **16.00**
Bowl, fruit; 5" **6.00**

Bowl, mixing; 5½", 7", or 8¾", ea. **125.00**
Bowl, salad; yellow.................. **55.00**
Bowl, vegetable; oval, 9½" L.. **25.00**
Bowl, 36s oatmeal................... **60.00**
Bud vase **400.00**
Butter dish, Chatham Gray .. **90.00**
Butter dish, colors other than
    Chatham Gray **50.00**
Cake plate............................... **70.00**
Calendar plate, 8", 9", or 10", ea. **40.00**
Chocolate creamer, after din-
    ner **92.00**
Chocolate cup, after dinner; straight
    sides **80.00**
Chocolate pot, after dinner; straight
    sides **400.00**
Chocolate sugar bowl, after dinner;
    w/lid **92.00**
Coaster/nut dish..................... **65.00**
Coffee cup, after dinner **20.00**
Coffeepot, after dinner......... **200.00**
Creamer................................... **8.00**
Creamer, after dinner............ **40.00**
Egg cup, double **30.00**
Epergne................................. **125.00**
Jug, footed **150.00**
Muffin cover........................... **140.00**
Muffin cover, w/8" underplate. **165.00**
Nappy, vegetable; round, 8½" . **25.00**
Pickle tray **28.00**
Pitcher, bulbous w/flat bottom, col-
    ors other than yellow.... **125.00**
Pitcher, bulbous w/flat bottom, yel-
    low.................................... **95.00**
Pitcher, juice......................... **200.00**
Plate, grill; 3-part **35.00**
Plate, 6" **3.00**
Plate, 7" **12.00**
Plate, 8" **25.00**
Plate, 9" **10.00**
Plate, 10" **25.00**
Plate, 15" **38.00**
Platter, 11½" **20.00**

Platter, 13"............................. **24.00**
Relish dish, 4-part **125.00**
Salt & pepper shakers, pr **18.00**
Sauceboat, fixed stand, colors other
    than yellow...................... **35.00**
Sauceboat, fixed stand, yellow. **22.50**
Saucer, coffee; after dinner...... **8.50**
Saucer, coffee/chocolate.......... **30.00**
Saucer, for cream soup........... **28.00**
Sugar bowl, after dinner; w/lid.. **40.00**
Sugar bowl, w/lid **15.00**
Teacup...................................... **8.00**
Teapot, curved spout............ **125.00**
Teapot, flat spout **160.00**
Tumbler, juice......................... **50.00**
Tumbler, water....................... **80.00**

Lunch Boxes

In the early years of this century, tobacco companies often packaged their products in tins that could later be used for lunch boxes. By the 1930s oval lunch boxes designed to appeal to school children were being produced. The rectangular shape that is now popular was preferred in the 1950s. Character lunch boxes decorated with the faces of TV personalities, super heroes, Disney, and cartoon characters are especially sought after by collectors today. Our values are for lunch boxes with bottles, and prices are ranged from excellent to near-mint condition. Deduct at least 20% if you have a lunch box without a Thermos. Refer to *Pictorial Price Guide to Vinyl and Plastic Lunch Boxes and Thermoses* and *Pictorial Price Guide to Metal Lunch Boxes and Thermoses* by Larry Aikens (L-W Book Sales) for more information. For an expanded listing, see *Schroeder's Collectible Toys, Antique to Modern* (Collector Books).

Addams Family, metal, 1970s, from $90 to **145.00**
Annie, vinyl, 1980s, from $50 to. **75.00**
Archies, metal, 1969, from $95 to **165.00**
Astrokids, plastic, 1980s, from $15 to **25.00**
Barbarino, vinyl, 1970s, from $125 to **150.00**
Barbie, vinyl, 1970s, from $65 to. **85.00**
Batman, vinyl, 1990s, from $15 to **25.00**
Battlestar Galactica, metal, 1970s, from $50 to **100.00**

Bionic Woman, metal, 1970s, from $40.00 to $80.00.

Care Bears, metal, 1980s, from $30 to **50.00**
Charlie's Angels, metal, 1970s, from $60 to **120.00**
CHiPs, plastic, 1970s, dome top, from $40 to **60.00**
Deputy Dawg, vinyl, 1960s, from $325 to **375.00**
Dick Tracy, plastic, 1990s, from $10 to **15.00**
Disney School Bus, plastic, 1990s, from $20 to **30.00**

Doctor Dolittle, metal, 1960s, from $95 to **165.00**
Fall Guy, metal, 1980s, from $30 to **60.00**
Fat Albert, plastic, 1970s, from $20 to **30.00**
Fire Station Engine Co #1, vinyl, 1970s, from $115 to....... **135.00**
Flintstones, metal, 1970s, from $120 to **190.00**
Garfield, plastic, 1980s, from $15 to **20.00**
GI Joe, metal, 1980s, from $35 to..**60.00**
Gremlins, metal, 1980s, from $25 to **45.00**
Gunsmoke, metal, 1959, from $150 to **300.00**
Hardy Boys Mysteries, metal, 1970s, from $30 to **65.00**
Heathcliff, metal, 1980s, from $25 to **40.00**
Hogan's Heroes, metal, 1960s, from $225 to **375.00**
Holly Hobby, plastic, 1989, from $20 to **25.00**
Holly Hobby, vinyl, 1970s, from $50 to **75.00**
Incredible Hulk, plastic, 1980s, dome top, from $40 to..... **50.00**
Indiana Jones, metal, 1980s, from $25 to **55.00**
Jet Patrol, metal, 1950s, from $250 to **400.00**
Jr Deb, vinyl, 1960s, from $100 to................................. **150.00**
Jurassic Park, plastic, 1990s, w/ recalled bottle, from $25 to.**30.00**
Kermit the Frog, plastic, dome top, 1980s, from $30 to **40.00**
Knight Rider, metal, 1980s, from $25 to **55.00**
Legend of the Lone Ranger, metal, 1980s, from $60 to **100.00**

Little House on the Prairie, metal, 1970s, from $75 to **125.00**

Little Old Schoolhouse, vinyl, 1970s, from $50 to **75.00**

Man From UNCLE, metal, 1960s, from $120 to **190.00**

Mary Poppins, vinyl, 1970s, from $75 to **100.00**

Masters of the Universe, metal, 1980s, from $35 to **70.00**

Mickey Mouse Club, metal, 1970s, from $35 to **75.00**

Mighty Mouse, plastic, 1970s, from $25 to **35.00**

Monkees, vinyl, 1960s, from $300 to **350.00**

Osmonds, metal, 1970s, from $65 to **100.00**

Pac-Man, metal, 1980s, from $25 to **50.00**

Pac-Man, vinyl, 1980s, from $40 to.................................... **60.00**

Peanuts, metal, 1960s, from $40 to.................................... **80.00**

Peanuts, metal, 1980s, from $20 to **40.00**

Pink Panther, vinyl, 1970s, from $75 to **100.00**

Popeye, plastic, 1979, dome top, from $30 to **40.00**

Porky's Lunch Wagon, metal, 1959, from $225 to **350.00**

Rifleman, metal, 1960s, from $325 to **450.00**

Rocky & Bullwinkle, plastic, 1990s, from $75 to **125.00**

Roy Rogers & Dale Evans, metal, 1950s, many versions, ea from $200 to **325.00**

Smurfs, plastic, dome top, 1980s, from $20 to **30.00**

Snoopy, vinyl, 1969, red, at mailbox, from $65 to **85.00**

Snoopy & Woodstock, plastic, dome top, 1970s, from $20 to **30.00**

Space: 1999, metal, 1970s, from $50.00 to $75.00.

Star Trek The Motion Picture, metal, 1980s, from $125 to **225.00**

Strawberry Shortcake, vinyl, 1980s, from $75 to **135.00**

Super Friends, metal, 1970s, from $50 to **100.00**

Superman, metal, 1970s, from $50 to **100.00**

SWAT, plastic, dome top, 1980s, from $30 to **40.00**

Thundercats, metal, 1980s, from $30 to **60.00**

Tic-Tac-Toe, vinyl, 1970s, from $50 to **75.00**

Waltons, metal, 1970s, from $65 to **105.00**

Welcome Back Kotter, metal, 1970s, from $50 to **100.00**

Wonder Woman, vinyl, 1970s, from $100 to **150.00**

Yogi Bear, plastic, 1990s, from $15 to **25.00**

Ziggy, vinyl, 1979, from $50 to . **75.00**

Magazines

Some of the most collectible magazines are *Life* (because of the celebrities and important events they feature on their covers), *Saturday Evening Post* and *Ladies' Home Journal* (especially those featuring the work of famous illustrators such as Parrish, Rockwell, and Wyeth), and *National Geographics* (with particularly newsworthy features). As is true with any type of ephemera, condition and value are closely related. Unless they're in fine condition (clean, no missing or clipped pages, and very little other damage), they're worth very little; and cover interest and content are far more important than age. For further information we recommend *Old Magazines*, by Richard E. Clear, published by Collector Books.

American Heritage, 1968, April, Mickey Mouse cover, VG **25.00**

Art Photography, 1956, April, Sophia Loren, VG **10.00**

Astounding Stories, 1931, December, EX.................. **40.00**

Bedtime Stories, 1937, August, EX.................................. **30.00**

Better Homes & Gardens, 1935, September, EX **30.00**

Better Homes & Gardens, 1960, October, EX **3.00**

Black Mask, 1931, March, VG. **45.00**

Camera Craft, 1925, July, EX. **15.00**

Campfire Girl, 1944 to 1959, ea from $3 to **5.00**

Car Craft, 1956, July, EX........ **5.00**

Co-ed, 1963, September, VG.... **4.00**

Collier's, 1945, June, Harry Truman, EX...................... **7.00**

Collier's, 1955, November 11, Agatha Christie, EX **10.00**

Cosmopolitan, 1932, March, Harrison Fisher cover, EX **25.00**

Cosmopolitan, 1969, August, Elizabeth Taylor, EX......... **8.00**

Cosmopolitan, 1979, April, Gia Carnagi, EX..................... **10.00**

Cycle World, 1968, August, EX **7.00**

Deep Sea Digest, 1950s, ea from $2 to **4.00**

Dime Adventure, 1935, June, EX.. **12.00**

Doc Savage, 1949, September, EX+ **20.00**

Ebony, 1953, Sophie Tucker article, EX **15.00**

Esquire, 1960, November, Lenny Bruce article, EX............. **10.00**

Fabulous Las Vegas, 1955, July 16, VG+, from $25 to **35.00**

Family Circle, 1946, April 26, Marilyn Monroe, EX **350.00**

Field & Stream, 1930-49, ea from $10 to **20.00**

Field & Stream, 1950-69, ea from $5 to **10.00**

Firehouse Magazine, 1976, August/September, EX **10.00**

Fortune, 1944, January, EX .. **12.50**

Garden & Home Builder, 1920s, VG, from $6 to................... **8.00**

Glamour, 1944, August, EX... **20.00**

Good Housekeeping, 1945, August, baby cover, EX+ **8.00**

Gourmet, 1965, April, Lucious Beebe & Along the Boulevards, EX **5.00**

Harper's Bazaar, New York NY, issues w/covers by Erte, ea from $40 to **80.00**

Harper's Bazaar, New York NY, 1940-50, ea from $7 to **15.00**

Hot Rod, 1949, December, NM..**12.00**

Hot Rod, 1952, June, EX **7.00**

House & Garden, 1954, November, EX **5.00**

House Beautiful, 1959, October, Frank Lloyd Wright, EX. **12.00**

Jack & Jill, 1959, August, EX. **4.00**

Jack & Jill, 1961, May, Roy Rogers, EX **10.00**

Jazz & Pop, 1971, March, Mick Jagger, EX+ **25.00**

Jet, 1965, July 1, Beatles, EX. **15.00**

Jungle Stories, 1950, Spring, VG..**7.00**

Ladies' Home Journal, 1934, January, reclining lady on cover, NM..**12.00**

Ladies' Home Journal, 1947, May, Eleanor Roosevelt article, EX+ **5.00**

Life, 1936, November 23, 1st photo issue, EX+ **100.00**

Life, 1939, December 11, Betty Grable, VG...................... **10.00**

Life, 1947, November 17, Howard Hughes, EX **15.00**

Life, 1950, June 12, Hopalong Cassidy, EX, $50.00.

Life, 1953, July 20, Senator John Kennedy, EX.................... **10.00**

Life, 1955, February 28, Shelly Winters in tub on cover, EX.**7.00**

Life, 1961, May 17, Alan B Shepard **12.00**

Life, 1963, August, 23, Sinatra cover, NM **8.00**

Life, 1964, February, Lee Harvey Oswald holding rifle on cover, EX **25.00**

Life, 1966, August 26, Strike Fever cover, EX.......................... **10.00**

Life, 1969, April 18, Mae West, VG.**10.00**

Life, 1969, July 25, Neil Armstrong cover, EX+.............................. **40.00**

Life, 1971, October 15, Disney World Opens! cover, EX.. **15.00**

Life, 1981, May, Reagan's attempted assassination, EX+ **12.00**

Life, 1992, 40 Years of Rock & Roll, EX **12.00**

Look, 1937, May, Jean Harlow, Prohibition, EX **15.00**

Look, 1940, February, 27, Superman Article, EX........................ **95.00**

Look, 1950, December 5, Esther Williams, EX **20.00**

Look, 1956, November, James Dean, EX **18.00**

Look, 1963, January, 9, Beatles article, EX **28.00**

Look, 1967, February 6, John Kennedy.............................. **6.00**

Look, 1970, July 28, Princess Anne cover, EX............................ **3.00**

Magic Magazine, 1993, September, Siegfried & Roy, NM+..... **75.00**

McCall's, 1965, November, EX . **4.00**

McCall's, 1968, June, Jacqueline Kennedy.............................. **6.00**

McCall's, 1969, September, EX.. **5.00**

Modern Screen, 1939, Deanna Durbin, EX **30.00**

Movie Life, 1968, October, Elvis, EX **20.00**

Movie Stars Parade, 1948, August, Shirley Temple & family on cover, EX.**15.00**

National Geographic, 1915-16, ea **15.00**

National Geographic, 1917-24, ea .**9.00**

National Geographic, 1925-29, ea .**8.00**

National Geographic, 1930-45, ea .**7.00**

National Geographic, 1946-55, ea .**6.00**

National Geographic, 1956-67, ea .**5.50**

National Geographic, 1968-69, ea .**4.00**

National Geographic, 1990-present, ea **2.00**

Newsweek, New York NY, 1950-59, ea from $2 to **5.00**

Newsweek, New York NY, 1960 to present, ea from $1 to **2.00**

Newsweek, 1975, October 27, Bruce Springsteen, EX **5.00**

People, 1982, John Belushi cover, EX **10.00**

Photoplay, 1975, August, Marilyn Monroe cover, Warhol article, NM **13.00**

Playboy, 1954, May, EX **60.00**

Playboy, 1972, Playboy's Vargas Girls, EX **6.00**

Rolling Stone, 1977, September 22, Elvis cover, EX **12.50**

Rolling Stone, 1981, October 1, Yoko Ono cover, EX **15.00**

Rolling Stone, 1992, April, NM.**11.00**

Rolling Stone, 1996, October, NM **8.00**

Saturday Evening Post, 1934, January 13, EX **22.50**

Saturday Evening Post, 1942, October 31, Halloween art by C Kaiser, VG **18.00**

Saturday Evening Post, 1962, June 16, Marlon Brando cover, EX **10.00**

Saturday Evening Post, 1976, April, Patty Hearst cover, EX **6.00**

Screen Album, 1964, Liz's Love Letters to Burton, EX **10.00**

Screen Guide, 1936, Ginger Rogers, EX **20.00**

Seventeen, 1959, September, EX **4.00**

Seventeen, 1967, June, EX **5.00**

Silver Screen, 1950s, ea from $5 to **10.00**

Skin Diver, 1964, June, EX ... **10.00**

Snowgoer, 1967, Fall, EX **15.00**

Time, 1967, July 7, Hippies Philosophy of a Subculture, EX **4.00**

Time, 1967, September 22, Beatles cover, EX **16.00**

Time, 1973, May 28, Nixon cover, EX **3.00**

Time, 1981, January 5, Reagan cover, EX **3.00**

Trains Magazine, 1940, November, VG+ **20.00**

TV Guide, May 8 – 14, 1965, Tina Louise and Bob Denver, EX, from $20.00 to $30.00. (Photo courtesy Greg Davis and Bill Morgan)

Vogue, 1952, May, Summer Fashion Issue, EX+ **17.00**

Vogue, 1970, March 1, Ali McGraw cover, EX **5.00**

Woman's Day, 1970, January, EX **3.00**

Wrestling Life, 1951, September, EX **25.00**

Marbles

Because there are so many kinds of marbles that interest today's collectors, we suggest you study a book that covers each type. Everett Grist (see Directory, Tennessee) has written several. In addition to his earlier work, *Antique and Collectible Marbles*, he has also written *Everett Grist's Big Book of Marbles*, which includes both antique and modern varieties. Both are published by Collector Books.

Remember that condition is extremely important. Naturally, chips occurred; and though some may be ground down and polished, the values of badly chipped and repolished marbles are low. In our listings, values are for marbles in the standard small size and in excellent to near-mint condition unless noted otherwise. Watch for reproductions of the comic character marbles. Repros have the design printed on a large area of plain white glass with color swirled through the back and sides. While common sulfides may run as low as $100.00, those with a more unusual subject or made of colored glass are considerably higher, sometimes as much as $1,000.00 or more. See Clubs and Newsletters for information concerning the Marble Collectors' Society of America.

Advertising, opaque white w/red Indian (Motorcycle) logo, 1", NM **45.00**

Akro Agate, oxblood, 16.31mm (larger than standard ⅝"), NM+ **48.00**

Akro Agate, Popeye corkscrew, red, white & blue, ⅝", NM+ . **125.00**

Akro Agate, Popeye corkscrew, yellow & purple, ¾", NM+ ... **65.00**

Akro Agate, sparkler, white, brown, yellow, green & red, ⅝", EX. **50.00**

Beetem, lg spiral swirl w/blue, white, yellow & red, 1½", EX **40.00**

Christensen Agate, flame swirl, ⅝", NM+ **150.00**

Christensen Agate, yellow oxblood flame, ¾", EX **185.00**

Clambroth, blue bands, ¹³⁄₁₆", EX .. **75.00**

End of Day, left-hand twist, multicolored, ⅞", NM+ **150.00**

Indian Swirl, black, blue & white, ¾", NM **45.00**

Joseph's Coat, multicolored w/green adventurine, ¹⁵⁄₁₆", M **130.00**

Lutz, clear w/white, light green & gold swirl, ⅝", EX **50.00**

Lutz, gold swirl w/black & white, ¾", NM **150.00**

Lutz, gold swirl w/green & white, ⅝", EX **115.00**

Marble King, blended Spider-Man w/red, blue & orange, ⅝", EX+ **38.00**

Mica, berry, ¾", G **42.00**

Onionskin, blue, pink w/white & yellow, 1¹¹⁄₁₆", NM **75.00**

Onionskin, green, blue & white swirl, ⅝", VG **45.00**

Onionskin, green, red, white & blue swirl, 2", NM **165.00**

Onionskin, pink, green, yellow & blue, 2¹⁄₁₆", EX **200.00**

Onionskin, red, white & blue swirl, 1⅜", NM+ **100.00**

Sulphide, angel w/wings spread, 1⅞", EX **175.00**

Sulphide, boy seated on stump, 1⅞", NM **125.00**

Sulphide, crucifix, 2¼", EX+ . **200.00**

Sulphide, girl w/hammer, 1⅝", NM **150.00**

Sulphide, sheep, 1¼", EX+... **175.00**

Transparent Swirl, divided core (multicolored), 1¹⁄₁₆", EX.. **75.00**

Transparent Swirl, latticino core, red, black, yellow swirl, ⅞", NM+ **150.00**

Transparent Swirl, latticinio core, red, white & blue swirl, 1½", VG **40.00**

Transparent Swirl, latticinio core, red & white swirl, 1¾", G. **45.00**

Transparent Swirl, latticinio core, ribbon swirl, 1¾", NM+. **145.00**

Transparent Swirl, solid core, blue w/red & white swirl, ¹³⁄₁₆", NM **130.00**

Transparent Swirl, solid core, multicolored, 1¼", EX **60.00**

Transparent Swirl, solid core, peppermint, 9¹⁄₁₆", NM **150.00**

Transparent Swirl, solid core, white & multi, yellow outer, 1¾", EX **40.00**

Matchbox Cars

Introduced in 1953, the Matchbox Miniatures series has always been the mainstay of the company. There were 75 models in all but with enough variations to make collecting them a real challenge. Larger, more detailed models were introduced in 1957. This series, called Major Pack, was replaced a few years later by a similar line called King Size. To compete with Hot Wheels, Matchbox converted most models over to a line called SuperFast that sported thinner, low-friction axles and wheels. (These are much more readily available from the original 'regular wheels,' the last of which was made in 1959.) At about the same time, the King size series became known as Speed Kings; in 1977 the line was reintroduced under the name Super Kings.

Another line that's become very popular is their Models of Yesteryear. These are slightly larger replicas of antique and vintage vehicles. Values of $20.00 to $60.00 for mint-in-box examples are average, though a few sell for even more.

Sky Busters, introduced in 1973, are small-scale aircraft measuring an average of 3½" in length. Models currently being produced sell for about $4.00 each.

To learn more, we recommend *Matchbox Toys, 1947 to 2003; The Other Matchbox Toys, 1947 to 2004;* and *Toy Car Collector's Guide,* all by Dana Johnson. There is also a series of books by Charlie Mack (there are three): *Lesney's Matchbox Toys Regular Wheels, SuperFast Years,* and *Universal Years.* To determine values of examples in conditions other than given in our listings, based on MIB or MOC prices, deduct a minimum of 10% if the original container is missing, 30% if the condition is excellent, and as much as 70% for a toy graded only very good.

King Size, Speed Kings, and Super Kings

Airport Rescue Fire Tender, #K-075, 1980, MIP, from $12 to **16.00**

Auto Transport, #K-010, 1976, MIP, from $20 to **30.00**

Camping Cruiser, #K-027, 1971, MIP, from $16 to **20.00**

Citreon SM, #K-033, 1972, MIP, from $12 to **16.00**

Dodge Custom Van, #K-080, 1980, from $18 to **24.00**

Fuzzy Buggy, #K-041, 1973, MIP, from $18 to **24.00**

KW Dart Dump Truck, #K-002, 1964, MIP, from $40 to ... **55.00**

Log Transport, #K-043, 1981, MIP, from $18 to **24.00**

Milligan's Mill, #K-039, 1973, MIP, from $12 to **18.00**

Motorcycle Racing Set, #K-091, 1982, MIP, from $45 to ... **65.00**

Pepsi Delivery Truck, #K-040, 1980, white, MIP, from $25 to.. **35.00**

Racing Car Transporter, #K-005, 1967, MIP, from $35 to ... **50.00**

Refuse Truck, #K-007, 1967, black wheels, MIP, from $35 to. **50.00**

Security Truck, #K-019, 1979, MIP, from $18 to **24.00**

Thunderclap Racer, #K-034, 1972, MIP, from $18 to **24.00**

Models of Yesteryear

Albion 6-Wheeler (1938), #Y-42, 1991, MIP, from $18 to ... **24.00**

Bugatti Type 35 (1932), #Y-11, 1987, MIP, from $20 to ... **30.00**

Cadillac (1913), #Y-6, 1967, gold-plated, MIP, from $225 to **275.00**

Garrett Steam Truck (1931), #Y-37, 1990, MIP, from $18 to ... **24.00**

Hispano Suiza (1938), #Y-17, 1973, green, MIP, from $24 to................................... **28.00**

Jaguar SS 100 (1936), #Y-1-C, silver & blue, MIP, from $16 to................................... **20.00**

Lincoln Zephyr (1938), #Y-64, 1992, MIP, from $30 to **45.00**

MG TC (1945), #Y-8, 1978, cream w/tan top, MIP, from $15 to............. **20.00**

Morris Pantechion Van (1933), #Y-31, 1990, MIP, from $18 to...... **24.00**

Packard Landaulet (1912), #Y-11, 1964, beige & brown, MIP, from $25 to **35.00**

Scania Vabis Postbus (1922), #Y-16, MIP, from $40 to **60.00**

Simplex (1912), #Y-9, 1968, pale gold w/black roof, MIP, from $50 to **70.00**

Unic Taxi (1907), #Y-28, 1984, maroon, blue & white, MIP, ea from $16 to **20.00**

Y-2-C, 1914 Prince Henry Vauxhall, 1970, MIP, $20.00. (Photo courtesy Dana Johnson)

Skybusters

Air Malta A300 Airbus, #SB-027, 1981, white, MIP, from $15 to................................... **20.00**

Alpha Jet, #SB-011, 1973, blue & red, MIP, from $10 to...... **15.00**

Boeing 747-400, #SB-031, 1990, any, MIP, from $7 to **9.00**

F-13, #SB-024, 1979, any, MIP, from $9 to **12.00**

James Bond Cessna 210 Float Plane, #SB-026, 1981, white, MIP, from $12 .... **16.00**

Junkers 87B, #SB-007, 1973, black w/swastikas, MIP, from $80 to **100.00**

Learjet, #SB-001, 1973, red w/Datapost decal, MIP, from $8 to **12.00**

Marine Phantom F4E, #SB-015, 1975, pink, MIP, from $7 to **10.00**

Mig 21, #SB-006, 1073, blue & white, MIP, from $8 to **12.00**

Ram Rod, #SB-016, 1976, red, MIP, from $7 to **10.00**

Royal Air Force Hawk, #SB-037, 1992, red, MIP, from $7 to..**10.00**

Spitfire, #SB-008, 1973, dark brown & gold, MIP, from $18 to . **24.00**

Tornado, #SB-022, 1978, light purple & white, MIP, from $7 to **10.00**

UTA Douglas DC-10, #SB-013, 1973, white, MIP, from $70 to..................................... **85.00**

Wild Wind, #SB-018, 1976, lime green & white, MIP, from $8 to **12.00**

1 – 75 Series

Aston Martin Racer, #19, 1961, gray or white driver, MIP, from $60 to **80.00**

Atlas Skip Truck, #37, 1976, orange w/red skip, MIP, from $90 to.......................... **120.00**

Beach Buggy, #30, 1971, pink & white, MIP, from $20 to.. **35.00**

Bedford Duple Long Distance Coach, #21, 1956, MIP, from $80 to **100.00**

Berkley Cavalier Travel Trailer, #23, 1956, pale blue, MIP, from $60 to **80.00**

Big Bull Bulldozer, #12, 1975, orange rollers, MIP, from $5 to **7.00**

Case Bulldozer, #16, 1969, dark red w/black treads, MIP, from $40 to **55.00**

Caterpillar DB Bulldozer, #18, 1956, red blade, MIP, from $80 to **110.00**

Cement Mixer, #3, 1953, blue w/gray plastic wheels, MIP, from $85 to **100.00**

Chevy Bel Air ('57), #4, 1979, metallic magenta, MIP, from $6 to **8.00**

Corvette ('97), #4, 1997, metallic blue, MIP, from $5 to **7.00**

Crane Truck, #49, 1976, red, MIP, from $80 to **100.00**

Crane Truck, #49, 1976, yellow, MIP, from $6 to **8.00**

DAF Girder Truck, #58, 1968, MIP, from $12 to **16.00**

Daimler Ambulance, #14, 1956, gray plastic wheels, MIP, from $80 to **100.00**

DeTomaso Pantera, #8, 1975, white w/blue base, MIP, from $10 to............................. **15.00**

Dodge Dump Truck, #48, 1966, MIP, from $10 to **15.00**

Dodge Stake Truck, #4, 1970, Super Fast, MIP, from $20 to.... **30.00**

Dumper, #2, 1953, green metal wheels, MIP, from $185 to **235.00**

Dune Man Volkswagen Beetle, #49, 1984, MIP, from $4 to **5.00**

Ergomatic Cab Horse Box, #17, 1969, w/2 horses, MIP, from $9 to..**12.00**

Euclid Quarry Truck, #6, 1964, yellow, MIP, from $15 to...... **25.00**

Field Car, #18, 1969, green plastic hubs, MIP, from $900 to.**1,200.00**

Field Car, #18, 1970, Super Fast, olive drab, MIP, from $75 to........**90.00**

Ford Capri, #54, 1971, MIP, from $12 to.............................. **18.00**

Ford Group 6, #45, 1970, Super Fast, metallic green, MIP, from $12 to.............................. **16.00**

Ford Mustang Fastback, #8, 1966, Super Fast, orange, MIP, from $320 to........................... **360.00**

Ford Mustang Wildcat Dragster, #8, 1970, MIP, from $25 to **40.00**

Ford Pickup, #6, 1968, white grille, MIP, from $10 to **15.00**

Ford Refuse Truck, #7, 1970, Super Fast, MIP, from $30 to.... **40.00**

Formula 1 Racing Car, #34, 1971, blue, MIP, from $12 to.... **16.00**

GMC Tipper Truck, #26, 1968, MIP, from $7 to **10.00**

Hay Trailer, #40, 1967, beige (rare color), from $175 to....... **225.00**

Hay Trailer, #40, 1967, common color, MIP, from $6 to...... **10.00**

Iron Fairy Crane, #42, 1969, MIP, from $45 to **75.00**

Jeep Hot Rod, #2, 1971, pink or red, MIP, from $16 to **20.00**

Jumbo Jet Motorcycle, #71, 1973, MIP, from $15 to **20.00**

Land Rover Fire Truck, #57, 1970, Super Fast, MIP, from $50 to **65.00**

London Bus, #5, 1954, red, MIP, from $80 to **100.00**

Lotus Europa, #5, 1969, Super Fast, black, MIP, from $16 to................................**20.00**

Massey-Harris Tractor, #4, 1954, w/ fenders, MIP, from $80 to .**100.00**

Mustang GT350, #23, 1979, MIP, from $12 to **16.00**

Pony Trailer w/Two Horses, #43, 1968, MIP, from $9 to **12.00**

Quarry Truck, #6, 1964, 6-wheeled, yellow, MIP, from $24 to. **28.00**

Rallye Royale, #14, 1973, MIP, from $8 to **12.00**

Saab 9000, #15, 1988, LW, metallic blue, MIP, from $9 to...... **12.00**

Standard Jeep CJ5, #72, 1966, red interior, MIP, from $16 to. **20.00**

Standard Jeep CJ5, #72, 1970, Super Fast, MIP, from $32 to **44.00**

T-Bird (1957), #42, 1982, red, MIP, from $6 to **8.00**

Toyman Dodge Challenger, #1, 1983, MIP, from $5 to **8.00**

Toyota Mini Pickup Camper, #22, 1983, MIP, from $6 to **8.00**

US Mail Jeep, #5, 1978, US Mail tampo, MIB, from $6 to.... **8.00**

Volkswagen 1600 TL, #67, 1970, Super Fast, MIP, from $35 to **50.00**

#23-D, Volkswagen camper with opening roof, 1970, MIP, from $18.00 to $20.00. (Photo courtesy Dana Johnson)

McCoy

A popular collectible with flea market goers, McCoy pottery was made in Roseville, Ohio, from 1910 until the late 1980s. They are most famous for their extensive line of figural cookie jars, more than 200 in all. They also made amusing figural planters, etc., as well as dinnerware, and vases and pots for the florist trade. Though some pieces are unmarked, most bear one of several McCoy trademarks. Beware of reproductions made by a company in Tennessee who at one time used a very close facsimile of the old McCoy mark. They made several cookie jars once produced by McCoy as well as other now-defunct potteries. Some of these (but by no means all) were dated with the number '93' below the mark. For more information refer to *McCoy Pottery Collector's Reference & Value Guide, Volumes I, II,* and *III,* by Margaret Hanson, Craig Nissen, and Bob Hanson; and *McCoy Pottery Wall Pockets & Decorations* by Craig Nissen. All are published by Collector Books. See also Cookie Jars. See Clubs and Newsletters for information concerning the newsletter *NM (Nelson McCoy) Xpress.*

Basket, Rustic, pine-cone decor, 6x8½", from $50 to **65.00**

Beverage server, Sunburst Gold, 1957, 11", from $60 to **80.00**

Bookends, birds (pr) on blossom branch, pastels, 1940s, pr from $175 to **250.00**

Bookends, horses rearing, white w/gold trim, 1942, 8", from $150 to **175.00**

Candleholder, leaf decor, matt, zigzag cup rim, footed, 1930s, from $35 to **50.00**

Centerpiece bowl, leaf decor, matt, zigzag rim, footed, 1930s, from $50 to **80.00**

Flower holder, cornucopia, any except gold, yellow or rose, 4", from $35 to **50.00**

Flower holder, cornucopia, gold, yellow or rose, 4", from $70 to **90.00**

Flower holder, turtle, any color except yellow or rose, 4", from $55 to **70.00**

Flower holder, turtle, yellow or rose, 4", from $90 to **110.00**

Flowerpot, Butterfly, any color except coral, w/saucer, 6½", from $80 to **100.00**

Flowerpot, Butterfly, coral, 1940s, w/saucer, 6½", from $125 to...................... **175.00**

Flowerpot, flower & leaf decor, matt, 1930s, w/saucer, 6", from $50 to **80.00**

Flowerpot, geometric bands, various colors, 1954, w/saucer, 6", from $20 to **30.00**

Hand dish, various colors, 1940s, 8½", from $100 to **150.00**

Hanging basket, leaves & berries, matt, 1930s, 6", from $40 to............. **60.00**

Jardiniere, broad leaves & fruit, brown & green matt, 1930s, 8", from $100 to **125.00**

Jardiniere, leaves on basketweave, pastel, 1940s, w/saucer, 4½"......... **65.00**

Jardiniere, leaves & berries on basketweave, w/pedestal, 21", from $300 to **400.00**

Jardiniere, Rustic, pine-cone decor, 7¼", from $40 to **55.00**

Jardiniere, Spring Wood (dogwood), pink, white or mint, 10", from $60 to **70.00**

Leaf dish, 3-part, 1952, 11x8", from $35 to **45.00**

Mug, Happy Face, Smile America, tan, white or yellow, 1971, 4", from $20 to **30.00**

Pitcher, Hobnail jug, pastel matt, 1940s, 48-oz, 6", from $100 to **150.00**

Pitcher, pine-cone decor, various colors, 1935, 6½", from $35 to **45.00**

Planter, frog & lotus blossom, green & yellow w/gold trim, 1943, 5" **40.00**

Planter, frog w/leaves on back, various styles/sizes, from $30 to **40.00**

Planter, gazelles & leaves, pastels, 1940s, 9½" L, from $40 to. **50.00**

Planter, grape cluster on attached leaf dish, 1950s, from $200 to **300.00**

Planter, Hobnail, pastel matt, 4-footed, 1940s, 5½" L, from $25 to **35.00**

Planter, leaf cornucopia, various colors, 3-footed, 1940s, 5", from $35 to **50.00**

Planter, log form, glossy chartreuse w/gold trim, 1954, 7½", from $30 to **40.00**

Planter, panther form, mouth closed, unmarked, 1950, 16" L, from $40 to **50.00**

Planter, panther form, mouth open, McCoy mark, 1960, 16" L, from $100 to **150.00**

Planter, Rustic, pine-cone foot, 1945, 7½" L, from $20 to.. **30.00**

Planter, Spring Wood (dogwood), pink, white or mint, 6-footed, 10½" **40.00**

Planter, turtle form, Floraline, white, 1960s, 5x3", from $12 to... **18.00**

Planter, Wild Rose, lavender, yellow, blue or pink, 1950s, 8", from $40 to **50.00**

Platter, Butterfly, leaf form, white or blue, 1940s, 14", from $300 to **400.00**

Platter, fish form, white, brown or rose, 1973, 18x8", from $40 to................................... **55.00**

Vase, Butterfly, any color but coral, handles, 1940s, 10", from $150 to................ **200.00**

Vase, Butterfly, any color except coral, cylindrical, 8", from $50 to **60.00**

Vase, Butterfly, coral, cylindrical, 940s, 8", from $70 to....... **80.00**

Vase, Butterfly, coral, handles, 1940s, 10", from $175 to.**225.00**

Vase, concentric circles, various colors, 1940s, 6¾", from $100 to **150.00**

Vase, cornucopia w/tassels, pastel matt, sq base, 1940s, 8", from $25 to **30.00**

Vase, dark green, footed, 1959, 14", from $75.00 to $100.00. (Photo courtesy Margaret Hanson, Craig Nissen, and Bob Hanson)

Vase, grape clusters (2) w/leaves, gold trim, 1951, 9", from $75 to **90.00**

Vase, green or white, ribbed cylinder, 1957, 10", 12" or 14", from $80 to **130.00**

Vase, handled urn w/wide ribs around middle, 1940s, 12", from $125 to **200.00**

Vase, heart shape w/roses, footed, 1940s, 6", from $60 to **80.00**

Vase, Hobnail, pastel matt gate type, 1940s, 6", from $150 to **200.00**

Vase, sailboats, sq base, 1942, 9", from $50 to **70.00**

Vase, swan form, pastels, 1940s, 6", from $35 to **45.00**

Vase, Wild Rose, lavender, yellow, blue or pink, 1950s, 8", from $80 to **100.00**

Vase, 2 6-sided vessels on berry & leaf base, matt, 1940s, 8", from $60 to **75.00**

Wall pocket, bananas on green leafy branch, 1950s, from $125 to **150.00**

Wall pocket, Butterfly, green, white or yellow, 7x6", from $250 to **350.00**

Wall pocket, fan shape, allover gold, 1950s, 8", from $70 to **90.00**

Wall pocket, fan shape, white, 1950s, 8", from $125 to. **150.00**

Wall pocket, violin form, aqua or brown, 1950s, 10", from $100 to **130.00**

Melmac Dinnerware

Melmac was a product of the postwar era, a thermoplastic material formed by the interaction of melamine and formaldehyde. It was popular because of its attractive colors and patterns, and it was practically indestructible. But eventually it faded, became scratched or burned, and housewives tired of it.

By the late '60s and early '70s, it fell from favor.

Collectors, however, are finding its mid-century colors and shapes appealing again, and they're beginning to reassemble melmac table services when pristine, well designed items can be found. For more information we recommend *Melmac Dinnerware* by Alvin Daigle Jr. and Gregg Zimmer (see the Directory under Minnesota).

Bowl, divided; dark peach, Watertown Lifetime Ware, 1950s, 10¼x7" **12.00**

Bowl, light green (resembles jadeite), rectangular, Texas Ware, 10" L. **12.50**

Bowl, mixing; Boontoon, orange speckled, 5¼x9⅜", NM **70.00**

Bowl, mixing; speckled earth tones, Boonton Texas Ware, 5⅛x11½", EX **55.00**

Bowl, salad; brown speckled, Boontone Texas Ware, 3x11" **65.00**

Butter dish, chartreuse, rectangular, Mallow Ware, 8" **7.50**

Creamer & sugar bowl, maroon, Mallow Ware, w/lid **10.00**

Cup & saucer, yellow cup w/patterned white saucer, Fashion Manor **5.00**

Pitcher, off white w/honeycomb texture, 4 mold seams, 8¼" . **16.00**

Plate, grill; salmon pink-orange, 3-compartment, Mallow Ware, 9½" **5.00**

Plate, Lassie portrait on white, 7¾" **30.00**

Salad-serving fork & spoon, chartreuse, marked Styson, 1", pr. **8.00**

Service, rooster, churn & coffee
mill design, 1970s, serves 4
(12 pc)............................ **20.00**
Tray, speckled multicolor on green, 6
compartments, 15x10", pr. **16.00**
Water set, Raffiaware, 2-tone pitcher w/lid & 8 tumblers in metal
frame............................... **85.00**

Metlox

Since the 1940s, the Metlox
company of California has been
producing dinnerware, cookie jars,
novelties, and decorative items, and
their earlier wares have become
very collectible. Some of their best-
known dinnerware patterns are
California Provincial (the dark
green and burgundy rooster), Red
Rooster (in red, orange, and brown),
Homestead Provincial (dark green
and burgundy farm scenes), and
Colonial Homestead (farm scenes
done in red, orange, and brown).

Carl Gibbs is listed in the
Directory under Texas; he is the
author of *Collector's Encyclopedia of
Metlox Potteries* (Collector Books).
His book is highly recommended if
you'd like to learn more about this
company. See also Cookie Jars.

Blueberry Provincial, bowl, veg-
etable; 7⅛", from $32 to.. **35.00**
Blueberry Provincial, pitcher, 2¼-
qt, from $65 to................. **70.00**
Blueberry Provincial, plate,
10½"............................. **13.00**
California Aztec, butter dish, from
$150 to.......................... **170.00**
California Aztec, coffeepot, from
$300 to.......................... **325.00**

California Aztec, platter, oval, 11",
from $75 to...................... **80.00**
California Ivy, coaster, 3¾".... **25.00**
California Ivy, cup, 6-oz......... **13.00**
California Ivy, platter/gravy liner,
oval, 9", from $35 to........ **40.00**
California Ivy, teapot, 6-cup, 36-oz,
from $115 to **125.00**

**California Provincial, candlehold-
er, from $40.00 to $45.00; chop plate,
12¼", from $70.00 to $75.00; and
teapot, seven-cup, from $110.00 to
$125.00.** (Photo courtesy Carl Gibbs Jr.)

California Provincial, casserole,
chicken lid, from $185 to. **200.00**
California Provincial, creamer,
6-oz.................................. **32.00**
California Provincial, pitcher, 1-qt,
from $75 to...................... **85.00**
California Provincial, plate, 9" ..**30.00**
California Strawberry, baker, oval,
11", from $45 to............... **50.00**
California Strawberry, creamer,
10-oz............................... **28.00**
California Strawberry, tumbler,
12-oz............................... **30.00**
California Tempo, bowl, vegetable;
9".................................... **30.00**
California Tempo, compote, from
$40 to.............................. **45.00**
California Tempo, cup & saucer . **12.00**
California Tempo, plate, barbecue;
12", from $35 to............... **40.00**
California Tempo, server, 3-part,
w/lid, 13½", from $45 to.. **50.00**

Colorstax, butter dish, 16-oz, from $30 to **35.00**

Colorstax, gravy boat, 1-pt **35.00**

Colorstax, plate, 10½" **15.00**

Grape Harbor, plate, 6⅜" **10.00**

Grape Harbor, salt & pepper shakers, pr **25.00**

Homestead Provincial, bowl, cereal; 7¼" **22.00**

Homestead Provincial, bowl, lug soup; 5" **35.00**

Homestead Provincial, egg cup, from $40 to **45.00**

Red Rooster, butter dish, decorated or red, from $60 to **65.00**

Red Rooster, cruet set, 2-pc, from $110 to **120.00**

Red Rooster, plate, 7½" **12.00**

Red Rooster, teapot, 6-cup, from $120 to **130.00**

San Fernando, baker, oval, 11¼", from $40 to **45.00**

San Fernando, cup, 6-oz **10.00**

San Fernando, plate, 7½" **10.00**

Sculptured Daisy, coffeepot, 8-cup, from $90 to **100.00**

Sculptured Daisy, cup & saucer, 6-oz **14.00**

Sculptured Daisy, salad fork & spoon, from $50 to **55.00**

Sculptured Grape, buffet server, 12" dia, from $75 to **80.00**

Sculptured Grape, compote, footed, 8½", from $75 to **80.00**

Sculptured Grape, plate, 10½". **18.00**

Sculptured Zinnia, coffeepot, 8-cup, from $90 to **100.00**

Sculptured Zinnia, mug **25.00**

Tickled Pink, baker, oval, 10¼", from $40 to **45.00**

Tickled Pink, tumbler, 14-oz . **28.00**

Vineyard, bowl, fruit; 6" **14.00**

Vineyard, bowl, vegetable; 8¼" .. **35.00**

Vineyard, pitcher, 1-qt, from $50 to **55.00**

Woodland Gold, plate, 10¼" ... **13.00**

Woodland Gold, salad bowl, 11", from $50.00 to $60.00; salad fork and spoon, from $50.00 to $55.00 for the set. (Photo courtesy Carl Gibbs Jr.)

Woodland Gold, salt & pepper shakers, pr **25.00**

Poppets

Casey, policeman **50.00**

Charlie, seated man, 5⅞" **60.00**

Colleen, 7¼" **50.00**

Doc, 7" **50.00**

Effie, cymbal lady, 7¾" **85.00**

Kitty, little girl, 6⅝" **50.00**

Mike, 5½" **50.00**

Mother Goose w/4" bowl **75.00**

Nellie, 8½" **60.00**

St Francis, 7¾" **65.00**

Miller Studio

Brightly painted chalkware plaques, bookends, thermometers, and hot pad holders modeled with subjects that range from Raggedy Ann and angels to bluebirds and sunfish were the rage during '50s and '60s, and even into the early 1970s you could buy them from the five-&-dime store to decorate your kitchen and bathroom walls with style and flair. Collectors who like this 'kitschy' ambience are snapping them up and using them in the vintage rooms they're re-creating with period appliances, furniture, and accessories. They're especially fond of the items marked Miller Studio, a manufacturing firm located in New Philadelphia, Pennsylvania. Most but not all of their pieces are marked and carry a copyright date. If you find an unmarked item with small holes on the back where stapled-on cardboard packaging has been torn away, chances are very good it's Miller Studio as well. Miller Studio is still in business and is today the only American firm that continues to produce hand-finished wall plaques. (Mr. Miller tells us that although they had over 300 employees back in the 1960s and 1970s, they presently have approximately 75.)

Thermometer, bird perched at birdhouse, ca 1984, M, $9.00.

Bird plaques, bluebirds w/yellow-orange breasts in flight, EX, 3-pc 15.00
Bird plaques, 2 birds & cherry branch, red w/green & white, 1972, EX 15.00

Bo Peep plaque, 1965, 7x4", VG.12.00
Cat head plaques, yellow, 1954, NM, 4x4", pr 15.00
Duck plaques, mother w/1 black & 3 yellow baby ducks, 1963, EX 20.00
Dutch girl toothbrush holder plaque, 1964, 7x4", EX ...35.00
Elephant plaques, cream w/pink hats, 1956, 7", EX, pr 15.00
Elf plaques, elf beside pink mushroom, 1979, EX, pr 15.00
Fish & bubbles plaques, pink & black airbrushing, 1970, EX, 4-pc 20.00
Fish & bubbles plaques, pink & blue w/black eyes & mouths, 1960, EX, 4-pc 20.00
Fish & bubbles plaques, white w/gold eyes & mouths, 1971, EX, 6-pc 18.00
Fish plaques, fish couple, parasol & top hat, 1969, 6" & 9", EX, pr 12.00
Fruit/vegetable plaques w/shaker & pepper mill, 1969, 5x9", VG, pr 12.00
Horse-head plaque, 1977, 6", M.12.50
Mermaid plaques, white w/gold highlights, 1968, 6", M, pr 20.00
Mushrooms on grassy base plaque, 1981, 5½", EX 10.00
Peacock plaques, larger: 17x10½", 2 smaller: 17x7", EX, 3-pc .25.00
Poodle head plaques, black w/gold detail, 1978, 6", EX, pr ... 10.00
Raggedy Ann & Andy face plaques, 5½", M, pr 15.00
Sad-face plaque, cut-out eyes & mouth, sm derby hat, 1963, 11", EX 35.00
Siamese cat plaques, pink bows, green eyes, 1976, 10½", EX, pr 22.00

Skunk plaque w/thermometer in tail, 1954, 6½x7", EX **10.00**

Swan plaques, 2 swans embossed on oval backgrounds, 1965, M, pr..................................... **15.00**

Turtle plaques, male & female, 1979, 5½", EX, pr **15.00**

Wishing well plaque w/thermometer, 1966, 6x5", EX **12.00**

Model Kits

The best-known producer of model kits today is Aurora. Collectors often pay astronomical prices for some of the character kits from the 1960s. Made popular by all the monster movies of that decade, ghouls like Vampirella, Frankenstein, and the Wolfman were eagerly built up by kids everywhere. But the majority of all model kits were vehicles, ranging from 3" up to 24" long. Some of the larger model vehicle makers were AMT, MPC, and IMC. Condition is very important in assessing the value of a kit, with built-ups priced at about 50% lower than one still in the box. Other things factor into pricing as well — who is selling, who is buying and how badly they want it, locality, supply, and demand. For additional listings we recommend *Schroeder's Collectible Toys, Antique to Modern* (Collector Books).

Addar, Evel Knievel, 1974, MIB. **50.00**

Airfix, Bigfoot, 1978, MIB **75.00**

Airfix, 2001: A Space Odyssey, 1970, Orion, MIB **75.00**

AMT, Flintstones Rock Crusher, 1974, MIB...................... **75.00**

AMT, Star Trek, Spock, 1973, NMIB (sm box) **150.00**

AMT, 62 Corvette Hardtop/Convertible, MIB, $55.00.

AMT/Ertl, A-Team Van, 1983, MIB **30.00**

Aurora, Alfred E Newman, 1965, unused, EXIB **165.00**

Aurora, Flying Sub, 1975, MIB **100.00**

Aurora, Frankenstein, 1971, glow-in-the-dark, MIB........... **150.00**

Aurora, Frankenstein, 1971, Monster Scenes, MIB.... **125.00**

Aurora, Incredible Hulk, 1974, Comic Scenes, MIB **100.00**

Aurora, Invaders, 1975, UFO, MIB **75.00**

Aurora, Jesse James, 1966, MIB...........................**200.00**

Aurora, John F Kennedy, 1965, MIB................................ **150.00**

Aurora, Lone Ranger, 1975, Comic Scenes, MIB (sealed)....... **65.00**

Aurora, Mummy, 1969, glow-in-the-dark, MIB **200.00**

Aurora, Pendulum, 1971, Monster Scenes, MIB **90.00**

Aurora, Prehistoric Scenes, 1971, Cro-Magnon Man, MIB .. **75.00**

Aurora, Prehistoric Scenes, 1972, Tar Pit, MIB **160.00**

Aurora, Robin, 1974, Comic Scenes, MIB.............................. **100.00**

Aurora, Spider-Man, 1974, Comic Scenes, MIB (sealed)..... **120.00**

Aurora, Superman, 1963, MIB.**350.00**

Aurora, Viking, 1959, Famous Fighters, MIB................ **250.00**

Aurora, Whoozis?, 1966, Suzie, MIB **75.00**

Bachmann, Birds of the World, Scarlet Tanager, 1990, MIB.............**20.00**

Billiken, Mummy, 1990, MIB. **175.00**

Dark Horse, King Kong, 1992, vinyl, MIB **75.00**

Horizon, Marvel Universe, 1988, Spider-Man, MIB **40.00**

Horizon, Robocop, 1992, Robocop #30, MIB **70.00**

Imai, Orguss, 1994, Spider-Man, new pose, MIB................. **30.00**

MOC, Sweathogs 'Dream Machine,' 1976, MIB **45.00**

Monogram, Blue Thunder Helicopter, 1984, MIB..... **30.00**

Monogram, Godzilla, 1978, MIB **100.00**

Monogram, Snoopy as Joe Cool, 1971, MIB...................... **100.00**

MPC, Alien, 1979, MIB (sealed).**100.00**

MPC, Fonzie & Dream Rod, 1976, NMIB **40.00**

MPC, Incredible Hulk, 1978, MIB (sealed) **50.00**

MPC, Incredible Hulk Van, 1977, MIB **25.00**

MPC, Star Wars, 1979, R2-D2, NMIB **35.00**

MPC, Strange Changing Vampire, 1974, MIB........................ **55.00**

Pyro, Restless Gun, 1959, Deputy Sheriff, MIB **70.00**

Revell, Alien Invader, 1979, w/lights, MIB (sealed)...................... **50.00**

Revell, Baja Humbug, 1971, MIB **85.00**

Revell, Cat in the Hat, 1960, MIB............................ **150.00**

Revell, CHiPs, 1980, Helicopter, MIB **35.00**

Revell, Code Red, 1981, Fire Chief's Car, MIB **20.00**

Revell, Dune, 1985, Sand Worm, MIB (sealed).................... **75.00**

Revell, Endangered Animals, 1991, Gorilla, MIB **30.00**

Revell, History Makers, 1983, Jupitor C, MIB (sealed)..**50.00**

Revell, Magnum PI, 1982, 308 GTS Farrari, MIB **60.00**

Revell, Moonraker Space Shuttle, 1979, MIB...................... **25.00**

Revell, Robotech, 1984, Commando, MIB (sealed).................... **50.00**

Revell, US Army Nike Hercules, 1958, MIB...................... **60.00**

Screamin', Contemplating Conquest, 1995, MIB (sealed). **50.00**

Screamin', Star Wars, Stormtrooper, 1993, MIB....................... **45.00**

Toy Biz, Ghost Rider, 1996, MIB..**30.00**

Toy Biz, Thing, 1996, MIB..... **20.00**

Tsukuda, Creature From the Black Lagoon, MIB................. **150.00**

Tsukuda, Frankenstein, 1985, MIB **100.00**

Tsukuda, Wolfman, MIB...... **100.00**

Mood Indigo

Quite an extensive line, this ware was imported from Japan during the 1960s. It was evidently quite successful, judging from the amount of it still around today. It's inexpensive, and if you're into blue, this is for you! It's a deep, very electric shade, and each piece is modeled to represent stacks of various fruits, with handles and spouts sometimes turned out as vines. All pieces carry a stamped number on the bottom which identifies the shape. There are more than 30 known items to look for, more than likely others will surface.

Ashtray, rest in ea corner, E-4238, 9" **25.00**
Bell, 5" **15.00**
Bowl, E-3870, 5x11½" **30.00**
Bud vase, E-3096, 8", ... **20.00**
Candleholders, goblet shape, 4½", pr **28.00**
Candy dish, 2 curved leaves w/fruit to side, 8" **20.00**
Cat figurine, E-2883, rare, 14½". **75.00**
Centerpiece, fruit stack, ribbed base, 12" **25.00**
Cigarette lighter, E-3100, 3¾" . **22.00**
Coffee cup, E-2431, 4" **6.00**
Cookie jar/canister, E-2374, 8". **18.00**
Creamer & sugar bowl, w/lid **12.00**
Cruet, E-3098 .... **25.00**
Dish, footed, E-2375, w/lid, 6". **15.00**
Gravy boat, E-2373, 6½" **15.00**
Jar, cylindrical, w/lid, 6½" **15.00**
Ladle, 9¾" **25.00**
Lavabo, vase w/spigot over half-bowl, E-3562, from $35 to **45.00**
Oil lamp, frosted shade, E-3267, 9½" **25.00**
Pitcher, E-2429, 6½" **18.00**
Pitcher, footed, E-2853, 6" **15.00**
Pitcher/Ewer & underplate, E-5240, 4" **15.00**
Planter, donkey pulling cart, 6x8" **18.00**
Planter, hexagonal foot, #3097, 4½x5" **12.00**
Plate, allover fruit, E-2432, 10"..**30.00**

Platter, 15x10" **40.00**
Salt & pepper shakers w/under-plate **18.00**

Snack set, 9½" plate with cup ring and 3½" cup, E-2615, from $20.00 to $25.00.

Teapot, E-2430, 8" **22.00**
Tray, 3-part shell shape, E-4555.**40.00**
Tray, 8½x6" **28.00**
Trivet, 6" dia **10.00**
Tureen/covered dish, E-3379 . **30.00**

Moon and Star

A reissue of Palace, an early pattern glass line, Moon and Star was developed for the market in the 1960s by Joseph Weishar of Island Mould and Machine Company (Wheeling, West Virginia). It was made by several companies. One of the largest producers was L.E. Smith of Mt. Pleasant, Pennsylvania, and L.G. Wright (who had their glass-ware made by Fostoria and Fenton, perhaps others as well) carried a wide assortment in their catalogs for many years. It is still being made on a very limited basis, but the most collectible pieces are those in red, blue, amber, and green — colors that are no longer in produc-tion. The values listed here are for pieces in red or blue. Amber, green

271

and crystal prices should be 30% lower.

Ashtray, round, allover pattern, scalloped rim, 4 rests, 8" dia... **25.00**

Ashtray, 6-sided, moons at rim, star in base, 5½"............. **18.00**

Ashtray, 6-sided, moons at rim, star in base, 8½"............. **25.00**

Banana Boat, allover pattern, scalloped rim, 12", from $35 to. **45.00**

Basket, allover pattern, scalloped rim, solid handle, 6", from $30 to **40.00**

Basket, allover pattern, scalloped rim, solid handle, 9", from $45 to **55.00**

Bowl, allover pattern, footed, crimped rim, 7½", from $20 to.................................... **25.00**

Bowl, allover pattern, footed, scalloped rim, 5x9½" **28.00**

Bud vase, 6½" **22.00**

Butter dish, oval, allover pattern, scalloped base, star finial . **65.00**

Butter/cheese dish, round, patterned lid, plain base, 7" dia........ **65.00**

Cake stand, 1-pc, allover pattern, scalloped rim & foot, 5x12" dia **55.00**

Cake stand, 2-pc, allover pattern, 11" dia............................. **70.00**

Candle lamp, patterned shade & base, plain insert, 9"....... **60.00**

Candleholder, bowl style w/ring handle, allover pattern, 2x5½", ea **12.00**

Candleholders, flared base, allover pattern, 4½", pr **25.00**

Candy dish, ball shape, footed, allover pattern, 6" **35.00**

Canister, allover pattern, 1-lb or 2-lb, ea from $15 to......... **20.00**

Canister, allover pattern, 3½-lb or 5-lb, ea from $18 to......... **28.00**

Cheese dish, patterned base, clear plain lid, 9½" **55.00**

Compote, allover pattern, scalloped, 5x6½".................... **15.00**

Compote, allover pattern, scalloped, 7x10" **35.00**

Compote, allover pattern, w/lid, 7½x6" **30.00**

Compote, allover pattern, w/lid, 8x4", from $25 to............. **38.00**

Console bowl, allover pattern, scalloped, flared foot, 8"........ **24.00**

Cracker jar/jardiniere, allover pattern, w/lid, 7½", minimum value **65.00**

Creamer & sugar bowl (open), disk foot, sm, from $20 to....... **25.00**

Cruet with stopper, 6¾", from $60.00 to $65.00.

Epergne, 2-pc, allover pattern, 9".................................... **60.00**

Fairy lamp, 6" **25.00**

Goblet, plain rim & foot, 5¾", from $9 to **12.00**

Jelly dish, patterned body & lid, plain flat rim, disk foot, 7x3½" ... **30.00**

Lamp, miniature, amber **125.00**

Lamp, miniature, blue, from $165 to **190.00**

Lamp, miniature, red, from $175 to **200.00**

Lamp, oil or electric, allover pattern, red or light blue, 24", minimum **275.00**

Nappy, allover pattern, crimped rim, 2¾x6", from $12 to .. **15.00**

Pitcher, straight sides, 1-qt, 7½", from $65 to **75.00**

Plate, patterned body & center, smooth rim, 8", from $30 to.............. **45.00**

Relish bowl, 6 lg scallops form allover pattern, 1½x8"......... **30.00**

Relish tray, rectangular, scalloped rim, star in base, 8" **35.00**

Soap dish, oval, allover pattern, 2x6" **9.00**

Sugar bowl, straight sides, allover pattern, w/lid, scalloped foot..... **40.00**

Syrup pitcher, allover pattern, metal lid, 4½x3½" **65.00**

Tumbler, plain rim & foot, 5-oz, 3½", from $10 to **12.00**

Tumbler, plain rim & foot, 6½", from $20 to **25.00**

Vase, pattern near top, ruffled rim, footed, 6", from $22 to **30.00**

Mortens Studios

Animal models sold by Mortens Studios of Arizona during the 1940s are some of today's most interesting collectibles, especially among animal lovers. Hundreds of breeds of dogs, cats, and horses were produced from a plaster-type composition material constructed over a wire framework. They range in size from 2" up to about 7", and most are marked. Crazing and flaking are nearly always present to some degree. Our values are for animals in excellent to near-mint condition, allowing for only minor crazing. Heavily crazed examples will be worth much less.

Arabian horse, wall plaque . **125.00**

Bengal tiger, 6x8"................. **175.00**

Boxer dog, head down on front paws, 4" long, from $60.00 to $75.00.

Chihuahua standing, light brown, 5½x6½" **70.00**

Cocker spaniel seated, black, 2¾". **40.00**

Collie lying down w/head up, 2x3" **55.00**

Collie pup seated, cream & white, 3¼x3½" **35.00**

Dachshund, black w/brown belly & nose tip, 2½x5½" **60.00**

Dalmatian puppy seated, 3¼x2½". **60.00**

Dalmatian seated, Royal Designs, 5x5" **60.00**

Dalmatian standing & looking forward, tail straight out, 6x7" **65.00**

German shepherd standing, tan & black, #755, 6½" **100.00**

Irish setter, reddish brown, 6⅛x10¾" **70.00**

Irish terrier puppy seated, w/sticker, 3" **50.00**

Kerry blue terrier w/head up, w/sticker, 5x7½"............... **60.00**

Persian cat, silver tabby, 3¾x4½" . **100.00**

Pomeranian standing w/head up, 2x2¾" **55.00**

Samoyed seated, cream colored, 4⅛" **42.00**

Wire-Haired fox terrier standing w/head & tail up, gray & white, 3½" **45.00**

Moss Rose

Though the Moss Rose pattern has been produced by Staffordshire and American pottery companies alike since the mid-1800s, the lines we're dealing with here are all from the twentieth century. Much was made from the late 1950s into the 1970s by Japanese manufacturers. Even today you'll occasionally see a tea set or a small candy dish for sale in some of the chain stores. (The collectors who are already picking this line up refer to it as Moss Rose, but we've seen it advertised as Victorian Rose, and some companies called their lines Chintz Rose or French Rose; but for now, Moss Rose seems to be the accepted terminology.

Rosenthal made an identical pattern, and prices are generally higher for examples that carry the mark of that company. The pattern consists of a briar rose with dark green mossy leaves on stark white glaze. Occasionally, an item is trimmed in gold. In addition to dinnerware, many accessories and novelties were made as well. Refer to *Garage Sale & Flea Market Annual* for more a more extensive listing.

Ashtray, 3 rests, Rosenthal, 4¼" dia **15.00**

Atomizer, Japan, EX working bulb............................... **22.00**

Bowl, Japan, 7½".......................**5.00**

Bowl, soup; scalloped rim, Japan, 7½" **10.00**

Bowl, vegetable; Royal Rose Fine China Japan, 10½x7¼" ... **25.00**

Bowl, vegetable; w/handles, Haviland, w/lid................ **35.00**

Butter dish, Japan, ¼-lb, 6¾x 3¾" **30.00**

Butter pat, 4 reticulated segments on rim, Rosenthal, 4" **8.00**

Cake plate, gold trim, Haviland Limoges, 9½" **90.00**

Child's tea set, 7½" pot, creamer & sugar, 6 cups & saucers.. **42.00**

Cigarette box, gold trim, Japan .**10.00**

Coffeepot, gold trim, red Japan mark, 9"........................... **30.00**

Creamer & sugar bowl, Royal Rose Fine China Japan, w/lid, 4"..**20.00**

Creamer & sugar bowl, Sealy China Made in Japan, w/lid **22.00**

Creamer & sugar bowl, w/lid, Ucago Japan **22.00**

Cup & saucer, demitasse; footed, Japan sticker................... **12.00**

Cup & saucer, pearlized w/gold trim, Japan, 3¾"................ **9.00**

Gravy boat, Sango Japan, w/attached undertray........................... **25.00**

Gravy boat, Haviland, w/undertray................................... **40.00**

Jam pot, rose finial, Japan, w/silver-plated spoon.............. **25.00**

Mustard jar, ovoid, Japan, w/lid & original spoon................... **15.00**

Pitcher, Aida shape, sterling base, platinum trim, Rosenthal, 8" **75.00**

Plate, Pomadour, Rosenthal, 6¼", 4 for.................................... **32.00**

Plate, Royal Rose China, Japan, 10", 4 for **50.00**

Platter, Haviland, 14½", from $35 to **45.00**

Platter, Rosenthal, 14" **50.00**

Salt & pepper shakers, footed, Royal Rose Japan, 4", pr **40.00**

Snack tray & cup, gold trim, unmarked Japan, 7¾" dia. **10.00**

Teapot, electric, Japan, 6½", $25.00.

Teapot, musical base, Norcrest, Japan **20.00**

Tidbit, 3-tier, Pompadour, Rosenthal, largest plate: 13½" . **85.00**

Tray, 3-part, Ucagco Japan, 10x7" **30.00**

Vanity set, sq jar & bottle w/matching atomizer (no bulb), Japan, 3-pc **45.00**

Music Boxes

So many of the music boxes you'll find at flea markets today are related to well-known characters or special holidays. These have a cross-over collectible appeal, and often are priced in the $75.00 to $100.00 range — some even higher. Many are animated as well as musical. Most modern music boxes are figural, but some have been made by children's toy companies to look like grandfather clocks or radios, for instance. Unless noted otherwise our values are for mint-condition examples.

Betty Boop, hula girl, resin, Aloha Oe, MIB **25.00**

Carousel horse, Carousel Waltz, Americana Collection, Tobin Fraley, EX **45.00**

Cat on Armchair, Fur Elise, Rosina Watchmeister/Goebel, MIB **45.00**

Coca-Cola, Emmett Kelly figure, numbered limited edition, MIB **75.00**

Coca-Cola, polar bear, Like To Teach the World To Sing, #272124, EX **30.00**

Coca-Cola, Santa's merry-go-round, Jingle Bells, Enesco, 1994, EX **30.00**

Curious George, figural, Up, Up & Away, Westland, MIB **75.00**

Disney, Lady & the Tramp, Oh What a Night, EX **80.00**

Disney, Little Mermaid snow globe, Under the Sea, 9", EX **70.00**

Disney, Mickey & Minnie atop grand piano, Gershwin's Havanola, MIB **60.00**

Disney, Mickey in hot-air balloon, Around the World..., Schmid, EX **55.00**

Disney, Snow White in jewelry box, resin, Braham's Waltz, MIB **55.00**

Disney, Tarzan snow globe, Two Worlds, 8", EX **65.00**

Dolphin snow globe, 3-D w/resin base, Some Where Out There, MIB **22.00**

Garfield, Swingin' in the Rain, Enesco, 1981, EX **20.00**

Hummel, Four Seasons/3rd edition, Anri, Goebel, 1988, EX.. **150.00**

Hummel, Ride Into Christmas, Winter Wonderland, Anri, Goebel, EX **150.00**

Little Drummer Boy, Lefton, M.**95.00**

Muppets, Kermit & Miss Piggy, Let Me Call You Sweetheart, Enesco, M **35.00**

Muppets, Kermit & Miss Piggy dancing, SF Music Box Co, 1998, MIB........................ **55.00**

National Geographic, mustangs, Chariots of Fire, SF Music Box Co, M **75.00**

Nightmare Before Christmas, 2-faced Mayor, Schmid, 1993, EXIB **110.00**

Peanuts, Charlie Brown, Take Me Out to the Ballgame, Anri, 1972, EX **135.00**

Peanuts, Linus & Snoopy, Release Me, Anri, 1968, EX **80.00**

Peanuts, Snoopy, When the Saints Go Marching In, Schmid, EX............... **175.00**

Peanuts, Snoopy as train conductor, Schmid #219, NM... **375.00**

Peanuts, Snoopy kissing frowning Lucy, Close to You, NM. **160.00**

Peanuts, Snoopy & Woodstock, socks in tree, O Tannenbaum, Schmid, 8", EX **75.00**

Penguin & baby, Lefton, EX.. **25.00**

Pink Panther, music conductor, UAC Geoffrey Japan, 1960s EX .. **30.00**

Pink Panther, snake charmer, ceramic, Royal Orleans, VG........ **40.00**

Rocky & Bullwinkle, figural, Ward Productions, 1961, MIB.. **40.00**

Santa, Santa Claus Is Coming to Town, Waco Melody in Motion, 1980s, M **285.00**

Smokey the Bear in yellow Jeep, Take Me Home Country Road, Lefton, EX **50.00**

Winnie the Pooh, Put a Little Spring in Your Step, You Are My Sunshine **50.00**

Yorkie & Friend, In the Good Old Summertime, SF Music Box Co, MIB **40.00**

Octoberfest, music and lights, 7½", M, from $45.00 to $55.00.

Niloak

Produced in Arkansas by Charles Dean Hyten from the early 1900s until the mid-1940s, Niloak (the backward spelling of kaolin, a type of clay) takes many forms — figural planters, vases in both matt and glossy glazes, and novelty items of various types. The company's most famous product and the most collectible is their Swirl or Mission Ware line. Clay in colors of brown, blue, cream, red, and buff are swirled within the mold, the finished product left unglazed on the outside to preserve the natural hues. Small vases are common; large pieces or unusual shapes and those with exceptional coloration are the most valuable. Refer to *The*

Collector's Encyclopedia of Niloak, A Reference and Value Guide, by David Edwin Gifford (Collector Books) for more information.

Note: The terms '1st' and '2nd art mark' used in the listings refer to specific die-stamped trademarks. The earlier mark was used from 1910 to 1924, followed by the second, very similar mark used from then until the end of Mission Ware production. Letters with curving raised outlines were characteristic of both; the most obvious difference between the two was that on the first, the final upright line of the 'N' was thin with a solid club-like terminal.

Figurine, donkey, brown, 2¾",
$75.00. (Photo courtesy David Edwin Gifford)

Ashtray, Mission, rolled rim w/3 rests, 5" dia **215.00**
Bowl, child peering into bowl, flat, glossy, 8x6" **90.00**
Candlestick, Mission, flared foot, blue, gray & cream, 1st mark, 10" **250.00**
Compote, Mission, footed, w/lid, 5½x6½" **395.00**
Cornucopia, Ozark Dawn, low-relief mark & gold foil label, 8" . **32.00**
Creamer, cow figure, tail handle, high gloss, unmarked, 4½" **55.00**
Figurine, elephant, Ozark Blue, hollow, unmarked, 2¼" ... **12.00**

Figurine, retreiver seated, 3-4"..**35.00**
Figurine, Southern Belle, Ozark Blue/Ozark Dawn, low-relief mark, 10" **185.00**
Flower frog, duck, Ozark Dawn II, unmarked, 6", from $45 to .**65.00**
Humidor, Mission, 2nd art mark, 5½", from $380 to **395.00**
Jug, Mission, dark blue, dark brown & tan, no handle, 2nd art mark, 7" **355.00**
Mug, various high-gloss colors, 3½", from $4 to **10.00**
Pitcher, bull's-eye decor, 1st Hywood by Niloak mark, 6" **67.00**
Planter, camel resting, attached bowl, glossy, block mark, 3½x6" **16.00**
Planter, circus elephant, Stars of the Big Top design, white, 7".. **40.00**
Planter, Fox Red, attached drip tray, rectangular, 6" **12.00**
Planter, Southern belle standing, tiered/ruffled skirt, 10".**165.00**
Powder jar, Mission, knob finial, 2nd art mark, 3x5"........ **385.00**
Salt & pepper shakers, geese, Ozark Dawn II, w/sticker, 2", pr..**40.00**
Salt & pepper shakers, penguins, Ozark Blue, w/sticker, 2¾", pr **22.00**
Tumbler, Mission, flared rim, Patent Pending, 5"........ **200.00**
Vase, maroon, tri-fluted, impressed mark, 7¾" **88.00**
Vase, Mission, cylindrical, tan, brown, cream & blue, 2nd art mark, 6" **130.00**
Vase, Mission, long cylindrical bottle neck w/flat round base, 8½" **115.00**
Vase, Ozark Blue, ewer form w/angular handle, marked, 8" **14.00**

Wall pocket, half-pitcher, Tobacco Spit, low-relief mark, 5½". **55.00**

Nippon

In complying with American importation regulations, from 1891 to 1921 Japanese manufacturers marked their wares 'Nippon,' meaning Japan, to indicate country of origin. The term is today used to refer to the highly decorated porcelain vases, bowls, chocolate pots, etc., that bear this term within their trademark. Many variations were used. Refer to *Van Patten's ABC's of Collecting Nippon Porcelain* by Joan Van Patten (Collector Books) for more information. See Clubs and Newsletters for information concerning the International Nippon Collectors Club.

Cheese dish, Oriental decor on white with cobalt and gold trim, M-in-wreath mark, 7¾", from $150.00 to $200.00. (Photo courtesy Joan Van Patten)

Ashtray, Dutch scene w/sailboats on sides, 3 rests, 2½x5" dia.. **95.00**

Ashtray, 3 rests, golfer, 4½" dia. **550.00**

Bowl, berry; rose pattern w/moriage at scalloped rims, w/liner, 7½". **95.00**

Bowl, ornate rose & lattice w/gold, open handles, 4-footed, 8". **80.00**

Celery dish, butterflies on blue, handles, 12" L **250.00**

Cup & saucer, blue & orange on white w/heavy gold trim, hexagonal **90.00**

Cup & saucer, chocolate; floral on white w/cobalt trim, beads & gold............................ **120.00**

Dresser tray, bird in tree, #106. **115.00**

Head vase, eyes closed, hand at neck, frosted updo, pearls, 7¼"................................. **80.00**

Humidor, Oriental style/allover moriage decor, light green tones, 7"......................... **300.00**

Jar, roses on gold, bulbous, 3-footed, Royal Kinran mark, w/lid, 7½................................. **230.00**

Jar, white floral branch on brown, beads at rim, cylinder, w/lid, 6".................................... **250.00**

Mug, tropical w/contrasting decorative rim & angled handle, 5½"................................. **100.00**

Napkin ring, cottage scene in oval w/floral & gold bead trim..**135.00**

Pitcher, white dragon on black, 5".................................. **300.00**

Plate, purple floral vine on shaded green w/moriage detail, 7½"........... **150.00**

Plate, roses w/gold moriage & trim on white, open handles, 10⅜", EX **75.00**

Ring holder, white 3-D hand on plate w/floral decor, 3¾" dia...... **135.00**

Shaving mug, red roses in grass, gold handle, 3½"............ **225.00**

Teapot, floral & filigree on white w/cobalt & bead trim, ball shape **200.00**

Teapot w/creamer & sugar bowl, angled handles, roses & checks, gold trim **90.00**

Vase, floral panels (4) w/gold, ornate handles at neck, 12½"..... **90.00**

Vase, floral w/gold, upturned handles at shoulders, 8" **100.00**

Vase, landscape & gold filigree, angled handles, 4-footed, 9½"............................. **300.00**

Vase, roses & white beading on gold, sm flared neck, 4". **285.00**

Vase, roses w/gold, sm ruffled rim, ear handles, bulbous, 9" . **80.00**

Noritake

Since the early 1900s, the Noritake China Company has been producing fine dinnerware, occasional pieces, and figural items decorated by hand in delicate florals, scenics, and wildlife studies. Azalea and Tree in the Meadow are two very collectible lines of dinnerware. We've listed several examples. Note: Tree in the Meadow is only one variant of the Scenic pattern. It depicts a thatched-roof cottage with a tree growing behind it, surrounded by a meadow and some water. Other variants that include features such as swans, bridges, dogs, windmills, etc. are not Tree in the Meadow.

Azalea

Basket, mint; #193, Dolly Varden........................ **150.00**

Bowl, #12, 10"......................... **38.00**

Bowl, deep, #310 .... **60.00**

Bowl, oatmeal; #055, 5½"....... **25.00**

Bowl, vegetable; #172, oval, 9¼". **42.00**

Bowl, vegetable; divided, #439, 9½"................................. **275.00**

Cake plate, #10, 9¾" **30.00**

Candy jar, w/lid, #313.......... **675.00**

Casserole, gold finial, #372.. **395.00**

Celery tray, closed handles, #444, 10".................................. **275.00**

Cheese/butter dish, #314 ..... **125.00**

Coffeepot, demitasse; #182.. **595.00**

Creamer & sugar bowl, gold finial, #401 .... **98.00**

Cup & saucer, bouillon; #124, 3½" **26.00**

Mustard jar, #191, 3-pc.......... **48.00**

Plate, #4, 7½"............................ **8.00**

Plate, #13, 9¾"........................ **18.00**

Platter, #311, 10¼" **185.00**

Relish, 4-section, #119, rare, 10". **160.00**

Salt & pepper shakers, bulbous, #89, pr............................... **38.00**

Syrup with underplate and lid, $110.00.

Teapot, #15 .... **110.00**

Vase, fan form, footed, #187 . **210.00**

Tree in the Meadow

Bowl, cream soup; w/handles. **75.00**

Bowl, oatmeal.......................... **25.00**

Bowl, soup **38.00**

Butter pat................................. **25.00**

Cake plate, open handles **35.00**

Celery dish............................... **35.00**

Compote................................... **95.00**

Creamer & sugar bowl, demitasse............................ **125.00**

Egg cup **30.00**

Lemon dish............................**15.00**
Mayonnaise set, 3-pc.............**35.00**
Plate, sq, rare, 7⅝"..................**80.00**
Platter, 13¾x10¼"....................**65.00**
Tea tile....................................**48.00**
Vase, fan form........................**95.00**

Miscellaneous

Ashtray, pipe sitting on club shape,
M-in-wreath mark, 5½"..**150.00**

Ashtrays: Deco lady, four rests, green mark, 5¼", $135.00; Egyptian portrait, three rests, 5", $95.00. (Photo courtesy Joan Van Patten)

Bowl, floral rim w/cobalt on white,
gold handles, M-in-wreath
mark, 8"........................**70.00**
Box, lady w/whippet, footed, gold finial,
M-in-wreath mark, 3" H....**200.00**
Cake plate, exotic birds, pink
border w/gold, M-in-wreath
mark, 8¼"......................**70.00**
Chamberstick, floral band on
orange lustre, M-in-wreath
mark, 4¾"......................**100.00**
Cigarette holder, flowers on bell
shape, bird finial, M-in-wreath
mark, 5"..........................**200.00**
Dresser tray, scenic reserves in gold
band on burgundy, marked, 13"
L..**120.00**
Egg cup, fruit compote & gold
on white, M-in-wreath mark,
3½"................................**45.00**

Humidor, horse w/in horseshoe
in relief, brown tones, M-in-
wreath mark, 7"............**575.00**
Mug, river scene, M-in-wreath
mark, 3¼"........................**80.00**
Mustard jar & undertray, floral,
blue on white w/gold, M-in-
wreath mark, 4"..............**40.00**
Sauce dish, roses w/orange lustre,
w/ladle & tray, M-in-wreath
mark, 5"..........................**80.00**
Spooner, river scene w/red-roofed
cottage, M-in-wreath mark, 8"
L..**70.00**
Teapot w/creamer & sugar bowl,
floral decor on black w/gold, 6"
pot..................................**165.00**
Vase, geometric band on orange
lustre, waisted, M-in-wreath
mark, 8¾"......................**145.00**
Wall pocket, musician w/wide ruffled collar, lustre, M-in-wreath
mark, 6"..........................**300.00**

Novelty Telephones

Novelty telephones representing well-known advertising or cartoon characters are proving to be
the focus of lots of collector activity — the more recognizable the
character, the better. Telephones
modeled after product containers
are collectible as well. For more
information refer to *Schroeder's
Collectible Toys, Antique to Modern*
(Collector Books).

AC Spark Plug, figural, black, green
& white, NM....................**75.00**
Alf, furry, M............................**75.00**
Alvin (Alvin & the Chipmunks),
1984, MIB........................**50.00**

Bart Simpson, seated, eyes light when phone rings, EX **35.00**

Bugs Bunny, Warner Exclusive, MIB **65.00**

Buzz Lightyear, MIB (sealed). **125.00**

Charlie the Tuna, MIB **60.00**

Darth Vader, 1983, MIB **200.00**

Garfield, receiver rests in Garfield's back, Tyco, unused, MIB . **50.00**

Ghostbusters, MIB.................**30.00**

Heinz Ketchup, bottle form, 8½", NM+...............................**55.00**

Hershey's Chocolate Milk, brown milk carton form, 9", EX. **20.00**

Little Sprout, 1984, NM **65.00**

M&M Candy, vintage-type dial, holds M&Ms, multicolored, MIB..................................**25.00**

Opus, Tyco, 1987, 14", EX **60.00**

Oscar Meyer Wiener, EX **65.00**

Pizza Inn, Pizza Man, 10½", NM.**55.00**

Roy Rogers, plastic wall-type, 1950s, 9", EX...................**50.00**

Raid Bug, M, from $65.00 to $80.00.

Seven-Up, can shape, Enterprex, 6", NM.............................**40.00**

Spider-Man, REC Sound, 1994, MIB.................................**30.00**

Star Trek Enterprise, 1993, NM..**25.00**

Strawberry Shortcake, MIB ..**75.00**

Thunderbird Coupe (1956), red & white plastic, 7¾" L, EX. **20.00**

Occupied Japan

Items with the 'Occupied Japan' mark were made during the period from the end of World War II until April 1952. Porcelains, novelties, paper items, lamps, silver plate, lacquer ware, and dolls are some of the areas of exported goods that may bear this stamp. Because the Japanese were naturally resentful of the occupation, it is felt that only a small percentage of their wares were thus marked. Although you may find identical items marked simply 'Japan,' only those with the 'Occupied Japan' stamp command values such as we have suggested below. For more information we recommend *Occupied Japan Collectibles* by Gene and Cathy Florence, published by Collector Books. Items in our listings are ceramic unless noted otherwise, and figurines are of average, small size. See Clubs and Newsletters for information concerning The Occupied Japan Club.

Ashtray, metal, hand form **10.00**

Ashtray, metal, peacock detail . **8.00**

Ashtray holder, elephant form, w/4 trays, glossy brown.........**20.00**

Candleholders, colonial figure seated between 2 flower cups, 4", pr.....................................**55.00**

Candy dish, metal, 3-part, center handle............................**10.00**

Child's tea set, 26 pcs w/6 place settings..............................**125.00**

Christmas nativity figures, 2½", 7-pc set............................**80.00**

Cigarette box, embossed roses on lid....................................**10.00**

Cigarette lighter, golf-ball form **18.00**

Cigarette lighter, Luckycar (brand name), green sedan, 3" L **125.00**

Creamer, white w/red flower ... **7.00**

Creamer and sugar bowl, ears of corn, from $25.00 to 30.00 for the pair. (Photo courtesy Gene and Cathy Florence)

Cup & saucer, white w/chintz-like floral decor, Merit............ **20.00**

Cup & saucer, yellow, flower inside.............................. **20.00**

Doll, celluloid, baby in snowsuit. **45.00**

Doll, celluloid kewpie, original feathers & gold hair, 7" .. **50.00**

Figurine, bird on stump, multicolored, 8"............................. **30.00**

Figurine, boy playing mandolin, 5" **15.00**

Figurine, boy w/accordion, 2½". **5.00**

Figurine, cat w/fiddle, 2" **7.50**

Figurine, colonial couple at piano, 4"...................................... **22.00**

Figurine, cowboy w/rope, 6½". **20.00**

Figurine, elf riding caterpillar. **20.00**

Figurine, flamingo w/head down, 5¼" **30.00**

Figurine, Mexican on donkey, 8¼" **30.00**

Incense burner, Mexican man seated, 4"................................ **25.00**

Leaf dish, white w/multicolored fruit decal in center, gold trim............................... **18.00**

Mug, elephant figure w/trunk forming handle, 4¾"................ **20.00**

Planter, Asian girl standing before lg shell, 6"........................ **30.00**

Planter, cow pulling cart, multicolored, 3x6¾"....................... **25.00**

Planter, donkey w/green cart.. **15.00**

Planter, girl w/cart, 2½"........... **8.00**

Planter, mallard duck, realistic, 4" L....................................... **28.00**

Plate, blackberries on stem, 6"..**12.00**

Platter, apples, 15"................. **25.00**

Salt and pepper shakers: seated middle-Eastern figures, Windmills, $22.00 for each pair.

Shelf sitter, ballerina, net skirt, 5" **30.00**

Teapot, windmill form............ **50.00**

Vase, swan form, multicolored, 5"................................... **20.00**

Vase, urn w/scrolled handles at neck, embossed flowers, 6¼"...... **25.00**

Wall pocket, teapot form w/flower decor, 6x8" **25.00**

Old MacDonald's Farm

Made by the Regal China Co., items from this novelty ware line were designed around characters and animals from Old MacDonald's farm. Recently prices have softened somewhat for all but the harder-to-find items, but due to the good quality of the ware and its unique styling, it's still very collectible.

Butter dish, cow's head........ **150.00**

Canister, cereal, coffee or flour; med, ea from $225 to **275.00**
Canister, chips, peanuts, popcorn, pretzels, tidbits, lg; ea from $325 to **350.00**
Canister, cookies or soap; lg, ea from $350 to **425.00**
Canister, salt, sugar or tea; med, ea, from $125 to **150.00**
Cookie jar, barn.................... **200.00**
Creamer, rooster, from $75 to. **85.00**
Grease jar, pig, from $125 to . **150.00**
Pitcher, milk; from $200 to.. **225.00**

Potato chips jar, from $200.00 to $250.00.

Salt & pepper shakers, boy & girl, pr...................................... **85.00**
Salt & pepper shakers, churn, gold trim, pr **100.00**
Salt & pepper shakers, feed sacks w/sheep, pr from $100 to. **125.00**
Spice jar, assorted lids, sm, ea from $125 to.......................... **150.00**
Sugar bowl, hen **95.00**
Teapot, duck's head.............. **225.00**

Paper Dolls

Though the history of paper dolls can be traced even farther back, by the late 1700s they were being mass produced. A century later, paper dolls were being used as an advertising medium by retail companies wishing to promote sales. But today the type most often encountered are in book form — the dolls on the cardboard covers, their wardrobe on the inside pages. These have been published since the 1920s. Celebrity and character-related dolls are the most popular with collectors, and condition is very important. If they have been cut out, even if they are still in fine condition and have all their original accessories, they're worth only about half as much as an uncut doll. In our listings, if no condition is given, values are for mint, uncut paper dolls. For more information, we recommend *Price Guide to Lowe and Whitman Paper Dolls* and *20th Century Paper Dolls*, both by Mary Young (see the Directory under Ohio) and *Paper Dolls of the 1960s, 1970s, and 1980s,* by Carol Nichols (Collector Books). For an expanded listings of values, see *Schroeder's Collectible Toys, Antique to Modern* (Collector Books). See Clubs and Newsletters for information concerning the *Paper Doll News.*

Junior Prom, Lowe #1042, 1942. **50.00**
Annette, Whitman #1971, 1960. **75.00**
Baby Beans & Pets, Whitman #1950, 1978 .... **12.00**
Baby-sitter, Saalfield, #2747, 1956.............................. **35.00**
Betty Boop Goes to Hollywood, Betty's Store LTD/Trina Robbins, 1984 .... **28.00**
Bewitched, Magic Wand, #114, 1956, boxed set................ **75.00**
Bobbsey Twins Play Box, GP Putnam's Sons #C2000, 1954.............. **50.00**
Cabbage Patch Deluxe Paper Dolls, Avalon #640, 1983........... **10.00**

Chitty-Chitty Bang-Bang Whitman #1982, 1968 .... **40.00**

Cinderella, Whitman #1992, 1965, from $30 to **55.00**

Connie Francis, Whitman #1956, 1963 .... **70.00**

Deana Durbin, Merrill #3480, 1940 .... **150.00**

Donna Reed, Artcraft #4412, 1959 .... **90.00**

Doris Day Doll, Whitman #1977, 1957 .... **100.00**

Elizabeth Taylor, Whitman #968, 1949 .... **175.00**

Finger Ding Paper Dolls, Whitman #1993, 1971 .... **15.00**

Flying Nun, Saalfield #1317, 1969.**60.00**

Francie, Whitman #4393/7420, 1976, from $9 to **16.00**

Gigi Perreau, Saalfield #2605, 1951 .... **75.00**

Green Acres, Whitman #4773, 1968 .... **55.00**

Haley Mills Summer Magic Cutouts, Whitman, #1966, 1963 ... **50.00**

It's a Small World, Whitman #1981, 1966 .... **30.00**

Jackie & Caroline, Magic Wand #107, 1969, from $25 to .. **45.00**

Lucille Ball/Desi Arnaz with Little Ricky, Whitman #2116, 1953, $100.00.
(Photo courtesy Rick Wyman)

Mickey & Minnie Steppin' Out, Whitman #1979, 1977 ....**25.00**

Munsters, Whitman #1959, 1966.......................... **100.00**

Oklahoma!, Whitman #1954, 1956 .... **100.00**

Pebbles & Bamm-Bamm, Whitman #4791, 1964, from $35 to **55.00**

Petticoat Junction, Whitman #1954, 1964 .... **100.00**

Pippi Longstocking, Whitman #4390/7409, 1976 .... **25.00**

Punky Brewster, Golden #1532, 1986, from $5 to **10.00**

Raggedy Ann, Milton Bradley #4106, copyright 1941 .. **100.00**

Ranch Family, Merrill #2585, 1957, $35.00.

Sandra Dee, Saalfield #4417, 1959 .... **65.00**

Shirley Temple, Whitman #1986, 1976, from $10 to **20.00**

Sleeping Beauty, Whitman #4723, 1958, from $75 to **100.00**

Sunshine Family, Whitman #1980, 1977 .... **12.00**

Tammy & Her Family, Whitman #1997, 1964 .... **60.00**

Tammy & Pepper, Whitman #11997, 1965, from $60 to **75.00**

That Girl, Saalfield #1351, 1967, from $45 to **75.00**

Walter Lantz Cartoon Stars, Saalfield, #1344, 1963 ..... **30.00**

Waltons, Whitman #1995, 1975, from $35 to **50.00**

Winnie the Pooh, Whitman #1977-24, 1980, from $25 to **30.00**

Woody Woodpecker & Andy Panda, Saalfield #1391, 1960s, from $25 to **40.00**

Pennsbury Pottery

From the 1950s through the 1970s, dinnerware and novelty ware produced by the Pennsbury company was sold through tourist gift shops along the Pennsylvania turnpike. Much of their ware was decorated in an Amish theme. A group of barbershop singers was another popular design, and they made a line of bird figures that were very similar to Stangl's, though today much harder to find.

Snack set, Rooster, $25.00.

Ashtray, Pennsbury Inn, 8" dia..**45.00**

Ashtray, Sommerset, 1804-1954, 5" dia **30.00**

Bookends, eagle, 8" **185.00**

Bowl, Dutch Talk, 9" **90.00**

Bread plate, Give Us This Day Our Daily Bread, 9x6" **40.00**

Butter dish, Folk Art, 5x4" **35.00**

Candleholders, Rooster, 4", pr.. **85.00**

Casserole, Hex, w/lid, 6½" **45.00**

Chip & dip, Rooster, 11" **85.00**

Coffeepot, Quartet, face of Olson, 5" dia **30.00**

Compote, holly decor, 5" **25.00**

Compote, Rooster, footed, 5".. **40.00**

Cookie jar, Red Barn **250.00**

Desk basket, National Exchange Club, 5" **40.00**

Desk basket, 2 women under tree, 5" **50.00**

Figurine, bluejay, #108, 10½" . **400.00**

Figurine, cardinal, #120, 6½" . **175.00**

Figurine, duckling pr, 6½" ... **295.00**

Figurine, Slick Chick, 5½" **50.00**

Mug, beer; Barber Shop Quartet.**25.00**

Mug, beverage; Rooster, 5" **20.00**

Mug, coffee; Amish, 3¼" **22.00**

Mug, coffee; Gay Ninety, 3¼". **35.00**

Mug, Red Barn, 3¼" **35.00**

Pie plate, Rooster, 9" **60.00**

Pitcher, Folk Art (later called Brown Dowry), 5" **50.00**

Pitcher, Yellow Daisy, 4" **32.00**

Plaque, Charles W Morgan, ship, 11x8" **110.00**

Plaque, Fishermen, 5" dia **26.00**

Plaque, Mercury Dime, 8" dia.. **65.00**

Plaque, Real Stinker, verse w/skunk, 6" dia **65.00**

Plaque, River Steamboat, 13½x10¼" **160.00**

Plaque, Swallow the Insult, 6" dia **25.00**

Plaque, United States Steel, 1954, 8" **40.00**

Plaque, Walking to Homestead, 6" dia **40.00**

Plate, Amish, 9" **40.00**

Plate, boy & girl, w/primary colors, 11" **95.00**
Plate, Eagle, 8" **50.00**
Plate, Harvest, 8" **40.00**
Plate, 2 birds over heart, 11" .. **85.00**
Salt & pepper shakers, Amish man & woman, pitcher form, pr from $30 to **45.00**
Sugar bowl, Rooster, w/lid **30.00**
Tray, Rooster, 7½x5" **30.00**
Tray, tulips, tree shape, 14½x11½". **40.00**
Tray, tulips, 7½x5" **30.00**
Wall pocket, floral heart shape w/blue border, 6½" **50.00**
Wall pocket, sailboat w/brown border, cut corners, 6½" sq ... **65.00**

Pez Dispensers

Originally a breath mint targeted for smokers, by the '50s Pez had been diverted toward the kid's candy market, and to make sure the kids found them appealing, the company designed dispensers they'd be sure to like — many of them characters the kids could easily recognize. On today's collectible market, some of those dispensers bring astonishing prices!

Though early on collectors preferred the dispensers with no feet, today they concentrate primarily on the character heads. Feet were added in 1987, so if you want your collection to be complete, you'll need to buy both styles. For further information and more listings, see *Schroeder's Collectible Toys, Antique to Modern* (Collector Books). Our values are for mint dispensers. Very few are worth collecting if they are damaged or have missing parts. See Clubs and Newsletters for information concerning *Pez Collector News*.

Football player, $175.00.

Aardvark, w/feet **5.00**
Batman, no feet **10.00**
Batman, no feet, w/cape **100.00**
Batman, w/feet, blue or black, ea from $3 to **5.00**
Bubble Man, w/feet **3.00**
Charlie Brown, Snoopy or Lucy, w/feet, ea from $1 to **3.00**
Charlie Brown, w/feet & tongue. **20.00**
Clown, w/feet, whistle head..... **6.00**
Daffy Duck, no feet **15.00**
Daffy Duck, w/feet, from $1 to. **3.00**
Donald Duck, no feet, from $10 to **15.00**
Donald Duck's Nephew, no feet .**30.00**
Fozzie Bear, w/feet, from $1 to.. **3.00**
Fred Flintstone, w/feet, from $1 to **3.00**
Gyro Gearloose, w/feet **6.00**
Jerry Mouse, w/feet, painted face.. **6.00**
Jerry Mouse, w/feet, plastic face. **15.00**
Lamb, no feet........................... **15.00**
Lamb, w/feet, from $1 to.......... **3.00**
Lamb, w/feet, whistle head ... **20.00**
Mickey Mouse, no feet, removable nose or cast nose, ea from $10 to **15.00**
Mickey Mouse, w/feet, from $1 to.. **3.00**

Miss Piggy, w/feet, ea from $1
to **3.00**
Miss Piggy, w/feet, eyelashes..**15.00**
Odie, w/feet............................**5.00**
Panda, no feet, die-cut eyes...**20.00**
Panda, w/feet, whistle head **6.00**
Pluto, no feet **15.00**
Pluto, no feet, red..................**15.00**
Pluto, w/feet, from $1 to **3.00**
Road Runner, no feet **25.00**
Road Runner, w/feet...............**15.00**
Smurf, w/feet...........................**5.00**
Smurfette, w/feet......................**5.00**
Tiger, w/feet, whistle head.......**6.00**
Tom, no feet............................**35.00**
Tom, w/feet, painted face.........**6.00**
Tom, w/feet, plastic face.........**15.00**
Zorro, no feet..........................**65.00**

Pfaltzgraff Pottery

Since early in the seventeenth century, pottery has been produced in York County, Pennsylvania. The Pfaltzgraff Company that operates there today is the outgrowth of several of these small potteries. A changeover made in 1940 redirected their efforts toward making the dinnerware lines for which they are now best known. Their earliest line, a glossy brown with a white frothy drip glaze around the rim, was called Gourmet Royale. Today collectors find an abundance of good examples and are working toward reassembling sets of their own. Village, another very successful line, is tan with a stencilled Pennsylvania Dutch-type floral design in brown. It was all but discontinued several years ago (they do make a few pieces for collectors

now), and Village fans are turning to secondary market sources to replace and replenish their services. The line is very extensive and offers an interesting array of items.

Giftware consisting of ashtrays, mugs, bottle stoppers, a cookie jar, etc., all with comic character faces were made in the 1940s. This line was called Muggsy, and it is also very collectible, with the more common mugs starting at about $35.00 each. For more information refer to *The Collector's Encyclopedia of American Dinnerware* by Jo Cunningham (Collector Books) and *Pfaltzgraff, America's Potter*, by David A. Walsh and Polly Stetler, published in conjunction with the Historical Society of York County, York, Pennsylvania.

Christmas Heritage, bowl, salad;
8½" **15.00**
Christmas Heritage, bowl, soup/cereal; #009, 5½", from $4 to **7.00**
Christmas Heritage, butter tub.**35.00**
Christmas Heritage, casserole, w/lid,
2-qt.....................................**50.00**
Christmas Heritage, gravy boat &
undertray.........................**20.00**
Christmas Heritage, mug, pedestal
foot, #290, 10-oz **5.00**
Christmas Heritage, plate, #004,
10", from $5 to...................**9.00**
Christmas Heritage, platter,
16¼x12" **25.00**
Christmas Heritage, tumbler,
glass w/red & green, 5½"", set
of 10.................................**35.00**
Gourmet Royale, ashtray, #069,
10" **15.00**

Gourmet Royale, ashtray, #618, 10".................................... **25.00**

Gourmet Royale, baker, #323, 9½", from $12 to **15.00**

Gourmet Royale, bean pot, #11-2, 2-qt, from $15 to **20.00**

Gourmet Royale, bean pot, w/lip, #30, lg, from $30 to......... **40.00**

Gourmet Royale, bowl, berry; 4⅝" **5.00**

Gourmet Royale, bowl, cereal; #934SR, 5½" **5.00**

Gourmet Royale, bowl, mixing; 6", from $8 to **12.00**

Gourmet Royale, bowl, mixing; 8", from $10 to **15.00**

Gourmet Royale, bowl, mixing; 10", from $20 to **25.00**

Gourmet Royale, bowl, soup; 7¼", from $6 to **9.00**

Gourmet Royale, bowl, vegetable; 8"....................................... **12.50**

Gourmet Royale, bread plate, #528, 12" L.................................. **20.00**

Gourmet Royale, canister set, 4-pc, from $50 to **60.00**

Gourmet Royale, casserole, stick handle, 1-qt, from $9 to.. **12.00**

Gourmet Royale, casserole, stick handle, 3-qt, from $15 to . **20.00**

Gourmet Royale, chip 'n dip, #306, 2-pc set, w/stand, from $22 to **25.00**

Gourmet Royale, creamer, #382..**4.00**

Gourmet Royale, cup & saucer. **5.00**

Gourmet Royale, egg/relish tray, 15" L.................................. **18.00**

Gourmet Royale, gravy boat, 2-spout, #426, w/underplate, from $9 to **14.00**

Gourmet Royale, jug, #385, 48-oz, from $20 to **25.00**

Gourmet Royale, mug, #286, 18-oz................................. **20.00**

Gourmet Royale, mug, #391, 12-oz **7.00**

Gourmet Royale, mug, #392, 16-oz **12.00**

Gourmet Royale, pie plate, #7016, 9½", from $10 to **15.00**

Gourmet Royale, plate, dinner; #88R, from $9 to **14.00**

Gourmet Royale, plate, salad; 6¾" **2.00**

Gourmet Royale, plate, steak; 12", from $10 to **15.00**

Gourmet Royale, platter, #16, 14"................................. **25.00**

Gourmet Royale, platter, #20, 14"................................. **25.00**

Gourmet Royale, relish dish, #265, 5x10", from $12 to........... **15.00**

Gourmet Royale, roaster, oval, #326, 16", from $25 to..... **32.00**

Gourmet Royale, sugar bowl... **6.00**

Gourmet Royale, teapot, #701. **25.00**

Gourmet Royale, three-part tray, 15½" long, $25.00.

Gourmet Royale, tidbit, 2-tier, from $10 to **14.00**

Heritage, butter dish, #002-028. **6.00**

Heritage, canisters, set of 4, from $55 to **60.00**

Heritage, cookie jar................ **50.00**

Heritage, ice bucket, #650..... **50.00**

Heritage, plate, chop; 12½"....**25.00**

Heritage, plate, dinner; 10".....**5.00**

Heritage, plate, salad; 7".........**3.00**

Heritage, quiche dish, 1¾x9". **25.00**

Heritage, water jug, 10" **38.00**

Muggsy, ashtray................... **125.00**

Muggsy, cookie jar, character face, minimum value **250.00**

Muggsy, mug, character face . **38.00**

Muggsy, tumbler **60.00**

Village, baker, oval, #024, 10¼", from $7 to **9.00**

Village, baker, oval, #241, 10" . **10.00**

Village, bean pot, 2½-qt, from $22 to **28.00**

Village, beverage server, #490, from $18 to **22.00**

Village, bowl, fruit; 5" **3.00**

Village, bowl, onion soup; stick handle **8.00**

Village, bowl, soup/cereal; 6" . **4.00**

Village, bread tray, 12" **15.00**

Village, chip 'n dip set, 2-pc, from $20 to **30.00**

Village, cookie jar, #540, 3-qt .. **20.00**

Village, creamer & sugar bowl, #020, from $9 to **12.00**

Village, cruets, vinegar & oil; pr. **60.00**

Village, cup & saucer, #001 & #002 .... **3.50**

Village, flatware, Oneida, service for 8, 40 pcs **235.00**

Village, ice bucket, metal liner. **55.00**

Village, pitcher, #416, 2-qt, from $20 to **25.00**

Village, plate, #004, 10", from $3 to **4.00**

Village, platter, #016, 14", from $12 to **18.00**

Village, quiche dish, 9" **16.00**

Pie Birds

What is a pie bird? It is a functional and decorative kitchen tool most commonly found in the shape of a bird, designed to vent steam through the top crust of a pie to prevent the juices from spilling over into the oven. Other popular designs were elephants and black-faced bakers. The original vents that were used in England and Wales in the 1800s were simply shaped like funnels.

From the 1980s to the present, many novelty pie vents have been added to the market for the baker and the collector. Some of these could be obtained from Far East Imports; others have been made in England and the US (by commercial and/or local enterprises). Examples can be found in the shapes of animals (dogs, frogs, elephants, cats, goats, and dragons), people (policemen, chefs with and without pies, pilgrims, and carolers), or whimsical figurals (clowns, leprechauns, and teddy bears). A line of holiday-related pie vents were made in the 1990s. Consequently, a collector must be on guard and aware that these new pie vents are being sold by dealers (knowingly in many instances) as old or rare, often at double or triple the original cost (which is usually under $10.00). Though most of the new ones can't really be called reproductions since they never existed before, there's a black bird that is a remake, and you'll see them everywhere. Here's how you can spot them: they'll have yellow beaks and protruding white-dotted eyes. If they're on a white base and have an orange beak, they are the older ones. Another basic tip that should help you distinguish old from new: older pie vents are air-brushed versus being hand painted. Please note that incense burners, one-hole pepper shakers, dated brass toy bird whistles, and ring holders (for instance, the elephant with a clover on his tummy) should not be mistaken for pie vents. See Clubs and Newsletters for information concerning *Pie Birds Unlimited Newsletter*.

Bear crying, brown, 4" **35.00**
Bear holding pie, green w/white striped pants, England, 4" .**70.00**
Bear in green jacket w/hat & shoes, England, 4½" **55.00**
Bird, black w/gold beak, Chic Pottery, 4½" **125.00**
Bird, pink on blue base, Shawnee for Pillsbury, 5½" **85.00**
Bird, white w/multicolored wings, Morton Pottery, 1950s, 4¾".**45.00**
Bird, yellow sleek design, England, 4" **85.00**
Bird, 2-headed, black & yellow, Devon **110.00**
Bird on nest, Artesian Galleries, copyright mark, 1950s, from $300 to **350.00**
Black chef, white coat & hat, blue pants, w/spoon................. **50.00**
Black chef, yellow holds white spoon, James Barry, 1945, 4"..... **110.00**
Blackbird on ear of corn, Four Rivers Pottery, EX **35.00**
Cardinal on base, unmarked, 3½" **25.00**
Clown, marked MB 90 inside, EX **45.00**
Eagle, golden color, marked Sunglow, from $75 to **85.00**
Elephant on drum, solid pink base, marked CCC, from $325 to. **350.00**
Elephant on hind legs on circus stand, England, 4" **65.00**

Funnel, white, plain, from $10 to **12.00**
Margaret Thatcher, jug shape, floral center, Wales, dated 1979-91 .... **110.00**
Nun, Made in England w/crown, 4", EX **65.00**
Pie Boy, w/green sombrero .. **400.00**
Policeman dressed in black, England, 4" **60.00**
Rooster, multicolored tail feathers, Cleminson, 4¼"................ **50.00**
Rooster, white w/red & black, Shade Tree Pottery.................... **45.00**

S-neck rooster, Pearl China Co., ca 1920 – 1950, 5", from $150.00 to $175.00.

Welsh lady, Cymru, from $75 to.............................. **95.00**
Witch holding pie, yellow bird on dress, marked England, 5" **65.00**

Pin-Back Buttons

Because most of the pin-backs prior to the 1920s were made of celluloid, collectors refer to them as 'cellos.' Many were issued in sets on related topics. Some advertising buttons had paper inserts on the back that identified the company or the product they were advertising. After the 1920s lithographed metal buttons were produced; they're now called 'lithos.' See also The Beatles; Elvis Presley; Political.

Associated Stamp Club, white Flying A logo on red, 1930s, 1" dia, NM **18.00**

Babe Ruth Baseball Club, 1970s, 1½", EX **6.00**

Dick Tracy Secret Service Patrol, blue & gold, 1980s, 3", EX. **5.00**

Dizzy Dean, ⅞" **100.00**

DuPont Smokeless Powder, bird in center, 1¼", EX **90.00**

Farrah, close-up photo image, 3", EX+ **20.00**

Green Hornet Agent, 1960s, 4", EX **15.00**

Healthy Me/Award Winner/Metro Life Foundation, Peanuts gang, 2½", M **6.00**

Hey Dude! I'm on FOX 49!, Bart Simpson on white, 1992, 2¼", M **12.00**

Hopalong Cassidy's Savings Rodeo, black & white on yellow, 1½", EX **35.00**

Huckleberry Hound for President, head on yellow, 1960s, 3", EX **20.00**

John Wayne, black & white photo on blue, 1940s-50s, 1¼" .. **14.00**

Mackenzie's Raiders, Fiery TV Action, Starring Richard Carlson, 3½" **75.00**

Matt Dillon's Favorite All Star Dairies, red, white & blue, 1960s, EX **30.00**

Mickey Mouse Club, 1970s, 3" . **8.00**

New Kids on the Block, image of Joseph, 6", NM **5.50**

Pebbles Flintstone, 1972, 2", EX.. **15.00**

Pride/Courage, image of Simba (Lion King), 2¼", MOC **4.00**

Snow White Jingle Club Member, red & black on white, 1930s, 1¼", EX **40.00**

Soupy Sales Society, Charter Member, 3½", EX **12.50**

Standard Red Crown Superfuel, More Live Power Per Gallon, 4", EX **100.00**

Superman of America, phrase encircles half-image, 1938-42, 1¼", VG **50.00**

Ted Williams, Boston Red Sox, w/portrait, 1950s, 1¼", EX **18.00**

Zorro/7-Up, Walt Disney Productions, 1957, 1¼", EX .. **20.00**

Rocky Jones Space Ranger, 1950s, Silvercup Bread Premium, EX, $35.00.

Pep Pins

In the late '40s and into the '50s, some cereal companies packed a pin-back button in each box of their product. Quaker Puffed Oats offered a series of movie star pinbacks, but Kellogg's Pep Pins are probably the best known of all. There were 86 different Pep pins. They came in five sets — the first in 1945, three more in 1946, and the last in 1947. They were printed with full-color lithographs of comic characters licensed by King

Features and Famous Artists — Maggie and Jiggs, the Winkles, and Dogwood and Blondie, for instance. Superman, the only D.C. Comics character, was included in each set. Most Pep pins range in value from $10.00 to $15.00 in NM/M condition; for more listings recommend *Garage Sale & Flea Market Annual* (Collector Books).

BO Plenty, NM 30.00
Corky, NM 16.00
Dagwood, NM 30.00
Dick Tracy, NM 30.00
Fat Stuff, NM 15.00
Felix the Cat, NM 60.00
Flash Gordon, NM 25.00
Flat Top, NM 23.00
Goofy, NM 10.00
Gravel Gertie, NM 15.00
Harold Teen, NM.................... 15.00
Inspector, NM......................... 12.50
Jiggs, NM 25.00
Judy, NM 10.00
Kayo, NM................................. 12.00
Little King, NM....................... 15.00
Little Moose, NM 15.00
Maggie, NM............................. 25.00
Mama De Stross, NM 30.00
Mama Katzenzammer, NM ... 25.00
Mamie, NM.............................. 15.00
Moon Mullins, NM 10.00
Olive Oyle, NM....................... 18.00
Orphan Annie, NM 25.00
Pat Patton, NM...................... 10.00
Perry Winkle, NM.................. 15.00
Phantom, NM.......................... 60.00
Pop Jenks, NM....................... 15.00
Popeye, NM 30.00
Rip Winkle, NM 20.00
Skeezix, NM 15.00
Superman, NM........................ 25.00

Toots, NM 15.00
Uncle Walt, NM...................... 20.00
Uncle Willie, NM.................... 12.50
Winkle Twins, NM 25.00
Winnie Winkle, NM 15.00

Pinup Art

Collectors of pinup art look for blotters, calendars, prints, playing cards, etc., with illustrations of sexy girls by artists who are famous for their work in this venue: Vargas, Petty, DeVorss, Elvgren, Moran, Mozert, Ballantyne, Armstrong, and Davis among them. Though not all items will be signed, most of these artists have a distinctive style that is easy to recognize.

Calendar, 1953, Sunny Skies, Brown & Bigelow, 32x16", $75.00.

Ashtray, metal w/painted image of nude blond by coffee table, 1950s, M 15.00
Blotter, Elvgren, Jill Needs a Jack, 1949, unused, EX............ 12.00
Blotter, Moran, Chief Attraction, Indian girl, 1944, NM..... 12.00
Book, Pin-Up Art, Walter T Foster, Earl MacPherson sketches, 1954, EX 50.00

Calendar, Elliot, 1950, Delectable Dishes, complete, NM..... 50.00

Calendar, Elvgren, 1946, A Pleasing Discovery, 11", complete, EX........................ 35.00

Calendar, Elvgren, 1946, Season's Greetings, complete, M in envelope........................... 55.00

Calendar, Pressler, 1934, Where Unimagined Beauty Dwells, complete, EX 85.00

Calendar, Randall, 1961, complete, NM.................................... 55.00

Calendar, Randall, 1968, Women of History, complete, EX..... 30.00

Calendar, Rolf Armstrong, 1941, Miss Advertising, 23", complete, EX........................... 70.00

Calendar top, Elvgren, Who Me?, 11x14½", EX 45.00

Fan, Armstrong, Queen of the Ball, 1980s repro, EX 15.00

Greeting card, MacPhearson, Nursery Rhyme for Grownups, 1950s, EX 25.00

Letter opener, Elvgren, plastic nude, painted dress, 1950s, 8½", NM........................... 35.00

Lighter, pocket; Vargas Girl (Windy, 1935), Zippo, 1993, unused, M 45.00

Magazine, Eyeful, DeVorss Girl on cover, 1945, EX................ 15.00

Magazine, Playboy's Vargas Girls, Playboy Press, 1972, EX. 80.00

Playing cards, Elvgren, nude & pelican, complete, MIB... 35.00

Playing cards, Elvgren, 52 American Beauties, complete, EXIB 80.00

Playing cards, Erbit, girl in hammock, 1950s, complete, MIB..............................25.00

Print, Armstrong, Adorable, brunette in red & white gown, 5x4", EX........................... 16.00

Print, DeVorss, Day Dreams, 5x3", EX 11.00

Print, Elvgren, cowgirl sits on fence w/smoking gun, 15x18", EX.................................. 50.00

Print, Elvgren, Miss Sylvania adjusting garter, 1961, 34x16", EX 65.00

Print, Erbit, Gorgeous, blond in white ermine, 1939, 8x6", EX 110.00

Print, Erbit, Happy Moments, blond w/puppy, 16x30", EX......... 30.00

Print, Moran, Diane, 1950, 16x20", EX 65.00

Print, Moran, nude redhead looking up, 1940s, framed, 11x15", EX 85.00

Print, Pressler, Carmelita, 15x12", EX 40.00

Tumbler, Petty, full-color illusion decal, 1940s, 4½", EX...... 15.00

Playing Cards

Here is another field of collectibles that is inexpensive, easy to display (especially single cards), and very diversified. Variations are endless. Some backs are printed with reproductions of famous paintings or pinup art. Others carry advertising messages, picture tourist attractions, or commemorate a world's fair. Early decks are scarce, but those from the 1940s on are usually more attractive anyway, so pick an area that interests you most and have fun! Though they're usually not dated, you may find some clues that will help you to determine an approximate date. Telephone numbers, zip codes, advertising slogans, and patriotic messages are always helpful. See also Pinup Art.

Alabama Crimson Tide, 1970s, M (sealed package)............... **15.00**

Cayman Airways, pirate turtle, MIB (sealed).................... **20.00**

Cunrad White Star Cruise Ship, ships on pink, complete, EX.........**30.00**

Dallas Cowboy Cheerleaders, Trans Media Inc, M (sealed box) . **8.00**

Doonesbury at Starbucks, complete double deck, NM+IB....... **35.00**

Epcot Center, M (sealed wrap). **6.00**

Game Birds, artwork by RC Bishop, complete double deck, MIB (sealed) **18.00**

Golden Nugget Gambling Hall, complete double deck, 1940s, MIB............................... **130.00**

Golden Nugget Gambling Hall, yellow & white on blue, 1963, M (sealed) **38.00**

Great Northern Railroad, Pinto Woman/Chief Middleman, double deck, NM **35.00**

Indians of the Southwest, Fred Harvey, complete, NMIB. **200.00**

It Pays To Plant Funk's G Hybrid, kitten spilling milk, complete, MIB................................. **25.00**

Looney Tunes, Warner Bros, 1990s, complete, NMIB................ **6.00**

Michelin, BP Grimund, complete, MIB................................. **15.00**

Mobile Oil, Pegasus flying past moon in starry sky, complete, EXIB...**30.00**

National Airlines, red & gray w/white lettering, complete, MIB..... **8.00**

Pennsylvania Railroad, pinochle deck, MIB (sealed).......... **10.00**

Quaker Old-Fashioned Oats, double deck, MIB (sealed packs).......................... **20.00**

Save the Dinosaurs, Conserve Energy, Chevron, complete, M (no box).............................. **8.00**

Scenes From Venice Italy, WPCC, gold edge, complete, MIB. **10.00**

Tiger Beer, complete, MIB....... **6.00**

TWA Airlines, Lockheed 1049G plane, 1955, complete, NMIB **10.00**

United Airlines, prop plane, complete double deck (1 red/1 blue), EXIB **110.00**

Van Camp's Pork & Beans, Dutch couple w/product, complete, MIB................................. **45.00**

Yellowstone National Park, scenes by JE Haynes, complete, 1930s, EXIB **40.00**

Moore-McCormack Lines, MIB, $50.00. (Photo courtesy Everett Grist)

Pocketknives

Knife collecting as a hobby began in earnest during the 1960s when government regulations required that knife companies mark their product with the country of origin. The few collectors and dealers cognizant of this change at once began stockpiling the older knives before this law was enacted. Another impetus to the growing interest came with the Gun Control Act of 1968, which severely restricted gun trading. Frustrated gun dealers transferred their attention to knives. Today there are collectors' clubs in many of the states. The most sought-after pocketknives are those made before WWII. However, Case, Schrade, and Primble knives of a more recent manufacture are also collected. Most collectors prefer knives 'as found.' It is best not to clean, sharpen, or try in any way to 'improve' an old knife.

The prices quoted here are for knives in used, excellent condition, unless otherwise noted. For further information refer to *Big Book of Pocket Knives*, by Ron Stewart and Roy Ritchie (Collector Books).

Shrade Old Timer, "USA 250-T," two blade, plastic handle, M in leather case, $25.00.

Barnett Tool Co, bone handle, blade, punch & pliers ... **175.00**

Case, Tested XX, 62031½, 2-blade, green bone handle, 3¾". **150.00**

Case, Tested XX, 8383, 2-blade, pearl handle, whittler pattern, 3½" **500.00**

Case, XX, 6231½, 2-blade, bone handle, 3¾" **75.00**

Case, XX 62009, 1-blade, bone handle, barlow pattern, 2⅜" . **40.00**

Cattaraugus, 22346, 2-blade, wood handle, jackknife, 3⅜"... **85.00**

Cattaraugus, 22929, 2-blade, bone handle, cigar pattern, 4¼" **300.00**

Diamond Edge, 2-blade, bone handle, jackknife, 3⅜" **75.00**

Hammer Brand, 2-blade, wooden handle, jackknife, 3¾"..... **85.00**

Henckels, JA; 3-blade, bone handle, whittler pattern, 3¼" **65.00**

Imperial Knife Co, 2-blade, bone handle, dog-leg pattern, 3⅜".... **50.00**

Ka-Bar, Union Cutlery, 2-blade, stag handle, Old Time Trapper, 4⅛" **85.00**

Keen Kutter, EC Simmons, 1-blade, bone handle, lockback, 4¼"................................. **200.00**

Keen Kutter, 1-blade, bone handle, TX toothpick, 5" **125.00**

Miller Bros, 2-blade, bone handle, jackknife, 3½" **100.00**

Napanoch Knife Co, 4-blade, bone handle, 3¼" **150.00**

Pal, 3-blade, bone handle, jacknife, 3⅜" **60.00**

Queen, #18, 2-blade, winterbottom bone handle, trapper, 4⅛".**150.00**

Remington, R775, 2-blade, red, white & blue handle, 3½" **185.00**

Robeson, Shuredge, 2-blade, strawberry bone handle, jackknife, 3½" **150.00**

Rodgers, Jos & Sons, multi-blade, stag handle, sportsman's...........**350.00**

Schatt & Morgan (current), 1-blade, bone handle, lockback, 5¼", M **100.00**

Shrade Walden, 3-blade, peach seed bone handle, 3⅜" **75.00**

Wards, 3-blade, bone handle, cattle pattern, 3⅝".....................85.00
Winchester, 2046 (old), 2-blade, celluloid handle, jackknife, 3¾"...............................85.00
Winchester, 3960 (old), 3-blade, bone handle, stockman, 4".......275.00
Winchester, 3971, 3-blade, bone handle, whittler pattern, 1989...............................75.00

Political Collectibles

Pennants, posters, badges, pamphlets — in general, anything related to a presidential campaign or politicians — are being sought by collectors who have an interest in the political history of our country. Most valued are items from a particularly eventful period or those things having to do with an especially colorful personality.

Celluloid pin-back buttons ('cellos') were first widely used in the 1896 presidential campaign; before that time medals, ribbons, and badges of various kinds predominated. Prices for political pin-backs have increased considerably in the last few years, more due to speculative buying and selling rather than inherent scarcity or unusual demand. It is still possible, however, to find quality collectible items at reasonable prices. In flea markets, recent buttons tend to be overpriced; the goal, as always, is to look for less familiar items that may be priced more reasonably. Most buttons issued since the 1964 campaign, with a few notable exceptions, should be in the range

of $2.00 to $10.00. Condition is critical: cracks, scratches, spots, and brown stains ('foxing') seriously reduce the value of a button.

Prices are for items in excellent condition. Reproductions are common; many are marked as such, but it takes some experience to tell the difference. For more information we recommend Edmund Sullivan's *Collecting Political Americana, 2nd Edition*. See Clubs and Newsletters for information concerning Political Collectors of Indiana.

Doll, Barry Goldwater, plastic nodder, Remco, 1964, 5½", MIB, $35.00.
(Photo courtesy Neal Auction Company)

Ashtray, Lyndon Johnson in gold on white cowboy hat, ceramic, 6½".....................18.00
Ashtray, President & Mrs John Kennedy color transfer, ceramic, 6", NM.........................12.00
Badge, Roosevelt/Barner, red, white & blue cello in brass frame, EX.....................................18.00
Balloon, Vote Kennedy, white on blue, unused...................10.00
Bank, FDR/Happy Days, barrel shape, 5", EX...................15.00
Banner, Franklin Roosevelt, red, white & blue cloth, 6x5", NM........15.00

Booklet, A Dozen Reasons To Elect Woodrow Wilson, 1944, NM. **10.00**

Bracelet, Nixon, pearl w/multicolor rhinestones, adult size, EX. **15.00**

Brochure, Ronald Reagan as Host of GE Theatre, 1954, EX **20.00**

Buckle, Carter on brass peanut shape, 3x2", NM **10.00**

Bumper sticker, Democrats for Nixon, EX **2.00**

Bumper sticker, Kennedy/Johnson jugate, orange & black, NM. **15.00**

Coloring book, Jimmy Carter, 1976, unused, EX **20.00**

Decal, window; Kennedy for President, shield shape w/JFK photo, 5½" **15.00**

Delegate's key, 1960 Chicago Republican Convention, EX .. **28.00**

Delegate's key, 1968 Democratic Convention, brass, lg, EX. **20.00**

Doll, Teddy Kennedy, cloth caricature, 1980, 5½", EX **15.00**

Doll, Tricky Dicky, rubber, 5", M (NM card) **25.00**

Game, Barrel of Clintons, NM. **12.00**

Invitation, Eisenhower-Nixon inaugural ball, 1957, EX **15.00**

Key chain, flasher, Kennedy/J Manford Core, black & white, EX **8.00**

License plate, California/Perot, yellow on black, 2x4", M **3.00**

License plate, Herbert Hoover for President, 3x5", VG **35.00**

Mask, Richard Nixon, rubber, natural colors, 1970s, NM **25.00**

Nodder, elephant, I'm for Ike, painted composition, 1950s, 6½", NM. **100.00**

Paperweight, bust of Herbert Hoover, copper paint on heavy metal, EX **28.00**

Pennant, Vote Dewey, Republican, green felt, 1948, 13", VG. **30.00**

Pin-back, Adlai Stevenson portrait, Best in View, 1952, 1½", EX. **70.00**

Pin-back, Harry S Truman, black & white portrait, 1884-1972. **5.00**

Pin-back, I'm With Magic (Johnson)!, People 1st, Clinton Gore, M **100.00**

Pin-back, Jimmy Carter for President, photo, 3" **6.00**

Pin-back, McGovern/Eagleton, NM **6.00**

Pin-back, Robert F Kennedy, full-color portrait, 1968, 3½" . **10.00**

Pin-back, Stop the Draft, white on green, 1½", VG **15.00**

Pin-back, We Want Mamie, portrait, red, white & blue, EX **12.00**

Pocket mirror, JFK portrait, black & white oval, 2¾", EX **25.00**

Postcard, George Wallace portrait, multicolored photo, M **2.00**

Poster, Nixon/Agnew w/25 celebrities (sketch), 1968, 25x20", M **28.00**

Salt & pepper shakers, JFK seated on chair, 2-pc, EX **90.00**

Snowdome, Douglas McArthur, 1940s, NM **38.00**

Stickpin, Ike embossed on side of elephant, NMOC **15.00**

Ticket, Democratic National Convention, F Roosevelt portrait, 1936, EX **20.00**

Token, dollar; Senator Goldwater, 1964 .... **5.00**

Princess House Glassware

The home party plan of Princess House was started in Massachusetts in 1963 by Charlie Collis. His idea was to give women an opportunity to have their own business by being a princess in their house, thus the name for this company. Though many changes have been made since the 1960s, the main goal of this company is to better focus on the home party plan.

Most Princess House pieces are not marked in the glass — they carry a paper label. Heritage is a crystal cut floral pattern, introduced not long after the company started in business. Fantasia is a crystal pressed floral pattern, introduced about 1980. Both lines continue today; new pieces are being added, and old items are continually discontinued.

Cake pan, Fantasia, frosted bottom, round, MIB **32.00**

Cake plate, Fantasia, high dome lid, #584, hostess gift...... **80.00**

Cake plate, Heritage, footed, deep scallops, dome lid, #076.. **75.00**

Candleholders, Heritage, crystal hurricane stems, 12", MIB, pr **20.00**

Canister set, Fantasia, sq, 4-pc, MIB................................. **60.00**

Canister set, Vintage Garden, ceramic, hostess gift, 3-pc............ **65.00**

Carafe, crystal w/copper warmer, lid & handle, 13½" overall...... **36.00**

Casserole dish, Fantasia, tab handles, w/lid, 5x14", MIB ... **30.00**

Champagne flutes, Heritage, 7.5-oz, 10", set of 8 .... **75.00**

Figurine, deer (buck), Wonders of the Wild, 6½x5" **42.00**

Figurine, fish, Pets Collection, 3x4"................................... **75.00**

Figurine, fish (bass), #989, Wonders of the Wild, MIB **45.00**

Figurine, lion in repose, Wonders of the Wild **35.00**

Figurine, Nativity, 3-pc set, MIB (individual boxes)............ **30.00**

Figurine, puppy, #812, 4½" long, $30.00. (Photo courtesy Debbie and Randy Coe)

Figurine, stallion rearing **40.00**

Flatware, Barrington, 20-pc, 18/10 gauge stainless steel, MIB. **125.00**

Goblets, iced-tea; Heritage, 6", set of 4 .... **35.00**

Gravy boat, Fantasia, w/underplate **35.00**

Heritage, roaster, w/dome lid, MIB **150.00**

Lamp, 3 glass tubes w/brass-tone top & base, hostess gift, rare, MIB................................. **50.00**

Measuring cup, Fantasia, 1-cup, MIB................................. **15.00**

Mugs, Heritage, #504, footed, 10-oz, set of 8, EX **65.00**

Pitcher, Heritage, 75-oz, 10", EX................................. **15.00**

Plate, Fantasia, 10", set of 4, EX............................... **40.00**

Platter, Fantasia, sq w/tab handles, frosted bottom, #536, 13", MIB **42.00**

Platter, 40th Anniversary, patterned crystal, 14x18"..... **45.00**

Rose bowl, #950, 5x6" dia, MIB **38.00**

Salad bowl, Fantasia, lg, MIB. **15.00**

Server, Heritage, round tray w/ high dome lid, #1554, 7x12½", MIB **70.00**

Snack server, Pavillion, stoneware, tray, 4 nesters & glass dome lid, MIB **75.00**

Soup/sandwich set, Fantasia, 12-oz cup/12" tray, plastic cup lid. **22.00**

Tea set, Hammersly Fine Bone China, Windsor Rose, 19-pc, MIB **175.00**

Teapot, Heritage, 3-pc w/pot, infuser & lid, 44-oz................. **65.00**

Tumblers, Heritage, 5½", set of 8 .... **65.00**

Vase, Heritage, cobalt, ball shape w/fluted rim, 5x4½" dia... **30.00**

Wine goblets, Heritage, #0892, 6-oz, 6", set of 4 .... **60.00**

Wine goblets, Heritage, #6173, 15-oz, 8½", set of 12 ...... **100.00**

Purinton

Popular among collectors due to its 'country' look, Purinton Pottery's dinnerware and kitchen items are easy to learn to recognize due to their bold yet simple designs, many of them of fruit and flowers, created with basic hand-applied colors on a creamy white gloss.

Apple, ashtray, center handle, 5½" **40.00**

Apple, bowl, cereal; 5¼" **10.00**

Apple, bowl, range; w/lid, 5½" . **65.00**

Apple, bowl, vegetable; divided, 10½" **35.00**

Apple, butter dish, 6½" **150.00**

Apple, canister, short, oval, 5", ea **55.00**

Apple, creamer & sugar bowl, miniature **30.00**

Apple, honey jug, 6¼".......... **150.00**

Apple, marmalade.................. **40.00**

Apple, pitcher, Rubel mold, 5". **75.00**

Apple, platter, 11" **15.00**

Apple, salt & pepper shakers, stacking; 2¼", pr **95.00**

Apple, tumbler, 12-oz, 5" **20.00**

Chartreuse, bowl, vegetable; 8½".**30.00**

Chartreuse, lap plate & cup.. **35.00**

Chartreuse, wall pocket, 3½". **50.00**

Fruit, canister, wooden lid, 7½".**65.00**

Fruit, cocktail dish, sea-horse handle, 11¾"........................... **55.00**

Fruit, coffeepot, 8-cup, 8" **65.00**

Fruit, creamer, 3".................. **15.00**

Fruit, jug, Dutch; 2-pt **15.00**

Fruit, relish, 3-part, pottery handle, 10"............................. **55.00**

Fruit, tumbler, 12-oz, 5" **20.00**

Heather Plaid, chop plate, 12". **35.00**

Heather Plaid, creamer, 3".... **20.00**

Heather Plaid, grease jar, 5½". **60.00**

Heather Plaid, pitcher, five-pint, $75.00. (Photo courtesy Susan Morris-Snyder)

Heather Plaid, sugar bowl, w/lid, 4"...................................... **30.00**

Intaglio, gravy pitcher, Taylor Smith & Taylor mold, 3¾".......... **65.00**

Intaglio, mug, beer; 16-oz, 4¾". **25.00**

Intaglio, pitcher, gravy; Taylor Smith & Taylor mold, 3¼" **65.00**

Intaglio, saucer, 5½"................ **3.00**

Ivy (red), biscuit jar, w/lid, 8" **45.00**

Ivy (red), coffeepot, 8-cup **25.00**

Ivy (red), honey jug, 6¼" **15.00**

Ivy (yellow), creamer, 3½"...... 15.00

Ivy (yellow), jug, Dutch; 2-pt. 20.00

Maywood, baker, 7"................ 25.00

Maywood, plate, 9½" 30.00

Morning Glory, honey jug, 6¼". 50.00

Morning Rose, plate, 9½"....... 40.00

Mountain Rose, plate, dinner; 9½" 40.00

Mountain Rose, teapot, 2-cup. 15.00

Normandy Plaid, bowl, vegetable; 8½" 20.00

Normandy Plaid, mug, beer; 16-oz, 4¾" 40.00

Normandy Plaid, mug, Kent; 1-pt, 4½" 30.00

Normandy Plaid, pitcher, beverage; 6¼" 45.00

Normandy Plaid, roll tray, 11". 35.00

Palm Tree, honey jug, 6¼"..... 75.00

Palm Tree, salt & pepper shakers, Pour & Shake, pr 75.00

Pennsylvania Dutch, baker, 7". 45.00

Pennsylvania Dutch, chop plate, 12"................................... 125.00

Pennsylvania Dutch, cup & saucer.................................. 20.00

Pennsylvania Dutch, jug, Rebecca; 7½" 75.00

Pennsylvania Dutch, star candleholder, ea 100.00

Petals, bowl, fruit; 12" 95.00

Petals, jug, Dutch; 5-pt.......... 50.00

Provencial Fruit, bowl, cereal; 5¼" 10.00

Provencial Fruit, grease jar, 5"..30.00

Saraband, bowl, fruit; 12" 25.00

Saraband, bowl, range; w/lid, 5½"............................... 20.00

Saraband, candleholder, 8-sided, 2x6", ea 20.00

Saraband, plate, dinner; 9¾".... 10.00

Saraband, plate, salad; 6¾"..... 8.00

Saraband, platter, 12"............ 20.00

Saraband, teapot, 6-cup, 6½". 25.00

Windflower, jardiniere, 5"...... 30.00

Woodflowers, relish tray, 8" ... 45.00

Puzzles

Of most interest to collectors of vintage puzzles are those made of wood or plywood, especially the early hand-cut examples. Character-related examples and those representing a well-known personality or show from the early days of television are coming on strong right now, and values are steadily climbing in these areas. For an expanded listing, see *Schroeder's Collectible Toys, Antique to Modern*.

Annie Oakley, frame-tray, #4508, EX 40.00

Babes in Toyland, frame-tray, Whitman #4454, 1961, EX .40.00

Banana Splits, frame-tray, Whitman #4534, 1969, EX 50.00

Ben Casey, jigsaw, Milton Bradley #4319, 1960s, NMIB 40.00

Broken Arrow, frame-tray, Built-Rite #1229, 1957, NM..... 55.00

Bugs Bunny 24 Carrots, jigsaw, Whitman #4605, 1977, MIB (sealed) 25.00

C'mon Scooby Doo, wooden frame-tray, Playskool, 1980, M . 35.00

Captain Kangaroo, frame-tray, Whitman #4446, 1960, EX.35.00

Circus Boy, frame-tray, Whitman #4428, 1958, NM............. 55.00

Daniel Boone Wilderness Scout, frame-tray, Jaymar #2722, EX................................... 40.00

Dr Kildare, jigsaw, Milton Bradley #4318, 1960s, NMIB 45.00

Dudley Do-Right, frame-tray, Whitman #4512G, 1975, NMIB **40.00**

Elmer Fudd Carrying Groceries, frame-tray, Jaymar, 1940s, G+ **30.00**

Felix the Cat, frame-tray, Built-Rite #1229, 1959, NM **65.00**

Flintstones, frame-tray, Whitman #4434, 1964, VG+ **40.00**

Gene Autry, frame-tray, Whitman #2962, 1950, unused, MIP .**65.00**

Gunsmoke, frame-tray, Whitman #4427, 1960, G **15.00**

Gunsmoke, jigsaw, Whitman #4609, 1969, 100 pcs, NMIB **25.00**

Hoppity Hooper, frame-tray, Whitman #4523, 1965, EX+ **50.00**

Huckleberry Hound, frame-tray, Whitman #4428, 1963, VG+..**35.00**

Jetsons, frame-tray, Whitman #4423, 1962, VG **38.00**

Josie and the Pussycats, jigsaw puzzle in green canister, United Kingdom, 1972, from $40.00 to $50.00.

Jungle Book, frame-tray, Whitman #4524, 1967, NM+ **40.00**

Jungle Jim, frame-tray, Built Rite #1229, 1956, NM **75.00**

Lassie, jigsaw, Whitman, #4505, 1966, MIB (sealed) **45.00**

Love Bug, frame-tray, Whitman #4510H, EX **40.00**

Mickey Mouse Club, frame-tray, Whitman #4428, 1950s, EX **35.00**

Pac-Man, Playskool, 15 pieces, from $7.00 to $10.00.

Peter Pan, frame-tray, Jaymar #2731, 1950s, NM **50.00**

Peter Pan Picture Puzzles, Whitman, 6 different, EX+IB **125.00**

Popeye, frame-tray, any Jaymar, 1950s-60s, 11x14", NM, ea from $30 to **35.00**

Rin-Tin-Tin, frame-tray, Whitman #4428, 1950s, VG **35.00**

Rin-Tin-Tin, jigsaw, Whitman, Rusty & Rinty, 63 pcs, NMIB...... **35.00**

Rocky & Bullwinkle, frame-tray, Whitman #4534A, 1976, EX+ **45.00**

Sleeping Beauty, frame-tray, Whitman, 1958, EX **35.00**

Snow White & the Seven Dwarfs, frame-tray, Whitman #2986, 1950s, EX **35.00**

Space Ghost, frame-tray, Whitman #4559, 1967, NM **50.00**

Super Circus, frame-tray, Whitman #2628, 1954, EX **38.00**

Tales of Wells Fargo, frame-tray, Whitman #4427, 1958, VG.**35.00**

Top Cat, frame-tray, Whitman #4457, 1961, scarce, G.... **20.00**

Uncle Scrooge/Puzzle Funnies, frame-tray, Whitman #451C, 1970s, NM **40.00**

Walt Disney's Adventureland, frame-tray, Whitman #4420, 1956, EX **40.00**

Radios

Novelty radios are those that carry an advertising message or are shaped like a product bottle, can, or carton; others may be modeled after the likeness of a well-known cartoon character or disguised as anything but a radio — a shoe or a car, for instance. It's sometimes hard to recognize the fact that they're actually radios.

Transistor radios are collectible as well. First introduced in 1954, many feature space-age names and futuristic designs. Prices here are for complete, undamaged examples in at least very good condition. If you have vintage radios you need to evaluate, see *Collector's Guide to Antique Radios* by John Slusser and the Staff of Radio Daze (Collector Books).

Novelty Radios

Ajax Laundry Detergent, product box style, AM/FM, Hong Kong, NM **65.00**

Annie w/Sandie, red & white plastic, AM, 1980s, MIB **75.00**

Bart Simpson, on skateboard, JPI, China, EX **50.00**

Batman, bust, 1973, NMIB ... **35.00**

Borden Milk Shake Chocolate Flavor (English & French), NM **50.00**

Bozo the Clown, flat-sided head & collar form, AM, 1972, NM **65.00**

Coors Light, can form, AM/FM, EX **25.00**

Fanta Orange, French/English, EX **35.00**

Firestone Steel Belted Radial - 721, made in Hong Kong, distributed by PRI, 5" diameter, from $35.00 to $50.00. (Photo courtesy Bunis and Breed)

Ghostbusters, FM, Concept 2000, China 1986-89, EX **25.00**

Helping Hand, lg white glove w/face, 6½", NM **75.00**

Incredible Hulk, Marvel Comics, 1978, 7", M **75.00**

Kodak Copy Machine, AM, EX **175.00**

Marlboro Cigarettes, pack form, Japan, EX **75.00**

McDonald's Big Mac, GE, AM, EX **60.00**

Miller High Life, can form, EX **25.00**

Mork From Ork Eggship, Concept 2000, 1979, MIB.............. **35.00**

Pinball Wizard, Astra, 1980s, AM, MIB.............................. **175.00**

Pink Panther, decaled image on 2-D plastic form, 9", NM....... **125.00**

Princess of Power, Power Tronic by Nasta, Mattel, 1985, NM **20.00**

Quick Quaker Oats, old style label, NM **100.00**

Radio Shack in red letters, plastic, strap handle, AM, 1979, EX............**50.00**

San Giorgio Elbow Macaroni, box style, made in Hong Kong, distributed by PRI, 3½x5", from $45.00 to $60.00. (Photo courtesy Marty and Sue Bunis)

Seven-Up Vending Machine, AM/FM, Markatron #2001, Hong Kong, EX **100.00**

Smurf's head, hand carried, 1982, EX **47.50**

Snoopy's Spaceship, Concept 2000, 1970s, EX **75.00**

Sonic Radio Man, robot form, MIB **75.00**

Spam, product can w/white top, NM....................................**50.00**

Starforce Robot, movable arms, Hong Kong, EX **50.00**

Superman Exiting Phone Booth, AM, Vanity Fair, 1970s, EX+....**50.00**

Texaco Gas Pump, Super Unleaded, EX **45.00**

Wilson NFL Football, w/kick-off stand, 6½", MIB **60.00**

Yoohoo Chocolate, AM/FM, China, EX **45.00**

Transister Radios

Admiral, Y2452, 1963, 10 transistors, AM/FM **20.00**

Admiral Super 8, #811B, 1959, 8 transistors, AM **15.00**

Airline, #GEN-125A, 1965, 7 transistors, AM......................**18.00**

Airline, GEN-1208A Eldorado, 1962, 6 transistors, AM ..**45.00**

Arvin, #61R16, 1961, 6 transistors, AM **25.00**

Arvin, #65R29, 1965, 6 transistors, AM **10.00**

Audition, #1069, 6 transistors, AM...............................**150.00**

Bulova, #672, 1962, AM........**65.00**

Channel Master, #6251, 1960, 7 transistors, AM **30.00**

Channel Master, #6479, 14 transistors, AM/FM **18.00**

Commodore, YTR-601, 6 transistors, AM **45.00**

Emerson, #849, 1955, AM....**175.00**

Emerson Titan, #888, 8 transistors, AM **72.00**

GE, #CT455A, 1960, 6 transistors, AM **15.00**

GE, #P776A, 1960, 7 transistors, AM **15.00**

GE, #P820, 1961, AM.............**15.00**

Hit Parade, #727, 6 transistors, AM **40.00**

Hitachi, #KH-915, 1963, 9 transistors, FM **95.00**

Hitachi, #WH-761B, 1962, 7 transistors, AM/FM................**55.00**

ITT, #600, 1963, 6 transistors, AM **55.00**

Jetstream, #JK29B-63A, 14 transistors, AM........................**20.00**

Lloyd's, #TR-10K, 1965, 10 transistors, AM **10.00**

Magnavox, #AM-81, 8 transistors, AM **125.00**

Motorola, #AX4B, 1961, 6 transistors, AM **25.00**

Motorola, #X11R, 1959, 6 transistors, AM **45.00**
Motorola, #6X28B, 1959, 6 transistors, AM **85.00**
Panasonic, #T-7, 1962, 7 transistors, AM **25.00**
Panasonic Tiny Tote, #R-111, AM..**50.00**
Philco, #NT-900, 1964, 9 transistors, AM **15.00**
Philco, #T-3-130, 1959, 3 transistors, AM **80.00**
RCA, #9-BT-9J, 1957, 6 transistors, AM **100.00**
RCA Jetstream, #1-BT-41, 1957, 6 transistors, AM **35.00**
RCA Thor Deluxe, #RGG 25B, 1965, 8 transistors, AM **15.00**
Realtone, #1443-5, AM........... **15.00**
Silvertone, #1203, 1961, 6 transistors, AM **30.00**
Silvertone, #2207, 1962, 6 transistors, AM **20.00**
Sony, #TFM-96, 9 transistors, AM/FM............................. **25.00**
Sony, #TR-710Y, 7 transistors, AM **45.00**
Sylvania, #5P11R, 1960, 5 transistors, AM **45.00**
Sylvania, #7P12T, 1959, 7 transistors, AM **20.00**
Toshiba Lace, #6TR-186, 6 transistors, AM **250.00**
Toshiba Rice Bowl, #6TR-92, 6 transistors, AM **350.00**
Vista, #G-1050, 1964, 10 transistors, AM/FM **20.00**
Westinghouse, #H-695P8, 1959, 8 transistors, AM **25.00**
Westinghouse, #H-712-P9, 1960, 9 transistors, AM **20.00**
Zenith, #TR-122, 1965, 12 transistors, AM **15.00**
Zenith, Royal, #750, AM **30.00**

Ramp Walkers

Ramp walkers date back to at least 1873 when Ives produced a cast-iron elephant walker. Wood and composite ramp walkers were made in Czechoslovakia and the USA from the 1920s through the 1940s. The most common were made by John Wilson of Watsontown, Pennsylvania. These sold worldwide and became known as 'Wilson Walkies.' Most are two-legged and stand approximately 4½" tall.

Plastic ramp walkers were manufactured primarily by the Louis Marx Co. from the 1950s through the early 1960s. The majority were produced in Hong Kong, but some were made in the USA and sold under the Marx logo or by the Charmore Co., a subsidiary of Marx.

The three common sizes are 1) small premiums about 1½" x 2"; 2) the more common medium size, 2¾" x 3"; and 3) large, approximately 4" x 5". Most of the smaller walkers were unpainted, while the medium and large sizes were hand or spray painted. Several of the walking types were sold with wooden or colorful tin lithographed ramps. For more extensive listings and further information, see *Schroeder's Collectible Toys, Antique to Modern* (Collector Books).

Astro & George Jetson, Marx. **75.00**
Bird, Czechoslovakian **35.00**
Bison w/native, Marx............. **40.00**
Camel w/2 humps, head bobs, Marx **20.00**

Chicks carrying Easter egg, Marx. **35.00**
Choo-Choo Cherry, w/plastic coin weight, Funny Face drink mix, Marx **60.00**
Dairy cow, Marx **20.00**
Donald Duck, Wilson **175.00**
Donald Duck pulling nephews in wagon, Marx.................... **35.00**

Donald's Trio, Disney, France, MOC, $150.00. (Photo courtesy Randy Welch)

Dutch boy & girl, Marx.......... **40.00**
Dutch girl, Czechoslovakian.. **60.00**
Eskimo, Wilson..................... **100.00**
Figaro the Cat w/ball, Marx.. **30.00**

Firemen, $35.00. (Photo courtesy Randy Welch)

Fred & Wilma Flintstone on Dino, Marx **60.00**
Frontiersman w/dog, Marx.... **95.00**
Hap & Hop soldiers, Marx..... **25.00**
Hippo w/native, Marx............ **40.00**
Minnie Mouse pushing baby stroller, Marx **35.00**

Mother Goose, Marx **45.00**
Nurse, Wilson........................ **30.00**
Pinocchio, Wilson **200.00**
Policeman, Czechoslovakian . **60.00**
Popeye pushing spinach can wheelbarrow, Marx.................. **30.00**
Rabbit, Wilson....................... **75.00**
Sailors SS Shoreleave, Marx. **25.00**
Santa Claus, Wilson.............. **90.00**
Santa w/gold sack, Marx **45.00**
Santa w/white or yellow sack, Marx, ea..................................... **40.00**
Sylvia Dinosaur, w/plastic coin weight, Long John Silver's, Marx, 1989 .... **15.00**
Top Cat & Benny, Marx......... **65.00**
Wimpy, Wilson..................... **175.00**
Yogi Bear & Huckleberry Hound, Marx **50.00**

Records

Records that made it to the 'top ten' in their day are not always the records that are prized most highly by today's collectors, though they treasure those which best represent specific types of music: jazz, rhythm and blues, country and western, rock 'n roll, etc. Many search for those cut very early in the career of artists who later became superstars, records cut on rare or interesting labels, or those aimed at ethnic groups. A fast-growing area of related interest is picture sleeves for 45s. These are often worth more than the record itself, especially if they feature superstars from the '50s or early '60s.

Condition is very important. Record collectors tend to be very critical, so learn to watch for loss of gloss; holes, labels, or writing on the label; warping; and scratches. In the listings that follow, the first condition code describes the record; the second, its jacket. To be judged 'like new' (near-mint), records must have a surface that retains much of its original shine, with only a minimal amount of surface noise. EPs (extended play 45s) and LPs (long-playing 33⅓ rpm 'albums') must have their jackets (cardboard sleeves) in nice condition free of tape, stickers, tears, or obvious damage. *The American Premium Record Guide* by Les Docks is a great source for more information. We also recommend *The Complete Guide to Vintage Children's Records* by Peter Muldavin, published by Collector Books.

Children's Records

Adventures of Mighty Mouse, Rocking Horse, 78 rpm, 1978, EX/EX 15.00

Alice in Wonderland, Disney, © 1979 Disneyland Records #306, EX (with sleeve), $15.00.

Alice in Wonderland, Golden, 45 rpm, 1950s, EX/EX 25.00

At Home With the Munsters, 33⅓ rpm, Golden LP139, 1960s, EX/EX 50.00

Batman's Pal Robin, 45 rpm, 1966, EX/NM figural sleeve 30.00

Bongo Fun & Fancy Free, Columbia, 3-record set, 78 rpm, 1940s, VG/EX 45.00

Bunny Easter Party, Voco EB½, picture disk, die-cut, 1948, NM 30.00

Charlie Brown's All Star, 33⅓ rpm, 1978, EX/EX 15.00

Felix the Cat, 45 rpm, Cricket Records, 1958, EX/EX 20.00

Flash Gordon, 33⅓ rpm, soundtrack, 1980, EX/EX 25.00

Flipper the King of the Sea, 45 rpm, MGM, 1960s, EX/EX 20.00

Gabby Hayes 1001 Western Nights, 78 rpm, RCA, 1950s, EX/VG 35.00

Jacob's Dream, Bible Story, picture disk, 1948, NM 15.00

Jumbo's Lullaby, 45 rpm, 1950s, red, EX/EX 10.00

Mary Poppins A Disneyland Record, WD Prod, 1964, LP, w/book, EX/EX 12.00

Mickey & the Beanstalk, 78 rpm, Capitol, 1949, EX/EX, from $15 to 20.00

Old McDonald Had a Farm, Voco, picture disk, 1948, 7", EX/EX 12.00

Paddington Bear Friends, 33⅓ rpm, 1982, M/NM 20.00

Popeye the Sailor Man, 33⅓ rpm, 1960s, VG/VG 10.00

Popeye the Sailor Man, 45 rpm, Golden, 1959, EX/EX 10.00

Rover the Strong Man, Vovo, 78 rpm, 1948, NM/EX, from $30 to 40.00

Roy Rogers Had a Ranch, 45 rpm, Golden, 1950s, EX/EX **45.00**

Scooby Doo Christmas Stories, 33⅓ rpm, 1978, EX/EX **25.00**

Smokey Bear, 45 rpm, Peter Pan, NM/NM **20.00**

Spidey Super Stories, 33⅓ rpm, Peter Pan, 1977, EX/EX . **25.00**

Three Little Kittens, 45 rpm, Disneyland, 1962, EX/EX. **10.00**

Uncle Wiggily, 33⅓ rpm, 1970, EX/ EX **25.00**

Wonder Woman, Christmas Island, 45 rpm, 1978, EX/EX **25.00**

Woody Woodpecker, Golden, 33⅓ rpm, 1963, EX/NM **30.00**

LP Albums

Allman Brothers Band, At Fillmore East, Nautilus NR-30, 2 LPs, NM/NM **110.00**

Beatles, Ain't She Sweet, Atco 33-169, 1964, VG/VG+. **85.00**

Beatles, Something New, Capitol ST 2108/Apple label, NM/NM.. **22.00**

Bill Haley & His Comets; Billy Haley's Chicks, Decca DL 78821, VG+/VG **40.00**

Brady Bunch, Meet the Brady Bunch, Paramount, 1972, M, $30.00.
(Photo courtesy Greg Davis and Bill Morgan)

Cash, Johnny; Sings Hank Williams, Sun 111, M/M . **55.00**

Cathy Jean & the Roomates, Great Oldies, Valmor 78, 1962, VG+/ VG+ **175.00**

Cochran, Eddie, Never To Be Forgotten, Liberty LRP-32201, NM/EX **25.00**

Crosby Stills & Nash, Deja Vu, Mobile Fidelity 1-088, NM/ VG+ **85.00**

Dave Clark Five, Glad All Over Again, EMI 0777078924913, EX/VG+ **26.00**

Diddley, Bo; Go Bo Diddley, Checker 1436, 1957, VG+/VG+ **28.00**

Doors, The Best of..., Elektra R-270407, 1985, 2 records, VG/ VG+ **35.00**

Hendrix, Jimi; Nudes, Polydor 2310269/70, 2-record gatefold, M/M **100.00**

Holly, Buddy; Buddy Holly Story, Coral CRL 757270, VG+/NM **35.00**

Holly, Buddy; The Buddy Holly Story, Coral 37279, VG/VG **35.00**

Honeycombs, Have I the Right, Inter-phon, 1965, M (sealed) **35.00**

John, Elton; Greatest Hits, LPZ-2013, limited edition, EX/ EX **110.00**

Kinks, Face to Face, Reprise RS-6228, EX+/VG+ **40.00**

Kinks, The Kink Kontroversy, Reprise RS-6197, 1966, M/M (sealed) **110.00**

Lewis, Jerry Lee; Sun 1230, VG+/ NM **85.00**

Nelson, Ricky; Imperial 9050, M/ M **40.00**

Nitty Gritty Dirt Band, self-titled, Liberty LST-7501, NM/EX . **22.00**

Olenn, Johnny; Just Rollin', Liberty 3029, M/M **180.00**

Orbison, Roy; At the Rock House, Sun 1260, 1961, VG+/VG+ **200.00**

Partridge Family, ...Album, Bell 6050, NM/NM.................. **25.00**

Perkins, Carl; Country Boy's Dream, Dollie, 1960s, M/M (sealed) **22.00**

Righteous Bros, You've Lost That Lovin' Feelin', Philles 4007, M/NM **28.00**

Ronettes, Presenting the Fabulous..., Phillies ST-90721, Stereo, VG/VG **200.00**

Shangri-Las, I Can Never Go..., Red Bird 20-104, NM/EX alternate cover **100.00**

Smashing Pumpkins, Mellon Collie..., limited edition, 1991, M/M............................... **175.00**

Steely Dan, Can't Buy a Thrill, ABC ABCX 758, 1972, promo copy, M/M **100.00**

Strawberry Alarm Clock, Incense & Peppermints, Uni 3014, 1967, NM/NM.......................... **100.00**

Toad, Tomorrow Blue, Hallelujah 19047, EX/EX gatefold cover/insert............................. **195.00**

Twitty, Conway; Saturday Night, MGM E3786, NM/EX...... **40.00**

Yardbirds, self-titled, Columbia SC6063, VG+/EX............. **30.00**

Young, Neil; Harvest, Nautilus NR 44, NM/NM.................... **170.00**

Anka, Paul; I Miss You So/Late Last Night, ABC 10011, signed, EX/EX **25.00**

Beach Boys, Kiss Me Baby/Help Me Rhonda, Capitol 5395, signed, VG/VG............................. **55.00**

Beatles, I Want To Hold Your Hand, Capitol 5112, NM/NM..... **90.00**

Beatles, Love Me Do/PS I Love You, Capitol, red vinyl, M....... **38.00**

Beatles, She Loves You, Swan S-4152, 1964, EX/EX.......... **48.00**

Boone, Pat; Sings the Sounds of Christmas, Vista, signed, EX/EX **45.00**

Brothers Four, Greenfields, Columbia 41571, 1960, VG/VG.......... **42.00**

Cash, Johnny; Folsom Prison Blues, Sun 232, VG **80.00**

DC Rand & the Jokers, Shake It Up, Candy C-003, 1959, VG+.. **32.00**

Deep Purple, Kentucky Woman, T-1508, VG/VG+ **30.00**

Diamonds, Honey Bird, w/3 others, Mercury EP-1-3357, EX/EX.**50.00**

Donovan, Riki Tiki Tavi, Epic 10649, 1970, picture sleeve only, EX **48.00**

Elvis, Christmas With Elvis, RCA EP 4340, 1965, VG+/VG+. **55.00**

Elvis, Do the Clam, RCA 47-8500, EX+/EX............................ **30.00**

Elvis, Good Rockin' Tonight, Sun Records 210, 1954, VG.. **260.00**

Elvis, I Forgot To Remember To Forget, RCA 47-6357, VG/G ...**100.00**

Elvis, Treat Me Nice/Jailhouse Rock, RCA 47-7035, EX/EX **28.00**

Facenda, Tommy; High School USA, Atlantic A-022, 1959, VG+..**33.00**

Flamingos, Golden Teardrops, Chance 1145, VG............. **45.00**

James, Elmore; Late Hours at Midnight, Flair 1062, VG+ ...**130.00**

Jan & Dean, Heart & Soul, Challenge 9111, 1961, EX.................. **22.00**

Lee, Brenda; Break It to Me Gently, Decca 3134, signed, EX/EX............................ **48.00**

Lewis, Jerry Lee; Good Golly Miss Molly, Sun 382, unused, M/M...............................**26.00**

Lewis, Jerry Lee; Lovin' Up a Storm, Sun, unused, M/M **28.00**

Martin, Janis; My Boy Elvis/ Little Bit, RCA 47-6652, 1950s, VG.....................**12.00**

Mellow Fellows, My Baby Needs Me, Dot 17135, NM..........**45.00**

Nelson, Ricky; I'm Walkin' Verve 10047, 1957, orange label, VG+.................................**22.00**

Paul Revere & the Raiders, Good Thing, Columbia 43907, 1966, VG+/VG+ **42.00**

Paul Revere & the Raiders, Ups & Downs, Columbia 44018, VG+/ M......................................**40.00**

Perkins, Carl; Blue Suede Shoes/ Honey Don't, Sun, VG **25.00**

Perkins, Carl; Glad All Over, Sun 287, M/M **22.00**

Rolling Stones, Paint It Black/ Stupid Girl, London 45 LON 901, EX/EX.......................**30.00**

Smith, Helene; Sure Thing, Deep City Records 2380 B, 1960s, NM...................................**28.00**

Valens, Richie; La Bamba/Donna, Del-Fi 4110, VG+ **32.00**

Williams, Jerry; Yvonne, Calla #116, M..........................**100.00**

Young, Neil; Down By the River, Reprise 0836, promo, VG.**25.00**

78 rpms

Arkansas Charlie, Texas Trail, Vocalion 5292 ....**15.00**

Arkansas Trio, Boll Weevil Blues, Edison 51373, EX/EX.....**10.00**

Astaire, Fred; Cheek to Cheek, Brunswick 7486, EX/EX.**10.00**

Baker, Buddy; Box Car Blues, Victor 40017, EX/EX.......**65.00**

Big Aces, Cherry, Okeh 41136, EX/ EX....................................**20.00**

Borton, Godfrey; Two Little Orphans, Bell 1187, EX/EX................**8.00**

Candy & Coco, China Boy, Vocalion 2849, EX/EX....................**30.00**

Carter, Floyd; Flemington Kidnap Trail Oriole 8847, EX/EX.**10.00**

Clarke & Howell, Birmingham Jail, Supertone 9536, EX/EX..**15.00**

Dells, Time Makes You Change, Vee-Jay 258, EX/EX........**30.00**

Duncan Sisters, Dusty Roads, Columbia 15745-D, EX/EX.**10.00**

Erby, Jack; Hey Peter, Columbia 14570-D, EX/EX..............**45.00**

Greene, Amos; Just a Lonely Hobo, Supertone 9709, EX/ EX...................................**15.00**

Grey, Wallace; Little Mamie, Champion 15832, EX/EX.**20.00**

Harmonians, Say It Again, Harmony 127-H, NM/NM **10.00**

Hudson, Hattie; Black Hand Blues, Columbia 14279-D, EX/EX.**50.00**

Jungle Kings, Friars Point Shuffle, Paramount 12654, EX/EX.**300.00**

Lymon, Frankie; I Want You To Be My Girl, GG-1-12, EX/EX.**28.00**

Maxwell, Claude; Bad Woman Blues, Sterling 3006, EX/EX..........**8.00**

Mercer, Johnny; The Tub Ran Over Again, Decca 142, EX/EX.**15.00**

Mills Brothers, Diga Diga Doo, Brunswick 6519, EX/EX.**15.00**

Mississippi Mudder, Meat Cutter Blues, Decca 7009, EX/EX.**42.00**

Pickett, Dan; Lemon Man, Gotham 201, EX/EX **20.00**

Radiolites, Sweet Loraine, Columbia 1432-D, NM/NM **10.00**

Riffers, Rhapsody in Love, Columbia 14677-D, EX/EX **40.00**

Smith, Bessie; Album (6-record), Columbia, 1937, M/G **130.00**

Stone, Jimmy; Midnight Boogie, Imperial 8137, EX/EX **8.00**

Tempo Kings, Rhythm of the Day, Perfect 14566, EX/EX **12.00**

Tennessee Drifters, Mean Ole Boogie, Dot 1002, EX/EX . **10.00**

Washboard Rhythm Band, Going Going Gone, Columbia 1480-D, EX/EX **75.00**

Red Glass

Ever popular with collectors, red glass has been used to create decorative items such as one might find in gift shops, utilitarian bottles and kitchenware, figurines and dinnerware lines such as were popular during the Depression era. For further information and study, we recommend *Ruby Glass of the 20th Century* by Naomi Over (Collector Books).

Ashtray, bowl shape w/scrolled end, gold decor, Venetian **10.00**

Ashtray, clown standing, Venetian, 1998, 4" **25.00**

Baby bootie, Daisy & Button, Summit, 1980, 4¼" **15.00**

Basket, bird-of-paradise pattern, LE Smith, 1980, 13½" **40.00**

Basket, Hobnail, ruffled rim, low foot, American Glass, 1990s, 7½" **20.00**

Bell, Victorian girl, Imperial, 1980s, 4" **95.00**

Bowl, ruffled rim, Blenko, 9½" **25.00**

Box, heart shape, bird in flight on lid, Mosser, 1980, 3" **8.00**

Cake plate, water lilies silver overlay, Cambridge, 14½" **95.00**

Candy dish, Eyewinker, pedestal foot, LG Wright, 1960s, 6" **35.00**

Candy dish, leaf form, Blenko, 1970s-80s, 6¾" **10.00**

Cookie cutter, star shape, Taiwan, 2½" **6.00**

Figurine, whale, solid, Rainbow Glass, ca 1980, 3½" **12.00**

Gravy pitcher, dolphin form w/dolphin finial, 2-pc, ca 1991 . **25.00**

Jack-in-the-pulpit vase, Italian, 13", from $40.00 to $45.00. (Photo courtesy Naomi Over)

Open salt, tulip form, Summit, 1980, 1" **6.00**

Open salt, wheelbarrow form, Summit Art Glass, 3½" W. **35.00**

Pitcher, cherry blossoms, AA Imports, 1980s, 6½" **25.00**

Plate, pineapple pattern w/floral decor, Indiana Glass, 1970, 8" **15.00**

Salt & pepper shakers, metal caps, Viking Glass, 1980s, 3½", pr.**20.00**

Tumbler, Georgian, handmade, Imperial Glass, 1930, 9-oz..**10.00**

Tumbler, Swirl, Cambridge, 1949-
53, 12-oz............................ **35.00**
Vase, twisted stem, Blenko, 1980,
13½" **20.00**

Red Wing

Taking their name from the
location in Minnesota where they
located in the late 1870s, the Red
Wing Company produced a variety
of wares, all of which are today
considered noteworthy by pottery
and dinnerware collectors. Their
early stoneware lines, Cherry Band
and Sponge Band (Gray Line),
are especially valuable and often
fetch prices of several hundred dollars per piece on today's market.
Production of dinnerware began
in the '30s and continued until the
pottery closed in 1967. Some of
their more popular lines — all of
which were hand painted — were
Bob White, Lexington, Tampico,
Normandie, Capistrano, and
Random Harvest. Commercial artware was also produced. Perhaps
the ware most easily associated
with Red Wing is their Brushware
line, unique in its appearance and
decoration. Cattails, rushes, florals, and similar nature subjects
are 'carved' in relief on a stone-
ware-type body with a matt green
wash its only finish. To learn about
Red Wing's stoneware production,
refer to *Red Wing Stoneware, An
Identification and Value Guide,* and
Red Wing Collectibles, both by Dan
DePasquale, Gail Peck, and Larry
Peterson. Both are published by
Collector Books.

Art Ware

Bowl, brown w/orange interior, flat,
#00414, 7"........................ **40.00**
Bowl, gray, rectangular, #5015,
1950s, 9", from $30 to..... **38.00**
Bowl, green w/brown trim, #937,
1950s, 10", from $40 to... **52.00**
Bowl, hyacinth, elongated, #64,
1960s, 14" L, from $34 to. **40.00**
Bowl, Nile Blue fleck, shell form,
#M1567, 1950s, 9", from $44
to **56.00**
Candleholders, green fleck
w/embossed ivy, #B2505,
1960s, 5", from $42 to. **54.00**
Candleholders, ivory, petal shaped,
#B1411, 1950s, 4", from $24
to **30.00**
Compote, green, pedestal foot,
#5011, 1950s, 4½x6¾", from
$30 to.............................. **36.00**
Figurine, Oriental lady, yellow,
#1308, 1950s, 10", from $100
to **130.00**
Jardiniere, scalloped, brass han-
dles, #M1610, 1960s, 10", from
$52 to.............................. **68.00**
Planter, deer form, turquoise,
#1338, 5½" **35.00**
Planter, green, embossed grid, #1616,
1950s, 7½", from $34 to..... **40.00**
Vase, bamboo on white w/green
interior, #1400, 1960s, 8", from
$36 to.............................. **46.00**
Vase, cornucopia, ivory w/embossed ivy,
#1097, 5¾", from $38 to.........**46.00**
Vase, crackled blue w/gunmetal
interior, #1301, 1950s, 5", from
$48 to.............................. **60.00**
Vase, ivory w/brass handles,
#M1609, 1950s, 10", from $46
to **60.00**

Vase, ivory w/green interior, fan form, #982, 1950s-60s, 7", from $36 to **48.00**

Vase, orchid fleck, fluted top, w/handles, #505, 1950s-60s, from $42 to **58.00**

Vase, salmon, petal shape, #1625, 1950s, 10", from $44 to...**56.00**

Vase, semi-matt green with ivory interior, 7½", from $32.00 to $42.00.
(Photo courtesy Brenda Dollen)

Vase, yellow w/brown leaves, #1204, 10", from $48 to...............**65.00**

Wall pocket, Magnolia, orange w/brown wash, #1630, 7".....................**125.00**

Dinnerware

Blossom Time, bowl, vegetable; divided, from $25 to........**30.00**

Blossom Time, butter dish, from $25 to..............................**30.00**

Blossom Time, coffee cup, from $32 to **37.00**

Blossom Time, teapot, from $65 to...................................**70.00**

Bob White, bowl, rimmed soup; from $25 to **30.00**

Bob White, butter warmer, w/lid, from $75 to **85.00**

Bob White, cruets, pr from $125 to................................ **135.00**

Bob White, lazy Susan, w/stand, tray & sauce bowls, from $225 to **250.00**

Bob White, plate, 6½", from $8 to...............................**10.00**

Bob White, platter, 13", from $50 to **60.00**

Bob White, teapot, from $85 to..**95.00**

Britanny, salt & pepper shakers, pr from $25 to **35.00**

Brittany, chop plate, from $60 to **70.00**

Brittany, creamer, from $35 to. **40.00**

Capistrano, bread tray, from $35 to **40.00**

Capistrano, buffet bowl, from $35 to **40.00**

Capistrano, plate, 10", from $18 to................................. **20.00**

Capistrano, salt & pepper shakers, from $20 to **25.00**

Lexington, bowl, rimmed soup; from $20 to **25.00**

Lexington, casserole, w/lid, from $30 to **35.00**

Lexington, plate, 10½", from $12 to **15.00**

Lotus, butter dish, from $20 to..**25.00**

Lotus, chop plate, from $35 to. **40.00**

Lotus, coffee cup, from $35 to. **40.00**

Lotus, gravy boat w/tray, from $20 to **25.00**

Lotus, pitcher, water; from $45 to....................................**55.00**

Lotus, relish, from $18 to......**20.00**

Lute Song, bowl, vegetable; from $22 to **27.00**

Lute Song, casserole, w/lid, from $35 to **40.00**

Lute Song, platter, lg, from $25 to...................................**30.00**

Lute Song, sugar bowl, w/lid, from $10 to **15.00**

Normandy, cup and saucer, from $15.00 to $18.00.

Orleans, bowl, coupe soup; from $20 to **25.00**

Orleans, gravy boat, from $75 to . **90.00**

Orleans, teacup & saucer, from $22 to **24.00**

Orleans, teapot, from $100 to .. **115.00**

Pepe, bean pot, w/lid, 1½-qt, from $30 to **35.00**

Pepe, cup & saucer, demitasse; from $15 to **20.00**

Pepe, plate, 7", from $10 to ... **12.00**

Pepe, relish dish, divided, from $20 to **25.00**

Picardy, beverage server, w/lid, from $60 to **70.00**

Picardy, bowl, salad; sm, from $20 to **25.00**

Picardy, creamer & sugar bowl, w/lid, from $35 to **40.00**

Picardy, cup & saucer **16.00**

Round-Up, bowl, rimmed soup; from $40 to **45.00**

Round-Up, bowl, salad; 12", from $100 to **125.00**

Round-Up, butter dish, from $65 to **75.00**

Round-Up, plate, 10½", from $50 to **60.00**

Round-Up, tray, cocktail; from $60 to **70.00**

Smart Set, bowl, vegetable; divided, from $40 to **45.00**

Smart Set, casserole, 4-qt, from $80 to **90.00**

Smart Set, cup & saucer, from $25 to **30.00**

Smart Set, platter, 13", from $70 to **80.00**

Smart Set, salt & pepper shakers, pr from $45 to **55.00**

Tampico, butter dish, from $35 to **40.00**

Tampico, mug, coffee; from $25 to **30.00**

Tampico, plate, 8½" **15.00**

Tampico, relish dish **25.00**

Tampico, teapot, from $90 to . **100.00**

Town & Country, baker, 11x7½", from $40 to **50.00**

Town & Country, bowl, cereal; 6", from $20 to **25.00**

Town & Country, mug, from $50 to **55.00**

Town & Country, plate, 12", from $30 to **40.00**

Town & Country, salt & pepper shakers, pr from $70 to .. **80.00**

Town & Country, soup ladle, from $175 to **200.00**

Restaurant China

Restaurant China is specifically designed for use in commercial food service. Not limited to restaurants, this dinnerware is used on planes, ships, and trains as well as hotel, railroad, and airport dining rooms. Churches, clubs, department and drug stores also put it to good use.

Good quality American-made heavy gauge vitrified china with traditional styling is very popular today. Some collectors look for transportation system top-marked pieces, others may prefer those with military logos, etc. It is currently considered fashionable to serve home-cooked meals on mismatched top-marked hotel ware, adding a touch of nostalgia and remembrances of elegant times past. For a more thorough study of the subject, we recommend *Restaurant China, Identification & Value Guide for Restaurant, Airline, Ship & Railroad Dinnerware, Volume 1* and *Volume 2,* by Barbara Conroy (Collector Books). She is listed in the Directory under California.

Cream pitcher, Canadian Pacific's Empress Hotel (Victoria, B. C.), 'Empress Hotel' pattern, Steelite bottom stamp, Ridgway, mid-1970s, from $15.00 to $20.00. (Photo courtesy Barbara Conroy)

Ashtray, Dudson, Binn's Limited, black logo & red line, 1968.**15.00**

Ashtray, Schonwald, Royal Caribbian Cruise Line, triangular, 1970s **10.00**

Ashtray, Wallace, Olympic Hotel, green logo on white, 1950s.**12.50**

Bowl, Homer Laughlin, Howard Johnson, Pie Man logo, 1960s-70s, 6" **12.00**

Bowl, Mayer, Metropolitan Life Ins, white w/blue logo, 2⅜x5⅜"..**12.00**

Bowl, Wallace, Grand Canyon Cafe, brown on tan, 1950s, 4".. **25.00**

Bowl, Wallace, plain white oval, 1930s, 8x10x2" **6.50**

Butter pat, unmarked, West Point, blue on white, 1930s, 3" . **25.00**

Cream pitcher, Jackson, Hawaii Kai, logo on white, 1970s, 3".... **15.00**

Cream pitcher, Jackson, Holiday Inn, H-I sign logo, 1960s, 3" **35.00**

Cream pitcher, Shenango, Mobil Oil, Pegasus logo, 1966, 3" **38.00**

Cream pitcher, Syracuse, American Legion Aux, blue logo, 1938, 9-oz...................................... **25.00**

Cup, Buffalo, Iowa Machine Shed logo on white, 3½" **6.50**

Cup, Hall, Hobo Joe, footed, #1272 backstamp, 1960s, 8-oz... **25.00**

Cup, Syracuse, brown airbrushed bear scene on tan, Econo-Rim, 1940 .... **35.00**

Cup, Syracuse, Sears Restaurants, green & brown on white, 1973 .... **15.00**

Cup, Syracuse, YMCA, gray logo on inside rim, 1950s, 4½"..... **25.00**

Cup, unmarked, Arizona Country Cafe/Shell logo, green on white, 4"...................................... **6.50**

Cup, unmarked, Sirloin Stockade, red logo on tan, 1980s, 3½". **8.00**

Cup, Wallace, Acey Ducey Club (US Navy), white w/blue top mark............................... **12.00**

Cup & saucer, demi; Jackson, Diamond Horseshoe Club, red logo, 1952........................ **45.00**

Cup & saucer, demi; Shenango, Howard Johnson, Pie Man logo, 1960s **25.00**

Cup & saucer, Syracuse, Purdue University, gold/black on white, 1960s **32.00**

Egg cup, double; McNicol, black & brown 'X' design on tan, 1940s-50s **20.00**

Plate, Canadian Pacific Railway 'Brown Maple Leaf' pattern, not railroad backstamped, 9", from $40.00 to $50.00. (Photo courtesy Barbara Conroy)

Plate, grill; Syracuse, Walgreen, brown & tan, 3-part, 1930s, 9½" **25.00**

Plate, Maddock Ultra, Chandris Lines, blue topmark, 9" .. **18.00**

Plate, Pyrex, MMG logo in gold on white, 5½" **5.00**

Plate, Shenango, Copper Penny, brown on ivory, 1960s-70s, 7" **16.00**

Plate, Shenango, Steak 'n Shake, black logo on white, 1970, 6½" **15.00**

Plate, Sterling, General Motors, black logo & stripe, 1968, 9" **55.00**

Plate, Tepco, The Cactus, siesta/cactus/name logo, 1960s, 8¼" . **20.00**

Plate, Walker, band of gray roses on white, 1950s, 9" **8.00**

Plate, Wallace, Denny's, donut crest, yellow rim, 1940s, 10½" .. **45.00**

Plate, Wallace, Grand Canyon Cafe, brown on tan, 1950s, 9¾". **75.00**

Plate, Wellsville, Del Webb's TownHouse, red on white, 1959, 7 " **12.00**

Platter, Mayer, Howard Johnson, 'Historical' in red, 1950s, 9½".**35.00**

Platter, Syracuse, Shriners, green & gold logo & bands, 1920s, 10" **15.00**

Platter, Wallace China, Bonanza, maroon logo on tan, 12¼".**35.00**

Relish tray, Iroquois, brown cowboy, horse & 3 lines on white, 12x6" **20.00**

Sauceboat, McNicol, US Army Medical Dept, white w/red logo **20.00**

Sauceboat, Shenango, Astroworld, mustard on white, 1970s, 6".........**25.00**

Sugar bowl, Shenango, Hilton Hotel, plain (no crest), 1950s-60s, 4" **20.00**

Sugar bowl, Shenango, Shamrock Hotel, green bands on white, 1950...**55.00**

Rock 'n Roll

Concert posters, tour books, magazines, sheet music, and other items featuring rock 'n roll stars from the '50s up to the present are today being sought out by collectors who appreciate this type of music and like having these mementos of their favorite performers around to enjoy. See also Elvis Presley; Records.

ABBA, annual, 1978, NM **25.00**

Aerosmith, guitar pick, blue on pearl, Joe Perry faux signature, 2001 .... **20.00**

Aerosmith, program, 1976 tour, 20 pgs, EX **30.00**

Alice Cooper, tour program, Mad House, 1978, EX.............. **35.00**

Beach Boys, tour book, 15 Big Ones, 1976, EX **25.00**

Beatles, dolls, w/metal stands, Applause, 1988, 22", set of 4, M **450.00**

Beatles, fan club booklet, black & white cover photo, 20-pg, 1970, EX .**30.00**

Beatles, magazine, Official Yellow Submarine, 49-pg, VG **45.00**

Beatles, paperweight, Official Beatles Fan Club, multicolor, 1970s, NM **35.00**

Beatles, three-ring binder, blue vinyl, 1960s, EX, $25.00.

Beatles, throw blanket, Sgt Pepper, 1990s, 53x65", M............. **35.00**

Bee Gees, puzzle set, On Stage, M (sealed) **24.00**

Bobby Vinton, poster, Surf Party, 1-sheet, 1964, NM.......... **70.00**

Buddy Holly, book, The Legend That Is Buddy Holly, 1990, VG . **20.00**

Chubby Checker, postcard, glossy black & white photo, 1960s, unused, M........................ **20.00**

David Cassidy, Colorforms, Partridge Family, 1972, NM (EX box). **80.00**

David Cassidy, photo badge, 1970s, 3", M (sealed) **24.00**

Everly Brothers, tour book, 1985, NM **25.00**

Hall & Oates, concert poster, 1976, 22x14", NM+ **50.00**

KISS, belt buckle, logo on brass, 1970s................................ **28.00**

KISS Colorforms, 1979, complete in excellent box, $85.00. (Photo courtesy June Moon)

KISS, pass, Revenge, laminated, 1992 .... **15.00**

KISS, pin, Gene Simmons face w/lg K overhead, from Hard Rock Cafe, MIP **50.00**

KISS, poster, group on Harleys, KISS logo upper left, 1979, 21x30", NM...................... **35.00**

Marie Osmond, Hair Care Set, Gordy, 1976, MOC........... **25.00**

Michael Jackson, phonograph, Sing Along..., Vanity Fair, MIB. **80.00**

Monkees, puzzle, Fairchild, 340 pcs, 1967, NMIB **60.00**

Ricky Nelson, Picture Patch, 1950s, MOC................................ **20.00**

Rolling Stones, concert ticket, New York, 1972, unused **165.00**

Rolling Stones, poster, Altamont, 22x14", M........................ **15.00**

Rolling Stones, rub-off transfers, 27 lip logos, unopened **5.00**

Rolling Stones, tour book, 1972 .**22.50**
Steve Miller Band, wall mirror, silk-screened logo, 1970s, 12x12", NM...................... **30.00**
Three Dog Night, poster, 1970s, 22x14", EX...................... **30.00**
Traveling Wilburys, poster, Vol 3, 23x35", NM...................... **25.00**

Rooster and Roses

Rooster and Roses is a quaint and provincial line of dinnerware made in Japan from the '40s and '50s. The rooster has a yellow breast with black crosshatching, a brown head, and a red crest and waddle. There are full-blown roses, and the borders are yellow with groups of brown diagonals. Several companies seem to have made the line, which is very extensive — more than 75 shapes are known. For a complete listing of the line, see *Garage Sale & Flea Market Annual* (Collector Books).

Ashtray, round or sq, sm, from $15 to....................... **25.00**
Basket, flared sides, 6", from $45 to....................... **65.00**
Bell, from $55 to...................... **95.00**
Bonbon dish, pedestal base, minimum value...................... **55.00**
Bowl, cereal; from $14 to....... **25.00**
Bowl, rice; on saucer, from $25 to **35.00**
Box, round, w/lid, from $25 to . **35.00**
Butter dish, ¼-lb, from $20 to.. **25.00**
Candy dish, w/3-D leaf handle, from $25 to...................... **24.00**
Canister, cylindrical, wooden lid, 7x5", from $160 to......... **195.00**

Canister, round, 4-pc, from $150 to **175.00**
Canister, sq, 4-pc, from $100 to. **150.00**
Canister set, stacking, rare, minimum value.................... **150.00**
Carafe, no handle, w/stopper lid, 8", from $65 to **85.00**
Carafe, w/handle & stopper lid, 8", from $85 to.................... **125.00**
Casserole dish, w/lid, from $65 to **85.00**
Cheese dish, slanted lid, from $40 to **55.00**
Coffee grinder, rare, minimum value **150.00**
Cookie jar, ceramic handles, from $85 to............................. **100.00**
Creamer & sugar bowl, w/lid, lg, from $25 to...................... **45.00**
Cruets, bottle shape w/bulbous bottom, lg handle, pr.......... **145.00**
Cruets, oil & vinegar, sq, lg, pr from $30 to............................. **45.00**
Cup & saucer......................... **25.00**
Egg cup, from $20 to.............. **25.00**
Instant-coffee jar, spoon-holder tube on side, rare............ **45.00**
Jam & jelly containers, cojoined, w/lids & spoons, from $35 to.......... **45.00**
Ketchup or mustard jar, flared cylinder, from $25 to............ **30.00**
Match holder, wall-mount, from $65 to **85.00**
Measuring cup set, 4-pc w/matching ceramic rack, from $45 to **65.00**
Napkin holder, from $30 to ... **40.00**
Pipe holder/ashtray, from $30 to. **50.00**
Pitcher, bulbous, 5", from $25 to. **30.00**
Planter, rolling pin shape, rare, minimum value............... **50.00**
Plate, bread; from $15 to....... **35.00**
Plate, dinner; from $25 to **35.00**

Platter, 12", from $55 to **60.00**

Relish tray, 2 round wells w/center handle, 12", from $35 to . **40.00**

Rolling pin, minimum value.. **50.00**

Salad fork & spoon, wood handles, ceramic wall rack, minimum, value **55.00**

Salt & pepper shakers, w/applied rose, sq, pr **23.00**

Salt & pepper shakers, 4", pr from $15 to **20.00**

Salt box, wooden lid **60.00**

Snack tray w/cup, oval, 2-pc, minimum value **65.00**

Tea set, stacking, $125.00. (Photo courtesy Jacki Elliott)

Toast holder, rare, minimum value **75.00**

Wall hanger, teapot shape, pr . **90.00**

Wall pocket, lavabo, 2-pc mounted on board, from $75 to ... **125.00**

Watering can, from $45 to **65.00**

Roselane Sparklers

A line of small figures with a soft shaded finish and luminous jewel eyes was produced during the late 1950s by the Roselane Pottery Company who operated in Pasadena, California, from the late 1930s until possibly the 1970s. The line was a huge success. Twenty-nine different models were made, including elephants, burros, raccoons, fawns, dogs, cats, and fish. Not all pieces are marked, but some carry an incised 'Roselane Pasadena, Calif.,' or 'Calif. U.S.A'; others may have a paper label.

Angelfish, 4½", from $40 to.... **25.00**

Basset hound pup, 2" **15.00**

Basset hound puppies (2), 1 sitting/1 recumbent, marked #98/#99, pr **50.00**

Basset hound sitting, 4" **15.00**

Bulldog looking up, jeweled collar, 3½" **22.00**

Bulldog puppy seated, blue eyes, 1¾" **12.00**

Cat holding babies, 5", from $40 to **45.00**

Cat lying down, head turned, tail & paws tucked under body, from $20 to **25.00**

Cat sitting, head turned, tail out behind **25.00**

Cat standing w/tail over back, jeweled collar, 5½", from $25 to **30.00**

Chihuahua sitting, looking straight ahead, paw raised, 7" **28.00**

Cocker spaniel, 4½", from $15 to.. **20.00**

Deer standing, head turned, 5½" . **25.00**

Deer standing, w/antlers, jeweled collar, 4½", from $22 to ... **28.00**

Elephant in stride trumpeting, jeweled headpiece, 6", from $35 to **40.00**

Elephant sitting on hind quarters, 6", from $35 to **40.00**

Fawn, legs folded under body, 4x3½" **25.00**

Fawn, upturned head, 4x3½" . **20.00**

Kangaroo mama holding babies, 4½", from $40 to **45.00**

Owl, very stylized, teardrop-shaped body w/lg round eyes, lg . **25.00**

Owl, 5¼".................................. **25.00**

Owl (baby), 2½", from $12 to . **15.00**

Pheasants (2) looking back, pink & blue, 3¾" & 5", pr from $30 to **35.00**

Pig, lg...................................... **25.00**

Raccoon standing, 4½", from $20 to..................................... **25.00**

Road Runner, 8½" L, from $30 to.**45.00**

Siamese cat, either style, from $22.00 to $25.00.

Siamese cat lying down, head resting on paw, jeweled collar, 5½" L.. **45.00**

Siamese cat sitting looking ahead, jeweled collar, 7", from $40 to.................................... **50.00**

Siamese mother cat & 2 babies, blue eyes, 9½" & 3¾"....... **75.00**

Squirrel eating a nut, lg bushy tail, blue & brown highlights, 4"..........**30.00**

Whippet sitting, 7½".......... **28.00**

Rosemeade

Novelty items made by the Wapheton Pottery Company of North Dakota from 1941 to 1960 are beginning to attract collectors of American pottery. Though smaller items (salt and pepper shakers, figurines, trays, etc.) are readily found, the larger examples are scarce and can be very expensive. The name of the novelty ware, 'Rosemeade,' is indicated on the paper labels (many of which are still intact) or by the ink stamp.

Figurine, circus horse (solid), 4¼x4¼", $350.00. (Photo courtesy Darlene Hurst Dommel)

Ashtray, pheasant on side, Corn Palace/Mitchell SD, 5"..**200.00**

Ashtray, tepee in bottom, 2 rests, Chihinkapa, 5½", from $150 to **200.00**

Ashtray, w/squatting mallard figure, 7", from $450 to.....**500.00**

Bank, black bear, 3¼x5¾", minimum value.................... **400.00**

Bank, fish, green or wine, 3x4½", from $300 to **350.00**

Bell, flower & leaf form, 3¾", from $125 to **150.00**

Candy dish, shell form, white & ice blue, 2¾x4½"..................... **50.00**

Cigarette box, horse embossed on lid, 2¼x4½", from $250 to......**300.00**

Cotton dispenser, rabbit, 4¾x2½", from $100 to **200.00**

Creamer & sugar bowl, cock pheasant, 9¼x14", from $250 to.**400.00**

Creamer & sugar bowl, twisted handles, from $200 to ... **225.00**

Figurine, cock pheasant, 9¼x14", from $250 to **400.00**

Figurine, cowboy boot, brown, 2x1¾", from $50 to **75.00**

Figurine, dolphin w/tail up, 2½", from $75 to **100.00**

Figurine, potato, 1½x2½", from $100 to **125.00**

Figurines, cocks fighting, 4¾x6" & 5¼x6½", pr from $150 to . **200.00**

Hors d'oeurves, cock strutting, 3¾x2¾", from $100 to **125.00**

Hors d'oeuvres, turkey, 6x6½", from $150 to **200.00**

Jam jar, barrel form w/strawberry finial, 5" **150.00**

Planter, lamb on knees, 6x6½", from $300 to **350.00**

Planter, wooden shoes, 2¾x4¾", from $45 to **65.00**

Plaque, Minnesota Centennial, 4½x3¾", from $75 to **100.00**

Plate, leaves embossed, 4½", minimum value..................... **200.00**

Salt & pepper shakers, badger, 1x2¾", pr, minimum value........... **600.00**

Salt & pepper shakers, cow & bull, 1¾", pr from $150 to **200.00**

Salt & pepper shakers, duckings, black, 2¼ & 2½", pr....... **100.00**

Salt & pepper shakers, flamingos on nests, 3" & 3¾", pr. **200.00**

Salt & pepper shakers, mallard ducks, 1x1¾", pr from $150 to **175.00**

Salt & pepper shakers, puppies begging, 3", pr from $75 to **85.00**

Salt & pepper shakers, swan, 2", pr from $75 to **100.00**

Salt & pepper shakers, wheat shock, 3¾", pr from $125 to **150.00**

Spoon rest, Prairie Rose, 4¼" dia, from $75 to **100.00**

Spoon rest, tulip, many colors, 5", ea from $80 to **100.00**

Tea bell, tulip, 3¾", from $125 to **150.00**

Wall pocket, dove, 4½x6¼", from $125 to **150.00**

Wall pocket, maid in crescent moon, 6½", minimum value..... **500.00**

Spoon holder, prickly pear with flower, 5½", $65.00. (Photo courtesy Darlene Hurst Dommel)

Roseville Pottery

This company took its name from the city in Ohio where they operated for a few years before moving to Zanesville in the late 1890s. The're recognized as one of the giants in the industry, having produced many lines in art pottery from the beginning to the end of their production. Even when machinery took over many of the procedures once carefully done by hand, the pottery they produced continued the fine artistry and standards of quality the company had always insisted upon.

Several marks were used along with paper labels. The very early art lines often carried an applied ceramic seal with the name of the line under a circle containing the words Rozane Ware. From 1910 until 1928 an Rv mark was used. Paper labels were common from 1914 until 1937. From 1932 until closure in 1952, the mark was Roseville in script or R USA, Pieces marked RRP Co Roseville, Ohio, were not made by Roseville Pottery but by Robinson Ransbottom of Roseville, Ohio. Don't be confused. There are many jardinieres and pedestals in a brown and green blended glaze that are being sold at flea markets and antique malls as Roseville that were actually made by Robinson Ransbottom as late as the 1970s and 1980s. That isn't to say they don't have some worth of their own, but don't buy them for old Roseville.

If you'd like to learn more about the subject, we recommend *The Collector's Encyclopedia of Roseville Pottery, Vols. 1* and 2, by Sharon and Bob Huxford and Mike Nickel. Mr. Nickel is listed in the Directory under Michigan.

Note: Watch for reproductions! They've flooded the market! Be especially wary at flea markets and auctions. These pieces are usually marked only Roseville (no USA), though there are exceptions. These have a 'paint by number' style of decoration with little if any attempt at blending. See Clubs and Newsletters for information concerning *Rosevilles of the Past* newsletter.

Apple Blossom, basket, #309, green or pink, 8", from $275 to. **325.00**

Apple Blossom, bud vase, #379, blue, 7", from $175 to ... **200.00**

Apple Blossom, window box, #368-8, green or pink, 11", from $175 to **200.00**

Baneda, candleholders, #1087, pink, 5½", pr from $500 to....... **550.00**

Baneda, center bowl, #233, pink, 3½x10", from $375 to **425.00**

Baneda, vase, #588, green, 6", from $600 to **650.00**

Baneda, vase, #610, 7", from $550 to **600.00**

Bittersweet, basket, #810, 10", from $250 to **300.00**

Bittersweet, cornucopia, #822, 8", from $125 to **150.00**

Blackberry, center bowl, #228, 13", from $700 to **750.00**

Blackberry, jardiniere, 7", from $650 to **750.00**

Bleeding Heart, plate, #381-10, green or pink, 10½", from $150 to **175.00**

Bleeding Heart, vase, #138, blue, 4", from $125 to............. **150.00**

Bushberry, bud vase, #152-7", blue, 7½", from $150 to **175.00**

Bushberry, double cornucopia, #155-8, 6", from $200 to **225.00**

Bushberry, pitcher, #1325, orange, 8½", from $375.00 to $425.00. (Photo courtesy David Rago Auctions)

Bushberry, vase, #29, blue, 6", from $150 to **175.00**

Cameo, double bud vase, gate type, 4x7½", from $350 to **400.00**

Cameo II, jardiniere, 8" H, from $450 to **550.00**

Capri, leaf dish, #532-16, 16", from $35 to **45.00**

Carnelian I, ewer, 15", from $400 to **500.00**

Carnelian I, fan vase, 6", from $70 to **80.00**

Carnelian I, vase, 6", from $100 to **125.00**

Carnelian II, basket, 4x10", from $225 to **275.00**

Carnelian II, planter, 3x8", from $125 to **150.00**

Clemana, bowl, #281, blue, 4½x6½", from $250 to **275.00**

Clemana, candleholders, #1104, green, 4½", pr from $300 to **325.00**

Clemana, vase, #280, tan, 6½", from $300 to **350.00**

Clematis, bowl, #445, brown or green, 4", from $60 to **75.00**

Clematis, candleholders, #1158, blue, 2½", pr from $110 to **130.00**

Clematis, wall pocket, #1295, blue, 8", from $225 to............. **250.00**

Columbine, cornucopia, #149-6, pink, 5½", from $175 to..**200.00**

Columbine, vase, #20, pink, 8", from $250 to **300.00**

Corinthian, ashtray, 2", from $175 to **200.00**

Corinthian, bowl, 3", from $75 to .**95.00**

Corinthian, jardiniere, 7", from $175 to..**200.00**

Cornelian, pitcher, 4", from $50 to...................................**60.00**

Cosmos, center bowl, #374-14, tan, 15½", from $250 to **300.00**

Cosmos, vase, #944, blue, 4", from $150 to **175.00**

Cremona, fan vase, 5", from $125 to **150.00**

Cremona, frog, from $50 to ...**75.00**

Cremona, urn, 4", from $150 to **175.00**

Dahlrose, candlesticks, #1969, 3½", pr from $175 to **225.00**

Dahlrose, pillow vase, #419, 5x7", from $250 to **275.00**

Dawn, ewer, #834-16, green, 16", from $650 to **750.00**

Dawn, vase, #826, green or pink, 6", from $200 to............. **250.00**

Dogwood I, vase, 12", from $350 to................................ **400.00**

Dogwood II, bowl, 4", from $125 to................................. **150.00**

Donatello, ashtray, 3", from $175 to **225.00**

Donatello, candlestick, 8", ea from $200 to **225.00**

Donatello, compote, 5", from $125 to **175.00**

Earlam, planter, #89, 5½x10½", from $400 to **450.00**

Falline, center bowl, #244, blue, 11", from $500 to........... **600.00**

Falline, center bowl, #244, tan, 11", from $350 to **450.00**

Ferella, vase, #505, tan, 6", from $700 to **800.00**

Florane, bud vase, 7", from $30 to.**35.00**

Florane, planter box, 6", from $25 to **30.00**

Florentine, ashtray, 5", from $150 to **175.00**

Florentine, jardiniere, 5", from $150 to **175.00**

Florentine, wall pocket, 7", from $175 to **200.00**

Foxglove, tray, #419, pink, from $150 to **175.00**

Foxglove, vase, #53-14, blue, 14", from $450 to **500.00**

Freesia, bowl, #465-8, green, 11", from $175 to **200.00**

Freesia, cookie jar, #3, green, from $550.00 to $650.00.

Freesia, ewer, #19, tangerine, 6", from $225 to **250.00**

Freesia, window box, #1392-8, green, 10½", from $200 to **225.00**

Fuchsia, candlesticks, #1132, green, 2", pr from $150 to **175.00**

Fuchsia, vase, #891-6, green, 6", from $200 .... **225.00**

Fuchsia, vase, #893-6, brown/tan, 6", from $175 to **200.00**

Futura, center bowl, #187, 3½", from $450 to **500.00**

Futura, frog for center bowl, #187, from $100 to **125.00**

Futura, vase, #382, 7", from $365 to **450.00**

Gardenia, basket, #610-12, 12", from $350 to **400.00**

Gardenia, hanging basket, #661, 6", from $300 to............. **350.00**

Gardenia, jardiniere, #600, 4", from $90 to **110.00**

Imperial I, compote, 6½", from $225 to **275.00**

Imperial II, bowl, 4½", from $300 to **350.00**

Iris, vase, #914, blue, 4", from $125 to **150.00**

Iris, vase, #924-9, pink or tan, 10", from $350 to **400.00**

Ivory II, dog, 6½", from $75 to..**100.00**

Ivory II, jardiniere, 6", from $50 to..................................... **75.00**

Ixia, basket, #346, 10", from $300 to **350.00**

Ixia, vase, #856-8, 8½", from $200 to **250.00**

Jonquil, candlesticks, #1082, 4", pr from $450 to **550.00**

La Rose, bowl, 3", from $125 to. **150.00**

La Rose, bowl, 6", from $100 to. **125.00**

Laurel, bowl, #252, gold, from $250 to **300.00**

Laurel, vase, #676, gold, from $450 to **550.00**

Lombardy, jardiniere, 6½", from $200 to **250.00**

Lotus, vase, #L3, 10", from $300 to................................... **350.00**

Lustre, candlestick, 5½", ea from $45 to **55.00**

Magnolia, ashtray, #28, blue, 7", from $150 to **175.00**

Magnolia, planter, #388-6, brown or green, 8½", from $85 to **95.00**

Mayfair, planter, #1113, 8", from $60 to **75.00**

Ming Tree, ashtray, #559, 6", from $75 to **85.00**

Ming Tree, ewer, #516, 10", from $150 to **175.00**

Ming Tree, hanging basket, 6", from $225 to **250.00**

Mock Orange, pillow vase, #930-8, 7", from $150 to............. **175.00**

Moderne, compote, #297-6, 6", from $250 to **275.00**

Morning Glory, center bowl, #270, ivory, 4½x11½", from $350 to........ **375.00**

Moss, bowl vase, #290, 6", pink & green or orange & green, from $350 to **400.00**

Moss, center bowl, #294, blue, 12", from $225 to **250.00**

Mostique, bowl, 7", from $175 to **200.00**

Mostique, compote, 7", from $350 to **375.00**

Orian, compote, #272, tan, 4½x10½", from $225 to **250.00**

Orian, vase, #733, yellow, 6½", from $250 to **275.00**

Peony, bowl, #661, 3", from $95 to **125.00**

Peony, planter, #387-8, 10", from $85 to **95.00**

Pine Cone, ashtray, #499, blue, 4½", from $200 to **225.00**

Pine Cone, mug, #960-4, brown, 4", from $250 to **450.00**

Pine Cone, pillow vase, #845-8, green, from $300 to....... **325.00**

Pine Cone, vase, #112, green, 7", from $175 to **200.00**

Poppy, bowl, #642-3, pink, 3½", from $125 to **150.00**

Poppy, vase, #368-7, tan, 7½", from $350 to **375.00**

Poppy, vase, #867, gray or green 6½", from $125 to **150.00**

Raymor, casserole, #183, med, 11", from $75 to **85.00**

Raymor, corn server, #162, 12½", from $45 to **50.00**

Raymor, cruet, 5½", from $65 to. **75.00**

Raymor, shirred egg, #200, 10", from $40 to **45.00**

Rosecraft Black & Colors, flowerpot, yellow, 4½", from $175 to **200.00**

Rosecraft Blended, vase, #35, 10", from $125 to **150.00**

Rosecraft Hexagon, candlestick, brown, 8", from $375 to . **425.00**

Rosecraft Panel, window box, green, from $550 to **600.00**

Rosecraft Vintage, bowl, 3", from $125 to **150.00**

Rozane, bud vase, #841/3, 7½", from $175 to **225.00**

Rozane, jardiniere, 9½", from $175 to **225.00**

Rozane, pillow vase, #904/7, 5", from $175 to **200.00**

Rozane Light, bowl, 3", from $250 to **300.00**

Rozane Light, sugar bowl, 4½", from $250 to **300.00**

Rozane 1917, compote, 8", from $150 to **175.00**

Russco, vase, 8½", from $125 to..**150.00**

Silhouette, planter, #731, 14" L, from $125 to **150.00**

Snowberry, tray, #1BL-12, green, 14", from $200 to........... **225.00**

Sunflower, bowl, 4", from $550 to **650.00**

Teasel, basket, #349, light blue or tan, 10", from $600 to... **650.00**

Teasel, vase, #888-12, light blue or tan, 12", from $450 to... **550.00**

Thornapple, bowl vase, #820-9, 9½", from $275 to **325.00**

Thornapple, hanging basket, 7" dia, from $300 to **350.00**

Topeo, bowl, red, 2½", from $150 to **175.00**

Topeo, center bowl, red, 3x11½", from $100 to **125.00**

Tourmaline, bowl, 8", from $75 to **100.00**

Tourmaline, ginger jar, 9", from $400 to **450.00**

Tourmaline, pillow vase, 6", from $100 to **125.00**

Tuscany, vase, gray/light blue, 4", from $75 to **100.00**

Tuscany, vase, pink, 8", from $200 to **225.00**

Velmoss, bowl, #266, green, 3x11", from $175 to **225.00**

Velmoss, vase, #718, blue, 8", from $300 to **35.00**

Velmoss Scroll, vase, 12", from $450 to **500.00**

Water Lily, cornucopia, #177, blue, 6", from $150 to **175.00**

Water Lily, vase, #78-9, brown, from $300 to **325.00**

White Rose, basket, #362-8, 7½", from $200 to **250.00**

White Rose, ewer, #993, 15", from $450 to **500.00**

Wincraft, cornucopoia, #221-8, 9x5", from $150 to **175.00**

Windsor, center bowl, blue, 3½x10½", from $450 to.. **550.00**

Windsor, vase, #546, rust, 6", from $300 to **350.00**

Wisteria, bowl vase, #632, tan, 5", from $350 to **450.00**

Zephyr Lily, fan vase, #205-6, blue, 6½", from $175 to **200.00**

Zephyr Lily, pillow vase, #206-7, brown, 7", from $200 to. **225.00**

Royal China

Several lines of the dinnerware made by Royal China (Sebring, Ohio) are very collectible. Their Currier and Ives pattern (decorated with scenes of early American life in blue on a white background) and the Blue Willow line are well known, but many of their others are starting to take off as well. Since the same blanks were used for all patterns, shapes and sizes will all be the same from line to line. Both Currier and Ives and Willow were made in pink as well as the more familiar blue, but pink is hard to find and not especially collectible in either pattern. See Club and Newsletters for information on Currier & Ives Dinnerware Collectors Club.

Blue Heaven, bowl, fruit nappy, 5½" **3.00**

Blue Heaven, creamer **8.00**

Blue Heaven, gravy boat **15.00**

Blue Heaven, plate, dinner; 10". **6.00**

Blue Heaven, sugar bowl **12.00**

Blue Willow, bowl, cereal; 6¼" . **15.00**

Blue Willow, bowl, soup; 8¼" . **15.00**

Blue Willow, butter dish, ¼-lb. **45.00**

Blue Willow, casserole, w/lid . **95.00**

Blue Willow, creamer **6.00**

Blue Willow, cup & saucer **6.00**

Blue Willow, pie plate, 10" **30.00**

Blue Willow, plate, bread & butter; 6½" **3.00**

Blue Willow, plate, dinner; 10". **8.00**

Blue Willow, plate, salad; rare, 7¼" **7.00**

Blue Willow, platter, oval, 13".. **32.00**

Blue Willow, salt & pepper shakers, pr **25.00**

Blue Willow, sugar bowl, w/lid . **15.00**

Blue Willow, teapot, unmarked, six-cup, $135.00. (Photo courtesy Mary Frank Gaston)

Buck's County, bowl, soup; 8½"..**18.00**

Buck's County, casserole, w/lid.**125.00**

Buck's County, cup & saucer... **8.00**

Buck's County, plate, bread & butter; 6¼"............................... **4.00**

Buck's County, plate, dinner; 10".**12.00**

Buck's County, platter, tab handles, 10½" **25.00**

Buck's County, salt & pepper shakers, pr............................. **35.00**

Buck's County, teapot **145.00**

Colonial Homestead, bowl, fruit nappy; 5½" **5.00**

Colonial Homestead, bowl, vegetable; 10"............................. **20.00**

Colonial Homestead, gravy boat, double spout **15.00**

Colonial Homestead, plate, dinner; 10"....................................... **8.00**

Colonial Homestead, plate, salad; 7¼" **8.00**

Colonial Homestead, platter, serving; tab handles, 11", $15.00.

Colonial Homestead, sugar bowl, w/lid **15.00**

Currier & Ives, bowl, lug soup; tab handles, 6¼" **50.00**

Currier & Ives, butter dish, summer scene, ¼-lb................ **45.00**

Currier & Ives, butter dish, winter scene, ¼-lb **35.00**

Currier & Ives, cake plate, flat, 10"..................................... **35.00**

Currier & Ives, cake plate, footed, 10".................................. **200.00**

Currier & Ives, candy dish, 7¾" **40.00**

Currier & Ives, casserole, angled handles, w/all white lid.**175.00**

Currier & Ives, casserole, angled handles, w/lid **100.00**

Currier & Ives, casserole, tab handles, w/lid **200.00**

Currier & Ives, chop plate, Getting Ice, 11½"........................... **35.00**

Currier & Ives, creamer, angled handle................................ **8.00**

Currier & Ives, creamer, round handle, tall, rare............. **75.00**

Currier & Ives, cup & saucer..**6.00**

Currier & Ives, pie baker, 10" (depending on print), from $25 to **45.00**

Currier & Ives, plate, calendar; 1969 – 1986, $20.00.

Currier & Ives, plate, dinner; 10"....................................**5.00**

Currier & Ives, plate, luncheon; very rare, 9" **20.00**

Currier & Ives, plate, salad; rare, 7"...................................... **15.00**

Currier & Ives, platter, oval, 13"..**35.00**

Currier & Ives, salt & pepper shakers, pr from $30 to **35.00**

Currier & Ives, sugar bowl, angled handles, from $15 to....... **18.00**

Currier & Ives, tumbler, glass, 4¾".................................. **15.00**

Currier & Ives, tumbler, glass, 5½".................................. **15.00**

Fair Oaks, bowl, divided vegetable.................................. **45.00**

Fair Oaks, bowl, vegetable; 9". **30.00**

Fair Oaks, creamer................ **12.00**

Fair Oaks, cup & saucer.......... **8.00**

Fair Oaks, plate, 10".............. **12.00**

Fair Oaks, sugar bowl, w/lid. **18.00**

Memory Lane, bowl, soup; 8½"..**12.00**

Memory Lane, bowl, vegetable; 10".**28.00**

Memory Lane, butter dish, ¼-lb.**35.00**

Memory Lane, creamer............ **8.00**

Memory Lane, gravy boat, double spout.............................. **24.00**

Memory Lane, plate, salad; rare, 7"...................................... **12.00**

Memory Lane, platter, oval, 13".**38.00**

Memory Lane, sugar bowl, w/lid..**15.00**

Memory Lane, tumbler, juice; glass.................................... **9.00**

Old Curiosity Shop, bowl, cereal, 6½" **15.00**

Old Curiosity Shop, bowl, vegetable; 9" or 10", ea.............. **25.00**

Old Curiosity Shop, cup & saucer **5.00**

Old Curiosity Shop, plate, dinner; 10"...................................... **8.00**

Old Curiosity Shop, sugar bowl, w/lid **15.00**

Royal Copley

Produced by the Spaulding China Company of Sebring, Ohio, Royal Copley is a line of novelty planters, vases, ashtrays, and wall pockets modeled after appealing puppy dogs, lovely birds, innocent-eyed children, etc. The decoration is airbrushed and underglazed; the line is of good quality and is well received by today's pottery collectors. For more information we recommend *Collecting Royal Copley Plus Royal Windsor & Spaulding* by Joe Devine; he is listed in the Directory under Iowa. See Clubs and Newsletters for information concerning *The Copley Currier.*

Ashtray, butterfly, paper label, USA on bottom......................... **25.00**

Bank, rooster, paper label, 8". **95.00**

Bank, teddy bear, black & white, 8"..................................... **175.00**

Candleholder, star & angel, paper label **30.00**

Candy dish, leaf form, impressed USA on bottom................ **25.00**

Coaster, hunting dog scene, 4½". **40.00**

Coaster, paintings of antique autos, unmarked, ea **40.00**

Figurine, Airdale, paper label.. **30.00**

Figurine, Blackamoor, 8½" **25.00**

Figurine, cockatoo, white w/gold trim, 7"........................... **40.00**

Figurine, cockatoo, 8¼", from $40.00 to $45.00.

Figurine, deer & fawn, signed w/raised letters, 8½" **45.00**

Figurine, finch, paper label, 5". **40.00**

Figurine, lark, paper label, 6½" .**24.00**

Figurine, little wren, paper label, variety of colors **32.00**

Figurine, pouter pigeon, paper label, 5¾" **25.00**

Figurine, sea gull, white w/gold trim, 8" **55.00**

Figurine, wren, paper label, 3½", from $20 to **24.00**

Lamp, clown, paper label, 8¼" .**100.00**

Lamp, cocker spaniel begging, 10" **125.00**

Pitcher, Floral Beauty, 8" **60.00**

Pitcher, Pome Fruit, tan, green stamp, 8" **65.00**

Planter, barefoot boy, tan hat, paper label, 7½" **45.00**

Planter, birdhouse w/bird, 8".. **110.00**

Planter, cat w/cello, 8", from $100 to **125.00**

Planter, Dogwood, oval, 3½" .. **25.00**

Planter, girl & wheelbarrow.. **30.00**

Planter, horse head, black, paper label, 6½" **90.00**

Planter, Indian boy & drum, paper label, 6½" **30.00**

Planter, kitten & boot **55.00**

Planter, kitten in cradle, paper label, 7½" **125.00**

Planter, Peter Rabbit, paper label, 6½" **65.00**

Planter, poodle sitting by basket, white, 7⅛" **50.00**

Planter, Water Lily, pink w/gray background, 6¼" **75.00**

Planter, white poodle, paper label, 5½" dia **45.00**

Plaque planter, Valentine, gold stamp, 5" **35.00**

Platter, big apple & finch, paper label, 6½" **45.00**

Sugar bowl, gray w/pink leaf-shaped handles, raised letters on bottom **35.00**

Vase, bamboo, cylindrical, paper label, 8" **20.00**

Vase, cornucopia, gold stamp, 8¼" **30.00**

Vase, Floral Elegance, cobalt blue, 8" **32.00**

Vase, Lord's Prayer, #339, decal on green **45.00**

Vase, trailing leaf & vine, paper label, 8½" **30.00**

Royal Haeger, Haeger

Manufactured in Dundee, Illinois, Haeger produced some very interesting lines of artware, figural pieces, and planters. They're animal figures designed by Royal Hickman are well known. These were produced from 1938 through the 1950s and are recognized by their strong lines and distinctive glazes. For more information we recommend *Haeger Potteries Through the Years* by David Dilley (L-W Books); he is listed in the Directory under Indiana.

Ashtray, leaf, #1382, 8", from $4 to **6.00**

Ashtray, leaf w/applied acorns, green, #2145, Haeger c 1976, 10"..**10.00**

Bookends, Calla Lily, amber, #475, 6" **75.00**

Bookends, Ram, #132, 8", minimum value **150.00**

Bowl, Petal, #343, 8" H, from $4 to **5.00**

Bowl, shell form, chartreuse & Silver Spray, #297, 14" ... **40.00**

Candleholder, double fish, Mauve Agate, #203, unmarked, 5", ea **35.00**

Candleholders, leaf form, ebony, #437, unmarked, 5", pr... **15.00**

Centerpiece, mermaid, 21" long, minimum value, $55.00. (Photo courtesy Lee Garmon and Doris Frizzel)

Compote, blue, 3-footed, #5 (unmarked), ca 1914, 2x6" dia................................... **35.00**

Cookie jar, Gleep, yellow-orange, head is lid, #8198.......... **200.00**

Dish, pheasant form, Gold Tweed, Royal Haeger USA, #329-H, 21".................................... **40.00**

Figurine, colt, #1404, 5½"...... **15.00**

Figurine, duck w/head up, white, #3, ca 1941, 5".................. **10.00**

Figurine, mare, #1405, 7½" ... **18.00**

Figurine, panther, #733, 13" L...**15.00**

Figurine, panther, ebony, #495, 24".................................... **40.00**

Figurine, pouter pigeon, #108, 7½", from $20 to **25.00**

Figurine, rabbit, blue, #3248, unmarked, 1940s, 5"....... **20.00**

Figurine, rooster, brown w/white drip glaze, #1762, 1970s, 20"............................. **150.00**

Figurine, tiger, amber, #313, 13" L **75.00**

Flower frog, nudes astride fish, yellow, #363, 10" **100.00**

Lamp, 2 fawns, #5195, 24", from $30 to **35.00**

Lavabo, pink, #1506/#1507, 2-pc..**75.00**

Lighter, fish form, vertical, Jade Crackle, #812-H, 1960s, 10"............................. **30.00**

Planter, dog in shoe, impressed Hound Dog Shoe Co (c) Haeger, 7½x10", from $40.00 to $50.00. (Photo courtesy Bill and Betty Newbound)

Planter, elephant, #563, 10½", from $20 to **25.00**

Planter, fish, #751, 6½"......... **10.00**

Toe Tapper, textured brown, #8296, 9", minimum value **40.00**

Vase, double leaf, Antique, #1460, unmarked, 11"............... **200.00**

Vase, rooster figure, #3220, unmarked, white, 14"..... **75.00**

Vase, Tulip, #616, 8" **10.00**

Russel Wright Dinnerware

Dinnerware with a mid-century flair was designed by Russel Wright, who was at one time one of America's top industrial engineers. His most successful lines are American Modern, manufactured by the Steubenville Pottery Company (1939 – 1959), and Casual by Iroquois, introduced in 1944. He also introduced several patterns of melmac dinnerware and an interesting assortment of spun aluminum serving and decorative items such as candleholders, ice buckets, vases, and bowls.

To calculate values for items in American Modern, at least double the low values listed for these colors: Canteloupe, Glacier Blue, Bean Brown, and White. Chartreuse is representd by the low end of our range; Cedar, Black Chutney, and Seafoam by the high end; and Coral and Gray near the middle. To price Casual, use the high end for Sugar White, Charcoal, and Oyster. Avocado, Yellow, Nutmeg Brown, and Ripe Apricot fall to the low side. Canteloupe commands premium prices, and even more valuable are Brick Red and Glassware prices are given for Flair in Crystal and Pink; other colors are higher. Add 100% for Imperial Pinch in Cantaloupe. Ruby is very rare, and market value has not yet been established.

Bowl, baker; American Modern, from $40 to **50.00**

Bowl, cereal or soup; Highlight, ea from $100 to **150.00**

Bowl, cereal; Iroquois, 5", from $12 to **15.00**

Bowl, fruit; Country Garden, from $100 to **115.00**

Bowl, fruit; Knowles, 5½", from $10 to **12.00**

Bowl, salad; Highlight, 52-oz, 10", from $35 to **45.00**

Bowl, serving; Knowles, round or oval, open, from $35 to ... **45.00**

Bowl, vegetable; American Modern, divided, from $135 to.... **150.00**

Butter dish, Iroquois, ½-lb, from $75 to **125.00**

Butter spreader, Pinch, from $100 to **110.00**

Casserole, American Modern, stick handle, from $35 to......... **40.00**

Centerpiece server, Knowles, from $150 to **200.00**

Chop plate, White Clover, 11", from $40 to **50.00**

Clock, White Clover, GE, from $75 to **85.00**

Coffeepot, demitasse; Iroquois Casual, 4½", from $100 to............... **125.00**

Coffeepot, Theme Formal, from $600 to **650.00**

Creamer, Flair, #711 .... **12.00**

Creamer, Highlight, from $40 to **55.00**

Creamer, Residential, from $10.00 to $12.00.

Cup, American Modern, from $10 to **12.00**

Cup, Residential, #701............. **6.00**

Cup, Sterling, 7-oz, from $13 to.**15.00**

Goblet, iced-tea, Old Morgantown, 15-oz, 5¼", from $25 to. **30.00**

Goblet, old-fashioned; Imperial Twist, rare, from $35 to.. **50.00**

Gravy boat, Spun Aluminum, from $150 to **200.00**

Ice bowl, Chase, #28002, w/tongs, from $175 to **185.00**

Mug, Iroquois, restyled, from $70 to **85.00**

Pitcher, Devonshire, #900025, from $225 to **250.00**

Pitcher, Iroquois, w/lid, 1½-qt, from $150 to **175.00**

Plate, American Modern, 6", from $6 to **8.00**

Plate, American Modern, 8", from $18 to **20.00**

Plate, compartment; Meladur, rare, 9½", from $15 to **18.00**

Plate, dinner, Highlight, from $35 to **40.00**

Plate, dinner; Sterling, 10¼", from $10 to **15.00**

Platter, American Modern, from $45 to **50.00**

Platter, Knowles, oval, 16", from $55 to **75.00**

Relish dish, Oceana, 1-handled, from $500 to **600.00**

Sugar bowl, American Modern, from $20 to **25.00**

Sugar bowl, Iroquois, stacking, from $20 to **25.00**

Teapot, Sterling, 10-oz, from $125 to **150.00**

Wastebasket, from $125 to .. **150.00**

Salt Shakers

You'll probably see more salt and pepper shakers during your flea market forays than T-shirts and tube socks! Since the 1920s they've been popular souvenir items, and a considerable number has been issued by companies to advertise their products. These advertising shakers are always good, and along with miniature shakers (1½" or under) are some of the more valuable. Of course, those that have a cross-

over interest into other categories of collecting — Black Americana, Disney, Rosemeade, Shawnee, Ceramic Arts Studios, etc. — are often expensive as well. There are many good books on the market; among them are *Florences' Big Book of Salt & Pepper Shakers* and *Florences' Glass Kitchen Shakers* by Gene and Cathy Florence, and *Salt and Pepper Shakers* by Helene Guarnaccia. All are published by Collector Books. See also Advertising Collectibles; Ceramic Arts Studio; Character Collectibles; Disney; Shawnee; Rosemeade.

Woody and Buzz Lightyear, Toy Story, Treasure Craft, copyright Disney Treasure Craft, from $45.00 to $65.00. (Photo courtesy Joyce and Fred Roerig)

Alligators, ceramic, realistic, Japan, 4" L, pr **10.00**

Amish couple, ceramic, Japan, #II763, 1950s, 4¾", pr **25.00**

Angel & devil, ceramic, unmarked Japan, 1950s, 4¼", 2-pc .. **24.00**

Bear & tall hive, ceramic, brown & yellow, Japan, 3¾", 2-pc .. **10.00**

Betsy Ross & Paul Revere, ceramic, Japan, 1960s, 4½", 2-pc .. **28.00**

Bible & gavel, ceramic, black & white, 1950s, 2½", 4", 2-pc.............**18.00**

Blue jays on stumps, ceramic, Japan, 3½", pr **15.00**

Boy & girl praying, ceramic, Japan, #C-2114, 3½", pr...............**12.00**

Brussel sprouts & celery people, ceramic, 3", 2-pc...............**15.00**

Bugs Bunny & Daffy Duck as cowboys, ceramic, WB '93...China, 4", 2-pc............................**30.00**

Cake & slice of cake, ceramic, 1", 2-pc..................................**12.00**

Camel w/2 humps (shakers), ceramic, 3¼" L............................**12.00**

Candlesticks, ceramic, white & brown, Japan, 3", pr **10.00**

Caramel apples, ceramic, 1½", pr.**7.00**

Cardinals, ceramic, Japan, 4¾", pr **18.00**

Carrots, ceramic, orange & green, c HH Japan, 3½", pr............**6.00**

Cat ice skaters, ceramic, 4½", pr from $8 to **18.00**

Chip 'n Dale, ceramic, New England Collector.../Disney, 1995, 2-pc **40.00**

Choir boys, ceramic, Japan, 1950s, 4¾", pr...............................**22.00**

Clown acrobats, ceramic, stacking, Japan, #115, 6¼", pr from $35 to **40.00**

Coffee mills, ceramic, Japan (embossed), 4", pr **10.00**

Colonial couple, ceramic, Occupied Japan, 3½", 2-pc..............**18.00**

Crabs, ceramic, Japan label, #H-762, 1½x3½", pr...............**18.00**

Dog musicians, ceramic, Japan, 2⅛", pr..............................**15.00**

Dogs (boy/girl) playing ping pong, ceramic, Japan, 1950s, 2¾", pr **20.00**

Dutch couple kissing, 4½", pr.**18.00**

Dutch girl & windmill, ceramic, Japan, 4¼", 2-pc..............**24.00**

Ears of corn w/smiling faces, plastic, Japan, 3", pr....**18.00**

Egg-head couple, ceramic, Japan, 4½", pr from $25 to **30.00**

Eggplants, ceramic, 3¼", pr ..**10.00**

Eskimo & igloo, ceramic, Japan, 1950s, 4½", 2-pc...............**24.00**

Famingos, ceramic, 1 head up/1 head down, Japan, 4", pr...........**24.00**

Fisherman/boat, ceramic, Elbee Art (unmarked), 1950s, 2¾x3", 2-pc......................................**26.00**

Gingerbread men, ceramic, brown & red, Japan (embossed), 4½", pr......................................**20.00**

Golf bag & ball, ceramic, brown & white, Japan, #H-151, 3¼" bag, 2-pc **18.00**

Graduation hat & scroll, ceramic, 1¾", 2-pc **20.00**

Great Smoky Moutains, ceramic mugs w/bear reserve on white, 2½", pr................................**4.00**

Hippo mother & baby, ceramic, browns, 1940s-50s, 2½x2½", 2-pc **28.00**

Hunter & rabbit, ceramic, unmarked, 1950s, 3½" hunter, 2-pc **22.00**

Ice cream cones, ceramic, pr .**10.00**

Indian boy & girl, ceramic, black, white & red, Japan, 1960s, 4½", pr..............................**22.00**

Indian couple, plastic, Watkins Glen NY, pr **8.00**

Indians seated, ceramic, Japan, 2½", pr.............................**12.00**

Iron & clothes basket, ceramic, white w/brown, 1¾", 2-pc.**18.00**

Irons, ceramic, 3¼", pr........**12.00**

John Kennedy & rocker, ceramic, Arrow, 1962, NYC/Japan, 4¾", 2-pc. **32.00**

Koala bears, ceramic, unmarked Japan, 1960s-70s, 2⅛", pr. **20.00**

Lambs, ceramic, Shawnee-like, 3", pr **12.00**

Lion tamer & lion, ceramic, Japan, 1950s, 4", 2-pc **26.00**

Man & fruit cart (shakers sit in cart), ceramic, Japan, 1950s, 3-pc **23.00**

Mexican man & cactus, ceramic, Japan, 3½", 2-pc **12.00**

Mice as baseball players, ceramic, Japan, 1950s, 3¼", pr...... **75.00**

Monkey huggers, ceramic, Japan, 3¼", pr from $12 to **15.00**

Monks w/beards, ceramic, brown tones, Japan, 2¼"............ **10.00**

Onions, porcelain, 3¼", pr..... **10.00**

Orange & lemon, ceramic, realistic, Japan, 1½", 2-pc **5.00**

Paul Bunyan & Babe the Blue Ox, ceramic, 2-pc, from $35 to. **42.00**

Peacocks, ceramic, c MK, 3¾", pr................................ **18.00**

Pears, ceramic, realistic, Japan, 2½", pr................................ **7.00**

Pheasant hen & cock, ceramic, Napco, 1940s, 4", 2-pc..... **22.00**

Phonographs, metal, 2" L, pr . **12.00**

Pig's heads, ceramic, S or P on forehead, 1950s, 4", pr **22.00**

Pigs, ceramic, I'm Salt/I'm Pepper, Japan, 3⅛", pr **12.00**

Pilgrim & turkey, ceramic, Japan, #20032, 5¼", 2-pc **15.00**

Pineapples, ceramic, realistic, 3⅛", pr... **6.00**

Pirate & treasure chest, ceramic, 1950s, 2-pc...................... **22.00**

Praying hands, plastic, bronze colored, Japan, 3¾", pr........ **12.00**

Pump & bucket, ceramic, purple & brown, Japan, 2¼", 2-pc.. **18.00**

Rabbit & cabbage, ceramic, Parkcraft mark, 4", 2-pc.**25.00**

Red & green peppers, ceramic, German (Sibs), 2½", pr ... **10.00**

Rocking chairs, metal w/painted detail, 2¼", pr......................**12.00**

Roosters, ceramic, Napco, 1950s, 4½", pr............................. **25.00**

Santa & Mrs Claus standing, ceramic, Japan, 4¼", 2-pc.**18.00**

Skillets, plastic, tan & black, marked Pat Pend, 4½", pr **4.00**

Snoopy on doghouse, ceramic, stack set, Benjamin & Medwin, 1994, 2-pc **35.00**

Statue of Liberty, ceramic, green, Copyright 1992, 5½", pr..**28.00**

Suitcases, ceramic, black, Japan, 2", pr **8.00**

Sunflowers w/faces, ceramic, Japan, 2½", pr **18.00**

Sweepers, metal, 3¾", pr **15.00**

Teddy bears (stacking set), ceramic, Japan, 4¼", 2-pc............. **18.00**

Telephone, old desk dial type w/painted numbers, 2-pc.. **15.00**

Thanksgiving pilgrim boy and girl, Hallmark, 1970s, $15.00 for the pair.

Toaster, plastic, divided in 2 w/1 having black toast, Carvanite, 2-pc **16.00**

Toy soldiers, ceramic, 4½", pr. **15.00**
Trout, ceramic, 5⅛" L **15.00**
Turkey in pan, ceramic, 2½", 2-pc,
    from $12 to **15.00**
Turkeys pecking, ceramic, 3",
    pr **15.00**
Umbrella stands, ceramic, yellow,
    3¾", pr **18.00**
Violins, cobalt glass w/plastic caps,
    4", pr **18.00**
Walnuts, ceramic, realistic, Arcadia
    Ceramics, 1½", pr **15.00**
Wolves dressed as grandma, lus-
    treware, Germany (unmarked),
    3½", pr **75.00**
Wooden shoes, ceramic, brown wash,
    Japan, 1965, 4", pr **12.00**

Scottie Dogs

An amazing array of Scottie
dog collectibles can be found in a
wide range of prices. Collectors
might choose to specialize in a
particular area, or they may enjoy
looking for everything from bridge
tallies to original portraits or paintings. Most of the items are from the
1930s and 1940s. Many were used
for advertising purposes; others are
simply novelties.

Ashtray, etched crystal, 1940s,
    4x2½", from $20 to **35.00**
Bank, Scottie sitting w/oversized
    head, ceramic, black & white,
    5" **20.00**
Bookends, cast iron, Hubley #263,
    1940s, from $125 to **150.00**
Cake pan, copper Scottie figure,
    1990s, 12x16" **75.00**
Cookie cutter, aluminum, Purple Puma
    Cookie Co, 1990s, 2½" **12.00**

Figurine, flocked plastic, 1950s,
    3½x3x1½", from $5 to **10.00**
Frame, ceramic, dog embossed in
    lower corner, 1980s, 5x4", from
    $5 to **15.00**
Letter holder, tin, Scottie decal, 1940s,
    6x4x6", from $30 to **50.00**

**Mug, Three Canny Scots, red
and black fired-on decoration,
Cambridge, 3", from $275.00 to
$350.000.** (Photo courtesy Candace Sten Davis
and Patrica Baugh/From the collection of Lesley and
Bill Connor)

Pitcher, juice; fired-on red & black
    Scotties, 1940s **40.00**
Salt & pepper shakers, silver-tone
    metal, 1940s, 2x3", pr from $25
    to **40.00**
Stuffed dog, vinyl, 1950s, 6x8x9",
    from $20 to **40.00**
Tie rack, figural head in profile
    w/rack, Soroco Wood, 1940s,
    7x9", EX **35.00**
Wall hook, pewter, dog w/shoestring in
    mouth, 1990s, 5", from $15 to.**25.00**
Wall plaque, Scottie face, ceramic, 1940s-
    50s, 4x2½", from $10 to **20.00**

Scouting Collectibles

Founded in England in 1907
by Major General Lord Baden-
Powell, scouting remains an impor-

tant institution in the life of young boys and girls everywhere. Recently scouting-related memorabilia has attracted a following, and values of many items have escalated dramatically in the last few years. Early first edition handbooks often bring prices of $100.00 and more. Vintage uniforms are scarce and highly valued, and one of the rarer medals, the Life Saving Honor Medal, is worth several hundred dollars to collectors. For more information we recommend *A Complete Guide to Scouting Collectibles* by Rolland J. Sayers; he is listed in the Directory under North Carolina.

Boy Scouts

Armband, Arena Staff, 1973 American National Jamboree, M....... **75.00**

Belt buckle, Boy Scouts Vietnam, brass, 2-pc, pre-1975, EX. **85.00**

Binoculars, ca 1960s, MIB, $25.00.
(Photo courtesy Don and Carol Raycraft)

Book, Boy Scout Book of Scout Stories, Crump, 1953, NM+ **5.00**

Book, Handbook for Boys, 1943, 16-pg, EX.......................... **15.00**

Calendar, 1945, Borden's Ice Cream, Scout pictured, 33", NM . **50.00**

Calendar, 1967 World Jamboree, complete, 42", EX............ **20.00**

Christmas cards, w/envelopes, 25 ea in red box.................... **10.00**

Flag, 1935 or 1937 Jamboree Troop Contingent, 36x60" **100.00**

Medal, Message Relay, w/blue ribbon holder, MIB **200.00**

Patch, Camp Zackwoods, 1947, EX................................ **175.00**

Pencil box, color scene of camp activities, 1930 .... **25.00**

Pennant, yellow felt w/BSA & Camp Lavigne emblem, 28" L, EX . **15.00**

Pocketknife, Official Boy Scout Knife, plastic, 1940s, 3½", EXIB **100.00**

Poster, Join the BSA, Scout/Smokey Bear, US Forest Service, 1954, 14".................................. **85.00**

Poster, 1935 Nat'l Jamboree, Rockwell art, 30x20".....**100.00**

Record, Morse Code Made Easy, 1950, 78 rpm **15.00**

Sleeping bag, regulation, 1950s, EX **40.00**

Tie bar, Eagle Scout, sterling, clip-on logo.............................. **5.00**

Woodburning kit, complete, EXIB **25.00**

Wristwatch, Timex, 1950s, w/original band........................... **15.00**

Yearbook, Official BSA, 1st edition, 1915, EX+ **18.00**

Girl Scouts

Barrette, gold-tone, 1950s, 2¼" L, NM **10.00**

Camera, Official GSA, Brownie box-type, 1949 .... **20.00**

Catalog, Girl Scout Equipment, 1957, 23-pg, EX............... **45.00**

Compass, US Gauge Co of NY, 1930, 1¼" dia, EX............ **55.00**

Cup, aluminum, collapsible, 1950 .... **5.00**

Doll, Girl Scout, Effanbee, 1965, MIB **30.00**

Flag, Official Brownie, 1930s, sm **25.00**

Handbook, Official Leaders, tan cover, 1920 .... **30.00**

Mess Kit, unused, EX (in poor original box), $27.50.

Patch, Treasurers, green twill, 1937 .... **10.00**

Pin, Mariner, 1940 .... **15.00**

Pin, wings, Brownie, 1926..... **15.00**

Uniform, Brownie dress, w/orange necktie, membership card, 1950s............................... **20.00**

Wallet, Brownies, 1940s, MIP. **10.00**

Whistle, Official, cylinder type, 1920s............................... **20.00**

Sears Kitchenware

During the 1970s the Sears Company sold several lines of novelty kitchen ware, including Country Kitchen, Merry Mushrooms, and Neil the Frog. These lines, especially Merry Mushrooms, are coming on strong as the collectibles of tomorrow. There's lots of it around and unless you're buying it from someone who's already aware of its potential value, you can get it at very low prices. It was made in Japan. Besides the ceramic items, you'll find woodenware, enamelware, linens, and plastics.

Country Kitchen

Butter dish **15.00**

Canister set, 4-pc **40.00**

Creamer.................................... **9.00**

Napkin holder **15.00**

Salt & pepper shakers, cylindrical, pr..................................... **15.00**

Spoon rest, rectangular, 4 rests .**10.00**

Merry Mushrooms

Deviled egg plate, $30.00.

Bowl, salad; w/original wooden fork & spoon, rare................... **60.00**

Butter dish, from $15 to **20.00**

Canister set, basketweave background, 4-pc..................... **65.00**

Canister set, mushroom shape, 4-pc **50.00**

Canister set, plastic, brown lids, 4-pc **32.00**

Canister set, smooth background, cylindrical, w/wooden lids, 4-pc **50.00**

Casserole, Corning Ware, glass lid, 1¾-qt **30.00**

Casserole, Corning Ware, glass lid, 2½-qt **40.00**

Clock, wall mount, battery-operated, from $25 to **30.00**

Coffee mug, textured backgound, 10-oz **9.00**

Coffee mug, thermo-plastic ... **16.00**

Coffee mug set, textured background, 4 on scrolling metal tree **45.00**

Coffeepot, yellow enamelware, clear glass lid, black handle **34.00**

Cookie jar **18.00**

Curtain valance, 12x66" **45.00**

Cutlery set, 4-pc **32.00**

Gravy boat, 5½" L w/7" undertray **30.00**

Napkin holder, from $20 to ... **25.00**

Place mats/napkins, quilted fabric, set of 4 ea, 8-pc **30.00**

Planter & undertray, textured background, brown tray . **30.00**

Plaque, mushrooms in relief on oval, 9½x7½" **60.00**

Salt & pepper shakers, 5", pr . **16.00**

Soup mug, hard to find, 3x4¾". **25.00**

Spice jar, paper label indentifies contents, sm **5.00**

Spice rack, 2-tier, 2 drawers in base, 12 spice jars, minimum value **65.00**

Spoon rest, 2 indents at bottom, 7½x5" **25.00**

Tea-light holder, mushroom shape, dated 1981, 7¾" **30.00**

Toaster oven, printed cloth.... **15.00**

Tureen, w/underplate & ladle, 2½-qt **58.00**

Utensil holder **35.00**

Wall pocket, pitcher & bowl shape **35.00**

Neil the Frog

Bell, green frog on yellow lily pad in relief on white, 1978, 4¾". **95.00**

Bowl, 2 3-D frogs play on rim, water lily leaves on sides, 3¾x7". **60.00**

Canister set, ceramic, 4-pc, from $50 to **60.00**

Canister set, plastic w/green lids, 4-pc, from $16 to **20.00**

Clock, lotus leaf shape, wall mount, battery-operated, from $20 to **25.00**

Coffee mug **8.00**

Cookie jar, frog finial, 10½" ... **35.00**

Creamer & sugar bowl, from $20 to **25.00**

Cruets, oil & vineger; 5", pr .. **30.00**

Kitchen towel, 24x15½" **9.00**

Miniature figurines, 1 w/flower, 1 w/ umbrella, 1¾" & 1⅝", pr...... **45.00**

Mustard jar, slot in lid for spoon. **20.00**

Napkin holder **15.00**

Skillet, enamel, 10" **20.00**

Teakettle, enamel, green lid .. **45.00**

Trivet, $20.00.

Sewing Items

Sewing notions from the 1800s and early twentieth century, such as whimsical figural tape measures, beaded satin pincushions, blown glass darning eggs, and silver and gold thimbles, are pleasant reminders of a bygone era — ladies' sewing circles, quilting bees, and beautifully hand-stitched finery. With the emphasis collectors of today have put on figural ceramic items, the pincushions such as we've listed below are coming on strong. Most were made in Japan; some were modeled after the likenesses of Disney characters. For more information we recommend *Sewing Tools & Trinkets,* by Helen Lester Thompson (Collector Books).

Kit, painted wood, mushroom darner, flower pincushion, thimble in bucket, 3", from $35.00 to $45.00.

Basket, pink basketweave w/black fuzzy poodle on smooth lid, 13" dia, EX.............................**30.00**

Basket, pink wicker w/decal on lid, 6¼x11" dia, NM+.............**50.00**

Basket, white wicker w/celluloid-covered cloth lid, ear handle, EX....................................**15.00**

Book, Needlepoint Made Easy, Mary Brooks Picken/Doris White, 1955, EX..............**15.00**

Booklet, Patchworker's Christmas, Rita Weiss, 1981, EX......**15.00**

Booklet, The Story of American Needlework (crewel work), 1961, EX+.........................**18.00**

Box, wood, 4-legged, hinged to fold out ea side, basket handle, EX..**60.00**

Buttons, mother-of-pearl, 7 on Miss America Pearls card w/graphics, NM...............................**6.00**

Darner, painted wood (worn stripes), 5½".....................**20.00**

Dress pattern, Vogue, 1940s, complete, MIP.........................**20.00**

Magazine, Needlecraft, March, 1926, 49 pgs, EX.............**14.00**

Pincushion, ceramic penguin beside cushion, Japan, 3"...........**32.00**

Pincushion, chalkware doll w/molded hair, cloth skirt/lace, 1930s, EX.....................................**55.00**

Pincushion, china cat w/cushion on back, 4" L............................**6.00**

Pincushion, taffeta heart w/pink ribbon & much crochet, 3½x5" **5.00**

Pincushion/tape measure, bisque donkey, Japan sticker, 4¾x3", EX.....................................**28.00**

Pincushion/tape measure, metal guitar w/fabric at body, VG....**30.00**

Scissors, electric, red and yellow plastic, early 1950s, $35.00. (Photo courtesy June Moon)

Scissors, gold-flashed w/stamped motif & enameling, Toledo, 3½", EX............................**35.00**

Scissors, red enameled handles, unmarked, 7½", NM........**12.50**

Scissors, sterling, marked USA LS&B, 5"..........................**50.00**

Tape measure, celluloid pink flamingo on green base, 2½", EX..................................**80.00**

Tape measure, celluloid pink pig w/red hat, Japan, 2½", VG..............**60.00**

Tape measure, ceramic Indian figure, Japan, 2", EX..........**42.00**

Tape measure, metal turtle, Pull My Head Not My Leg on back, 2" L, EX..........................**100.00**

Tape measure, plastic red apple w/green leaf that pulls out, EX..................................**36.00**

Tape measure, tin antique auto, tape pulls from front, 1930s, EX..................................**150.00**

Tatting shuttle, Bakelite, marbleized pink, EX...................**12.50**

Tatting shuttle, sterling, Webster, EX.....................................**75.00**

Thimble, china, Country Roses, Royal Albert, 1", MIB.....**18.00**

Thimble, plastic, Reach for Sunbeam Bread, white, M.................**35.00**

Thimble, sterling, Greek Key design on band, marked Sterling, EX..................**26.00**

Travel kit, egg shape w/Calvert Blended Whisky ad, Germany, 2", EX..............................**25.00**

Shawnee

The novelty planters, vases, cookie jars, salt and pepper shakers, and 'Corn' dinnerware made by the Shawnee Pottery of Ohio are attractive, fun to collect, and still available at reasonable prices. The company operated from 1937 until 1961, marking their wares with 'Shawnee, U.S.A.,' and a number series, or 'Kenwood.' Refer to *Shawnee Pottery,* by Jim and Bev Mangus (Collector Books) for more information. See also Cookie Jars. See Clubs and Newsletters for information concerning the Shawnee Pottery Collectors' Club.

Baker, Lobster, open, 195, 5".**40.00**

Bowl, batter; w/handle, Lobster, 928, from $50 to..............**55.00**

Bowl, fruit; Valencia, from $15 to...................................**20.00**

Bowl, mixing; King Corn, Shawnee 8, 8", from $40 to.............**50.00**

Butter dish, King or Queen Corn line, from $55.00 to $65.00.

Canister, Dutch decal, USA, 2-qt.**50.00**

Carafe, patio; Kenwood USA 945, from $75 to......................**80.00**

Casserole, King Corn, Shawnee 74, lg, from $50 to.................**60.00**

Chop plate, Valencia, 13".......**27.00**

Coaster, Valencia, ea..............**18.00**

Coffeepot, regular, Valencia...**50.00**

Cookie jar, King Corn, Shawnee 66....................................**250.00**

Creamer, White Corn, USA, 12-oz, from $25 to......................**30.00**

Egg cup, Valencia....................**18.00**

Grease jar, Flower & Fern, from $40 to..............................**45.00**

Hors d'oeuvres holder, Lobster, USA, 7¼"........................**275.00**

Mug, Lobster, Kenwood USA 911, 8-oz, from $75 to **85.00**

Nappy, Valencia, 8½" or 9½" .. **20.00**

Pie server, Valencia **55.00**

Pitcher, Boy Blue, gold, Shawnee 46, 20-oz **200.00**

Pitcher, ice; Valencia, from $30 to **35.00**

Planter, girl & mandolin, USA 576 .... **24.00**

Planter, Irish setter, USA **10.00**

Plate, Queen Corn, Shawnee 93, 8", from $28 to **32.00**

Platter, King or Queen Corn, Shawnee 96, 12" **55.00**

Relish tray, King Corn, Shawnee 79, from $30 to **40.00**

Salt & pepper shakers, King or Queen Corn, 3¼", pr **28.00**

Salt & pepper shakers, Muggsy, lg, pr from $55 to **50.00**

Salt & pepper shakers, Smiley & Winnie, green collar, sm, pr **75.00**

Spoon holder, double, Lobster, USA 935, 9", from $225 to..... **250.00**

Sugar bowl, clover bud, USA. **55.00**

Sugar bowl, Lobster, w/lid, 907 .**26.00**

Sugar shaker, White Corn, USA, from $70 to **80.00**

Teacup & saucer, Valencia **22.00**

Teapot, Flower & Fern, 6-cup. **45.00**

Town & Country snack set, King Corn **225.00**

Wall pocket, red feather **45.00**

Sheet Music

The most valuable examples of sheet music are those related to early transportation, ethnic themes, Disney characters, a particularly popular actor, singer, or composer, or with a cover illustration done by a well-known artist. Production of sheet music peaked during the 'Tin Pan Alley Days,' from the 1880s until the 1930s. Covers were made as attractive as possible to lure potential buyers, and today's collectors sometimes frame and hang them as they would a print. Flea markets are a good source for sheet music, and prices are usually very reasonable. Most are available for under $5.00. Some of the better examples are listed here. Refer to *The Sheet Music Reference & Price Guide* by Anna Marie Guiheen and Marie-Reine A. Pafik (Collector Books).

All Right Louie Drop the Gun, Carter & Johnson, Arthur Godfrey cover **10.00**

Autumn Serenade, Sammy Gallop & Peter DeRose, 1945 .... **5.00**

Bible Tells Me So, Dale Evans, Roy Rogers & Dale on cover, 1945.**16.00**

Breakfast at Tiffany's, Henry Mancini, Audrey Hepburn cover, 1961 .... **8.00**

Calypso, John Denver, John Denver cover, 1975 .... **15.00**

Cool, Sondhiem & Bernstein, from West Side Story, 1957 .... **5.00**

Do It While You're Young, Lampert & Loring, from The Snow Queen, 1959 .... **4.00**

Dreamer's Holiday, Kim Gannon & Mabel Wayne, Perry Como on cover, 1949 .... **10.00**

Evelina, Harold Arlen & EY Young, 1944 .... **12.00**

Everybody Loves Somebody, I Taylor & K Lane, Peggy Lee cover, 1948 .... **10.00**

Fire & Rain, James Taylor, James Taylor cover, 1969 .... 5.00

Forever, Buddy Kellen, Little Dippers cover, 1960 .... 5.00

Goodnight My Love, Mack Gordon and Harry Revel, 1936, from the movie Stowaway, Shirley Temple, Robert Young and Alice Faye photo, $20.00. (Photo courtesy Guiheen and Pafik)

Green Beret, PG Fairbanks & CWD Ken Whitcomb, 1964 .... 5.00

Guys & Dolls, Joe Swerling, Abe Burrows & Frank Loesser, 1950 .... 5.00

Homework, Irving Berkin, from Miss Liberty musical, 1949 .... 6.00

House I Live In, Lewis Allen & Earl Robinson, Sinatra cover, 1942 .... 18.00

I Just Called To Say I Love You, Stevie Wonder, 1984 .... 5.00

Indiana Moon, Benny Davis & Isham Jones, Perret cover artist, 1923 .... 10.00

Just a Prayer Away, C Tobias & D Kapp, Kate Smith cover, 1944 .... 6.00

Just Walking in the Rain, Johnny Bragg & Robert S Riley, 1953 .... 12.00

Katie, Cole Porter, from DuBarry Was a Lady, 1943 .... 10.00

Kiss Me Sweet, Milton Drake, 1959 .... 7.00

Lady Bird Cha Cha Cha, Norman Rockwell cover art, 1968 . 25.00

Lullaby of Birdland, George Shearing, 1952 .... 3.00

Meet Me in Seattle Suzie, Lassers, 1962 .... 5.00

Mule Train, Johnny Lang, Hy Heath & Fred Glickman, 1949 .... 6.00

Near to You, Richard Adler & Jerry Ross, from Damn Yankees, 1955 .... 6.00

Night & Day, Cole Porter, from Gay Divorce, Sinatra cover, 1932 . 10.00

On the Street Where You Live, Lerner & Lowe, from My Fair Lady, 1956 .... 5.00

One Boy, Lee Adams & Charles Strouse, from Bye Bye Birdie, 1960 .... 5.00

Paper Roses, Janice Torre & Fred Spielman, Marie Osmond cover, 1962 .... 8.00

Peppermint Twist, Joey Dee & Henry Glover, 1961 .... 5.00

Quiet Cathedral, Iris Mason & Hal Saunders, 1945 .... 3.00

Quit Cryin' the Blues, Felix Lewis, 1931 .... 15.00

Ramblin Rose, Noel Herman & Joe Sherman, Nat King Cole cover, 1962 .... 4.00

River Kwai March, Arnold, from Bridge Over River Kwai, 1957 .... 6.00

Second Hand Rose, Grant Clarke & James Hanley, Streisand cover, 1965 .... 14.00

Seventy Six Trombones, Meredith Wilson, from Music Man, 1957 .... 8.00

Since I Kissed My Baby Goodbye, Cole Porter, 1941 .... **5.00**

Tequila, Chuck Rio, The Champs photo cover, 1958 .... **4.00**

There's No Business Like Show Business, Irving Berlin, 1946 .... **10.00**

They Can't Take That Away From Me, Gershwin, Fred Astaire & Ginger Rogers **12.00**

Three Coins in the Fountain, Sammy Cann and Jule Styne, 1954, from the movie Three Coins in the Fountain, Clifton Webb, Dorothy McGuire and other stars in photo, $5.00. (Photo courtesy Guiheen and Parfik)

Volare, Mitchell Paris & Domenico Modugno, McGuire Sisters cover, 1958........................ **3.00**

Voyage to the Bottom of the Sea, Faith, W Pidgeon, etc cover, 1961 .... **8.00**

Wake Me When It's Over, Chan & Van Heusen, cast photo cover, 1960 .... **4.00**

Where Is the Life I Led? Cole Porter, from Kiss Me Kate, 1948 .... **6.00**

Yellow Rose of Texas, Don George, Johnny Desmond cover, 1955 .... **3.00**

Your Cheatin' Heart, Hank Williams, Hank Williams photo cover, 1952........................ **8.00**

Zana Zaranda, Mort Greene & Harry Revel, Call Out the Marines, 1942 .... **5.00**

Zigenuer, Noel Coward, 1941 .. **5.00**

Shot Glasses

Shot glasses, old and new, are whetting the interest of today's collectors, and they're relatively easy to find. Basic values are given for various categories of shot glasses in mint condition. These are general prices only. Glasses that are in less-than-mint condition will obviously be worth less than the price given here. Very rare and unique items will be worth more. Sample glasses and other individual one-of-a-kind oddities are a bit harder to classify and really need to be evaluated on an individual basis. For more information we redcommend *Shot Glasses: An American Tradition* by Mark Pickvet; he is listed in the Directory under Michigan. See Clubs and Newsletters for information concerning the Shot Glass Club of America.

Barrel shaped, from $5 to........ **7.50**

Black porcelain replica, from $3.50 to **5.00**

Carnival colors, plain or fluted, from $100 to **150.00**

Culver 22k gold, from $6 to..... **8.00**

Depression, colors, from $10 to..**12.50**

Depression, colors w/patterns or etching, from $17.50 to... **25.00**

Depression, tall, general designs, from $10 to...................... **12.50**

Depression, tall, tourist, from $5 to.. **7.50**

European design, rounded w/gold rim, from $4 to.................. **6.00**

Frosted w/gold designs, from $6 to..................................... **8.00**

General, advertising, from $4 to................................ **6.00**

General, enameled design, from $3 to.. **4.00**

General, etched design, from $5 to..................................... **7.50**

General, frosted design, from $3.50 to.. **5.00**

General, gold design, from $6 to **8.00**

General, porcelain, from $4 to . **6.00**

Inside eyes, from $6 to............. **8.00**

Iridized silver, from $5 to **7.50**

Mary Gregory or Anchor Hocking Ships, from $150 to....... **200.00**

Nineteenth-century cut patterns, from $35 to **50.00**

Nude, from $25 to **35.00**

Plain, w/or w/out flutes, from 50¢ to .... **.75**

Planet Hollywood/Hard Rock Cafe, sm, from $10 to **12.50**

Pop or soda advertising, from $12.50 to **15.00**

Ruby flashed, from $35 to...... **50.00**

Sayings & toasts (1940s & 1950s), from $5 to **7.50**

Sports (Professional Teams), from $5 to.................................... **7.50**

Square, general, from $6 to..... **8.00**

Square, w/etching, from $10 to..**12.50**

Square, w/pewter, from $12.50 to **15.00**

Square, w/2-tone bronze & pewter, from $15 to **17.50**

Standard glass w/pewter, from $7.50 to............................ **10.00**

Steuben or Lalique crystal, from $150 to **200.00**

Tiffany, Galle or fancy art, from $600 to **800.00**

Tourist, colored glass, from $4 to . **6.00**

Tourist, general, from $3 to..... **4.00**

Tourist, porcelain, from $3.50 to .**5.00**

Tourist, Taiwan, from $2 to..... **3.00**

Tourist, turquoise or gold, from $6 to **8.00**

Whiskey or beer advertising, modern, from $5 to **7.50**

Whiskey samples, M, from $75 to **350.00**

Silhouette Pictures

Silhouettes and reverse paintings on glass were commercially produced in the US from the 1920s through the 1950s. Some were hand painted, but most were silkscreened. Artists and companies used either flat or convex glass. Common subjects include romantic couples, children, horses, dogs, and cats. Many different styles, sizes, colors, and materials were used for frames. Backgrounds also vary from textured paper to foils, colorful lithographs, wildflowers or butterfly wings. Sometimes the backgrounds were painted on the back of the glass in gold or cream color. These inexpensive pictures were usually sold in pairs, except for the advertising kind, which were given by merchants as gifts. For more information we recommend *The Encyclopedia of Silhouette Collectibles on Glass* by Shirley

Mace (Shadow Enterprises); she is listed in the Directory under New Mexico.

**Benton, convex, no title, #160, 4x5",
$20.00.** (Photo courtesy Shirley Mace)

Art Publishing, flat, Dutch wind-mill against multicolored back-ground.............................**12.00**

Art Publishing, flat, flowers & but-terfly on oval **18.00**

Art Publishing, flat, windblown lady w/whippet................**22.00**

Benton, convex, couple by lamppost, multicolored floral border...**40.00**

Benton, convex, couple courting against cottage background...............**40.00**

Benton, convex, couple holding music between them & sing-ing.....................................**25.00**

Benton, convex, couple in horse-drawn carriage w/autumn background.....................**40.00**

Benton, convex, couple push-ing child in wheelbarrow in autumn scene..................**40.00**

Benton, convex, lady beside arbor w/umbrella in rain..........**30.00**

Benton, convex, lady playing piano as dog watches **42.00**

Benton, convex, man in chair w/pipe & book & cat at feet.........**25.00**

Benton, convex, man in gondola against Venetian scene...**35.00**

Benton, convex, Scottie dog w/leaf in mouth..........................**30.00**

Benton, convex, ship sailing on rough sea.........................**25.00**

Buckbee Brehm, flat, Good Night (couple kissing), 1924.....**24.00**

Buckbee Brehm, flat, Spanish lady dancing w/musicians beyond...........................**22.00**

Buckbee Brehm, flat, The Love Letter (lady kissing note), 1930.................................**23.00**

C&A Richards & Co., flat, Per Aspera Ad Astra, by C. & A. Richards Co., 3x7", $45.00. (Photo courtesy Shirley Mace)

Deltex, flat, Hearts (couple carving hearts in tree) **35.00**

Deltex, flat, lady w/Scottie dog los-ing hat in wind................**35.00**

Flowercraft, flat, couple kiss-ing, pressed flowers in back-ground **22.00**

Newton, flat, lady at spinning wheel................................**20.00**

Reliance, flat, Little Red Riding Hood & wolf in woods.....**35.00**

Reliance, flat, Lucky April Shower (man w/umbrella)............**20.00**

Reliance, flat, Tulip Time (Dutch boy & girl) **30.00**

Stanwood-Hillson, flat, dog begs to girl in chair w/cottage back-ground..............................**35.00**

Snow Domes

Snow domes are water-filled paperweights. The earliest type was made in two pieces with a glass globe on a separate base. First made in the mid-nineteenth century, they were revived during the 1930s and 1940s. the most common snow domes on today's market are the plastic half-moon shapes made as souvenirs or Christmas toys, a style that originated in West Germany during the 1950s. Other shapes such as round and square bottles, tall and short rectangles, cubes, and other simple shapes are found as well.

Character, Betty Boop, by Bully Inc., Fleischer Studios Inc., M, $18.00.

Advertising, Coca-Cola Polar Bear, glass w/resin base, musical, 6", EX **20.00**
Advertising, Texaco tanker truck against cityscape in round dome, EX **65.00**
Bank, souvenir scene on plastic, sq base, slit in back, EX **8.00**
Birth announcement, babies on see-saw w/stork in middle, plastic dome, M **8.00**

Birthday, It's Down Hill From Here, Garfield/floating numbers, Enesco, M **20.00**
Character, Creature From the Black Lagoon, figural, MIB **15.00**
Character, Grumpy Care Bear w/umbrella, musical, 6", MIB **55.00**
Character, Lone Ranger Round-Up, glass dome, Driss, 1950s, 4", VG+ **50.00**
Character, Lone Ranger Round-Up, plastic w/decal on base, 4", EX **38.00**
Character, Raggedy Ann & Andy in moving sled, Bobbs-Merrill, 1980, 3", M **35.00**
Character, Road Runner/Wile E Coyote in globe, desert base, 1995, MIB **55.00**
Christmas, Olde World Village, musical, Partylites, 2003, 7", MIB **50.00**
Christmas, Santa or snowman roly-poly figure, 1970s, EX, ea. **20.00**
Christmas, tree in globe on white plastic stand, Austria, 1950s, 7", M **75.00**
Disney, Beauty & the Beast, 1991, MIB **45.00**
Disney, C Robin holds globe w/dragon, Pooh, Eeyore & Tigger watch, MIB **75.00**
Disney, Donald Duck w/globe in tummy, plastic, 1960s-70s, VG+ **45.00**
Disney, Mickey & Minnie Wedding, glass w/resin base, 9x6", MIB **70.00**
Disney, Woody's Round-Up, characters from Toy Story, MIB. **90.00**
Easter, rabbit w/eggs standing next to pine tree, Austrian glass dome, M **10.00**

Figural, animal draped across lg plastic dome, EX **10.00**

Figural, clown w/water ball tummy, 1970s, EX **30.00**

Figural, orange w/leaves, NM. **30.00**

Graduation, Congratulations, cap cocked stop dome, EX **8.00**

Halloween, Trick or Treat!, witch atop house w/skeletons in dome, EX **10.00**

Religious, saint in glass globe, decal on plastic base, 1930s, EX..**40.00**

Souvenir, Amish Farm and House, Lancaster, PA, calendar in base, M, $25.00.

Souvenir, Art Institute of Chicago, replica of lion at entrance, M **48.00**

Souvenir, Boston MA, Madonna & child in globe, porcelain base, 4", EX **32.00**

Souvenir, Cedar Point, dolphin atop dome on water wave, EX. **15.00**

Souvenir, Crystal Cave PA, plastic half dome, 2¼" H, M **12.00**

Souvenir, Florida, alligator w/dome belly, plastic, 1970s, 5", M.**12.00**

Souvenir, Florida, frog w/dome belly, plastic, #353R, 1970s, 4", EX **15.00**

Souvenir, Great Smoky Mountains, bear in woods w/bear stop, EX................................... **18.00**

Souvenir, Memphis, paddle wheeler & street scene, black base, EX................................... **10.00**

Souvenir, Mexico, 2 on seesaw, plastic dome, #354V, 1970s, 3x4", EX **20.00**

Souvenir, New York, black & white dog, Made in USA, 4x3", EX **55.00**

Souvenir, New York World's Fair, 1964-65, NM.................... **35.00**

Souvenir, Paris, cityscape, 2x3", EX **18.00**

Souvenir, Wildwood by the Sea NJ, plastic footed half dome, 2½x3", EX **18.00**

Soda Pop

Now that vintage Coca-Cola items have become rather expensive, interest is expanding to include some of the less widely known flavors of soda — Dr. Pepper, Nehi, and Orange Crush, for instance. For more information we recommend *Collectible Soda Pop Memorabilia* by B.J. Summers (Collector Books).

Dr. Pepper

A young pharmacist, Charles C. Alderton, was hired by W.B. Morrison, owner of Morrison's Old Corner Drug Store in Waco, Texas, around 1884. Alderton, an observant sort, noticed that the drugstore's patrons could never quite make up their minds as to which flavor of extract to order. He concocted a formula that combined many flavors, and Dr. Pepper was born. The name was chosen by Morrison in honor of a beautiful young girl with whom he had once been in love. The girl's father, a Virginia doctor by the name of Pepper, had discouraged the relationship due to their youth, but Morrison had never forgotten her. On December 1, 1885, a U.S. patent was issued to the creators of Dr. Pepper.

Bottle, miniature, embossed clear glass, 1940s, 3½", EX **80.00**
Bottle carrier, cardboard 6-pack, 1940s, EX **125.00**
Bottle crate, wood, yellow w/red logo, 12x18x4", EX **35.00**
Bottle topper, Virginia Kavanagh, NM, from $215 to **245.00**
Calendar, 1951, complete, NM . **125.00**
Clock, plastic bottle-cap style, 11" dia, EX **50.00**
Clock, plastic w/chrome trim, logo under numbers, Pam, 1970s, EX **110.00**
Fan pull, cardboard, beach girl w/umbrella, VG **125.00**
Key holder, rubber, oblong, gold & black, 1940s-50s, 1½x2", NM **15.00**
Light, stained glass-like plastic, 7x8" dia, EX **100.00**
Match holder, light green tin, 1930s, 6", EX+ **100.00**
Radio, wooden cooler form, electric, 1940s, VG **525.00**
Sign, cardboard, Try a Frosty Pepper..., w/graphics, 1960s, 15x25", NM **50.00**

Sign, embossed tin, red oval above gold V on white, 1960s, 12x28", EX **125.00**
Sign, paper, Have a Picnic at NY World's Fair on Us!, 1964, 25x15", M **100.00**
Thermometer, dial type w/glass front, Hot or Cold, Pam, 1950s-60s, NM **125.00**
Thermometer, plastic bottle shape w/10-2-4 logo on white, 11" dia, NM **125.00**

Thermometer, red and white, 26x7¼", EX, $175.00.

Tray, Drink a Bite To Eat, girl holding 2 bottles, 1939, EX . **325.00**
Tumbler, Good for Life, tapered, applied label, 1940s, EX. **150.00**
Watch, metal case w/leather strap, Fossil, 1980s, MIB **80.00**

Hires

Did you know that Hires Root Beer was first served to fairgoers at the Philadelphia Centennial in 1876? It was developed by Charles E. Hires, a druggist who experimented with roots and herbs to come up with the final recipe.

The company originally chose the Hires boy as their logo, and if you'll study his attire, you can sometimes approximate a guess as to when an item he appears on was manufactured. Very early on he appeared in a dress, and from 1906 until 1914 it was a bathrobe. He sported a dinner jacket from 1915 until 1926.

Sign, tin, Bracing — Delicious, 1923, 28x11", $325.00. (Photo courtesy Craig Stifter)

Blotter, Real Root Juices Make...Avoid Imitations, 1920, EX................... 15.00

Clock, plastic, Genuine Hires Root Beer on white, Neon Products, EX....................................55.00

Door push bar, porcelain, red & blue on aqua, 3x31", EX+ 175.00

Door push/pull handle, tin, vertical, blue & white stripes/bottle, NM.................................150.00

Hires, sign, tin, R-J logo/In Bottles/Ice Cold on blue, 10x28", NM 50.00

Menu board, cardboard, image of moustached man, 1950s, 28x15", VG+ 75.00

Menu board, tin chalkboard, Drink..In Bottles, blue & white stripes, NM....................145.00

Pocket mirror, celluloid, Hires boy pointing, 2¼" dia, EX......25.00

Sign, cardboard, shows Hires w/food specials, 1950s, 8x24", NM..................................60.00

Sign, die-cut cardboard, With Lunch 5¢, graphics, 1940s, 11x10", NM+..............................100.00

Sign, metal, Say! Drink Hires 5c/It Is Pure, 9½x17", VG........85.00

Sign, tin, Enjoy Hires, Healthful/ Delicious, 1930s, 27½x9½", EX...................................50.00

Sign, tin, Hires R-J Root Beer In Bottles Ice Cold, 10x28", NM 50.00

Sign, tin bottle shape, 1950s, 22", M....................................200.00

Syrup dispenser, front spout, stainless steel w/tin signs, 8½" 135.00

Thermometer, metal, blue & white stripes, bottle at bottom, 27", VG....................................25.00

Tray, Drink...Honest Root Beer, 2 girls, Haskell Coffin, 14x10", EX 15.00

Nehi

Banner, paper, NE above bottle/HI below, 1940s, 19x40", VG..100.00

Bottle, clear w/red & white painted label, 10-oz, EX...............12.50

Bottle carrier, cardboard 6-pack for 7-oz bottles, Take Me Home, EX...................................35.00

Bottle opener, engraved Drink Nehi, Consolidated Cork Co, EX...................................15.00

Calendar, 1935, Rolf Armstrong art, complete, NM+.......500.00

Nehi, clock, round, glass front, metal frame, yellow dot, 15" dia, NM..........................325.00

Paperweight, glass, pinup-style sailor girl, NM.................25.00

Sign, metal, Curb Service..., blue on yellow, 1940s, 28x20", EX.65.00

Sign, metal, Drink Nehi Beverages, legs & bottle, 1940s, 21x13", NM **215.00**

Tray, beach girl on wave w/bottle in foreground, G **150.00**

Nesbitt's

Thermometer, tin, four-color, 1950s, 24", $135.00. (Photo courtesy Craig Stifter)

Bottle, clear w/white painted label, EX, 9½" **10.00**

Bottle carrier, cardboard 6-pack, 1940s, EX **25.00**

Bottle opener, embossed metal, Drink Nesbitt's, 3¼", EX.. **20.00**

Calendar, 1953, complete, EX. **65.00**

Clock, fluourescent tube light, Drink Nesbitt's Orange, 26x12x4", EX **50.00**

Door push bar, porcelain, Take Home a Carton/bottle, 32½", EX .**150.00**

Menu board, tin, 1950s, 20x28", from $50 to **75.00**

Picnic cooler, 1950s, EX......... **65.00**

Shot glass, clear w/orange & white painted logo, 2¼", EX...... **12.00**

Sign, cardboard, clown w/2 kids drinking Orange, 16x24", EX......**25.00**

Sign, die-cut cardboard, lady in hat & gloves w/bottle, 1950s, 21", EX **75.00**

Sign, tin, Drink & 5¢ above bottle, 1950s, 49x16", EX......... **275.00**

Sign, tin bottle shape, 84x24", NM+.............................. **850.00**

Thermometer, metal, black & yellow, red & white letters, 1938, 27", NM.......................... **200.00**

Orange-Crush

Bottle, aqua w/embossed letters, 6-oz, EX **22.50**

Bottle, clear w/embossed letters, ribbed, 24-oz, 1920s, EX. **25.00**

Bottle, dark amber w/applied orange & white painted label, 6-oz, EX **40.00**

Bottle opener, metal wall-mount w/embossed lettering, 1950, 3", NM **30.00**

Calendar, 1946, complete, 31x16", VG.................................. **125.00**

Door push, porcelain, 1950s, 9⅜x3½", EX.................... **925.00**

Menu board, logo & bottle at top, Stout Sign, 1940s-50s, 27x19", EX+ **100.00**

Menu board, tin over cardboard w/slots flanking bottle cap, 23x35", VG.................... **175.00**

Sign, cardboard hanger, ca 1920s, EX, $250.00.

Sign, celluloid button hanger, Enjoy...Naturally..., 9" dia, NM+................................. **150.00**

Sign, celluloid over cardboard orange button, Crushy/phrase, 9", EX **165.00**

Sign, reverse-painted glass, round, Fresh/Drink O-C/Crushy, 9½", EX **200.00**

Sign, self-framed cardboard, beach couple/phrase, 1950s, NM **225.00**

Thermometer, dial, white w/ orange background, 12" dia, EX **350.00**

Tray, 6 bottles arranged like spokes of a wheel, 1940s, 10" dia, NM **150.00**

Pepsi-Cola

Pepsi-Cola has been around about as long as Coca-Cola, but since collectors are just now beginning to discover how fascinating this line of advertising memorabilia can be, it's generally much less expensive. You'll be able to determine the approximate date your items were made by the style of logo they carry. The familiar oval was used in the early 1940s, about the time the two 'dots' (indicated in our listings with '=') between the words were changed to one. But the double dots are used nowadays as well, especially on items designed to be reminiscent of the old ones — beware! The bottle cap logo was used from about 1943 until the early to mid-'60s with variations. For more information refer to *Pepsi-Cola Collectibles* by Bill Vehling and Michael Hunt and *Introduction to Pepsi Collecting* by Bob Stoddard.

Bank, vending machine w/miniature bottles, Louis Marx, EXIB **115.00**

Book cover, paper, Come Alive!, teen couple in gym, 1960s, M **5.00**

Bottle, Fountain Syrup, clear w/red & white painted label, 12-oz, EX **65.00**

Bottle carrier, plastic 6-pack, bottle cap logo, 16-oz, 1960s-70s, EX+ **30.00**

Bottle carrier, wood, holds 6 bottles, EX **150.00**

Bottle opener, wall mount, red logo on yellow, 5x2¼", EX+ **75.00**

Calendar, 1945, pinup girls, complete, M **65.00**

Change receiver, rubber, Say Pepsi Please, geometric trim, 1960s, NM **25.00**

Clock, light-up, double-bubble, Say Pepsi Please, 1950s, EX+ .. **600.00**

Clock, light-up, Drink Pepsi Ice-Cold, bottle caps as numbers, 15", EX **700.00**

Clock, light-up, Swihart, 1940s, 15", EX+, from $375.00 to $450.00.

Door push bar, porcelain, yellow & white, 2x31", EX+ **125.00**

Frisbee, white w/Diet Pepsi logo, 1980s, 9" dia, EX **4.00**

Hat, hot neon pink ball-cap style w/P-C logo, adjustable, EX. **5.00**

Lighter, logo cap on white, musical, 1950s, 2¾x2", EX 100.00

Matchbook, #7 WWII Disney military insignia on P=C cover, 1940s, EX 15.00

Ornament, white flat plastic star w/P-C logo, gold-trim, 3", MIB 3.00

Sign, cardboard, Pepsi's Best Take No Less, lady & bottlecap on red, 1940s, EX 575.00

Sign, die-cut cardboard standup, Pepsi cop/5¢ sign, 7½x6½", EX+ 150.00

Sign, die-cut cardboard standup, Santa w/bottle, 1956, 20", EX 60.00

Sign, flicker disk, Take Home..., Reach for..., bottle cap, 10" dia, EX 200.00

Sign, light-up, plastic oval, rotates, 2-sided, 1950s-60s, 10x20", NM 200.00

Sign, tin bottle cap, 19¼" dia, NM 375.00

Tap knob, musical bottle-cap type, chrome & plastic, 1940s, EX+ 90.00

Thermometer, metal, Bigger/Better, bottle graphic, 16", EX+ . 250.00

Thermometer, metal, The Light Refreshment, dated 1956, 27", NM 175.00

Tray, Enjoy P=C/Hits the Spot, w/musical notes, 1940s, 11x13", NM 100.00

Wristwatch, white bottle-cap face, Armitron, 1988, MIB (can-shaped box)...................... 45.00

Royal Crown Cola

Bottle crate, wooden, red w/yellow lettering, EX.................... 30.00

Bottle display, cardboard & foil, pleated fan shape w/button, 1930s, M 135.00

Bottle opener, wall mount, raised letters in red on silver, Star X, EX 30.00

Bottle topper & bottle, cardboard, Santa w/wreath & bottle, NM+ 20.00

Calendar, 1951, Ann Blyth w/dog, complete, 24", EX.......... 160.00

Clock, metal and plastic, lights up, 34x37", VG, $1,000.00.

Clock, triangular, white letters on orange, white border w/numbers, EX 100.00

Fan, cardboard, all-American girl, 1950s, EX 30.00

Fan, cardboard, Shirley Temple w/bottle, 12x8", EX 20.00

Lighter, can shape, red logo on white, 1950s, 1½x¾", M .. 25.00

Radio, can shape, GE/Hong Kong, EX 20.00

Sign, cardboard, Gene Tierney, phrase & logo, 1940s, 11x28", NM 300.00

Sign, cardboard, image of Barbara Stanwyck, 1940s, 11x28", NM 75.00

Sign, cardboard, You'll Flip... ZZZip..., lady in hat, 11x28", NM+ 30.00

Sign, metal, Drink..., red & white, 1950s, 17x34", EX **125.00**

Sign, porcelain, couple picnicking, 12x15½", EX **25.00**

Sign, self-framed embossed tin, lg bottle graphic, 36x16", VG **175.00**

Sign, tin bottle shape, 1950s, 12", NM+ **350.00**

Thermometer, dial, red, white & blue w/blue border, 12", EX **85.00**

Thermometer, tin, Better Taste Calls for RC, red & white, 21", EX **200.00**

Thermometer, tin, bottle next to gauge on blue, 1960s, 17", NM **230.00**

Trolley sign, cardboard, Lucille Ball says RC Tastes Best!, 1940s, EX+ **200.00**

Seven-Up

Though it was originally touted to have medicinal qualities, by 1930 7-Up had been reformulated and was simply sold as a refreshing drink. The company who first made it was the Howdy Company, who by 1940 had changed its name to 7-Up to correspond with the name of the soft drink. Collectors search for the signs, thermometers, point-of-sale items, etc., that carry the 7-Up slogans.

Ashtray, brown glass w/white lettering, 3 rests, 5½" dia, NM .. **15.00**

Ashtray, round glass dish w/logo in center, 1950s-60s, 4½" dia, EX+ **25.00**

Bill hook, celluloid button, I'd Hang for a Chilled 7-Up, EX+.. **35.00**

Bottle topper, Top O' the Mornin', leprechaun & shamrocks, NM **12.00**

Calendar, 1953, complete, EX+ .**75.00**

Clock, First Against Thirst/logo, vertical w/bowed sides, EX.... **75.00**

Clock, glass face, wood frame, 1940s, 15½", $225.00. (Photo courtesy Buffalo Bay Auctions)

Clock, plastic 'mod' flower shape w/multicolored graphics, 17", VG **65.00**

Display bottle, plastic, 1960s, 28", EX **85.00**

Doll, Fresh-Up Freddie, painted rubber, 1959, VG **125.00**

Doll, Fresh-Up Freddie, stuffed cloth w/rubber head, Canada, 15", EX............................. **75.00**

Doll, Spot, plush, red/black/white, w/suction cups, 7-Up tags, 6", NM **5.00**

Drinking glass, 'The Unglass,' upside down bell shape, EX............ **5.00**

Hat, green ball-cap style w/rope cord trim & 7-Up w/red dot logo, EX **5.00**

Menu board, tin chalkboard, hand-held bottle, 27x19", EX+. **70.00**

Menu board, tin chalkboard, Squirt boy & lg bottle, 1954, 27x19", EX+ **250.00**

Ornament, Spot figure, plush w/Santa hat, sunglasses & present, NM **5.00**

Sign, cardboard, All-Family Drink!, baby in highchair, gold frame, NM+ 100.00

Sign, cardboard, We're Fresh Up Family, 1948, 11x21", EX 10.00

Sign, cardboard hanger, hand-held bottle, 1947, 5x9½", EX 40.00

Sign, flange, You Like It, It Likes You, 12x10", EX 40.00

Sign, plastic light-up, Fresh Up..., Nothing Does..., 1950s , 11" sq, EX 200.00

Sign, tin, hand-held bottle, rolled raised rim, 1947, 20x28", EX 225.00

Sign, tin, Nothing Does It Like Seven-Up, 1950s, 13x44", EX 150.00

Sign, tin bottle shape, wet-look, 2-sided, 44x13", EX 300.00

Telephone, Red Spot figure, 7-Up Co, 1990, EX.................... 18.00

Thermometer, dial, Fresh Clean Taste, 1960s, 12" dia, EX. 50.00

Thermometer, dial, glass w/metal frame, yellow sunburst, 12" dia, VG........................... 150.00

Thermometer, porcelain, The Fresh-Up Family Drink/bottle, 15", NM........................... 85.00

Tie clip, enameled logo on bar, EX 15.00

Miscellaneous

A&W Root Beer, plush bears, 2 different, 1997-98, NM, ea from $15 to 20.00

A-Treat, menu board, tin chalkboard, red, white, & blue, 20x18", NM+ 40.00

Big Red, bottle, clear, 10-oz... 10.00

Birchola, fan, cardboard w/stick handle, gazing couple on reverse, EX...................... 75.00

Bubble Up, sign, celluloid, green oval, Just Pure Pleasure!, 9x13", NM..................... 150.00

Canada Dry, kick-plate sign, name & logos, 10x30", EX+ 50.00

Canada Dry, sign, die-cut tin shield, crown, black, red & white, 14", NM 125.00

Cliqout Club Ginger Ale, calendar, 1942, complete, EX 100.00

Dad's Root Beer, menu board, tin chalkboard, bottle cap, 28x20", NM 75.00

Dad's Root Beer, thermometer, tin, Just Right.../bottle cap, 27", NM ..80.00

Dad's Root Beer, thermometer, tin, sq corners, 27", NM 75.00

Diet-Rite Cola, lighter, aluminum w/flip top, VG 15.00

Donald Duck Cola, sign, die-cut cardboard standup, 22x26", EX. 85.00

Double Cola, menu board, tin chalkboard, red, white & blue, 2x820", NM..................... 100.00

Double Cola, sign, cardboard hanger, hot-air balloon, 1950s, 9", NM 18.00

Frostie, menu board, tin, Real Taste Treat, slotted, 1950, 12x36", NM 500.00

Frostie, mugs, glass w/painted logo, 1950s-60s, set of 4, EX ... 30.00

Frostie, thermometer, tin, mascot, bottlecap & 6-pack on white, 26", EX............................. 185.00

Grapette, mechanical pen, plastic, 1950s, 5", EX+.................. 30.00

Grapette, mirror framed by advertising, 1940s-50s, 16x8", NM 300.00

Grapette, sign, cardboard, Thirsty or Not!, girl & flowers, 28x24", NM+ **175.00**

Grapette, sign, cardboard standup, lady in raincoat & dog, 1940s, 19" **125.00**

Grapette, themometer, tin, Remember To Buy.., bottle graphics, 15", EX **100.00**

Grapette, thermomter, dial, bottle cap form, 11" dia, EX **100.00**

Kist, calendar, 1951, Lou Gehrig/ boy on pitcher's mound, complete, EX **250.00**

Kist, clock, red, white & black on white, wood box frame, 16" sq, NM+ **200.00**

Mission Beverage, bottle, clear, 1-qt **15.00**

Moxie, ashtray, aluminum w/ embossed logos, 3 rests, 1960s, 5½" dia, EX **20.00**

Moxie, bottle, aqua, 7-oz, EX . **20.00**

Moxie, sign, die-cut cardboard standup of hand-held bottle, 1950s, NM **100.00**

NuGrape, blotter, image of blotter, EX+ **30.00**

NuGrape, thermometer, dial, phrase & bottle on white, 12" dia, NM **100.00**

NuGrape, tray, A Flavor You Can't Forget, hand-held bottle, 13x11", VG **60.00**

Orange Kist, sign, tin, Drink... & Other Flavors, 6x13", NM **60.00**

Sprite, figure, Lucky Lymon, vinyl, 1980s, MIB **35.00**

Squirt, change mat, plastic, hologram logo, 9x12", EX+ **75.00**

Squirt, clock, light-up, Switch to..., Pam, 15" dia, EX+ **375.00**

Squirt, doll, Squirt Boy, vinyl w/cloth outfit, 1960s, 17", VG **200.00**

Squirt, Party Fun Book, 1953, EX **25.00**

Sun Crest, calendar, 1949, complete, NM **150.00**

Sun Crest, clock, light-up, round, numbers around bottle, NM **375.00**

Vernor's, bank, metal can shape, 1960s, M **15.00**

Whistle, clock, die-cut pressed board, electric, #Wc 6-92, EX, $1,100.00. (Photo courtesy Collectors Auction Service)

Whistle, pocket mirror, rectangular, 2 elves w/sign, 1940s, 2x3", NM **150.00**

Whistle, sign, die-cut cardboard, boy on bike, 21x21", NM **425.00**

Whistle, whistle, blue metal, Thirsty? Just Whistle, NM............. **10.00**

Souvenir Spoons

Originating with the Salem Witch spoons designed by Daniel Low, souvenir spoons are generally reasonably priced, easily displayed, and often exhibit fine artwork and craftsmanship. Spoons are found with a wide range of subject matter including advertising, commemorative, historic sites, American

Indians, famed personalities, and more. Souvenir spoons continue to capture the imaginations of thousands of collectors with their timeless appeal. For further information we recommend *Collectible Souvenir Spoons, Books I* and *II,* by Wayne Bednersh (Collector Books).

Alaska, sterling, transfer print enamel finial, demitasse, from $5 to.**15.00**

Apostles, figural handle, plain bowl, Gorham, reissue, 1974, ea from $50 to **75.00**

California, bear/poppies figural handle, plain bowl, Shiebler, from $75 to **125.00**

Carnegie Library Rockford IL, Chantilly handle, Gorham, from $30 to **50.00**

Century of Progress, 1833-1933/ Chinese Temple, Deco style, from $25 to **50.00**

Colorado Gateway to Garden of the Gods, scene on handle & bowl, from $40 to **75.00**

Daniel Boone, tobacco leaf handle, image on round bowl, Gorham **100.00**

DAR & temple scene in bowl, Krider, from $50 to **70.00**

Flatiron Building, New York embossed in bowl, various handles, from $20 to **75.00**

Fort Sumter Charleston SC, gold-washed bowl, Towle, from $25 to **50.00**

Gerber Baby embossed on handle, silver plate, from $5 to ... **10.00**

Golden Gate International Exposition, sterling, demitasse, from $20 to............ **40.00**

Hershey's, name enameled on handle, silver plate, from $5 to........**10.00**

High Water Mark Gettysburg in bowl, Baronial pattern, Smith, from $40 to **75.00**

Indian scout kneeling, various bowls, Manchester/Baker, from $30 to **75.00**

Japanese painted porcelain scene on sterling, sq finial, from $20 to **30.00**

Miner standing w/pan of gold, Grass Valley Cal & image in bowl................................. **150.00**

Monte Carlo, mechanical enameled roulette wheel finial, from $40 to **85.00**

New Casino, Santa Cruz Cal, Irving pattern, Wallace, from $35 to............................. **60.00**

Niagara Falls, embossed handle, waves in bowl, WE Glenn & Sons, from $50 to **70.00**

Pinocchio enameled figure on handle, plain bowl, stainless steel **10.00**

Rip Van Winkle, image on handle, pear-shaped bowl, Durgin, from $40 to **70.00**

Stork handle, engraved bowl, Lunt, from $30 to **60.00**

Tampa FL, skyline handle w/pierced bonbon bowl, from $150 to..**300.00**

Teddy Roosevelt, enameled bust image on bowl, Mechanic, from $40 to **60.00**

Waikiki Hawaii, ornate handle w/boat scene in long bowl, from $140 to **200.00**

Wisconsin Dells, Chimney Rock image on cut-out handle, from $10 to **20.00**

Yellowstone Park, Great Falls image on cut-out handle, Robins, from $15 to........ **30.00**

Sports Collectibles

When sports cards became so widely collectible several years, other types of related memorabilia started to interest sports fans. Now they search for baseball uniforms, autographed baseballs, game-used bats and gloves, and all sorts of ephemera. Although baseball is America's all-time favorite, other sports have their own groups of interested collectors.

Autographed baseball, Pete Rose, 9-11-85, 4,192 (hits), from $50.00 to $60.00.

Baseball, Detroit Tigers, Official Ball, 19 signatures, NM . **75.00**

Baseball, Ted Williams Wilson Speed, 1960s, NMIB **90.00**

Baseball glove, Don Drysdale, Spaulding, 1960s, VG **25.00**

Baseball glove, Mark Balenger, VG **25.00**

Bat, Stan Musial autograph, NM **175.00**

Book, Baseball's Immortals, The Story of Dizzy Dean, 1953, EX **35.00**

Book, Official Rule, All American, International Soap Box Derby, 1947 .... **45.00**

Book, 1953 NASCAR Record; softcover, 120 pages, VG+..... **65.00**

Cap, Troy Aikman autograph, NM **45.00**

Catcher's mitt, Spaulding's #42-789, Andy Etchebarren's, 1960s, NM+ **85.00**

Clock, Joe Lewis, copper molded, lightweight, electric, United Self Starting, $1,000.00. (Photo courtesy Collectors Auction Service)

Doll, Joe Montana, stuffed print cloth in 49ers' uniform, NM **30.00**

Hat, Ricky Rudd #27 (NASCAR), Coca-Cola Racing Family, M **15.00**

Hockey puck, Wayne Gretzky autograph, EX **100.00**

Key chain, Roberto Clemente, shows 1960 Topps card, M **15.00**

Lighter, Dale Earnhardt, photo-holographic image, Zippo, M **40.00**

Magazine, Basketball's Best, NBA Pictorial Review, 1955-56, EX **18.00**

Magazine, Sport, Lou Gehrig cover, October 1948, EX.......... **120.00**

Media guide, 1963 Rose Bowl, EX **40.00**

Media guide, 1973 University of Florida Gators, NM **55.00**

Pennant, LA Angels, red on dark blue, 26x8½", EX............. **50.00**

Pennant, LA Dodgers, blue & white, early 1960s, 14x5", EX ... **20.00**

Pennant, New York Mets (1965), team photo, EX **150.00**

Photo, Jeff Gordon, NASCAR, 8x10", M........................... **35.00**

Pin, Ted Williams of Boston Red Sox, image on yellow, Topps, 1956, EX **200.00**

Pin-back button, Harlem Globe-trotters team picture, M. **20.00**

Pin-back button, Oscar Robertson portrait w/ball, Specs International **20.00**

Pit badge, Indianapolis 500, bronze helmet shape, 1953, EX+..**100.00**

Poster, 1967 Indy (500) Pace Car, Camaro SS, 23x18", EX.. **25.00**

Program, Harlem Globetrotters, 31st season, 1957, EX..... **25.00**

Program, Indy 500, 1961, 7 flags on tan cover, EX................... **30.00**

Radio, plastic baseball shape w/strap, San Diego Padres, China, 3", M................... **35.00**

Tie bar, Indianapolis 500, race car in gold-plated metal, 1940s, EX **40.00**

Wallet, Joe Dimaggio, leather w/cartoon image, zippered, 1950s, EX **300.00**

Wristwatch, NASCAR's Richard Petty, Hope Industries, 1992, unused, MOC **25.00**

Yearbook, Detroit Tigers, 1955, EX.................................. **75.00**

Yearbook, Indianapolis 500, 1975, EX+ **25.00**

Stangl

The Stangl Company of Trenton, New Jersey, produced many striking lines of dinnerware from the 1920s until they closed in the late 1970s. Though white clay was used earlier, the red-clay patterns made from 1942 on are most often encountered and are preferred by collectors. Decorated with both hand painting and sgraffito work (hand carving), Stangl's lines are very distinctive and easily recognized. Virtually all is marked, and most pieces carry the pattern name as well.

In addition to the dinnerware, Stangl is famous for their lovely bird figurines, which they made from 1940 until as late as 1978. Nearly all are marked and carry a four-digit number used to identify the species. For more information we recommend *Collector's Encyclopedia of Stangl Artware, Lamps, and Birds* by Robert C. Runge, Jr. (Collector Books).

Soup mug, Fruit and Flowers 14-ounce, from $65.00 to $80.00.

Ashtray, Town & Country #5287, blue bathtub shape, from $35 to **60.00**

Bean pot, Colonial #1388, lg, from $40 to **50.00**

Bowl, coupe soup; Americana #2000, 7½" **10.00**

Bowl, coupe soup; Fruit #3697, from $25 to **35.00**

Bowl, lug soup; Golden Harvest #3887 .... **10.00**

Bowl, salad; Country Garden #3942, 12", from $80 to. **100.00**

Bowl, salad; Sunflower #3340, extra deep, 10", from $75 to **85.00**

Bowl, vegetable; Americana #2000, oval, 8", from $10 to........ **15.00**

Bowl, vegetable; Blueberry #3770, divided oval, from $40 to.. **45.00**

Bowl, vegetable; Fruit #3697, divided oval, from $35 to **40.00**

Bread tray, Star Flower #3874, from $20 to **25.00**

Butter dish, Fruit #3697, from $50 to **60.00**

Cake stand, Bittersweet #5111, from $10 to **15.00**

Cake stand, Colonial #1388, from $20 to **25.00**

Cake stand, Orchard Song #5110, from $10 to **15.00**

Carafe, Americana #2000, wooden handle, from $40 to......... **50.00**

Carafe, Magnolia #3870, shape #2000, from $150 to **200.00**

Casserole, Amber-Glo #3899, skillet shape, 6", from $10 to **15.00**

Casserole, Magnolia #3870, skillet shape, 8", from $20 to..... **25.00**

Coffeepot, Golden Harvest #3887, 4-cup, from $50 to **65.00**

Cup & saucer, Sunflower #3340, from $15 to **20.00**

Egg cup, Colonial #1388, from $10 to **15.00**

Flowerpot, Town & Country #5287, blue, 5", from $25 to **35.00**

Gravy boat, Colonial #1388, from $20 to **25.00**

Gravy boat, Country Garden #3942, from $35 to **40.00**

Gravy boat, Yellow Tulip #3637, w/ underplate, from $35 to... **40.00**

Mug, stacking; Bittersweet #5111, from $20 to **25.00**

Mug, stacking; Orchard Song #5110, from $25 to **30.00**

Napkin ring, Town & Country #5287, black or crimson, from $15 to **20.00**

Pickle dish, Star Flower #3864, from $10 to **15.00**

Pitcher, Country Garden #3942, 1-qt, from $50 to **60.00**

Pitcher, Magnolia #3870, 1-qt, from $40 to **50.00**

Pitcher, Yellow Tulip, 1-pt, from $20 to **25.00**

Plate, Blueberry #3770, from $20 to **25.00**

Plate, grill; Kiddieware, Campfire, 1955, 9", from $200 to. **250.00**

Plate, Kiddieware, Goldilocks, 1946, 9", from $100 to... **125.00**

Plate, Wild Rose #3929, 10" .. **22.00**

Relish dish, Colonial #1388, 3-part, 12", from $25 to............... **35.00**

Salt & pepper shakers, Golden Harvest #3887, pr **12.00**

Sherbet, Fruit #3697, from $25 to.................................... **30.00**

Sugar bowl, Colonial #1388, bird finial, from $35 to **45.00**

Sugar bowl, Wild Rose #3929, from $15 to **20.00**

Teapot, Amber-Glo #3899, from $40 to **50.00**

Teapot, Sunflower #3340, from $120 to **145.00**

Tidbit, Town & Country #5287, black or crimson, 10½", from $15 to **20.00**

Birds

#3250D, Duck grazing, 3¾" ... **75.00**
#3275, Turkey, 3½" **350.00**
#3400, Lovebird, old version, 4"..**100.00**
#3402, Oriole, beak down, old style,
3½" **125.00**
#3405D, cockatoos (pr), revised,
9½" **110.00**
#3443, Duck flying, gray, 9".**225.00**
#3448, Blue-Headed Vireo, 4¼".**65.00**
#3454, Key West Quail Dove, single
wing up, 10" **200.00**

#3580, Cockatoo, medium, 8⅞", $125.00.

#3583, Parula Warbler, 4¼"... **35.00**
#3591, Brewer's Blackbird, 3½".**170.00**
#3597, Wilson Warbler, yellow &
black, 3".......................... **40.00**
#3715, Blue Jay w/peanut, Fulper
black & blue glaze...... **2,000.00**
#3746, Canary (right), rose flower,
6¼" **235.00**
#3750, Scarlet Tanager, 8½".**375.00**
#3752D, Red-Headed Woodpeckers
(pr), glossy pk, 7¼" **400.00**
#3810, Black-Throated Warbler,
3½" **150.00**
#3848, Golden-Crowned Kinglet,
4¼" **80.00**

#3922, European Goldfinch.**1,200.00**
#3925, Magnolia Warbler.**2,800.00**

Star Wars

Capitalizing on the ever-popular space travel theme, the movie *Star Wars* with it's fantastic special effects was a mega box office hit of the late 1970s. A sequel called *Empire Strikes Back* (1980) and a third adventure called *Return of the Jedi* (1983) did just as well, and as a result, licensed merchandise flooded the market, much of it produced by the Kenner company. The last two films were *Star Wars Episode I* and, of course, *Episode II* soon followed. *Episode III* was released in 2004.

Original packaging is very important in assessing a toy's worth. As each movie was released, packaging was updated, making approximate dating relatively simple. A figure on an original *Star Wars* card is worth more than the same character on an *Empire Strikes Back* card, etc.; and the same *Star Wars* figure valued at $50.00 in mint-on-card condition might be worth as little as $5.00 'loose.' Especially prized are the original 12-back *Star Wars* cards (meaning 12 figures were shown on the back). Second issue cards showed eight more, and so on. For more information we recommend *Star Wars Super Collector's Wish Book* by Geoffery T. Carlton; and *Schroeder's Collectible Toys, Antique to Modern*. Both are published by Collector Books.

Note: Because space was limited, SW was used in our descriptions for Star Wars, ROTJ was used for Return of the Jedi, ESB for Empire Strikes Back, and POTF for Power of the Force.

Figure, Amanaman, POTF, w/coin, M (EX 92-back card)..... **280.00**

Figure, Darth Vader/Lightsaber Attack, Revenge of the Sith, NRFP **15.00**

Figure, Death Star Droid, SW, MOC **230.00**

Figure, Han Solo, SW, lg head, NM+ (M 20-back card).. **510.00**

Figure, Lenni the Ewok, plush, Kenner, 1983, EX **35.00**

Figure, Luke Skywalker, SW, X-Wing Pilot, NM+ (NM 20-back card) **375.00**

Figure, Neimoidian Warrior #42, Revenge of the Sith, NRFP. **15.00**

Figure, Princess Leia Organa, SW, M (EX+ 12-back card)... **275.00**

Figure, R2-D2, POTF, w/pop-up light saber & coin, M (NM+ 92-back card) **215.00**

Figure, R2-D2, SW, MOC (21-back card) **225.00**

Figure, Snaggletooth, SW, blue body, EX **300.00**

Figure, Storm Trooper, SW, M (EX 12-back card) **260.00**

Figure, Storm Trooper, SW Collection Series, Kenner, 12", EXIB **25.00**

Figure, Yoda, talker, 500 phrases, Revenge of the Sith, NRFB. **20.00**

Figure, Zuckess, ESB, M (NM 48-back card) **35.00**

Figure, Zuckess, POTF, w/coin, M (NM 92-back card) **45.00**

Figure set, Bounty Hunters, Previews Exclusive, complete, M (VG box) **35.00**

Figure set, Six Pack #93390, ESB, complete, M (EX box).... **400.00**

Lego set, Darth Vader #7251, NRFB **15.00**

Lego set, Jabba's Palace #4480, NRFB (sealed) **45.00**

Lego set, Twin-Pod Cloud Car #7119, 2002, NRFB **20.00**

Lego set, W-Wing Fighter #7140, SW, MIB **32.00**

Lego set, Yoda #7194, NRFB (sealed) **150.00**

Model kit, Star Destroyer, ESB, MPC, M (sealed contents)/EX box **35.00**

Mug, Chewbacca figural head, Rumph!, California Originals, 1977, MIB, $75.00. (Photo courtesy June Moon)

Photograph, Mark Hamill as Luke Skywalker, autographed, 8x10", EX **28.00**

Plate, Han Solo collage, Hamilton, 1997, MIB **25.00**

Playset, Bespin Control Room, Micro Collection, MIB **60.00**

Playset, Cloud City, ESB, complete, EX **135.00**

Playset, Creature Cantina, 1977, MIB, $360.00.

Playset, Dagobah, Darth Vader & Luke Battle, ESB, complete, EX **25.00**

Playset, Hoth Ice Planet, ESB, MIB **335.00**

Playset, Rebel Command Center, ESB, complete, EX **80.00**

Playset, Watto's Box #84159, Episode I, NRFB **25.00**

Vehicle, AT-ST w/driver, ROTJ, complete, EX **35.00**

Vehicle, Droids A-Wing Fighter, complete, EX (VG box).. **275.00**

Vehicle, Ewok Battle Wagon, POTF, complete, EX (VG box).. **300.00**

Vehicle, Imperial Shuttle, ROTJ, NRFB (NM box) **300.00**

Vehicle, Obi-Wan's Jedi Star-fighter, Revenge of the Sith, NRFB **20.00**

Vehicle, Super Star Destroyer (Electronic), POTF 2, 1990s, M (EX box) **215.00**

Vehicle, X-Wing Fighter, SW, Kenner, G **15.00**

Vehicle, X-Wing Starter Set, Estes #1490, 1996, MIB (sealed) **20.00**

Video DVD Star Wars Trilogy set, 4-disc wide screen, EXIB . **40.00**

Video game, Bounty Hunter, EXIB **32.00**

Swanky Swigs

Swanky Swigs are little decorated glass tumblers that once contained Kraft Cheese Spread. The company has used them since the Depression years of the 1930s up to the present time, and all along, because of their small size, they've been happily recycled as drinking glasses for kids and juice glasses for adults. Their designs range from brightly colored flowers to animals, sailboats, bands, dots, stars, checkers, etc. There is a combination of 223 verified colors and patterns. In 1933 the original Swanky Swigs came in the Band pattern, and at the present time they can still be found on the grocery shelf, now a clear plain glass with an indented waffle design around the bottom.

They vary in size and fall into one of three groups: the small size sold in Canada, ranging from 3¹⁄₁₆" to 3¼"; the regular size sold in the United States, ranging from 3⅜" to 3⅞"; and the large size also sold in Canada, ranging from 4³⁄₁₆" to 5⅝".

A few of the rare patterns to look for in the three different groups are small group, Band No. 5 (two red and two black bands with the red first); Galleon (two ships on each glass in black, blue, green, red, or yellow); Checkers (in black and red, black and yellow, black and orange, or black and white, with black checkers on the top row); and Fleur-de-lis (black with a bright red filigree design).

In the regular group: Dots Forming Diamonds; Lattice and

Vine (white lattice with colored flowers); Texas Centennial (cowboy and horse); Special Issues with dates (1936, 1938, and 1942); and Tulip No. 2 (black, blue, green, or red).

Rare glasses in the larger group are Circles and Dots (black, blue, green, or red); Star No. 1 (small stars scattered over the glass in black, blue, green, or red); Cornflower No. 2 (dark blue, light blue, red, or yellow); Provincial Cress (red and burgundy with maple leaves); and Antique No. 2 (assorted antiques on each glass in lime green, deep red, orange, blue, and black).

Antique #1, any color, Canadian, 3¼", ea............................... **8.00**

Antique #1, any color, 1954, 3¾", ea from $4 to **5.00**

Antique #2, any color, Canadian, 1974, 4½", ea **20.00**

Bachelor Button, red, white & green, Canadian, 1955, 3¼"........... **6.00**

Band #1, red & black, 1933, 3⅜".**3.00**

Band #2, red & black, 1933, 3⅜".**3.00**

Band #4, blue, 1933, 3⅜" **3.00**

Blue stars & red hearts, US, 2003 .... **5.00**

Bustlin' Betty, any color, Canadian, 1953, 3¼", ea **8.00**

Bustlin' Betty, any color, 1953, 3¾", ea.. **4.00**

Checkerboard, white w/blue, green or red, 1936, 3½", ea **20.00**

Circles & Dot, any color, Canadian, 1934, 4¾", ea **20.00**

Coin, coin decor around base, 1968, 3¾" **1.00**

Colonial, waffle decor around middle & base, 1976, 4⅜"........ **1.00**

Cornflower #1, light blue & green, Canadian, 1941, 3¼"......... **8.00**

Cornflower #2, dk blue, lt blue, red or yellow, Canadian, 1947, 3¼". **8.00**

Cornflower #2, dk blue, lt blue, red or yellow, 1947, 3½", ea..... **4.00**

Dots forming diamonds, any color, 1935, 3½" **50.00**

Forget-Me-Not, any color, Canadian, 3¼", ea............................... **8.00**

Galleon, any color, Canadian, 1936, 3⅛", ea............................. **30.00**

Hostess, indented grooved base, Canadian, 1960, 5⅝", ea..... **5.00**

Kiddie Kup, any color, Canadian, 1956, 4¾", ea **20.00**

Lattice & Vine, white w/blue, green or red, 1936, 3½", ea **100.00**

Petal Star, indented star base, Canadian, 1978, 3¼", ea ... **2.00**

Petal Star, indented star base, 1978, 3¾", ea .... **.50**

Posy Jonquil: yellow, 4½", $20.00 – 25.00; yellow, 3¼, $20.00 – 25.00; yellow, 3½", $7.00 – 8.00. (Photo courtesy Gene and Cathy Florence)

Special Issue, Cornflower #1, 1941, 3½" **410.00**

Stars #1, any color, Canadian, 1934, 4¾", ea.............................. **20.00**

Stars #1, yellow, 1935, 3½", ea. **25.00**

Texas Centennial, any color, 1936, 3½", ea............................. **30.00**

Train, engine, Holiday, wine, 2004 .... **5.00**

Tulip (Posy Pattern), red & green, 1941, 3½", ea **4.00**

Tulip (Posy Pattern), red & green, 4½", from $20 to **25.00**

Tulip #1, any color, 1937, 3½", ea.................................. **4.00**

Tulip #2, any color, 1938, 3½", ea.............................. **25.00**

Tulip #3, any color, Canadian, 1950, 3¼", ea................................ **8.00**

Violet (Posy Pattern), blue & green, Canadian, 1941, 3¼" **8.00**

Wildfire Series, any in series, Canadian, 1975, 4⅝", ea . **20.00**

Syroco

From the early 1940s until 1962, Syroco items were replicas of wood carvings cast from wood fibre, but most of what you'll find today are made of resin. They're not at all hard to find; and because they were made in so many shapes and designs, it's easy and inexpensive to build an interesting collection. Some are hand painted, and others are trimmed in gold. You may also find similar products stamped 'Ornawood,' 'Decor-A-Wood,' and 'Swank.' These items are collectible as well.

Bookends, buck in trees, 7x5¼" . **40.00**

Bookends, Scottie dogs, 5", pair from $35.00 to $50.00. (Photo courtesy Candace Sten Davis and Patricia J. Baugh)

Clock, #4580, with label, gold, 15" square, $40.00. (Photo Courtesy Lee Garmon)

Clothes brush holder, Scottie dog by brick & wood fence, 5½x4" **25.00**

Corkscrew, Indian chief bust as handle, 7" **200.00**

Figurines, peacocks, 13" L female & 14" H male, pr **35.00**

Mirror w/shelf below, rococo swirls & flowers, gold, 22x11" ... **32.00**

Sconce, 2-light, 3-leaf clover top w/rococo scrollwork arms, gold, 18", pr **42.00**

Sconce, 5 votive cups supported by open rococo swirls, gold, 35x16" **80.00**

Shelf, sq fluted supports w/arched apron, gold, Home Interiors, 20" L................................. **25.00**

Tray, 2 lg maple leaves w/branch handles, gold, 12x7" **15.00**

Wall clock, star shape (12-point), wood-tone, 1967, 25" **40.00**

Wall clock, starburst style w/multi layers of closely spaced rays, 23" **65.00**

Wall clock, wide frame w/openwork fruit & vegetables, gold, 21" dia **30.00**

Wall decor, flying figural Canadian goose, natural colors, 18x24" **35.00**

Wall decor, key shape w/crown-like top & lion w/in rococo scrolls, gold, 18" **60.00**

Wall decor, spoon & fork w/fruit & vegetables, multicolored, 18", pr **35.00**

Wall mirror, round gold-framed mirror w/lg eagle surmount, 17x11" **40.00**

Wall pockets, fluted bowl w/rococo scrolls ea side, ivory, 10", pr **35.00**

Tea Bag Holders

These are fun and inexpensive to collect. They were made, of course, to hold used tea bags, but aside from being functional, many are whimsical and amusing. Though teapots are the most commonly found shape, you can find fruit, bird, and vegetable shapes as well.

Cottage form, thatched roof, 3½x5" **15.00**

Cup form, white w/floral decoration, strainer on top, #435, 2¼" . **15.00**

Flower form, Desert Rose, Franciscan **18.00**

Flower form, Moss Rose, gold trim, w/drain basin, Japan, #T-103 .... **25.00**

Flower form, pink w/green center, Stangl, 3¾x4" **20.00**

Leaf form, white w/floral spray, gold trim, Japan **6.00**

Rooster form, multicolored, Holt Howard, 1960, 5½" **15.00**

Swan form, white, Lenox, 2x2½"..**15.00**

Teapot form, Blue Paisley, Lefton #2354 .... **18.00**

Teapot form, Blue Willow, set of 6 .... **35.00**

Teapot form, butterfly, blue on white w/green trim, Raynaud Limoges **20.00**

Teapot form, floral design, Lefton #8282, from $5 to **10.00**

Teapot form, gray parrot on white, English China 5⅛" **25.00**

Teapot form, Hawaii the 50th State, hula dancer, gold trim **15.00**

Teapot form, Miss Cutie Pie, 2 birds on top, Napco, 1950s **35.00**

Teapot form, Rose Chintz, lavender, Lefton................................. **8.00**

Teapot form, roses on white, Lefton #6672, 4½" **10.00**

Teapot form, smiling faces, I Will Hold the Bag, set of 4 in rack, 1950s............................... **45.00**

Teapot shape, I Will Hold the Tea Bag, Japan, $10.00.

Teapots

The popularity of teatime and tea-related items continues, and vintage and finer quality teapots have become harder to find. Those from the 1890s and 1920s reflect their age with three and four digit prices. Examples from the 1700s and 1800s are most often found in museums or large auction houses. Teapots listed here represent examples still available at the flea market level. Most collectors begin with a general collection of varied teapots until they decide upon the specific category that appeals to them. Collecting categories include miniatures, doll or toy sets, those made by a certain manufacturer, figurals, or a particular style (such as Art Deco or English floral). Some of the latest trends in collecting are Chinese Yixing (pronounced yee-shing — teapots from an unglazed earthenware in forms taken from nature), 1950s pink or black teapots, Cottageware teapots, and figural teapots (those shaped like people, animals, or other objects). While teapots made in Japan have waned in collectibility, collectors have begun to realize many detailed or delicate examples are available. Of special interest are Dragonware teapots or sets. Some of these sets have the highly desired lithophane cups — where a Geisha girl is molded in transparent relief in the bottom of the cup. When the cup is held up to the light, the image becomes visible.

Arthur Wood & Sons, violets on white porcelain w/gold trim, 7½x6" 48.00

Avon, cat dressed in finery holds teapot (spout), 6" 70.00

Cortendorf/Germany, cat figure, black & white w/red collar 100.00

Crawford Pottery, holly leaves on white, 1950s, sm 20.00

Fitz & Floyd, bear figure holding candy cane, paw is spout. 75.00

Fitz & Floyd, Jefferson Memorial form, limited edition, 7", from $175 to 200.00

Gloria Vanderbilt, cat figure w/black & white stripes, 10" 55.00

Golden Crown/W Germany, elf figure on knees 85.00

Heritage Mint Ltd, carousel horse 25.00

Heritage Mint Ltd, Mother Goose holds ear of corn, 8½x7".. 22.50

India, brass, 6", $25.00; 8½", $20.00.

Japan, elephant form, howdah forms lid, lustreware, 8-cup........ 55.00

Japan, mirror brown on redware, Deco-style handle, 4x8x5½"........... 25.00

Japan, painted dots form flowers on brown, angled handle, 5x8". 20.00

Japan, rabbit form, brown & white, 1930s, 6½"........................ 45.00

Japan, tomato form, red w/green handle & spout, stem finial, 4x5" 50.00

Japan, tree shown in sunset, 5x8" 30.00

Nasco/Japan, pink roses w/gold on white, 4x5"....................... 32.50

Ransburg Pottery, asters on red stoneware, 6x9½x6" 75.00

Russ/China, Nutcracker, 1980s..30.00

Sadler, dragons & pagodas, 6-sided, footed, 6".......................... 45.00

Sadler, floral on white, 4¾".... 15.00

Sadler, pink & blue flowers on white w/gold trim, ribbed, 6½"..45.00

Sadler, roses on white w/gold trim, cylindrical, 8" 60.00

SCC/China, cottage form w/thatched roof, 1950s, 6½x7½" **32.50**

Superior Ceramics/England, daisies & blue flowers on swirled body, 5" **17.50**

Tiara Exclusives

Collectors are just beginning to take notice of the glassware sold through Tiara in-home parties, their Sandwich line in particular. Several companies were involved in producing the lovely items they've marketed over the years, among them Indiana Glass, Fenton, Dalzell Viking, and L.E. Smith. In the late 1960s Tiara contracted with Indiana to produce their famous line of Sandwich dinnerware (a staple at Indiana Glass since the late 1920s). Their catalogs continue to carry this pattern, and over the years, it has been offered in many colors: ruby, teal, crystal, amber, green, pink, blue, and others in limited amounts. We've listed a few pieces of Tiara's Sandwich below, and though the market is unstable, our values will serve to offer an indication of current values. Unless you're sure of what you're buying, though, don't make the mistake of paying 'old' Sandwich prices for Tiara. To learn more about the two lines, we recommend *Collectible Glassware from the 40s, 50s, and 60s,* by Gene and Cathy Florence (Collector Books). Also refer to *Collecting Tiara Amber Sandwich Glass* by Mandi Birkinbine; she is listed in the Directory under Idaho.

Basket, Amber, tall & slender, 10¾x4¾", from $40 to **50.00**

Bowl, salad; slant sides, Chantilly Green, 3x8⅜", from $15 to..**20.00**

Bowl, slant sides, Amber, 1¾x4¾", from $4 to **5.50**

Butter dish, Chantilly Green, 6½x7½", $30.00.

Butter dish, domed lid, Bicentennial Blue, 6" H, from $25 to... **35.00**

Butter dish, domed lid, Teal Green, 6" H, from $25 to **35.00**

Cake plate, Chantilly Green, footed, 4x10", from $60 to **75.00**

Candleholders, Amber, 3¾", pr from $10 to **20.00**

Candleholders, Sea Mist (light), 8½", pr from $35 to **45.00**

Canister, Amber, 26-oz or 38-oz, 7½", ea from $12 to **20.00**

Clock, wall hanging, Amber or Peach, 12" dia, from $12 to **18.00**

Compote, Amber, 8", from $18 to.**25.00**

Cup, Amber, 9-oz, from $3 to... **4.00**

Dish, club, diamond, heart or spade, clear or Amber, 4", ea from $3 to **5.00**

Egg tray, Amber or Spruce Green, 12", ea from $15 to **20.00**

Egg tray, Peach, 12", from $20 to.**35.00**

Fairy (Glo) lamp, Chantilly Green or Horizon Blue, 6", ea from $20 to **25.00**

Goblet, Amber, 8-oz or 8½-oz, 5¼" or
 5½", ea from $6 to **8.00**
Gravy boat, Amber, from $35
 to **45.00**
Mug, footed, Amber, 5½", from $6
 to **8.00**

**Pitcher, Amber, 8½", from $25.00
to $40.00.**

Pitcher, Peach, 8½", from $20
 to **30.00**
Plate, Amber, 8", from $5 to **8.00**
Plate, Amber, 10", from $9 to . **15.00**
Plate, Chantilly Green, 8¼", from
 $4 to **8.00**
Plate, Chantilly Green, 10", from
 $8 to **12.00**
Platter, sawtooth rim, Amber, 12",
 from $8.50 to **12.00**
Relish tray, 4-part, Amber, 10",
 from $15 to **20.00**
Salt & pepper shakers, Amber, 4¾",
 pr from $18 to **25.00**
Tray, 3-part, Chantilly Green,
 12" **19.00**
Tumbler, Amber, 10-oz, 6½" **8.00**

Tobacco Collectibles

Even though the smoking
habit is frowned upon nowadays,
related items still have collector
appeal. The tobacco industry used
to widely advertise their products, and retail companies turned
out many types of smoking accessories, such as pipes, humidors,
lighters, and ashtrays to accom-
modate smokers. Vintage tins,
store bins, cigarette packs, tobacco
pouches, signs, and thermometers
are among the more sought-after
items.

Box, Log Cabin, wood w/graphic
 paper label inside hinged lid,
 16x14x9" **700.00**
Box, Shaw's Short Sweet Smokes,
 cardboard, white on red,
 4x3x1", G **25.00**

**Carton, Marvels Mild Cigarettes,
G, $40.00.** (Photo courtesy B.J. Summers/Chief
Paduke Antique Mall)

Cigar clipper/fob, bulldog-shaped
 brass fob, John Merriam's...,
 EX **300.00**
Cigar pack, Tish-I-Mingo Cigar
 Clippings, red on tan, 1926, 5",
 G...................................... **75.00**
Cigarette pack, Lucky Strike, green
 w/red logo, gold trim, EX . **55.00**
Cigarette papers, Broads/The
 Working Man's Cigarette
 Paper, 1960s, NM............ **25.00**
Cigarette rolling machine, Premier,
 hand crank, 3 settings, 1960s,
 MIB.................................. **50.00**
Crate, wood w/Duke's Mixture
 advertising stamped on sides,
 9x23", G **50.00**

Lunch box, Dan Patch Cut Plug, swing handles, red & black on yellow, EX **275.00**

Lunch box, Pedro Smoking Cut Plug, tin, red on yellow, 4x8x5", NM **300.00**

Lunch box, Satisfaction Cut Plug, gold on red, 4½x7½", EX. **225.00**

Pin-back, Smoke Bagley's Sun Cured, sun w/features, celluloid, G **55.00**

Pipe, meerchaum, horse jumping fallen tree, amber mouthpiece, 4½" long, $85.00.

Pipe tamper, leprechaun, brass, 1960s, 2½", EX **20.00**

Pocket tin, Briggs Pipe Mixture, vertical, brown, 1920s, 4½", G **60.00**

Pocket tin, Charm of the West, flat, yellow, 2⅜x3⅝", EX+ **325.00**

Pocket tin, Coach & Four, vertical, black & red, 4½", EX+ .. **175.00**

Pocket tin, Hand Made, vertical, light green, 4", EX **300.00**

Pocket tin, Lucky Strike Roll Cut, vertical, green, 1910, 4½", EX **240.00**

Pocket tin, Prince Albert Crimp Cut, vertical, red, 1960s, EX+ **18.00**

Shakers, Kool's Willie & Millie penguins, plastic, 3½", EX, pr. **20.00**

Sign, George Washington Cut Plug, die-cut tin lunch box shape, 9", EX+ **550.00**

Sign, Imperial Club 5cts Cigar, tin, cigar box graphic, 10x14", EX+ **125.00**

Snuff dispenser, Copenhagen, metal, cylindrical, 15½", EX **40.00**

Spittoon, sample, white porcelain w/Beco Ware label, 3½" dia **400.00**

Store bin, Tiger Chewing Tobacco 5¢ Packages, tin, sq, 11½", EX+ **800.00**

Thermometer, Chesterfield, metal, They Satisfy!, 13½", VG. **100.00**

Thermometer, L&M, metal, Check Today's Change, 13", NM .**110.00**

Tin, Country Club 5¢, outdoor club graphics, sq, slip lid, 5½", EX **200.00**

Tin, Dill's Best Smoking Tobacco, 1920s-30s, 3x5" dia, EX+. **100.00**

Tin, Dixie Queen Plug Cut, round, smaller gold slip lid, 6½", EX+ **300.00**

Tin, Gobblers (Cigars), round, slip lid, 5", EX+ **425.00**

Tin, Lucky Strike, green & red logo, oblong, 1910S, 4½x3", EX .**100.00**

Tin, Popper's 10¢ Ace, biplane graphics, sq, slip lid, 5½x5x5", EX+ **400.00**

Tin, Sunset Trail 5¢, vertical oblong, slip lid, 5½x6x4", EX+... **425.00**

Tin, Whip Ready Rolled, red & green, octagonal, slip lid, 5½", EX **350.00**

Tip tray, El Verso Havana Cigars, man in chair, 6½x4½", EX. **85.00**

Tobacco pack, Lime Kiln Club, paper, black ethnic graphics, 1920, EX+ **350.00**

Tobacco tag, Grape Wine Twist, tin, purple grape cluster on cream, NM **50.00**

Tobacco tag, One in a Hill, red on yellow, EX......................... **25.00**

Tradecard/calendar, Gold Coin Chewing Tobacco/Victory, 1887, 3½", G............................... **50.00**

Tools and Farm Implements

Old farm tools and implements have been long sought after by collectors. Some like to decorate their country-inspired rooms with these primitives, while others appreciate them for their their enduring quality and the memories they evoke of times gone by. For whatever reason you may be collecting them, flea markets can be a treasure trove of great old tools.

Anvil, hollow cast iron, circular back opening, 4 fastening holes, VG.......................... **50.00**

Auger, EC Stearns No 4, VG. **60.00**

Auger, 17" long metal 1¼" bit w/16" straight wooden handle, G. **15.00**

Axe, Keen Kutter, NY Yankee pattern, from $25 to............. **30.00**

Barbed-wire staple puller, marked JACUZZI/1740/T 102 C, 14", EX...................... **12.00**

Barn beam hook, Roger & Nellis Pat'D 1870, all metal, VG............ **115.00**

Bee smoker, metal container w/attached bellows, 1903, 9" H, EX..................... **18.00**

Brace, Stanley No 923-6, 6", NM............................ **75.00**

Buck saw, reddish-stained wood w/metal blade & tension, 30" L, VG.................................. **45.00**

Bung cutter, metal, 10" straight wooden handle, 1⅛" drill, 13", EX... **120.00**

Calf-weaning tool, metal, 4½x3", VG.................................... **12.00**

Chisel, Buck Bros, ¼" socket firmer, 12", VG **25.00**

Chisel, Buck Bros, ⅜" bevel edge socket firmer, NM **45.00**

Chisel, Stanley No 720, ¼" bevel-edge socket firmer, 6" blade, 12"...**40.00**

Chisel, Whitherby, ¾" socket firmer, 6¼" blade, 13¼", VG........ **40.00**

Clevis/coupler, John Deere, No TC & 123A, EX **35.00**

Clock, Rotary International embossed on gear shape, electric, 7" dia....................... **28.00**

Clothes-washing stomper, galvanized metal end w/wooden handle, 23", EX............... **16.00**

Corn dryer, metal rod w/spikes to dry up to 10 ears, early 1900s, 19".................................... **22.00**

Corn knife/scythe, 10" curved blade w/13" curved arm & wooden handle............................. **15.00**

Corn planter, garden; American Standard, Pat'd ..1891/1893, 33" L, EX **65.00**

Corn sheller, R&H/Root-Heath Mfg Co, cast iron, 12x11", VG. **55.00**

Cow/goat bell, metal, 6x4½", VG............................. **18.00**

Doweling jig, Stanley No 59, NMIB.............................. **45.00**

Draw knife, Keen Kutter, beech handles, 8", VG **40.00**

Draw knife, L&IJ White, 8", G..**35.00**

Egg basket, rubber-coated wire w/bail handle, 10½x14" dia, EX................................**25.00**

Fence wire crimper, Fence Tight No FT-9, 17x8", EX+............. **65.00**

Hammer, claw; EL Brown No 18, VG...................................**25.00**

Hatchet, Genuine Plumb, 6x3½" head, 13" overall, VG......**22.00**

Hay knife, Keen Kutter, serrated edge, from $75 to **100.00**

Hay knife/saw, 3-tooth cutting head, wood handle, pre-1900, 46" L, EX **35.00**

Hay spear (used to lift bales into barn lofts), 36x18", VG...**50.00**

Hog holder, all metal w/2 open handles, 12" L, EX........**140.00**

Hog ringer tool, marked Pat'd Apr 21 1880, EX......................**15.00**

Horse clippers, Priest's Clippers New Market Pattern, 12", EX....................................**50.00**

Ladle, blacksmith/tinsmith; metal, 6" cup w/2 side spouts, 18" L, VG.....................................**16.00**

Level, CF Richardson, japanned cast iron, 6", VG..............**75.00**

Level, Standard Tool Co, Patent May 11 1897 stamped on top, VG...................................**300.00**

Padlock & key, Miller Pat 12-19-05, 2½", VG.............................**18.00**

Pitch fork tines, 3-tine, no handle, ironwork, VG...................**12.00**

Plane, tongue and groove; Stanley #48 Model SW Sweetheart, $165.00.

Plow wrench, No 83, 12", VG.**85.00**

Pliers, duckbill; Sargent, Bernard's patent style w/parallel jaws, NM..................................**20.00**

Potato planter, cast iron, wood handle w/open grip, 30" L, VG.......**30.00**

Pulley, marked RM Co No 12, all cast iron, 11", EX **50.00**

Pulley, marked 3 285, wooden wheel w/cast iron housing, EX...................................**45.00**

Riveter (hand) for harness, brake & clutch lining repair, cast iron, VG....................................**40.00**

Saw, crosscut; Atkins No 59, 26", VG....................................**38.00**

Saw, crosscut; Henry Disston & Sons D-8, 1940s medallion, 26", EX...............................**60.00**

Saw, pruning; Atkins No 13, 14", VG....................................**25.00**

Scale, Hansen's Dairy Scale, 60-lb capacity, 8" dia face, VG.**18.00**

Screwdriver, spiral ratchet; Yankee No 135A, VG **25.00**

Sheep sheers, Keen Kutter, metal, 12" L, VG.........................**15.00**

Sickle sharpener, IHC logos, cast iron, crank handle & gears, VG....................................**65.00**

Skidder logging tongs, hammered & shaped metal, 14" L, 20" W (open), VG......................**110.00**

Sledgehammer, 14" wood handle w/6x2" dia cast-iron head, unmarked, EX.................**85.00**

Square, bevel; Stanley No 25 6" Sliding T, NM..................**35.00**

Square, combo w/level & scribe (12"), Fitching Tool Co, VG.........**20.00**

Steelyard (scale), metal, 3 hooks & solid weight on rod, EX..**65.00**

Steer horn cutter, cast iron, 37x8", VG....................................**12.00**

Tool box, cast iron w/John Deere embossed on sides, open, 10" L, G......................................**45.00**

Wrench, crescent; P&C Co, 4",
VG **20.00**

Wrench, H&E Wrench Co, Pat Mar
27 1923, G **35.00**

Wrench, John Deere, Deere lettered in
open handle, 7½" L, EX.....**100.00**

Wrench, John Deere, DM, straight
handle, VG **20.00**

Wrench, John Deere, E782, solid
wavy handle, EX.............**32.00**

Wrench, John Deere, SC/25, open
sq handle, 6", VG **30.00**

Wrench, pipe; Sheffy Mfg Co, self-
adjusting, Pat's Jan 24 1896,
VG **125.00**

Wrench, South Bend Chilled Plow,
curved handle, 9½", G **28.00**

Toothbrush Holders

Children's ceramic toothbrush
holders represent one of today's
popular collecting fields, with some
of the character-related examples
bringing $150.00 and up. Many were
made in Japan before WWII. For
more information we recommend
*A Pictorial Guide to Toothbrush
Holders* by Marilyn Cooper; she
is listed in the Directory under
Texas.

Annie Oakley, Japan, 5¾", from
$125 to **150.00**

Bear beside tree stump (holder),
ceramic, multicolored, 2½" .**20.00**

Bird on branch, wall-pocket style,
ceramic, lustre, Japan, 5", from
$100 to **150.00**

Bonzo-type dog, Goldcastle,
4¼x2¾" **75.00**

Brother, boy reading book, Japan,
1930s, 7" **70.00**

Candlestick maker, Goldcastle,
5¼" **165.00**

Chef, slots at arms, lustre, Japan,
5½", from $100 to **150.00**

Children (2) in open auto, holders
in back, tray in front, Japan,
5"....................................**200.00**

Clown holding mask, arms extended, tray at feet, wall hanger,
6"....................................**100.00**

Clown juggling, Japan, 5"......**75.00**

Doctor w/satchel, Japan, 5¾"..**90.00**

**Dog with bas-
ket, Japan, 5¾",
$100.00.** (Photo cour-
tesy Marilyn Cooper)

Donald Duck, Mickey & Minnie
Mouse, bisque, Japan,
Disney **175.00**

Dutch boy & girl kissing, Goldcastle, 6" **145.00**

Dutch girl, 2 holders at apron pockets, California pottery, 7".**50.00**

Elephants (3) sitting upright,
Japan, 2¼x3¾"................**55.00**

English bobby w/hands in pockets,
Nayo/Japan, 1930s, 5¼x2½".**80.00**

Little Red Riding Hood, Germany
(DGRM), 5½", from $200 to..**250.00**

Lone Ranger, chalkware, 1 hole, no
tray, 4" **75.00**

Mailman w/open pouch, lustre, Japan,
5¾", from $100 to.............**150.00**

Old King Cole, Japan, 5¼", from
$85 to **100.00**

Three Bears w/bowls, 3 holes in
back, Imperial China/Japan,
4x4½" **145.00**

Three Little Pigs w/instruments,
Disney/Japan................. **120.00**

Tom Tom the Piper's Son, Japan,
5¾", from $100 to **150.00**

Toys

Toy collecting remains a very popular hobby, and though some areas of the market may have softened to some extent over the past two years, classic toys remain a good investment. Especially strong are the tin windups made by such renowned companies as Strauss, Marx, Lehmann, Chein, etc., and the battery-operated toys made from the '40s through the '60s in Japan. Because of their complex mechanisms, few survive.

Toys from the 1800s are rarely if ever found in mint condition but should at least be working and have all their original parts. Toys manufactured in the twentieth century are evaluated more critically. Compared to one in mint condition, original box intact, even a slightly worn toy with no box may be worth only about half as much. Character-related toys, space toys, toy trains, and toys from the '60s are very desirable.

Several good books are available, if you want more information: *Collector's Guide to Tootsietoys* by David E. Richter; *Matchbox Toys, 1947 – 2003* by Dana Johnson;

Hot Wheels: The Ultimate Redline Guide, Volumes I and *II*, by Jack Clark and Robert Wicker; *Star Wars Super Collector's Wish Book* by Geoffrey T. Carlton; *Big Book of Toy Airplanes* by W. Tom Miller; *Toy Car Collector's Guide* by Dana Johnson; and *Schroeder's Collectible Toys, Antique to Modern.* (All are published by Collector Books.) See also Action Figures; Breyer Horses; Hartland; Character Collectibles; Rampwalkers; Star Wars; Western Heroes; Club and Newsletters.

Battery-Operated

Acro-Chimp Porter, YM, 1960s, 9",
NMIB **100.00**

Alley the Roaring Stalking Alligator,
Marx, 18", NMIB **275.00**

Antique Fire Car, TN, 1950s, 10",
EXIB **350.00**

Astro Dog, Y, remote control, 1960s,
11", EXIB **175.00**

Barber Bear, TN, plush, tin base,
1950s, 10", EXIB........... **450.00**

Baseball Pitching Game, Marx,
EXIB **75.00**

Batman Flying Batplane, Remco,
1966, remote control, 12",
EXIB **125.00**

Bear Target Game, MT, litho tin,
1950s, 9", NMIB............ **300.00**

Beauty Parlor, S&E, 1950s, 9½x6½"
L, EX............................. **525.00**

Big Wheel Ice Cream Truck, Taiyo,
1970, 10", EX................. **100.00**

Bobby Drinking Bear, Y, plush,
remote control, 1950s, 10",
VGIB **600.00**

Brewster the Rooster, Marx, plush,
10", EXIB....................... **75.00**

Bubble Blowing Musician, Y, 1950s, 10", EXIB......................250.00

Busy Secretary, Linemar, 1950s, 7½", MIB, $300.00.

Calypso Joe, Linemar, remote control, 1950s, 10", EX.......350.00

Chap the Obedient Dog, Rosko, 1960s, MIB.....................150.00

Chee Chee Chihauha, Mego, 1960s, 8", EX................................50.00

Chippy the Chipmunk, Alps, 1950s, 12", MIB........................125.00

Circus Queen (Seal), Kosuge, 1950s, rare, 11", MIB................375.00

Dancing Merry Chimp, Kuramochi, 1960s, 11", NM..............150.00

Dandy Turtle, DSK, 1950s, 8", M...............................150.00

Donald Duck Locomotive, MT, tin & plastic, 1970, 9", M...175.00

Dream Boat (Rock 'n Roll Hot Rod), TN, tin, 7", NMIB.........400.00

El Toro, TN, litho tin, 1950s, NMIB............................225.00

Excalibur Car, Bandai, litho tin, 1960s, 10", EX...............125.00

FBI Godfather Car, Bandai, 1970s, 10", MIB.........................125.00

Fighting Bull, Alps, 1960s, 10", MIB...............................175.00

Fire Tricycle, TN, litho tin, w/driver, 10" L, EXIB..............650.00

Frankenstein (Monster), TN, 1960s, 13", VG+........................100.00

Fred Flinstone's Bedrock Band, Alps, 1960s, 10", VGIB.365.00

Funland Cup Ride, Sansco, 1960s, 7", NM+IB.....................350.00

Go Stop 'Benz Racer #7, Marusan, 10", EXIB......................250.00

Grasshopper, MT, 1950s, 6", M.350.00

Green Hornet Secret Service Car, ASC, 1960s, 11", EX+...700.00

Hong Kong Rickshaw, PMC, 1960s, EXIB................................90.00

Jig-Saw Magic, Z Co, 1950s, 7x5x9", MIB................................100.00

Journey Pup, S&E, 1950s, 8" L, M....................................50.00

Jumbo the Bubble-Blowing Elephant, Y, 1950s, 7", GIB..............125.00

King Size Fire Engine, Bandai, 1960s, 13", M.................150.00

Light House, Alps, litho tin, 1950s, 6½x8½", EX....................600.00

Linemar Music Hall, 6", EXIB.325.00

Lucky Cement Mixer Truck, MT, 1960s, 12", M.................150.00

Magic Beetle, Linemar, 7", EXIB...........................55.00

McGregor, TN, 1960s, 12", EXIB..........................115.00

Mickey Mouse Locomotive, MT, 1960s, 9", NM................175.00

Miss Friday the Typist, TN, 1950s, 8", EXIB.........................175.00

Mumbo Jumbo Hawaiian Drummer, Alps, 1960s, 10", VG................................150.00

Nutty Mad Indian, Marx, VG+IB........................175.00

Peppy Puppy w/Bone, Y, 1950s, 7", M.....................................75.00

Pipie the Whale, Alps, 1950s, 12", NM................................325.00

Robo Tank TR2, TN, 1960s, 6",
NM+ **175.00**
Shutter-Bug (Eyes Open), TN,
1950s, 9", VGIB **400.00**
Swimming Fish, Koshibe, 1950s,
11", NM **125.00**
Tom Tom Indian, Y, 1960s, 11",
M **75.00**
Wal-Boot Hobo, Tomy, 1960s, 20",
NM **100.00**
Xylophone, Ace, 1950s, 6" L,
NM **60.00**

Train Sets

American Flyer, Burlington Zephyr,
silver & black, VG **225.00**
American Flyer, Comet, VG.. **450.00**
American Flyer, Golden State,
VGIB **575.00**
American Flyer, Minnie Ha-Ha,
VG **300.00**
American Flyer, Reliable Freight
#30705, EXIB **150.00**
American Flyer, Tru-Model Freight
#101, VGIB **250.00**
Lionel, Burlington Northern
Limited #8585, NMIB... **300.00**
Lionel, Conrail Limited #18200,
MIB **250.00**
Lionel, CSX Freight Train #11779,
MIB **275.00**
Lionel, Maple Leaf Limited #8152,
MIB **200.00**
Lionel, Midnight Flyer #1960, MIB
(sealed) **100.00**
Lionel, New Englander #1050,
NM **200.00**
Lionel, SSS Santa Fe Work Train
#1632, MIB **275.00**
Marx, Happi-Time Santa Fe
Freight/Passenger #05944,
VGIB **200.00**

Marx, Santa Fe Passenger #44544,
VGIB **225.00**
Marx, Western Passenger #44464,
MIB **600.00**

Vehicles

**Corgi, Aston Martin DB4 Saloon,
1960, MIB, $110.00.** (From the Al Rapp
Collection)

Bandai, Ford T-Bird (1959), tin,
friction, 8", M **260.00**
Bandai, Mercedes-Benz Convertible,
tin, friction, 8", EX+ **125.00**
Buddy L, Boat Hauler, blue w/
white grille, 2 boats, 1960s,
27", VG **200.00**
Buddy L, Fast Freight Semi, open
trailer, 6-wheeled, 1950s, 20",
NMIB **650.00**
Buddy L, Merry-Go-Round Truck,
1960s, 13", NM **325.00**
Buddy L, Sand & Stone Dump Truck,
6-wheeled, 1950s, 14½", EX. **200.00**
Cor-Cor, DeSoto Sedan, pressed
steel, windup/battery-op lights,
18", G **550.00**
Corgi, Chevrolet Police Patrol Car,
#481, MIB, from $110 to. **140.00**
Corgi, Porsche 924 Poleizei, #430,
MIB, from $30 to **45.00**
Dinky, Rolls Royce Phantom V,
diecast, from $165 to **180.00**

Dinky, Triumph TR2, diecast, from $225 to **260.00**

Ertl, Pontiac Trans Am Coupe (1996), diecast, metallic red, 1:18 scale **30.00**

Hubley, Poultry Truck, diecast, w/accessories, 10", from $265 to **300.00**

Johnny Lightining, Custom XKE, diecast, doors open, 1969. **125.00**

Johnny Lightning, Jet Powered Screamer, diecast, 1970 .. **35.00**

Keystone, Greyhound Bus, pressed steel, 18", VG **350.00**

Keystone, Steam Shovel #46, pressed steel, 21", G **100.00**

Kingsbury, Cadillac Sedan, pressed steel, windup, 1940s, 14½", VG **350.00**

Majorette, Toyota Truck & Trailer, diecast, from $12 to **15.00**

Marx, A&P Super Markets Semi, 8-wheeled, 1950s, 27", G ... **100.00**

Marx, Delivery Pickup Truck, 1950s, 14", EX **325.00**

Marx, Dump Truck, flat-top cab, swinging side dump, 1940s, 10½", VG **125.00**

Marx, Lumar Construction End Loader, 1950s, 16", EX ... **35.00**

Metalcraft, Heinz Delivery Truck, pressed steel, b/o lights, 12", G **300.00**

Ny-Lint, Bronco w/Safari Animal Trailer, w/3 animals, 1960s, 23", EX **75.00**

Ny-Lint, Cannon Truck, 4-wheel, 1960s, 23", complete, VG+ .**75.00**

Ny-Lint, Payloader, pressed steel, 4-wheeled, 1960s, 17", EX . **150.00**

Ny-Lint, Truck & Horse Van, pressed steel, 1960s, 23", EXIB **200.00**

Smith-Miller, Dump Truck, GMC, pressed steel, crank-op, 1950s, 12", NM **275.00**

Smith-Miller, Dump Truck, GMC, pressed steel, crank-op, 1950s, 8", EX **175.00**

Smith-Miller, Official Tow Car (MIC), Mack, pressed steel, 17", EX. **300.00**

Steelcraft, City Trucking Co Dump Truck, 4-wheel, 1940s, 21", VG **325.00**

Tonka, Allied Van Lines, cabover w/aluminum trailer, 1950s, 24", VG **140.00**

Tonka, Auto Transport, metal, 2-tier, side lever, 1960s, 28", VG **100.00**

Tonka, Cement Truck, metal, 10-wheel, 1960s, 16", EX.. **85.00**

Tonka, Rescue Squad, metal, 1960s, 13", VG+ **125.00**

Tonka, Tanker, pressed steel cab w/plastic trailer, 1950s, 27", G **65.00**

Tootsietoy, Pan American Airport Set, 1950s, NMIB **300.00**

Turner, Dump Truck, pressed steel, 6-wheel, 1940s, 27", VG **150.00**

Wind-Ups, Friction, and Other Mechanicals

Artie the Clown in Crazy Car, Unique Art, litho tin, 7" L, G **250.00**

Big Top Tent, Chein, 1961, 10", EXIB **200.00**

BO Plenty, Marx, 9", EX **250.00**

Bombo the Monk, Unique Art, litho tin, VGIB **125.00**

Bruno, Alps, bear w/plush head, cloth jacket, tin pants, 6", EXIB **150.00**

Capitol Hill Racer, Unique Art, litho tin, 11" L, EXIB....**135.00**

Casper the Friendly Ghost Rollover Tank, Linemar, litho tin, VG **325.00**

Charlie McCarthy Walker, Marx, 9", EX..............................**325.00**

Choo Choo Train, Linemar, litho tin, 12", EXIB................ **115.00**

Circus Trio Clown, Alps, plastic w/cloth outfit, 6½", VGIB....................**30.00**

Cowboy on Rocking Horse, Cragstan, litho tin, 7" L, EXIB **250.00**

Dick Tracy Police Station, Marx, w/car, 9" L, G+...............**250.00**

Donald Duck Climbing Fireman, Linemar, litho tin, 12" (w/ladder), EX **300.00**

Donald Duck the Drummer, Linemar, litho tin, 6", EX...............**425.00**

Donald Duck w/Whirling Tail, Marx, plastic, 7", EX.....**100.00**

Drum Major, Wolverine, litho tin, 14", EX............................**275.00**

Ferdinand the Bull, Linemar, litho tin, 6", VG......................**125.00**

Flintstone Pals on Dino, Marx, any character, 8", EXIB.......**350.00**

GI Joe & His K-9 Pups, Unique Art, litho tin, 9", EXIB.........**275.00**

GI Joe & Jouncing Jeep, Unique Art, litho tin, 7", EXIB .**275.00**

Huckleberry Car, Marx, friction, tin w/vinyl head, 4" L, any, NMIB, ea **250.00**

Humphery Mobile, Wyandotte, litho tin, 9", G **200.00**

Li'l Abner & His Dogpatch Band, Unique Art, litho tin, 6x9", EX................................**400.00**

Lincoln Tunnel, Unique Art, litho tin, 24" L, EXIB **350.00**

Marine Sergeant, Chein, 1960s, 5", EX **250.00**

Mickey Mouse Dipsey Car, Linemar, litho tin, 5", VG+IB.......**400.00**

Mickey Mouse Roller Skater, Linemar, litho tin w/cloth pants, 6", EX **650.00**

Mickey's Delivery, Linemar, friction, litho tin, 5½" L, EX..........**300.00**

Minnie Mouse Seated in Rocking Chair Knitting, Linemar, tin, EXIB.**550.00**

Mr Machine, Ideal, plastic, VGIB **200.00**

Olive Oyl Ballet Dancer, Linemar, friction, w/pull rod, 5½", EXIB............................ **600.00**

Rodeo Joe, Unique Art, litho tin, 8" L, EX..............................**225.00**

Shy-Anne (Indian Chief), Linemar, WDP, litho tin w/cloth outfit, 6", EX..............................**300.00**

Skin Diver, Chein, 11½", NMIB.................... **200.00**

Steam Roller, Lindstrom, tin, 11½" L, VG+IB **200.00**

Sweeping Mammy, Lindstrom, litho tin, 8", EXIB, $325.00.

Tambourine Clown, TN, cloth costume, 6", EXIB.................**50.00**

XP-1960 Dream Car, Mattel, friction, 8½", EXIB **225.00**

Yogi Bear in Cadillac, Linemar, 1961, friction, 9", NM ...**350.00**

Trolls

The first trolls to come to the United States were molded after a 1952 design by Marti and Helena Kuuskoski of Tampere, Finland. The first to be mass produced in America were molded from wood carvings made by Thomas Dam of Denmark. They were made of vinyl, and the orignal issue carried the mark 'Dam Things Originals copyright 1964 – 1965 Dam Things Est.; m.f.g. by Royalty Designs of Fla. Inc.' (Other marks were used as well; look on the troll's back or the bottom of his feet for Dam trademarks.) As the demand for these trolls increased, several US manufacturers became licensed to produce them. The most noteworthy of these were Uneeda doll company's Wishnik line and Inga Dykin's Scandia House True Trolls. Thomas Dam continued to import his Dam Things line.

The troll craze from the '60s spawned many items other than dolls such as wall plaques, salt and pepper shakers, pins, squirt guns, rings, clay trolls, lamps, Halloween costumes, animals, lawn ornaments, coat racks, notebooks, folders, and even a car.

In the '70s, '80s, and '90s, more new trolls were produced. While these trolls are collectible to some, the avid troll collector still prefers those produced in the '60s. Condition is very important worth-assessing factor; our values are for examples in EX to NM condition. To evaluate trolls in only G to VG condition, decrease these numbers by half or more.

Lion, Dam Things, 1960s, 5", NM, $125.00.

Bank, clown, Dam, thin white hair, red nose, red outfit, 1988, 7",' EX **20.00**

Baseball player, Dam, striped outfit, cap & felt glove, 1977, 9", NM **20.00**

Batman, complete silkscreened costume, 5½", EX **18.00**

Black nurse, Russ, pink hair, in uniform & hat w/red cross, 5", M **55.00**

Boy, Dam, white hair, felt cap, outfit & neck scarf, 1982, 10½", M **22.00**

Boy, Dam, white hair, yellow shirt, purple pants, 1984, 6", EX **35.00**

Boy, Dam/Norfin, yellow hair, red & green T-shirt, jeans, 8", 1990, M **20.00**

Boy, Dam/Norfin #604, orange hair, orange & green outfit, 1977, 9", EX **28.00**

Bride & Groom, Ace/Dam, 1986, 4½" ea, M, pr **18.00**

Caveman, Dam, orange hair, leopard outfit, fuzzy slippers, 8", EX **15.00**

Chef Norfini, Dam/Norfin, all white, 1977, 9", M **18.00**

Clown, Dam/Norfin, black hair, colorful outfit & hat, 1977, 9½", EX 20.00

Donkey, Dam, blond mane, gold glass eyes, pink skin tone, 9", EX 100.00

Dr Olav, Dam/Norfin #6058, green surgeon's outfit, 1977, 9½", EX.................................. 30.00

Elephant, Dam, purple hair, amber eyes, wrinkle-look skin, 6½", EX 100.00

Fire Chief, Dam/Norfin, red felt hat, yellow slicker, 1980s, 10", VG 25.00

Giraffe seated looking up, Dam, white hair, amber eyes, 12", VG+ 75.00

Girl, Dam, blond, amber eyes, swimsuit & hat, w/fish, 1960s, 2½" 45.00

Girl, Dam, orange hair, amber eyes, green dress, 1979, 17½", EX. 85.00

Girl, Dam, pink hair, amber eyes, cat on outfit, pearls, 1960s, 2½" 100.00

Girl, Dam/Norfin #520, white hair, amber eyes, felt outfit, 5", EX............................. 45.00

Girl, Dam/Peachy, yellow hair & eyes, Luna Creations outfit, 3", NM 30.00

Girl, Scandia, purple, hair, blue spiral eyes, tutu, 1960s, 2¾", EX 110.00

Girl, Scandia, red hair & eyes, purple outfit w/lace, 1960, 2½", NM 28.00

Grandma/Grandpa, Norfin, white hair, amber eyes, felt outfits, 14", pr 75.00

Hanna Elf, Norfin, white hair, blue & yellow felt outfit, 1980, EX 35.00

Horse, Dam, blond mane & tail/pink skin tone, 3" H, EX 45.00

Ice Skater, Scandia, blue hair, spiral eyes, felt outfit, 3", EX..... 75.00

Iggy, Dam, blond hair, green eyes (rare), street clothes, 11", EX 125.00

Iggy, Dam, clown outfit, black hair, orange eyes, 12", EX..... 125.00

Iggy, Dam, Tartan Boy overalls, black hair, amber eyes, 11", G 32.00

Monk, Dam/Norfin, brown hair, eyes & felt outfit, 1972, 10", EX 30.00

Monkey in swing, England, hot pink hair, black eyes, 3" troll, EX 75.00

Mouse, Dam/Norfin, lime hair, gray & pink mouse outfit, 1986, 3" 12.00

Prisoner #51538, Dam/Norfin, purple hair, prison outfit, 1977, 9", EX 22.00

Scuba diver, yellow hair, blue suit, green mask & fins, 4", EX.. 22.00

Stressed Out, Dam, hot pink hair, gray sweater, 1986, 4½", EX 18.00

Ye Ye, Dam, yellow hair, blue eyes, felt outfit, 12", EX 100.00

Universal Potteries

Located in Cambridge, Ohio, Universal Potteries Incorporated produced various lines of dinnerware from 1934 to the late 1950s, several of which are very attractive, readily available, and therefore quite collectible. Refer to *The Collector's Encyclopedia of American Dinnerware* by Jo Cunningham (Collector Books) for more information. See also Cat-Tail Dinnerware.

Fruit, refrigerator pitcher, from $30.00 to $40.00.

Baby's Breath, bowl, coupe soup; 7¾" 12.00

Baby's Breath, cup & saucer . 15.00

Baby's Breath, sugar bowl, w/lid, from $25 to 30.00

Ballerina, bowl, salad; from $15 to 20.00

Ballerina, cake plate, w/handles, 10", from $25 to 30.00

Ballerina, egg cup, from $15 to .20.00

Ballerina, plate, dinner; 10", from $10 to 15.00

Ballerina, salt & pepper shakers, pr from $15 to 20.00

Bittersweet, creamer, 3⅝", from $20 to 25.00

Bittersweet, platter, 13½" L, from $28 to 32.00

Bittersweet, salt & pepper shakers, 3½", pr from $30 to 35.00

Blue & White, canteen jug, from $35 to 40.00

Blue & White, syrup pitcher, God Bless America, from $55 to.60.00

Broadway Rose, plate, Atlas Glove mark, 10" 10.00

Calico Fruit, custard cup, 2½" . 15.00

Calico Fruit, plate, dessert; 6" .. 9.00

Calico Fruit, salt & pepper shakers, pr from $30 to 35.00

Calico Fruit, saucer 5.00

Calico Fruit, tray, 11½", from $25 to 30.00

Circus, spoon, from $30 to 35.00

Circus, teapot, 6-cup, from $55 to 60.00

Holland Rose, bowl, 4" 5.00

Holland Rose, plate, dessert; 6". 7.00

Hollyhocks, bowl, salad; from $25 to 30.00

Iris, casserole, w/lid, from $45 to..50.00

Iris, pie baker, from $25 to 30.00

Iris, plate, luncheon; 9" 11.00

Largo, plate, dessert; 6" 5.00

Largo, salt & pepper shakers, pr from $16 to 20.00

Laurella, bowl, cereal; lug handles, solid colors, 7" 10.00

Laurella, chop plate, 13¾" 25.00

Laurella, cup & saucer, solid colors 14.00

Mod Flower, cookie jar, from $55 to 60.00

Rambler Rose, gravy/sauceboat, from $20 to 25.00

Rambler Rose, plate, dessert; 6", from $4 to 5.00

Red & White, ball jug, from $60 to 75.00

Red & White, bean pot, w/lid, from $35 to 40.00

Red & White, teapot, 6-cup, from $40 to 45.00

Red Poppy, plate, chop; 11½" . 13.00

Rosette, bowl, 9" 13.00

Rosette, coffeepot, 9½", from $40 to 45.00

Rosette, refrigerator jar, w/lid, 3", from $20 to 25.00

Shasta Daisy, plate, dinner; 10½", from $8 to 11.00

Shasta Daisy, platter, 13" L, from
$40 to **50.00**
Woodvine, bowl, flat soup **9.00**
Woodvine, bowl, vegetable; oval,
from $12 to **15.00**
Woodvine, creamer, from $15 to. **20.00**
Woodvine, gravy/sauceboat.... **20.00**
Woodvine, sugar bowl, w/lid, from
$20 to **25.00**

Valentines

Valentine's Day is every day
of the year for valentine collectors
who are always on the endless
search for that special one to add to
their collection. Advertising, party
favors, paper dolls, comic characters, transportation, and postcards
represent just a few of the varied
categories in this field.

All valentines are collectible.
Remember the cards you gave to
fellow students, and the boxes you
used to put them in? The new baby
boomers are now starting to search
for their childhood memories and,
yes, that includes valentines. How
about trolls, Disney, and 'for the
teacher' valentines? All of them are
unique in their own special way.

Whatever you collect, chances
are good there will be a valentine
that relates to it, whether it might
be antique lamps, Black Americana,
record players, dolls, track and field,
dogs, cat, sewing machines, etc.
Please keep in mind these seven factors before purchasing a card: condition, size, manufacturer, category,
scarcity, artist signature, and age.
For more information we recom-

mend *Valentines with Values, One
Hundred Years of Valentines,* and
Valentines for the Eclectic Collector,
all by Katherine Kreider.

Key:

D — dimensional
HCCP — honeycomb paper puff
PIG — Printed in Germany

**Flat, Flintstones,
1962, 4¾x3", EX,
$5.00.** (Photo courtesy
Katherine Kreider)

Dimensional, big-eyed child playing
piano, 2-D, Germany, 4x2¼",
EX **10.00**
Dimensional, Campbell Soup Kids
at fireplace, 1920s, 3½x3½",
EX **10.00**
Dimensional, cherubs in sailboat,
Germany, early 1900s, 4x4½",
EX **15.00**
Dimensional, Cupid Air Line, diora-
ma, 1920s, 4½x6x2", EX . **15.00**
Dimensional, Victorian lady w/sham-
rocks, 5-D, Germany, 1900s, 7",
EX **25.00**
Dimensional, wishing well among
trees, 2-D, Hallmark, 1960s,
9", EX **10.00**
Flat, archer, heart-shaped, Gibson,
USA, 4x3", EX **3.00**
Flat, boy troll, USA, 1960s, 6x5½",
EX **5.00**
Flat, double ice-cream cone,
unmarked USA, 1960s, 3x2½",
EX **3.00**

Flat, elephant in boxing ring, USA, 1940s, 3½x2½", EX............ **3.00**

Flat, frog couple, side easels, USA, 1920s, 5x4", EX................. **4.00**

Flat, Polly Prinkup, Art Deco, 1920s, 4x4", EX............... **20.00**

Flat, spaceman, USA, 1940s, 6¼x3", EX.. **3.00**

Flat, Uncle Sam, chromolitho, early 1900s, 3½x3", EX **10.00**

Folded-flat, army WAC, USA, 1940s, 6x4", EX............... **10.00**

Folded-flat, school kids w/chalkboard, To My Teacher, USA, 4½", EX **3.00**

Folded-flat, Snow White & Happy caricature, USA, 1940s, 5¾x4", EX **25.00**

Hold-to-light, big-eyed kids climbing apple tree, USA, 9½x6", EX **10.00**

Hold-to-light, steamboat, Germany, early 1900s, 10½x6x3¼", EX..**20.00**

Honeycomb paper puff, hippo playing ice hockey, Germany, 1920s, 5", EX................................. **3.00**

Honeycomb paper puff, kids w/teddy bear, Germany, 1920s, 7½", EX **10.00**

Honeycomb paper puff, shaving razor, Beistle, USA, 1920s, 8x2x8", EX....................... **15.00**

Mechanical-flat, English bulldog driving car, Germany, 1920s, 6", EX............................... **10.00**

Mechanical-flat, frying pan, USA, 1950s, 5¼x2½", EX............ **5.00**

Mechanical-flat, kangaroo, USA, 1940s, 9x5", EX................. **5.00**

Mechanical-flat, pilgrims, USA, 1950s, 5¾x3½", EX............ **4.00**

Mechanical-flat, reamer, USA, 1940s, 6x4", EX............... **10.00**

Mechanical-flat, turtle, 1940s, 6x4", EX **10.00**

Novelty, Charlie McCarthy lollipop card, Rosen, 1930s, 8½x6", EX.................................. **25.00**

Novelty, die-cut heart w/football charm, USA, 1930s, 5½x5", EXIB **25.00**

Novelty, paper doll bathing beauty, 1930s, 4½x4½", NM......... **15.00**

Novelty, real hair valentine, easel-back, Germany, 1930s, 6½", EX.... **10.00**

Penny Dreadful, baseball player, USA, 1920s, 9½x6", EX..... **3.00**

Penny Dreadful, Dieter, USA, 1930s, 8½x9", EX **10.00**

Postcard, Kewpie, Rose O'Neill, Gibson Co, 1910-20s, EX. **25.00**

Postcard, Whitney children holding hands, Worcester Mass, 1920s, EX **2.00**

Mechanical-flat, cigar-smoking man with top hat, Germany, early 1900s, 6½x3¾", EX, $45.00. (Photo courtesy Katherine Kreider)

Van Briggle

The Van Briggle Pottery of Colorado Springs, Colorado, was established in 1901 by Artus Van Briggle upon the completion of his quest to perfect a complete flat matt glaze. His wife, Ann, worked with him and they, along with George Young, were responsible for the modeling of the wares. Known for their flowing Art Nouveau shapes, much of the ware was eventually made from molds with each piece carefully trimmed and refined before the glaze was sprayed on. Their most popular colors were Persian Rose, Ming Blue, and Mustard Yellow.

Van Briggle died in 1904, but the work was continued by his wife. With new facilities built in 1908, tiles, gardenware, and commercial lines were added to the earlier artware lines. Reproductions of some early designs continue to be made, The Double AA mark has always been in use, but after 1920 the dates and/or shape numbers were dropped. The Anna Van Briggle glaze was developed for a later line that was made between 1956 and 1968.

Ashtray, sq dish w/center handle, turquoise, 1950s-60s **55.00**
Bookends, owl w/wings spread on open book, turquoise, 1922-26, pr **300.00**

Bowl, Lady of the Lake, blue and green matt, post-1920s, 9x14", **$275.00.** (Photo courtesy Treadway Galleries)

Candlesticks, tulip form w/leafy stem, Golden Rod, 1980s, pr **50.00**
Cowboy boot, turquoise, late 1980s **45.00**
Creamer & sugar bowl, hexagonal, turquoise, 1930s-40s, ea . **35.00**
Figurine, elephant in stride & trumpeting, turquoise, late 1980s **75.00**
Figurine, girl holding shell in lap, white, 8" **100.00**
Figurine, Indian maiden grinding corn, Golden Rod, 1980s-91 .... **115.00**
Flower frog, duck in pond, turquoise, 2⅞x9¾" frog & 6x14" bowl **150.00**
Lamp, woman kneeling w/pot on shoulder, mulberry, no shade, 1940s-50s **350.00**
Leaf dish, maple leaf form w/embossed veins, glossy brown, 1971 .... **45.00**
Mug, wooden barrel form w/2 bands, brown w/gray rim, 1968-70s. **25.00**
Planter, swan design, mulberry, scalloped, footed, oblong, 1930s-40s **120.00**
Vase, crescent moon shape, Persian Rose, 7½x7¾" **100.00**
Vase, dragonflies, dark turquoise, 2⅜x8" **175.00**
Vase, leaves embossed on turquoise ball form, rimless, 1980s. **100.00**
Vase, leaves form body, blue & aqua mottling, post-1930s, 3½" **100.00**
Vase, triple cornucopia, turquoise, 1960s-70s **40.00**
Vase, twisted design, red w/purple overspray, 7½" **110.00**
Wall plaque, Indian's face, Ming Green, 5½x3½" **125.00**

Vernon Kilns

From 1931 until 1958, Vernon Kilns produced hundreds of patterns of fine dinnerware that today's collectors enjoy reassembling. They retained the services of famous artists and designers such as Rockwell Kent and Walt Disney, who designed both dinnerware lines and novelty items. Examples of their work are at a premium. (Nearly all artist-designed lines utilized the Ultra Shape. To evaluate the work of Blanding, use 200% of our high range; for Disney lines, 700% to 800%; Kent — Moby Dick and Our America 250%; for Salamina, 500% to 700%.) For more informtion, we recommend *Collectible Vernon Kilns* by Maxine Nelson (Collector Books). Our values are average. The more elaborate the pattern, the higher the value.

Chatelaine, decorated Jade, dinner plate, $25.00; cup and saucer, $25.00.

Anytime, bowl, chowder; 6", from $8 to **12.00**
Anytime, bowl, vegetable; 9", from $12 to **18.00**
Anytime, gravy boat, from $18 to.. **20.00**
Anytime, platter, 13½", from $18 to **25.00**

Anytime, relish dish, 3-compartment, from $20 to **25.00**
Anytime, teapot, from $35 to.. **65.00**
Butter dish, from $30 to **40.00**
Chatelaine, bowl, serving; bronze or topaz, 9", from $25 to .**35.00**
Chatelaine, chop plate, bronze or topaz, 14", from $40 to.... **45.00**
Chatelaine, creamer, bronze or topaz, from $20 to **25.00**
Chatelaine, plate, dinner; 10½", platinum, from $20 to... **25.00**
Chatelaine, plate, salad; 7½", bronze or topaz................ **14.00**
Chatelaine, salt & pepper shakers, bronze or topaz, pr from $20 to **25.00**

Homespun, salt and pepper shakers, 3", $18.00 for the pair.

Lotus, bowl, vegetable; divided, from $20 to **25.00**
Lotus, butter dish, oblong, from $35 to **45.00**
Lotus, mug, 9-oz, from $15 to. **20.00**
Lotus, salt & pepper shakers, pr from $20 to **25.00**
Melinda, bowl, fruit; 5½", from $6 to **10.00**
Melinda, casserole, w/lid, 8", from $45 to **75.00**
Melinda, egg cup, from $18 to . **25.00**
Melinda, plate, luncheon; 9½" . **14.00**
Melinda, tidbit, 2-tier, wooden fixture, from $20 to **30.00**

Montecito, bowl, mixing; 6", from $20 to **25.00**

Montecito, bowl, salad; angular, 13", from $40 to **65.00**

Montecito, chop plate, 17", from $50 to **95.00**

Montecito, coaster, ridged, 3¾", from $18 to **22.00**

Montecito, creamer, angular or round, open, from $15 to . **20.00**

Montecito, pepper mill, w/metal fitting, lg, from $40 to **50.00**

Montecito, plate, dinner; 10½", from $15 to **25.00**

Montecito, teapot, angular or round, from $45 to **95.00**

Pan American Lei, bowl, mixing; 7", from $30 to **40.00**

Pan American Lei, creamer, from $20 to **25.00**

Pan American Lei, plate, coupe; 6", from $10 to **12.00**

Pan American Lei, sauceboat, from $30 to **35.00**

San Marino, bowl, fruit; 5½" ... **7.00**

San Marino, bowl, serving; 9", from $15 to **20.00**

San Marino, flowerpot, scarce, 3", from $18 to **25.00**

Transitional (Year 'Round), buffet server, trio, from $35 to .. **50.00**

Transitional (Year 'Round), butter dish, from $25 to **35.00**

Transitional (Year 'Round), creamer, from $8 to **10.00**

Transitional (Year 'Round), plate, dinner **12.00**

Transitional (Year 'Round), teacup & saucer, from $8 to **12.00**

Ultra, bowl, cereal; 6", from $10 to.................................... **15.00**

Ultra, bowl, salad; 11", from $45 to **85.00**

Ultra, coffeepot, regular, 6-cup, from $65 to **125.00**

Ultra, plate, dinner; 10½", from $12 to **20.00**

Ultra, plate, luncheon; 8½", from $15 to **20.00**

Ultra, tumbler, Style #4, 13-oz, 5", from $25 to **40.00**

Vietnam War Collectibles

There was conflict in Vietnam for many years before the United States was drawn into it during the Eisenhower years, and fighting raged until well into 1975 when communist forces invaded Saigon and crushed the South Vietnamese government there. Today items from the 1960s and early 1970s are becoming collectible. Pins, booklets, uniforms, patches, and the like reflect these troubled times when anti-war demonstrations raged and unsound political policies cost the lives of many brave young men.

Belt buckle, I Served My Time in Hell — Veteran, 1959-1975, EX **15.00**

Beret, Ranger; black w/yellow lining, metal badge, EX **130.00**

Booklet, Operation & Preventive Maintenance of Colt M16A1 Rifle, EX+ **12.00**

Boots, jungle; leather w/green cloth uppers, Genesco, EX, pr . **75.00**

Compass, Airpath MS 17983-2, M.................................. **110.00**

Compass, US Army, Union Instrument Corp, dated 1967, EX in pouch..................... **60.00**

Cookstove, Rogers M-1950, uses gasoline, EX **30.00**

Hammock, jungle green, 1966, EX **25.00**

Helmet, US Airborne, captain's, camo w/liner, strap & band, EX **90.00**

Helmet, US M-1, w/riot face shield, dated 5/31/67, EX............ **30.00**

Jacket, camo w/silk liner, zippered, made by S Vietnamese, ca 1968, EX **215.00**

Jacket, field; green cloth, hood inside collar, 4 flap pockets, NM **75.00**

Jacket, flight; green, zippered, EX **85.00**

Knife, Camillus, 5" blade, leather w/sharpening stone, dated 5/67, EX **30.00**

Knife, Gerber Mark II Dagger, 1969, 11½", M (M leather sheath) **770.00**

License plate, Back Our Boys in Vietnam, red, white & blue, 6x12", EX........................ **40.00**

Lighter, Zippo, River Section 512 PBR/gunboat, EX.......... **475.00**

Lighter, Zippo, Viet Nam Chu Lai 68-69/Airborne emblem, EX .. **90.00**

Lighter, Zippo, Viet Nam 67-68 Tuy Hoa USMC Getting Short, G **265.00**

Medal, Cross of Gallantry, w/matching lapel pin, EX **35.00**

Medal, South Vietnam Air Service, w/original ribbon, EX...... **65.00**

Patch, MAAG Viet-Nam, blue & white stars, EX **35.00**

Patch, River Rats, 3x3", VG .. **75.00**

Playing cards, Death Cards, message for Vietnamese on back, NM **75.00**

Radio, Raythenon, green & orange camo, EX.......................... **50.00**

Survival cards, For Southeast Asia, dated 4/1/68, MIB **15.00**

Survival kit, Hot-Wet Environment, FAASS Surgical Mfg Co, EX.**55.00**

Survival vest, 11 pockets, Lankford Mfg Co, 1974, VG+.......... **35.00**

Uniform, WAC; green pinstripe skirt & blouse, ca 1962, EX **95.00**

Wings, Command Pilot, Sterling, 3", EX............................. **115.00**

Wristwatch, Benrus military issue, olive green nylon band, EX.**75.00**

Wristwatch, DTU-2A/P, stainless steel w/black 24-hour face, VG **125.00**

Patch, USAF, from $90.00 to $100.00.
(Photo courtesy Michael Dougerty)

Wall Pockets

Here's a collectible that is easily found, relatively inexpensive, and very diversified. They were made in Japan, Czechoslovakia, and by many, many companies in the United States. Those made by companies best known for their art pottery (Weller, Roseville, etc.) are in a class of their own, but the novelty, just-for-fun wall pockets stand on their own merits. Examples with large, colorful birds or those with unusual modeling are usually the more desirable. For more information we recommend *Collector's Encyclopedia of Made in Japan Ceramics* by Carole Bess White (published by Collector Books), who is listed in the Directory under Oregon. See also California Pottery, Cleminson; McCoy; Shawnee; other specific manufacturers.

Basket (oval) w/grape cluster & 2 flowers, Japan, 6¾" **15.00**
Bird & fruit basket, multicolored lustre, 8" **225.00**

Bird on flowering tree branch, Made in Japan, 10", from $35.00 to $40.00. (Photo courtesy Carole Bess White)

Blue bird against tree trunk w/blossoms, lustre, 8" **75.00**
Cone form w/Deco flower, lustre trim, Japan, 7¼" **35.00**
Cornucopia & fruit, basketweave w/multicolored embossing at rim **15.00**
Creamer & sugar bowl, white w/painted flowers, sponged rim, 8" L **12.00**
Cup & saucer, bright yellow, Camark, 7½" **20.00**
Dutch boy w/goose beside stone wall, Japan, 6" **18.00**
Dutch girl w/basket, Japan, 6½" **15.00**

Elf leaning on stone wall, Treasure Craft, 5" **25.00**
Fan, embossed bow/applied flowers, white w/gold trim, Lefton, 8" **22.00**
Fruit embossed on cone shape, multicolored w/blue lustre .. **325.00**
Girl in yellow dress & hat, 4½" .. **25.00**
Grandfather clock, embossed/airbrushed, USA 1267, 6¾" . **15.00**
Japanese lady w/basket on her back, multicolored, Banko, 9" **85.00**
Lady dancing, blue dress, Japan, 8½" **55.00**
Man's head w/mustache, airbrushed detail, 4¼" **22.00**
Monkey w/pot on tree trunk, white w/painted & embossed detail, 6¾" **12.00**
Pine cone form, Cortney, 4¾"... **8.00**
Radishes, bunch tied w/string, Portugal, 11½" **32.00**
Sailboat, white w/gold lustre, Brown China Co, 5¾" **20.00**
Straw hat, brown w/white wash, Stanford Pottery, 9" **12.00**
Strawberries & leaves, airbrushed leaves, glossy, 7½" **28.00**
Telephone, early wall type w/woodgrain detail, gold trim, 5" . **15.00**
Umbrella w/painted berries & leaves on white, Orion sticker, 6½" **12.00**
Violin w/pansies, gold trim, 6½" . **12.00**

Weeping Gold

Weeping gold was produced by many American potteries during the 1950s. It is characterized by the irregular droplets of lustrous gold that covers its surface. On some items the gold may be heavy; sometimes it is applied in random swirls. Real gold was actually used, and some examples will be stamped '22k (or 24k) gold.' You may see silver used in this manner as well. Figural items, larger vases, and serving pieces are most marketable. Cups and saucers are scarce, so they ofen sell in the higher ranges as well.

Ashtray, hands, 3-footed, Hand Painted 22k Gold USA..., 1½x5x3¾" **25.00**
Bell, w/original clapper, 5¾".. **20.00**
Candy dish/compote, 3¾x5⅝".. **22.00**
Cup & saucer, demitasse; Hand Decorated 22k Gold USA, Weeping Bright Gold **25.00**
Ewer, Holly Ross Distinguished China 22k gold, 11⅜" **30.00**
Figurine, elephant, 8¾x10x3½" .**55.00**
Figurine, panther, 6x11" **35.00**
Pitcher, Jim Beam label on rectangular body, from $25 to ... **40.00**
Vase, bud; stick neck, 8" **25.00**
Vase, embossed floral, slim & waisted, slightly scalloped rim, 12" **40.00**

Vase, Savoy label, 12½", from $50.00 to $60.00.

Wall pocket, fan shape, Sunburst, McCoy, 8x8½" **75.00**

Western Heroes

As children, baby boomers often spent Saturday mornings watching television shows featuring Roy Rogers, Sky King, and the Lone Ranger, to name only a few. Davy Crockett and Daniel Boone were regulars on the Wonderful World of Disney on Sunday nights. One western hero after another struggled with the 'bad guys' every day of the week on radio. As a result of all those popular TV and radio shows, vast amounts of merchandise and premiums were sold or given away to ardent fans. Many of those fans (all grown up) are on the hunt today for items relating to their favorite western heroes. For more information, we recommend *The W.F. Cody Buffalo Bill Collector's Guide* by James W. Wojtowicz and *Schroeder's Collectible Toys, Antique to Modern,* published by Collector Books. See also Character and Promotional Drinking Glasses; Children's Books; Coloring Books; Comic Books; Games; Puzzles.

Davy Crockett

Davy Crockett had long been a favorite in fact and folklore. Then with the opening of Disney's Frontierland and his continuing adventures on 1950s television came a surge of interest in all sorts of items featuring the likeness of Fess Parker in a coonskin cap. Millions were drawn to the mystic excitement surrounding the settlement of our great country. Due to demand, there were many types of items produced for eager fans ready to role play their favorite adventures.

Binoculars, plastic, Harrison, MIB **175.00**
Doll, painted plastic, cloth outfit & hat, Fortune Toy, 1950s, 7", NMIB.............................. **100.00**
Lamp, chalkware figural base w/mountain scene on shade, 18", VG **100.00**
Lamp, rotating cylinder, Econolite, 11", EX............................ **275.00**
Marionette, composition w/complete cloth outfit, Peter Puppet, 14", EX............................. **150.00**
Nightlight, figural head, Kupfer, 1950s, MIB **115.00**
Pencil case, Frontierland, brown vinyl holster w/gun-shaped case, VG........................... **50.00**
Stick horse, Pied Piper Toys, MIB.............................. **125.00**
Tent, brown & white graphics on tan canvas, Empire/WD Prod, 1950s, NM **135.00**
Towel, white terry, Cannon/WD Prod, 1950s, 37x20", NM+ **40.00**
Woodburning set, Frontier..., ATF, USA, MIB...................... **175.00**

Gene Autry

First breaking into show business as a recording star with Columbia Records, Gene went on to become one of Hollywood's most famous singing cowboys. From the late 1930s until the mid-'50s, he rode his wonder horse Champion through almost 90 feature films. He

did radio and TV as well, and naturally his fame spawned a wealth of memorabilia originally aimed at his young audiences, now grabbed up just as quickly by collectors.

Doll, composition w/cloth outfit & felt hat, Terry Lee, 16", NM+ **500.00**
Flashlight, Cowboy Lariat, EXIB......................... **100.00**
Guitar, plastic, Emenee, 32", NMIB............................. **225.00**
Outfit, shirt & pants (not for play), California Ranchwear, M..**300.00**
Pistol horn, Metal Products, 6½", NM+IB........................... **175.00**
Record player, plastic, 'Flying A' decal, Columbia, 13" L, VG **250.00**
Rug, tan chenille, name & Champ above & below horse head, 37x25", EX+..................... **75.00**
Spurs, Official Cowboy..., Leslie-Henry, EXIB.................. **100.00**
Wallet, leather w/zipper closure, Gene & Champion, Aristocrat, VGIB............................... **75.00**

Hopalong Cassidy

One of the most popular western heroes of all time, Hoppy was the epitome of the highly moral, role-model cowboys of radio and the silver screen that many of us grew up with in the '40s and '50s. He was portrayed by Bill Boyd who personally endorsed more than 2,200 items targeting Hoppy's loyal followers.

Bank, plastic bust figure w/removable hat, Savings Club..., 4", EX **50.00**

Coin, Hoppy/Good Luck From Hoppy, 1¼" dia, VG **15.00**

Crayon & stencil set, Transogram, 1950s, complete, some use, EXIB **50.00**

Dinner plate, 9½", $48.00.

Doll, rubber head, cloth outfit, w/gun & holster, 1950s, 21", NM. **300.00**

Drinking straws, cut-out photo of Hoppy on back, 1950s, NMIB **75.00**

Figure & Paint Set, Laurel Ann, complete, EXIB **250.00**

Hand puppet, cloth body w/vinyl head, 1950s, scarce, NM . **200.00**

Night light, figural glass gun in holster, Aladdin, 1950s, NM **350.00**

Pocketknife, black w/black & white image, 2", NM+ **85.00**

Scrapbook, vinyl hardcover w/embossed image, string-bound, NM .. **125.00**

Stationery folio, complete w/paper & envelopes, VG+ **50.00**

Wallet, brown leather w/color head images, zipper closure, 1950s, VG+ **50.00**

The Lone Ranger

Recalling 'those thrilling days of yesteryear,' we can't help but remember the adventures of our hero, The Lone Ranger. He's been admired since that first radio show in 1933, and today's collectors seek a wide variety of his memorabilia; premiums, cereal boxes, and even carnival chalkware prizes are a few examples. See Clubs and Newsletters for information on *The Silver Bullet.*

Binoculars, plastic, Harrison, EX+IB **135.00**

Horseshoe set, rubber, Gardner, NMIB **85.00**

Push-button puppet, on Silver, Press Action Toys, 1939, NMIB **150.00**

Record player, wooden case, Decca Lone Ranger Inc, EX **350.00**

Ring Toss, die-cut cardboard, complete, Rosebud Art, MIB. **250.00**

School bag, canvas w/plastic handle, image on side pocket, 1950s, EX **100.00**

Soap figure, Kerk Guild, 1939, 4½", EXIB **65.00**

Target, litho tin w/metal support, Marx/TLP Inc, 1930s, 9½" sq, EX **50.00**

Toothbrush holder, Lone Ranger on Silver, Syrocco, 1939, 4", EX................................. **50.00**

Roy Rogers

Growing up during the Great Depression, Leonard Frank Sly was determined to make his mark in the entertainment industry. In 1938 after landing small roles in films featuring Gene Autry and others, Republic Studios (recognizing his talents) renamed their singing cowboy Roy Rogers and placed him in his first leading role in *Under Western Stars.* By 1943 he had become America's 'King of the Cowboys,' and his beloved wife Dale Evans and his horse Trigger were at the top with him. See Clubs and Newsletters for information on the Roy Rogers — Dale Evans Collectors Association.

Archery set, Ben Pearson, scarce, 37", NMOC **175.00**
Branding set/ink pad, tin container, 1950s, EX **65.00**
Crayon set, Standard Toykraft #940, 1950s, VGIB **75.00**
Flashlight, Signal Siren, tin, Usalite, 7", MIB **150.00**
Fountain pen, name on black plastic barrel, gold trim, 1950s, 5", VG **50.00**

Guitar, Roy, Dale, and Trigger, 28", EX, $125.00. (Photo courtesy Dunbar Gallery)

Guitar, wood & pressed wood, Range Rhythm/Rich Toys, 31", NMIB **200.00**
Hand puppet, cloth w/vinyl head & hat, 1950s, 7", EX+ **75.00**
Lamp base, plaster figure on rearing Trigger, Plasto, 10½", EX+ **100.00**
Lantern, litho tin, 8" (w/handle up), EX **50.00**

Modeling clay set, NM (in box w/Roy & Trigger) **150.00**
Pencil case, vinyl w/white stitching, graphics, snap closure, 8", EX **50.00**
Woodburning set, Burn-Rite, complete, EXIB **175.00**

Miscellaneous

Andy Devine, hand puppet, cloth w/vinyl head, 1950s, EX **100.00**
Annie Oakley & Tag, belt, tooled leather w/name & rope design, MOC................................ **85.00**
Cisco Kid, belt, black leather w/brown embellishments, 1950s, NM **55.00**
Dale Evans, wash mitt, terry cloth, color image/name/Queen of the West **25.00**
Dale Evans, Western Dress-Up Kit, Colorforms/R Rogers Ent, 1959, EXIB **50.00**
Daniel Boone, figure, plastic w/vinyl head, fur cap, powder horn, 6", NM................................... **50.00**
Daniel Boone, Super Slate From the ...TV Show, Saalfield, 1964, EX **75.00**
Daniel Boone, Woodland Whistle, Autolite premium, EXIB **100.00**
Gabby Hayes, doll, stuffed cloth w/fur beard & felt hat, 1960s, 13", M **40.00**
Gabby Hayes, hand puppet, cloth w/vinyl head, JVZ, 1949, EX **200.00**
Gunsmoke, notepad, Amanda Blake (Miss Kitty) hugging Matt's horse, EX **40.00**

Gunsmoke, slippers, black vinyl, yellow/red images, Columbia, M **200.00**

Johnny Ringo, hand puppet, Laura (girlfriend), Tops in Toys, 10", EX+ **40.00**

Kit Karson, 3-Powered Binoculars, 1950s, EXIB **150.00**

Maverick, Oil Paint-by-Numbers, Hasbro, 1958, complete, EX. **40.00**

Red Ryder, medallion, embossed brass, Daisy Mfg Co 1938 Red Ryder, 2" dia **75.00**

Red Ryder, Playmates Gloves, multi-colored cloth, 1950s, NM .. **30.00**

Rin-Tin-Tin, Corporal Rusty 101st Cavalary Outfit, complete, NMIB **175.00**

Tales of Wells Fargo, Paint-by-Numbers, 1959, partially used, EX **55.00**

Tonto, doll, stuffed body w/compo head, complete, 20", EX. **500.00**

Virginian, Movie Viewer, Chemtoy, 1956, MOC (sealed) **45.00**

Wanted Dead or Alive, Mares Laig cap gun, Marx, MOC **100.00**

Wild Bill Hickok, wallet, fastens w/Western buckle, NM+ . **75.00**

Zorro, hand puppet, vinyl head w/cloth body, felt hat, Gund, 1950s, EX+ **75.00**

Zorro, magic slate, Watkins-Strathmore, 1950s-60s, complete, EX **75.00**

Westmoreland

Originally an Ohio company, Westmoreland relocated in Grapesville, Pennsylvania, where by the 1920s they had became known as one of the country's largest manufacturers of carnival glass. They are best known today for the high quality milk glass which accounted for 90% of their production. For further information we recommend *Westmoreland Glass, The Popular Years,* by Lorraine Kovar (Collector Books); see the Directory for information on the Westmoreland Glass Society, Inc., listed in Clubs and Newsletters. See also Glass Animals and Birds.

Basket, Daisy or Ruby, 6x9".. **75.00**

Basket, Della Robbia, crystal, 9" dia **70.00**

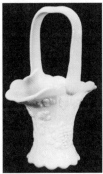

Basket, Panelled Grape, milk glass, #1881, 8", $77.50. (Photo courtesy Ruth Grizel)

Bell, Mary Gregory on crystal w/ruby stain, plain rim, 5" **30.00**

Bonbon, Beaded Bouquet, milk glass, handled, w/lid **50.00**

Bowl, American Hobnail, cupped, milk glass, 8 .... **40.00**

Bowl, Beaded Grape, milk glass, footed, w/lid, 7".............. **40.00**

Bowl, Paneled Grape, milk glass, cupped, #1881, 8" **45.00**

Candleholders, Beaded Grape, Golden Sunset, 4", pr......**50.00**

Candleholders, starfish, Almond, 5" wide, pr from $45 to **55.00**

Candleholders, Thousand Eye, crystal w/stain, 5", pr **60.00**

Candy dish, green frost, dolphin feet, shell finial, 6½", $40.00.

Cigarette box, English Hobnail, milk glass, 4½x3½"..........**17.50**

Compote, Mary Gregory decor on any Mist, w/lid **90.00**

Covered animal dish, camel, Antique Blue, Green or Yellow Mist.**125.00**

Covered animal dish, chick on oval 2-handled basket, milk glass, 4"......................................**30.00**

Covered animal dish, duck on wavy base, milk glass or Milk Glass Mist..................................**60.00**

Covered animal dish, eagle & babies on basketweave, milk glass, 8" **125.00**

Covered animal dish, fox on diamond or lacy base, milk glass............................**125.00**

Covered animal dish, hen on basketweave, Pink Mist or ruby, 3½" **40.00**

Covered animal dish, lamb on picket-fence base, Purple Marble, 5½" **150.00**

Covered animal dish, lion on lacy base, Antique Blue, 8" ..**190.00**

Covered animal dish, lovebirds on base, milk glass, 6½".......**50.00**

Covered animal dish, rabbit on diamond nest, purple slag, limited edition of 150, 1978, $190.00. (Photo courtesy Ruth Grizel)

Covered animal dish, robin on twig nest, ruby carnival, 6¼"..**95.00**

Covered animal dish, rooster on diamond or lacy base, milk glass, 8" **45.00**

Covered animal dish, swan (closed neck) on diamond, milk glass, 5½".**70.00**

Covered animal dish, swan (open neck) on diamond, milk glass, 5½" **50.00**

Covered animal dish, swan (raised wing) on lacy base, cobalt, 9½"..................................**340.00**

Doorstop, bulldog, Amber Mist, 7 lbs **350.00**

Egg cup, double; American Hobnail, milk glass **17.50**

Figurine, bulldog, Electric Blue, #75, 2½", from $25 to......**35.00**

Figurine, butterfly, Almond, Mint Green or Mint Green Mist, 2½" **25.00**

Figurine, owl on tree stump, any color, 5½", ea from $35 to.**50.00**

Figurine, Porky Pig, crystal, Dark Blue Mist or Mint Green, 3".........**30.00**

Figurine, pouter pigeon, Amethyst
Mist #9, 2½", from $25 to.**35.00**

Figurine, robin, all Mist colors or
ruby, solid, 5¼"................**25.00**

Jardiniere, Daisy on any Mist,
straight, footed, 5"..........**30.00**

Lamp, candle; owl, red or yellow,
metal latticework base, #110,
4¼"...................................**24.00**

Lamp, fairy; Wakefield, crystal
w/silver trim, footed........**75.00**

Lamp, mini-lite, any Mist w/any
decal, w/shade.................**30.00**

Lamp, mini-lite, any Mist w/out a
decal, w/shade.................**27.50**

Lamp, mini-lite, milk glass w/Roses
& Bows, w/shade...........**135.00**

Mayonnaise plate, Lotus, Crystal
Mist, 7"..............................**7.50**

Napkin ring, milk glass w/holly
decor, 6-sided...................**50.00**

Paperweight, turtle, dark blue,
Green Mist or Lilac Mist, no
holes..................................**50.00**

Paperweight, turtle, milk glass, no
holes..................................**75.00**

Pitcher, water; Old Quilt, crystal or
moss green, 5-pt, 8½"......**55.00**

Planter, Paneled Grape, sq, footed,
milk glass, 4½"................**40.00**

Plate, dinner; Beaded Grape, milk
glass, 10½"......................**55.00**

Plate, dinner; Paneled Grape, milk
glass, 10½"......................**55.00**

Plate, luncheon; English Hobnail,
crystal w/black stripe, sq,
8¾".................................**22.50**

Relish dish, Old Quilt, milk glass,
round, 3-part...................**35.00**

Salt & pepper shakers, Colonial,
Laurel Green, pr.............**40.00**

Sugar bowl, Colonial, Golden
Sunset, Keystone mark..**22.50**

Toothpick holder, owl, crystal,
3"................................. **15.00**

Toothpick holder, owl, milk glass,
#62, 3", from $20 to........**25.00**

Tumbler, English Hobnail, crystal,
footed, 12½-oz, 6¼"..........**15.00**

Vase, bud; Beaded Bouquet, any
color, plain, flat, 6"..........**50.00**

Vase, English Hobnail, milk glass,
crimped rim, 4½".............**12.50**

Wexford

Wexford is a diverse line of
heavy-gauge glassware that Anchor
Hocking has made since 1967. It
was an extensive line at one time,
and a few pieces still being produced today. It's very likely you'll
see it at any flea market you visit.
Right now, it's not only plentiful,
but inexpensive, so it's a good time
to start collecting. There are 77
pieces listed in *Anchor Hocking's
Fire-King & More* written by Gene
and Cathy Florence, and he says
that others will no doubt be report-
ed as collectors become more familiar with the market.

Ashtray, 5½"............................**4.00**

Bowl, fruit; footed, 10"...........**14.00**

Bowl, trifle; plain top.............**10.00**

Butter dish, ¼-lb.....................**6.00**

Cordial, 3-oz............................**2.50**

Creamer, 8-oz..........................**2.50**

Goblet, 10-oz............................**3.50**

Mug, 15-oz..............................**15.00**

Pitcher, footed, 18-oz.............**10.00**

Plate, dinner; scalloped edge, 9½"..**20.00**

Platter, 14" dia........................**5.00**

Relish tray, 3-part, 8½"............**4.00**

Salt & pepper shakers, 2-oz, pr.**3.00**

Saucer, 6"................................... **1.00**
Sugar bowl, w/lid, 8-oz............. **3.00**
Tidbit, 2-tier **10.00**
Tumbler, 16-oz.......................... **3.50**

**Decanter, 32-ounce, $12.00; Bowl, 5",
$3.00; Vase, 10½", $12.50.** (Photo courtesy
Gene and Cathy Florence)

Wilton Pans

Wilton started mass merchandising the shaped pans in the early 1960s, and the company has been careful to keep up with trends since then. Thus, many of the pans are limited production which adds to the collectible factor. You've probably seen several of these as you made your flea-market rounds. Especially good are the pans that depict cartoon, story book, or movie characters. Of course, condition is vital, and examples with the paper inserts/instructions, and accessory pieces bring the highest prices.

As with any collectible, future demand is impossible to predict, but since many Wilton pans can be found at garage sales, thrift stores, and flea markets for just a few dollars, right now it doesn't take a lot of money to start a collection.

Barbie, 1995, w/insert, plastic figure & face, used, EX....... **10.00**
Barney, #2105-6713, 1993, w/insert, used, EX **25.00**
Batman (waist up/before moon), 1989, pan only, used, EX . **25.00**
Batman oval emblem, 1964, pan only, used, VG **22.00**
Bert & Ernie, #502-7423, 1971, w/insert, used, EX........... **18.00**
Blues Clues (full body), w/insert, used, EX **25.00**
Blues Clues (head/front paws), 2003, w/insert & instructions, unused, M........................ **12.00**
Bob the Builder, w/insert, unused, EX **14.00**
Boba Fett, 1983, w/insert & instructions, unused, EX............ **45.00**
Charlie Brown (baseball), w/insert & plastic face plate, unused, EX **22.00**
Cookie Monster, w/insert & instructions, used, EX, from $10 to . **15.00**
Country Goose, w/insert & instructions, unused, EX.............. **5.00**
Cowboy/Sheriff w/lasso, pan only, used, EX **15.00**
Donald Duck head (in profile), #515-1503, 1977, pan only, unused, VG..................................... **25.00**
Dora the Explorer, w/insert & instructions, used, NM ... **18.00**
Dumbo, #515-434, 1976, pan only, used, EX **30.00**
Elmo head (Sesame Street), w/insert, used, EX+......... **30.00**
Friendly Dinosaur, 1988, w/insert, used, EX **5.00**
Frog w/smiling face, #502-1816, 1979, pan only, used, VG . **35.00**
Garfield w/slice of birthday cake, 1984, w/insert, unused, EX........... **12.00**

Good Cheer Mug, #502-3965, 1984, w/insert, used, EX........... **25.00**

Haunted House, 2000, w/insert & instructions, unused, M.. **10.00**

Itsy Bitsy Baby, 2000, pan only, used, EX **25.00**

Minnie Mouse, #2105-3502, 1998, pan only, EX **30.00**

My Little Pony, #2105-2914, 1986, pan only, used, EX **45.00**

Mystical Dragon, 1984, w/insert, unused, M........................ **75.00**

Mystical Dragon, 1984, w/insert, used, VG **55.00**

Number 1, 1979, #502-1905, used, EX...................................... **20.00**

Playboy Bunny head, #502-2994, pan only, used, EX **15.00**

Pluto head, 1976, pan only, sm, used, NM **7.00**

Power Ranger (Jason), #2105-5975, 1994, w/insert, used, EX .. **22.00**

Power Ranger (Saban), 1994, pan only, used, EX.................. **20.00**

Precious Moments, #2105-9365, 1993, pan only, used, EX . **22.00**

Rainbow Brite, 1983, w/insert & instructions, used, EX **20.00**

Smiling Skull, w/insert & instructions, unused, M, from $15 to **20.00**

Smurfette, 1983, w/insert, unused, EX **25.00**

Snoopy (Red Baron), w/insert & instructions, unused, M.. **60.00**

Spider-Man, w/insert, used, EX. **10.00**

Stand-up Holiday Tree, w/instructions & box, used, EX **22.00**

Superman/Batman (waist up), 1977, w/instructions & faces, used, EX **25.00**

Tractor, w/insert & instructions, unused, M........................ **10.00**

Veggie Tales, w/insert, used, EX. **25.00**

Western Boot, 1995, #2105-1238, w/insert & instructions, used, VG **28.00**

Winnie the Pooh holding #1, 1998, pan only, unused, G **20.00**

Wonder Woman, 1978, MIB (sealed) **45.00**

Pillsbury Doughboy, 1974, pan only, $55.00.

World's Fairs and Expositions

Souvenir items have been issued since the mid-1800s for every world's fair and exposition. Few fairgoers have left the grounds without purchasing at least one. Some of the older items were often manufactured right on the fairgrounds by glass or pottery companies who erected working kilns and furnaces just for the duration of the fair. Of course, the older items are usually more valuable, but even souvenirs from the past 50 years are worth hanging on to. See Clubs and Newsletters for information concerning the World's Fair Collectors' Society, Inc.

1933 Chicago

Astray, copper, 3-legged pot sits on cross-stick frame **30.00**

Book, Official Book of Views, 60 pages, 9x12", EX 20.00

Bracelet, gold-tone metal cuff w/ornate Chicago skyline, EX.............25.00

Handkerchief, fair scenes in orange & gray on white, 12" sq, EX 25.00

Pencil holder, metal bulldog figure, pencil fits in mouth, 2", EX.25.00

Salt & pepper shakers, Tea Time, clear glass w/black letters, EXIB 75.00

Tie bar, 1933 Chicago & logo in silver on blue, silver band, EX 15.00

1939 New York

Compact, brass and plastic with rhinestones, from $60.00 to $75.00.

Board game, Going to the World's Fair, complete, EXIB 150.00

Brochure, Heinz 57, color fold-out, 20x14", EX.......................10.00

Coaster set, Trylon & Perisphere center, 4 ea of 4 colors, 3" dia.................................50.00

Comb, amber plastic in embossed gold-tone metal case w/fair medallion.........................30.00

Figurine, cast iron, terrier seated w/fair symbols, 3"............35.00

Mug, ceramic, NYWF in blue w/fair symbols in white sq on green, 5"......................................25.00

Pennant, Aviation Building, fair scenes on blue, 24", EX...50.00

Postcard, Trylon & Perisphere, color on linen, unused, EX......500.00

Salt & pepper shakers, Trylon & Perisphere in orange on blue base...................................15.00

Tray, fair scenes in aqua & white on red, 17½x13", VG 25.00

1939 San Francisco

Book, Treasure Island, fair photos, 32 pages, EX....................35.00

Bookmark, butterfly form, yellow on acetate w/paper, MIP.............................25.00

Guide, Official Guide Book, Betty Crocker, 116 pages, 5½x8", VG 25.00

Guide, Southern Pacific RR, pictorial, 12 pages, EX............15.00

Ice pick, World's Fair marked on wooden handle, 8"...........22.00

Pillow case, black scenes on white w/yellow border, white fringe, 18".....................................12.00

Pocketwatch, Official Souvenir on face, logo on back, silver, EX 125.00

Sun Tower, bronze finish, 4¼", minimum value 75.00

Ticket, Cavalcade of the Golden West, 2x1¼"......................4.00

Token, aluminum, Road of Streamliners & Challengers, EX .8.00

1962 Seattle

Charm bracelet, gold metal, 10 charms, 7"........................25.00

Coin, 1939-S Walking Liberty half-dollar, EX........................15.00

Compact, Clarice Jane, brushed brass, sq w/fair logo, MIB. **30.00**

Earrings, embossed copper, SWF, logo, 21 & Space Needle, 1" dia, pr...................................... **25.00**

Plate, fair overview, blue-green border w/silver stripe, 10¾". **16.00**

Punch-out kit, Space Needle, 3-D **25.00**

Spoon, Space Needle & logo, sterling, 1", EX **20.00**

Tumblers, frosted glass w/scenes, set of 6, from $30 to........ **40.00**

Tumblers, white plastic w/colored scenes, set of 8, NMIB.... **70.00**

Umbrella, child's, pink w/fair buildings, Space Needle finial, EX................................. **50.00**

1964 New York

Booklet, Vatican Pavilion at the World's Fair..................... **12.00**

Brochure, Monorail, 7 pgs, EX. **25.00**

Calendar, perpetual, blue & white logo on white, Japan, 3½"............................... **35.00**

Charm, world globe in frame, 14k gold **125.00**

Coin purse, green vinyl, Unisphere & logo, oval..................... **25.00**

Cowboy hat, white w/black & white band, Arlington, EX........ **25.00**

Figurine, flute player from It's a Small World, Disney, 7½", NMIB............................. **40.00**

License plate, Unisphere in center on blue & orange............. **50.00**

Paperweight, clear cube w/red horse, Swedish Pavillion, 2x1⅜x1¾"........................ **15.00**

Paperweight, Unisphere, on metal base, US Steel, 2½x5½"..... **6.00**

Pin-back button, Meet Me at the Smoke Ring, EX.............. **12.00**

Postcard, Caribbean Pavilion, unused **2.00**

Program, Progressland, 10 pages, 8½x11"............................. **45.00**

Tumbler, frosted w/Shea Stadium on green & brown, info on back, 6½" **10.00**

View-Master reel pack, Federal & State Area, 3 reels, MIP. **40.00**

Visitor's Guide & Map, Squibb & Sons **6.50**

Medal, bronze, 2½", $25.00 to $30.00.

1982 Knoxville

Coin, commemorative; gold-tone, logo/aerial view, ½" dia ... **10.00**

Creamer, brown glaze w/cream speckled rim, Hull, 4½" .. **15.00**

Mirror, bar; Stroh's Official Beer at the Fair, oval, 14x11"...... **50.00**

Pen, floaty; fair scene, Denmark on pocket clip, EX **15.00**

Pocketknife, white Bakelite w/red Coca-Cola logo, 2-blade... **10.00**

Pocketwatch, logo in red, white & blue, Westclox, MIB........ **50.00**

Postcard, United States Pavilion. **2.50**

Directory

The editors and staff take this opportunity to express our sincere gratitude and appreciation to each person who has in any way contributed to the preparation of this guide. We believe the credibility of our book is greatly enhanced through their participation. Check these listings for information concerning their specific areas of expertise.

If you care to correspond with anyone listed here in our Directory, you must send a SASE with your letter. If you are among those listed, please advise us of any changes in your address, phone number, or e-mail.

Alabama
Cataldo, C.E.
4726 Panorama Dr. SE
Huntsville, 35801
256-536-6893
genecams@aol.com

California
Ales, Beverly L.
4046 Graham St.
Pleasanton, 94566-5619
925-846-5297
Kniferests@sbcglobal.net
Specializing in knife rests; editor of
Knife Rests of Yesterday and Today

Conroy, Barbara J.
P.O. Box 2369
Santa Clara, CA 95055-2369
Author of *Restaurant China, Restaurant, Airline, Ship & Railroad Dinnerware, Vol I* and *II* (Collector Books).

Elliott, Jacki
9790 Twin Cities Rd.
Galt, 95632
209-745-3860
Specializing in Rooster and Roses

Harrison, Gwynne
11566 River Heights Drive
Riverside, 92505
951-343-0414
morgan99@pe.net

Buys and appraises Autumn Leaf; edits newsletter

Hibbard, Suzi
849 Vintage Ave.
Fairfield, 94585-3332
Dragon_Ware@hotmail.com
www.dragonware.com
Specializing in Dragonware and 1000 Faces china, other Orientalia; related

Needham, Leonard
MacAdam's Antiques
screensider@sbcglobal.net
Specializing in automobilia, advertising

Utley, Bill; Editor
Flashlight Collectors of America
P.O. Box 40945
Tustin, 92781
714-730-1252 or fax 714-505-4067
Specializing in flashlights

Colorado
Diehl, Richard
5965 W Colgate Pl.
Denver, 80227
303-985-7481
Specializing in license plates

Connecticut
Sabulis, Cindy
P.O. Box 642
Shelton, 06484
203-926-0176

www.dollsntoys.com
Specializing in dolls from the '60s
– '70s (Liddle Kiddles, Barbie, Tammy,
Tressy, etc.); co-author of *The Collector's Guide to Tammy, The Ideal Teen,*
and author of *Collector's Guide to Dolls
of the 1960s & 1970s* (Collector Books)

Florida
Kuritzky, Lewis
4510 NW 17th Pl.
Gainesville, 32605
352-377-3193
lkuritzky@aol.com
Author of *Collector's Guide to Bookends*

Poe, Bill and Pat
220 Dominica Cir. E
Niceville, 32578-4085
850-897-4163 or fax 850-897-2606
BPOE@cox.net
Buy, sell, trade cartoon character glass-
es, PEZ, Smurfs, California Raisins,
M&M items

Posner, Judy
P.O. Box 2194
Englewood, 34295
judyposner@yahoo.com
Specializing in figural pottery, cookie
jars, salt and pepper shakers, Black
memorabilia, and Disneyana; sale lists
available; fee charged for appraisals

Snyder-Haug, Diane
St. Petersburg, 33705
Collector Book author specializing in
women's clothing

Idaho
Birkinbine, Mandi
P.O. Box 121
Meridian, 83680-0121
tiara@shop4antiques.com
www.shop4antiques.com

Author of *Collecting Tiara Amber
Sandwich Glass,* available from the
author for $18.45 ppd. Please allow 4 to
6 weeks for delivery

McVey, Jeff
1810 W State St. #427
Boise, 83702-3955
Author of *Tire Ashtray Collector's
Guide* available from the author

Illinois
Garmon, Lee
1529 Whittier St.
Springfield, 62704
217-789-9574
Specializing in Borden's Elsie, Reddy
Kilowatt, Elvis Presley, and Marilyn
Monroe

Jungnickel, Eric
P.O. Box 4674
Naperville, 60567-4674
630-983-8339
Specializing in Indy 500 memorabilia

Kadet, Jeff
TV Guide Specialists
P.O. Box 20
Macomb, 61455
Buying and selling of *TV Guide* from
1948 through the 1990s

Karman, Lori and Rich
Editors of *The Fenton Flyer*
815 S. Douglas
Springfield, 62704
Specializing in Fenton art glass

Klompus, Eugene R.
Just Cuff Links
P.O. Box 5970
Vernon Hills, 60061
847-816-0035
genek@cufflinksrus.com
Specializing in cuff links and men's
accessories

399

Stifter, Craig
218 S. Adams St.
Hinsdale, 60251
cstifter@collectica.com
Specializing in soda memorabilia such
as Coca-Cola, Hires, Pepsi, 7-Up, etc.

Indiana
Dilley, David
Indianapolis
317-251-0575
glazebears@aol.com or bearpots@aol.com
Author of book on Royal Haeger; available from the author

McQuillen, Michael and Polly
P.O. Box 50022
Indianapolis, 46250-0022
317-845-1721
michael@politicalparade.com
www.politicalparade.com
Specializing in political memorabilia

Iowa
Devine, Joe
D&D Antique Mall
1411 3rd St.
Council Bluffs, 51503
712-232-5233 or 712-328-7305
Author of *Collecting Royal Copley Plus
Royal Windsor & Spaulding*

Kentucky
Hornback, Betty
707 Sunrise Ln.
Elizabethtown, 42701
Specializing in Kentucky Derby and
horse racing memorabilia; send for
informative booklet, $15 ppd.

Louisiana
Langford, Paris
415 Dodge Ave.
Jefferson, 70121-3311
504-733-0067
bbean415@aol.com.

Author of *Liddle Kiddles*; specializing
in dolls of the 1960s – 70s

Maine
Hathaway, John
Hathaway's Antiques
3 Mills Rd.
Bryant Pond, 04219
207-665-2214
Specializing in fruit jars, mail-order a
specialty

Maryland
Raven'tiques
27965 Peach Orchard Rd.
Easton, 21601-8203
410-822-5441
Specializing in walking figures and tin
wind-up toys

Massachusetts
Porter, Richard T.
Porter Thermometer Museum
Box 944
Onset 02558
thermometerman@aol.com
Specializing in thermometers

Wellman, BA
P.O. Box 673
Westminster, 01473-0673
BA@dishinitout.com
Specializing in all areas of American
ceramics; researches Royal China

White, Larry
108 Central St.
Rowley, 01969-1317
978-948-8187
larrydw@erols.com
Specializing in Cracker Jack; author of
books; has newsletter

Michigan
Nickel, Mike; and Cindy Horvath
P.O. Box 456
Portland, 48875-0456

517-647-7646
mandc@voyager.net
Specializing in Ohio art pottery, Kay
Finch, Author of *Kay Finch Ceramics,
Her Enchanted World,* available from
the authors; co-author of *Collector's
Encyclopedia of Roseville Pottery Re-
vised Edition, Vol I* and *Vol II* (Collector
Books)

Pickvet, Mark
5071 Watson Dr.
Flint, 48506
Author of *Shot Glasses: An Ameri-
can Tradition,* available for $12.95
plus $2.50 postage and handling from
Antique Publications, P.O. Box 553,
Marietta, OH 45750

Ross, Michele
P.O. Box 94
Berrien Center, 49102
279-925-6382
motherclay2@aol.com
Specializing in Van Briggle and other
American pottery

Whitmyer, Margaret and Kenn
P.O. Box 30806
Gahana, 43230-2704
Authors (Collector Books) specializing
in children's dishes, Christmas collect-
ibles, Hall china

Nebraska
Johnson, Donald-Brian
3329 S 56th St. #611
Omaha, 68106
donaldbrian@webtv.net
Specializing in Ceramic Arts Studio

New Hampshire
Holt, Jane
P.O. Box 115
Derry, 03038
Specializing in Annalee dolls

New Jersey
Litts, Elyce
P.O. Box 394
Morris Plains, 07950
973-361-4087
happy.memories@worldnet.att.net
Specializing in Geisha Girl (author of
book); also ladies' compacts

Palmieri, Jo Ann
27 Pepper Rd.
Towaco, 07082-1357
201-334-5829
Specializing in Skookum Indian dolls

Sparacio, George
P.O. Box 791
Malaga, 08328
609-694-4167; fax 609-694-4536
mrvesta@aol.com
Specializing in match safes

Visakay, Stephen
P.O. Box 1517
W Caldwell, 07007-1517
SVisakay@aol.com
Specializing in vintage cocktail shakers
(by mail and appointment only); author
of *Vintage Bar Ware*

New Mexico
Mace, Shirley
Shadow Enterprises
P.O. Box 1602
Mesilla Park, 88047
505-524-6717; fax 505-523-0940
shadow-ent@zianet.com
www.geocities.com/MadisonAvenue/
   Boardroom/1631
Author of *Encyclopedia of Silhouette
Collectibles on Glass* (available from
the author)

New York
Beegle, Gary
92 River St.
Montgomery, 12549

914-457-3623
Liberty Blue dinnerware, also most lines of collectible modern American dinnerware as well as character glasses

Dinner, Craig
39-74 45th St.
Sunnyside, 11104 or
P.O. Box 184
Townend VT 05353 (Summer)
718-729-3850
Specializing in figural cast-iron items (door knockers, lawn sprinklers, doorstops, windmill weights, etc.)

Schleifman, Roselle
16 Vincent Rd.
Spring Valley, 10977-3829
212-534-7933
Specializing in Duncan & Miller, New Martinsville glass

Weitman, Stan and Arlene
P.O. Box 1186
Massapequa Park, 11758
scrackled@earthlink.net
www.crackleglass.com
Authors of *Crackle Glass, Identification and Value Guide, Volumes I* and *II* (Collector Books)

North Carolina
Brooks, Ken and Barbara
4121 Gladstone Ln.
Charlotte, 28205
Specializing in Cat-Tail Dinnerware

Sayers, Rolland J.
Southwestern Antiques and Appraisals
P.O. Box 629
Brevard 28712
Researches Pisgah Forest pottery; author of *Guide to Scouting Collectibles,* available from the author for $32.95 pp.

North Dakota
Farnsworth, Bryce L.
1334 14 1/2 St.
S Fargo, 58103
701-237-3597
Specializing in Rosemeade

Ohio
Benjamin, Scott
P.O. Box 556
LaGrange, 44050-0556
440-355-6608
www.oilcollectibles.com
Specializing in automobilia, gas globes

China Specialties, Inc.
Box 471
Valley City, 44280
Specializing in high-quality reproductions of Homer Laughlin and Hall china, including Autumn

Graff, Shirley
4515 Grafton Rd.
Brunswick, 44212-2005
Specializing in Pennsbury

Mangus, Beverly and Jim
4812 Sherman Church Ave. SW
Canton, 44706
Authors (Collector Books) specializing in Shawnee pottery

Young, Mary
P.O. Box 9244
Wright Bros. Branch
Dayton, 45409
937-298-4838
Author of books; specializing in paper dolls

Oklahoma
Boone, Phyllis Bess
14535 E 13th St.
Tulsa, 74108-4527
9918-437-7776
Specializing in Frankoma pottery

Ivers, Terri
Terri's Toys and Nostalgia
206 E. Grand
Ponca City, 74601
580-762-8697
toylady@cableone.net
Specializing in character collectibles,
lunch boxes, advertising items, Breyer
and Hartland figures, etc.

Moore, Shirley and Art
4423 E. 31st St.
Tulsa, 74135
918-747-4164
Specializing in Lu-Ray Pastels and
Depression glass

Oregon
Brown, Marcia "Sparkles"
P.O. Box 2314
White City 97503
541-826-3039
Collector Books author specializing in
jewelry

Coe, Debbie and Randy
Coes Mercantile
P.O. Box 173
Hillsboro, 97123
Specializing in Elegant and Depression
glass, art pottery, Cape Cod by Avon,
Golden Foliage by Libbey Glass Com-
pany, Gurley candles, and Liberty Blue
dinnerware

White, Carole Bess
2225 NE 33rd Ave.
Portland, 97207-5116
Specializing in Japan ceramics; author
of books

Pennsylvania
BOJO/Bob Gottuso
P.O. Box 1403
Cranberry Twp., 16066-0403
phone or fax 724-776-0621
www.bojoonline.com

Specializing in the Beatles and rock 'n
roll memorabilia

Cerebro
P.O. Box 327
East Prospect, 37317-0327
www.cerebro.com
Specializing in advertising labels

Greenfield, Jeannie
310 Parker Rd.
Stoneboro, 16153-2810
724-376-2584
Specializing in cake toppers and egg
timers

Kreider, Katherine
Kingsbury Antiques
P.O. Box 7957
Lancaster, 19604-7957
717-892-3001
katherinekreider@valentinesdirect.com
Specializing in valentines

South Carolina
Belyski, Richard
P.O. Box 14956
Surfside Beach, 29587
Specializing in Pez

Cassity, Brad
2391 Hunter's Trail
Myrtle Beach, 29574
419-283-8697
Specializing in Fisher-Price pull toys
and playsets up to 1986 (author of book)

Greguire, Helen
79 Lake Lyman Heights
Lyman, 29365
864-848-0408
Author (Collector Books) specializing in
Graniteware

Fields, Linda
230 Beech Lane
Buchanon, 38222

Fpiebird@compu.net.
Specializing in pie birds

Texas
Cooper, Marilyn M.
8408 Lofland Dr.
Houston, 77055-4811
713-465-7773
Or summer address:
P.O. Box 755
Douglas, MI 49406
Author of *The Pictorial Guide to Toothbrush Holders* ($22.95 postpaid)

Docks, L.R. 'Les'
Shellac Shack; Discollector
Box 691035
San Antonio, 78269-1035
docks@texas.net
Author of *American Premium Record Guide;* specializing in vintage records

Gibbs, Carl, Jr.
1716 Westheimer Rd
Houston, 77098
Author of *Collector's Encyclopedia of Metlox Potteries* (Collector Books); specializing in American dinnerware

Jackson, Joyce
900 Jenkins Rd.
Aledo, 76008-2410
817-441-8864
jjpick@firstworld.net
Specializing in Swanky Swigs

Nossaman, Darlene
5419 Lake Charles
Waco, 76710
Specializing in Homer Laughlin China information and Horton Ceramics

Pogue, Larry
L and J Antiques & Collectibles
8142 Ivan Ct.
Terrell, 75161-6921
972-551-0221

LandJAntiques@direcway.com
Specializing in head vases, string holders, general line

Woodard, Dannie
P.O. Box 1346
Weatherford, 76086
371-594-4680
Author of *Hammered Aluminum, Hand Wrought Collectibles*

Utah
Spencer, Rick
Salt Lake City
801-973-0805
Specializing in Shawnee, Roseville, Weller, Van Telligen, Regal, Bendel, Coors, Rookwood, Watt; also salt and pepper shakers, cookie jars, etc., cut glass, radios, and silver flatware

Wisconsin
Helley, Phil
Old Kilbourn Antiques
629 Indiana Ave.
Wisconsin Dells, 53965
608-254-8770
Specializing in Cracker Jack items, radio premiums, dexterity games, toys (especially Japanese wind-up toys), banks, and old Dells souvenir items marked Kilbourn

Wanvig, Nancy
Nancy's Collectibles
P.O. Box 12
Thiensville, WI 53092
Author of book; specializing in ashtrays

West Virginia
Apkarian-Russell, Pamela
Halloween Queen Antiques
577 Boggs Run Rd.
Benwood 26031-1001
Specializing in Halloween collectibles, postcards of all kinds, and Joe Camel

Clubs and Newsletters

Akro Agate Collectors Club
Clarksburg Crow
Roger Hardy
10 Bailey St.
Clarksburg, WV 26301-2524
304-624-4523
www.mkl.com/akro/club
Annual membership fee: $25

Antiques Coast to Coast
Mark Chervenka, Editor
P.O. Box 12130
Des Moines, IA 50312-9403
800-227-5531 (subscriptions only) or
515-274-5886
acrn@repronews.com
12- monthly issues: $32 US, $41
Canada, $59 foreign

The Antique Trader Weekly
Nancy Crowley, Editor
P.O. Box 1050
Dubuque, IA 52004-1050
collect@krause.com
www.collect.com
Subscription: $38 (52 issues) per year;
sample: $1

Autographs of America
Tim Anderson
P.O. Box 461
Provo, UT 84603
801-226-1787 (afternoons, please)
www.AutographsOfAmerica.com
Free sample catalog of hundreds of
autographs for sale

Autumn Leaf
Bill Swanson, Editor
807 Roaring Springs Dr.
Allen, TX 75002-2112

972-727-5527
www.nalcc.org

Avon Times
c/o Dwight or Vera Young
P.O. Box 9868, Dept. P.
Kansas City, MO 64134
AvonTimes@aol.com
Send SASE for information

Bookend Collector Club
Louis Kuritzky, M.D.
4510 NW 17th Place
Gainsville, FL 32650
352-377-3193
lkuritzky@aol.com
Membership (includes newsletter): $25
per year

Candy Container Collectors of America
The Candy Gram Newsletter
c/o Jim Olean
115 Mac Beth Dr.
Lower Burrel, PA 15068-2628
www.candycontainer.org

CAS Collector's
206 Grove St.
Rockton, IL 61072
www.cascollectors.com
Ceramic Arts Studio history website:
www.ceramicartsstudio.com
Established in 1994 as the Ceramic Arts
Studio Collectors Association, CAS
Collectors welcomes all with a common
interest in the work of Ceramic Arts
Studio of Madison, Wisconsin. The club
publishes a quarterly newsletter and
hosts an annual convention in Madison
each August in conjunction with the
Wisconsin Pottery Association Show &

Sale. Family membership: $25 per year. Information about the club and its activities, as well as a complete illustrated CAS history, is included in the book *Ceramic Arts Studio: The Legacy of Betty Harrington by Donald-Brian Johnson, Timothy J. Holthaus, and James E. Petzold (Schiffer Publishing, 2003).*

Fiesta Collector's Quarterly
P.O. Box 471
Valley City, OH 44280
www.chinaspecialties.com

Cookie Crumbs
Ruth Capper, Secretary/Treasurer
PO Box 245
Cannon Falls, MN 55009
www.cookiecuttercollectorsclub.com
Subscription $20 per year (4 issues, payable to CCCC).

Currier & Ives Dinnerware Collector Club
Charles Burgess, Membership
308 Jodi Dr.
Brownstown, IN 47220-1523
812-358-4569
annmah2@aol.com
www.royalchinaclub.com
Membership: $15

Czechoslovakian Collectors Guild
    International
Alan Badia, Membership Chairman
15006 Meadowlake St.
Odessa, FL 33556-3126
www.czechartglass.com

Doll News Magazine
United Federation of Doll Clubs
Ann Seymour, Secretary-Treasurer
110762 W. Crestview Lane
Laurel, MD 20723

301-725-5041
www.ufdc.org

Doorstop Collectors of America
Jeanie Bertoia
2413 Madison Ave.
Vineland, NJ 08630
609-692-4092
Membership: $20 per year, includes 2 newsletters and convention; send 2-stamp SASE for sample

Dragonware Club
c/o Suzi Hibbard
849 Vintage Ave.
Fairfield, CA 94585
Dragon_Ware@hotmail.com

FBOCC (Figural Bottle Opener Collectors)
John T. Fitzsimmons
9697 Gwynn Park Drive
Ellicot City, MD 21042
johnf129@aol.com

Fenton Art Glass Collectors of America, Inc.
Butterfly Net newsletter
P.O. Box 384
702 W. 5th St.
Williamstown, WV 26187
faqcainc@wirefire.com
Membership: $20; Associate member: $5

Fiesta Collector's Quarterly
P.O. Box 471
Valley City, OH 44280
www.chinaspecialties.com
Subscription: $12 per year

Fisher-Price Collector's Club
Jeanne Kennedy
1442 N Ogden
Mesa, AZ 85205
gasper_b@bellsouth.net

www.fpclub.org
Monthly newsletter with information and ads; send SASE for more information

Flashlight Collectors of America Newsletter
Bill Utley
P.O. Box 4095
Tustin, CA 92781
714-730-1252
flashlight@worldnet.att.net
Flashlights, Early Flashlight Makers of the 1st 100 Years of Eveready, full color, 320 pages, now available; quarterly flashlight newsletter, $12 per year

Frankoma Family Collectors Association
c/o Nancy Littrell
P.O. Box 32571
Oklahoma City, OK 73123-0771
www.frankoma.org
Membership dues: $35 (includes quarterly newsletter and annual convention)

The Front Striker Bulletin
Bill Retskin
P.O. Box 18481
Asheville, NC 28814-0481
704-254-4487 or fax 704-254-1066
bill@matchcovers.com
www.matchcovers.com
Membership: $10 per year

Griswold & Cast Iron Cookware Association
G&CICA Secretary
P.O. Box 33688
Portland, OR 97292
Membership: $20 per individual or $25 per family (2 members per address) payable to club

Hall China Collectors' Club Newsletter
Virginia Lee
P.O. Box 360488
Cleveland, OH 44136

Head Hunters Newsletter
c/o Maddy Gordon
P.O. Box 83 H
Scarsdale, NY 10583
For collectors of head vases; subscription: $26 yearly for 4 quarterly issues. Ads free to subscribers

International Nippon Collectors Club (INCC)
Jennifer Cavedo, Membership Chair person
8490 Palace Dr., Kelseyville, CA 95451
www.nipponcollectorsclub.com
Publishes newsletter 6 times a year; Holds annual convention; Membership: $30

International Perfume and Scent Bottle Collectors Association
c/o Randall B. Monsen
P.O. Box 529
Vienna, VA 22183
fax 703-242-1357
www.perfumebottles.org

Just Cuff Links
Eugene R. Klompus
PO Box 5970
Vernon Hills, IL 60061
847-816-0035; fax: 847-816-7466
genek@cufflinksrus.com

Knife Rests of Yesterday and Today
Beverly L. Ales
4046 Graham St.
Pleasanton, CA 94566-5619
Subscription: $20 per year for 6 issues

Marble Collectors' Society of America
51 Johnson St.
Trumbull, CT 06611
blockschip@aol.com
www.blocksite.com

McDonald's® Collector Club
PMB 200
1153 S. Lee St.
Des Plains, IL 60016-6503
www.mcdclub.com
Membership: $25 individual per year;
$30 family

National Association of Avon Collectors
c/o Connie Clark
6100 Walnut, Dept. P,
Kansas City, MO 64113
Information requires LSASE

National Depression Glass Association
P.O. Box 8264
Wichita, KS 67208-0264
Membership: $20 per year
www.ndga.net

National Fenton Glass Society
P.O. Box 4008
Marietta, OH 45750
Membership: $20; includes *The Fenton Flyer* newsletter

National Graniteware Society
P.O. Box 9248
Cedar Rapids, IA 52409-9248
www.graniteware.org
Membership: $20 per year

National Imperial Glass Collectors'
Society, Inc.
P.O. Box 534
Bellaire, OH 43906
www.imperialglass.org
Membership: $18 per year (+$3 for each
associate member), quarterly newsletter

National Milk Glass Collectors' Society
Opaque News, quarterly newsletter
Barb Pinkston, Membership Chairman
1306 Stowe St.
Inverfness, FL 34450-6853
membership@nmgsc.org.
www.nmgcs.org
Please include SASE

National Reamer Association
c/o Wayne Adickes
408 E. Reuss, Cuero, TX 77954
adickes@sbcglobal.net
www.reamers.org
Membership: $25 per household

National Society of Lefton Collectors
The Lefton Collector Newsletter
Loretta DeLozier
P.O. Box 50201
Knocksville, TN 3795-0201
leftonlady@aol.com

National Valentine Collectors Association
Nancy Rosen
P.O. Box 1404
Santa Ana, CA 92702
714-547-1355
Membership: $16

NM (Nelson McCoy) Xpress
Carol Seman, Editor
8934 Brecksville Rd., Suite 406
Brecksville, OH 44141-2318
McCjs@aol.com

www.nmXpress.com
Subscription: $26 per year

The Occupied Japan Club
c/o Florence Archambault
29 Freeborn St.
Newport, RI 02840-1821
florence@aiconnect.com
Publishes *The Upside Down World of an O.J. Collector,* a bimonthly newsletter;
Information requires SASE

On the LIGHTER Side
International Lighter Collectors
Judith Sanders, Editor
136 Circle Dr.
Quitman, TX 75783
903-763-2795 or fax 703-763-4953
Annual convention held in different cities in the US; send SASE when requesting information

Paden City Glass Collectors Guild
Paul Torsiello, Editor
42 Aldine Road
Parsippany, NJ, 07054
pcguild@yahoo.com

Paper & Advertising Collectors' Marketplace
PO Box 128
Scandinavia, WI 54977-0128
715-467-2379 or fax 715-467-2243
pacpcm@eagleonline.com
www.engleonline.com
Subscription: $19.95 in US (12 issues)

Paper Doll News
Emma Terry
P.O. Box 807
Vivian, LA 71082
Subscription: $12 per year

Peanut Pals
Judith Walthall, Founder
P.O. Box 4465
Huntsville, AL 35815; 205-881-9198
Associated collectors of Planters Peanuts memorabilia, bimonthly newsletter
Peanut Papers; annual directory sent to members; annual convention and regional conventions. Dues: $20 per year; membership associate memberships available); Membership information: 246 Old Line Ave., Laurel, MD 20724, or check with peanutpals.org; Sample newsletter: $2

Pez Collector's News
Richard Belyski, Editor
P.O. Box 14956
Surfside Beach, SC 29587
peznews@juno.com
www.pezcollectorsnews.com

Pie Birds Unlimited Newsletter
Rita Reedy
1039 NW Hwy. 101
Lincoln City, OR 97367
ritazart@lycol.com

Political Collectors of Indiana
Michael McQuillen
P.O. Box 50022
Indianapolis, IN 46250-0022
317-845-1721
michael@politicalparade.com
www.politicalparade.com
Official APIC (American Political Items Collectors); chapter comprised of over 100 collectors of presidential and local political items

The Prize Insider Newsletter for Cracker Jack Collectors
Larry White

108 Central St.
Rowley, MA 01969
978-948-8187
larrydw@erols.com

Rosevilles of the Past Newsletter
Nancy Bomm, Editor
P.O. Box 656
Clarcona, FL 32710-0656
407-294-3980
rosepast@worldnet.att.net
Send $19.95 per year for 6 to 12 news-
letters

Roy Rogers – Dale Evans Collectors
  Association
Nancy Horsley, Exec. Secretary
P.O. Box 1166
Portsmouth, OH 45662-1166
www.royrogers.com

Shawnee Pottery Collectors' Club
c/o Pamela Curran
P.O. Box 713
New Smyrna Beach, FL 32170-0713
Send $3 for sample copy

The Shot Glass Club of America
Mark Pickvet, Editor
P.O. Box 90404
Flint, MI 48509

The Silver Bullet
Lone Ranger Fan Club
P.O. Box 9561
Longmont, CO 80502
806-373-3969
www.lonerangerfanclub.com
Membership: $36

Stretch Glass Society
P.O. Box 3305 Society
Quartz Hill, CA 93586

stretchglasssociety.org
Membership: $22 (US); $24 (International); holds annual convention

Tea Talk
P.O. Box 860
Sausalito, CA 94966
415-331-1557
teatalk@aol.com

The TeaTime Gazette
P.O. Box 40276
St. Paul, MN 55104
612-227-7415
info@teatimegazette.com

Tiffin Glass Collectors
P.O. Box 554
Tiffin, OH 44883
www.tiffinglass.org
Membership: $15

Toy Shop
700 E State St.
Iola, WI 54990-0001
715-445-2214
www.toyshopmag.com
Subscription (3rd class) $33.98 (US) for
26 issues

The Trick or Treat Trader
Pamela E. Apkarian-Russell
C.J. Russell and The Halloween Queen
PO Box 499, Winchester, NH 03470;
603-239-8875
halloweenqueen@cheshire.net
Subscription: $15 (4 issues)

Vintage Fashion & Costume Jewelry
  Newsletter/Club
P.O. Box 265
Glen Oaks, NY 11004
718-969-2320 or 718-939-3095

Yearly subscription: $20 (US) for 4 issues; sample copy available by sending $5

Westmoreland Glass Society
Steve Jensen
P.O. Box 2883
Iowa City, IA 52240-2883
www.westmorelandglassclubs.org
Membership: $15 single or $25 household

The Willow Review
P.O. Box 41312
Nashville, TN 37204
Send SASE for information

World's Fair Collectors' Society, Inc.
Fair News newsletter
Michael R. Pender, Editor
P.O. Box 20806
Sarasota, FL 34276-3806
941-923-2590
wfcs@aol.com
Dues: $20 (US), $25 (Canada), $30 (overseas)

Index